ENDORSEMENTS

The most basic freedom of all is freedom of religion. Michael P. Farris, in his volume *From Tyndale to Madison*, has given to every lover of liberty one of the most thoughtful and helpful volumes in recent generations. My own conviction is that there will be no volume published this year that demands as careful a reading as this book. Especially do I wish that every member of the congress and the judiciary, together with every pastor in America, would read this volume and apply it to their life and work.

—Paige Patterson, President
Southwestern Baptist Theological Seminary
Fort Worth, Texas

A tour de force of extraordinary magnitude and unusual importance. Only rarely does a book posses the significance of *From Tyndale to Madison*. Drawing upon a remarkable array of primary and secondary sources, Michael P. Farris meticulously and successfully debunks the myths that "the Enlightenment is responsible for the American Bill of Rights" and that "Enlightenment philosophies were chiefly responsible for opening people's minds to the error of religious persecution and paving the way for a society in which 'heretics' are not tortured and burnt in town squares." *From Tyndale to Madison* is a "must read" for everyone interested in history.

—Charles W. Dunn, Dean
Regent University
Virginia Beach, Virginia

This fascinating account of where the American dream of liberty of conscience that produced the religious freedom we all so freely enjoy in this country today, originated in the heart of William Tyndale. He was helped of course by other heroic men of faith who also have their lives to translate and distribute the Word of God into English so that every man, even "the ploughman" could read the Bible for himself. Tyndale was right. Bible reading in one's own language did transform religion in Europe and became the driving force that produced religious freedom in the American colonies.

This book proves beyond doubt that the "enlightenment" had little or no influence on our treasured religious freedom. Instead it was fostered by men like John Witherspoon, the president of Princeton College, a Scottish Presbyterian preacher and legal scholar who by his teaching educated many of the founders who went as delegates to the Continental Congress, particularly James Madison, who was considered "the father of the Constitution."

In this exciting history, Mike Farris traces the story of how familiarity with the Bible and the faith it inspires is what really produced the religious freedom that is the bedrock foundation of our country. Once I began reading it, I could not lay it down. I heartily recommend this book to anyone who would want to know the truth about the history of America!

—Tim LaHaye
Tim LaHaye Ministries

From Tyndale To Madison

MICHAEL FARRIS

From TYNDALE *To* MADISON

HOW THE DEATH OF AN ENGLISH MARTYR LED TO THE AMERICAN *Bill of Rights*

B&H
PUBLISHING GROUP
Nashville, Tennessee

ISBN: 978-0-8054-2611-3

Published by B&H Publishing Group,
Nashville, Tennessee

Dewey Decimal Classification: 261.72
Subject Heading: FREEDOM OF RELIGION—HISTORY \
CHURCH HISTORY \ PROTESTANTISM

Images in the book are used by permission of The Bodleian Library,
Oxford University and The Library of Virginia.

1 2 3 4 5 6 7 8 9 10   11 10 09 08 07

To J. Michael Smith, my
co-laborer in the battle for
religious and parental liberty.

ACKNOWLEDGMENTS

Naomi Harralson, my invaluable researcher and associate, has lived up to the accolades bestowed upon her at Patrick Henry College. She was awarded the 2005 Beverly LaHaye Leadership Award as the outstanding female graduate. Without her this book would not have been possible. My two assistants, Amanda Taylor and Rachel Kozlowski, help keep my life organized so that projects of this magnitude are even possible. John Vinci helped in the early stages of research and discovered the critical collection of Early English Books Online.

Helen Marie Taylor, a relative of James Madison and a Virginia patriot, first alerted me to the possible family relationship between William Tyndale and James Madison. This opened up an entire new venue for research that paid numerous dividends in finding out the full story of the history of religious freedom.

CONTENTS

INTRODUCTION

*M*y own college textbook from a political philosophy class espoused a common view regarding the source of contemporary religious liberty. Enlightenment philosophies, it taught, were chiefly responsible for opening people's minds to the error of religious persecution and paving the way for a society in which "heretics" are not tortured and burnt in town squares.

This conception has not gone away. I recently served as a judge for a national essay contest in which the contestant instructions explained that religious liberty is a concept derived from the European Enlightenment. After all, the general argument goes, devoted Christians have often been the chief persecutors in Western history and therefore cannot be said to have had a positive role in advancing the idea that the civil magistrate should not interfere with matters of conscience. On the contrary, it is said, the forces most inimical to genuine Christian faith—a general religious apathy among the populace, relativism in regard to truth, a growing secularist mind-set, and Enlightenment-influenced skepticism among intellectual leaders—were the primary forces behind the triumph of religious liberty in the West.

Examples come from diverse sources. Firuz Kazemzadeh, an esteemed Ivy League scholar who has been appointed and reappointed to the U.S. Commission on International Religious Freedom, attributes the failure of Muslim nations to embrace religious liberty to the fact that they have neither "gone through the Enlightenment" nor "developed any of the attitudes that formed the minds of the founding fathers of this country, including deism and a measure of skepticism in matters of religion which permitted the kind of tolerance which we all seek today."[1] Historian Merrill D. Peterson has called the 1787 Virginia Statute for Religious Liberty "the supreme expression of the eighteenth-century Enlightenment," which was driven by "skepticism toward all received truths and of untrammeled free inquiry in the pursuit of knowledge."[2] The introduction to the audio edition of Joseph J. Ellis's

His Excellency: George Washington refers to the United States of America as "the greatest achievement of the Enlightenment."[3] Even Larry Schweikart and Michael Allen, who wrote *A Patriot's History of the United States* to counteract the effect of a popular Marxist interpretation of American history entitled *A People's History of the United States*, say that "the overall molding of America's Revolution in the ideological sense" was derived from Enlightenment thinkers Thomas Hobbes and Charles de Montesquieu.[4] And the colorful 2003 edition of Joy Hakim's *Freedom: A History of US*, which sports a foreword written by President George W. Bush and the First Lady, discusses the freedom born out of the Age of Reason, concluding, "And that's when we were lucky enough to be born."[5]

We have to recognize the truth of the claim that professing Christians were indeed the principal persecutors during the relevant era in which religious liberty emerged. But is it necessarily true that the heroes who stood against persecution and brought liberty of conscience to the forefront in America were avowed skeptics and unorthodox secularists? The goal of this book is to answer this question by undertaking a detailed account of the troubling history of religious persecution from the sixteenth through the eighteenth centuries, chiefly in England, and by exploring the ideas that brought religious liberty to America.

Today all Christian denominations embrace religious liberty as an ideal. But it was not always so. It is improper to judge today's adherents of a particular branch of Christianity by the acts of their distant theological cousins. Moreover, it is unfair to denigrate entirely the life's work of significant religious reformers for their failure to embrace religious liberty.

Yet the sad truth is that some giants of the faith were religious persecutors. The story that follows is told with unflinching honesty. However, it must be borne in mind that this book is limited to a discussion of religious liberty. The scope affords no opportunity to praise these individuals' many other positive achievements. It is similar to a discussion of the founding fathers and slavery: even those who owned slaves and defended slavery, as regrettable as this was, made significant contributions to the founding of this nation. Indeed, the foundations they laid were chiefly responsible for slavery's eventual eradication.

In a similar way, religious liberty arose gradually. Catholics, Anglicans, Calvinists, and Lutherans persecuted each other and other smaller groups of dissenters. It would be erroneous to castigate men or entire movements for their failures without recognizing their achievements in other areas. At the end of the road, an Anglican, James Madison, trained in liberty by a Calvinist Presbyterian, John Witherspoon, worked with the persecuted Baptists of Virginia to turn a broken theory of religious toleration into the robust experience of religious liberty that has changed America and the world.

We must tell the story of the Christian persecutors so that we can put to the test the claim that people who cared little about faith and religion were the heroes of liberty. The true heroes are not to be found among the salons of the Enlightenment philosophers but in the cells in King's Bench Prison and tied to the stake at Smithfield.

This is the story of those who lived and died believing that God is the author of liberty.

PART I

FROM OUT OF THE SHORT FIRE

Chapter One

SCRIPTURE FOR PLOUGHBOYS

Tyndale's Mission

"If God spare my life many years, I will cause a boy that driveth the plough to know more of Scripture than you do."
WILLIAM TYNDALE

There are times when profound ideas are most clearly articulated in the heat of debate. A simple statement, designed to make a small point, suddenly illuminates the mind in a way that changes the course of lives and sometimes the course of civilization.

In the western shire of Gloucester stands yet today a grand stone manor house in the Cotswold tradition, Little Sodbury Manor. It is strategically perched on the edge of a hillside, revealing an idyllic view of the vale of the Severn. The square tower of the ancient parish church in the village of Little Sodbury lies in the near distance. In 1522, an Oxford scholar named William Tyndale secured a position in this home as the tutor for the children of the lord of the manor, Sir John Walsh, and his wife, Lady Anne.

Walsh was an important figure in the county, having twice held the post of high sheriff of the shire, among other important offices for both church and crown. The family's social standing was significant, evidenced by a visit to their home by Henry VIII and then queen Anne Boleyn on the evening of

August 23, 1535. Anne Walsh was the sister of Sir Nicholas Poyntz of Acton Court, who was a close friend of both Henry and Anne.

Tyndale, like the Walshes, came to have strong Protestant leanings in an age when religious conformity was expected and violently enforced. While living at Little Sodbury, Tyndale had an argumentative encounter with a traveling "learned man," undoubtedly a priest of indeterminate rank. A theological debate erupted between Tyndale and the cleric, in which Tyndale demonstrated that the priest's position was contrary to the teachings of the Bible.

To this the learned man replied, "We were better to be without God's laws than the pope's!"

Tyndale swiftly declared, "I defy the pope and all his laws." The famous martyrologist Foxe notes that Tyndale went on to assert that "if God spared him life, 'ere many years, he would cause a boy that driveth the plough to know more of the Scripture than he did."[1] (In the original versions of Foxe's *Actes and Monuments*—now known as *Foxe's Book of Martyrs*—he uses third-person pronouns to describe Tyndale's statement, but it is clear that Tyndale is speaking of himself.)

With these few words Tyndale not only declared the central purpose of his own life but also unknowingly set into motion a long chain of events that would ultimately lead to the religious liberty of the American people.

Impediments to Biblical Literacy

For Tyndale to achieve his goal of giving the Bible to ploughboys the worlds of religion, law, and politics would all have to dramatically change. The Bible was essentially unknown in a nation where the Roman Church was so dominant that the pope's annual revenue from England was comparable to that taken by the king.[2] Even the clergy were largely scripturally illiterate. Tyndale made a practice of conversing with everyone from archdeacons to children about matters of faith, and his simple and plain explanations of passages of the Bible frequently revealed the error of even the most learned. Despite everyone's common acknowledgement of Tyndale's "virtuous disposition" and "life unspotted," some began fervidly to resent him.[3]

After a while, clamoring on the part of area priests led to charges of heresy and a trial. The official in charge of the proceeding railed viciously against Tyndale. Yet none of the priests in attendance would stand as his accuser, and Tyndale was able to return to the Walshes after his examination. "This I suffer," he said, "because the priests of the country be unlearned."[4] And indeed they were—at least in the Scriptures. Even thirty years later, when the bishop of Gloucester surveyed the knowledge of the 311 priests, deacons, and archdeacons in the diocese, 168 were unable to name the

Ten Commandments (nine didn't even know how many commandments there were); thirty-nine did not know where the Lord's Prayer appeared in the Bible, and thirty-four were unable to name the author of the Lord's Prayer.[5]

Around the same time that Tyndale was at Little Sodbury, Thomas Cranmer, who would later become the first Protestant archbishop of Canterbury, introduced a radical new practice at Cambridge University that demonstrated the breadth of biblical illiteracy even among those at the top of religious society. Those who were being examined for a doctorate in divinity at Cambridge would now, thanks to Cranmer's innovation, be examined on the Bible. Cranmer's 1694 biography, written by John Strype, describes the situation:

> For he used to examine these Candidates out of the Scriptures. And by no means would he let them pass, if he found they were unskillful in it, and unacquainted with the History of the Bible. So were the Friars especially, whose Study lay only in School-Authors. Whom therefore he sometimes turned back as insufficient, advising them to study the Scriptures for some years longer, before they came for their Degrees, it being a shame for a Professor in Divinity to be unskilled in the Book, wherein the Knowledge of God, and the Grounds of Divinity lay. Whereby he made himself from the beginning hated by the Friars.[6]

The impediments for a ploughboy or any other layman to obtain Bible knowledge in Tyndale's day were daunting. As a result of the Constitutions of Oxford of 1408, it was illegal to translate any portion of the Bible into English without permission from a bishop. This enactment also prohibited anyone from owning such an English Bible. Violation of the law was considered heresy, a crime traditionally punishable by being burned at the stake. It had been passed in reaction to the efforts of John Wycliffe to translate the Bible into English for the people of the nation. In addition to these formidable legal barriers, a ploughboy would simply not be able for practical reasons either to obtain a copy of the Latin Bible or to read it if he could. Moreover, Cardinal Thomas Wolsey issued a general prohibition on May 14, 1521, against any books that proclaimed the doctrines of the Reformation.[7]

Common literacy, a free press, and the free exercise of religion would be needed before an English translation would be practical. All were utterly out of the question when Tyndale declared his purpose to help ploughboys know the Scriptures. Yet he apparently still believed that all these barriers could be overcome and the Bible be made available to all the people of England.

Tyndale's Quest

Tyndale ultimately left the employment of the Walsh family in pursuit of this goal. He went to London to seek an audience with the bishop of London, Cuthbert Tunstall, to obtain permission to translate the New Testament from the original Greek into English. Schooled on the continent and highly admired by some contemporaries as a man of learning and charity, Tunstall was a close friend and supporter of the man whose work had made a fresh translation possible: the great scholar Erasmus.

Looking at the rest of Europe in 1523, Tyndale saw that England stood alone in its lack of a vernacular translation of the Bible. (Wycliffe's earlier translation from Latin was in a form of English so archaic that it was virtually unreadable in the early sixteenth century.) The first vernacular translation were printed in Germany in 1466, France in 1474, Italy in 1471, and Spain (Catalan) in 1478.[8] All these were translated from the Latin Vulgate into the local tongue, but Luther's 1522 New Testament in German was the first translation to be based on the Greek text produced by Erasmus. Erasmus had recently published a New Testament with the original Greek and a new Latin translation in a side-by-side format. His purpose was to provide a new Latin translation of the Bible to replace the venerable but error-ridden Vulgate translated by Jerome in the fourth century. To prove the accuracy of his *Novum Testamentum omne*, Erasmus placed the Greek text alongside the Latin. This Greek text would enable Tyndale to work from the original language into English.

Tyndale's request to Tunstall for permission to translate the New Testament exemplified a certain naiveté that would ultimately prove disastrous.[9] He often approached matters as if all others would make decisions as he did—by simply looking at the Word of God and applying its clear directives to the situation at hand. Tyndale often acted in apparent obliviousness to the political realities of his situation. Tunstall's friendship with Erasmus might have given Tyndale hope that the bishop would be favorable to his request. The Tyndales were also a highly respected and wealthy family of nobility, while Tunstall himself had no such background. These were but few positive factors against so many to the contrary.[10]

Three powerful reasons made it highly unlikely that Tunstall would approve Tyndale's proposition. First, the stigma of the Wycliffe translation was not completely forgotten. Twenty-two Lollards, the followers of Wycliffe, were burned at the stake between 1506 and 1519.[11] Rather than fading from memory, the ashes of the Lollard martyrs were still warm. Second, Tyndale's reputation as a troublemaker in Gloucestershire may well have reached the bishop's ears. Even though he had survived the heresy proceeding, Tyndale had still been charged and was likely viewed as a potentially serious menace to the peace. The third obstacle was the most important: Luther's translation of the New Testament had quickly become synonymous with heresy. Giving sanction to an English Luther was an idea simply not to be countenanced by the Catholic bishop of London.

By the time of Tyndale's request, Luther was considered the arch-heretic in England. In April 1521, Henry VIII began work on a book denouncing Luther. (The king seemed to have an equal passion for intellectual pursuits and frivolous pleasures and was always as eager to read Aquinas or write his own discourses as he was to make merry with the youths in his company.[12]) Henry's book was called *Assertio septem sacramentorum* (i.e, *A Defense of the Seven Sacraments*) and was published that July. Although he likely completed a large part of the work himself, some portions were written by scholars such as Thomas More, who acknowledged a minor role.[13] The book contains scathing personal attacks on Luther, as well as a defense of the Catholic Church's infallibility, the Pope's authority, and the claim that ceremonies and practices based on the oral traditions of the church were from Christ Himself.

Henry wrote of Luther:

> The most greedy wolf of hell has surprised him, devoured and swallowed him down into the lowest part of his belly, where he lies half alive and half dead in death: and whilst the pious pastor calls him, and bewails his loss, he belches out of the filthy mouth of the heathen wolf these foul inveighings, which the ears of the flock detest, disdain and abhor.[14]

The pope was pleased with Henry's attack, awarding him the title *Fidei Defensor*—defender of the faith. The title is still used by the British monarch today, with the abbreviation F.D. appearing on modern coins of the realm.

In 1522, Luther replied to the king, somewhat intemperately himself, calling the king "more a trivial buffoon than a king," among other *ad hominem* attacks.[15] Thomas More was given the task of replying to Luther, and he set to work on this task in early 1523. More's replies to Luther were vicious, though sometimes expressed in humorous mocking, and laced with scatological attacks that sound more like a twenty-first century comedian too filthy for network television than a sixteenth-century saint:

> Since he has written that he already has a prior right to bespatter and besmirch the royal crown with s***, we will not have the posterior right to proclaim the bes****ed tongue of this practitioner of posterioristics most fit to lick with his anterior the very

posterior of a p***ing she-mule until he have learned more correctly to infer posterior conclusions from prior premises.[16]

C. S. Lewis rightly described More as almost obsessed with harping
on Luther's "abominable bichery" to the point where he "loses himself in a
wilderness of opprobrious adjectives."[17]

In this atmosphere, there was no chance that Tyndale's request, made in
the spring of 1523, would be granted. Tunstall turned Tyndale down with
some formal courtesies but little warmth. Tyndale later wrote:

> And so in London I abode almost a year, and marked the
> course of the world . . . and saw things whereof I defer to speak
> at this time and understood at the last not only that there was
> no room in my lord of London's palace to translate the New
> Testament, but also that there was no place to do it in all England,
> as experience doth now openly declare.[18]

Tyndale left for the continent, intent on finding a place to translate the
Bible into English in order to send the printed Word of God back to ploughboys, laborers, merchants, and even the clerics of England. The first stops
on his journey are not known with certainty, but he ended up in Cologne,
Germany. The details of his early work in translating the New Testament
are also obscure, but Tyndale was engaged in the actual printing of the first
twenty-two chapters of the book of Matthew during the summer of 1525.
After receiving a threat from a Catholic spy, he and an assistant were forced
to leave Cologne immediately with their printed sheets and manuscripts.
This was no mere act of paranoia but a response to a genuine danger.
Escaping to Worms, Tyndale successfully completed and printed his first
translation of the New Testament early in 1526. Copies of Tyndale's work
were openly sold in London by February of the same year.

Book Burning and Heretic Hunting

On February 11, a large anti-Luther demonstration was held at St. Paul's
Cathedral, complete with the burning of Luther's books and copies of his
translation of the New Testament. The books had been seized in a raid led by
Thomas More on a German section of London. More arrested three heretics
on the spot and returned the following day for further searches.[19] Sometime in
March, officials became aware that a new source of heresy was in circulation:
Tyndale's English New Testament printed without any of the traditional indi-
cia of the translator or publisher. Cardinal Wolsey, who as vice-regent often
seemed more in charge of the nation than Henry VIII, convened the bishops

Page from the book of Acts in the 1536 edition of Tyndale's translation of the New Testament, *The Newe testament yet once agayne corrected by William Tyndale*; courtesy of Bodleian Library, University of Oxford, Douce N. T. Eng. F. 1536, image 212.

that summer to consider the new threat. Unsurprisingly, they concluded that the "error-ridden" translation (of Tyndale) should be burned. Orders were issued to booksellers to stop selling the work. In connection with a public burning of copies of the English New Testament, Bishop Tunstall preached a sermon at St. Paul's on October 26 denouncing the translation as having more than two thousand errors—a highly unlikely claim, given the

painstaking and thorough process Tyndale endured throughout its preparation as well as the esteem with which later scholars have viewed his work.[20]

At first, officials seemed content to find books and burn them. But it
would not be long before the 150-year tradition of hunting, arresting, and
burning the Lollards began to be applied to the Lutherans and others coming to a new form of Christian faith after reading the New Testament in
English. The first notable arrest was that of Thomas Bilney in November
1527 in Cambridge. Bilney, a scholar trained in both civil and canon law,
renounced his newfound faith but was nevertheless imprisoned in the
Tower of London for twelve months starting that December. In the words
of David Daniell, the highly esteemed Tyndale biographer, Bilney's arrest
"heralded an onslaught," and Tunstall's prisons were full beyond capacity
by March.[21] Many of those arrested recanted their heresy; and many, like
Bilney, seemed genuinely confused since still they held to many central
Catholic doctrines, including the doctrine of transubstantiation and the
authority of the pope.

John Tewkesbury, a leather seller (according to martyrologist Foxe)
or a haberdasher (according to seventeenth-century historian Strype), was
one of those arrested in this wave of heretic hunting. In April 1529, he was
twice examined by Tunstall and subsequently taken by Thomas More to his
house in Chelsea, where he was so badly tortured at the rack that he was
nearly unable to walk. He recanted his new faith but later abjured and was
burned at the stake. Foxe reports that this tradesman was so well versed in
"the doctrine of justification and all other articles of faith . . . that Tunstall
and all his learned men, were ashamed that a leather-seller should so dispute
with them, and with such power of the Scriptures and heavenly wisdom, that
they were not able to resist him."[22] With a boldness reminiscent of that of
Peter and John when they stood before the religious authorities of their day,
Tewkesbury caused his persecutors to marvel. This episode demonstrated
that Tyndale was already succeeding in his mission to train the common,
laboring class to be superior to the professional clerics in scriptural understanding.

In addition to his heresy for possessing and knowing the Bible in
English, Tewkesbury was also closely examined on Tyndale's second important work, a book entitled *The Treatise of the Wicked Mammon*. This treatise
expounds upon the central Reformation doctrine of justification by faith,
warning readers that many "philosophers and worldly wise men" have arisen
who hold to the "belief that they shall be justified in the sight of God by
the goodness of their own works and have corrupt[ed] the pure word of
God to confirm their Aristotle."[23] *Wicked Mammon* was printed in Antwerp

(where Tyndale had moved) on May 8, 1528, and was distributed in England soon thereafter.

Two Men and Their Missions

In that fateful year of 1528, Henry's highest officials were vigilantly engaged in the discovery, arrest, prosecution, torture, and imprisonment of heretics. Six years earlier the king had intemperately castigated Luther, but now Lutheran heretics suffered from far more than a war of words. Some of Henry's officials—particularly Thomas More—sincerely believed they were serving God as they brutalized religious dissenters.

Henry began to be distracted. A young woman entered the swirl of court life who captured the king's complete attention. For several years she had lived in the French court as an attendant of Henry's sister, Mary, the wife of Louis XII. The attendant's name was Anne Boleyn.

Tyndale was on a mission to educate all men in the rich truths of the Bible so that they would know God; Henry was on an entirely different mission—one driven by ego and hormones. The well-known story of his lust and power had an incredible impact on the role of the Bible in England and the Western world. As when Joseph's brothers sold him into slavery in Egypt, however, evil may have been intended, but God caused the good ultimately to prevail.

Chapter Two

THE KING, THE POPE, AND THE WORD

Henry's Great Matrimonial Cause

"This fellow Cranmer has the right sow by the ear."

HENRY VIII

atherine of Aragon was seven years old when Christopher Columbus departed from the court of her parents, Ferdinand and Isabella, headed for the New World. Several years earlier, at age three, she had been betrothed to marry Arthur, the crown prince of England. She was about ten months his senior. Arthur and Catherine were married on November 14, 1501, when both were a mere fifteen years old. Arthur died six months after their wedding day, leaving Catherine in a difficult position for several years while her superiors deliberated about how and with whom her future should be spent. Catherine steadfastly claimed that her marriage had never been consummated, which had significant implications for her marital eligibility.

Arthur's younger brother Henry was not quite eleven when the crown prince died. Characteristically, King Henry VII promised the young widow that she could marry his second son when he was of age. If her first marriage had never been consummated, no religious law would have forbidden Catherine from marrying Henry since the first marriage would be viewed as a nullity. Nevertheless, to remove any doubt—and at the insistence of

Catherine's mother, Isabella—the pope issued a special decree authorizing the second marriage. But by the time the younger Henry was old enough to marry (or at least old enough by the standards of European royalty), his father had lost interest in a political alliance with Spain. Henry VII consequently forbade the marriage with Catherine.

Just a few years later, the king died, and in 1509 the newly crowned Henry VIII married Catherine of Aragon. She was twenty-three years old. Henry was just shy of his eighteenth birthday and the seeming epitome of English royalty. Catherine was likewise praised by contemporaries for her "mind and goodness" and exalted as an example of a godly and able queen.[1] Henry and Catherine were, of course, devout Catholics.

Although the couple was said to have had happy early years together, Henry apparently took many lovers during his marriage to Catherine— including Mary Boleyn, the sister of Anne Boleyn—and all hope that she would bear her husband a son ended an unfulfilled dream. Henry and Catherine had one surviving child—a daughter named Mary.

They were nineteen years into their marriage when Anne Boleyn first appeared in the British court in 1528. For several years Anne had served as an aide to Henry's sister, who was married to the king of France. When Henry tried to secure Anne Boleyn as yet another lover, she refused to be a mere mistress but made clear that she was willing to be his queen. The allure of the unobtainable Anne led Henry to seek a divorce. His lust for Anne conveniently coincided with his frustration with Catherine's inability to give birth to a male heir—a problem that was not likely to be remedied with the passing of time as Catherine was nearly forty-three when Anne surfaced in the court. However, Henry would need permission from the pope since divorce was not normally permitted by Catholic doctrine.

The pope faced a couple of major difficulties in granting Henry's wishes, even if he had desired to permit the king to have a second wife. First, the only basis upon which he could grant an annulment—divorce was never a real possibility—was that Henry was ineligible to marry Catherine since she had been his brother's wife. This theory was based on a scriptural passage forbidding one man from having sexual relations with his brother's wife. Although it was facially doubtful that this passage was talking about remarriage of a widow, the important thing for the story of religious liberty is that Henry asserted that he should not have been allowed to marry Catherine in the first place because it was in violation of the standards of the Bible. Since he had received a papal dispensation to marry her, granting his present wish would require a tacit acknowledgement that the Bible was superior to the edicts of the pope—an outcome that was not likely to occur.

Even though Henry had dispatched the ultra-powerful Cardinal Thomas Wolsley to make his appeal to the pontiff, there were pressing practical reasons that prevented the pope from granting Henry's wish. Among other factors, Rome was in serious distress because Charles V, the Holy Roman emperor, and his military forces were occupying the city. Even though Charles was a devout Catholic, as were the majority of his German troops, the city was in chaos. In a recent biography of Tyndale, Brian Monynahan describes the scene:

> [The troops] did delight in humbling the pope and his priests.
> Blasphemers in the Eternal City, they wore cardinals' robes,
> drank from sacred chalices, stabled their horses in St. Peter's and
> the Sistine Chapel, daubed Luther's name on paintings, stole
> jewels and offerings from the shrines, and, tearing the bones of
> saints from reliquaries, threw them for dogs to devour. Cardinal
> Giovanni del Monte, the future Pope Julius III, was hung by his
> hair until a ransom was paid for him.[2]

Wolsley: *Ipse Rex*

Although Wolsley held incredible power and wealth, his own fate and the fate of the Catholic Church in England became tied to his efforts to secure a papal sanction for Henry's annulment.

An examination of Wolsley's career reveals a remarkable rise through the ranks of England's church as well as the royal court. He was born a butcher's son but received an education at Magdalen College, Oxford—some years before Tyndale's schooling there—and received his degree at a young age, earning him the title "boy-bachelor."[3] He was ordained a priest and became a chaplain at the royal court sometime around 1507. Along the way Wolsey amassed an amazing fortune that rivaled that of the king. Part of this fortune came from the practice of awarding leading clerics multiple offices from which were obtained multiple salaries.

While holding royal office, Wolsley simultaneously held church positions at Hereford Cathedral, Limington in Somerset, Redgrave in Suffolk, Lydd in Kent, and Torrington in Devonshire, among others.[4] This does not mean that Wolsley actively preached or shepherded these congregations or dioceses; the typical practice was similar to that of an absentee landlord: collecting lucrative salaries while providing little, if any, direct service. Wolsey was not alone in this practice. For example, Tyndale's home of Gloucester county contained the diocese of Worcester, which was among the most abused bishoprics in England. Few of its principal pastors had lived there since 1476, and after 1512 "the diocese had enjoyed three Italian bishops, who lived at ease in Rome, and never set foot in England at all, yet drawing meanwhile, ample stipends."[5]

On November 18, 1515, Wolsley was consecrated a cardinal at a ceremony in Westminster Abbey and just over a month later, on December 24, was made the lord chancellor of England—the highest rank in the land other than king. It is said that "his power with the king was so great that the Venetian Ambassador said he now might be called '*Ipse rex*' (the king himself)."[6] Wolsley had tried to climb an even higher ladder: he was twice considered for election as pope between 1521 and 1523 but failed on both occasions because of intrigues involving the Holy Roman emperor, Charles V.

For all of his influence and accomplishment, Wolsley's downfall came as the result of his inability to deliver a papal decree allowing Henry to divorce Catherine of Aragon. The final episode in the series of frustrating failures was an ecclesiastical trial sanctioned by Pope Clement VII to determine the legality of Henry's first marriage. Cardinal Campeggio was appointed along with Wolsley to decide the matter as a legatine court—that is, a court empowered to act in the name of the pope and with his full authority. Campeggio, however, was under papal instruction to delay the matter as long as possible.

Having arrived at Dover on September 20, 1528, the cardinal proved himself to be a master of delay. He first met with Henry to try to convince him to reconcile with Catherine, but the monarch made clear that he would accept nothing less than annulment. Campeggio then tried to persuade Catherine to retire to a convent, which would have given Henry a different, yet authorized, ground for a divorce. She refused his request in a meeting held in late October.

Henry decided to apply pressure of his own on the queen. In November she was prohibited from seeing her daughter, Mary, as punishment for refusing to obey the king. In January 1529, Catherine challenged the jurisdiction of the legatine court, demanding that the matter be transferred to Rome for a personal decision by the pope. Despite her pleas the trial finally began at Blackfriars, a Dominican monastery at Oxford, on June 18, 1529. Henry argued that his failure to have a male heir was the result of God's punishment for having violated God's law by marrying his sister. This was not the only time that Henry employed this argument, under the pretense of a grief-stricken conscience from the sin of marrying his brother's wife. If he had also expressed grief over his many acts of adultery and had Anne Boleyn not been waiting in the wings, perhaps Henry's pangs of conscience could be given more credence.

Catherine again challenged the jurisdiction of the legatine court, but this motion was denied. She then argued that she had never consummated her marriage with Henry's brother and steadfastly defended her marriage to Henry. After being rebuffed on a second motion to have the matter removed to Rome for trial, Catherine left the hearing for good. On July 16, however, the pope granted her wish and ordered the trial moved to Rome—a decision that infuriated Henry, especially when he was summoned in August to appear before the pope in Rome.

Quieting the King's Conscience

In the midst of this messy, soap opera-like intrigue, Henry was offered an alternative path to dissolve his marriage with Catherine. A new approach had been suggested by Thomas Cranmer, a Cambridge scholar and priest who heretofore had not been associated with the cadre of clerics serving in Henry's royal court.

Cranmer had been trained in divinity at Cambridge, a training that was unusual in his day. He spent three years in the study of Scripture to determine if the claims of Luther were true. His motive was uncommon, as was his intensive study of the Bible, even among those seeking advanced degrees in divinity. As we saw earlier, Cranmer introduced the practice of questioning Cambridge divinity students on their knowledge of Scripture. As a leading scholar at the university, he was appointed to serve on one of the panels of clerics that were consulted about the religious question of the king's "great matrimonial cause." Cranmer, however, had left the university because of an outbreak of the plague and was not present at the university at the time needed.[7] The remaining religious scholars at both Oxford and Cambridge unanimously concluded that the marriage was lawful, and thus could not be dissolved, because it had been sanctioned by the pope.

A short time later, two of Henry's chief aides—his almoner, Edward Fox, and his clerk, Stephen Gardiner (a person who would figure prominently in the reign of Bloody Mary)—happened to meet Cranmer at a home in Essex. They posed their theological questions concerning the lawfulness of the marriage to the Cambridge man. Obviously, Fox and Gardiner were looking for a way to provide theological cover for the outcome desired by Henry. Cranmer delighted them with his reply. He argued for the supremacy of Scripture over a decree of the pope and suggested a new methodology for making the determination of the king's "great Matter."

Submit the question to the professors of religion at the great colleges of Europe, Cranmer argued. Since they were trained to understand the

Bible, they could give the best advice on the meaning of Scripture. Then the king could receive their scriptural interpretations and decide for himself whether the Word of God permitted him to marry Catherine in the first place.[8] This was a truly radical idea, and it was well received by the king. Cranmer was immediately brought before the royal court. The seventeenth-century historian strype describes Henry's reaction to this new scholar: "Having heard him discourse upon the Marriage, and well observing the Gravity and Modesty, as well as Learning of the Man, [the king] resolved to cherish and make much of him. This was about August 1529, the King having commanded him to digest in Writing, what he could say upon the foresaid Argument."[9] Strype is eloquent in his description. Henry is more earthy. This fellow Cranmer, the king said, had "the right sow by the ear."[10] Cranmer was thus commissioned to write a book on the lawfulness of the marriage, which would then be reviewed by other university professors to collectively advise the king. Cranmer's book argued that the Bible made clear that no man could marry his brother's wife and that the "Bishop of Rome by no means ought to dispense to the contrary."[11]

While writing his book, Cranmer was assigned to live in the home of one of his noblemen: Thomas Boleyn, the father of Anne. Boleyn was doubly sympathetic to Cranmer's approach. Obviously, he was in favor of his daughter's marriage to the king. Boleyn also appeared to have a previous love and appreciation for the Scriptures. Strype records of Boleyn, "He was also much addicted to the Study and Love of the Holy Scriptures, as the same *Erasmus* in an Epistle to him mentioneth, and commendeth him for."[12] Boleyn had also been a patron of Erasmus, commissioning three of his publications. While he was in this home, "a great Friendship was contracted between [Cranmer] and that Noble Family; especially the chief Members of it, the Countess, and the Lady *Ann*, and the Earl himself."[13] It is well-known that Anne had strong Protestant leanings which she would, in due course, bring to bear upon Henry. The period of time she spent with the learned Protestant theologian in her own family home appears to have been a significant force in the development of such views.

Cranmer's ideas had an even more radical implication which he may have realized but certainly did not disclose: If the king of England could decide what was right in God's eyes after consulting with Scripture, then so could any other person. Not only did Cranmer express an idea that led to the supremacy of the king over the pope, but it was also fully consonant with the idea being expressed at the same time by Tyndale—that each man could come directly to God through faith in Jesus Christ, guided by the final authority of the Word of God.

The Rise of Thomas More

Thomas Cranmer and his notions came to Henry's attention sometime in the fall of 1529, coinciding with the king's growing impatience with his pompous Cardinal Wolsley. Failing to achieve Henry's desires with Rome, Wolsley was removed from office on October 18. Eight days later, Thomas More, who had served in a variety of increasingly important offices, was appointed the Lord Chancellor of England. Even though More was a thoroughly devout Catholic, as he was later to prove with his own life, he became lord chancellor just as the king began to pursue Cranmer's theory of the supremacy of Scripture over Rome.

The king and queen were fond of More's company because of both his scholarly knowledge and "merry and pleasant disposition."[14] Both of these characteristics were in fact present in More from a young age. As a youth he would give witty and articulate *ex tempore* performances in the middle of Christmastide plays held at the cardinal's house where he boarded, causing the cardinal to predict that, in time, More would "prove a marvelous Man."[15]

Deep Catholic devotion on the part of the new lord chancellor, however, was not enough to keep England within Rome's grasp forever. In November 1529, Parliament passed the first in the series of Acts that eventually led to the break with the pope and the church in Rome. This bill was relatively modest in scope and aimed at curing some of the worst abuses of the church practices. For example, no person could hold more than four church offices at once—a practice that would have cramped the ability of the favored clergy, like Wolsley, to amass vast personal wealth.

Meanwhile, in early 1530, Henry dispatched Cranmer to the continent "to dispute these Matrimonial matters of his Majesty at Paris, Rome, and other places."[16] Although politics and bribes may have helped to pave the way, Cranmer must have been incredibly persuasive in his disputations, as evidenced by a book entitled *The determinations of the most famous and most excellent universities of Italy and France, that it is so unlawful for a man to marry his brother's wife, that the pope hath no power to dispense therewith.*[17] This volume records the decisions by the faculties of divinity at seven French and Italian universities—all of which supported the key principles of Cranmer's argument: that Scripture prohibited the marriage of a brother's wife and that the pope had no authority to override Scripture.

Henry's matrimonial cause had the potential to engulf all of Europe in an ideological dispute that could undermine the dominance of the Roman Church by the simple assertion that Scripture is supreme over the authority of the Roman Church. Obviously, this idea was being promulgated elsewhere by Luther for entirely different purposes. And this is not to say that Henry or his new lord chancellor was warm to the ideas of the reformers; indeed, Thomas More had aided Henry about seven years earlier in his celebrated book castigating Luther. And More had already begun to take up the pen against William Tyndale in one of the most celebrated theological debates of all time—a matter we will consider in full in the next chapter. For the moment, More was willing to walk the tightrope between the king and the pope.

The Break with Rome

Henry VIII might never have pursued breaking with the Catholic Church if he could have obtained papal sanction to divorce Catherine. Yet even though no genuine resolution between the king and the pope was truly possible, Henry and Clement VII chose not to engage in meaningful diplomacy but rather proceeded to exchange hostile proclamations that served only to harden their mutual opposition.

In December 1530, Clement ordered Henry to Rome to answer Catherine's appeal of his proposed divorce. The next month the pope added a second official demand that Henry have no contact with Anne. Henry retaliated in February by securing an act from Parliament that declared him the "Supreme Head and Sole Protector" of the Church of England. Despite this clear denial of papal authority, Thomas More continued to serve as lord chancellor for fifteen more months—a position that allowed him to conduct a vicious purge of Protestant dissenters.

Pope Clement declared in January 1532 that the appeal of Henry's request for a divorce would be postponed for yet another year. In March, Henry responded by gaining parliamentary approval to reduce severely the payment of "annates"[18] to the pope. He suspended the operation of this act which, in effect, dangled the purse before the pope. The financial threat produced no positive response from Rome, so in May 1532 Henry forced a Convocation of the Church of England—the body that had the authority to make canonical law—to agree to a document known as "the Submission of the Clergy."[19] It should be remembered that the Convocation was the body that had issued the Constitution of Oxford of 1408, which banned the printing or possession of an English Bible. Any new proclamations of this sort would now require the approval of the king. This proved too much for Thomas More. The next day he resigned as lord chancellor of England.

Sometime in December 1532, Anne apparently succumbed to Henry's sexual demands because in January she informed the king that she was pregnant. It is generally thought that she and the king were married secretly on

January 25. In the spring Henry used Parliament to terminate Catherine's appeal to the pope. On April 7, Parliament passed the Act in Restraint of Appeals, which forbade the appeal of religious matters to any foreign tribunal. On April 12, Thomas Cranmer, now the archibishop of Canterbury, was officially authorized to determine the legality of Henry's marriage to Catherine—a decision that was a foregone conclusion given Cranmer's longstanding view on the matter. Also, the mere fact that Cranmer was appointed archbishop was a de facto break with Rome. Cranmer, who had been widowed as a young man, had remarried, and a married archbishop was by definition a Protestant cleric.

On May 13, Cranmer declared the marriage between Henry and Catherine to have been void from the beginning because it was contrary to God's law. One of the most significant consequences of this decision was that their daughter, Mary, was thereby determined to be an illegitimate child—a stigma that would greatly embitter her and drive her even deeper into her devotion to the Catholic faith. Mary, known to posterity as "Bloody Mary" for her actions that would follow after Henry's death, for now lost her title as princess and was referred to instead simply as "Lady Mary." Furthermore, a new princess was born four months after Cranmer's declaration: On September 7, 1533, Anne gave birth to Elizabeth, who would eventually rule England as Elizabeth I.

Chapter Three

WAR OF THE WORDS

Skirmishes over the Vernacular Bible

And now the spirit of error and lying hath taken his
wretched soul with him straight from the short fire
to the fire everlasting.

Sir Thomas More, describing the execution of
a man for owning a Tyndale New Testament

Thomas More and William Tyndale would engage in one of the most prolific debates in human history; more than a million words were exchanged in less than five years. Most of these came from the sarcastic, and often vile pen of Saint Sir Thomas More. From 1529 to 1533, More wrote three tomes aimed at discrediting Tyndale, resulting in an explosive series of charges and countercharges. The first work contains four books with a total of seventy-seven chapters, the second has nine books (the modern version constitutes a three-volume set), and the third is fifty chapters long. In response to More's *Dialogue Concerning Heresies*, Tyndale wrote *An answere unto Sir Thomas Mores dialoge* in 1531. More's *Confutation* follows a common pattern of the time in which he quotes a passage from Tyndale's *Answer* and then follows it by a lengthy opposing argument. The two men debated a whole range of doctrinal issues, but the central dispute concerned the role of Scripture and the propriety of an English translation.

It is a massive understatement to say that neither was cordial to the other; harsh attacks were employed by both. This is not to say, however, that the written works were equal—either in length or abusive language. Tyndale slips in an occasional verbal jab with a harsh epithet, while More spews hundreds of words at a time that hardly bear any semblance to his reputation as a humanist scholar. To use another description by C. S. Lewis, More "cannot denounce like a prophet; he can only scold and grumble like a father in an old-fashioned comedy."[1] For example, More described the effect of Tyndale's and Luther's books on readers with these words:

> So great a pestilent pleasure have some devilish people caught, with the labor, travail, cost, charge, peril, harm, and hurt of them self, to seek the destruction of other. As the devil hath a deadly delight to beguile good people, and bring their souls into everlasting torment without any manner winning, and not without final increase of his own eternal pain: so do these heretics the devil's disciples beset their whole pleasure and study to their own final damnation, in the training of simple souls to hell by their devilish heresies.[2]

By contrast, anyone who spends time reading Tyndale will discover the aptness of David Daniell's analysis: "Every phrase comes from a mind steeped in both Testaments. . . . The steady beat of Scripture sounds throughout Tyndale's book. Scripture's phrases and echoes are everywhere, and there is hardly a page without two or three quotations at least."[3] The dangerous and demanding work of Bible translation had driven its words deep into Tyndale's soul as he labored to find the best English equivalent for each phrase from the original languages.

The most readily accessible example of Tyndale's writing is *The Obedience of a Christian Man*, newly edited by Daniell. Consider one example to see the magnificence of Tyndale's mastery of scriptural phrases:

> Husbands, love your wives, as Christ loved the congregation, and gave himself for it, to sanctify it and cleanse it. Men ought to love their wives as their own bodies. For this cause shall a man leave father and mother and shall continue with his wife and shall be made both one flesh. See that every one of you love his wife even as his own body: All this saith Paul (Ephesians 5 and Colossians 4). He saith husbands love your wives and be not bitter unto them, and Peter in the third chapter of his first epistle saith, men dwell with your wives according to knowledge (that is according to the doctrine of Christ) giving reverence unto the wife,

as unto the weaker vessel (that is, help her to bear her infirmities) and as unto them that are heirs also of the grace of life, that your prayers be not let. In many things God hath made the men stronger than the women, not to rage upon them and to be tyrants unto them but to help them to bear their weakness. Be courteous therefore unto them and win them unto Christ and overcome them with kindness, that of love they may obey the ordinance that God hath made between man and wife.[4]

The reader is left with no doubt that this was the man who crafted scores of the familiar phrases later to appear in the King James Bible, such as "let there be light," "fight the good fight," "a law unto themselves," and "the powers that be."

Thomas More, on the other hand, almost never quotes Scripture. He asserts the statements of Scripture in indirect paraphrases, and then only infrequently. For example, in his *Confutation*, he has but ten indirect references to specific passages in the Bible in his forty-page introductory argument.[5]

Although More was one of the ablest minds of his day and his logic sometimes clearly gets the better of Tyndale, his use of Scripture in argument is superficial at best. When Tyndale argued that "the pith and substance in general of every thing necessary to our souls' health, both of what we ought to believe, and what we ought to do was written"[6] in the Bible, More counters with an argument of the supremacy of the Roman Church over Scripture:

We say that since our savior hath him self promised in the gospel, that him self and his holy spirit shall be with his church all days unto the end of the world: yet followeth say we thereof, that his church shall never fail as long as the world lasteth. And because our savior saith in likewise, that his holy spirit ever abiding in his church, shall teach his church all things, and lead them into every truth, and put them in remembrance of all that he himself had or would say unto them: we deduce thereupon yet he will not suffer his church to fall in to the erroneous belief of any damnable untruth / but lead them into the truth yet is the contrary of that untruth. And since he said not the holy ghost shall write unto you all things, nor shall write you all truth / but shall lead you into all truth: we deduce thereupon that the belief where into the spirit of god leadeth us and planteth it in our heart, is as good and as sure to salvation of our souls without any writing at all, as if it were written in parchment with golden letters and Christ's own hand.[7]

More made a fascinating suggestion to his readers to help them resolve whether he or Tyndale was correct on these issues. In the paragraph after the one previously quoted, More tells his readers that "every man may see that we draw it not far off, but that the scripture well and clearly maintaineth our deducting thereof."[8] It is a mystery how the reader was supposed to evaluate More's argument. Owning a Bible in English was a crime. Few could read Latin, and fewer yet had immediate access to the Latin text. And More himself was the very person vigorously hunting to discover and exterminate those who possessed the very book they would need to validate his argument. A Bible was simply too dangerous for the common people, More believed.

This leads to the central question: What justification did Tyndale offer for a vernacular translation? And why did More think that it was dangerous for the English public to have a Bible in their own language?

Tyndale's Argument for the Bible in English

Tyndale made an extensive argument for the propriety of translating Scripture into the mother tongue of his people in *Obedience of a Christian Man*. He begins with a criticism of the Catholic Church's motives in denying such freedom:

> That thou mayest perceive how that the scripture ought to
> be in the mother tongue and that the reasons which our [spiritual
> leaders] make for the contrary are but sophistry and false wiles to
> fear thee from the light, that thou mightest follow them blindfold
> and be their captive, to honor their ceremonies and to offer to
> their belly.[9]

This theme is important to Tyndale's argument. Throughout his writings he demonstrates how the ceremonies that the Roman Church contends were revealed by God to the church authorities are better understood as money-making opportunities for the clergy. The sale of indulgences is the best known of these practices. People are denied the freedom to know God's Word, Tyndale suggests, because if they could read it for themselves they would stop paying for religious services that are contrary to the teaching of Scripture.

After this criticism Tyndale's positive argument for a vernacular translation begins with Scripture: "First God gave the children of Israel a law by the hand of Moses in their mother tongue."[10] Following this is a quotation from Deuteronomy 6 concerning Israel's duty to teach God's Word to their children: "Hear Israel let these words which I command thee this day stick fast in thine heart, and whet them on thy children and talk of them as thou sittest in thine house, and as thou walkest by the way."[11] He then comments, "This was commanded generally unto all men. How cometh it that God's word pertaineth less unto us than unto them? . . . How can we whet God's word (that is put it in practice, use and exercise) upon our children and household, when we are violently kept from it and know it not?"[12]

Anticipating the arguments of More and others, Tyndale answers this criticism: "If the scripture were in the mother tongue they will say, then would the lay people understand it every man after his own ways."[13] Tyndale suggests that this would be no problem if the teachers were honest with their use of the Word although in reality the priests were "abominable schoolmasters." "If ye would teach," he asks, "how could ye do it so well and with so great profit, as when the lay people have the scripture before them in their mother tongue? For then should they see by the order of the text, whether thou jugglest or not. And then would they believe it, because it is the scripture of God."[14] Rather than promoting the idea of spiritual anarchy, Tyndale's purpose in having men read the Bible was to help them know God and obey His precepts. He emphasized that "we may apply the medicine of scripture, every man to his own sores" and that, in the Bible, "thou shalt find therein spirit and life and edifying."[15]

After presenting these proofs drawn from the Old Testament, Tyndale then turns to the New with the declaration, "Christ commandeth to search the scriptures (John 5)."[16] Moreover, Tyndale notes that when Paul preached to the Berean church, as recorded in Acts 17, the people "searched the scriptures daily, whether they were as he alleged them."[17] Then he makes the obvious comparison: "Why shall not I likewise, whether it be the scripture that thou allegest? . . . Or whether thou be about to teach me or to deceive me."[18]

Tyndale's argument goes to the heart of the principle of freedom of conscience: every man has the right to look in the Word of God and decide for himself whether what is being taught is true. Although Tyndale's arguments are directed against the church hierarchy, there are clear political implications as well:

> Now when we look on your deeds, we see that ye are all sworn together and have separated yourselves from the lay people, and have a several kingdom among yourselves and several laws of your own making, wherewith ye violently bind the lay people that never consented unto the making of them.[19]

Here Tyndale not only advocates freedom of conscience, as well as the related rights of freedom to speak and to publish, but also endorses the ultimate principle of democracy in which all laws require the consent of the laypeople.

In a later section entitled "The duty of kings and judges and officers," Tyndale advances several other principles that we recognize as parallel to provisions within the American Bill of Rights. Judges should not, he says, "break up into the consciences of men, after the example of Antichrist's disciples, and compel them either to forswear themselves by the almighty God and by the holy gospel of his merciful promises or to testify against themselves."[20] He also argues for equal protection and due process for all—including those of completely different faiths:

> Moses (Deuteronomy 17) warneth judges to keep them upright
> and to look on no man's person, that is, that they prefer not the
> high before the low, the great before the small, the rich before the
> poor, his acquaintance, friend, kinsman, countryman or one of his
> own nation before a stranger, a friend or an alien; yea, or one of
> their own faith before an infidel: but that they look on the cause
> only to judge indifferently.[21]

His basis for advocating this advanced form of equal justice was that all men are "under the testament of the law natural which is the laws of every land made for the common wealth there and for peace and unity that one may live by another."[22] Using Scripture alone, he reached the conclusion that God demands religious equality before the law. Thus, "whosoever therefore hindereth a very infidel from the right of that law, sinneth against God and of him will God be avenged."[23]

Tyndale's concepts of law by consent of the governed, even-handed justice, religious equality before the law, due process, fair trials, the freedom to speak, publish, and to decide for one's self the truth about God were prescient and profound. He advanced these concepts into the English system at a time when, at least in practice, they were utterly foreign. These conclusions were the necessary outgrowth of his belief that men should have the Scripture in their own language so they could come to God directly as individuals by their own choice rather than according to the dictates of either government or the hierarchical church.

More's Opposition to the Bible in English

More made a frontal attack on Tyndale's argument. "Of all wretches," he wrote, "worst shall he walk that, forcing [caring] little of the faith of Christ's church, cometh to the scripture of God, to look and try therein whether the church believe aright or not."[24] Tyndale's translation of the New Testament was labeled the "father" of all "evil sects," worse than all the heretical books in Latin, French, and "Douch."[25]

In More's view anything that questioned the Catholic Church was anathema. His vehemence was so extreme on this point that he repeatedly suggests it would be better if the Bible had never been written since it was being used to question the Roman Church:

> And finally thus ye see that Tyndale and such other as would have us reject and refuse all that God hath taught his church, but if it be proved by scripture: be not only unable to prove or defend that heresy / but also do handle the scripture itself in such a shameful wise, that if other men whom they reprove did not handle it better, it had been better to have left all together unwritten, and never had scripture at all.[26]

Again, More wrote: "Then have we from Tyndale the first epistle of saint John in such wise expounded, that I dare say that blessed apostle rather than his holy words were in such a sense believed of all Christian people, had lever [rather] his epistle had never been put in writing."[27]

When Tyndale read these words of More, he may well have recalled his early confrontation back in his days at Little Sodbury with the traveling cleric who declared, "We were better to be without God's laws than the pope's!"

More goes on to argue that Tyndale's translation contained heresies because the words he used called into question doctrines of the Catholic Church.[28] This was not a mere conjecture, the lord chancellor reasoned, because the remainder of Tyndale's writings revealed his heretical intent. More boldly claims that if another man, without heretical intent, had made the same translation, it would be "without evil meaning or suggestion thereof."[29] Tyndale's heretical intent "was the very thing for which his translation was very well worthy to be burned."[30]

Although Bishop Tunstall made preposterous claims of thousands of errors in Tyndale's translation, and although More treats Tyndale's work as being utterly beyond redemption, More's substantive criticism of the translation boils down to six disputed words. Among the foremost of these is Tyndale's translation of the Greek word *ecclesia* as "congregation" rather than "church." This, of course, was a crucial matter because the Catholic claim to a worldwide hierarchical structure would evaporate if indeed Scripture introduced the idea that a church is a local, independent congregation.

In Tyndale's *Answer*, he makes some interesting arguments about the Greek word *ecclesia*. Before the era of the apostles, *ecclesia* was used by Greek authors to indicate an assembly or congregation of people. Moreover,

Tyndale points out that in Acts 19 Luke uses the word *ecclesia* three times to describe the pagan mob in Ephesus that rioted in the defense of the goddess Diana and threatened to kill the apostle Paul and his companions.[31]

Jesus used this Greek word only three times. One instance is in the famous reference to Peter where He says, "On this rock I will build my *ecclesia*." The other uses are both in Matthew 18:17, where Jesus tells his disciples how to resolve disputes among themselves. Tyndale did not argue that *ecclesia* always meant local congregations; he believed it had a variety of meanings. Sometimes it indicated a local congregation, and on other occasions it was the whole body of true believers. More insisted that *ecclesia* was *always* properly understood to mean the Roman Catholic Church—a hard argument in light of its application to the Ephesian mob in Acts 19.

The second challenged word, *presbyter* in Greek, was initially translated as "senior" by Tyndale, but in his later editions he corrected it to the word "elder." More was incensed that Tyndale failed to use the word "priest" instead. If Tyndale was right, the office of human priest does not explicitly exist in the New Testament—a development that would counter the foundation of the Catholic clerical structure.

Likewise the dispute over the Greek word *agape* had serious implications for Catholic practices. Translated "charity," as More desired, the word has clear financial implications. If Tyndale is correct and the word is rendered "love," then 1 Corinthians 13 indicates that the highest duty of the Christian is to love others rather than to give gifts of charity to the church. The other challenged words were Tyndale's translation of "favor" for "grace," "knowledge" for "confession," and "repentance" for "penance"—the latter two with clear implications for Catholic practices.

More was known as a humanist scholar because earlier in his career he supported the "new learning"—that is, the classical revival that challenged the traditions of scholasticism. Scholasticism had produced some notably perverse arguments, such as one that centered on the doctrine of transubstantiation—the belief that the bread in the Lord's Supper becomes the literal body of Christ during the Mass—and asked whether Christ's body was clothed or unclothed after the bread had been transformed.[32] After an incident at Oxford in which one scholastic called the new Greek lecturers "archdevils," More wrote to the Oxford authorities and pleaded with them to curtail the older crowd who were supposedly "cavorting, guffawing and monkeying around in the pulpit" instead of devoting themselves to serious study.[33]

Now that the Catholic Church was challenged, however, More, the former advocate of learning, became an advocate of ignorance. Rather than letting truth cure the poison of heresy, he argued that it would be better if readers read neither side of the argument because the poison would have some effect, regardless of the value of the medicine:

> And likewise would I counsel every good Christian man, and specially such as are not groundedly learned / to cast out the poisoned draft of these heretic's books, which when they be drunken down infect the reader and corrupt the soul unto the everlasting death / and therefore neither vouchsafe to read their books nor any thing made against them neither, but abhor to hear their heresies so much as named.[34]

He was especially contemptuous of the idea that ordinary people could correctly understand the Scripture:

> For though the Scripture be true in itself: yet since it is not so plain but that many great difficulties arise thereupon / in which though he, which upon the study thereof hath bestowed many years, may perceive the true part from the false: yet unto the unlearned it shall likely full oft, that in such dispositions the false part may seem truest.[35]

As is apparent, More's argument proves too much if his objection was simply to the accuracy of Tyndale's translation. The Bible is just too difficult, he says, for laymen who have not undertaken years of formal study. More willed them to be ignorant of the written Word of God lest they ever doubt the Catholic Church on any point. He was opposed to the general circulation of the Bible no matter how it was translated because unlearned men would be confused thereby. In fact, More blamed Tyndale for those that the lord chancellor put to death for their heresy against the Church of Rome.

The First to Be Burned

Early in 1529, a priest named Thomas Hitton was arrested for heresy after preaching in Kent. He was interrogated—we can assume without mercy—and confessed to have smuggled an English New Testament into England from the continent. He was condemned by Archbishop Warnham and Bishop Fisher. By standard practice the ecclesiastical condemnation was enforced by the secular authorities to maintain the pretense that the church itself did not shed blood. On February 23, 1529, Hitton was burned at the stake in Maidstone. Those professing to love and serve God ceremoniously executed another professing Christian in a slow, agonizing, and brutally painful death—all for the express purpose of sending this "heretic" straight into the fires of hell.

Hitton is generally considered the first English martyr of the Reformation to suffer this fate although the followers of Wycliffe, the Lollards, had been burned at the stake as recently as 1519.[36] Considerable insight into More's contemptuous view of the rights of conscience, not to mention Protestant dissenters, can be derived from his detailed discussion of Hitton's execution in his 1532 publication entitled *The co[n]futacyon of Tyndales answere made by syr Thomas More knyght lorde chau[n]cellour of Englonde.*

More is often exalted as one of the earliest champions of religious tolera-tion because of the system he devised for Utopia, the imaginary kingdom in his book by the same name. The first Utopian king, Utopus, allowed citizens of his state to hold diverse religious opinions, and the priests in the estab-lished church were elected to their positions. More wrote *Utopia* in 1516, prior to the religious upheavals and rampant "heresy" brought about by the Reformation, which were unlike anything he had hitherto witnessed. In the words of W. K. Jordan, the "horrors" of the religious disorder and "strange sects which he saw springing up mushroom-like all over Europe profoundly altered his views."[37]

By the time More wrote the *Confutation* sixteen years later, the tone of his writings bore little resemblance to the calm, measured qualities charac-terizing his earlier work. As with Augustine before him, and Luther around the same time, experience had radically transformed his theories about lib-erty of conscience. In the *Confutation* More first attacked Tyndale, alleging that he was responsible for both Hitton's death and his damnation to hell: "Then they boast that they have done a great mastery, and say they have made a martyr / when their poisoned books have killed the crysteman[38] both in body and soul."[39] In the next paragraph More taunted Tyndale, claiming that he had never met a heretic who would not confess his error to save his life—despite the obvious fact that Hitton did no such thing. More chided Tyndale for issuing a calendar with the date of Hitton's death to be memo-rialized in the place of a Roman Catholic saint. To More this meant that Tyndale had granted Hitton *de facto* sainthood. More then recited Hitton's doctrinal views in exhaustive detail, which were ascertained through mul-tiple interrogations to mockingly demonstrate that Tyndale had created an inglorious "saint."

From More's perspective it was self-evident that no person could accu-rately be described as a saint who rejected the authority of the church. It was on this point that More began his recitation of the heresies of Thomas Hitton:

> Now be it he said that he had always as his leisure would give
> him leave, and as he could find opportunity in places where he

came, taught the gospel of god after his own mind and his own
opinion, not forcing of the determination of the church / and said
that he intended to his power so to persevere still.[40]

This passage describes the central battle of the ongoing battle between
More and Tyndale. Does man come directly to God? Or must he come
through the sacraments and ceremonies of the church? Is there a right of
individual conscience?

Hitton incensed More by his views that, while baptism was necessary and
marriage was good, neither had to be done by a priest or in the church—and
that the baptism would be much "better if it were spoken in english."[41] We
shall omit More's crude language employed to describe his antipathy toward
Hitton's views on the necessity of a church marriage. Hitton also denied the
validity of most of the other sacraments of the church as well as the existence
of purgatory. More condemned all of Hitton's "errors" as he reviewed them
one by one.

Hitton understood the centrality of Scripture in the determination of
man's duty of obedience to God, as More described when he wrote that
Hitton "held that what so ever the pope[42] or the general council make, beside
that that is expressly commanded in scripture / ever man may lawfully break
it without any manner sin at all mortal or venial either."[43] Hitton specifically
denied that any Christian prince could lawfully "make any law or statute for
the punishment of any theft or any other crime by which law any man should
suffer death. For he said that all such laws be contrary to the gospel, which
will no man to die."[44] Because of Hitton's belief in a general prohibition of
the death penalty, More contended that Hitton deserved to die. The irony
seems to have been lost on the lord chancellor.

More was astonished that despite the fact Hitton held all these "abominable heresies," the Bible smuggler was convinced "that he had the grace of
god with him, and that the holy ghost was within him."[45] More triumphantly
described the judgment and execution of such a rank heretic:

> And so was he after much favor showed him, and much labor
> charitably taken for the saving of him / delivered in conclusion
> for his obstinacy to the secular hands, and burned up in his false
> faith and heresies, wherof he learned the great part of Tyndale's
> holy books / and now the spirit of error and lying, hath taken his
> wretched soul with him straight from the short fire to the fire
> everlasting.[46]

Hitton was not the only one to suffer during the leadership of Thomas
More, a fact which makes the current claim that he is a great hero of the right

of conscience not just a little hypocritical. More gleefully oversaw the fiery execution of numerous heretics and kept a personal torture chamber in his home to aid in his interrogation of religious dissenters.

But there was more. The lord chancellor also forcefully argued that it is simply wrong to dissent from the law on the basis of conscience. He contended that those guilty of heresy were also guilty of sedition. His words against those who advocate the right of conscience are remarkable:

> They bid the people for a countenance to be obedient. But they say therewith that the laws & precepts of their sovereigns do nothing bind the subjects in their consciences, but if the things by them commanded or forbidden, were before commanded or forbidden in scripture. And all the words of scripture whereby they be commanded to obey their governors, would they restrain unto those things only that are expressed already within the corps [body] of scripture. So that if they can beguile the laws and precepts of their sovereigns unaware to other men, and thereby flee from the peril of outward bodily punishment: their evangelical liberty should serve them sufficiently for discharge of their conscience, and inwardly make them in their souls clear angelical hypocrites.
>
> Now when they falsely tell them that they be not bound to obey their governors' lawful commandments / and then holily counsel them to obey their unlawful tyranny (for by that name call they the laws) what effect wene [suppose] ye they would that their advice should have? They know themselves well enough and the manner of the people too / and be not so mad I warrant you but that they perceive full well, that if they can persuade the people to believe that they be not in their conscience bound to obey the laws and precepts of their governors / themselves be no such precious apostles, that folk would forbear their own ease or pleasure, for the faint feigned counsel of a few false apostates. And thus is it sure, that by their false doctrine they must if they be believed, bring the people into the secret contempt, and spiritual disobedience, & inward hatred of the law / whereof must after follow the outward breach, and thereupon outward punishment & peril of rebellion / whereby the princes should be driven to sore effusion of their subjects blood, as hath already . . . happened in Almayne [Germany] and of old time in England.[47]

More defended his many executions by describing "heretics" that were "justly" burned at the stake.[48] Tyndale was threatened with a similar fate: "Tyndale if he do[es] not amend in time, he is like to find him when they come together, an hot firebrand burning at his back, that all the water in the world will never be able to quench."[49]

Chapter Four

TYNDALE'S TRIUMPH

Shame on Those Who Think Evil of It

But still ye will say, I cannot understand it. What marvel?
How shouldest thou understand, if thou wilt not read nor
look upon it? Take the Books into thine hands,
read the whole story, and that thou understandest not,
read it again, and again.

THOMAS CRANMER

*I*n 1534, a series of acts was passed to finalize the break with Rome, many of which were aimed directly at stifling any criticism of the king's action in divorcing Catherine and marrying Anne. For example, the Treason Act of 1534 made any publication which labeled the king a "heretic, schismatic, tyrant, usurper, or infidel" an act of treason punishable, of course, by death. The Act of Succession was passed in March to ensure that Anne's children, not Catherine's daughter, Mary, would inherit the throne. Set forth in the Act was a clear denunciation of the principle that the pope could override the written Word of God. Claims to the contrary, Parliament decreed, "shall be void and of none effect."[1]

Each person in England, starting with the king's councilors, was required to take an oath swearing to the principles contained in this act. Thus, the oath required far more than recognition of the legitimacy of Henry's marriage with Anne. It also implicitly—but unmistakably—required the English leaders, clergy, and people to embrace the idea that the written Word was superior to the decisions of the pope. Thomas More's modern biographer and defender, Peter Ackroyd, explains the implication of this provision of the Act when he writes, "In one sentence the Act thereby destroyed the jurisdiction and authority of the Pope."[2]

The Death of Thomas More

Thomas More had been attempting to live in quiet seclusion prior to the passage of the Oath of Succession. But with the legal requirement that officials acknowledge the superiority of the Word of God over the dictates of the pope, More could no longer feign indifference. The oath required him to swear his allegiance to principles he disbelieved. On Sunday, April 12, 1534, he was served with a summons on his way home from attending Mass at St. Paul's Cathedral. It required him to appear at Lambeth Palace the next day to take the oath. After requesting copies of the oath and the act, he meticulously read both, then replied to Archbishop Cranmer and the other commissioners who waited for his response:

> My purpose is not to put any fault either in the Act or any man that made it, or in the oath or any man that swears it, nor to condemn the conscience of any other man. But as for myself in good faith my conscience so moves me in the matter, that though I will not deny to swear to the succession, yet unto the oath that here is offered to me I cannot swear, without the jeopardizing of my soul to perpetual damnation. . . . If you doubt whether I refuse the oath only for the grudge of my conscience, or any other fantasy, I am ready here to satisfy you by my oath. Which, if you do not trust it, why should you be the better to give me any oath? And if you trust that I will herein swear true, then I trust of your goodness you will not move me to swear the oath you had offered me, perceiving that for to swear it is against my conscience.[3]

As Ackroyd notes, "He was invoking the dicates of his conscience for his refusal, but at no stage did he explain what they were."[4] Taken in isolation, More's action makes a compelling case for the freedom of conscience. The echoes of More's vindictive words against Tyndale's claim of freedom of conscience, however, shatter his saintly image. If More repented of his attitude toward Tyndale and the other Protestants he had jailed, tortured, and burned, the judgment of history might be different. But More's story

contains no Damascus-like turnabout. He argued for a right for himself that
he had previously denied to others.

More was thrown into prison where he lingered for fifteen months. He
endured the imprisonment with patience, and his married daughter, Meg,
was able to gain permission to visit him. They recited psalms and litanies,
as they were accustomed to doing together, and discoursed about the state
of his wife and household.[5] On July 1, he was tried and convicted of treason.
On July 6, he was beheaded at the Tower of London. A small act of Henry's
grace saved him from being hanged, disemboweled, and then drawn and quartered—the standard punishment for treason.

Between More's first and second interrogations, on May 21, 1535,
William Tyndale was arrested at Vilvorde Castle near Brussels due to the
actions of a traitorous friend named Henry Phillips. He was held in prison
for "one year, one hundred thirty-five days."[6] Only one item written by
Tyndale while in prison has survived. It was a note handwritten in Latin, to
an unnamed person in authority, in which Tyndale pleaded:

> I believe, right worshipful, that you are not unaware of what
> may have been determined concerning me. Wherefore I beg
> your lordship, and that by the Lord Jesus, that if I am to remain
> here through the winter, you will request the commissary to
> have the kindness to send me, from the goods of mine which he
> has, a warmer cap; for I suffer greatly from cold in the head, and
> am afflicted by a perpetual catarrh, which is much increased in
> this cell; a warmer coat also, for this which I have is very thin; a
> piece of cloth too to match my leggings. My overcoat is worn out;
> my shirts are also worn out. He has a woolen shirt, if he will be
> good enough to send it. I have also with him leggings of thicker
> cloth to put on above; he has also warmer night-caps. And I ask
> to be allowed to have a lamp in the evening; it is indeed weari-
> some sitting alone in the dark. But most of all I beg and beseech
> your clemency to be urgent with the commissary, that he will
> kindly permit me to have the Hebrew bible, Hebrew grammar,
> and Hebrew dictionary, that I may pass the time in that study. In
> return may you obtain what you most desire, so only that it be for
> the salvation of your soul. But if any other decision has been taken
> concerning me, to be carried out before winter, I will be patient,
> abiding the will of God, to the glory of the grace of my Lord Jesus
> Christ: whose Spirit (I pray) may ever direct your heart. Amen W.
> Tindalus[7]

There is no reason to believe that Tyndale's request was granted, at least insofar as it enabled him to translate more of the Old Testament.[8] It is unknown whether he even received the warmer clothing he so clearly needed.

In August 1536, Tyndale was formally judged to be a heretic by the Roman Catholic Church and handed over to the secular authorities for execution. Two months later, in early October—perhaps on the sixth day of the month[9]—William Tyndale was strangled to death while tied at the stake, and then his dead body was burned in the ritualistic fashion then in vogue. Tyndale's last words were, "Lord, open the king of England's eyes!"[10]

Kindling the Fire of God's Word

Henry VIII never did become a true advocate of either Protestantism or religious freedom. But, just as Thomas More feared and William Tyndale wished, through Henry the door was opened for the Word of God to be published in English.

Both of the king's two chief advisors in the post-More period were staunch advocates for the publication of the Bible in English. Thomas Cromwell rose from a humble family to a series of offices and honors. He was appointed chancellor of the exchequer in 1533, vicar general (a senior administrative office in the new independent English Church) in 1535, and the following year he was named lord of the privy seal, succeeding Thomas Boleyn in that office. He spent his young adulthood tramping through Italy with the French army and gaining practical experience in diverse trades but quickly won favor with Cardinal Wolsey upon his return to England. After entering the king's service, he became one of the most influential individuals pressing for the break with Rome. Likewise, Thomas Cranmer, the archbishop of Canterbury, was a committed Protestant who sincerely advocated the public circulation of an English Bible as the logical conclusion of his personal spiritual convictions.

Cromwell had made some attempt, albeit unsuccessful, to secure Tyndale's release through the Holy Roman emperor. As one of the chief architects of Henry's divorce from the emperor's niece, Cromwell was most ill-suited to be an advocate for this Protestant "heretic." But, after a series of delays due to hostility from both nobles and clerics, Cromwell and Cranmer together were able to secure Henry's "license" for a Bible translated by "Thomas Matthew." No such translator existed. In reality the Bible was chiefly the work of Tyndale—a name too heretical to appear in print. It was assembled by an English exile in Antwerp named John Rogers, a graduate of Pembroke Hall at Cambridge in 1526.

The New Testament in the "Thomas Matthew" Bible is entirely Tyndale's. Tyndale also translated the Pentateuch and the nine historical books of the Old Testament ending at 2 Chronicles.[11] For the remainder of the Old Testament, Rogers used a 1534 translation by Miles Coverdale. Coverdale, also an exile on the continent at the time, was the first to print a full Bible in English, but he was a Latinist who knew neither Hebrew nor Greek. His translation suffers from its failure to work from the original languages, even though it was an accomplishment of great courage and historical significance. When Cranmer reviewed the Bible at Cromwell's request, he concluded, "I like it better than any other translation heretofore made."[12]

The cover page of the Matthew's Bible is incredibly interesting. It is adorned with the same set of illustrations as the 1534 Coverdale Bible. At the top of the page, God is represented by a shining circle with the name of God in Hebrew characters. He is flanked by Adam and Eve (discreetly covered with fig leaves) on the left and a triumphant Jesus on the right with the words "This is my dear son in whom I delight, hear him" emblazoned in a scroll.

There are four scriptural stories depicted in the center of the page, two from each of the testaments. At the bottom, a resplendent Henry VIII sits on an elevated throne with a group of bishops kneeling on the left and a kingly-looking group of nobles kneeling on the right. This was clearly designed to appeal to Henry's perception that he had become supreme ruler of both church and state.

The most fascinating item on this cover page is found at Henry's feet. It is the crest of the Order of the Garter, the oldest and highest order of British chivalry founded by Edward III in 1348. At the time the shield in the center of the crest contained four sections: two representing Henry's (highly disputed) claim to the French throne, symbolized by three fleur-de-lis, and two sets of three stylized lions, symbolizing England. The crest of the Order of the Garter has been slightly modified since England no longer claims the throne of France, but it is still today a part of the iconography of British royalty. However, it is the slogan of the order, circling the shield, that is the real source of irony: "Hony soyt qui mal y pense." (The modern French spelling is *honi soit qui mal y pense*.) It means, "Shame on those who think evil of it."

These words have now appeared as a part of British royal symbols for nearly seven hundred years, but perhaps never were they put to better use than on this first legally authorized Bible in English. It was a clear (albeit unintentional) repudiation of the legacy of repression of the Bible from the Constitutions of Oxford in 1408 to the still smoldering fires set by the late lord chancellor, Thomas More.

It would not be long before a more elaborate apologetic argument for the translation of Scripture would appear in official print. In 1539,

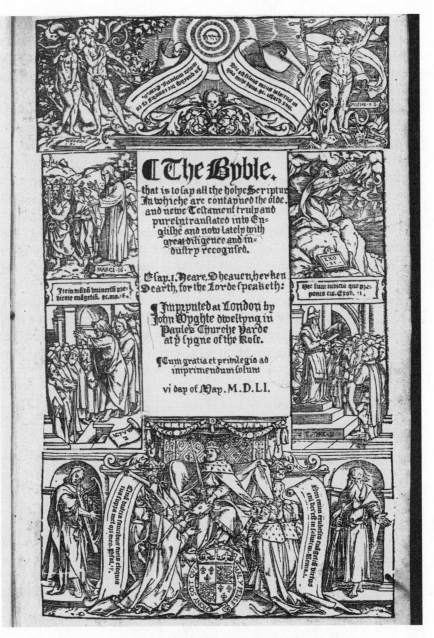

Title page of the 1551 edition of the "Thomas Matthew" Bible,
courtesy of The Bodleian Library, University of Oxford,
Denyer Bib. Eng. C. 1551.

Cromwell succeeded in getting his friend Miles Coverdale appointed to oversee this work that would come to be known as the "Great Bible," an English translation geared toward the common reader and authorized by the king of England.[13] Coverdale used basically the same text as that of the Matthew's Bible. Coverdale's version was finally printed with slight revisions but only after great difficulty involving both political and diplomatic interference. The 1539 copy of the Great Bible, currently accessible thanks to the British Library, does not contain an important preface written by Thomas Cranmer. However, copies of the Great Bible from 1540 and 1541 in the British Library and the New York Public Library contain Cranmer's lengthy preface concerning the people's right to read the Word of God. It is a several-page argument that was later reprinted as a separate document under the apt title *The Judgment of Archbishop Cranmer Concerning the Peoples Right to, and Discreet Use of the H. Scriptures*. A handful of brief portions from the prologue give clear insight into the value that Cranmer placed on the Word of God in the life of each person: I would marvel much that any man should be so mad, as to refuse in darkness, light; in hunger, food, in cold, fire: for the Word of God is light. . . . Thy word is a lantern unto my feet. It is food. . . . Man shall not live by bread only, but by every word of God. It is fire. . . . I am come to send fire on the earth, and what is my desire, but that it be kindled.[14]

Let no man make excuse and say (saith he) I am busied about matters of the Commonwealth, I bear this office, or that, I am a craftsman, I must apply mine occupation, I have a wife, my children must be fed, my household must I provide for, briefly I am a man of the worlde, it is not for me to read the Scriptures, that belongeth to them that have bidden the world farewell, which live in solitariness, and contemplation, and have been brought up and continually counseled in learning and religion. To this answering, What sayest thou man (saith he?) It is not for thee to study and to read the Scripture, because thou are encumbered and distract[ed] with cares and business. So much more it is behovefull for thee to have defense of Scriptures, how much thou are the more distressed in worldly danger. They that be free and far from trouble and intermeddling of worldly thing, live in safeguard and tranquility, and in the calm, or with a sure haven. Thou art in the middle of the sea of worldly wickedness, and therefore thou needest the more of ghostly [i.e., spiritual] succor and comfort. They sit far from the strokes of battle, and far out of the gun shot, and therefore they be but seldom wounded. Thou that standest in the forefront of the host, & nighest to thine enemies, must needs take now and then many strokes, and be grievously wounded, and therefore thou hast most need to have thy remedies and medicines at hand.[15]

But still ye will say, I cannot understand it. What marvel? How shouldest thou understand, if thou wilt not read nor look upon it? Take the Books into thine hands, read the whole story, and that thou understandest not, read it again, and again: if thou can neither so come by it, counsel with some other than it better learned.[16]

The reading of the Scriptures is a great and strong bulwark or fortress against sin: the ignorance of the same is a greater ruin and destruction of them that will not know it. That is the thing that bringeth in heresy, that is it that causeth all corrupt and perverse living, that is it that bringeth all things out of good order.[17]

Here may Princes learn how to govern their subjects: subjects obedience, love and dread to their Princes: husbands how they should behave themselves unto their wives, how to educate their children and servants. . . . Here all manner of person, men, women, young, old, learned, unlearned, rich, poor, priests, laymen, lords, ladies, officers, tenant, and mean men, virgins, wives, widows, lawyers, merchants, artificers, husbandmen, and all manner of persons, of what estate or condition soever they be, may in this book learn all things what they ought to believe, what they ought to do, and what they should not do, as well concerning Almighty God, as also concerning themselves and all other.[18]

This last section of Cranmer's argument is particularly significant. Lord Chancellor More and other defenders of the restriction of scriptural knowledge argued that, at most, a few select laymen—and never women—should have limited access to the Scriptures in English. Cranmer's listing of all manner of men and women as persons deserving to read the Scriptures for themselves was truly revolutionary in concept and scope.

It is sad, perhaps, that Cranmer used the term "husbandmen" instead of "ploughboy" in his list of those needing access to the Bible, but the point is not lost. Neither did Tyndale go entirely unrecognized. In one of the series of initials which decorate this edition of the Bible, the initials "W T" appear in an ornate fashion, taking up half a page in a conspicuous spot between books. There is no explanation offered.

Within five years of Tyndale's execution, his translation of the Word of God was placed before the entire English population. Husbandmen—and their fellow farm workers the ploughboys—were urged by the archbishop of Canterbury to read the Scriptures from a Bible in their native tongue, licensed by the king of England.

Tyndale and More: An Epilogue

Thomas More and William Tyndale engaged in one of the greatest published debates of all time. In the words of David Daniell, who brilliantly summarizes their dispute, "More gave us three quarters of a million words of scarcely readable prose attacking Tyndale. Tyndale outraged More by giving us the Bible in English, England's greatest contribution to the world for nearly five hundred years."[19]

Both men suffered a martyr's death. Thomas More, indeed, was a man for all seasons—an advocate of learning and an advocate of ignorance, the persecutor and the martyr. William Tyndale gave his life so that all men might read God's Word in their own language. If that seminal achievement were not enough, Tyndale's efforts laid the groundwork for scriptural arguments that would inspire generations in their pursuit of religious liberty, democracy, and human rights for all.

Chapter Five

THE BIBLE AND
THE BOY KING

The Reign of Edward VI

---

*Unto a Christian man, there can be nothing either
more necessary or profitable than the knowledge of holy
Scripture.*

THOMAS CRANMER

enry VIII believed that a male heir would provide stability and longevity to the throne. Like many of the other desires associated with his multiple marriages, however, the reality proved far less satisfying than the dream.

Edward VI, child of Henry's third wife, Jane Seymour,[1] became king of England at the death of his father on January 28, 1547. Jane had died a scant two weeks after Edward's birth. Despite his sorrow over the loss of his young wife, Henry finally had the son for whom he had wished for so long, and it went without question that the boy would receive an education from England's finest tutors. The young prince responded with such remarkable ease to his lessons in French, Latin, philosophy, logic, music, and astronomy that even visiting philosophers were impressed. He was just nine years old when his father died. He and his half sister Elizabeth were said to have cried unsparingly when they were told of their father's death, moving the hearts of all who witnessed and causing "the most iron eyes" to share their tears.[2]

Gifted though he was, even those committed to the political theory of monarchy recognized that the nation could not be governed by a nine-year-old child. A council was thus appointed to govern in the king's stead during Edward's minority, but his maternal uncle, Edward Seymour, dominated. Seymour, who held the title of Duke of Somerset, was a committed Protestant. He was selected by the council as Lord Protector—the de facto king.

Archbishop Cranmer believed that the death of Henry would serve to advance the cause of the Reformation.[3] Cranmer began his reforming efforts with his own position. To reinforce the idea that the ecclesiastic authorities were subject to the king, Cranmer sought reappointment as Archbishop of Canterbury from Edward. He was recommissioned for this position on February 7, 1547.[4] Thirteen days later he performed the coronation of Edward in an elaborate ceremony involving the placement of three crowns on the young boy's head.

The ceremony was noteworthy for its many conspicuous Protestant references. In Cranmer's coronation speech, he began by repudiating any claim of authority the pope might make over the king:

> Most Dread and Royal Sovereign: The Promises your
> Highness hath made here, at your Coronation, to forsake the Devil
> and all his Works, are not to be taken in the Bishop of Rome's
> sense, when you commit any thing distasteful to that See, to hit
> your Majesty in the Teeth, as Pope Paul the Third, late Bishop of
> Rome, sent to your Royal Father, saying, *Didst thou not promise, at*
> *our permission of thy Coronation, to forsake the Devil and all his Works,*
> *and dost thou run to Heresy? For the Breach of this thy Promise, know-*
> *est thou not, that 'tis in our Power to dispose of thy Sword and Scepter to*
> *whom we please?*[5]

Cranmer went on to reassure Edward that his duty to forsake the devil was not a promise that gave any ecclesiastical authority, either in Rome or England, to remove him from his royal office.

There were deliberate Protestant overtones in the ceremony itself. When the king was anointed with oil, Cranmer informed the boy monarch that the oil "is but a ceremony." God's "election" of Edward was in his person—that is, in his birth—which God confirmed with "the Gifts of his Spirit, for the better ruling and guiding of his people."[6] Cranmer admonished Edward to follow the example of Josiah, the boy king of Israel. In this connection, Edward was urged to see "that God [is] truly worshipped, and

Idolatry destroyed; the Tyranny of the Bishops of Rome banished from your subjects, and Images removed. These Acts be Signs of a second Josias, who reformed the Church of God in his Days."[7]

Reformation Efforts Begin

After the coronation, both the archbishop and Seymour pursued an aggressive policy to ensure that the newly separated Church of England remained faithful to the Reformation. This course of action met with resistance by certain bishops, rank-and-file clergy, and even segments of the populace. The bishop of Winchester, Stephen Gardiner, was the leader of the Catholic forces. (Gardiner, it should be remembered, had been instrumental in helping Henry seek a divorce from Catherine and had, in fact, introduced Cranmer to the king.) In order to slow the progress of the Reformation, Gardiner argued that no changes to the laws of religion should be made during the period of Edward's minority.[8] Gardiner's resistance was unavailing and ultimately landed him in prison—first in Fleet, then later in the Tower of London, where he was incarcerated for about five years.

In order to bring sound Protestant teaching to the people, Archbishop Cranmer had to do an end run around many of the established clergy. In addition to the problem of active resistance, the gross biblical illiteracy of many of the clergy made it impossible for them to teach sound, Bible-based doctrine to the people. One Protestant bishop, John Hooper, bishop of Gloucester, devised a program of scriptural education for the clerics in his diocese. For example, they had to be trained to answer the following questions:

1. Concerning the Commandments
   —How many Commandments.
   —Where they are written.
   —Whether they can recite them by Heart.
2. Concerning the Christian Faith
   —What are the Articles of the Christian Faith.
   —Whether they can recite them by Heart.
   —That they corroborate them by Authority of Scripture.
3. Concerning the Lord's Prayer
   —Whether they can say the Petition by Heart.
   —How they know it to be the Lord's Prayer.
   —Where it is written.[9]

Cranmer's seventeenth-century biographer commented on the knowledge of the clerics on these matters:

Which Demands, how easy soever they were, many Curates and Priests (such was the Ignorance of those Days) could say but little to. Some could say the *Pater Noster* in Latin, but not in English. Few could say the Ten Commandments. Few could prove the Articles of Faith by Scripture. That was out of their way.[10]

To combat scriptural illiteracy, Cranmer had to resort to a book of homilies to supply the needed teaching for the churches. The priests were ordered to read these homilies in Sunday services. When they finished reading the entire group of messages, they were to begin again. The bishops were supposed to collaborate in the preparation of the book of homilies, but due to Fisher's resistance, Cranmer ended up having a "great hand" in the actual preparation of these sermons.[11]

Cranmer's book of homilies began with a strong admonition for each individual to read and study the Bible for himself:

Unto a Christian man, there can be nothing either more necessary or profitable, than the knowledge of holy scripture: forasmuch as in it, is contained God's true word, setting forth his glory, and also man's duty. And there is no truth, nor doctrine, necessary for our justification and everlasting salvation, but that is (or may be) drawn out of that fountain, and well of truth. Therefore, as many as be desirous to enter into the right and perfect way unto God must apply their mindes to know holy scripture without which, they can neither sufficiently know God and his will, neither their office and duty.[12]

It should not be forgotten how radical such teaching would have seemed to many in England at the time. A decade earlier, men and women were being burned at the stake for owning such a Bible. Now churchgoers were being admonished to view the Scriptures as the sole source of spiritual truth.

In fact, some churchgoers did *not* accept Cranmer's efforts to promote the use of the Bible in English. Rebellions broke out in 1549, particularly in the county of Devon. The people had two central complaints: One was against the nobility for "enclosing of their Commons from them,"[13] a land-use dispute; the other was a protest of the "laying aside the old Religion."[14] Their particular demands concerning religion were the restoration of Latin masses, the use of images, worshipping the Sacrament, purgatory, the abbies, and the removal of the English Bible.[15]

Yet such rebels were hardly universally acclaimed. A ballad entitled "Defeat of the Devon and Cornwall rebels of 1548" proclaimed:

There hartes ware so coted in the popes lawes
They begane the laste yere when they slew bodye
All Englande rejoysethe at ther over throwse
For only the Lorde is oure kynges victorye.[16]

Nor should it be thought that a majority of the clergy embraced the old view. In one crucial ecclesiastical debate concerning the permissibility of marriage by the clergy, the pro-married clergy viewpoint prevailed by a vote of 53–22.[17]

In addition to the book of homilies, Cranmer appointed a team of "Visitors"—traveling preachers whose theology he trusted.[18] These visitors went throughout the land to teach people sound doctrine from the Protestant perspective. Among those appointed were Nicholas Ridley and Dr. Rowland Taylor, both of whom were later martyred by Edward's half sister, Bloody Mary.

Protestants as Persecutors

Cranmer's approach to the treatment of his theological enemies was somewhat more restrained than those who preceded him and those who followed. The bishop of Winchester, Stephen Fisher, was jailed for his dissent from the efforts to reform the church; but he was not burned, as surely would have happened to a similarly prominent dissenter in the years of Henry VIII and Thomas More. The archbishop tried to reason with Fisher by telling him that his purpose for reforms was simply to "set out the freedom of God's mercy."[19] In dealing with another recalcitrant bishop, Cranmer refused to impose any harsh punishment, which drew a sharp rebuke from his friends, who warned him that the dissenters would not return the favor should they regain power.[20]

Cranmer was not the only one who showed mercy to the ousted Catholic clerics. When Nicholas Ridley was made the bishop of London, he treated his imprisoned predecessor with a form of civility that was uncommon for the era. Rather than confiscate all of Bishop Boner's personal possessions, Ridley guarded Boner's goods and even supplied food and shelter to members of his family.[21]

This is not to say that no one was burned at the stake during the reign of Edward VI and the last years of Thomas Cranmer's service as archbishop. While the friends of Rome were shown comparative mercy, those who preached new doctrines—some of which were clearly heretical by any measure—were dealt with more severely. John Atherton, a priest who preached a denial of the Trinity and of the deity of both Jesus and the Holy Spirit, was forced to abjure his beliefs.[22] Another was forced to abjure on two matters: Michael Thombe, a butcher from London, believed and taught that "Christ took no flesh of our Lady; and that Baptism of Infants is not profitable, because it goeth before faith."[23] He escaped the fires by signing an oath declaring his former opinions to be "Errors and Heresies, and damnable Opinions."[24]

Even a Protestant bishop ran into legal difficulty when he went further than the Anglican Church was willing to go. In July 1550, John Hooper returned from exile in Germany and Switzerland and was made bishop of Gloucestershire. Hooper, however, refused to wear the same formal vestments as the Catholic bishops because he believed the clothing represented the false teachings that were being thrown out. Cranmer ultimately had him jailed until he relented. Hooper was then consecrated in his bishopric and gained a reputation as a great preacher.[25]

Not all declared heretics escaped. Cranmer personally pronounced sentence over Joan Bocher, also known as Joan of Kent, who expressed doubts that Jesus "took flesh" of the Virgin Mary since she had been conceived in sin and thus, apparently, would give Jesus a sin nature. With Hugh Latimer assisting Cranmer in the ecclesiastical trial, Joan was convicted, turned over to the secular authorities, and cruelly burned at the stake.[26] She was described by some as an Anabaptist,[27] but this was employed generally as a derisive name for anyone who went beyond the reforms sanctioned by the Church of England.

Inroads of the Reformation

In the study of religious liberty, there is a temptation to skip over the short reign of Edward VI and proceed from the religious violence of Henry VIII to the religious violence of Queen Mary. But despite the failures of Cranmer and the king's protectors to embrace liberty on a broad scale, they unleashed powerful forces and ideas that could not be extinguished from England even under the extreme and massive killing spree that followed under Mary.

During the years of Edward's reign, Cranmer produced and secured the ratification of the Book of Common Prayer, launching a tradition of liturgy for the Church of England that survives, although modified, nearly five hundred years later. He also sponsored influential reformed scholarship at Cambridge and Oxford and assigned the notable foreign theologians Martin Bucher and Peter Martyr to teach at these universities.[28]

Strype records, "Protestants began more freely to put forth Books, and to disperse such as were formerly printed beyond Sea, in behalf of Religion against Popery, and concerning such as had suffered under the Cruelties of the Church of Rome."[29] This is not to say that true freedom of the press existed; the Anglican Church continued to practice the previous Roman view in which it was the duty of the state to preserve the purity of Church doctrine. Although methods of repression were somewhat moderated, a review of the available books printed in the years of Edward's reign demonstrates that books on religion dominated all publications and the reformers' viewpoint was, for all intents and purposes, the only one that found its way into print.

Edward died just shy of his sixteenth birthday in 1553. Had he lived, the Reformation certainly would have made even deeper inroads into England. Indeed, according to Strype, influential continental reformers "took such great Joy and Satisfaction in this good King, and his Establishment of Religion, that the Heads of them, Bullinger, Calvin, and others, in a Letter to him, offered to make him their Defender, and to have Bishops in their Churches as there were in England, with the tender of their Service to assist and unite together."[30]

While such a potential union alarmed the Catholic hierarchy meeting at the Council of Trent,[31] it is unlikely that such a union would have resulted in religious freedom. For as we will soon see, the continental reformers, like the Anglicans, rejected any reform of the central tenet that fosters religious persecution.

Chapter Six

MARY'S FIVE YEARS OF TERROR

A Catholic Monarch Returns

"Be of good comfort, Master Ridley, and play the man; we shall this day light such a candle by God's grace in England as I trust never shall be put out."

HUGH LATIMER

parliamentary enactment of 1543 had allowed Henry to choose his successors in his will. Edward was named first, followed by Mary, then Elizabeth, and then the Lady Jane Grey, granddaughter of Henry's sister. Not many years later Edward also attempted prior to his death to pass the crown by his will. There were two problems with this. First, despite the fact that he was the ruling monarch of England, he was a minor and thus legally incapable of making a will. Second, the law of succession did not normally permit designation of a successor by will; such permission had to be specifically granted by Parliament, as had been done in Henry's case.

Nonetheless, Edward attempted to pass the crown to his Protestant cousin, Jane Grey. She was arguably the only one eligible to succeed the throne of England since Mary and Elizabeth had both been declared illegitimate when, in turn, in lieu of divorce, Henry had his marriages to Catherine and Anne Boleyn declared unlawful and void. (Under English law, an illegitimate child of the monarch was ineligible to assume the throne.) However, Henry's will and Parliament's enabling legislation were followed, and Mary and Elizabeth's prior declarations of illegitimacy were ignored.

Thomas Cranmer and other key leaders acted in obedience to Edward's wishes as well as to their own theological viewpoints, pledging their support for Jane Grey and declaring her to be queen in lieu of Mary. Such leaders would become doubly doomed—their Protestant theology would prove sufficient to cost them their lives even aside from their offense in backing Lady Jane's attempt at succession.

Mary established her claim to the throne rapidly, buoyed by the overwhelming support of the English people. While some supported her because of their desire to return the nation to the Roman Catholic faith, numerous faithful Protestants also supported her claim to the throne simply because she was the designated successor as authorized by the law of Parliament.

Mary's approach to religious matters cannot be understood in doctrinal terms alone. The personal humiliation she had suffered—the public repudiation of her mother, her parents' marriage, and her own "illegitimacy"—gave rise to a desire for revenge. These personal affronts were inextricably joined with England's rejection of Catholicism. Mary had lived for years in constant fear of losing her life. Moreover, she never seemed able to command respect or maintain the same regal air that her younger sister, Elizabeth, seemed to possess naturally.

Mary came to power in late July 1553 and entered London on August 3. Her first declaration in regard to religion was relatively modest: She declared that it was illegal to refer to anyone's opponent as a "papist or heretic."[1] But it was quickly understood that all of the Reformation was now overturned. Priests began openly to celebrate the Mass, although it was still technically illegal under the Act of Uniformity of 1552.[2] This shocked some and caused open unrest. Mary also released Bishop Stephen Gardiner from the Tower and immediately made him the lord chancellor.

Archbishop Cranmer's friends had earlier warned him that his relative leniency to Gardiner and his fellow dissenters would not be repaid with kindness. This was an understated prophecy.

On August 13, Mary ordered "Dr Bourn, a canon of St Paul's, who was a Catholic supporter, to preach at Paul's cross."[3] His sermon was a denunciation of the Protestants, causing an outcry from some of the Protestant laymen. Someone even threw a dagger at Bourn, but it was wide of its mark. Leading Protestant clergymen John Bradford and John Rogers (who had helped Tyndale with his translation efforts) were present. In an effort to avoid a dangerous riot, Bradford and Rogers successfully urged the crowd to become quiet. Despite their calming actions, the two pastors were charged with provoking the disturbance. When they insisted that they had actually prevented it from becoming any worse, Gardiner replied that since the crowd had listened to their instructions, this demonstrated that they were, in fact, the leaders of the uprising. Both men were arrested and imprisoned.[4]

As with Rogers and Bradford, the initial arrests of other leading clergymen were not for heresy but were based on absurd and obscure charges. Protestant bishops John Hooper and Miles Coverdale, the great Bible translator, were arrested "apparently because they had not paid some dues [to the Queen] which had been obsolete for many years."[5] Hugh Latimer was sent to the Tower for his "seditious demeanor."[6]

Transubstantiation and Clerical Marriage

It was not long, however, before Gardiner would level two principal charges against all` Protestant clergy to convict them of heresy. First was their view on the doctrine of transubstantiation. The second issue was the marriage of the clergy. To many people the difference between Catholic and Anglican doctrine on the practice of the sacraments seems minimal. The truth is, however, that the difference is rather significant, especially as it pertains to the role of the official church in obtaining salvation.

Both Catholics and the early Anglicans—as judged by the theology of Cranmer—believed that a person is initially brought into the Christian faith upon his baptism as an infant. It would be fair to note that Catholics did not recognize baptism by any church that had departed from Rome's orb as having any spiritual effect. At least initially, Anglicans could not take the same view of Catholic baptisms since all Anglican leaders had been baptized as Catholics. Beyond the centrality of infant baptism, however, the two views on how a person ultimately obtains salvation were radically different.

In the Catholic viewpoint, the role of the church was central to salvation. Specifically, the celebration of the Mass was viewed as an ongoing sacrifice of the body and blood of Jesus for forgiveness of the people's sins.[7] The priest, by his pronouncements during the Mass, turned the bread into the literal body of Jesus, and the wine into His literal blood. The priest alone drank the wine, but he offered the bread-transformed-to-divine-flesh to the people. When they consumed Jesus' body, the people received the grace of God for continued salvation. Grace was not available outside the sacraments of the church, and without the church's grace salvation was impossible. Salvation was viewed as an ongoing process, never resulting in absolute certainty for the practicing Catholic. Any mortal sin, for example, would cause a baptized person to forfeit his or her salvation, no matter how many times one had previously taken communion.

To obtain forgiveness for any sin, an adherent had to approach God solely through the organs of the church. Specifically, the sacrament of confession in which the adherent would confess sin to the priest was the singular method of obtaining forgiveness, although the church did occasionally allow alternative paths—such as through the sale of indulgences. The priest played two roles in the forgiveness of sin. First, he received the confession and pronounced conditional forgiveness. Second, he would assign acts of penance, which often included some financial assessment for the benefit of the church to complete the process of forgiveness.

As the first Anglican archbishop of Canterbury, Cranmer taught that infant baptism initially brought a person into the Christian faith. After that, however, a person was saved by faith. He shared Calvin's view that faith was not a free decision made by an individual in response to the offer of salvation but rather an irresistible gift from God. While eliminating any role for man's free will, Cranmer also eliminated the necessity for the official church to produce additional acts of grace that could effect salvation.

Thus, beyond infant baptism, the Anglican and Catholic views of salvation were radically different. In the most basic sense, the central issue was whether man came to God by the acts of God or the acts of the church.

One aspect of soteriology that Anglicans and Catholics shared in common was that unless one believed the "correct" theology, one's erroneous views would preclude salvation. Both views embraced the phrase "damnable heresies." Both believed, for example, that those who rejected infant baptism were unsaved heretics. Catholics and the early English Reformers were indistinguishable in their embrace of the doctrinal view that it was pleasing to God to punish and kill those who deviated from official church doctrine. Such punishment of damnable heretics was designed to send the heretic to hell and send a warning to others—with the hope of encouraging their salvation.

It is interesting to note that Erasmus, whose Greek New Testament served as a catalyst for the Reformation, thought that the scope of belief necessary for salvation was narrow according to Scripture. These essentials could be understood and believed by the multitudes, not just the scholars. Thus, recondite doctrinal conclusions drawn from disputes concerning matters like the sacraments should not be forced on anyone. Since they are not essential, they cannot lead to damnation regardless of which side of the dispute an individual is on.[8] Neither the Catholics nor Anglicans embraced this far more tolerant view.

The second major "heresy" Mary used to pursue the Protestant clergy was the issue of clerical marriage. As on other points of theology, coerced conformity was demanded. A priest could easily profess to have "seen the light" on the issue of transubstantiation and claim to come back to the

Catholic view. But for married clergymen, many with children, the issue was far more problematic. Under Mary and Gardiner the church and state united to demand, upon pain of a fiery death, that the married clergy put away their wives and children. The church pronounced a divorce of the marriage and forbade any rehabilitated clergyman to contact or support his family. As a result of these edicts, many families were set adrift without any means of support. The official acts of persecution, besides being inhumane, were often in defiance of the civil law as well. Strype describes Gardiner's tactics in the earliest days of Mary's reign:

> He was purposed to stifle the Religion as speedily and as vig-
> orously as he could. And one way he had to do this, was to send
> his Spies into all the Churches in London. And these would come
> into the Churches, and disturb the Ministers with rude Words and
> Actions in their very Ministration; and then go to the Bishop and
> make their Informations. And so the Ministers were fetch'd up by
> the Officers before him, and then committed, unless they would
> comply. And this in the very beginning of the Queen's Reign,
> when the Preachers did but according to the Laws then in Force,
> before the Parliament had repealed the Book of Common-Prayer,
> and the rest of K. Edward's Reformation.[9]

Mary's driving desire was that all her subjects believe as she did, and her will alone was enough to restore what her opponents called "Popish Priests and Popish Usages everywhere" without the need for Parliamentary acquiescence.[10]

Rounding up the Protestant Leadership

By September 13, Thomas Cranmer, the archbishop of Canterbury, was summoned to the Star Chamber and then committed to the Tower of London. Certainly, Cranmer was a heretic in the minds of Mary and Gardiner, the new judges of orthodoxy. He was married, for one thing, but he had an additional fatal flaw. The "chief reason" given for his imprison-ment was "the inveterate malice his enemies conceived against him for the divorce of K. Henry from the Queen's Mother: the blame of which they laid wholly upon him, though Bishop Gardiner and other bishops were con-cerned in it as deep as he."[11]

Many of Cranmer's fellow Protestants were quickly arrested.

> The Tower, as well at the Fleet and the Marshalsea, was
> crowded with prisoners. All that were supposed to favour Religion,

or that made any whisper against the Popish Religion, or that had any the least Hand in Q. Janes' Business, being taken up and committed.[12]

Initially, Cranmer was in the same cell with Hugh Latimer, Nicholas Ridley, and John Bradford, which, while very crowded, was at least a source of mutual encouragement.

While Mary's regime implemented a return to Catholicism prior to and apart from Parliamentary authorization, she eventually employed Parliament to change the underlying laws to conform to her viewpoint. The first step, according to Strype, was to secure the election of new, compliant members of Parliament. In 1554, "great Care was [then taken] of getting Parliament-men, that might do what was to be laid before them."[13] Having succeeded at this task, Mary saw to it that laws were passed that again recognized the primacy of the pope and repealed the key provisions of all Cranmer's reforms. The pope gladly reinstated the English Church into the Catholic fold and sent as his official envoy a man named Reginald Pole, an English exile who had been made a cardinal despite the fact that he had never been a priest.

With the church leadership secure, the time to eradicate heresy was at hand. The burnings began with Bibles and other heretical books. Cranmer's treatise against transubstantiation, the Book of Common Prayer, and all "heretical" translations of the Bible—that is, all translations not authorized by the Catholic Church—headed the lists of banned books. It was once again illegal to possess any English Bible. Bishops were given the authority to search any home or business for such books and seize them from their owners.[14] Early warnings of these sanctions had been seen only weeks after Mary's accession when she declared that reading and preaching from the Bible were universally banned and "all men were to refrain from interpreting 'the word of God after their own brain in churches and other places both public and private.'"[15]

According to Strype, the burning of heretics started before the laws had been properly changed to permit this punishment:

> For Protestants were already not only imprisoned, but
> put to Death, without any Warrant of Law, but only by virtue
> of Commissions from the Queen, and the Lord Chancellor.
> Whereupon, when one in the Convocation stated this Objection,
> That there was no Law to condemn them: Weston, the Prolocutor,
> answered, "It forceth not for a Law: We have a Commission to
> proceed with them: and when they be dispatched, let their Friends
> sue the Law."[16]

The first Protestant victim of Mary's fires was John Rogers, who had tried to stop the disturbance at St. Paul's. He was a graduate of Cambridge, the more radical of the two ancient British universities, and had gone to Antwerp as a chaplain for English merchants. There he met William Tyndale, the man under whose influence he was converted to the Protestant faith.

Although Rogers's work in publishing the Great Bible in 1539 was a sufficient reason for Gardiner to conclude that the man deserved death, the fact that he was married and the father of ten children provided indisputable grounds for his condemnation. Rogers's final request to see his wife and children one last time was summarily denied. Even without permission he did see them briefly as he was being marched from prison to his death at Smithfield, the notorious site of numerous prior executions by fire.[17]

On February 4, 1555, Rogers was tied to a wooden stake surrounded by piles of wood called "faggots." The wood was apparently dry as the fire burned quickly—a relative form of mercy. His legs were completely burned off. Nonetheless, he rubbed his hands in a washing motion in the fire as if the fire was little more than cold water. Raising his hands into the air in prayer, he quickly died.[18] A flock of doves flew overhead, which many of those present took as a sign that the Holy Spirit had carried his soul to heaven.[19]

Rowland Taylor and His Legacy

The third to be burned was Rowland Taylor. Taylor's last position had been as the rector of Hadleigh in the county of Sussex—a position roughly equivalent to that of a modern "senior pastor." Previously, Taylor, who possessed Cambridge degrees in law, had been especially close to Cranmer and served for a time as one of his domestic chaplains.[20] He was arrested at the Council's command even before Mary arrived in London, within a week of her proclamation as queen.[21]

Taylor's marriage and his genealogy have been the source of a great deal of historical comment, both professional and amateur. Numerous sources, including Web sites authored by Taylor's descendants, claim that his wife was Margaret Tyndale, the sister of *the* William Tyndale. She may indeed have been his sister, but the record is less than conclusive. The best evidence, perhaps, comes from a biography of Taylor written by William James Brown, who in 1959 held Taylor's prior pastorate as the rector of Hadleigh. Possessed with the local church records and other firsthand sources, Brown states:

> In regard to his marriage, when Taylor was questioned on oath before Dr. Harvey, he stated that he had contracted a marriage

with a certain Margaret, a single woman, about twenty-nine years previously (that is, 1554) in the house of John Tyndale, a merchant tailor of London, not in the face of the Church, but in the presence of Benet a priest, John Tyndale, and his wife. . . . But who was John Tyndale? We have no certain knowledge; but it is interesting to note that Foxe, under the year 1550, gives a list of persons "abjured in the Diocese of London," and among them is a certain John Tyndale. His offence was "sending five marks to his brother William Tyndale beyond the sea and receiving and keeping with him certain letters from his brother." . . . Most likely Taylor knew him and his brother, especially as the Tyndale family came from Northumberland [the region of Taylor's childhood]. It may therefore be conjectured that the marriage took place in John Tyndale's house, the brother of William, the translator of the Bible.[22]

Two specific aspects of this story remain in doubt. First, it cannot be conclusively proven that the John Tyndale, in whose house Taylor was married, was actually the brother of William rather than a man merely having the same name. Tyndale was not a common name but was not necessarily unique, either. Second, we do not have any direct evidence that Margaret was a Tyndale at all, much less John and William Tyndale's sister.

It would make sense, however, that Margaret had some relationship to John Tyndale or his wife since the marriage took place in their home and no one else was present besides a priest. Moreover, Taylor's failure to give his wife's maiden name during his examination for heresy or in any other surviving church record would seem to be nothing more than a desire to shield his wife's family. The danger his wife and children would face if the authorities believed she was William Tyndale's sister are self-evident.

The children and descendants of Rowland and Margaret Taylor are also a matter of intense speculation and many competing claims. Jasper Ridley states, as do many other sources, that the couple had three children, including one grown son who was Catholic.[23] However, relying on the record of Taylor's interrogation before the Catholic tribunal in 1554, William James Brown states that Taylor testified that he had nine children—a claim that also appears on a number of family Web sites and other sources.[24]

Foxe tells us that there was a son named Thomas at Taylor's execution. It is Thomas who is the source of intense genealogical interest. Many sources, including a 1985 book entitled *From Log Cabins to the White House: A History of the Taylor Family*, claim that five generations after Thomas Taylor, in his line of direct descendants, was born a woman named Frances Taylor. We know with certainty that Frances Taylor was the grandmother of

James Madison and the great-aunt of Zachary Taylor. What is uncertain, but supported by a great number of claims from family Bibles and the like, is the claim that Frances Taylor was indeed a descendant of Thomas Taylor. If true, Rowland Taylor would be the great-great-great-great-great-great-grandfather of James Madison.

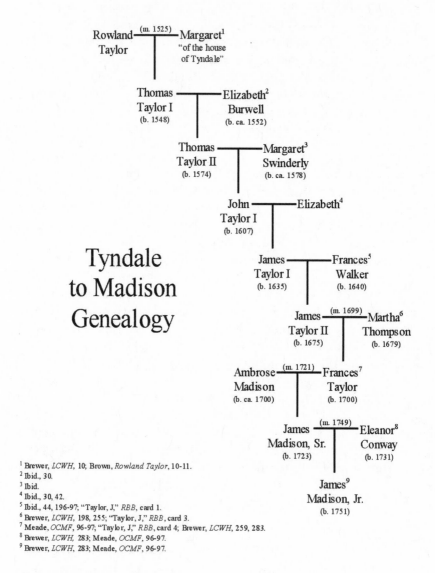

Tyndale to Madison Genealogy

Rowland Taylor —(m. 1525)— Margaret[1] "of the house of Tyndale"

Thomas Taylor I (b. 1548) ——— Elizabeth[2] Burwell (b. ca. 1552)

Thomas Taylor II (b. 1574) ——— Margaret[3] Swinderly (b. ca. 1578)

John Taylor I (b. 1607) ——— Elizabeth[4]

James Taylor I (b. 1635) ——— Frances[5] Walker (b. 1640)

James Taylor II (b. 1675) —(m. 1699)— Martha[6] Thompson (b. 1679)

Ambrose Madison (b. ca. 1700) —(m. 1721)— Frances[7] Taylor (b. 1700)

James Madison, Sr. (b. 1723) —(m. 1749)— Eleanor[8] Conway (b. 1731)

James[9] Madison, Jr. (b. 1751)

[1] Brewer, *LCWH*, 10; Brown, *Rowland Taylor*, 10-11.
[2] Ibid., 30.
[3] Ibid.
[4] Ibid., 30, 42.
[5] Ibid., 44, 196-97; "Taylor, J," *RBB*, card 1.
[6] Brewer, *LCWH*, 198, 255; "Taylor, J," *RBB*, card 3.
[7] Meade, *OCMF*, 96-97; "Taylor, J," *RBB*, card 4; Brewer, *LCWH*, 259, 283.
[8] Brewer, *LCWH*, 283; Meade, *OCMF*, 96-97.
[9] Brewer, *LCWH*, 283; Meade, *OCMF*, 96-97.

LCWH - From Log Cabins to the White House
OCMF - Old Churches, Ministers, and Families of Virginia, vol. 2
RBB - R. Bolling Batte Papers Biographical Card Files, Library of Virginia

The familial relationship between the great martyrs of the faith, William Tyndale and Rowland Taylor, and the great hero of religious liberty, James Madison, is certainly possible, and some published sources claim it is proven.[25] One can hope that further research may yield the evidence that would make the story as conclusive as it is tantalizing.

But there is no doubt that Taylor suffered a martyr's death at the stake. Rather than being burnt at Smithfield like other leading martyrs, Taylor was sent to be burned within sight of the church in Hadleigh to serve as an object lesson of the terrors awaiting those who clung to the Protestant faith. While being led to the place of his execution on February 9, 1555, Taylor removed his boots and outer clothing and called out to the crowd of his parishioners, "Good people! I have taught you nothing but God's holy word, and those lessons that I have taken out of God's blessed book the holy Bible, and I am come hither today to seal it with my blood."[26] After Taylor was fastened to the stake, a local butcher was commanded to light the fire. He refused to do so, claiming he was lame. Another lit the fire, but a guard who had been incensed by Taylor's bold declaration struck the martyr on the head so fiercely that he died instantly. Thus, Taylor did not suffer long in the flames.

Bishop Hooper, who initially refused his Anglican bishopric because he did not wish to wear Catholic vestments, was not so fortunate. On the same day that Taylor was executed in the east of England, Hooper was led to the stake in the west at Gloucester, where he had served as bishop. The faggots carried by horses to the place of execution were green, so the fire "kindled not by and by."[27] Adding to the difficulty, it was a cold and windy day in that part of England. After burning off Hooper's legs, the fire nearly died out completely. Crying for the fire to come and finish his agony, Hooper stood on the remaining stumps praying in anguish. Eventually one of his arms was burned off as well. The hellish torture lasted forty-five minutes before Hooper, retaining consciousness the entire time, finally succumbed to the brutally slow flames.[28]

The Execution of "Ordinary" Protestants

In addition to these leading reformers, an enormous number of lesser-known believers, executed at Mary's command, included many women. The stories of two such martyrs shall suffice to illustrate the depth of cruelty of the queen and her willing accomplices.

Perotine Gosset, together with her mother and sister, was convicted of heresy in the summer of 1556 in Guernsey, in the Channel Isles. Perotine did not reveal to the authorities that she was pregnant. The heat of the flames caused her to give birth to a living son, who was snatched from the flames by bystanders. The sheriff grabbed the baby and threw him back into the burning mass of wood and human flesh. His apparent reason was that the baby had been in the mother when she was convicted to die, and so the death sentence applied to him as well.[29]

In 1557, near the eastern coast of England in the town of Colchester, a young woman named Rose Allin was suspected of heresy. A local justice of the peace, Edmund Tyrrel, began to harass her on the subject of her parents' religious beliefs as she was in town to draw some water. She replied with bold words, saying, "Sir, with that which you call heresy, do I worship my Lord God, I tell you truth."

These words angered the petty official, who responded, "Then I perceive you will burn, gossip, with the rest, for company's sake."

Rose added, "No sir, not for company's sake, but for my Christ's sake, if so I be compelled, and I hope in His mercies, if He call me to it, He will enable me to bear it."

Calling her a "whore," Tyrrel placed her hand in a candle in an attempt to demonstrate the pain of the fires that would engulf her and her family if they did not recant. She did not flinch when he first burned her hand, so he kept the flames hard against her until the hand was burned to the point of revealing bone. Even then she did not give him the satisfaction of crying in agony. A few months later, along with her mother and stepfather, Rose Allin was sent to the stake, and her entire body was burned.[30]

Of the 283 Protestant martyrs burned by Bloody Mary, however, none were more famous than three men burned just outside the entry gate of Balliol College at Oxford University.

The Deaths of Latimer, Ridley, and Cranmer

Hugh Latimer was approximately seventy years old when he was arrested by Mary's officials. Oft described as a second Saul, he had been a leading contender against the Reformation in his early days at Cambridge. In fact, he made a habit of going to meetings of Reformed thinkers to engage them in disputations. Many Catholics believed he was going to be their champion after receiving his doctorate in studies designed to refute the claims of the reformers. However, one of the early leading Protestants, Thomas Bilney, approached Latimer, and by personal testimony convinced Latimer that he could have confidence that God had forgiven his sins by the simple matter of personal faith in Jesus. Experiencing this new birth and forgiveness of sins, Latimer became an instant advocate for the cause he had previously attempted to best in debate.

During the reign of Henry VIII, Latimer served for a period as the bishop of Worcester but was arrested for heresy when Henry reacted against some reforms that he believed strayed too far from the truth of the Catholic Church. During Edward's reign Latimer was a leading preacher, very popular for his sermons that stressed prayer, righteous living, and a personal faith in God fed by the reading of Scripture. Some excerpts from a sermon of Latimer entitled "Thou Canst Make Me Clean" give insight into the spirit of his ministry:

> There cometh a leper unto him, saying: "Lord, if thou wilt, thou canst help me." This leper took Christ to be a Savior, and therefore he cometh unto Him for help and succor. So let us come unto Him, for He is the Savior of mankind, and He is the only Helper that succoreth both our bodies and souls. He saveth our souls by His Word, if when we hear the same and believe it. The salvation of our bodies shall appear at the last day, where soul and body shall come together. So that if the soul be saved, the body is saved, for soul and body shall go together. And so He saveth both our bodies and souls.
>
> Note here also the behavior of this leper man, for by his example, the best doctor in divinity need not to be ashamed to learn, for in him appeareth a marvelous strong faith and confidence that he had in Christ, for he doubted not but that Christ was able to help him, neither mistrusted he His goodness and mercy. Therefore faith hath moved him to come to Christ, and to desire help of Him.[31]

In the same sermon Latimer spoke, almost prophetically, of what would happen to the faith of some should the Catholic Church regain its ascendancy:

> You may note also the inconstancy of the people, who now greatly esteemed and regarded our Savior and His Word, and shortly after consented to His death, by persuasion of the church leaders, which was a great and heinous wickedness in the sight of God. Therefore let us not follow their example, neither let us be persuaded by any man living to forsake God and His Word, but rather let us suffer death for it. Howbeit, I fear that if there should come a persecution, there would be a great number of those which now speak fair of the gospel who would be like this people, for I fear they would soon be persuaded by the papistical priests, to do and speak against Christ, to forsake His Word, and deny the

gospel as these people did, clean forgetting, and setting aside all
that which they had heard of our Savior upon the mountain.[32]

Considerably younger than Latimer, Nicholas Ridley was about fifty-
two years old at the time of his arrest. Another Cambridge man, he had been
promoted by Cranmer first to the position of bishop of Rochester and then
to that of bishop of London. Like Cranmer, he had sided with Lady Jane
Grey in her failed claim to the throne.

After their arrests Ridley and Latimer were taken to Oxford for formal
disputations on their doctrinal deviations from the teachings of Rome. The
sessions were marked with hisses and other loud interjections from the audience of scholars loyal to the pope. There was no question as to the outcome;
the disputations were show trials, nothing more.

Condemned as heretics, Ridley and Latimer were taken to their execution in front of the Balliol College gate in Broad Street on October 16, 1555.
It is lore among some students at Balliol today that the black discoloration on
that portion of the outer walls of the college is from the fires that consumed
these martyrs. (Indeed, the blackness on the immediate walls is different
from the color of those surrounding.) After the two men were tied to the
stake, Ridley's brother was able to tie a bag of gunpowder around each of
their necks to hasten their death and avoid long suffering. As the fire was
lit, Latimer spoke to Ridley in the midst of their ordeal these famous words:
"Be of good comfort, Master Ridley, and play the man; we shall this day light
such a candle by God's grace in England as I trust never shall be put out."[33]

Cranmer suffered greatly in the months following the execution of his
close friends and allies. Like Ridley and Latimer, Cranmer was forced to
go through a process of ecclesiastical trials to determine his guilt of heresy.
Since he had been an archbishop and at one time had been confirmed in this
position by the pope, the tribunal ordered him to appear in Rome within
eighty days to make his answer in person.[34] He said that he would go if the
queen allowed him to do so.[35] Mary naturally refused to let so big a prize
leave her kingdom. Accordingly, he was held in contempt of the ecclesiastical court in Rome and was convicted without a trial in that locale upon his
failure to appear.[36] There were other irregularities in the English proceedings as well. Cranmer was denied the right to counsel and the right to review
and correct the written transcript of his argument, which was a recognized
right of litigants.[37] There was no chance that Cranmer could have been
found innocent of heresy even if the church tribunals had followed the law,
but these irregularities only marked the base spirit of vengeance that drove
Mary and the Council to secure the death of their archenemy.

Under the law of the Roman Church, a person who recanted his heresy would be subjected to severe acts of penance but would have his life spared on the first conviction. A second conviction could not be mitigated in this fashion. Certain persons within the church began to believe that it would be a great advantage if the greatest heretic in England—the archbishop of Canterbury—would return to the fold. Thus, Cranmer was subjected to intense psychological pressure to force him to recant. He was treated harshly, then with leniency; during good times he would be kept under house arrest in pleasant homes, but then he would be returned to prison. Suffering from severe loneliness after the deaths of Ridley and Latimer, he began to trust his jailer.[38] Eventually, he succumbed to the program of pressure and signed a recantation, which was rejected on the grounds that it was not sufficient. He was clearly operating under the impression that the recantation would save his life. Thus, Cranmer, now a broken man, signed a repeated series of confessions and recantations, each more detailed and humiliating than the previous. Mary, however, gave utterly no credence to the proposition that Cranmer should be allowed to live.

A final church service was scheduled at Saint Mary's in Oxford. Cranmer may have been given the impression that he would be allowed to live after this service and his last confession of guilt, but Mary and Gardiner were determined to have him executed for heresy regardless of whether his sentence was lawful. There is no better way to experience this last church service and his execution than to read the dramatic testimony of an unknown Catholic eyewitness:

> On Saturday last, being the 21st of March was his Day
> appointed to die. And because the Morning was much Rainy, the
> Sermon appointed by Mr. Dr. Cole to be made at the Stake, was
> made in S. Mary's Church. Whither Dr. Cranmer was brought
> by the Mayor and Aldermen, and my Lord Williams. With whom
> came divers Gentlemen of the Shire, Sir T. A. Bridges, Sir John
> Browne, and others. Where was prepared over against the Pulpit,
> an high Place for him, that all the People might see him. And
> when he had ascended it, he kneeled down and prayed, weeping
> tenderly: which moved a great number to Tears, that had conceived
> an assured hope of his Conversion and Repentance.
>
> Then Mr. Cole began his Sermon. The sum whereof was this.
> First, He declared Causes, why it was expedient, that he should
> suffer, notwithstanding his Reconciliation. The chief are these,
> One was, for that he had been a great cause of all this Alteration
> in this Realm of England. And when the Matter of the Divorce,

between King Henry VIII, and Queen Katherine, was commenced
in the Court of Rome, he having nothing to do with it, set upon
it, as Judg, which was the entry to all the Inconveniences that followed. Yet in that he excused him, that he thought he did it not
of Malice, but by the Persuasions and Advice of certain Learned
Men. Another was, that he had been the great setter forth of all
this Heresy received into the Church in this last Time; had written in it, had disputed, had continued it, even to the last Hour:
and that it had never been seen in this Realm, (but in the time of
Schism) that any Man continuing so long, hath been pardoned: and
that it was not to be remitted for Examples-sake. Other Causes he
alleged, but these were the chief, why it was not thought good to
pardon him. Other Causes beside, he said, moved the Queen and
the Council thereto, which were not meet and convenient for every
one to understand them. . . .

He comforted and encouraged to take his Death well, by many
places of Scripture. And with these, and such, bidding him nothing
mistrust but he should incontinently receive that the Thief did: To
whom Christ said [Today you will be with me in Paradise (This
phrase was in Latin in the original.)]. . . . He glorified God much
in his Conversion; because it appeared to be his only Work. . . . In
discoursing of which place, he much commended Cranmer, and
qualified his former Doing.

And I had almost forgotten to tell you, that Mr. Cole promised
him, that he should be prayed for in every Church in Oxford, and
should have Mass and Dirge Sung for him; and spake to all the
Priests present to say Mass for his Soul.

When he had ended his Sermon, he desired all the People to
pray for him: Mr. Cranmer kneeling down with them, and praying for himself. I think there was never such a number so earnestly
praying together. For they, that hated him before, now loved him
for his Conversion, and hope of Continuance. They that loved him
before could not sodenly hate him, having hope of his Confession
again of his Fall. So Love and Hope encreased Devotion on every
side.

I shall not need, for the time of Sermon, to describe his
Behaviour, his Sorrowful Countenance, his heavy Cheer, his Face
bedewed with Tears; sometime lifting his Eyes to Heaven in Hope,
sometime casting them down to the Earth for Shame; To be brief,
an Image of Sorrow. . . .

When Praying was done, he stood up, and having leave to speak, said, Good People, I had intended indeed to desire you to pray for me; because Mr. Doctor hath desired, and you have done already, I thank you most heartily for it. And now will I pray for my self, as I could best devise for mine own comfort, and say the Prayer, word for word, as I have written it. And he read it standing: and after kneeled down, and said the Lord's Prayer; and all the People on their Knees devoutly praying with Him. His Prayer was thus:

O Father of Heaven; O Son of God, Redeemer of the World; O Holy Ghost, proceeding from them both, Three Persons and one God, have Mercy upon me most wretched Caitiff, and miserable Sinner. I who have offended both Heaven and Earth, and more grievously than any Tongue can express. . . . Wherefore have Mercy upon me, O Lord, whose Property is always to have Mercy. For although my Sins be great, yet thy Mercy is greater. I crave nothing, O Lord, for mine own Merits, but for thy Name's Sake, that it may be glorified thereby: and for thy dear Son Jesus Christ's sake. . . .

Then rising, he said, Every Man, desireth, good People, at the time of their Deaths, to give some good Exhortation, that others may remember after their Deaths, and be the better thereby. . . .

First, It is an heavy case to see, that many Folks be so much doted upon the Love of this false World, and so careful for it, that for the Love of God, or the Love of the World to come, they seem to care very little or nothing therefore. . . .

The Second Exhortation is, That next unto God, you obey your King and Queen, willingly and gladly, without murmur or grudging. . . .

The third Exhortation is, That you Love all together like Brethren, and Sisters. For alas! pity it is to see, what Contention and Hatred one Christian-Man hath to another: Not taking each other, as Sisters and Brothers; but rather as Strangers and mortal enemies. . . .

The fourth Exhortation shall be to them that have great Substance and Riches of this World. . . . For if ever they had any Ocassion to shew their Charity, they have now at this present the poor People being so many, and Victuals so dear. . . .

And now for so much as I am come to the last End of my Life, whereupon hangeth all my Life passed, and my Life to come,

either to live with my Savior Christ in Heaven, in Joy, or else to
be in Pain ever with wicked Devils in Hell, and I see before mine
Eyes presenting either Heaven ready to receive me, or Hell ready
to swallow me up; I shall therefore declare unto you my very Faith,
how I believe, without Colour of Dissimulation. For now is no
time to dissemble, whatsoever I have written in Times past.

First, I believe in God the Father Almighty, Maker of Heaven
and Earth, etc. and every Article of the Catholic Faith, every
Word and Sentence taught by our Saviour Christ, his Apostles and
Prophets in the Old and New Testaments.

And now I come to the great Thing that troubleth my
Conscience more than any other thing that ever I said or did in
my Life: and that is, the setting abroad of Writings contrary to
the Truth. Which here now I renounce, and refuse, as things written with my Hand, contrary to the Truth, which I thought in my
Heart, and writ for fear of Death, and to save my Life, if it might
be: and that is, all such Bills, which I have written or signed with
mine own Hand, since my Degradation: wherein I have written
many things untrue. And forasmuch as my Hand offended in writing contrary to my Heart, therefore my hand shall first be punished. For if I may come to the Fire, it shall be first burned. And as
for the Pope, I refuse him, as Christ's Enemy and Antichrist, with
all his false Doctrine.

And here being admonished of his Recantation, and
Dissembling, he said, Alas, my Lord, I have been a Man, that all
my Life loved Plainness, and never dissembled now against the
Truth; which I am most sorry for. He added hereunto, That for
the Sacrament, he believed as he had taught in his Book against the
Bishop of Winchester. And here he was suffered to speak no more.

So that his Speech contained chiefly three points, Love to
God, Love to the King, and Love to the Neighbour. In the which
talk he held Men very suspense, which all depended upon the
Conclusion. Where he so far deceived all Mens Expectations, that
at the hearing thereat, they were much amazed, and let him go on
a while, till my Lord Williams had him play the Christian Man,
and remember himself. To whom he answered, That he so did: For
now he spake Truth.

Then he was carried away; and a great number, that did Run
to see him go so wickedly to his Death, ran after him, exhorting
him, while Time was, to remember himself. And one Friar John,
a godly and well-learned Man, all the way traveled with him to

reduce him. But it would not be. What they said in particular I cannot tell, but the Effect appeared in the End. For at the Stake he professed, that he died in all such Opinions as he had taught, and oft repented him of his Recantation.

Coming to the Stake with a cheerful Countenance, and willing Mind, he put off his Garments with haste, and stood upright in his Shirt: and a Bachelor of Divinity, named Elye, of Brazen-nose College, laboured to convert him to his former Recantation. . . . Unto whom he answered, That as concerning his Recantation, he repented it right sore, because he knew it was against the Truth; with other words more. Whereupon the Lord Williams cried, Make short, Make short. Then the Bishop took certain of his Friends by the Hand. But the Bachelor of Divinity refused to take him by the Hand, and blamed all others that so did, and said, He was sorry that ever he came in his Company. And yet again he required him to agree to his former Recantation. And the Bishop answered, (showing his Hand) This is the Hand that wrote it, and therefore shall it suffer first Punishment.

Fire being now put to him, he stretched out his right Hand, and thrust it into the Flame, and held it there a good space, before the Fire came to any other Part of his Body; where his Hand was seen of every Man sensibly burning, crying with a loud Voice, This Hand hath offended. As soon as the Fire got up, he was very soon Dead, never stirring or crying all the while.[39]

Although he wavered, in the end Cranmer demonstrated that true courage is not fearlessness; it is doing what is right even when you have good reason to be afraid.

Chapter Seven

DEBATING FREEDOM INSIDE THE KING'S BENCH PRISON

The Freewiller Conventiclers

If the gospel should reign again . . . the true church might shed blood for believers' sake.

THREAT FROM A REFORMED PASTOR WRITTEN
TO FREEWILL LAYMEN IN PRISON

he next important step in the battle for religious liberty arose not from the educated religious elites such as Cranmer, Ridley, and Latimer, but from a group of ordinary laymen who dared to defy both Bloody Mary *and* the Reformed leadership. Although most of the dissidents were artisans, primarily from the weaving and cloth trade, as ordinary laborers they were in a general sense Tyndale's "ploughboys." The common people whose lives were dramatically changed after a personal confrontation with the living Word of God were the first to resist religious tyranny.

In order to understand the historical context in which these individuals lived, we must first return briefly to the era before Bloody Mary to set the stage for a significant theological dispute that would later erupt between two groups of Protestants held in Her Majesty's prisons.

68

Bibles and Conventicles

Even though the Reformers generally advocated widespread availability of the Bible during the reigns of Henry VIII and Edward VI, the educated and ruling elites consistently objected when the laity—particularly the lower classes—asserted any religious opinion contrary to their own. This drive to keep the common people's understanding of the Bible subjugated to the educated elite began in Henry's time. In 1543, two years after Henry ordered that the Great Bible be made available in every church for public reading, Parliament enacted a statute to delineate when, how, and by whom it could be read, excluding the lower classes entirely.[1] Regardless of these official pronouncements, neither the distribution of Bibles nor the limitation on who could read them ever gained much ground in practice.[2]

In churches where public Bible reading was implemented, parishioners' lives were transformed. One twenty-year-old young man, William Mauldon, left a written account of how he "returned 'everie sundaye' to hear more of the Bible read till his father prevented him."[3] He and another young man combined their funds to buy a New Testament. William appears to have become a Protestant simply by reading the Scriptures, as evidenced by his later attempt to convince his mother that some of the practices of the Catholic Church were "plain idolatry."[4]

Foxe records the spiritual impact of Tyndale's translation upon a farmer named John Maundrel from Wiltshire in southwest England who "became a diligent hearer and a fervent embracer of God's true religion."[5] Maundrel never learned to read, but whenever he was in the company of a willing reader, he asked to have his personal copy of the Scriptures read to him over and over to the point where he had memorized substantial portions. The inference from Foxe's account was that it was the Bible itself that impacted Maundrel's spiritual formation and doctrinal views rather than the teaching of learned clerics—and perhaps even in spite of them.

During Henry VIII's reign, Maundrel was accused of speaking against "holy water and holy bread and such like ceremonies" and thus was made to wander about the market wearing a white sheet and holding a candle. Later, after Mary came to the throne, Maundrel continued to take a bold stand against clerics and their practices, even though he was armed only with his knowledge of the Scriptures. One day when Maundrel and two companions objected to a Vicar's prayers for souls in Purgatory, they were placed in stocks, then carried away to be imprisoned and examined by the chancellor of the diocese. The chancellor demanded that they give an account of how they believed. Maundrel and his friends answered, "As Christian men should and ought to believe . . . in God the Father, and in the Son, and in the holy

Ghost, the Articles of the Creed, the holy Scripture from the first of Genesis to the last of the Apocalypse."

"But that faith," Foxe notes, "the Chancellor would not allow," for he proceeded to question them on the Sacraments, transubstantiation, the authority of the pope, purgatory, and the worshipping of images, to which Maundrel responded that wooden images are "good to roast a shoulder of mutton, but evil in the church: whereby idolatry [is] committed."[6]

Exasperated, the Chancellor turned instead to Maundrel's companion, John Spicer, a bricklayer by trade, and said, "Come on, come on, thou Spicer art to blame, for . . . thou has marred this poor man and hast taught him all these heresies."

"No, M. Chancellor," Spicer replied, "I have not taught him, but I have read to him, and he is able, thanks be to God, to teach both you and me."[7]

Maundrel and Spicer were later burnt at the stake.[8]

It was a similar group of laymen from Essex who set the stage for an important development in religious liberty. This group of religious dissenters, whom Strype would later describe as "Men of strict and holy Lives, but very hot in their Opinions and Disputations,"[9] first came to the attention of officials during Edward's reign. Their controversial leader, Henry Hart, had attracted unfavorable attention as early as 1538, when he was indicted for "unlawful assembly."[10] Thirteen years later, in 1551, another unlawful assembly was held in the village of Bocking in the county of Essex. Authorities who became aware of its presence dubbed it a "conventicle," the name they gave to all such unauthorized religious gatherings.

Conventicles were apparently similar to the flavor of a modern home Bible study, although a comparison to a home church might be more apt. Many of these gatherings were a de facto substitute for attending the local official church. One of the most significant differences between these home gatherings and the official church, whether Catholic or Protestant, was the absence of ordained pastoral leadership sanctioned by the recognized church. The leaders of these coventicles were not appointed by church officials but rather held their positions by virtue of their scriptural knowledge, their spiritual character, and the common consent of the congregation. Lay leadership was a necessity since there is no record of an ordained clergymen among their group. However, these dissenters also rejected the idea that a university-educated, officially ordained minister was necessary to lead a local congregation. First, they contended that Scripture was sufficient to teach all doctrinal matters without guidance from any but the witness of the indwelling Spirit of God in the heart of the individual believer. Second, they believed that the accepted methods of higher learning had a negative effect on the ability of the clergy to lead them aright.

One author of their persuasion, John Champneys, published a tract in 1548 entitled *The harvest is at hand, wherein that tares shall be bound, and cast into the fire and brent.* In it Champneys rebuked the educated clergy, whom he compared to the scribes and Pharisees, for holding their congregations as prisoners to their own "clerkly sophistical doctrines" apart from the power of the Spirit of God.[11] Their deeds revealed, he explained, that these were unregenerate men. Champneys argued that even though "neither reason nor learning can declare the true religion in Christ," these clergy nevertheless "thinketh to minister the gospel by their outward learning" rather than according to the Word of God and the gospel of Christ, for they "are puffed up with the delusion of the devil, and knoweth nothing that is good, but wasteth their brains about questions and arguments and strife of words, with many vain disputations after their corrupt minds, being clearly destitute of all true knowledge."[12]

The extant works of Henry Hart emphasize a similar theme. Hart called for genuine repentance and reformation, even in the midst of a people whom he described as praising God with their lips while their hearts were far from Him. "For the fear that they owe unto [Him]," Hart declared, "turn they unto men's laws and doctrines."[13] Instead of fearing God, the clerics became proud, prompting Hart to warn, "Truly knowledge is dangerous, where love, and obedience is lacking, for it tickleth the mind of fools, and lifteth them up into vanity," while those who "seek to increase in virtue, walk surely." Search the Word of God reverently, he urged, "lest ye stumble in your way, and take a sudden fall."[14] In a tone echoing the biblical prophets, Hart comforted and cautioned his readers with these words:

> Woe be to those bishops, pastors / and lawyers / of what name and place so ever they be, which boast of power and authority to rule and govern another / and yet have no respect to their own souls: for . . . miserably shall they be rewarded that bear the name of christian people which seek holiness only by outward sacraments and signs, not regarding what the heart and inward conscience be / and also say in your selves, tush we be well enough, for the holy laws ceremonies / and Sacraments of God are remaining among us and thereby we are known to be his people. Nevertheless be thou of good comfort, O thou little worm Jacob, and thou despised Israel, for thy redeemer liveth: fear neither the proud boasting nor threatening of thine enemies. . . .
>
> S. Paul saith, where are the wise? Where are the scribes? Where are the disputers of this world, hath not God made the wisdom of the world foolishness? For the foolishness of God, saith

he, is wiser than men, and the weakness of God, is stronger than men . . . for God hath chosen the foolish before the world, that he might confound the wise, and the weak before the world hath God chosen, saith Paul, that he might confound the mighty and the vile and despised before the world hath God chosen, yea, and that which is nothing saith he, that he might destroy that which is ought, that no flesh should rejoice in his presence.

Therefore, do not justify your selves as pharisees, neither exalt anything in flesh and blood, for the things which men highly magnify, saith the Lord, be abominable in the sight of God. Lay away your high reasons, and let God's word although it seem simple and rude lead you, seek not to join your wisdom with God, lest in coveting to climb so high, ye take a great fall[;] obedience is an acceptable offering.[15]

The Freewillers and the Predestinators

Champneys, Hart, and their colleagues were ordinary laymen and women who took to heart Cranmer's admonition to read the Scripture. When they did, they reached doctrinal conclusions quite different from those of the Anglican hierarchy. Naturally enough, they sought religious fellowship with those who were like-minded. The historical significance of these independent gatherings was noted by John Strype who called them "the first that made separation from the Reformed Church of England."[16] They are commonly identified today as the "Freewillers," a name Strype gave them because they engaged in a key dispute with reformed Anglicans over the doctrine of predestination. Modern historians also confirm their importance. British scholar Thomas Freeman concurs with Strype, stating, "The Freewillers were historically significant: they were the first English Protestants to establish organised congregations which not only repudiated, but also challenged, the authority of the Protestant clerical leadership."[17]

The Freewillers held a service in a home in Bocking on Christmas Day in 1550. News of this came into the hands of the Privy Council, who requested the lord chancellor, Richard Rich, to apprehend the owner of the home, identified as "one 'Upcharde,'" to bring him forward for interrogation.[18] Upcharde's testimony revealed that about sixty persons had met in his home to discuss "'thinges of the Scripture, speciallie wheather it were necessarie to stand or kneele, barehedde, or covered at prayer.' The assembly eventually concluded that it was the attitude of the heart which mattered before God, and not external appearances at ceremonies."[19] Eventually twelve additional members of the coventicle were arrested and taken before the officials for interrogation on February 3. They were treated with relative leniency, however, when the nature of their views was revealed.[20] Although discussion of the doctrine of election was touched upon in these custodial interrogations, it does not appear to have been a major focus of the inquiry.

The most heated exchanges between these lay conventiclers and the Edwardian Anglican leadership erupted a few years later around 1555—when both sides were in the King's Bench prison awaiting their fates at the hands of Bloody Mary. One faction in this theological fight was composed of some of the leading Anglican clergymen of the Edwardian years. This included John Bradford, the clear leader of the "Predestinators," along with Rowland Taylor, John Philpot, and Robert Ferrar, who had been bishop of St. David's. The Freewillers in prison were led by a layman named John Trewe, but their most significant leader, Henry Hart, apparently remained outside the prison walls even though he was clearly involved in the dispute.

The principal evidence concerning this dispute is from a short book published in 1819 by an Oxford scholar, Richard Laurence, who researched all available documentation regarding the combatants in the King's Bench prison and subsequently republished two of these original manuscripts. The first section of his publication is a defense of predestination by John Bradford called *A Treatise on Predestination, with an answer to certain Enormities Caluminously Gathered of one to slander God's Truth*. The second document was entitled *John Trewe, the unworthy marked Servant of the Lord, being in bands for the testimony of Jesu, signifieth the cause of contention in the King's Bench, as concerning sects in religion, the 30th of January, Anno Dom. 1555*.

Bradford's treatise was written in response to the document of a "calumnious calumniator,"[21] whom historians believe was none other than Henry Hart.[22] Hart's tract evidently began to require the attention of Bradford, who served a pastoral role while in prison by maintaining correspondence with a diverse "network" of Protestants.[23] Two prominent women among this group had begun to express doubts about the doctrine of predestination as Bradford had taught it to them.[24] Their doubts were apparently fueled, in part, by Hart's tract.

Bradford, like most other leading Anglicans of the period, taught that God chose two groups of people before the foundation of the world. One group, the elect, would receive salvation as a result of God's irresistible grace. The elect would be saved with absolute certainty, while those not chosen would receive eternal damnation. In *A short and pithie defence of the doctrine of holy election and predestination of God*, Bradford writes that God's heirs "are elect and predestinate to the praise of God's glory, which we should more care for, than for the salvation of all the world":

This glory of the Lord is set forth as well in them that perish and are reprobates, as in the elect, and therefore S. John bringing in the place of Isaiah speaking of the reprobate saith, that Isaiah spake that he when he saw the glory of the Lord. . . . Let not [the reprobates'] eyes be evil because God is good, and doth good to whom it pleaseth him. . . . Let us therefore labour, study, cry, and pray for repentance and faith, and then cannot we be damned, because we are the blessed of the father before all worlds, and therefore we believe, therefore we repent.[25]

While the women who corresponded with Bradford appeared to believe that his teaching was correct, they feared that they might not be part of the elect. The freewill position, as espoused by Hart and John Trewe, had substantial appeal to people who aspired to be believers but who were uncertain whether God had included them among the elect. Hart and Trewe taught that anyone who wanted to be a believer in Christ could obtain salvation by receiving salvation through faith. It was possible to lose salvation, they taught, but this would only happen for those who deliberately repudiated God in their hearts and in their actions. In Trewe's own words:

[The predestinators] affirm, that Christ hath not died for all men. Whereby they make Christ inferior to Adam and grace to sin, and doth destroy faith, and the certainty of our election; and it is enough to drive as many, as believe it, to despair, for lack of knowledge whether Christ died for them or not. . . . For we, that do hold and affirm the truth, that Christ died for all men, as appeareth Gen. iii. c. xii. a. xxii. d. Psal. lxxxii. b. Psal. cxlv. Esay liii. John i. c. Rom. v. c. 1 Cor. xv. C. 2 Cor v. c. 1 Tim. ii. a. 1 John ii. a. Heb. ii. c.; we do by the holy Scriptures satisfy every man that doth repent and unfeignedly believe with a lively faith [that he] is in the state of salvation, and one of God's elect children, and shall certainly be saved, if he do not with malice of heart, utterly forsake God, and despise his word and ordinance, and become a persecutor of his children.[26]

Bradford was concerned that Hart and Trew's view might appeal to these women's desire for assurance that Jesus had died for them. He could not stand by while these lay preachers misled women with what he believed to be false doctrine.

Bradford quoted the words that Hart had written to try to convey the idea that Jesus died for all, not just the elect: "The Holy Ghost saith, 'The Lord is loving to every man, and his mercy over all his works.' And again by

St. John, 'that Christ is the true light that lighteneth every man that cometh into the world.'"[27] Bradford, who was a trained religious scholar, answered Hart with an *ad hominem* attack: "These be the words wherein a man may easily see he hath not learned his A B C concerning the Scriptures, or else his judgment could not be so base."[28]

Trewe mourned the attitude of his learned prisonmates toward those who had not received formal education:

> Moreover we saw in that they did hold and affirm, that none but great learned men could have the true understanding of the word of God; and in that they would not nor could not answer us how they approved their doctrine; and in forbidding us to ask how they could approve that, which they taught; and in the defacing, displacing, and washing away of the holy Scriptures, and such like, they do jointly agree with the Papists, that do the like to maintain their superstition, idolatry, and blasphemy, and their wicked beastly living . . . affirming, that no simple man without the tongues can truly understand them . . . also it doth cause all such as believe to neglect reading of the holy Scriptures, and to fall to other vanities and wickedness, because *they* are so manifestly and flat *against that most wicked and false opinion.*[29]

It was common to attack all such religious dissenters for their lack of formal education and official ordination. John Champneys's work was ridiculed in a similar manner. One John Veron, in his work *A fruteful treatise of predestination*, wrote, "For, there be none so great enemies unto learning, as they that be altogether unlearned, and without godly knowledge, as this valiant champion of the free will men is, who is so rude and ignorant, that he can not construe 2 lines of Saint Augustine."[30]

While the jabs of Veron and the concerns raised by Bradford's female correspondents demonstrated that the conflict between free will and predestination existed outside the walls of the King's Gate prison, it was inside the prison that the soteriological debate became the most heated. The conflict between the two camps, however, did not begin with the doctrine of salvation, but erupted over *gambling*. The predestination faction within the prison apparently spent time in gambling contests with cards, dice, and "bowls." The freewill group challenged this as sinful behavior and a misuse of time that could otherwise be better used in spiritual preparation for their likely upcoming martyrdom. Perhaps the freewill faction also took offense with the fact that the predestinators had extra money for gambling, while the freewill group lacked money for basic necessities since all prisoners were dependent on outside sources of money for food and essentials to make their lives bearable.[31] The predestinarians had aristocratic connections and monetary support from the societal elite. The freewill faction voiced a long-standing accusation that the predestinarians showed "respect of persons preferring the wealthy, which if they be liberal, though they be drowned in many vices."[32] It would have been a simple solution for the wealthier faction to have used their gambling money to buy food for their poorer brothers.

The response of the predestinarians to this complaint about gambling led this group into an intense debate over the doctrines of salvation. They argued that an elect believer would never repudiate the faith, so they need not be concerned about preparing for martyrdom. Nor could they commit a serious sin that would lead to questions about their salvation, so any argument that gambling was a sin was in error. God would preserve them, as the elect, from committing serious sin. Bradford wrote in a letter to "certain men, which maintain the heresy . . . concerning man's free-will":

> For whom [God] loves he leaves not, but loves them unto the end, (John xiii.) so that perseverance is proper to them, and distinguishes them from hypocrites and such as seem to others, and sometimes to themselves also, that they are God's children, which if they once were indeed, then, as St John says, they should not sin the sin unto death, nor should they go out of God's church, but as Paul says, should persevere to the end.[33]

Each of the warring factions did its best to convince the other Protestants in the hellish prison to convert to their viewpoint. The scholarly advocates of Reformed theology were far more effective in securing converts. There were efforts to try to find a method of peaceful reconciliation through the signing of mutually agreeable statements of belief, although no such accord was ever achieved. Invariably, each side accused the other of dealing in bad faith.

One of the most notable differences between Bradford's and Trewe's styles in their arguments over election and holy living concerns the use of Scripture. The only Scripture directly quoted in Bradford's whole response to Henry Hart is in a passage quoted from Hart's work. Although he sporadically paraphrases recognizable passages of the New Testament, he never gives a direct citation to any particular chapter, usually simply saying "as St. Paul sayeth" or the like. In contrast, Trewe's short work contains several direct citations of passages of Scripture, making clear to the reader which passages are claimed to support his arguments.

Both sides clearly believed that the other camp's errors amounted to heresy. As we discern the history of religious liberty, the important question is, "What is to be done with 'heretics'?" The freewiller Trewe reports the views of the Reformers on this critical issue:

> They did not only fall out with us, and after their accustomed manner call and report us heretics, cast dust in our faces, and give judgment of damnation on us, and otherways ungodly handled us; *but also threatened us, that we were like to die for it, if the Gospel should reign again, affirming that the true church might shed blood for believers' sake, of the which we brought to disprove them.*[34]

In other words, the pro-gambling faction told the antigambling dissenters, *If we return to power, watch out; we will put you to the sword ourselves for your heresy.* Since the evidence of this threat comes from the alleged victim, one must consider the possibility that the report of the threat was an exaggeration or an angry declaration made in the heat of argument. Unfortunately, however, the threat is generally consistent with views expressed by all the major Reformers of the era: Heretics must be punished.

Knox's Answer to His "Adversarie"

One of the most important figures of the Reformation, John Knox, writing from the safety of exile in Geneva, entered into this debate against the King's Bench freewillers sometime prior to 1560. Knox, along with hundreds of other Reformed leaders, had escaped to Geneva in the early days of Mary's reign. It appears that he may have had some earlier dealing with the freewill faction in Kent, having been sent there to preach in 1551.[35] Somewhere along the way, Knox obtained a copy of a pamphlet on the freewill doctrine commonly referred to as *The confutation of the errors of the careless by necessity*, which provoked alarm upon its arrival in Geneva. The only surviving portions of this freewill work are the passages quoted by Knox in his reply entitled *An answer to a great number of blasphemous cauillations written by an Anabaptist, and aduersarie to Gods eternal predestination.*

Knox quoted his "adversarie" concerning a theme familiar to the King's Bench dispute—namely, the freewillers' criticism that the predestinarians were libertine in their approach to sin. "What can the devil wish his member to teach more for the advancement of his kingdom," the adversarie asked, "than if they be persuaded that neither well doing availeth or pleaseth God, nor evil doing hindreth unto salvation?"[36] Knox's response to this charge is especially pertinent to the study of religious liberty:

> Before I have required, and yet again do require of God's
> faithful lieutenants in earth, I mean of lawful Magistrates, who

rule in God's fear, whom ye utterly study to abolish, and deprive, of them I say, I have required justice to be ministered betwixt us, and you, without respect of persons.[37]

Knox went on to suggest that if the Reformers were the ones in doctrinal error, then let them "without mercy die the death."[38] He nevertheless made clear that he believed his freewill opponents were the ones guilty of heresy, saying, "Then can we not cease to desire that this your former blasphemy may be revenged upon your own heads."[39] The idea that believers could be friends by agreeing to disagree on the specifics of the doctrine of election was foreign to his line of argument. Heresy demanded punishment by the magistrate, Knox argued.

Knox then turned quickly to defend Calvin's Geneva, which had already acquired infamy for the execution of the heretic Servetus in 1553:

> What maketh the poor city of Geneva, poor I say, in man's
> eyes, but rich before God, by the plentiful abundance of his heav-
> enly graces, what maketh it, I say, so odious to the carnal men of
> this world? Assuredly not this doctrine, wherewith ye charge us.
> For that could well please the carnal man, to let him live at his
> pleasure, without all punishment. Is it not the just rigor of justice,
> and the severity of discipline executed therein, in such sort, that
> no manifest offender, where soever he hath committed his offense,
> doth there escape punishment? Is not this it, that so doth offend,
> not only the licentious of the world? But even you dissembling
> hypocrites, can not abide, that the sword of God's vengeance shall
> strike the murderer, the blasphemer, and such others, as God by
> his word commandeth to die. Not so by your judgments, he must
> live, he may repent. And those commonwealths, do ye highly
> praise, where men may live as they list [i.e., wish], be subject to no
> law, nor order, yea where the drunkard and such others abomi-
> nable persons are permitted, to live quietly & find favor to escape
> punishment & shame. But because in the streets of Geneva dare
> no notable malefactor more show his face (all praise and glory be
> unto God) than dare the owl in the bright sun therefore it is hated.
> Therefore it is called blood thirsty, and thus blasphemously tra-
> duced, as after ye write.[40]

Like Calvin before him, Knox repeatedly justified the use of the death penalty for those who blaspheme God and for those who "obstinately . . . maintain and defend doctrine & diabolical opinions, plainly impugning to God's truth."[41]

Knox defended the apparent harshness of punishing a dissenter on a matter of conscience:

> We say the man is not persecuted, for his conscience, that declining from God, blaspheming his majesty, and condemning his religion obstinately defendeth erroneous and false doctrine. This man I say lawfully convicted, if he suffer the death, pronounced by a lawful Magistrate, is not persecuted (as in the name of Servetus ye furiously complain) but he suffereth punishment according to God's commandment pronounced in Deuteronomy, the 13th chapter.[42]

In a laundry list of those deserving the death penalty for their blasphemies, heresies, and diabolical opinions, Knox listed the Jews, both of his day and of old, as the "fifth sort" who deserve this condemnation. Knox was not alone in his anti-Semitic views. Luther wrote a book *On the Jews and Their Lies* in 1543; its title is a sufficient summary of its contents.

In the course of his defense of the death penalty for heretics and blasphemers, Knox attacked a little-known scholar by the name of Sebastian Castellio.[43] He labeled Castellio as the "champion" of the freewillers' belief that it was wrong to punish heretics by the imposition of the death penalty, although Knox does not quote any material by his "adversarie" that mentions Castellio, an important critic of Calvin in Switzerland.[44] We will examine the dispute between Calvin and Castellio in detail in the next chapter. For now it is important to note that Knox clearly believed that the debate in the King's Bench prison and the debates in Geneva were intertwined.

The Conventiclers' Legacy

Almost all of the freewillers were executed by Mary, died in prison, or disappeared from view after the succession of Elizabeth. There is no record of the re-creation of any of their congregations after this period. However, the debate they started—that it was sinful for Christians to take the lives of other Christians for doctrinal differences—would continue to percolate, if through no other medium than the writings of John Knox, who published their views in the process of refuting them.

These were the first Protestants to separate from the reformed Church of England, thereby declaring that they did not need leaders who had been formally educated or ordained by the official church. There are two key ideas implicit in the arguments of these "lowly" Christians: first, that individual believers had the right to interpret the Scriptures for themselves; and second, that the Scriptures did not require people to attend a church sanctioned by either the government or an ecclesiastical hierarchy. Both the idea of individual free exercise and objections to official establishments of religion were thus introduced into the British system by laymen lacking real education but who had, in fulfillment of Tyndale's dream, learned the Scriptures for themselves.

Chapter Eight

DEFENDING A DOCTRINE, KILLING A MAN

Religious Liberty in Calvin's Geneva

The defense of doctrine is not the affair of the magistrate but of the doctor. What has the sword to do with doctrine?
SEBASTIAN CASTELLIO

Geneva, Switzerland, played a vital role in the development of English and American concepts of religious liberty. This is true, in part, because many English Reformers fled there during Bloody Mary's persecutions. It was during this period that some of these English refugees developed the Geneva Bible, the translation the Pilgrims carried with them to Plymouth Rock. Even without these years of sojourn, however, Geneva would have been important to the religious heritage of England and America because the theology of Geneva's most famous citizen had an enormous impact on the development of Protestant Christianity.

Calvin on Liberty

John Calvin. His name provokes intense reactions nearly five hundred years after his death. To many, he is a great hero of the faith. Others view him from the opposite perspective. Regardless, there is no doubt that he was a profound thinker whose influence is nearly impossible to overstate.

Calvin placed great emphasis on what he referred to as a *duplex regimen*, or "twofold government." This may be understood as "two worlds, over which different kings and different laws have authority."[1] A correlative idea was the independence of the institutional church from the state. (This view clearly differed from the English Reformation, which was *predicated* on state control of the church.) Magistrates, Calvin wrote, are "invested with divine authority, and are wholly God's representatives . . . acting as his vice regents," and yet they must not "make laws according to their own decision concerning religion and the worship of God."[2] Despite some parallels to the Catholic view of the independence of the church, Calvin stopped well short of ecclesiastical supremacy in the papal tradition that claimed the power to name and depose kings.

The independence of the institutional church is undoubtedly an important component of religious liberty, and on this score, Calvin was an advocate. He did much to defend the authority of the church over the state in spiritual matters and simultaneously overthrow the dominance of the Roman Catholic Church, along with the demand of adherence to its particular creed. "Geneva," John Adams wrote, "which had shaken off the yoke of its bishop and the Duke of Savoy, and erected itself into a republic, under the title of a free city, for the sake of liberty of conscience," should never be "forgotten or despised. Religious liberty owes it much respect, Servetus notwithstanding."[3]

However, when it came to the liberty of the individual to worship God as he wished—in Geneva or elsewhere—Calvin was an adamant opponent in both theory and practice. He often wrote of "liberty of conscience," especially in his earlier works, but there is little question that this refers only to spiritual freedom, not political. A foretaste of his approach can be found in his sermon commentaries on Deuteronomy 13, which describe Israel's duty to put to death those individuals who urged the nation to follow false gods. "Now at first sight," Calvin granted, "this Law seemeth to be over-straight: for is it meet that a man should be punished so sore for speaking his mind?" The answer was unequivocal: "Let us not think that this law is a special law for the Jews; but let us understand that GOD intended to deliver us a general rule, to which we must tie ourselves."[4] He reasoned that the purpose of such laws is the honor and glory of God; since men are punished for speaking against another person, how much more should they be punished for blaspheming the eternal God of the universe.

Calvin did not face pagans who forthrightly called for the worship of foreign gods; rather, his concern was with professing Christians who dared to hold a doctrine he found to be heretical. He told his Geneva congregation, "There is a man that goes about to pervert the truth through fond devotion; and to turn it into untruth: the same man ought to die"—along with idolaters, blasphemers, Muslims, and other deviant individuals.[5] Who did Calvin think was responsible for carrying out the sentence of death in order to preserve the "purity" of religion?

> It is said in the Psalm, that kings shall come to submit themselves to him that was to be sent to be the redeemer. And again that they shall be as foster fathers to the Church, and that Queens shall give her suck; that is to say, that such as have the sword of Justice in their hand, shall take God's Church into their protection to maintain it in the pure doctrine, and in the same Religion that is set down in God's word. Since it is so, it is to be concluded, not only that it is Lawful for all Kings and Magistrates, to punish heretics and such as have perverted the pure truth: but also that they be bound to do it, and that they misbehave themselves towards GOD if they suffer errors to roost without redress, and employ not their whole power to show a greater zeal in that behalf than in all other things.[6]

Calvin's teachings of political religious intolerance influenced English theories for a considerable period. Moreover, his views on this score were, as we will see in later chapters, put into practice with an unflinching hand in colonial Massachusetts. To understand Calvin's ideas and doctrines, we must not only examine the infamous incident regarding the execution of the heretic Servetus but also the ensuing debate with Calvin's lieutenant-turned-critic, Sebastian Castellio.

Calvin and Servetus

Michael Servetus was a Spaniard born in 1511 who became a student at the University of Toulouse, which had a reputation for Catholic orthodoxy. As young Servetus quickly discovered, however, "the very citadel of doctrinal rectitude harbored evangelicals" and had turned into a "hotbed of radicalism"—which meant that students were literally risking their lives to read the Bible in its original languages late into the night, eagerly discussing the texts and their implications.[7]

Historian Roland Bainton suggests that Servetus was perplexed by the refusal of Spanish Moors and Jews to embrace the Trinity—which would, of course, require recognition of the deity of Jesus Christ.[8] After studying Scripture and the early church fathers at Toulouse, Servetus found to his amazement that the word *Trinity* is not mentioned in the Bible even though it was punishable by death, according to the Code of Justinian, to deny that God exists in three persons. Servetus ended up with a self-concocted amalgamation of truth and error. He denied that the Holy Spirit was a separate person of the Godhead and believed that there was indeed a preexistent Word, with God forever. The Son, on the other hand, was "produced by the union of this Word with the man Jesus" whose personality existed not eternally, but from the time of his conception.[9] Servetus likewise held idiosyncratic views concerning the capacity of man to become unified with deity through the sacraments.[10] No orthodox Christian of any stripe could conclude otherwise: Servetus was a heretic.

In 1531, Servetus published his views in *The Errors of the Trinity* near Strasbourg.[11] He attempted to set up residence in both Bern and Strasbourg, only to be rejected because of his refusal to confess to the eternal personhood of the Son of God. He began to live in France under an assumed name, eventually turning to the study of medicine in Paris. He had obvious talent in this arena and is credited with first discovering the pulmonary circulation of the blood.[12] While practicing medicine in France, he became acquainted with Anabaptists and adopted their view that baptism of infants was of no effect because it preceded personal faith.[13]

Fully convinced of his own ability to argue theology, Servetus began corresponding with Calvin. Eventually Calvin refused further answer and simply sent him a copy of the *Institutes*. Servetus returned it with insulting comments in the margins. This caused Calvin to remark in 1546 that if Servetus came to Geneva, he would never let the heretic escape alive if it was within his power to prevent it.[14]

In early 1553, Servetus was arrested for heresy by Catholic officials in Lyons, where he had been living under the assumed name of Michael Villanovanus. To aid the inquisition, Calvin sent the Catholic officers (albeit reluctantly, some say) the copy of his *Institutes* containing Servetus's handwritten contemptuous comments. As one author remarks, "Thus Calvin collaborated with the Inquisition."[15] However, Servetus escaped from the jailer's house and made his way out of the city on foot, leaving his accusers to burn him in effigy, along with his books. After spending a short time elsewhere in France, he planned to journey to Naples where he could work as a physician. His intent was to get there via Geneva and Zurich. This plan was quickly frustrated. As Servetus later testified during his trial, he arrived in Geneva on a Saturday night. The next morning he had no choice but to attend the mandatory church service where he was recognized by some who knew him from Lyons. They revealed his presence to John Calvin, who immediately instigated Servetus's arrest on a capital charge of heresy.[16]

Since Servetus had spread no heresy *in* Geneva, there was a serious question of the city's jurisdiction for any prior offense committed elsewhere. Moreover, the normal practice of Geneva was to banish heretics in the first instance. In fact, the law under which the council prosecuted him was not the code of Geneva but the Code of Justinian, which ordered death for both the denial of the Trinity and the denial of infant baptism. Servetus's views on the Trinity at his multiple hearings were somewhat equivocal. He stated that "he did believe in the Trinity, that is, in the Father, the Son, and the Holy Spirit, three persons in God. But he interpreted the word 'person' . . . to mean simply a mode of the divine manifestation."[17] On baptism, there was no attempt at confusion or compromise. Infant baptism was, he said, "a diabolical invention—an infernal falsehood to destroy the whole of Christianity."[18]

Servetus was not allowed a lawyer at his trial, but he was clever enough on his own to challenge the jurisdiction to try him under the Code of Justinian since Calvin disbelieved Justinian in regard to many matters of religion and the church, which Calvin considered corrupt.[19] Servetus also urged that Calvin be brought to trial for having betrayed him to the Inquisition.[20] These petitions were useless. Servetus was convicted by the Council of Geneva on the charges of denying both the Trinity and the efficacy of infant baptism. Calvin served only as his accuser. On October 27, 1553, Servetus was chained to the stake, where he was heard to cry out, "O Jesus, thou Son of the eternal God, have pity on me!" He was slowly burned along with a copy of his writings. William Farel, a theologian who had accompanied him to the stake, noted that if he had been willing to confess Jesus as the eternal Son of God, he could have avoided the flames.

The execution of Servetus was not unusual in its time, perhaps save for the procedural and jurisdictional irregularities already noted. Calvin's embrace of the death penalty for heresy was in essence no different from either Catholic or Anglican practices, although both of these denominations executed a far greater number of religious dissenters.

Calvin's involvement with and endorsement of this execution is notable for two significant reasons. First, this execution prompted one of Calvin's associates, Sebastian Castellio, vigorously and openly to attack the doctrine of death for heresy. Castellio began to write and publish a series of books castigating both Calvin's theories and actions but still maintaining the supremacy of Scripture. One of these, titled *De Haereticis* (*Concerning Heretics*), became what some consider the century's most significant work on the continent advocating religious toleration.[21] Second, Calvin and one of his important associates, Theodore Beza, undertook a written defense of Geneva's execution of Servetus. Calvin's theological arguments related to this matter were also carried on by John Knox, the famed Scottish reformer, and many others both on the continent and across the English Channel for a considerable period of time.

Calvin and Castellio

The argument between Castellio and Calvin over religious liberty is perhaps one of the most important in history, at least symbolically speaking. And it is clear that both men's views were significant in the development of British views on the matter. As we saw in the prior chapter, the views of Castellio were attributed to the freewillers in King's Bench prison in the mid-1550s. As later chapters will reveal, advocates for religious liberty ranging from Roger Williams to John Locke to Leonard Busher, a seventeenth-century English Baptist, included quotations from Castellio in their own works or possessed copies of Castellio's discourses in their libraries. One scholar writes, "At a time of extreme dogmatism, Castellio was the first to emphasize and place a firm and enduring foundation for the principle of tolerance."[22] Castellio's arguments are now readily available, but surprisingly Calvin's complete work in opposition to religious liberty is found only in the original languages of Latin and French. A full English text of John Knox's case against religious liberty does exist, published in 1560, which can be construed as an authoritative contemporary voice from the Reformed perspective.

Sebastian Castellio was born in the Duchy of Savoy in 1515 to a peasant and his wife. Despite his humble beginnings his academic aptitude was undoubtedly significant, allowing him the opportunity to receive a good education. He studied as a young man at the Collège de la Trinité in Lyon, where he likely witnessed the execution of Protestant heretics at the hands of a cardinal in 1540.[23] It soon became clear that as a newly converted Protestant, he either had to flee or else meet the same fiery death. Castellio chose to journey to Strasbourg, a city where the Reformation had met with a warm welcome. At the time Calvin was also in Strasbourg during his exile from Geneva by the city fathers. Castellio lived in Calvin's home for a short period and was drawn into the Genevan exile's circle of friends.

Castellio moved to Geneva in June 1541, a few months before Calvin's triumphant return at the request of the city. Upon Farel's recommendation, he was hired as the head teacher of the Collège de Rive, which existed to provide solidly Protestant and humanist instruction.[24] In addition to his teaching duties, Castellio started a translation of the Bible into French, wrote a relatively popular children's book combining the teaching of Latin with Christian instruction, and preached in some of the nearby villages. He sought permission to be a pastor, but this request was rejected by Calvin and the church he headed. This dispute soured their relationship to a considerable degree although Calvin did write a letter of reference for Castellio when he left for Basel in 1545.[25]

Calvin and Castellio had disputed over two doctrinal points prior to the latter's departure for Basel. One centered on the question of whether the Song of Solomon was an allegory (as Calvin believed) or a shameful love poem (as Castellio thought). The other involved a point in the Apostle's Creed which says that after Christ was buried He "descended into hell." Calvin contended that this should be understood to express an allegorical truth—that Christ's death included the spiritual punishment by God on our sins—that is, the sins of the elect. Castellio took it to be a literal statement.[26]

While in Basel, Castellio finished two significant Bible translations. One, a Latin version translated from Hebrew that displayed Castellio's talent as a scholar and classical linguist, was published in 1551. Four years later he completed a French translation "based on the common speech and designed for the ordinary uneducated reader."[27] In his desire to place a French Bible within the reach of the ordinary layman, he appears to have shared in the vision of Tyndale and his ploughboys.

Of special interest to this study of religious liberty is Castellio's dedication of his Latin Bible to England's Edward VI and the preface of his French Bible, addressed to both the king of France and the nation's Catholics and Protestants as a whole. The first work unveils his earliest plea for religious toleration, which predates the Servetus incident by two years; it introduced themes on which he later expounded in his numerous writings.[28] To the French king, he wrote:

> Hitherto the world has always made this mistake. The prophets, the apostles, so many thousands of martyrs, and even the Son of God were put to death under color of religion. An account must be given for all this blood by those who have been striking at random in the night of ignorance. . . . Believe me, your Majesty, the world today is neither better nor wiser nor more enlightened than formerly. It were better, therefore, in view of so much doubt and confusion to wait before shooting until the dawn, or until things are better disentangled, lest in the darkness and confusion we do that of which afterwards we shall have to say, "I did not intend to."[29]

And to the Catholics, he urged:

> Recall how you have treated the Evangelicals. You have pursued and imprisoned them and left them to be consumed of lice

and rot in foul dungeons in hideous darkness and the shadow
of death, and then you have roasted them alive at a slow fire to
prolong their torture. And for what crime? Because they did not
believe in the pope, the mass, purgatory, and other things, which
are so far from being based on Scripture that even the very names
are not to be found there. Is that a good and just cause for burning
men alive?[30]

Interestingly, Calvin had used almost the exact same language in
the prefatory address to King Francis in his 1536 edition of the *Institutes.*
Referring to the "order of priests," he wrote, "Why, therefore, do they fight
with such ferocity and bitterness for the Mass, purgatory, pilgrimages, and
trifles of that sort . . . even though they prove nothing of them from God's
Word?"[31] Yet rather than pleading with the king to be an example of tolerance and charity, as Castellio did repeatedly, Calvin advocated tolerance
only for what he considered the true church. "Our doctrine must tower
unvanquished above all the glory and above all the might of the world," he
declared.[32] And it was none other than the king himself who must wield his
earthly sword on its behalf.[33]

Castellio, on the other hand, was fond of pointing out how error in
religious matters is best corrected by means of the written or spoken word
instead of force:

> Here are the three remedies which you employ: to shed blood,
> to force consciences, and to condemn as infidels those who do not
> agree with your doctrine. . . . But rationalize as much as you please
> before men and draw as many fine distinctions as you please, nev-
> ertheless we know well, and I call your own consciences to witness,
> that you are doing to others what you would not have done unto
> you. . . .
> When Jesus disputed with the Jews, though they were highly
> opinionated, he was sometimes able to reduce them to silence
> with a single word. . . . We need only to ask those who force con-
> sciences, "Would you like to have yours forced?" And immediately
> their own conscience, which is worth more than a thousand wit-
> nesses, will convict and make them dumb.[34]

Castellio expanded further his appeal by explaining that the precise
punishment for heresy required in Scripture is excommunication, not death,
and that "to extend the law of Moses to cover those who err in the interpretation of Scripture is to be too ingenious in shedding blood."[35]

Just five months after the execution of Servetus—after the publication of the Latin translation and prior to the publication of the French—Castellio, using the pseudonym Martin Bellius, published an anthology of works denouncing the burning of this heretic in Geneva.[36] The preface of the book contains a long dedication to a German prince, Duke Christoph of Wurttemberg. This dedication begins with an allegorical question: Castellio asks the prince what he would do if he went on a journey, leaving his subjects with instructions to make robes ready for his return, only to find upon his arrival that his people were engaged in vicious disputes, in which some were killing others over their views of the nature of his return:

> Would you, O Prince, commend such citizens? Suppose, however, that some did their duty and followed your command to prepare the white robes, but the others oppressed them on that account and put them to death. Would you not rigorously destroy such scoundrels?
>
> But what if these homicides claimed to have done all this in your name and in accord with your command, even though you had previously expressly forbidden it? Would you not consider such outrageous conduct deserved to be punished without mercy?[37]

Castellio then turned quickly from the allegory to a description of the situation at hand in Geneva and the rest of Europe. He identified pride as the root reason persecution was so rampant:

> Men are puffed up with knowledge or with a false opinion of knowledge and look down upon others. Pride is followed by cruelty and persecution so that now scarcely anyone is able to endure another who differs at all from him. Although opinions are almost as numerous as men, nevertheless there is hardly any sect which does not condemn all others and desire to reign alone. Hence arise banishments, chains, imprisonments, stakes, and gallows and this miserable rage to visit daily penalties upon those who differ from the might about matters hitherto unknown, for so many centuries disputed, and not yet cleared up.[38]

As indicated in this passage, Castellio took the position that many of the disputed points of theology are difficult questions of scriptural interpretation, but none of these are necessary to be known with certainty for salvation. For example, he denied that differences over forms of communion or baptism should justify any professing Christian putting to death one who disagreed on such matters.[39]

Importantly, Castellio disclaimed that he somehow agreed with heretics or embraced a form of relativism. As he himself put it, "Now I say this not because I favor heretics. I hate heretics."[40] Throughout the work Castellio nevertheless made clear that the proper response to a heretic is limited to actions by the church to instruct and admonish rather than to imprison or kill the dissenter:

> It is absurd to wage spiritual war with earthly arms. The enemies of Christians are the vices which are to be cured by virtues. Diseases are to be healed by contrary remedies; learning must drive out ignorance; patience overcome injury; modesty resist pride; diligence oppose laziness; clemency fight against cruelty; and insincerity is to be laid low by a mind transparent, religious, pure, and devoted to God. These are the true arms and true victories of the Christian religion. The office of the doctor is not to be committed to the executioner, nor the outside of the cup to be cleansed before the inside.

Rather than arguing for a libertarian morality, he simply argued that no one should be forced to conform to a government-prescribed theology. "This I say only with regard to religion," he said, "for when it comes to crimes, murder, adultery, theft, false witness, and the like, which God has commanded to be punished and for which He has prescribed the penalty, these are not called into controversy."[41]

Castellio's anthology of twenty chapters contains the works of several prominent Catholic and Protestant theologians, including Augustine, Luther, and Calvin. All three of these men had argued for some form of religious liberty early in their careers, but experience changed their perspective, causing them later to embrace laws and judgments that sanctioned punishment of heretics even to the point of death.[42] Castellio argues that their earlier views should be the ones to be believed because they were "written in a time of tribulation when men are the more accustomed to write the truth, and because it is especially consonant with the meekness and the mercy of Christ."[43]

One of the most interesting selections in this work is a chapter written by Basil Montfort, which is generally accepted to be another pseudonym for Castellio.[44] In this essay titled "Refutation of the Reasons Commonly Alleged in Favor of Persecution," Castellio reviewed all of the passages of Scripture commonly used to justify the burning of heretics. Nearly all the arguments in favor of persecution are from the Old Testament. For example, Castellio contended that Deuteronomy 13, commanding the death of false prophets, cannot be interpreted to justify the death of someone who merely disagrees with the ecclesiastical or magisterial authority over the meaning of Scripture:

> I ask, to begin with, who is a false prophet? Moses teaches in this passage that the false prophet is one who predicts something that does not come to pass, and also one who teaches the people to serve strange gods. But today false prophets or heretics are not judged by these tests, but by their opinions.[45]

Calvin, on the other hand, taught that the penalty prescribed in this chapter of the Pentateuch should apply even to "homebred battles" in which a professing Christian deviated from "pure doctrine" and caused "diversity of opinions."[46]

Castellio systematically revealed what he considered the logical error of the persecutors, together with their hypocritical practices, for punishing heretics while allowing those who commit open moral sins to walk the streets unpunished. Using the biblical example of Achan, whose whole family was stoned to death for his sin, Castellio ridiculed the persecutors' selective use of the Old Testament: "If we wish to imitate this example let us kill the entire families of the heretics, or rather let us return to Moses and be circumcised. Let us reject Christ and with the Jews await another under the shadow of the law."[47]

Turning then to the New Testament, Castellio took issue with the persecutors' use of the example of Ananias and Sapphira, whom they contended were killed by Peter. He made the self-evident point that this couple was not killed by human execution but by the direct act of God and not for heresy but for lying to the Holy Spirit: "And how many are there today who lie against the Holy Spirit. When they repeat after you these words, 'Our Father who art in heaven?' How many are there who conduct themselves as becomes the children of God?"[48]

Castellio argued that in New Testament times, the sword to be used in spiritual battles is the Word of God, not a physical weapon; Christ took away Peter's sword in the garden, but the magistrate is clearly entrusted with wielding the sword to punish clear moral violations such as murder and theft. He advanced the principle that the sword of the magistrate and the sword of the church are to be separate and distinct in their jurisdiction. In making this argument, Castellio directly quoted from Calvin's *Institutes* in condemnation of the recent actions against Servetus in Geneva.[49]

One of the most frequently cited texts on both sides of the religious tolerance debate during the sixteenth and seventeenth centuries is the parable of the wheat and tares found in Matthew 13:24–30:

Another parable He put forth to them, saying: "The kingdom
of heaven is like a man who sowed good seed in his field; but while
men slept, his enemy came and sowed tares among the wheat and
went his way. But when the grain had sprouted and produced a
crop, then the tares also appeared. So the servants of the owner
came and said to him, 'Sir, did you not sow good seed in your
field? How then does it have tares?' He said to them, 'An enemy
has done this.' The servants said to him, 'Do you want us then to
go and gather them up?' But he said, 'No, lest while you gather
up the tares you also uproot the wheat with them. Let both grow
together until the harvest, and at the time of harvest I will say
to the reapers, 'First gather together the tares and bind them in
bundles to burn them, but gather the wheat into my barn.'"

The use of this passage to justify persecution by Christians against
heretical Christians began with Augustine. Even though he initially taught
that no one should come to the faith except through their voluntary consent, he changed his opinion after encountering the Donatists.[50] Augustine
wrote:

When the Lord . . . said to his servants who wanted to gather
the cockle: "Allow them to grow until the harvest," he gave the
reason by adding: "Lest perhaps gathering up the cockle, you root
up the wheat also together with it." Thereby he shows plainly
enough that when that fear does not exist and one is quite sure
of the soundness of the good seed, i.e., when someone's crime
is known and appears so foul that he finds no defender (or such
defenders that no schism need be feared), then severe discipline
must not remain dormant, for the more diligently charity is preserved, the more efficacious is the correction of perversity.[51]

A straightforward reading of the parable would seem to indicate that
the admonition to "leave the crop alone" was given *because* it is too difficult for humans to discern with accuracy who belongs to the tares; only an
omniscient God can perform faultless weeding, particularly among those
who profess to believe in Him. Augustine essentially turned the parable on
its head, however, and concluded, "If the bad seed is known, it should be
uprooted."[52] This interpretation would be cited for centuries "not only to
justify the Roman government's repression of the Donatists but to provide a
wider reason for religious persecution by the civil authorities."[53]

Castellio offered his interpretation of the parable. Speaking to princes
and begging for mercy, he says, "Take counsel with the merciful, who advise

you to leave the tares until the harvest, for those who wish to pull them up before, eradicate also the command of Christ, who directs that they be left."[54] Luther had concurred with this explanation of the parable in favor of tolerance when he was young, but in later years, he presented the following commentary instead:

> "Suffer both to grow [the tares and the good grain]": this does not refer to the authorities, but to the preachers who should not under pretext of their function exert any physical compulsion. But, according to what has been said, it is clear that the public authority is bound to repress blasphemy, false doctrine and heresy, and to inflict corporal punishment on those that support such things.[55]

Calvin's *Defensio*

It has already become clear that Calvin desired to show no mercy to anyone who dared to "pervert the truth," but he likewise had no kind words for those who promoted religious toleration. "To be short," he said, "whoever he is that speaketh for he [i.e., the heretic] is not to be taken for an ignorant person, seeing he would that false doctrines should be unpunished: but rather he is to be counted a despiser of GOD, and an upholder of the devil, which seeketh nothing else but the turning of all things upside down in the world."[56] Needless to say, Castellio's writings did not help put him on friendly terms with the Genevan reformer.

A month prior to the publication of Castellio's *Concerning Heretics*, Calvin had issued a book titled *Defensio Orthodoxae Fidei* (Defense of the Orthodox Faith) as a vindication of his actions in the death of Servetus. The Latin version was printed in February 1554, and the French version the following month. It is curious, however, given the intense devotion of the enthusiasts of John Calvin to his work, that Calvin's defense of his theories of religious intolerance has apparently never been published as a complete work in English. Small snippets of Calvin's *Defensio* in English do appear in various modern authors' works.[57]

All the ministers of Geneva signed the *Defensio*, but it was not immune to criticism even from Calvin's associates. Heinrich Bullinger was concerned that it would trouble "simple-minded persons."[58] Calvin already knew that he could criticize philosophical opponents by deriding their lack of education, a common tactic in his day, so he offered preemptive advice: "Let untrained men, therefore, and those not sufficiently taught, stop denying that penalties must not be extracted from the corrupters of true doctrine, unless they wish to openly clamor at God."[59]

Another well-respected individual, Nicolaus Zurkinden, wrote in a letter to Calvin, "I wish the former part of your book, respecting the right which the magistrates may have to use the sword in coercing heretics, had not appeared in your name, but in that of your council, which might have been left to defend its own act."[60] Zurkinden knew that Calvin's good name was at stake.

The passage Zurkinden referred to is of special interest to students of religious liberty. It is titled, "Whether It Is Permissible for Christian Judges to Punish Heretics." Calvin did not contend here that every religious error should be punished by death. For minor offenses, forgiveness should be offered. For others, a moderate chastening is sufficient. Blatant impiety, however, must receive the punishment of death.[61] Elaborating on the category deserving death, Calvin wrote:

> But where religion is subverted from its foundations, where
> some go so far as to utter blasphemy against God, where they are
> carried away by impious and pernicious teachings to the destruc-
> tion of their souls, where finally their doctrine openly ascribes
> error to the only and blameless God, it is necessary to resort to the
> most extreme remedy, in order to prevent the deadly venom from
> spreading any further.[62]

While Calvin made strained arguments from the New Testament to support his conclusions, there is no doubt that his viewpoint was rooted and grounded in the Old Testament. He saw no difference between the laws given for the governance of Israel and those that should be applied when Christian magistrates govern a nation. In his own words, "the coming of Christ did not change the political order, nor take anything away from the duty of the magistrates."[63]

Calvin vigorously rejected the idea that the execution of Servetus could be equated with the execution of true Christian martyrs like Cranmer, Ridley, and Latimer. This opinion had precedent, so Calvin quoted it: "Augustine rightly sums up the same thing: the cause makes the martyr, not the punishment."[64]

Moreover, Calvin appeared unaware of the irony that if he returned to Catholic France, he would face the same charges and penalties. The only explanation is that he believed he possessed the correct theology, all others notwithstanding. Thus, he viewed his participation in the burning of a heretic as justified, but a burning by the pope was *un*justified—a murderous persecution of the godly.

Many of Calvin's modern supporters try to distance him from the controversy surrounding Servetus's execution. Respected Christian author David W. Hall defends Calvin's involvement in the Servetus affair by writing:

Servetus was the only person tried and executed for heresy during Calvin's tenure in Geneva, while the nearby city of Toulouse
arraigned 208 people for heresy in one year (1554) alone. Calvin
pled for leniency in the mode of punishment, and the Genevan
council consulted with other Swiss cities and leading theologians,
who unanimously concurred with its decision. In contrast to Calvin,
Thomas Aquinas, the towering medieval thinker, had favored burning heretics at the stake. He wrote that certain heretics were not
only to be excommunicated but also should be handed over to secular officials "to be exterminated from the world by death."[65]

Nothing in this analysis is untruthful in itself, but it does leave a false
impression. Calvin *did* plead for "leniency" in the mode of punishment—he
requested that Servetus *be put to death by the sword instead of by fire.*[66] Calvin
also made no effort to disclaim his role in Servetus's death, though he
remained aloof for a time after Servetus's conviction.[67] He openly admitted
that he was responsible for Servetus's arrest: "Let me suppose that I may be
charged on the point, which I do not hide, that it may be represented by my
authorship, he, having been detected in this city, was brought to plead his
case."[68] Calvin also acknowledged that he was in charge of the prosecution's
strategy ("nor do I deny that the legal form was dictated by my counsel").[69]

Two final exchanges between Calvin and Castellio suffice to highlight
the two strains of argument that would prove influential in later centuries.
Servetus may not have lived to defend himself against Calvin's *Defense*, but
Castellio did not let it go unanswered. He quoted Calvin's opinions regarding religious toleration and answered them in the form of a dialogue:

[Calvin:] Now we see that the ministers of the Gospel must
be prepared to bear the cross and enmity and whatever pleases
the world, and the Lord equipped them with no other arms than
patience. Nevertheless, kings are commanded to protect the doctrine of piety by their support.

[Castellio:] To kill a man is not to defend a doctrine, but to kill
a man. When the Genevans killed Servetus they did not defend
a doctrine; they killed a man. The defense of doctrine is not the
affair of the magistrate but of the doctor. What has the sword to
do with doctrine?[70]

[Calvin:] What will become of religion? By what marks will
the true Church be discerned? What will Christ himself be if the
doctrine of piety is uncertain and in suspense?

[Castellio:] Religion will be based on an assured faith concerning things which are hoped for, not known, as Abraham, when he

was called to go out, obeyed not knowing whither he went. . . .
The true Church will be known by love which proceeds from faith,
whose precept is certain. "By this shall all men know that ye are my
disciples if ye have love one to another." . . . The doctrine of piety
is to love your enemies, bless those that curse you, to hunger and
thirst after righteousness, and endure persecution for righteousness'
sake.[71]

Calvin's theories of persecution carried great weight for many years in
the Protestant world. A century after his death, eminent personae in England
and America still referred to him as an authority and justification for their
opinion that the state has the responsibility to root out religious error by
force.[72]

"A Perpetual Memory of Cruelty"

This battle of words did not end with Calvin and Castellio, nor were
their arguments confined to the walls of Geneva. As we have seen, John
Knox took up Calvin's mantle, and his work against the "blasphemous cavil-
lations" of the "Anabaptist" likely found eager readers not only in Geneva
but also in the British Isles, where the King's Bench debates over free will
and predestination had taken place a few years prior. Knox ultimately left it
to history to judge the episode of Servetus's execution and Calvin's theories
of using capital punishment against heretics: "John Calvin hath besides committed to writing, the examination of Servetus, and the cause of his miserable death, which books albeit to you, they be a perpetual memory of cruelty,
yet I have good hope, that to our posterity, they shall be profitable."[73]

Many generations of persecutors would follow before the prevailing
opinion changed. But has posterity found Calvin's book justifying his execution of Servetus to be profitable in determining our course on matters of the
rights of conscience? The fact that no scholar of Calvin has ever bothered
to translate and publish in English the very work cited by Knox gives us the
definitive reply: When it comes to the propriety of Calvin's views on individual religious liberty, honest history has not judged them fondly.

Chapter Nine

AT THE ICY BLAST OF THE TRUMPET

Puritans and Separatists Under the Elizabethan Settlement

Those who have the true gospel doctrine and faith will persecute no one, but will themselves be persecuted.

HENDRICK TERWOORT

wo and a half years after Thomas Cranmer was burned at the stake after stating, "As for the Pope, I refuse him, as Christ's Enemy and Antichrist, with all his false doctrine," England became officially Protestant once more. On Thursday, November 17, 1558, Queen Mary Tudor died. The following January, Mary's younger half sister was crowned Elizabeth I at twenty-five years of age amidst shouts of "God save Queen Elizabeth! Reign she most long, reign she most happily."[1]

An art critic once described the portraits of Elizabeth as depicting a woman of little warmth but much majesty. Indeed, this could readily serve as a description of her deliberate policy toward the religious affairs of her beleaguered nation.

From the vantage point of her own time, Elizabeth undoubtedly chose the best realistic alternative for the settlement of the religious controversies that had preceded her. As the daughter of Anne Boleyn, whose marriage to Henry was the chief cause of England's rift with Rome, Elizabeth could not be expected to choose to keep England a Catholic nation. After all, accepting the pope's authority would require her implicitly to confess her own illegitimacy. In fact, many expected her to exact revenge upon the Catholic loyalists for the public persecution of Protestants. And while she did eventually pursue anti-Catholic policies, her initial steps were moderate, even kindhearted, compared to those of her sister.

Elizabeth was so insistent that she would not seek revenge on her sister's officials that even the sheriff of Guernsey escaped punishment for his inhumane act of cruelty; it was he who had thrown Perotine Gosset's baby, born in the flames, back into the fire to join his mother in death. Elizabeth determined that those who were acting in obedience to their prior queen would not be punished.

Rejecting both Catholicism and revenge, Elizabeth pursued a policy demanding outward conformity with the rituals of the reinstituted Protestant church. Her policy purported not to coerce the conscience. It was not a violation of the law simply to believe the wrong doctrine. Yet failure to conform to the ritualistic practices of the Church of England could result in arrest, imprisonment, banishment, or death.

It is important to note that the justification for this insistence on religious unity was primarily grounded in political reasoning rather than on the claim that it was necessary to have one true church singularly qualified to be the channel through which a person might obtain eternal salvation. W. K. Jordan puts it this way: "The Government steadfastly maintained that it did not propose to persecute conscience, and that it dictated modes of worship for political ends."[2]

By demanding religious acts for a secular purpose, Elizabeth unwittingly sowed seeds of destruction to the concept of a Christian nation that had prevailed unbroken since the days of Augustine. Augustine, Calvin, Luther, More, Cranmer, and countless others believed that a commonwealth was coextensive with the church. All people residing in the nation were in fact members of the one true church by virtue of their participation in its sacraments. Of course, these men held widely disparate views of what constituted the one true church, but they all were incapable of separating the church from the entire nation in their theological understandings.

Without the one true church teaching proper doctrine and administering the sacraments in the correct manner, it was thought that the people would be unable to attain salvation. Thus, uniformity was utterly essential for the salvation of all. Anything less would result in eternal damnation for those under their charge. Such a theological approach embraced a doctrine of coercion since earthly coercion was far better than the alternative of eternal damnation. So reasoned Augustine and all who followed him.

But there were those in Elizabeth's England who loudly objected to this theory on doctrinal grounds. The separatist Henry Barrowe, in one sarcastic sentence, summarized the theological problem inherent in the idea that the monarch could determine the religious views of an entire nation: "All this people, with all these manners, were in one day, with the blast of Queen Elizabeth's trumpet, of ignorant papists and gross idolaters, made faithful Christians, and true professors."[3]

Elizabeth's insistence on outward conformity only (and that upon political grounds) would eventually "alienate and antagonize men of deeply spiritual character who [had] become cognizant of the secular character of the State Church."[4] Far from producing true peace, her religious policies produced seditious plots by Catholics both foreign and domestic, as well as adverse reactions from two sets of more conservative believers who steadfastly maintained their political loyalty to the queen. Puritans agreed with the church's doctrine but were repulsed by its failure to purge itself fully of Catholic trappings. Far more important to the development of the theory of religious liberty were the Elizabethan Separatists, who insisted as a matter of biblical doctrine that the state had no authority to create a state with compelled worship.

The Legal Framework of Elizabethan Religious Policy

Forty days after the death of her sister, Elizabeth issued her first order regarding the practice of religion. On December 27, 1558, the young monarch made a proclamation forbidding public preaching until new laws could be enacted to establish fully her ecclesiastical polity. Citing occurrences of "unfruitful dispute[s] in matters of religion," Elizabeth found it necessary to "charge and command . . . all manner of her subjects, as well as those that be called to the ministry in the Church as all others, that they do forbear to preach, or teach, or to give audience to any manner of doctrine or preaching."[5] She granted only a limited exception to permit the reading of designated portions of the Gospels, epistles, or Ten Commandments, provided they were read "in the vulgar tongue, without exposition or addition of any manner, sense, or meaning to be applied and added."[6]

The queen's stated purpose for this ban on all manner of preaching? She sought to promote "the due honour of Almighty God, the increase of virtue and godliness, with universal charity and concord among her people."[7] But silencing all voices for a season was more likely a means to achieve political stability among discordant religious factions.

Parliament was convened on January 25 of the new year to begin consideration of Elizabeth's proposed resolution of the religious disputes.

Nicholas Bacon, the lord keeper, opened the session with a lengthy speech that dealt "tenderly and wisely" with the dispute at hand.[8] Members were admonished to avoid "all manner of contention, reasonings, and disputes . . . comelier for scholars than counselors."[9] Moreover, such railings "were causes of much expense of time, and bred few good resolutions."[10]

In April of the following year, the Act of Supremacy was enacted, reviving ten acts of Henry VIII and one of Edward VI. It also repealed Mary's Heresy Act and those enactments that had nullified several of Henry and Edward's Protestant-oriented statutes.[11] In short, a complete barrier to the pope's jurisdiction over the land of England was again erected. England was once again a Protestant nation.

As was typical, an oath was required of all manner of officials, ecclesiastical and civil. Each was required to swear:

> The queen's highness is the only supreme governor of this realm, and of all other her highness's dominions and countries, as well in all spiritual or ecclesiastical things or causes, as temporal, and that no foreign prince, person, prelate . . . has or ought to have any jurisdiction . . . or authority ecclesiastical or spiritual, within this realm.[12]

No one was forced to swear to believe in particular religious doctrines. Only teachings related to the authority of the pope had to be repudiated.

Immediately on the heels of this act of supremacy, Parliament enacted the Act of Uniformity. Its principal purpose was to reinstate the Book of Common Prayer and its connected liturgy from the reign of Edward VI, although several changes were incorporated within the act. In addition, mandatory attendance at an official church every Sunday and holy day was demanded of every person in the realm.[13] Interrupting these mandatory services with criticism or presentation of alternative religious views was prohibited. The act required that the first and second offenses be punished by fines. For a third offense, the offender would have to forfeit all property to the crown and be placed in prison for life.[14]

Again, no person was required to believe or endorse a particular religious doctrine. The law merely demanded that each person in the realm sit silently in the pew of the Church of England every Sunday and keep any dissenting thoughts safely unsaid. Even Catholics were not forced to commit to particular religious creeds. So long as Catholics swore allegiance to the queen, they could long all they wished for the Mass and other components of Catholic services and doctrine. In reality, the only material difference between Elizabeth's approach and that of Mary was the forced swearing to a particular belief.

Protests to the intolerant nature of this "settlement" were raised in Parliament. One member argued, "Though in the old law idolatry was punished with death; yet, since the coming of Christ, who came to win the world by peace, the greatest punishment taught by the Apostle was that of excommunication."[15] The parliamentarian's views were perhaps prophetic but without any practical political effect since they were in the extremely small minority.

This left England with a national church that was, in the words of Tennyson, "faultily faultless, icily regular, splendidly null."[16] The queen abhorred "loose ends" or anything else that disturbed a set pattern, and her nature was reflected perfectly in the silent majesty of coercive patterns of worship.[17] Dissenters were less than satisfied. They considered it a "patent legal fiction" that the queen's system did not coerce consciences.[18]

While Elizabeth was overwhelmingly popular throughout her reign, the evidence suggests that the public implicitly rejected her idea that the state could settle all religious practices for the people. There was, however, widespread consensus that religious truth could be discovered and known by means of studying the Bible.[19] Given this broad support for the authority of the Bible and the truth it was believed to contain, Elizabeth and her officials walked away from their strongest argument when they found it necessary to "disclaim any divine sanction for their orders" as well as the corresponding prerogative to bind consciences.[20] In a spiritual sense, perhaps it was best that she did not attempt to misuse Scripture to contend, as so many had done before, that it sanctioned the murderous path of coerced uniformity.

The Catholic Problem

While Elizabeth is praised for her moderation toward Catholic recusants by secular historians such as Harvard's W. K. Jordan, she is viewed by many Catholic scholars as a brutal tyrant who unjustly persecuted the faithful.[21] The *Catholic Encyclopedia* claims that "the total number of Catholics who suffered under her was one hundred and eighty-nine, one hundred and twenty-eight of them being priests, fifty-eight laymen, and three women. To them should be added . . . thirty-two Franciscans who were starved to death."[22]

Likewise, it is hotly disputed that Catholics were not persecuted for their faith but rather for their treasonous political views. Again, the *Catholic Encyclopedia* asserts:

> By the Act of Supremacy Catholics offending against that statute had been made liable to capital punishment as traitors, the queen hoping thereby to escape the odium attaching to the

infliction of death for religion. Few will now dissent from the words of Green in his "Short History": "There is something even more revolting than open persecution in the policy which brands every Catholic priest as a traitor, and all Catholic worship as disloyalty." But, for a time, the policy succeeded, and the martyrs who suffered for no other cause than their Catholic faith were commonly believed to have been put to death for treason.[23]

Jordan disagrees. He maintains that the Elizabethan state had always made clear that it would "punish only those actions on the part of Catholics which by its own interpretation it considered harmful to the safety of the realm."[24] Catholics, he writes, were free to believe whatever they wished— except that the pope was supreme over the monarch and possessed the right to remove the monarch for heresy. This was a religious belief with obvious political implications. The Catholic church called it faith; Elizabeth called it treason.

Elizabeth's effort to pursue a plan of comparative toleration for Catholics was completely eviscerated by hostile actions taken by the current pope. Pius V, selected as the pontiff in 1566, was persuaded soon thereafter that he should begin an aggressive policy to secure the reconversion of England. In 1569, a papal representative was sent to the northern counties of England along with twelve thousand crowns for the purpose of encouraging resistance or rebellion.

Late that fall, Thomas Percy, earl of Northumberland, and Charles Neville, earl of Westmoreland, led an armed rebellion in the northern counties of England. Their motives were diverse, but one primary purpose was to restore the Catholic Church. To achieve this aim they intended to replace Elizabeth with Mary, Queen of Scots, who was Catholic. But Elizabeth's forces succeeded in quelling the Catholic rebellion, and Neville and Percy only succeeded in cementing the view that Catholicism was to be equated with treason.

Hard on the heels of the armed Catholic uprising, on February 25, 1570, Pius V issued a Papal Bull declaring that all of Elizabeth's subjects were absolved from any allegiance to her. Moreover, anyone who obeyed any of her orders was declared "anathema"—that is, eternally condemned. For establishing a heretical kingdom, Elizabeth was excommunicated and declared to be deprived of her "pretended title" to the throne.[25] Thus, all faithful Catholics in England were given an irreconcilable choice: obey the Queen and go to hell by order of the pope, or obey the pope and be sent to heaven immediately by the order of the queen.

Catholic threats continued throughout Elizabeth's reign. Beginning in 1580, Jesuit priests were sent to England for expressly subversive purposes. Robert Persons and Edmund Campion, the two former Oxford scholars who served as their leaders, were viewed with great suspicion and hostility. Campion was charged with treason and executed in 1581. Shortly thereafter, Persons left England to run the mission in exile. Even Catholic advocates acknowledge that Persons played a role in organizing the attempted invasion of England by the Spanish Armada in 1588.[26] Understandably, Elizabeth took increasingly severe steps against Catholic intrigues, including the execution of her cousin and rival, Mary, Queen of Scots.

Nevertheless, the Elizabethan persecution of Catholics, whether for political or religious motives, had little direct effect on the development of the concept of religious liberty in England. Its *indirect* effect, on the other hand, was substantial. For at the same time that Elizabeth faced these clear political and military threats from internal and external Catholic enemies, there was clamor among Puritans and Separatists for religious change. To Elizabeth, this was not a time for change. Uniformity was needed to stabilize the nation and defend against the Catholic threat.[27]

The Elizabethan Puritans

Many today hold an oversimplified view of the early Puritans and Separatists. Hundreds of Web sites today offer descriptions of Puritans and Separatists that correspond nearly word for word with a recent Fourth of July sermon given by a Baptist preacher:

> Remember, the Church of England was in chaos; it needed cleaning up. Out of its crisis emerged two groups: Separatists and Puritans. Now, this might be hard to remember but just try: Separatists wanted to SEPARATE from the church. Puritans wanted to PURIFY the church but remain in it. Got it?[28]

This summary is unsatisfactory if the goal is to understand the roles played by the Church of England, the Puritans, and especially the Separatists in the advancement of religious liberty.

To understand the Puritans' role, we must first understand the scope of their criticism of the Anglican church. No significant doctrinal issues were raised by Elizabethan Puritans, and their chief "purifying" aims centered on the removal of vestiges of Catholicism from the formal ceremonies of the church, which the Puritans considered to represent popish superstition. Of particular concern were the wearing of Roman-style clerical vestments, the use of wafer bread and the sign of the cross in worship, the rite of confirmation, kneeling at communion, the giving of rings in marriage, the purification of women after childbirth, the terms "priest" and "absolution," the observation of saints' days, ritualistic bowing at the name of Jesus, and exquisite singing in harmonic parts accompanied by organs.[29]

Elizabeth, however, loved ritual and majesty and was unsympathetic to such requests for change. She refused to have the altar and crucifix removed from her own chapel.[30] Undaunted, the Puritans continued to clamor for greater reform in these public matters in order to bring the English church into line with the practices of "the best reformed churches" on the continent.[31] The more important issue raised by the Puritans, at least insofar as religious liberty is concerned, was that they believed in "an ideal Calvinistic state . . . [with] a civil power controlled and directed by the ecclesiastical organization; a system which approached a theocracy and whose obvious model was Geneva."[32] It is not surprising that these ideas would be introduced into England, given the numerous religious refugees who fled to Geneva and Lutheran Germany during Mary's reign but returned after Elizabeth's accession.

Like the Church of England, the Puritans embraced the concept of national uniformity of religion. Indeed, there was an assumption that the entire nation was the "people of the Lord"—that is, the elect.[33] Unlike the church leaders, the Puritans believed that the ecclesiastical body should be allowed to make its independent determinations as to religious matters, which would then be enforced by the power of the crown.[34] One leading Puritan argued:

> For as it is not lawful for the prince to preach nor administer the Sacraments; no more is it lawful for him to make laws in ecclesiastical matters contrary to the knowledge of his learned pastors.
>
> [To that end, the prince ought] to make civil laws to bind the people unto the confession of true faith, and the right administering and receiving of the Sacraments and to punish infractions of the same. But in these capacities the prince should be guided by the advice of his clergy.[35]

Other Puritan writers made it unmistakably plain that the duty of the prince was to punish heretics "by the sword of justice," lest the government perish.[36] The fingerprints of Calvin are easily seen in such beliefs. Both as to the organization of the relationship between the prince and the church, and as to the duty to demand religious uniformity, with an unwavering punishment of heretics, the Elizabethan Puritans had learned their lessons well from the school of Geneva.

In the midst of Elizabeth's troubles with the Catholics, her government determined that it was time to crack down on Puritan dissent. In 1583, John Whitgift was elevated to the position of archbishop of Canterbury. Within three weeks of his installation, he issued a series of strict orders in the hope of curtailing Puritan teaching.[37] One of the results of this controversy was the removal of several highly qualified Puritans from ministerial service. Some Puritans simply refused to accept positions that were offered. Notably, several refused to accept bishoprics.[38] Others were removed for carrying their dissent too far. Moreover, the removal of many Catholic clergy helped to thin the ranks of qualified personnel.

During this period, individuals from Cornwall sent a petition to Parliament complaining of the lack of proper pastors:

> We have about 160 churches, the greatest part of which are supplied by men who are guilty of the grossest sins; some fornicators, some adulterers, some felons, bearing the marks in their hands for the said offence; some drunkards, gamesters on the Sabbath day. . . . There were 140, scarcely any of whom could preach a sermon, and most of whom were pluralists and non-residents.[39]

The Puritan demand for a "learned preaching ministry" was meritorious yet appears to have remained essentially unresolved.[40] The conduct at many local parish churches had to have been amazingly wild to prompt the following injunction issued in Grindal in 1570:

> No peddler shall be admitted to sell his wares in the church porch in divine service; that parish clerks shall be able to read; that no lord of misrule, or summer lords and ladies, or any disguised persons, or morris-dancers, or others, shall come irreverently into the church, or play any unseemly parts with scoffs, jests, wanton gestures, or ribald talk, in the time of divine service.[41]

The church's reaction to Elizabethan Puritans largely consisted of public criticism and the denial or removal of Puritan leaders from positions of influence. In 1593, with Whitgift's manipulation, Parliament passed a law to silence Puritan criticisms.[42] Still, no Puritan was ever executed during Elizabeth's reign.

Despite noble efforts to remove objectionable practices and rituals, Puritans failed to understand the central problem with the Elizabethan church: No one could be coerced to love and serve God no matter how pure the external ceremonies might be.

Swarms of Satanists, Broods of Bishops

One of the rare things that united Catholics, Anglicans, and Puritans was their utter contempt for Anabaptists and other Separatists. The bishop of London, John Aylmer gives a glimpse of the Anglican viewpoint. He described them as "Anabaptists, with infinite other swarms of Satanists," continuing, "and in these latter days, the old festered sores newly broke out, as the Anabaptists, the free-willers, or rather the forward-willers, with infinite other swarms of God's enemies."[43] Completing his litany, these dissenters were called "ugglie monsters" and "brodes of the devvil's brotherhood."[44] Whitgift also cited Zwingli, Calvin, Bullinger, and others to demonstrate that Anabaptists were a sect hated by "all estates and orders of the realm."[45]

One of the chief complaints by such critics was that these separatists denied the concept of a Christian nation as defined by Augustine and his followers—that is, a church that is composed of the entire population of a nation, willing or not. Those who desired to be fully separated from the national church were often compared to Augustine's theological enemies, the Donatists, whose rejection of the Catholic Church on the grounds of its impurity had caused him to formulate his doctrine sanctioning persecution in the name of unity. An Anglican bishop, for example, wrote to a colleague and complained that some refused to enter the official church, baptize their children, partake of the Lord's Supper, or hear sermons. He bristled that these dissenters sought "bye-path" and "establish[ed] a private religion, and assemble in private houses . . . as the Donatists of old."[46]

During a debate in 1573 with Thomas Cartwright, a leading Puritan, Archbishop Whitgift falsely accused his opponent of holding Anabaptist views. Despite the mistaken application to Cartwright, Whitgift accurately summarized the views of the Anabaptist movement on matters of governance and religious liberty:

> They taught that the civil magistrate had no authority in
> ecclesiastical matters . . . that he ought not to meddle in causes of
> religion and faith. That no man ought to be compelled to faith,
> and to religion. That Christians ought to punish faults, not with
> imprisonment, not with sword, or corporal punishments, but only
> with excommunication.[47]

In fact, the first to face the fires of persecution in Elizabeth's reign were a group of Flemish (Dutch) Anabaptists who were arrested on Easter Sunday, April 3, 1575, while worshipping in a private house just outside the city gates of London. A total of twenty-five people were arrested and taken before the magistrate.[48] Five of the group quickly relented and were released. Fourteen women and one youth from the group were deported, though the young man was beaten while being transported from the prison to the wharf. The remaining five were incarcerated. One individual soon died from the horrid conditions of the prison—where the religious prisoners were kept separated from the ordinary criminals, lest the latter be infected by the religious views of dissenters.[49]

To his credit, John Foxe, the great martyrologist, petitioned the queen to spare the lives of these religious prisoners. He did admit, however, that Anabaptists had no right to hold their opinions and deserved some sort of punishment but urged that the sentence be other than death.[50] Foxe's plea was disregarded. Two of the remaining five were sentenced to death in a warrant signed by Elizabeth on July 15, 1573. A Baptist scholar of the eighteenth century compared the warrants for these executions with warrants used by Bloody Mary and concluded, "These warrants are substantially alike. In fact, they are almost couched in the same language, word for word."[51] Both queens claimed to be "defenders of the . . . faith" and possess the requirement to "root out and extirpate heresies and errors."[52]

One of those scheduled for execution was Hendrick Terwoort, a twenty-five-year-old who had been married only two months before his imprisonment. The other was Jan Pieters, a much older man with nine dependent children. His first wife had been martyred in Flanders. His second wife was the widow of a martyr. A special petition urging leniency for Pieters in light of his family was unavailing with the presiding bishop. Terwoort's and Pieters's pleas to the queen are an eloquent memorial to religious liberty:

> May it also please your majesty in your wisdom and innate
> goodness to consider, that were it not right, but hypocrisy in us to
> speak otherwise than we in our consciences think; and also that
> it is not in our power to believe this or that, as evil-doers who do
> right or wrong as they please. But the true faith must be implanted
> in the heart of man by God; and to him we daily pray, that he
> would give us his Spirit to understand his word and gospel.[53]

The fires of Smithfield, so notorious under Mary, were rekindled.

Separatist Ideas of Church and the Sacraments

Not all separatists were foreign Anabaptists, although it is evident that there was some influence from such quarters. The principal origins of English Separatism were doctrines of pietism—the desire for increased personal devotion and practical Christianity—and "the searching of the Bible for the true pattern of ecclesiastical organization."[54]

The Separatists of the Elizabethan era possessed many of the views of Henry Hart and the other freewillers who had surfaced during the Marian persecution. Under the leadership of Robert Browne, the movement became significantly more widespread. Browne rejected the central theory of governmental control over religion and wrote, "For the Scepter and kingdom of Christ is not of this world, to fight with dint of sword."[55]

Like virtually every other Protestant movement, the Brownists, as they came to be called, professed that the sole authority for both doctrine and church governance was the Bible itself. This claim was vastly different in practice when not backed by the power of the state to enforce one's scriptural interpretations. The Brownists relied instead on the approach described in the book of Isaiah: "Come now, let us reason together, says the Lord."

The Separatist theology concerning the role of the church in the process of salvation also differed radically. The Anglican view was that the entire nation was drawn into salvation through the true church; salvation was accomplished by participation in the church's sacraments, particularly baptism. The Separatists' criteria for the true church were different:

It consists of a company and fellowship of faithful and holy
people gathered in the name of Christ Jesus their only King,
Priest, and Prophet; worshipping him aright, being peaceably and
quietly governed by his officers and laws keeping the unity of faith
in the bond of peace and in love unfeigned.[56]

Another Separatist writer combined these ideas with the important notion of a voluntary confession of faith to define the true church as "a company of faithful people by the Word of God called out and separated from the world and the false ways thereof, gathered and joined together in fellowship of the Gospel, by a voluntary profession of the faith and obedience of Christ."[57] Efforts by the prelates to use the power of the state to coerce worship, it was believed, only hindered the exercise of true worship.[58] Henry Barrow wrote, "It is not in the power of princes or any man whatsoever, to persuade the conscience and make members of the church: but . . . this must be left to God alone, who only can do it."[59]

While these particular Separatists did not yet articulate a mature understanding of religious liberty, they clearly proclaimed its central tenet: At the heart of any theory of religious liberty lies the belief that true worship of God is given voluntarily by each person. Jordan concurs with this assessment and comments, "This conception [of the church, held by the Separatists] emphasized the spiritual character of worship and would seem to minimize the importance of the Church as an agency of salvation. It reduced to an absurdity the thesis that persecution could be of any possible assistance in the attainment of salvation or in the construction and functioning of the true Church."[60]

These Separatist works were published by a congregation pastored by Francis Johnson and John Greenwood, the congregation's teacher. For disseminating these independent-minded views, these Brownists were condemned in print as "Full Donatists."[61] Worse, they were persecuted like the Donatists by arrest, imprisonment, and execution. In 1592 or 1593, Greenwood was arrested and executed. Johnson was arrested in 1593, along with around fifty other members of the church, and was still in prison in 1594.[62] Many of the group migrated to Holland, where they formed a small church.

Voices of Liberty and Voluntary Consent

The words of Terwoot, the young Anabaptist executed in 1573, were perhaps the finest of the era in proclaiming that God was on the side of liberty.

> Observe well the command of God; Thou shalt love the stranger as thyself. Should he who is in misery, and dwelling in a strange land, be driven thence with his companions, to their great damage . . . oh! That they would deal with us according to natural reasonableness and evangelic truth, of which our persecutors so highly boast. . . . From all that it is clear that those who have the true Gospel doctrine and faith will persecute no one, but will themselves be persecuted.[63]

It is of considerable interest that Robert Browne, one of the first voices for religious liberty in England, also proclaimed a clear theory of the right of self-government in matters of both ecclesiastical and civil government. In the appendix of his 1582 book is a series of questions and answers regarding various controversial questions:

> *What agreement must there be of men?*
> For Church governors there must be an agreement of the church. For civil Magistrates, there must be an agreement of the people or Commonwealth.
> Church governors are persons receiving their authority and office of God, for the guiding of his people the church, received and called thereto, by due consent and agreement of the Church. . . .

Civil Magistrates, are persons receiving their authority and office of God, for the due guiding of the commonwealth, whereto they are duly received and called by consent and agreement of the people and subjects.[64]

Magistrates, he continued, are to "make and execute laws by public agreement in all outward justice."[65] Here, at the close of the sixteenth century, in the voice of a persecuted leader of a despised minority sect, is a clear articulation of the basic concept of religious liberty and self-government—that voluntary consent lies at the heart of every form of liberty. Browne got these ideas from his reading of the Word of God. Tyndale's ploughboys had become the prophets of liberty.

Elizabeth died at the age of sixty-nine in the forty-fifth year of her reign. Outward conformity was by then diligently enforced in England, but the Puritans, Catholics, and Separatists still yearned for change.

Chapter Ten

THE "VERY WISEST FOOL IN CHRISTENDOM"

King James I

That it is one of the principal parts of that duty which appertains unto a Christian king, to protect the true church within his own dominions, and to extirpate heresies, is a maxim without all controversy.

JAMES I

nglish Puritans were expecting one of their own when King James arrived from Scotland, where he had been king for thirty-six years—since the year after his birth. After all, he had been raised and tutored by the Knox Presbyterians who forced his Catholic mother, Mary Stuart, to abdicate the Scottish throne in a whirl of contention and scandal. Moreover, Elizabeth had ordered his mother's execution, so they assumed that he would not be especially inclined to continue her religious policies.

Puritans were not the only ones who were hopeful about James's reign. Catholics had built their hope upon comments James had made in Scotland that led them to believe he would permit "a considerable enlargement of their liberties."[1] Other dissenters would naturally have been encouraged to believe the same when, in the last days of Elizabeth's reign, James intervened—in the name of religious freedom—several times on behalf of jailed ministers.[2]

"Moderates," who desired greater "liberality of mind and objectivity in point of view," thought that the king's scholarly interests would have cultivated these attributes—and indeed he was well taught and well read—but they too were disappointed.[3] Each faction looked with eager anticipation to the arrival of the new monarch based on some aspect of James's prior history or conduct. They soon found him complicated and clearly his own guide.

Family History and Childhood

At James's birth his mother, Mary, is reputed to have said to one of her soldiers, "This is the prince whom I hope shall first unite the two kingdoms of England and Scotland." James was, indeed, descended from the royal line of both nations. His great-grandmother Margaret was the sister of Henry VIII. Even though Scotland had long been an ally of France against England, the king of Scotland, James IV, had agreed to marry Margaret at the urging of her father. Relations with England quickly soured, however, after Henry VIII instigated an invasion of France. When James IV was killed in battle against the English in 1513, his son became King James V at one year of age.

James V's second marriage after the death of his first wife, a French princess, was to Mary of Guise, another member of the French nobility. James died without a male heir in 1542. His daughter, who is now referred to as Mary, Queen of Scots, was six days old at the time of his death. Henry VIII attempted to arrange a marriage treaty between the infant Scottish queen and his son Edward. Some Scottish nobles joined forces to support the plan, but this was an explosive move—not only because of the traditional alliance with France but also because of the religious implications if Edward married a French Catholic after Henry's break with Rome. In the end Henry VIII's efforts at a marriage treaty failed once again, and little Mary was sent to France. Instead of Edward, she married the French dauphin in 1558, who became Francis II the following year.

Even though the pro-English and pro-Reformation forces in Scotland lost Mary to her mother's country, they were far from defeated. Scottish Protestants joined ranks officially in 1557 to form the first of their famous covenants and were henceforth referred to as the "Lords of the Congregation."[4] Protestant clergy and congregations multiplied under Mary of Guise, who governed Scotland as her daughter's regent. The proliferation of such churches paralleled the increasing political strength of the Protestant nobility. The Protestant religious "crisis" soon morphed into a "rebellion."[5]

John Knox had been feeding the fire from abroad. In 1556, he wrote a letter to the Catholic queen regent in which he urged her to turn her realm away from idolatry and damnation to the "true worshipping of God."[6] In 1558, he wrote his *Letter to the Commonalty of Scotland*, in which he maintained that he and his learned colleagues had shown by the Scriptures that Catholicism was "vain, false, and diabolical." Therefore, he said, "we require, that by your power the tyranny of those cruel beasts (I mean of priests and friars) may be bridled, till we have uttered our minds in all matters this day debatable in Religion."[7]

And then Knox returned to Scotland. He preached a sermon at Perth in May 1559 that resulted in an iconoclastic riot and the destruction of church property. Tensions continued to escalate into armed conflict. The French supported the queen regent while Elizabeth sent troops to support the Protestant lords. The lords were able to gain control of Edinburgh within a year of the riot; and after Mary of Guise's death in June 1560, their power was consolidated by the Treaty of Edinburgh, which succeeded in removing all foreign troops. During this time, "numerous leading churchmen abruptly and seemingly without difficulty deserted to the protestant cause."[8]

The Scottish parliament that met in August repudiated the jurisdiction of the Catholic Church and adopted a confession drafted by Knox and other reformers that was pronounced as "grounded upon the infallible truth of God's word."[9] Knox also assisted in the preparation of both a directory of public worship and the *First Book of Discipline*, which outlined a Presbyterian form of government for the new Scottish Kirk, the national church. Organizationally, authority was to flow from the individual congregations up through synods to the General Assembly. Thus, Scotland became a Protestant country—not modeled after England's Episcopal form of church government, but after the Presbyterian standard of Geneva.[10] And it was utterly intolerant of any religion save its own brand of Protestantism.

Meanwhile, Scotland's young Queen Mary was still in France, where she was expected to stay. But when her husband died just two years after their marriage, this arrangement was put in jeopardy. Mary's Protestant half brother and one of the most powerful men in Scotland, the Lord James Stuart, went to France to counsel her to return to Scotland to rule in person and, once there, to acquiesce to the radical changes recently wrought in her country. Protestant nobility were eager to assure Mary of their loyalty, but they were understandably wary of the religious influence of the Guises, who were the effectual rulers of France.

Eighteen-year-old Mary returned to Scotland in 1561 to face an awkward situation: the celebration of Mass was illegal in a country with a Catholic queen. James Stuart had assured Mary that she could still participate in her private Masses, so she worshipped at her own service the Sunday after her return. When a group of angry Protestants attempted to break into the chapel, James prevented them from doing so, much to Knox's chagrin.[11] The queen issued a proclamation stating that she would not interfere with the existing religious arrangement in exchange for her freedom to practice Catholicism, even though she was forced to acknowledge that her Catholic subjects had no equivalent right.

Shortly thereafter, a series of conferences between Knox and the queen commenced. The first took place on August 26, 1561. As Knox records in his *Ecclesiastical History of Scotland*, Mary had four principal charges against him:

> That he had raised a part of her subjects against her Mother and her self; That he had written a Book against her just Authority; [she meant the *Treatise against the Regiment of Women*] which she had and would cause the most learned in *Europe* to write against it; That he was the cause of great sedition, and great slaughter in *England*; And that it was said to her, That all that he did was by Necromancy.[12]

While the latter two accusations were highly suspect, it was certainly true that Knox had written a book in 1558 entitled *The First Blast of the Trumpet against the Monstrous Regiment of Women*. It was aimed chiefly at the Catholic Mary Tudor, but clearly had negative implications for all women rulers. In it, Knox wrote:

> For who can deny but it repugneth to nature, that the blind shall be appointed to lead and conduct such as do see? That the weak, the sick, and impotent persons shall nourish and keep the whole and strong, and finally, that the foolish, mad and frenetic shall govern the discrete, and give counsel to such as be sober of mind? And such be all women, compared unto man in being of authority. For their sight in civil regiment, is but blindness: their strength, weakness: their counsel, foolishness: and judgment, frenzy, if it be rightly considered.[13]

Mary, Queen of Scots, understood the threat that this theory posed. "You think," she exclaimed, "that I have no just authority!"

Knox quickly backpedaled: "And my hope is, that so long as ye defile not your hands with the Blood of the Saints of God, that neither I nor that Book shall either hurt you or your Authority; for in very deed Madame, that Book was written most especially against that wicked *Mary* of *England*."

The queen corrected him, noting that the book was written against "women in general."

"Now Madame," Knox reassured her, "if I had intended to trouble your State, because you are a woman; I might have chosen a time more convenient for that purpose than I can do now, when your own presence is within the Realm."

Mary was not going to let Knox get away with beating around the bush, so she queried, "But yet you have taught the people to receive another Religion than their Princes can allow: And how can that Doctrine be of God? Seeing that God commandeth Subjects to obey their Princes?"

Knox replied that religion derived not from princes but from God alone. So he said:

> There is neither greater Honour, nor greater Obedience to be given to Kings and Princes, than God hath commanded to be given to Father and Mother: But so it is, That the Father may be stricken with a Frenzy, in the which he would slay his own Children; Now, Madame, if the children arise, join themselves together, apprehend the Father, take the Sword or other Weapon from him; and finally, bind his hands, and keep him in Prison till that his Frenzy be over-past, think ye, Madame, that the children do any wrong? Or think ye, Madame, that God will be offended with them that have stayed their Father from committing wickedness?

Knox then applied the analogy to princes and their subjects:

> It is even so, Madame, with Princes that would murder the children of God that are subject unto them. Their blind zeal is nothing but a very mad frenzy; and therefore to take the sword from them, to bind their hands, and to cast them into prison, till that they be brought to a more sober mind, is no disobedience against Princes, but just obedience, because it agreeth with the Word of God.

Mary stood dumbfounded until her half brother James, who was also present in the room, began to ask her what was wrong. After a long period of silence, she answered, "Well, then I perceive that my Subjects shall not only obey you, and not me; And shall do what they list, and not what I command, and so must I be subject unto them, and not they to me."

Knox's reply was, "Yea, God craves of Kings, That they be, as it were, Foster-Fathers to the Church, and commands Queens to be Nourishers unto his people. And this subjection unto God, and to his troubled Church, is the greatest dignity that flesh can get upon the face of the earth."

"Yea," she retorted, "but ye are not the Church that I will nourish; I will defend the Church of *Rome*, for I think it is the true Church of God."[14]

Remarkably, Mary took no vengeance with the sword as her English counterpart certainly would have done.

But Knox's pronouncements were, to a degree, prophetic. After the death of the queen regent, he was known to pray, "God, for his great mercy's sake, rid us from the rest of the Guisian brood. Amen, amen."[15]

His prayer was answered—and Mary's fear realized—when in 1567 she was imprisoned and deposed after a series of scandals, then beheaded by Elizabeth nearly twenty years later on charges of treason. Her infant son by her second husband, Lord Darnley (another great-grandson of Henry VII) became King James VI of Scotland upon her deposition. Mary's half brother, the Lord James Stuart, became regent, and the young king was subjected to the competing interests and pressures of Scottish nobility throughout his childhood.

King James and the Puritans

As a young man, James was an excellent student with wide-ranging interests and the intellect to master many subjects. In fact, he would eventually write many books. However, the lessons he took most to heart sprouted from the political intrigues that had resulted in the imprisonment and death of both his parents. James was especially affected by his mother's tragic downfall. Despite her faults and serious blunders, he carried a deep bitterness toward the religious faction that he held responsible for her death and which would shape his own approach to religious matters when he became King James I of England upon the death of Elizabeth.

A boy king, raised in opulence under the tutelage of the Puritan strangers who had overthrown his mother, acquired more than a distrust of the ecclesiastical and political theories of his tutors; thus he was a prime candidate for personal and moral failure. While in his teens, James was seduced by a Frenchman named Esmé Stuart d'Aubigny.[16] D'Aubigny took advantage of a young man who had been deprived of his parents and raised with the strange combination of Puritan strictness and the indulgences that are naturally bestowed upon an absolute monarch. However, the emoluments of the Scottish court were relatively meager in comparison to the throne of England, to which James would ascend at the age of thirty-seven. He had married Anne of Denmark, a Catholic, in 1589, and she bore him eight children. Like many kings before him, James was not a faithful husband. But unlike those who kept mistresses, James came to prefer male lovers.

On his way from Scotland to assume the English throne, James was presented with a petition purportedly signed by a thousand Puritan members of the Anglican clergy asking for certain modest reforms in the forms of church ceremony and minor alterations in the Articles of Religion. The exact number of signers is uncertain, but from the claim that the document garnered a thousand pastoral signatures, it became known as the Millenary Petition.

This petition reveals an interesting array of requests. The first three items related to baptism and its role in the salvation of children. The Puritans requested that the sign of the cross no longer be used in the performance of infant baptism because it had too strong a Catholic appearance. They also requested that infants no longer be questioned as to their personal faith in the baptismal service.[17] The trio of demands ended with a request that children not be put through the process of confirmation when they were older.

The latter two demands were interrelated. The Puritans objected to any implication that a child's consent formed any part of his or her salvation. Children were brought irresistibly into the covenant community of the elect by the grace of God without any necessity for the prior consent of the person being saved. The Puritan objection was *not* that it was inherently silly to ask an infant about his or her personal faith. (Indeed, the implication of the ceremony was that the question of personal faith was asked of the child during baptism, and then during the confirmation process the much older child, after years of instruction, would give the answer that counted.) The objection to these aspects of baptism and confirmation were designed to make the ceremonies match the doctrines of Calvinism. While the Anglican leadership, at this stage, was as thoroughly Calvinist in doctrine as the Puritans, they were also traditionalists who saw no harm in retaining a select number of the ceremonies and practices inherited from Rome.

Other ceremonies and practices smacked a little too much of popish behavior for the Puritans. For example, the petition voiced opposition to the priestly ceremonial garb of the cap and surplice, as well as the use of terms such as "priest" and "absolution." Another objection was to the use of a ring in the marriage ceremony, and another request was that the music in church services be "moderated to better edification."[18] The Puritans found the high-church style of Anglican music too showy.

The petitioners further demanded that clerics be limited to collecting one "living"—that is, one salary. The Anglican Church had continued to follow Catholic tradition of loading multiple pastoral salaries upon high-office holders, many of whom never once appeared in the jurisdiction for which they were being paid. A related request sought to impose a requirement that "none hereafter be admitted into the ministry but able and sufficient men, and those to preach diligently and especially upon the Lord's day."[19] The remaining complaints were a hodgepodge of relatively trivial matters which generally aimed to trim some of the Roman pomp from the Anglican services. No significant doctrinal issues were raised.

James decided to dispose of the concerns raised by the petition in grand style. A conference was to be held at the magnificent palace at Hampton Court on January 14, 1604. The church was to be represented by the archbishop of Canterbury, John Whitgift, as well as eight bishops, five deans, and two other clergymen. The Puritans were represented by four clerics: John Reynolds, Thomas Sparks, Laurence Chaderton, and John Knewstubs. While James was utterly confident in his own skills of theological disputation, he nonetheless weighted the panel strongly in favor of the established church. Neither group knew what to expect from this Scottish king who had been steeped in Puritan traditions.

The king surprised all sides by excluding the Puritans from the first day of the conference. He began the proceedings by revealing to the Anglican elite his contempt for the Scottish religious order:

> It pleased him both to enter into a gratulation to almighty
> God, (at which words he put off his hat) for bringing him into the
> promised land, where Religion was purely professed; where he sate
> among grave, learned and reverend men; not, as before, elsewhere,
> a King without State, without honor, without order; where beard-
> less boys would brave him to his face: and to assure us, that he
> called not this assembly for any Innovation, acknowledging the
> government Ecclesiastical, as now it is, to have been approved by
> manifold blessings from God himself, both for the increase of the
> Gospel, and with a most happy and glorious peace.[20]

Episcopal leaders had to be ecstatic at James's opening comments concerning his intentions for the Puritans. Noting that while it was possible that "corruptions might insensibly grow," his intent was nevertheless "like a good Physician, to examine & try the complaints, and fully to remove the occasions thereof, if they prove scandalous, or to cure them, if they were dangerous, or, if but frivolous, yet to take knowledge of them, thereby to cast a sop into *Cerebus* his mouth, that he may never bark again."[21]

Without Puritan observers, James questioned the Anglican leadership on the matters contained within the Millenary Petition that actually seemed to bother him. His stated purpose in proceeding in this fashion was "that if anything should be found meet to be redressed, it might be done . . . without any *visible alteration*."[22] He first turned his attention to the issue raised by the Puritans about confirmation. If the term *confirmation* meant that it was confirming the validity of baptism, he said, "as if this Sacrament without it, were of no validity, then were it blasphemous."[23] James may have rejected the trappings of the Scottish Presbyterians, but he was clearly affected by their Calvinist doctrines. He likewise sought a response to the Puritan objection relative to the questions asked of infants at their baptisms, which were to be answered by the child's own volition upon their profession of faith at confirmation. Since this tended to raise questions about whether the child was actually saved upon baptism, James made clear that he abhorred this "abuse in Popery."[24]

The bishops, having the advantage of seeing the Millenary Petition well in advance, were prepared. The bishop of London defended the practice of confirmation out of the ancient church fathers and, for special effect, employed Calvin's commentary on Hebrews 6:2, where Calvin defended the practice of confirmation and made clear that the child's baptism in a believing family settles the issue of his salvation.

Upon hearing this defense, James "called for the Bible, read the place of the Hebrews, and approved the exposition."[25] James decided that although confirmation could be kept as a practice, it should no longer be called a "sacrament"—which would imply that it contained the actual grace of God necessary for salvation. It should be renamed "an Examination with a Confirmation,"[26] lest it be confused with the truly sacramental nature of infant baptism.[27]

The issue of baptism and its role in salvation, along with the doctrine of free will, would prove to be central issues in the quest for religious liberty, as would become more apparent a few years into James's reign. Infant baptism, coerced by the state, was the easiest mechanism whereby to achieve a universal Christian state—that is, a national church that includes every member of the body politic. A church consisting only of voluntary members, an idea essential to religious liberty, was counterintuitive to the idea of infant baptism. This was especially true when the process of confirmation was deemed to come dangerously close to introducing the idea of voluntariness into the church's practices. James, the Anglicans, and the Puritans were of one mind on the necessity of a coercive, national church despite their surface disagreements over confirmation. Their minds were entirely closed to theological principles that might lead to a belief in a voluntary church membership based on personal faith.

James ended the first day of the Hampton Court Conference with words that would leave the Anglican leaders with no doubt of his loyalty. The Anglican note taker recorded that:

> his majesty should profess howsoever he lived among *Puritans*, and
> was kept, for the most part, as a Ward under them, yet, since he

was of the age of his Son, 10 years old, he ever disliked their opinions; as the Saviour of the world said, *Though he lived among them, he was not of them.*[28]

Four days later, on "Monday, January 16, between 11 and 12 of the Clock, were the four Plaintiffs called into the Privy Chamber."[29] The Puritans were to have their opportunity to present their case. The Anglican entourage was present, along with the young crown prince, Henry, who was to receive a live lesson in statecraft from his father.

The king noted that he had received "many grievous complaints" and that he thought it "best to send for some" whom he "understood to be the most grave, learned, and modest of the aggrieved sort."[30] Dr. Reynolds was the acknowledged leader of the dissenting delegation. He grouped their requests into four categories: (1) conforming the doctrine of the church to God's Word; (2) planting good pastors capable of teaching in all churches; (3) modifying church government to conform to the Bible; and (4) modifying the Book of Common Prayer to increase piety.

The first doctrinal objection raised was against Article 16 of the Articles of Religion. This article said, "After we have received the holy Ghost, we may depart from Grace."[31] This was a contradiction of Article 17, which set forth the Calvinist principle of the perseverance of the saints—a corollary to the doctrine of election and predestination. The second objection concerned the limitation that only those properly ordained could perform pastoral functions. The third was the anticipated topic of confirmation that James and the bishops had already settled between themselves, unbeknownst to the Puritan faction.

The bishop of London's defense of Article 16 was not consistent with authentic Calvinism. While purporting to believe in predestination in an orthodox sense, he nevertheless labeled the Puritan view on the matter a "desperate doctrine" which "presumed too much of persisting in Grace."[32] The argument that salvation was assured regardless of subsequent sinful behavior was too much for the bishops to agree to. James's reply demonstrated that he was far closer to the Anglican view on the matter. He said that he "wished that the doctrine of Predestination might be very tenderly handled, and with great discretion, lest on the one side, God's omnipotence might be called in question, by impeaching the doctrine of his eternal predestination; or on the other, a desperate presumption might be arreared, by inferring the necessary certainty of standing and persisting in grace."[33]

On the other subjects, the conclusions reached the prior day on private baptisms and the modest restatement of the purposes of confirmation were given piecemeal to the dissenters. However, when the matter strayed into the area of church governance, James quickly rejected any notion of Presbyterian government as being utterly antithetical to the principles of a monarchy. In a famous line he proclaimed, "No Bishop, no King."[34] Episcopal church structure was needed to sustain the political theory of a monarchy, James believed. Once congregational governance became the standard, the nation would inevitably drift toward a democracy. If the people could rule themselves in matters of religion, why not in matters of politics as well? The Puritans denied the implication, and perhaps at this time they genuinely believed that a Puritan monarchy would be the best means to enforce their desired version of national religious uniformity. But James was prescient in his understanding of the long-range political implications of Presbyterianism and congregationalism.

James clearly thought that some of the Puritan objections were simply straining at gnats. One such objection related to the precise wording of the standard declaration that the pope had no spiritual authority over England. The Puritans wanted to add words to make it unmistakably plain that he ought not to possess such power. James rebuked them by saying that the language was plain enough as it was. After this exchange, one of the participants, most likely an Anglican leader, quoted the words of "M. Butler of Cambridge," who declared that "a Puritan is a Protestant frayed out of his wits."[35]

Coercing the Petitioners

James repeatedly ridiculed the Puritans, and his derision increased in volume as the conference proceeded. When the Puritans objected to yet another ceremony because of its overtones of papal influence, James replied, "By this argument, we might renounce the Trinity, and all that is holy, because it was abused in Popery: Merrily they used to wear hose & shoes in Popery, therefore, you shall, now, go barefoot."[36]

The king even ridiculed the courage of the Puritans when compared to their Scottish counterparts. He asked the dissenters whether they had any objection to the papal-styled cornered caps worn by the Anglican bishops. They all approved them. Turning to the bishops, the king said, "You may now safely wear your Caps, but I shall tell you, if you should walk in one street in Scotland, with such a Cap on your head, if I were not with you, you should be stoned to death with your Cap."[37]

Rejecting any claim that the Puritans should receive accommodation for their religious consciences, James stingingly denounced the request as "smelling very rankly of Anabaptism."[38] Indeed it did. The idea of freedom of conscience for anyone contained a necessary rejection of the idea of religious uniformity. And at this stage it was true that only the Anabaptists held such views.

James blustered, "I will have none of that, I will have one Doctrine and one discipline, one Religion in substance, and in ceremony: and therefore I charge you, never speak more to that point."[39] Not long afterwards, he added, "If this bee all . . . that they have to say, I shall make the[m] conform themselves, or I will harry them out of the land, or else do worse."[40]

He left no doubt about what he meant when he said that the weak were to be informed, while the willful were to be punished.[41]

A New Translation of the Bible

As the objections droned on, finally Dr. Reynolds brought up an idea that would prove to be the unintended but momentous consequence of the Hampton Court conference:

> After that, he moved his Majesty, that there might be a new translation of the Bible, because, those which were allowed in the reigns of Henry the eight, and Edward the sixth, were corrupt and not answerable to the truth of the Original. Reynolds followed with a list of mistranslated sections that the Bishops dismissively rejected as known and trivial problems. However, James saw an opportunity to drive an additional stake into the heart of Puritanism. Knowing well, that they believed that the Geneva translation—which had never been authorized for use in England—was the proper version, James proclaimed his desire for a new translation in a manner sure to displease the Puritans:

> Whereupon his Highness wished, that some especial pains should be taken in that behalf for one uniform translation (professing that he could never, yet, see a Bible well translated in English; but the worst of all, his Majesty thought the Geneva to be) and this to be done by the best learned in both the Universities, after them to be reviewed by the Bishops, and the chief learned of the Church.[42]

The Puritans had to recognize that their theological enemies—the Anglican hierarchy—had just been given the task to translate the Scripture in a manner pleasing to them. Both James and the Bishops were especially pleased with the opportunity to eliminate the Geneva's marginal comments that repeatedly gave the standard Calvinist interpretation in passage after passage. James wanted a Bible unadorned by such comments.

James's next remarks make clear that he had no idea how significant the translation project would prove to be. For immediately after this subject, James declared that "if these be the greatest matters you be grieved with, I need not have been troubled with such importunities and complaints; as have been made unto me; some other more private course might have been taken for your satisfaction."[43]

The evidence that James sanctioned the beginning of the translation project is beyond dispute. However, when the work was done seven years later, there is no historical evidence to demonstrate that he approved the final product, thus calling into question the traditional claim that this Bible was "authorized."[44] David Daniell's seminal work, *The Bible in English*, concludes that the phrase "our authorized version" first appeared in connection with the King James Bible in 1824.[45] While such an authorization was at least implied and while the cover of even the earliest editions say "*appointed* to be read in churches," no edict from James approving the final product of the translators has ever been discovered.

Inference of the king's approval is strong since censorship of the press was still in vogue. When any book was authorized to be read, it was a sign that it had survived the government's policy of prior censorship. There were no Puritan voices raised against such censorship. Indeed, at the Hampton Court Conference the Puritan faction had urged James that "unlawful and seditious books, might bee suppressed, at least restrained, and imparted to a few: for by the liberty of publishing such books, so commonly, many young Scholars, and unsettled minds in both Universities, and through the whole Realm were corrupted and perverted."[46]

Nevertheless, the greatness of this enduring translation lies in the accuracy and beauty of its words, not in any sanction from an English king who by 1611 was engaged in openly immoral conduct. Indeed, modern computer analysis demonstrates that approximately eighty-five percent of the words of the King James Version originated with William Tyndale.[47] (Obviously, this applies only to those books translated into English by Tyndale prior to his execution.)

The Aftermath of Hampton Court

James and the Anglican elite overwhelmingly bested the Puritan objectors during the conference, although the arrangements for the affair can hardly be called a fair fight on a level playing field. Nonetheless, the upshot of the conference was a crushing setback for Puritanism during James's reign. The Anglican leaders followed James's example by heaping opprobrium on their opponents at every convenient opportunity with jabs such as,

"A puritan is such a one as loves God with all his soul, but hates his neighbor with all his heart."[48] The king's ham-fisted tactics were to have long-range consequences, for "James chose immediately to drive Puritanism into a state of dull resentment which was to grow into flaming opposition before his life was out."[49]

While the Puritans continued some efforts to bolster their position in Parliament, the Anglican leadership employed the nation's official ecclesiastical body, Convocation, to cement their dominance over the objectors. The Canons of 1604 announced that the clergy and laity would both be required to conform to the Book of Common Prayer, "which was declared to be in complete accord with the Word of God."[50] Anyone who denied the truth of this position was to suffer excommunication, which implied far more than removal from the church—in theory, it resulted in the eternal damnation of the expelled dissenter. Dissenting clergymen were given until November 30 to conform or be expelled from their ministerial positions.[51]

The House of Commons had, in the interim, passed a resolution insisting that all laws—ecclesiastical and temporal—necessarily required their consent. This was not an effort to protect religious liberty for the Puritans or any other faction. With explicit language repudiating the concept of toleration, Parliament proclaimed that its goal was that "such laws may be enacted as by the relinquishment of some few ceremonies of small importance" in order that "a perpetual uniformity may be enjoined and observed."[52]

By March 1605, the key leaders of the Puritan faction had been deprived of their ministerial positions. An estimated three hundred members of the clergy refused to conform to James' demands and were ejected from the ministry.[53] Some would escape to Holland. Not long afterward, many would escape to the New World.[54]

All the relevant factions—James, the bishops, the Puritans, and the Parliament—held to the Augustinian position of compelled uniformity of religious practice. While they professed to believe that only "persuasion and reason can alone make a man a good Christian,"[55] they nonetheless thought that if this should fail, "the magistrate must compel."[56] James himself wrote:

> That it is one of the principal parts of that duty which appertains unto a Christian King, to protect the true Church within his own Dominions, and to extirpate heresies, is a Maxim without all controversy; in which respect those honorable Titles of . . . *Keeper and Avenger of both the Tables of the Law*, and . . . *Nursing Father of the Church*, do rightly belong unto every Emperor, King, and Christian Monarch.[57]

Even though the Anglican leadership was all too eager to follow the king's edict to "harry" the Puritans and other dissenters out of the land, some became uncomfortable with the path of persecution. Rather than advancing a theory of religious liberty, some Anglican thinkers began to water down their theology in order to reduce friction over religious matters. The church should not declare every truth to be fundamental, one Anglican author contended, and it should avoid any coerced uniformity on nonfundamental matters.[58] Eventually, by declaring more and more matters to be nonfundamental, it was thought, religious controversy could be made extremely minimal. Yet once a matter was declared not to be important enough to require uniformity, lay members of the church were prone to think that such matters were simply not worth believing.

Although many (including the worthy religious history historian W. K. Jordan) view minimization of the importance of religious tenets as "half the struggle for toleration,"[59] in reality it had no such outcome. Religious liberty would require a total rejection of any power of government to define orthodoxy and punish those who dissent. Whether the range of punishable heterodoxy was limited or extensive, use of this weapon was always tyrannical. The ruler who sent only a *few* to prison or to the stake could not claim to be a friend of liberty. A friend of liberty is not merely "moderate" on the matters he views as worthy of punishment; rather, *in spite of* his own strongly held convictions, he refuses to punish anyone at any time for disagreeing.

King James and His "Favourites"

Modern historians have a decided penchant for researching and writing about "gender and sexuality" in every imaginable manifestation and with reference to every generation and culture group that has walked the face of the earth. Any careful reader has reason to be suspicious when authors begin to uncover the "suppressed gay identities" of historical figures. Nevertheless, there does seem to be considerable evidence that King James I had homosexual leanings and, in fact, did little to hide his affections—to the great disgust of some members of his court.

One author named Francis Osborne grew up in England during the latter days of Elizabeth I and lived through the reigns of both James I and his son, Charles. During the period known as the Interregnum, Osborne retired to Oxford to write. While there, he produced some historical memoirs that shed unfavorable light on the late King James:

> [The Earl of Carlisle] lay always under the comfortable
> aspect of King *James* his favor, though I never found him in his

bosom, a place reserved for younger men and of more endear-
ing Countenances: and these went under the appellation of his
Favorites or *Minions*. . . . Now as no other Reason appeared in favor
of their choice but *handsomeness*, so the love the K. showed was as
amorously conveyed as if he had mistaken their Sex, and thought
them Ladies. Which I have seen *Somerset* and *Buckingham* labor
to resemble, in the effeminateness of their dressings. Though in
. . . wanton gestures they exceeded any part of Woman-kind my
Conversation did ever cope withal. Nor was his love, or what else
posterity will please to call it (who must be the Judges of all that
History shall inform) carried on with a discretion sufficient to
cover a less scandalous behavior; for the King's kissing them after
so lascivious a mode in public, and upon the Theater as it were of
the World.[60]

King James had a series of these male "favourites" who shared a similar
appearance and were showered with gifts, honors, and titles from the king.[61]
This was said to have provoked, quite understandably, jealousy on the part of
both his wife, Queen Anne, and his son, Prince Charles.[62]

The earl of "Somerset" and duke of "Buckingham" whom Osborne
referred to were Robert Carr and George Villiers. Both young men were
given grand titles and the riches that accompany them not from a family
inheritance but as reward for their private relationship with James.

Villiers, in particular, had a special place in the king's affections, as evident from the many extant letters they exchanged.[63] James addressed Villiers
as "My only sweet and dear child," "sweet heart," and "Steenie," a nickname
that has been referred to as a "half-profane allusion" to St. Stephen, whose
face was said to look like the face of an angel in Acts 6.[64] James went so far
as to call Villiers his "wife."[65]

Seventeenth-century historian Arthur Wilson records how Villiers cap-
tivated the king's attention just as Carr's power and influence was reaching
its peak due to the favors of the king:

> About this time the King cast his eye upon a young
> Gentleman, so rarely *moulded*, that he meant to make him a
> *Masterpiece:* His name was *George Villers*. . . . The King stricken
> with this new object, would not expose him to so much hazard as
> the *malice* of a jealous *Competitor* [i.e., Carr], nor make him self to
> so much censure, as to be thought changeable, and taken again
> with a sudden affection.[66]

Thus, the king instructed his confidants to introduce Villiers to his inner circle slowly, beginning in the position of cupbearer.

While James's actions and terms of endearment are open to differing interpretations, it is well-known that he bestowed excessive honor where it was open to question. After Carr's fall from power due to his implication in a murder plot, the king did not hesitate in replacing him with Villiers as "his new *Favourite*":

> To speak of [Villier's] Advancement by *Degrees*, were to lessen the King's Love; for *Titles* were heaped upon him, they came rather like *showers* than *drops*. For as soon as *Somerset* declined, he mounted. *Such is the Court motion!* Knighthood, and Gentleman of the Bed-Chamber, were the first sprinklings. . . . He now reigns sole *Monarch* in the King's affection, every thing he doth is admired for the *doers* sake. . . . But the King is not well without him, his company is his solace.[67]

Not all subjects acquiesced to the king's bestowals but were rather repulsed by his behavior in more ways than one.[68] Not only were there moral objections; his favorites came at an exorbitant price. Osborne wryly remarks, "For the setting up of these *Golden Calves* cost *England* more than Queen *Elizabeth* spent in all her Wars."[69]

Despite his tremendous intellect and the legacy of his "authorized" translation of the Bible, James's personal improprieties led to much contemporary disdain and criticism. Henry IV of France perhaps said it best when he declared James to be "the very wisest fool in Christendom."

Guy Fawkes and the Catholic Problem

Early in his reign, James I showed himself comparatively tolerant of Catholic dissenters and at times appeared to come down far more harshly on the Puritans. After all, his wife, Anne of Denmark, was Catholic. Nonetheless, any Catholic hopes for increased toleration were not likely to be fulfilled in an atmosphere where the Puritan branch of Anglicanism was suffering increased persecution.

Sometime in 1604, Robert Catesby, a Catholic whose father had been imprisoned for harboring a priest and who was forced to leave the university without a degree for refusing to take the oath of supremacy, concocted a plot to blow up the entire Parliament while King James was present. The plot involved a core group of about thirteen men including Guy Fawkes, who rented a house in the immediate vicinity of Westminster. In the basement was stored sufficient gunpowder to blow up everything and everyone in the area. Fawkes intended to light the fire and escape to the continent. However, an anonymous letter warning one member of Parliament to stay away from the chambers led to a search of the area and the discovery of the plotters and their explosives around midnight on November 4, 1604—the day before the scheduled reopening of Parliament and the intended deadly attack. Some plotters were killed in the action taken to capture them; the rest were tried and brutally executed for high treason.

In retaliation, Parliament enacted two laws that led to long-term persecution of English Catholics. The first required that all Englishmen not only attend Anglican services, but also partake of the communion.[70] The second placed a series of civil disabilities on Catholics, excluding them from serving in the Court and barring them from holding public office[71] or even voting in Parliamentary elections. The ban on voting was not lifted until 1829.[72]

In 1606, James attempted to lighten the load somewhat by distinguishing between "political" and "spiritual" Catholics. Spiritual Catholics were those who swore allegiance to England while holding to Roman Catholic views on spiritual matters. Political Catholics not only embraced the doctrinal tenets of Catholicism but also believed in the supremacy of the pope over political leaders, including his right to remove any king from the throne and to urge faithful Catholics to overthrow his rule. An oath of allegiance was prepared to try to distinguish between the two groups—a meager but important effort to seek some sort of accommodation with rank-and-file Catholics. The pope, however, denounced the Oath of Accommodation for containing "many things obviously contrarient to faith and salvation."[73]

The Fires of Smithfield Kindled Once More

No Catholic or Puritan was ever executed for heresy during the reign of James I. Two commoners possessing idiosyncratic, if not delusional, religious beliefs were not so fortunate.

Bartholomew Legate rejected the deity of Christ and refused to subscribe to any of the ancient creeds. James took a special interest in Legate and tried various means to convince Legate of his theological error, but Legate persisted. Under the bishop's lead, an ecclesiastical court pronounced Legate "an obdurate, contumacious, and incorrigible Heretic."[74] The bishop turned him over to King James, who ordered Legate to be burned. The burning took place at Smithfield on March 18, 1612. In the words of a seventeenth-century historian, "Never did a scare-fire at midnight summon more hands to quench it, that this noon-day did eyes to behold" Legate's execution.[75]

Edward Wightman was likely insane—or, as Jordan phrases it, was "the victim of religious mania."[76] Possessing some views that could be called mainstream Anabaptist, he also believed that he was the prophet promised to the world by Moses and, if that was not enough, was also the "comforter" that Christ promised to His disciples.[77]

After a public trial, Wightman was led to the stake in the city of Lichfield, about one hundred miles north of London. As the flames began to eat away at his body, he shouted out his intention to recant.[78] Members of the crowd rushed to save him. He was given a document to sign, which secured his release for the moment. However, when taken back to court to enter a formal recantation, he refused to do so. James ordered the execution, which took place on April 11, 1612, in Lichfield.[79]

Wightman is considered the last person to have been executed for heresy in England. Public reaction to these two burnings was overwhelmingly negative—a reaction that was not without effect on James. He decided that "heretics [there]after, though condemned, should silently, and privately waste themselves away in the Prison" because this was undoubtedly better than "to grace them and amuse others with the solemnity of a *public Execution*, which in popular judgments usurped the honor of a *persecution*."[80]

In keeping with James's decision, many more would be arrested for their views after the Wightman incident. Many would die in prison—a less expeditious method of execution but fully effective.

King James I embraced no version of liberty. He was no less a tyrant of the soul than his predecessors.

Chapter Eleven

THE BRAVEST VOICES OF LIBERTY

The First English Baptists

For our lord the king is but an earthly king, and he hath no authority as a king but in earthly causes . . . for men's religion to God is betwixt God and themselves.

THOMAS HELWYS

*I*n the early seventeenth century, there were two widely divergent views within Christianity concerning the desirability of religious liberty. The line of demarcation was not between Catholic and Protestant, as many may suppose or perhaps wish. The key philosophical question dividing the two camps was this: Are saving faith and church membership entirely voluntary matters of the human will, or can these be compelled?

Those who taught that both faith and church membership were involuntary acts followed the teachings of Augustine, while those who believed that both faith and church membership must be truly voluntary categorically rejected Augustinian theology on these matters.[1] Augustine believed that the church, the visible institution, was to be universally adhered to by all within the state. After all, did not Jesus say that all believers were to be one? Dissent was to be silenced with the aid of the magistrate and his sword. Of course, Augustine believed that the Roman Catholic Church was the one true church, and schism or heresy—any form of contradiction or departure from the teachings of Rome—was to be decisively handled by the magistrate.[2] The Reformers, both Anglican and Puritan, rejected Augustine's singular devotion to Rome, but otherwise faithfully followed his teaching concerning the appropriateness of coerced membership in the national church. This was also consonant with Augustine's teachings on predestination and election, which the Reformers followed more faithfully than Rome.[3]

In the era of King James, all the major religious factions—Anglican, Puritan (Presbyterian), and Catholic—were Augustinian in terms of the voluntariness of church membership. They did not merely fail to achieve religious liberty; they rejected the very concept as a dangerous heresy.[4] However, a tiny group of dissenters argued that all of these groups were in error. Each of the major groups believed that theirs was the one true church. So did the dissenters. Yet while the major factions all wanted to control the levers of power of both the state and national church and to compel all within England to adhere to their particular theology, the dissenters rejected the notion that God was pleased by such acts of coercion. These dissenters were the first English Baptists.

The Baptist View on Religious Liberty: An Overview and Contrast

An assessment of the early English Baptists' contribution to the development of religious liberty, written by Harvard's esteemed historian of the early twentieth century, W. K. Jordan, bears repeating:

> It is with the Baptists that the tolerant implications of Protestant sectarianism become most fully apparent. Their doctrinal and institutional beginnings antedated Calvinism, and, with the exception of various schismatic groups, the main body of Baptists was but slightly influenced by the teachings of Calvinism respecting both the nature of the Church and the necessity of a highly organized and rigidly imposed doctrinal system. Their religious teachings were revolutionary and anarchistic, and for well over a century they were persecuted throughout Protestant Europe. Few sects have survived such contempt and hatred as that to which the Baptists were subjected. It is to their great credit that, though persistently persecuted, they maintained steadily the doctrine of religious liberty and denied that any human power, whether civil or ecclesiastical, exercised any legitimate authority over the human conscience.[5]

Jordan continues by answering the charge that the Baptists were like all other sects who simply wanted religious toleration for themselves alone:

> It is true that every persecuted sect which holds that it teaches divine truth and follows the divine will maintains that the State cannot justly punish its members for beliefs which are held in conscience. But such groups, unless their underlying philosophy rests upon the assertion of the religious necessity of freedom for every Christian man, will not be likely to argue for the toleration of groups which differ both from them and from the established order. . . .
>
> The Baptists taught even more consistently than the Congregationalists that the true Church was a voluntary congregation of believers, and they were never confused by the Calvinistic teaching, which tended to persist in Congregationalism, that it was the duty of the prince to encourage the true religion and to repress the false. The Baptists not only regarded the Church as a voluntary organization, but insisted that the regenerated alone could be admitted to it with adult baptism as the outward badge of the state of grace.[6]

Jordan also describes the Anabaptist/Baptist unique stance relative to the teachings of Augustine:

> The sect rejected the Augustinian theology of the reformers and insisted vehemently upon the complete freedom of the will and the moral responsibility of the individual not only for his conduct but for his salvation. Hoffman had taught as early as 1525 that though all men were sinful, they were all called by God to salvation since Christ had died for them. All men have been given sufficient grace to achieve salvation if they will.[7]

Thus, the Baptist view of religious liberty arose directly from their view of how a person can obtain salvation. The Augustinian camp that opposed religious liberty and practiced coercion likewise reasoned to their conclusions as the result of their soteriological beliefs. Moreover, each group's theory of religious liberty was inseparable from its view on membership in the universal church. The Baptist interpretation was that the church is made up of those who have believed in Christ as Savior as the result of a free and voluntary decision, evidenced by their own decision to be baptized as a confessing believer. The Augustinian view held that all those residing in a nation where the ruler had declared Christianity to be the religion of the state were required to be members of the church, as evidenced by universal, compelled infant baptism. This difference on the subject of baptism was of considerable significance. After all, it was this distinctive that gave the Anabaptists— a term which means "rebaptizers"—their name.

Those who practiced infant baptism, as we have seen, saw in this practice a true effusion of the grace of God which causes, assures, or leads to salvation. As much as the Baptists would dispute the soteriological effect of infant baptism, the real key was its involuntary nature.[8] The Baptists believed that membership in Christ's true church, the invisible association of all true believers, comes as the result of a voluntary choice and genuine faith. At the heart of the Baptist criticism of "paedobaptism" was the contention that it resulted in an involuntary induction of a person into supposed membership in Christ's universal church. Saving faith could be neither the result of compelled grace, they argued, nor the result of the involuntary baptism of an infant who is totally unaware of the nature and meaning of the act.

The Baptists, like the Anabaptists before them, held strong views concerning the financial support of the established church through government-mandated church taxes. They rejected all "forms of State support and maintained their preachers by their free-will offerings."[9] Anabaptists were also generally pacifists who believed it was inappropriate for Christians to serve in the office of civil magistrate. On these latter matters, there arose a key difference between Baptists and Anabaptists. Baptists thought it was fully appropriate for Christians to serve as magistrates as well as in the military. Baptists also taught, just as Tyndale had proclaimed in *The Obedience of the Christian Man*, that it was the duty of all Christians to obey the magistrate—provided, however, that the magistrate did not stray into the jurisdiction of the conscience.

It must be remembered that the debate over the voluntary nature of saving faith and church membership was not merely theoretical differences debated within the confines of a university disputation. These were matters of life and death for the simple reason that those who held the reins of power believed it was their God-given duty to coerce all others to join in their beliefs and practices. Beginning in Zurich in 1525, "thousands of Anabaptists were either beheaded or burned at the stake or drowned—drowning being deemed an appropriate punishment for such criminals."[10] Thus, when an English Baptist argued for religious liberty, he knew that public advocacy of liberty could cost him his freedom, his property, and his life.

Origins of the English Baptists

While the early English Lollards held many views parallel to those of the first Baptists, the chain of history does not run in a direct path between these two groups. Likewise, the Kent Conventiclers of the Bloody Mary era held to most of the views of the first English Baptists, but it is not easy to find direct linkage between these two sets of dissenters.[11] There is good reason to suspect some influence on Baptist thinking from both Wycliffe and the Lollards as well as the Kent Freewillers, but again, to demonstrate these connections is difficult. Constructing this particular chain of theological heritage is complicated by the fact that it involves an attempt to trace the ideas and movements of those who were considered by their government to be dangerous criminals.

However, there are certain portions of the path followed by these brave dissidents that are familiar to students of early American history. The first English Baptists were directly connected to other dissidents who, as a little party of Pilgrims, sailed for America in 1620 in a small sea vessel called the *Mayflower.*

The Baptists can trace their line of theological belief to the Brownists of the Elizabethan era. In the 1580s, sectarian groups formed congregations in Norwich, London, Gainsborough, and Scrooby.[12] These "independent congregations" were "Calvinistic in theology and life, but congregational and democratic in church government."[13] Elizabeth had succeeded in driving most of these people to the Netherlands, although some of the leadership returned to England only to be hung by her in 1593.[14]

The exodus of these sectarian dissenters continued in the early years of King James. In 1606, John Smyth, Thomas Helwys, and John Murton—all of whom became significant leaders of the English refugees—found their way to Amsterdam. By this time any hope that James might institute a more tolerant policy had completely evaporated. Smyth, the initial leader of the group, made alliances with other English refugee congregations in Amsterdam, including one from London led by Francis Johnson and another from Scrooby led by John Robinson. As is common among those who have broken the shackles of orthodoxy, Smyth's small splinter group shattered into even smaller groups, dividing over idiosyncratic issues such as the question of whether Bible teaching in church should be done straight from the original languages, translated on the spot by the pastor, or whether it was acceptable to use prior English translations.[15] One historian claims that Smyth had "considerable influence over Robinson before they both went to Holland, with the result that Smyth's language and ideas passed, by way of Robinson, to the Pilgrim Fathers."[16]

While in Holland, Smyth became convinced that believer's baptism was correct and convinced most of his church to follow him. His change in regard to believer's baptism was directly connected to his rejection of Calvinist views on salvation. Smyth and his group rapidly moved in the

Arminian direction on the question of free will. Smyth had already separated from Robinson and the former Scrooby congregation before these new views were adopted; thus, the group which ultimately headed to Plymouth did not embrace these particular changes concerning either baptism or free will.

Smyth's congregation, however, became convinced that their own baptisms as infants were invalid; accordingly, the believers set out to baptize themselves properly. After some debate as to who was qualified to perform the first baptism, they finally implemented the idea that their pastor, Smyth, would baptize himself and then the rest of the congregation. This 1609 believer's baptism—the first by an English-speaking congregation—was not done by immersion. The pastor took a basin of water and drenched the head of the person being baptized.[17]

After a while, the group began to have doubts over the legitimacy of their baptism since it had not been sanctioned by any person who had been previously baptized in the proper manner. They turned to the Dutch Anabaptists and ultimately to the Waterland Mennonites, asking them to sanction yet another baptismal service.[18]

Thomas Helwys and about ten others refused to go along with this move. They rejected the idea that there must be a succession of properly sanctioned elders in order to administer baptisms. This, they argued, was a destruction of the liberty of the gospel and tantamount to a return to the Catholic position on the necessity of apostolic succession. Accordingly, Helwys and the small minority who refused to join Smyth's latest modification of his own views excommunicated him. Among their considerations was the deep concern that the Anabaptist Mennonites failed to embrace an important doctrine concerning the nature of Christ. While the Mennonites endorsed the idea that Jesus was fully God, they rejected the notion that He was also fully man. Helwys and the remaining congregation believed strongly that Jesus was both fully God and fully man.[19]

By 1612, Helwys and his small following had become convinced that they had been in error to leave England. Perhaps Helwys was motivated in part by personal guilt over his own family situation. He was from a notable family from Broxtowe Hall, near Nottingham, and was educated at Gray's Inn in London, where he had received both general instruction and a legal education. When he fled to Holland, he left his wife and children behind in the apparent belief that their relatively high social status would grant them exemption from the Anglican persecutions underway under King James. He was mistaken, and his wife was thrown into prison.[20]

Whatever else may have motivated their return, this first group of English Baptists returned to London near the end of 1612, saying that there were "thousands of ignorant souls in our own country [who] were perishing for lack of instruction."[21] They returned as missionaries to their homeland.

There is no doubt they understood the dangers they faced, but Helwys did not choose clandestine evangelism as his mode of operation. In 1612, he published a 212-page treatise titled *A Short Declaration of the Mistery of Iniquity* that was pointedly written to King James. The copy that remains in Oxford's Bodleian Library contains this hand-written dedication on the inside cover:

> Hear, O King, and despise not the counsel of the poor, and let their complaints come before thee. The king is a mortal man and not God: therefore hath no power over the immortal souls of his subjects, to make laws and ordinances for them, and to set spiritual Lords over them. If the king have any authority to make spiritual Lords and laws, then he is an immortal God, and not a mortal man. O King, be not seduced by deceivers to sin against God whom thou oughtest to obey, nor against thy poor subjects who ought and will obey thee in all things with body, life and goods, or else let their lives be taken from the earth. God save the King. Spittlefield, near London. Tho: Helwys.

Although Smyth had written an earlier treatise eloquently calling for full religious liberty—the first such work in the English language—it was written from the relative safety of exile in Holland. Helwys dared to publish this new advocacy for complete religious liberty from the outskirts of London. And just to be sure that he was not mistaken for someone desirous of simply stirring up public opinion, he sent his book directly to the king of England, whom he hoped to convince to join the cause of religious liberty. Of this work, Jordan says, "Helwys gave to religious toleration the finest and fullest defence which it had ever received in England."[22] But Jordan understates the case. Helwys did not call for mere toleration, which implies the continuation of compelled orthodoxy with official permission for certain dissenters to differ in certain particulars. Helwys called for religious freedom for everyone—not just Baptists and not just Protestants but Catholics as well. And he went even further than that: "Let them be heretics, Turks, Jews or whatsoever, it appertains not to the earthly power to punish them in the least measure."[23]

This little known book is not only one of the most important works on religious freedom in the English language, but it is without doubt one of the most courageous acts of conscience in the annals of mankind. Helwys was asking King James to consider the cause of liberty. But his ideas were far too dangerous. He was promptly thrown into prison where he remained until his

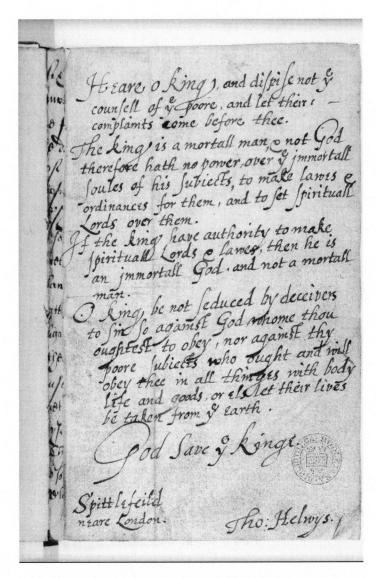

Handwritten dedication page from Thomas Helwys. A short
declaration of this mystery of iniquity (1612), courtesy of
The Bodleian Library, 8° H 105 Th.

death. Helwys's case was yet another example of why the anti-Augustinians
had such difficulty finding a great champion who could produce the massive
theological treatises to match those of Calvin and other Reformers: The

leaders of the freewill group were systematically executed by their theological opponents.

Undaunted, the church founded by Helwys continued with other lay leaders, and by 1626 there were four sister churches in London and the home counties.[24] Eventually, others would be convinced by various aspects of the message of these first Baptists. A group of Calvinistic Baptists, known as Particular Baptists, would form in later decades and become important in their own right. The original freewill Baptists henceforth became known as General Baptists. While the Particular Baptists held to the teaching of religious freedom with tenacity, theirs was an attempt to patch together the theology that advocated liberty and the Augustinian views which taught and practiced persecution.

The writings of Thomas Helwys were the starting point of an open call for religious liberty in England. His arguments deserve to be fully known and understood since these same principles, advocated by his Baptist descendents, would prove to be a critical factor in the achievement of religious liberty in America. First, let us examine *A Declaration of Faith of English People*, drafted by Helwys and his congregation and published in Amsterdam in 1611. This is generally acknowledged as being the earliest Baptist confession.

Having established the religious tenets that led these people to embrace the principle of religious liberty for all, we will then look at two subsequent works which boldly proclaimed to King James the biblical necessity of religious freedom.

The First Baptist Confession

Containing twenty-seven articles, *A Declaration of Faith of the English People* clearly rejected some of the more troubling aspects of Anabaptist thinking. The first article embraced an orthodox understanding of the Trinity, while the eighth article proclaimed that Jesus is "one person in two distinct natures, TRUE GOD, and TRUE MAN."[25]

The first Baptists' view on original sin was similar to that of the other Reformers: Adam's disobedience is imputed to all men, and thus "death went over all men."[26] But unlike the other Reformers, the first Baptists did not embrace the idea that the work of Christ was limited by God's choice of the elect; rather, they understood the work of Christ as being as extensive as the result of Adam's sin. They taught, in their third and fifth articles, that just as Adam's sin is imputed to all men, the righteousness of Christ through His obedience on the cross is available to all men, but only those who respond in faith are actually justified.

Another critical issue was the Baptist view of the church. The articles stated that it is the "company of faithful people" who are joined together unto the Lord and one another by baptism; that is, that baptism is an outward manifestation of dying unto sin and walking in newness of life "and therefore in no wise appertains to infants."[27] Although the church is one in Christ, Helwys wrote, "Yet it consists of diverse particular congregations."[28] Such a congregation has full authority to administer the ordinances of the church—baptism and communion—and otherwise engage in all the ministries of a local church. Moreover, no congregation may dictate to any other congregation how it should conduct its affairs since "as one congregation hath Christ, so hath all."[29] By definition these views of the church were a cry for religious liberty since they removed the possibility of a coercive national church.

Two items in this document are of special interest to modern Christians. First, the original Baptists had an article of faith that would prohibit today's mega-church movement: They held that the members of every congregation ought to know each other so they can perform the duties of love one to another, and the elders especially should know the whole flock. That this tiny handful of persecuted people even contemplated the day when their number would be so large as to require such an article was a testimony to a vision that was both large and bold.

The second interesting item held that the Baptist churches were to be governed by elders and deacons. Elders were to be the men who taught the flock and tended to spiritual needs. Deacons, both men *and* women, were to tend to the needs of the poor.[30] These leaders were to be chosen by the local congregation according to the qualifications listed in the New Testament— which by implication rejected the necessity of a university-educated pastorate. Moreover, no congregation had any say over the selection of another congregation's leadership.[31]

Finally, these first Baptists proclaimed the role of the Word of God in their belief system:

> That the scriptures off the Old and New Testament are written for our instruction, 2. Tim 3.16 & that wee ought to search them for they testify of CHRIST, Io. [John] 5.39. And therefore to bee used withal reverence, as containing the Holy Word off GOD, which only is our direction in all things whatsoever.[32]

The Mistery of Iniquity

Helwys began his 1612 publication, *A Short Declaration of the Mistery of Iniquity*, with an explanation of his actions that seem extraordinarily coura-geous. Why would he return to England from the relative safety of Holland? And why on earth would he write a treatise urging the king to change his religious policies in light of the known dangers of so doing? Helwys answered these questions with the first sentence of his book:

> The fear of the Almighty (through the work of his grace) having now at least overweighed in us the fear of men, we have thus far by the direction of God's word and Spirit stretched out our hearts and hands with boldness to confess the name of Christ before men, and to declare to the Prince and People plainly their transgressions, that all might hear & see their fearful estate and standing, and repent, and turn unto the Lord before the decree come forth.[33]

It was not an unusual beginning for a religious treatise in the prophetic tradition, being a call to the king and his people to repent from their sin. But it was the description of their sin that was unusual. The "mistery of iniquity" exposed was that the king and his bishops were usurping the place of God by demanding rule over the consciences of men.

Helwys's subtle intellectual humility is worth noting. Like all those who believed they had discovered God's truth, Helwys unashamedly urged others of differing views to repent, for they were in error. But note how he condi-tioned his call to repentance: "And our continual prayers unto the Lord are, and shall be that the Lord will enlighten your understandings, and raise up all the affections of your souls and spirits, that you may apply yourselves unto these things, so far as his word and spirit doth direct you."[34]

Helwys was willing to sacrifice his freedom and his life to offer others the truth, yet he was so solicitous of the idea that no one should usurp the role of God, that Helwys added the caveat "so far as his word and spirit doth direct you." This was a man who truly believed that every person had the right and responsibility to come directly to God to determine the truth in light of the written Word and the inner ministry of the Holy Spirit.

Early in the book, Helwys made the charge that the king and bishops were usurping the place of Christ by arrogating to themselves the power to rule over the souls of men. Religious laws and ceremonies not found in the Bible constitute usurpation, he wrote, because Jesus demands total domin-ion over spiritual matters. Using the highly volatile question of freedom for Catholics, Helwys demonstrated his total commitment to religious liberty while at the same time making clear that he believed the king has rightful authority to demand the political loyalty of all his subjects:

> We still pray our lord the king that we may be free from sus-
> pect, for having any thoughts of provoking evil against them of
> the Romish religion, in regard of their profession, if they be true
> & faithful subjects to the king for we do freely profess, that our
> lord the king hath no more power over their consciences than over
> ours, and that is none at all: for our lord the king is but an earthly
> king, and he hath no authority as a king but in earthly causes,
> and if the king's people be obedient and wise subjects, obeying all
> human laws made by the king, our lord the king can require no
> more; for men's religion to God, is betwixt God and themselves;
> the king shall not answer for it, neither may the king be judged
> between God and man. Let them be heretics, Turks, Jews, or
> whatsoever it appertains not to the earthly power to punish them
> in the least measure.[35]

Helwys directly confronted the notion that all kings have been given by God the authority to rule over spiritual matters. If the king has the authority to set the religious policy for the nation, he argued, then both Christ and the apostles should not have been permitted to teach, since they were not in conformance with the religion of those who ruled their lands.[36]

As for the bishops whom the king had set up as spiritual authorities over the nation, Helwys used an innovative analogy to challenge their author-ity to interpret Scripture for the entire nation. Suppose, he suggested, that Christ and His apostles were to appear in England and preach and proclaim the gospel before thousands of people. The bishops were in attendance, and so were thousands of people who likewise heard the words of Christ. What would happen, he asked, if after Christ and the apostles had departed, there arose a dispute between the bishops and the people over what had really been said in the hearing of all?

> Can our lord the king (that is accounted a most wise and just
> Prince in his judgment); judge that we are all bound to cast away
> our own understandings of Christ's speaking and are compelled to
> believe and understand Christ to speak, as the lord Bishops under-
> stand Christ's speaking? Oh let our lord the king with compassion,
> consider, whether ever since the heavens and earth were created,
> there was a more unequal extreme cruelty than this, that the king's
> people should be compelled (in a cause that concerns the everlasting

condemnation of their souls and bodies to hell) of force submit their souls and bodies to the understanding of the Lord Bishops.[37]

At the heart of the idea of religious freedom is the belief in the right of private judgment here so eloquently defended by Helwys. How would it be just for God to send people to hell if they were forced by the king's power to believe that which the bishops taught if the bishops were in error? Only free men can be held accountable for their choices by a just God.

While the Augustinian theorists weighted their arguments heavily on the Old Testament, Helwys turned to the examples of coercion by temporal rulers as contained in the New Testament. He argued that wherever "the professors of the faith in Jesus were adjudged by earthly rulers and Governors, for any thing that they did or held of conscience to God and of faith to Jesus Christ, if earthly rulers and Governors took the cause in hand by their power, the judgment was always wicked and abominable."[38]

Helwys then addressed a defense raised by those who supported the coercive national church. Those who punished Christ and the disciples were heathen kings, and heathen kings have no power to punish Christians, they might argue. Helwys answered with admirable restraint. He asked, "Have you the power to imprison, banish, and put to death anyone simply because you are a disciple of Christ?" These powers reside only in a king because of his temporal office, not because of his relationship to Christ. And either these powers belong to all kings—including those heathens who punished Christ and the apostles—or they belong to no king at all. The Christian king has no such power because "Christ the king did not so himself: he never appointed to be punished any one man for disobeying his Gospel with the least bodily punishment."[39]

> For Christ and Apostles had no such power given them: neither taught they the disciples to take upon them any such power, and to execute it upon the contrary minded, but taught them to the contrary to instruct them with meekness, and by preaching the word seek their conversion, with all long suffering, and not to destroy them by severe punishments.[40]

Unlike Luther, Knox, and Calvin, Helwys strongly urged that it was improper for Christians to take harsh action against the Jews and "all infidels." Rather, Christians "should go in and out with holiness and all meekness before his people to win them to Christ."[41]

At the core of the persecuting establishment was the fundamental belief that the bishops spoke not merely as teachers and spiritual leaders, but with the spiritual authority of God Himself. Or as Helwys put it, "as though with them only remained the oracles of God."[42] To this, Helwys answered:

> Yea if they can but prove that we ought to rest or depend upon their judgments and understandings in the exposition of any one part of God's word: or that they have power to ordain and appoint any one Ordinance, or the manner of administering any one Ordinance in the worship of God and Church of Christ, we profess unto our lord the king we will yield them all the obedience they require. But if they will prove these things only by Convocation Canons, how can our lord the king require that the king's servant should dishonor God, by casting his holy truth away and with it the salvation of our souls and depend upon their Canons, and yield them obedience, and perish in both souls and bodies.[43]

Then Helwys added these poignant words: "We have rather chosen thus to lay down our lives at the feet of our lord the king in presenting the cause into the king's presence. Saying with Esther: If we perish, we perish for running thus boldly uncalled into the king's presence: but we will wait with hope and expectation."[44]

Esther was saved in her encounter with the pagan king of Babylon. The "Christian" king of England had, by this time, lost his nerve in terms of sentencing people to be burned at the stake. James instead had Thomas Helwys arrested and thrown into Newgate prison where he was kept until his death.

Religions Peace

Leonard Busher, another early English Baptist, advocated religious liberty for all men in a 1614 plea written to King James and the Parliament. *Religions Peace; or A reconciliation between Princes & Peoples & Nations* is recognized as the first book in English devoted solely to the topic of religious liberty. The book contained two sections. The first was a biblical argument that religious persecution is the tool of the devil and the Antichrist and that no true Christian can engage in deadly persecution. It addressed the necessity of each individual being born again as a result of being taught from the Word of God rather than being forced to embrace the religion of their King or Queen:

> In all humility I give you to understand, that no Prince or People can possibly attain that one true Religion of the Gospel,

which is acceptable to God by Jesus Christ, merely by birth, for Christ saith, *Except a man be born again he cannot see the kingdom of God.* . . .

Therefore Christ commanded this word to be preached to all nations, that thereby they may attain the new birth. [45]

A deep immersion in the writings of this era is necessary to appreciate fully the rarity of this argument. References to being "born again" were uncommon among the Reformers. The idea that a true church could consist of an entire nation leaves scant, if any, theological room for thinking of the necessity of being born again. The focus of the era was the turning of nations into a unified "true church," not the conversion of individual souls via a new birth.

With his focus on preaching the gospel and seeking individual conversions, Busher contended that religious liberty for all was essential to the success of such efforts. His was no secular plea for tolerance or diversity of opinion. Rather, it was his love for the gospel of Christ and his soul-compelled duty to preach it to willing ears that urged this man from Gloucestershire to argue for liberty of conscience. Busher believed that the conscience, under the conviction of the Holy Spirit, would be used to bring men to Christ. A free conscience was therefore the *sine qua non* of a true conversion, and thus a true Christian. Those who argued that heretics should be burned, banished, or imprisoned were not following the directives of Christ, he contended. Rather, "that is Antichrist's ordinance."[46]

Echoing the arguments of Sabastian Castellio some eighty years earlier, Busher argued that the true Church never persecutes but is always persecuted by the false.[47] Moreover, the demand of the bishops that the people listen only to their voices contradicts the clear teaching of the apostle John that believers are to test the spirits of the teachers gone out into the world to see if they be of Christ or the Antichrist.[48]

Although Busher did not cite Castellio's name, there is a nearly word-for-word quotation of a section of Castellio's dedication to Duke Christoph from his book *Concerning Heretics.* In it Busher described an episode when the bishop of Rome was attempting to convert a Turkish emperor. The emperor responded to the bishop by noting that even as Christ did not use the sword to coerce people into believing Him, neither did he force Islam on unwilling subjects. Busher then asked:

How much more ought Christians not force one another to Religion? *and how much more ought Christians to tolerate Christians when as the Turks tolerate them? Shall we be less merciful than the Turks? Or shall we learn the Turks to persecute Christians? It is not*

only unmerciful, but unnatural and abominable, yea, monstrous for
one Christian to vex and destroy another for difference and questions of
Religion, and though tares have overgrown the wheat, yet Christ will
have them let alone till harvest.[49]

The italicized text here appears in a different typeface in the 1646 edition of the book in the manner used to indicate quoted material. The source of the quotation is not cited, yet it is unmistakably from the above-referenced work of Castellio.[50] Given the fact that Castellio was not working in English, the minor differences in text can be attributed to the process of translation.

Just as Castellio wrote in legitimate fear for his life due to the threats of Geneva, so too Busher had every reason to fear James and the English bishops—especially since he unrelentingly described the bishops as tools of the devil for killing innocent people in the name of God.

Objections Answered

In 1615, while Helwys languished in Newgate, yet another tract on religious freedom was anonymously published by Baptist dissenters with the lengthy but informative title *Objections Answered by way of Dialogue, wherein is proved by the Law of God; by the law of our Land: and by his Majesty's testimonies, That no man ought to be persecuted for his religion, so he testify his allegiance by the Oath, appointed by Law.* Whether it was written by Helwys or John Murton, his successor, is unknown. But it is certain to be the work of one or more in their Baptist congregation.

In the format of a dialogue between three persons named Christian, AntiChristian, and Indifferent, the major arguments that had been raised against religious liberty since the days of Augustine were systematically and decisively answered using powerful scriptural exegesis and, at times, humorous logic.

From the time of Elizabeth, the Church of England had ceased to claim that anyone had to believe official doctrine although all were still required to worship in the established church. Speaking to this arrangement, the character of Christian answers that John 4:24 (NIV) makes plain that "God is spirit, his worshipers must worship in spirit and in truth." But the Church of England did not require true worshippers—just compelled ones. Compelled worship by those who do not believe in the ceremonies could not possibly be worshipping God, the tract argued, because they did not view it as the truth, and hypocritical worship cannot possibly please God.[51]

Focusing on the bishops' claims of authority, Christian points to the work of the Holy Spirit and the present ministry of Christ to disprove the bishops' claim to be Christ's vice-regents in His absence. Christ "hath left no Vice-regent in that his Office, for he is never absent from his Church. Mat. 18.20 and 28.20."[52] In this same vein Christian also takes on the claim of apostolic succession from the apostle Peter, saying "Christ did not promise before his ascension to leave Peter with them, to direct and instruct them in all things; but he promised to send the Holy Ghost unto them for that end."[53]

Continuing with the claimed authority of Peter, Christian addresses the episode between Peter and Ananias and Sapphira. The deaths of these two early disciples were often cited by persecutors, including Thomas More and others, as authority for their execution of heretics. The character of Christian says:

> But for your Argument of Peter's extraordinary smiting of Ananias and Saphira, he neither laid hand upon them, nor threatened them by word, only declared what should befall them from God; and therefore serveth nothing to your purpose. Also that Paul to Elmyas, he laid no hands upon him, but only declared the Lord's hand upon him, and the judgment that should follow. If you can so pronounce, and it so come to pass upon any, do it, and then you may be accounted Master-builders and layers of a new foundation, or another Gospel.[54]

Christian then focuses his attention on the Catholic problem, concentrating on the understandable fear arising from papal edicts that released Catholics from obedience to kings who were out of favor with Rome and even commanded such Catholic subjects to kill their kings. Christian comments that "one of the chief cause of all their treasons hath been because of all the compulsions that have been used against their consciences."[55] But then he turns this argument against the English establishment with biting logic. Referring to the pope's advice that excommunicated kings be killed by their subjects, Christian states:

> For that damnable and accused Doctrine, as we abhor it with our souls, so we desire all others may: and therefore all the Laws that can be made for the prevention of such execrable practices are most necessary. But now I desire all men to see, that the Bishops and we justly cry out against this accused doctrine and practice in the Pope and his associates, That Princes should be murdered by their Subjects for contrary-mindedness in Religion, yet they teach the King to murder his Subjects for the self-same thing, viz, for being contrary-minded to them in their Religion.[56]

No one, the tract argued, should kill another for religious differences, whether they be pope, king, bishop, or commoner.

One final argument in the tract is worthy of special note. The character AntiChristian raises the familiar refrain, "Hath not the King the same power that the Kings of Israel had, who compelled men to the observation of the Law of God?"[57] To this Christian answers:

> Yes, Christ alone is King of Israel, that sits upon David's throne, and therefore mark the true proposition: In the time of the Old Testament the Kings of Israel had power from God to compel all to the Ordinances of God, or to cut them off by their Sword from the earthly Land of Canaan, and the Promises thereof: So in the New Testament the King of Israel, Christ Jesus, hath power from the Father to compel all to the Ordinances of God, or to cut them off by his Sword from the heavenly Land of Canaan, and the Promises thereof. The Kings of Israel only had this power under the Law, and the King of Israel only hath this power under the Gospel: And therefore whosoever will challenge this power under the Gospel, he must be the King of Israel in the time of the Gospel, which is peculiar only to Jesus Christ, unto whom all Power in Heaven and Earth is given.[58]

Helwys could not have been clearer.

Such arguments never convinced King James, nor the Anglican bishops, nor the Puritans of the era. But judging these arguments by the test of history, the Baptist dissenters had a far better understanding of what the Bible teaches about freedom, compulsion, and persecution. The power to change the world was not to be found in the pomp of the court of James, nor in the cathedrals of coercion, but in the chapels of liberty that faithfully argued for freedom for all from the pages of the Word of God.

Chapter Twelve

THE ENGLISH
REHOBOAM

Charles I

---

*But the external worship of God in his church is
the great witness to the world, that our heart states
right in that service of God. Take this away, or bring
it into contempt, and what light is there left to shine
before men, that they may see our devotion,
and glorify our Father which is in Heaven?*

WILLIAM LAUD, ARCHBISHOP OF CANTERBURY

I n the Old Testament, Rehoboam inherited the throne of Israel from his father, Solomon. The people came to Rehoboam and pleaded with him to "lighten the load" that Solomon had required of them. Rehoboam sought counsel from the friends of his youth who advised him to reply, "My little finger is thicker than my father's waist. My father laid on you a heavy yoke; I will make it even heavier. My father scourged you with whips; I will scourge you with scorpions."[1] The people of Israel were dismayed by this reply and proclaimed:

What share do we have in David,
what part in Jesse's son?

To your tents, O Israel!
Look after your own house, O David![2]

Rehoboam's ill-advised harshness divided the kingdom, causing a split between the lands of Israel and Judah that was never repaired.

Charles I could aptly be called England's Rehoboam. Inheriting his father's hatred of Puritans and falling under the spell of his father's "favourite," George Villiers, now styled the Duke of Buckingham, Charles adopted a policy of severity against Puritan dissenters so vicious that it plunged England into civil war and later cost him his life.

Charles I was twenty-four years old when, in 1625, he inherited the kingdoms of England, Scotland, and Ireland from his father. Of eight brothers and sisters, only Charles and his older sister, Elizabeth, were still living at the time of his accession.[3] James's firstborn son, Henry, who had accompanied his father to his famous confrontation with the Puritans at Hampton Court, had died from typhoid fever in 1612 at the age of eighteen. The other five siblings all died in infancy.

Charles's future troubles with Parliament over religious questions were foreshadowed by his father's efforts to secure a wife for him from among the European royalty. Since the vast majority of the continental monarchies were still associated with the Roman Catholic Church, the likelihood of finding a suitable Protestant princess was small indeed. In 1623, James dispatched both the twenty-three-year-old prince and the Duke of Buckingham (Villiers) to Spain to broker a marriage agreement with the Spanish Infanta, the seventeen-year-old princess, Maria Anna. Catholic Spain made toleration of English Catholics a prerequisite for giving the Infanta's hand.[4] At first James was all too ready to acquiesce to this demand, but his Parliament, the populace, and eventually even Charles himself showed such strong and heated opposition that the strategy collapsed. This failed negotiation contributed to the increasing public distrust and hatred of Villiers, who was already despised for his unscrupulous use of the largess of the throne to enrich and empower his friends. Yet a permanent friendship was forged between Charles and Villiers during the trip to Spain.

After the Spanish treaty collapsed, James turned to Catholic France and Princess Henrietta Maria, the sister of Louis XIII, as the next choice for a wife for his son. Like Spain, France demanded toleration of English Catholics as a condition for the marriage treaty. But this time Buckingham, Charles, and then James were successfully pressured to consent. The Venetian Ambassador in Paris recorded that the final agreement stated that English Catholics "shall be allowed to live in the profession of their faith, without molestation, and shall not be persecuted or compelled in any matter of conscience."[5] This, however, was in direct contradiction to a speech James had given to Parliament less than a month before in which he had assured its wary members that he was indeed concerned about the spread of popery and "would make no pledge of immunity to the Catholics in any marriage treaty."[6] Once arrived in England, Henrietta Maria, still a confirmed Catholic, openly celebrated the Mass to the great distress of many—particularly the Puritans within both the Church of England and Parliament.

Charles's personal troubles with Parliament began even before his coronation ceremony. James died in March 1625, but the formal celebration of Charles's ascension to the throne did not take place until February 2 of the following year. In the meantime Parliament met during the summer of 1625 in the midst of a deadly outbreak of the plague. The sickness was so pervasive in London that the second session of this Parliament had to be moved to the comparative safety of Oxford. The king's principal objective for this Parliament was to raise money for a war against Spain. Among other objectives, the intended war was apparently designed to help his sister, Elizabeth, and her husband, Frederick, regain the Palatinate along the Rhine, which had been lost to the Holy Roman Emperor.[7]

Parliament was dubious of these foreign policy objectives as well as the king's new Catholic bride. The marriage treaty with France, which promised too many concessions to Catholicism, did not sit well with Puritan elements. Accordingly, Parliament refused to allow Charles the traditional lifetime grant of authority to impose a customs levy on shipping, which constituted a principal source of the throne's revenue. Instead, Parliament allowed Charles to collect this "tonnage and poundage" tax for one year only.

Moreover, Parliament began to make moves to impeach Buckingham from office. Charles dissolved this first Parliament on August 12, 1625, to forestall any attack on his trusted counselor.

The atmosphere of mutual distrust between Charles and the Puritan-leaning Parliament made the king especially open to the ideas of Anglo-Catholicism, a rising faction within the Church of England.[8] This small but influential group of leaders within the Anglican Church, like the king, was focused on the objective of eradicating the influence of the Puritans. The essence of the Puritan complaint against the Church of England was that it retained too many symbols and reminders of Catholicism. The response of the anti-Puritan segment was to push the church even more strongly in the direction of Rome. They reasoned that if more Catholic symbols and practices could be reintroduced, the Puritans would be increasingly unable to conform to the mandated standards of church policy and would be forced for reasons of conscience to resign from positions of leadership. The Anglo-Catholics were not opposed to physical coercion to help secure the desired end. In this way the church could be "purified" from Puritan influence.

But the Anglo-Catholics went too far toward Rome—not only for the Puritan leaders but also for the comfort of the English populace. Memories of Bloody Mary's reign had been ingrained too deeply in the English psyche to permit even the appearance of reconciliation with Rome. Anti-Catholic paranoia ended up causing otherwise moderate Anglicans to run for cover to the Puritan camp.[9] Thus, a steely wedge was driven between the king and the Church on the one hand and the Parliament and the bulk of the populace on the other. Within two decades after James's death, England was embroiled in religious strife that would shortly lead to open war.

The First Voice of Anglo-Catholicism

In 1624, the year before Charles assumed the monarchy, a little known cleric named Richard Montague published a book titled *A Gagg for the new Gospell? No: A New Gagg for an Old Goose*. It was one of the first written exposés of Anglo-Catholicism.

Montague's book centered on Catholic missionary activity in England, which had become increasingly common due to the French marriage treaty and James's corresponding efforts to relax penal laws against Catholics. One of these "Romish Rangers," as the missionaries were called, had given Montague a pamphlet titled *A Gagg for the new Gospell*, which used a translation of the English Bible to prove that the Roman Church is the one true church—the Anglican Church and others notwithstanding.[10] Montague was unimpressed and sarcastically remarked that if he had not been a Protestant, the little book would have made him one by virtue of its poor quality.[11]

Central to the Catholic "Gagger of Protestantism's" argument was the claim that the Scriptures are difficult to understand, and therefore people need the church to act as an authoritative interpreter; vernacular translations tend only to breed heresy.[12] One Protestant respondent countered the gagger's arguments by using the "Rheims New Testament."[13] As the Rheims Bible's preface emphasized, and the Catholic Gagger hotly asserted, the institutional church was still supposed to function as the gateway to Scripture as well as to salvation; the ability to investigate spiritual truth by means of God's Word and Spirit was reserved for the "Lord Bishops," as Thomas Helwys called them. The Protestant *Rhemes against Rome* used the Rheims translation itself to reach the commonsense conclusion that even though some Bible passages are easy and others more challenging, heresy is caused primarily by ignorance of the Scriptures as opposed to the misuse of them.[14] Therefore, the laity should not be restricted in their access to the

Bible.[15] For his part Montague did not condemn the availability of Scripture to commoners in *A New Gagg*, but he did claim that the Anglican Church was like Rome because it could issue official interpretations of Scripture.

It may seem ironic that Montague, in writing against the Catholic gagger, would be suspected of secretly advocating the Roman faith, but this is precisely what happened. In claiming to leave all "private opinions" of his own and others aside in order to defend the Church of England proper, he opened himself to the vigorous criticism of those who believed that his true intent was quite the contrary.[16]

The country reacted fiercely. After Montague published another work named *Appello Caesarem* that seemed to hint even more strongly of Catholic tendencies, one Anthony Wotton decided to take Montague to task in his publication *A dangerous plot discovered*. In keeping with this sentiment, the House of Commons passed a resolution in 1629 which cited Montague's works as a "great danger" to "Church and State" and recommended that they be burned and the "authors or abettors" sufficiently punished.[17]

Montague abandoned all moderation in referring to the Puritans, whom he denounced as "Bastards," "Vagabonds," and "Urchins."[18] In his preface to *Appello Caesarem*, he wrote:

> My direct dealing herein . . . hath very much and highly discontented some *Private Divines*, who desire to have those opinions, which are controverted among ourselves, to be taken and defended for the common and public doctrine of the *Church*: but more especially hath it incensed those *Classical Puritans*, who were wont to pass all their Strange Determinations, Sabbatarian Paradoxes, and Apocalyptical Frenzies under the Name and Covert [sic] of *The True Professors of Protestant Doctrine*.[19]

As this quotation demonstrates, the crux of the matter was that both Puritans and Anglo-Catholics viewed their own party as the sole defender of the true church of England, making the tension between them fundamentally irresolvable.[20] Furthermore, in regard to religious liberty, "neither side was willing or, because of its ideology, able to embrace religious toleration as a solution for the difficulties."[21] They each claimed the exclusive right to implement an English Church according to their own interpretations of Scripture and to compel all others to conform. The only question was, Which side would hold the reins of political power?

The King, the Catholics, and the Commons

When Charles's first Parliament convened in 1625, the House of Commons made an investigation of Montague's works its top priority in discussing the Anglo-Catholic problem. After the Commons finally decided by vote that Montague should be imprisoned, the king rebuffed the decision by notifying Parliament that the "insufferable" Anglo-Catholic had been honored with the position of royal chaplain instead.[22] But members had little opportunity to react; Charles abruptly adjourned Parliament after deliberations had begun, heightening suspicions that the king was up to no good.

To suppress the bitter indignation that was starting to spread beyond Westminster's gates—particularly after the arrival of Henrietta Maria and her French Catholic entourage—the government outlawed divisive religious disputes by proclamation, and Charles also issued a plea to the bishops entreating them to assist the state "by preaching peace and unity at home" in light of foreign threats.[23] The "breach of Unity," he explained, "is grown too great and common among all sorts of men. The danger of this goes far: for in all States it hath made way for enemies to enter."[24]

Charles's appeal only created more acrimony in light of his actions. He and Buckingham were heavily involved in unpopular military campaigns against Spain and France and were struggling to pay for them, even through extralegal means. In an effort to wrangle money from Parliament, Charles reneged on his toleration promises to the French and promised to enforce Catholic recusancy laws. Even though the Commons was pleased by this anti-Catholic move, Charles continued to rankle the Puritans by aligning himself with Anglo-Catholicism and appointing its advocates to important church positions.

Charles's third Parliament, which assembled in March 1628, decided to make their own demands of the king and assert their rights and prerogatives as a legislative body. This assertion of authority was called the Petition of Right, which drew on ancient precedent to insist on the necessity of parliamentary consent in matters of taxation. It also articulated some basic rights of English "freemen," such as the right of due process.[25] Even though Charles correctly viewed the document as an assault on his power, he gave his consent to these measures in Parliament in order to receive sorely needed funds in return.

When Parliament reconvened the following year, its members launched a verbal attack on Anglo-Catholicism. A committee on religion prepared a resolution that made the bold claim that the Anglo-Catholics' "combined counsels, forces, attempts, and practices, together with a most diligent pursuit of their designs" were aimed at "the subversion of all the Protestant

Churches in Christendom."[26] The resolution likewise decried the "weak resistance" made against religious innovators and the increase of Catholic recusants.[27]

After a brief adjournment, a resolution was introduced in the whole House naming two kinds of people as "capital enem[ies] to this kingdom and commonwealth."[28] The first category included "whosoever shall bring in innovation of religion, or by favour or countenance seek to extend or introduce popery or Arminianism, or other opinion disagreeing from the true and orthodox church."[29] The second category included anyone who counseled the king to levy the tonnage and poundage taxes without Parliament's consent, contrary to the supposed agreement spelled out in the Petition of Right.

Charles was outraged and announced to the Speaker of the House that Parliament should be dissolved before the resolution could be passed. Not to be outdone, a handful of members forcibly held the speaker in his chair until voting on the resolution had concluded and the members had voted to adjourn themselves.

It would be eleven years, however, before the king would permit Parliament to convene again. Charles entered a period of personal rule that placed him squarely in the category of persons just denounced as "capital enemies" by the Commons. He not only continued to receive money through the despised tonnage and poundage taxes but also appointed one of the nation's foremost Anglo-Catholics, William Laud, to the archbishopric of Canterbury in 1633. With the Parliamentary buffer between the English Church and Anglo-Catholicism dissolved, Laud, Montague, and their allies launched their reformation efforts with a vengeance.

The Laudian Framework of Anglo-Catholic Reformation

Archbishop Laud was ruthless in his campaign to force his concept of the English Church on the nation and mitigate Puritan influence as much as possible. Even though Laud, like the Catholic Church, rejected the Augustinian teachings on predestination, he nevertheless saw coercion as a useful and necessary tool. Rather than emphasize uniformity of belief to the glory of God as the goal of suppressing heterodoxy, as Calvin did, Laud and the Anglo-Catholics chose to emphasize the unity of the church in matters of worship, ceremony, hierarchy, and external conformity.

As mentioned earlier, one of the foremost goals driving Anglo-Catholicism was the eradication of Puritanism. In prior decades, doctrinal Calvinism—at least in regard to theological questions like predestination—had been the glue that prevented an open rift from developing between the Puritans and the Anglican Church.[30] For example, over a thousand "Orthodox Ministers of the Gospel in the Church of England" subscribed to a 1629 letter condemning Montague's now notorious books. For support of their position, they enlisted the agreement of "the Church of Geneva" and even the Scottish Kirk.[31] But when the highest positions in the church began to be filled by those who rejected Calvinist views of election and salvation and tended toward Rome in matters of worship, any previous affinity between the Puritans and the institutional church quickly dissolved.

With this dissolution came increased opposition to Episcopal church structure, in which the power of ordination rested solely in the hands of the bishops.[32] Laud clearly believed that episcopacy—governing of the church by the hierarchy of bishops—was by divine right. In a 1637 speech, he went so far as to say, "From the Apostles' times, in all ages, in all places, the Church of CHRIST was governed by Bishops: And Lay-Elders never heard of, till Calvin's new-fangled device at Geneva."[33] Even though Parliament had long supported the Episcopal form of church government, Archbishop Laud's claim of divine right, together with the bishops' alliance with a king who thought nothing of usurping legislative power, drove Parliament into the waiting arms of the Puritans and their desire for a Presbyterian church structure, in which appointed or elected elders make decisions for the local church.[34]

In some respects Anglo-Catholicism might have had the makings of moderation. Laud showed an openness to Rome that could have led to toleration. Neither Laud nor Montague claimed that the Roman church was a *false* church and *for that reason* to be suppressed. Montague asserted, "I am absolutely persuaded, and shall be till I see cause to the contrary, that the Church of Rome is a true, though not a sound Church of Christ."[35] This view was antithetical to everything Puritan.

The archbishop's embrace of a more Arminian view on predestination might have suggested a more lenient view since Arminianism in Holland stood for toleration.[36] Dutch Arminians allowed the civil magistrate some degree of latitude in overseeing the affairs of the public church, but they disliked the rigid and comprehensive nature of Calvinism because it tolerated no dissent, even in areas that could be seen as nonessential.[37] The Arminians' influence in Holland, combined with the decentralized political situation there, allowed it to become a haven for persecuted religious minorities. When "Arminianism" arrived in England, however, it had a very different implication. The rejection of the Calvinist version of the doctrine of predestination entailed not so much a desire to narrow the scope of "orthodox" belief as a desire to create greater affinity between the English Church and Catholicism abroad.[38]

But none of these factors produced even the slightest hint of toleration in the actions of Laud. He was simply a brutal tyrant. The Star Chamber was a favorite weapon in Laud's arsenal. A secret court that had been used to intimidate dissenters in earlier times, the Star Chamber was employed more aggressively by Charles I and his advisors. (Frequently nobles considered too powerful to be prosecuted in ordinary courts were brought before this secret tribunal.)

It could be said that Archbishop Laud and his allies were not concerned with doctrinal purity at all when they engaged in the worst of their coercion. Although they indeed "distrusted the fundamental Protestant teachings of the right of private judgment and the necessity for every man to find religious truth for himself,"[39] this was largely because of the outward implications of inward nonconformity, not because it necessarily opened the door to heresy. Laud wrote:

> This I have observed farther: That no One thing hath made Conscientious men more wavering in their own minds, or more apt, and easy to be drawn aside from the sincerity of Religion professed in the Church of England, then the Want of Uniform and Decent Order in too many Churches of the Kingdom. . . . 'Tis true, the Inward Worship of the Heart, is the Great Service of God, and no Service acceptable without it: But the External worship of God in his Church is the Great Witness to the World, that Our heart states right in that Service of God. Take this away, or bring it into Contempt, and what Light is there left to shine before men, that they may see our Devotion, and glorify our Father which is in Heaven?[40]

For Archbishop Laud, *unity* expressed through the outward uniformity of the church was the goal, and discipline was the best tool to be used in pursuit of this aim. Laud disclaimed that his actions amounted to persecution, saying:

> God forbid that I should ever offer to persuade a Persecution in any kind, or practice it in the least. . . . But on the other side, God forbid too, That your Majesty should let both Laws and Discipline sleep for fear of the Name of Persecution. . . . If I can help on to Truth in the Church, and the Peace of the Church together, I shall be glad, be it in any measure. Nor shall I spare to speak Necessary Truth, out of too much Love of Peace. Nor thrust on Unnecessary Truth to the Breach of that Peace. . . . And if for Necessary Truth's sake only, any man will be offended, nay take,

nay snatch at that offence, which is not given, I know no sense of that. 'Tis Truth, and I must tell it. 'Tis the Gospel, and I must preach it.[41]

Like many others before him, Laud engaged in the fiction that when the belief of "true doctrine" was punished, it was persecution. The punishment of "false doctrine" was merely the execution of justice, he claimed. Yet to the Puritans and Separatists who suffered at Laud's bloody hands, his "discipline" was persecution indeed.

Pilloried Puritans and Cropped Ears

It is obvious from Laud's justifications why the Puritans were, in his mind, the worst offenders and why they bore the brunt of Laudian intolerance. The Puritans created division and cried foul whenever "popish" ritual crept into public worship—ritual which Laud understood as a sign of devotion to the church universal.[42]

Catholics did not suffer to the same degree. Penal laws against them were alternately relaxed and enforced throughout the reign of Charles I. Public outcry over a specific incident, such as when Queen Henrietta Maria made a public spectacle of her faith by praying at the site of a Jesuit martyr's death, was followed by a tightening of enforcement.[43] After a gradual increase in laxity, the cycle would begin again.

Puritan lecturers, on the other hand, were consistently forbidden from public preaching at certain times and on certain subjects.[44] The pillory and public whippings were mandated for those who published books without approval from proper authority.[45] The Court of High Commission demanded that those who held conventicles would be subject to its punishment. And when a stonemason named John Trendall used the Bible in his home to teach "sundry opinions repugnant to the doctrine of the Church of England," officials came close to burning him, as they had done to Legate and Wightman had been twenty-seven years before.[46]

One Sunday morning conventicle met at a brewer's clerk's house in London. Its members were discovered, imprisoned, and hauled before the High Commission, Laud, and the bishop of London in 1632. The preacher, Mr. Latropp, was interrogated: "How many women sat cross-legged on the bed whilst you sat on one side and preached and prayed most devoutly? . . . How [are you a minister] and by whom qualified?"

Latropp responded, "I am a minister of the gospel of Christ, and the Lord hath qualified me."

After he refused to take the oath, other members of the conventicle were brought forward and questioned as to why they were acting in contempt of the Church of England. One Samuel Eaton explained that they did what they did "in conscience to God" and that they merely "read the Scriptures and catechized [their] families." The bishop called Latropp and his company "dangerous men" with "heretical tenets," and the archbishop sent the whole party to prison.[47]

Laud also attacked those who dared to differ with him in printed articles. Alexander Leighton, whose *Sions Plea against the Prelacy* denounced episcopacy as "unlawful and Antichristian," was cruelly tortured in accordance with a Star Chamber decree.[48]

For writing a supposedly libelous book about how "popular stage-plays . . . are sinful, heathenish, lewd, ungodly spectacles," William Prynne was "sentenced to pay a fine of £5000, to be perpetually imprisoned, to be deprived of his degree . . . to stand in the pillory at Westminster and Cheapside, to have an ear cut off at each place, and to wear a paper declaring his offense."[49] The only mitigation was a "cropping" of the ears instead of entire removal.[50]

Prynne still wrote from prison, however, and in June 1637, he and two fellow Puritans, John Bastwick and Henry Burton, lost whatever ear remained for publishing anti-episcopal sentiments. Prynne also received the branding "S. L." on both cheeks, which stood for "seditious libeler," though he preferred to think of it as "stigmata Laudis."[51] In spite of popular outcry over the treatment of these men, Laud gave a Star Chamber speech for the occasion that accused the three men of being "the greatest innovators that the Christian world hath almost ever known."[52] Innovation, of course, being improper and heretical.

Breach of Peace

Laud's Puritan-leaning enemies in Parliament asserted their own claims of authority over the power of the church, sometimes accompanied by fanatical recommendations. A 1629 resolution drafted by a committee on religion recommended, among other things:

> (1) Due execution of laws against Papists. (2) Exemplary punishments to be inflicted upon teachers, publishers, and maintainers of popish opinions, and practicing of superstitious ceremonies, and some stricter laws in that case to be provided. (3) The orthodox doctrine of our Church, in these now controverted points by the Arminian sect, may [be] established and freely taught, according

as it hath been hitherto generally received, without any alteration or innovation; and severe punishment, by the same laws to be
provided against such as shall, either by word or writing, publish
anything contrary thereunto. (4) That the said books of Bishop
Montague and Cosin may be burned. (5) That such as have been
authors or abettors of those popish and Arminian innovations in
doctrine may be condignly punished. (6) That some good order
may be taken for licensing books hereafter.[53]

The Commons even went so far as to suggest that children of Catholics
should be seized and given a Protestant education instead, far away from the
influence of their parents. This measure failed in the House only because
common sense indicated that the king would reject it.[54]

Ironically, Laud's actions achieved the "Breach of Peace" he most hated.
His immoderate measures ended up turning the nation against him and
contributed to antipathy toward the king, who had given Laud his full support. Riots became commonplace. Parliament had been alienated. Droves of
Puritans were escaping to America. And as Laud hardened his position, his
opposition hardened theirs, resulting in extremism on both sides.[55] Moderate
Anglicans became Puritans; Puritans became radical Puritans or Separatists;
and eventually Parliament abandoned all restraint.

The Laudian ideal of coerced religious uniformity, implemented
through a national church structure with the support of the civil magistrate,
bore only bitter fruit.

Chapter Thirteen

"THE LORD HATH NOW SOME CONTROVERSY WITH ENGLAND"

The Westminster Assembly and English Civil War

---

*After all our pangs and dolor and expectations, this real
and thorough Reformation, is in danger of being strangled
in the birth by a lawless Toleration that strives to be
brought forth before it.*

AN OPEN LETTER FROM LONDON MINISTERS

*J*ames I once remarked, "No bishop, no king." His words were a proclamation of support for the Anglican Church's existing structure of rule by bishops serving under royal appointment. The phrase "no bishop, no king" could also be considered a hauntingly violent prophecy that was fulfilled during the reign of James's son, Charles. Both Archbishop Laud and Charles I would meet a violent death as the people of England, fed up with the abuses of power from church and state, rose up to overthrow both systems of government, episcopacy and monarchy.

The English Civil War cannot be separated from the religious strife of the day—strife that was chiefly a question of who would control the reins of government and thereby impose their preferred religious system on the people of England. All of the major factions embraced the Augustinian notion of a "Christian nation" where all people in the political state were required by force of law to belong to the "one true church."

The influential Westminster Confession of Faith would be drafted and promulgated to clarify correct doctrine and method of appropriate church government for the entire nation. But even this highly regarded statement could not hold the nation together. War was inevitable to determine which religious faction could impose their will on all.

Charles's Troubles with Scotland

Even though Charles had been born in Scotland, he had moved with his family to London when he was only two years old. Charles therefore had learned little of Scottish ways and, in due course, attempted to push the Scots much further than they were willing to go when he dared to meddle with their beloved national church, the Scottish Kirk.

James had done his best to push episcopacy in Scotland through his bishops, but his efforts to assert his royal right to manage the nation's religious matters never gained much ground. His physical absence from the country after 1603 gave Scotch Presbyterians the opportunity to strengthen their position among the people and through the nation's general assembly.

Charles was not officially crowned king of Scotland until 1633 during a visit to Edinburgh. Somewhat shocked by what he saw in the Scottish churches, he attempted to impose a prayer book in 1637 that reflected Laud's Anglican views, not Geneva's Presbyterian ideals. Charles's mandate was met with unbridled defiance. Everyone from commoners to nobility, ministers and laity, joined together in signing a National Covenant. The signers of the document pledged to defend the Presbyterian Scottish Kirk and Confession of Faith—as the embodiment of true Reformed religion—from all outside imposition of authority, especially in the form of bishops.

Charles ordered troops into Scotland in early 1639 to quell the rebellion. But the king's troops were no match for the well-trained and highly motivated "Covenanter" army of Scots, and he was obliged to sign a truce within a few months. The following year he mobilized troops once again but met with even greater disaster. Charles's inadequate forces and lack of funds forced him to reconvene the English Parliament for the first time in eleven years. Unsurprisingly, however, members were stubbornly intransigent to his demands for money to fight the Scots, so he promptly dissolved the body again within three weeks.

By mid-October of 1640, the Treaty of Ripon ended the battle to impose episcopacy in Scotland. With insufficient funds to pay the indemnities demanded by the victorious Scots, Charles was again desperate for help. Just as the winter chill had begun to settle quietly over London in late 1640, he summoned the infamous "Long Parliament" that would prove to be his undoing.

Rooting Out Episcopacy

Charles's pleas for money were bound to fall on cropped ears. Expecting Anglo-Puritans in Parliament to fund an Anglo-Catholic war against Scotch Presbyterian Puritans was an ill-considered policy maneuver.

The Puritan-dominated Parliament and the Scots were united in their opposition to episcopacy in the tradition of Archbishop Laud, which would become apparent as soon as Parliament reconvened in London. More than fifteen hundred men arrived at Westminster to present a petition containing fifteen thousand signatures and addressed to the House of Commons. The preamble of the petition made clear the signers' intention:

> And whereas the said government [of archbishops and lord bishops, deans, and archdeacons, &c.] is found by woeful experi-ence to be a main cause and occasion of many foul evils, pressures and grievance of a very high nature unto his majesty's subjects in their own consciences, liberties and estates . . . we therefore most humbly pray . . . that the said government with all its dependen-cies, roots and branches, may be abolished, and all laws in their behalf made void, and the government according to God's word may be rightly placed among us.[1]

The Puritan petitioners expressed frustration over the "pride and ambi-tion of the prelates," the suppression of Calvinist doctrine, and the "great conformity and likeness both continued and increased of our Church to the Church of Rome."[2] Fed up with the excesses of Laud and encouraged by the spirit of their Scottish brethren, the petitioners identified Laudianism with episcopacy and concluded that since the former had to go, the latter had to, too—roots, branches, and all. Within months nineteen counties besides London had joined the petitioning efforts.[3]

Parliament responded quickly. On December 18, 1640, by order of the House of Commons, Laud was impeached for high treason, chiefly for his role in provoking the disastrous war with Scotland. Laud was arrested and placed in the Tower of London in early 1641 where he would remain for over three years. Even though his prosecution in 1644 was headed by William Prynne, who had been a victim of Laud's persecution, the evidence was insufficient to sustain a verdict on the charge of treason. Undeterred, the Parliament passed a bill of attainder sentencing Laud to death for his misdeeds even though they could not make the case for conviction of an ordinary criminal charge. Laud was beheaded on Tower Hill, January 10, 1645.

Soon after Laud was thrown in prison, Parliament made clear that it was not content with removing this one errant bishop. The members were set on finding a path for institutional reform. Formal debate over episcopacy began in the Commons in February 1641. Animosity toward church "government by bishops" grew more animated and intense as summer approached, both within Parliament and without.

The various parties joined in opposition were far from agreed on what should be established in its place, however, and shifting alliances were frequent as developments with king and country unfolded. From the days of Thomas Cranmer, the Anglican Church had been Calvinist on the issues of election and predestination. Consequently, the Anglican Church was like Geneva in this important doctrinal matter while different from their Swiss counterpart on the matter of church government. Laud, however, had led the Church of England away from Calvinist views of salvation. Thus, the Calvinists remaining in the Church of England looked to their Scottish Presbyterian allies. English Puritans quickly shifted their stance to purport that Presbyterianism—congregational selection of church leaders and governance by synods and assemblies—was the best solution to all the threats they faced. They wanted to stop abuses by royally appointed bishops in the tradition of Laud as well as the prospect of "religious anarchy" in the form of sectarianism.[4] Scotland served as positive proof that this balanced approach would work for an entire nation.

The threat of sectarianism grew in magnitude as the harsh discipline of previous decades began to crumble with Parliament's abolition of the Star Chamber and the Court of the High Commission.[5] These courts had served as the enforcement mechanism whereby the government and church could control licensing and printing. With these obstacles to a free press removed, scores of pamphlets began to flood the country, many of which argued for religious liberty. But members of Parliament were not pleased by the public's newfound liberty of printing and preaching. The House of Lords heard grim forebodings of chaos when Bishop Hall informed them that sectaries[6] were being "instructed by guides fit for them, cobblers, tailors, felt-makers, and such like trash, which all were taught to spit in the face of their mother, the Church of England, and to defy and revile her government."[7]

Presbyterianism and its system of rigorous discipline offered the most obvious solution to the sectarian problem, but moderates in the Commons were unwilling to move quickly to abolish the tradition of royally appointed bishops. They wanted nothing of Laud, but their defense of the historic church structure became untenable in light of his abuses.[8] The moment for compromise with the Puritan forces passed, never to return.

An Impasse Turns into Armed Conflict

By late fall of 1641, an impasse was reached among members of Parliament concerning the kind of religious settlement that would best meet the needs of the nation. So, under the leadership of John Pym, the Commons passed the *Grand Remonstrance* by a vote of 159–148 as a resentful reiteration of grievances against Anglo-Catholicism.[9] It also served as a declaration of Parliament's intention to rectify the abuses that had occurred under Laud.

There was no call for toleration or religious liberty. The Commons affirmed that they had no desire to "let loose the golden reins of discipline and government in the Church, to leave private persons or particular congregations to take up what form of divine service they please."[10] Rather, they insisted that "there should be throughout the whole realm a conformity to that order which the laws enjoin according to the word of God"—in other words, a national church with no more toleration for dissent than previously.[11] The *Remonstrance* further recommended that Protestant divines from both home and abroad should be assembled into a general synod to advise Parliament on the particulars of the "intended reformation."[12]

The *Remonstrance*—along with Charles's foolhardy attempt to breach Parliamentary privilege and arrest five members of the Commons—was effective in pushing the tide of already excited public opinion toward the adoption of a bill in February 1642 that excluded all bishops from the House of Lords. Charles was in a precarious position, so he gave his *pro forma* assent to the exclusion bill and a host of other demands. One bill he simply could not countenance, however, was one that authorized Parliament to raise and train its own troops supposedly "for the safety and defence of the kingdom of Wales."[13] Firing back a reply in the form of a royal proclamation on May 27, 1642, Charles ordered the country not to comply in order "to prevent that some malignant persons in this our kingdom do not by degrees seduce our good subjects from their due obedience to us and the laws of this our kingdom."[14]

The Lords and Commons counterattacked by turning the militia bill into an ordinance, which held official legal status even though it lacked the king's assent. On the same day as the king's proclamation, they issued a joint declaration in which they claimed that the royal office was distinct from the king's person, and since the latter had been "seduced by evil counsel," the "high court of parliament" was obliged to "provide for the necessities, prevent the imminent dangers, and preserve the public peace and safety of the kingdom, and to declare the king's pleasure in those things"—even if contrary to the king's actual will and pleasure.[15] By this time, it was obvious who held the position of strength, for Charles had already fled from London with his family and decided shortly thereafter to send Henrietta Maria to the continent to enlist support for his cause.

On June 1, Parliament further capitalized on the king's weakness and presented him with the Nineteen Propositions, which essentially demanded that he turn over the reins of government entirely to Parliament. By the terms of the propositions, Parliament would have the final say over all members of the Privy Council and other members of state, the marriages of Charles's children, the reformation of the Church of England, pardons, and the military, among other things.[16] One section demanded that "the laws in force against Jesuits, priests, and popish recusants be strictly put in execution, without any toleration or dispensation to the contrary."[17]

These radical demands placed Charles in the welcome position of being able to appear a beacon of moderation and stability among those alarmed by the recent upheavals and Parliament's extreme temper.[18] While the king began to garner support and recruit "royalist" troops with the help of loans from some wealthy earls, Parliament was busy mobilizing its own army.[19] Armed conflict was finally at hand.

Neither side could find a quick path to victory. The Parliamentary army controlled London from the outset which gave it a decided advantage, although the lack of central command and control hampered the army's effectiveness. Several attempts by the royal army to capture London were rebuffed by the Parliamentary forces. The war would continue to grind on indecisively for several years with the fighting confined to a season of relatively good weather each year.

The Assembly of Divines

There had been many proposals in the months before the fighting began to convene a grand assembly of clerical leaders to debate and decide correct doctrine and church governance as a means to find a "settlement" of the growing religious strife. Before such an official assembly could be gathered, however, war had erupted. The influence of the Scottish Kirk would come to play a crucial role in the nature of the assembly and the confession of faith that was ultimately written. But there were far more pressing reasons than doctrinal affinity for seeking the participation of the Scots.

The Scottish Kirk's General Assembly first heard rumors of Parliament's intent finally to convene the oft-proposed assembly of divines as a means of handling England's religious matters and curbing civil war shortly after the fighting commenced.[20] Since both Charles and Parliament stood to gain or lose significantly from Scotland's military support, the Scots decided to go ahead and set forth their prerequisites for assistance. The trade-off for both English parties was clear: either face political and military defeat, or make a deal with the Scots at the price of making the English Church Presbyterian.

"The Lord hath now some Controversy with *England*," the Scottish General Assembly declared, "which will not be removed, till first and before all the Worship of His Name and the Government of His House be settled according to His own Will."[21] They proceeded to assert in no uncertain terms that Presbyterian polity was "perpetual" and by divine right, and therefore England would know no peace until it followed Scotland's example of establishing "Government of the Reformed Kirks by Assemblies."[22] The General Assembly had to wait nearly a year before Parliamentary commissioners arrived in Scotland to negotiate the terms of the alliance with some Scotch counterparts, who then sent a draft to the General Assembly and the Scottish Estates for approval.

Meanwhile, Parliament had passed a legally binding ordinance that brought the Assembly of Divines into existence at last—without, of course, the assent of the king.[23] Its members had been selected and had taken their seats in the summer of 1643 under the magnificent fan-vaulted ceiling of Henry VII's chapel at Westminster Abbey, next door to where Parliament met, and debate on the Thirty-Nine Articles was in progress.

The title of the agreement that was forged between Parliament and the Scots was the Solemn League and Covenant. It was a "league" insofar as it reflected Parliament's need for political and military assistance. It was a "covenant" insofar as it reflected the spirited Scottish demands for "true" reformation of the English church and subsequent unification with their Kirk. Whether Parliament knew exactly how much it was potentially surrendering is open for speculation, but the Scots certainly had a clear idea of where they were headed.

The document contained the predictable pledge to "endeavor the extirpation of popery, prelacy . . . superstition, heresy, schism, profaneness, and whatsoever shall be found to be contrary to sound doctrine and the power of godliness" and the somewhat disingenuous promise to "preserve and defend the king's majesty's person and authority."[24] It was the first article, however, that left the most room for maneuver on all fronts. Those taking the oath (which by February 1644 included all Englishmen over the age of eighteen) agreed to:

sincerely, really, and constantly, through the grace of God, endeavor in our several places and callings, the preservation of the reformed religion in the Church of Scotland, in doctrine, worship, discipline, and government, against our common enemies; the reformation of religion in the kingdoms of England and Ireland, in doctrine, worship, and government, *according to the word of God and the example of the best reformed Churches*; and we shall endeavor to bring the Churches of God in the three kingdoms to the *nearest conjunction and uniformity in religion, confession of faith, form of Church government, directory for worship and catechizing*, that we, and our posterity after us, may, as brethren, live in faith and love, and the Lord may delight to dwell in the midst of us.[25]

The shrewd Sir Henry Vane of England had succeeded in making sure that "according to the word of God" was inserted so as to make Presbyterian polity less inevitable, but beyond this loophole the proposed reformation was heavily in favor of the Scotch interpretation.[26]

Furthermore, the four Scotch divines who joined the Westminster Assembly as commissioners in September 1643, amidst pomp and circumstance appropriate to the occasion, found themselves in good company among the 121 divines already gathered.[27] If the future of episcopacy had been questionable up to this point, its doom in the Assembly was quickly sealed after the Scots arrived. The Puritan-dominated body of divines had still been trying to find its feet in the vast morass of ideas about church government and discipline, so with a little encouragement from the influential Scots at a moment of golden opportunity, Presbyterianism quickly achieved dominance among Assembly members.[28]

Once Parliament, moderates and all, had taken the oath to subscribe to the Covenant, the "Presbyterians had been led to believe that England was now prepared to embrace the tenets and discipline of Geneva."[29] The idea foremost in everyone's mind was to establish a new orthodoxy that would prevent a recurrence of the abuses suffered under Laud (who was at this time a resident of the Tower London). Since the system of bishops seemed to have been the chief cause of corruption and coercion, it was concluded that changing the church's form of ecclesiology would be the best solution.

Despite this agreement, there remained two tightly knit dissenting groups within the Assembly of Divines that offered persistent, and at times vociferous, opposition to the implementation of national Presbyterianism. Those in the first group were called Independents.[30] Their differences with the rest of the Assembly came to the forefront in discussions on church discipline—whether a synod or local congregation should hold the power of enforcement. Whereas the Presbyterians saw themselves as occupying a middle-of-the-road position between "popish and prelatical tyranny" and "Brownistical and popular anarchy," the Independents saw themselves as defending the middle position between the Presbyterians and the sectaries.[31]

The influence of the Erastians, who composed the second small group, would have been negligible had it not been for the fact that Parliament was almost entirely Erastian. Although Erastianism is susceptible to diverse explanations (many of which are at odds with the views of its sixteenth-century namesake, Erastus), its fundamental tenet during the civil war era was that no single form of church government could claim to be by divine right, but each "depend[ed] on the will of the magistrates."[32] Parliament held to the belief that "the Church derived all its authority and jurisdiction from the State; and it [i.e., Parliament] identified the State with itself."[33] In fact, the Westminster Assembly itself rested on an Erastian foundation, for Parliament had been the one to call the Assembly into existence, and it would be the one to approve or reject the Assembly's work once completed. If an official, established Presbyterian Church existed in England at all, it would hold its position by virtue of Parliamentary right, not because it was God's *de facto* divine will.

The Independent Controversy

By the time the Assembly had completed its revision of the Thirty-Nine Articles and moved on to consider the government and discipline of a reformed English Church, it had moved from the chapel to the medieval-era "Jerusalem Chamber" in another section of Westminster Abbey. The Jerusalem Chamber is the room where translators, working at the behest of James I some three decades earlier, had completed their English version of the Scriptures. Now, as formerly, biblical scholars wrangled about words and the interpretations of passages both in committee and as a whole.

The debates were relatively private and temperate until the group of Independents led by Thomas Goodwin, Philip Nye, William Bridge, Jeremiah Burroughs, and Sidrach Simpson caused a major explosion with the publication of their *Apologeticall Narration* in early 1644. All five ministers had been exiled in Holland during the Laudian persecution and had only recently returned to England.[34] They explained that they felt no animosity toward other churches at home or abroad, even though they belonged officially to none but simply desired to glean truth from the experiences of all and be directed by "that sacred pillar of fire" of the "first Apostolic directions" contained in the New Testament.[35]

From the five ministers' study of the early church, they concluded that discipline should be exercised within each congregation by its own elders and not, as the majority of divines in the Assembly believed, by the authority of the combined elders of many congregations.[36] Every congregation, the Independents said, should possess through its elders full power over itself, until such time as they should "be challenged to err grossly."[37]

The Independents did not claim any divine-right status for their interpretation of church government. Instead, they resolved neither "to make [their] present judgment and practice a binding law unto [themselves] for the future" nor commit the error of their Presbyterian brethren in alleging that their system alone possessed the stamp of God's approval.[38] In perhaps the harshest criticism contained in the *Apologeticall Narration*, Goodwin and his allies wrote:

> We do professedly judge the Calvinian Reformed Churches
> of the first reformation from out of Popery, to stand in need of a
> further reformation themselves; And it may without prejudice to
> them, or the imputation of Schism in us from them, be thought,
> that they coming new out of Popery (as well as England) and the
> founders of that reformation not having Apostolic infallibility,
> might not be fully perfect the first day.[39]

Apart from this critique, the "dissenting brethren," as they were soon to be labeled, maintained a defensive tone similar to a plea for mercy. The conclusion of the *Apologeticall Narration* expressed some trepidation at the "opposition and reproach of good men" who intimidated the Independents "even to the threatening of another banishment."[40] It also pleaded for the quiet pursuit of subsistence as a human "birth-right," the "enjoyment of the ordinances of Christ" as their Christian "portion," and the "allowance of a latitude to some lesser differences with peaceableness."[41]

It does not require a huge logical leap to reach the conclusion that it was the intolerance—perceived or actual—of the other divines in the Westminster Assembly that caused the Independents to feel the need to take their arguments outside the walls of the Jerusalem Chamber. Their "narration" was not addressed specifically to other divines but to Parliament and, hence, the nation at large. The effect was explosive. Not only did it touch off a heated exchange of published works between the Independents and the advocates of "Presbyteriall Government," but it also stoked the flames of agitation for religious liberty.

William Prynne, the hearty Puritan whose ears had been chopped off under Laud's regime, ironically became an advocate for a national church (though not necessarily a Presbyterian one). He also called for the severe punishment of heresy by the sword of the civil magistrate.[42] His 1644 *Twelve Serious Questions touching Church Government* offered no concrete solutions to the controversy developing in the Assembly, but it does reveal the degree to which the church government debates had begun to turn into a controversy over toleration of dissent. Among the central issues needing resolution were, in his estimation:

> Whether, if any Kingdom or Nation shall by a National Council, Synod, and Parliament, upon serious debate, Elect such a public Church Government, Rites, discipline as they conceive to be most Consonant to God's Word . . . and settle them by a general law; all particular Churches Members of that Kingdom & Nation, be not thereby *actually obliged in point of Conscience & Christianity, readily to submit thereto,* and no ways to seek an exemption from it, under pain of being guilty of Arrogance, Schism, Contumacy, and liable to such penalties as are due to these offenses?
>
> Whether that independent [church] Government which some contend for if positively and fully agreed on . . . be not of its own nature a very Seminary of Schisms, and dangerous divisions in Church, State? A flood-Gate to let in an inundation of all manner of Heresies, Errors, Sects, Religions, destructive opinions, Libertinism and lawlessness among us, without any sufficient means of preventing or suppressing them when introduced? Whether the final result of it (as Master [Roger] *Williams* in his late dangers *Licentious book* [i.e., *A Bloudy Tenent*] determines) will not really resolve itself into this detestable conclusion, *That every man . . . ought to be left to his own free liberty of conscience, without any coercion or restraint, to embrace and publicly profess what Religion, Opinion, Church-Government he pleaseth, & conceiveth to be truest though never so erroneous, false, seditious, detestable in itself?*[43]

At first the Independents made a point of distancing themselves from the various nonconformist groups burgeoning all over England. They claimed they abhorred the "proud and insolent title of Independency" given by critics because it had the inaccurate connotation of raising "a trumpet of defiance against what ever Power, Spiritual or Civil."[44] Equally odious in their eyes was the charge of "Brownism," which had become a catch-all term to describe the beliefs and practices of non-Presbyterian, non-Episcopal Christians.[45] Nevertheless, Assembly members accused the Independents of advocating principles that implicitly suggested religious toleration, and some sectaries, making the same observation, began to consider the Independent divines as allies in the quest to defeat yet another potentially oppressive national church.

In the meantime there were important developments on the field of war in the year 1644. While the Scottish army crossed the border from the north, Oliver Cromwell led a Parliamentary cavalry unit to a surprising victory over a highly effective royal cavalry unit. However, Cromwell was frustrated with the inability to follow up for a more decisive victory because of the independent decisions of other generals.

That winter Cromwell returned to Westminster and demanded that Parliament make a clean sweep of the military high command and establish a national army with central command and control. Cromwell was initially placed as second in command of the "New Model Army." Sir Thomas Fairfax was commander in chief.

In June 1645, the New Model Army destroyed the main forces under the command of the king at a battle at Naseby. The following year, Charles was unable to raise sufficient forces; and Oxford, Charles's *de facto* capital, was forced to surrender in June 1646. Charles had personally surrendered to the Scottish army in May of that year in hopes of cutting yet another deal with the Scots, who had become impatient with the progress of the Westminster Assembly. But in January 1647, the Scots handed the king over to the New Model Army. He was promptly imprisoned to await trial.

"God-Provoking, Truth-Defacing, Church-Ruinating, & State-Shaking Toleration"

The Westminster Assembly was still in full debate when the New Model Army began to emerge victorious in 1645. Their work continued through the last year of battle and was not yet complete when royalist Oxford surrendered.

Just as the Scottish army played a crucial role in the final days of the war, so too the Scottish commissioners were especially influential in the final months of the work of the Westminster Assembly of Divines. One of the main points of Scottish frustration with the progress of the Assembly and the English Parliament was the growing number of voices calling for some form of religious toleration.

In the heat of the argument over religious toleration, a group of London ministers closely associated with the Scottish delegates published an open letter to their "Reverend, Learned, and Religious Brethren the Prolocutor and the rest of the Divines assembled."[46] In this letter "against toleration," the authors hotly criticized the dissenting Independents. The desire for toleration was dismissed as being "extremely unreasonable and preposterous" for multiple reasons, "partly because no such toleration hath hitherto been established (so far as [they knew]), in any Christian State by the civil Magistrate."[47]

The Londoners classified Independency as a schism. As such, they said, toleration of it would be harmful to the church because, among other things:

> 8. The whole work of Reformation especially in discipline and Government will be retarded, disturbed, and in danger of being made utterly frustrate and void, whilst every person shall have liberty upon every trivial discontent at Presbyterial Government and Churches to revolt from us and lift themselves in separated Congregations.
> 9. All other Sects and Heresies in the Kingdom will be encouraged to endeavor the like toleration . . .
> 10. All other Sects and Heresies in the Kingdom will safe-guard and shelter themselves under the wings of *Independency*, and some of the *Independents* in their books have openly avowed, that they plead for liberty of conscience as well for others as themselves.[48]

Schism would be harmful to the commonwealth, as well, they argued, because "it is much to be doubted, lest the power of the Magistrate [to dictate religious matters], should not only be weakened, but even utterly overthrown" if toleration were granted.[49]

After providing a list of reasons toleration of Independency would also be contrary to the Solemn League and Covenant, the London ministers made a final plea to the Assembly to disregard the Independents' and sectaries' requests:

> These are some of the many considerations which make deep impression upon our Spirits against that great *Diana* of *Independents*, and all the Sectaries so much cried up by them in these distracted times, *viz., A Toleration, A Toleration. . . .* Our bowels, our bowels are stirred within us, and we could even drown ourselves in tears, when we call to mind how sharp a travail this Kingdom hath been in for many years together to bring forth that blessed fruit of a pure and perfect Reformation, and now at last after all our pangs and dolor and expectations, this real and thorough Reformation, is in danger of being strangled in the birth by a lawless Toleration that strives to be brought forth before it.[50]

Having come so close to achieving reformation of the English Church in accordance with the "best Reformed churches," these men were not about to let dissenters or advocates of tolerance get in the way of ecclesiastical purity. Two of the most influential Scots in the Assembly, George Gillespie and Samuel Rutherford, stepped to the front to lend their considerable support to the arguments raised in opposition to religious toleration.

Gillespie preached a sermon before the House of Lords in August 1645 at the Abbey Church at Westminster. His text was a verse from Malachi: "But who may abide the day of his coming? For he is like a refiner's fire, and like fuller's soap." After discussing its meaning, Gillespie proceeded to expound on its application. The second application to Parliament dealt with liberty of conscience:

> In the second place, think of the extirpation of Heresy, and of unsound dangerous Doctrine, such as now springeth up apace, and subverteth the faith of many. There is no Heretick nor false Teacher, which hath not some one fair pretext or another: But bring him once to be tried by this refining fire, he is found to be *like a potsherd covered with silver dross. What is the chaff to the wheat*, saith the Lord? And what is the dross to the silver? If this be the way of Christ which my Text speaketh of, then (sure) that which now passeth under the name of *Liberty of Conscience*, is not the way of Christ. . . . If *Liberty of conscience* ought to be granted in matters of Religion, it ought also to be granted in matters Civil or Military. But *Liberty of conscience* ought not to be granted in matters Civil or Military, as is acknowledged; Therefore neither ought it to be granted in matters of Religion.[51]

Gillespie extrapolated on this topic in his work *Wholesome Severity reconciled with Christian Liberty. Or, The true Resolution of a present Controversy concerning Liberty of Conscience*, in which he discussed "pernicious, God-provoking, Truth-defacing, Church-ruinating, & State-shaking toleration."[52] He was responding to some of the recent publications advocating religious liberty, such as Roger Williams's *Bloudy Tenent*. Gillespie did not skirt the issue, but carried on in the tradition of Calvin—whose *Refutation of the Errors of Servetus* and "Whether Christian Judges May Lawfully Punish Heretics" he referenced for support.[53]

"I have endeavored in this following discourse," Gillespie wrote in the preface, "to vindicate the lawful, yea necessary use of the coercive power of the Christian Magistrate in suppressing and punishing heretics and sectaries, according as the degree of their offence and of the Church's danger shall require."[54] He acknowledged that the "less discerning" sort might be persuaded to embrace liberty of conscience, but "those of the godly who have their senses exercised to discern good and evil" are not so gullible when under "fair colors and handsome pretexts [the] sectaries infuse their poison."[55] Quoting extensively from Augustine against the Donatists, Calvin against Servetus, Beza against Castellio, and "the Reformed Churches in their public Confessions of Faith," Gillespie made the case that the magistrate must guard "both Tables" of the Ten Commandments by force and that the judicial laws of Moses are still applicable.[56]

Numerous tolerationists had cited the fifth chapter of Acts for support for their position, when Gamaliel exhorts to the council who wanted to stone Peter and the apostles to "refrain from these men & let them alone: for if this counsel or this work be of men, it will come to naught. But if it be of God ye cannot overthrow it, lest haply ye be found even to fight against God."[57] Gillespie attacked their use of this passage, arguing that Calvin "takes Gamaliel to be a godless Politician, and a Neutralist, and his speech to have a great error in it," just as Beza "thinks Gamaliel spake not from love to the Apostles, but from fear of the Romans."[58]

Samuel Rutherford expressed his opinion of religious toleration in a tome entitled *A free disputation against pretended Liberty of Conscience*. While acknowledging that "religion and faith cannot be forced," Rutherford said that it does not follow that "the magistrate can use no coercive power in punishing heretics and false teachers."[59] The sword may lawfully be used "to punish acts of false worship in those that are under the Christian Magistrate and profess Christian Religion, in so far as these acts come out to the eyes of men and are destructive to the souls of these in a Christian society."[60]

These statements reveal why Independents and other sectaries had good reason to fear Presbyterianism's ascendancy. The concept of a national church possessing something akin to "Apostolic infallibility," in the words of the dissenting brethren, with the magistrate equipped with civil sword to root out suspicious doctrine and maintain unity, was a chilling proposition to some and indubitable orthodoxy to others. The battle over religious liberty thus played a crucial role in the English civil war.

Unsuccessful Accommodation

Before long the dissenting brethren's fierce refusal to be identified with either religious toleration or the sectaries had turned into an alliance with these very groups.[61] The Independents in the Commons, led by Sir Henry Vane, and the Independents in the army, led by Oliver Cromwell, had already committed themselves to religious toleration—at least for those within a widely defined scope of orthodoxy.[62] Vane was finding ways to increase the number of sympathetic allies in Parliament, while Cromwell naturally drew sectaries into the army by virtue of his tolerationist stance.[63] Cromwell's approach to leadership was "to Cry up Liberty of Conscience, and be very tender of Men differing in Judgment, by which he drew all the Separatists and Anabaptists to him."[64] As the Puritan Richard Baxter observed, "In all this Work, the Vanists in the House, and Cromwell in the Army, joined together, out-witted and over-reached the rest, and carried on the Interest of the Sectaries."[65] The Independents and Erastians, along with all the others interested in defeating a too-rigid national religious policy, joined forces and cooperatively strategized while it suited their purposes.[66] Furthermore, the clout of the Parliament's New Model Army increased significantly as they were closing in on victory in the battles with the royalists, and this placed a significant obstacle in the way of the Assembly's program for reform.

One typical pamphlet arguing for religious liberty is an anonymous work with the lengthy title *Strong motives, or Loving and modest advice, unto the petitioners for presbiterian government. That they endeavour not the compulsion of any in matters of religion, more then they wish others should endeavour to compell them. But with all love, lenitie, meekenesse, patience, & long-suffering to doe unto others, as they desire others should doe unto them.*[67] This pamphlet illustrates how Cromwell was viewed by those who feared the effect of a national church dictated by the Assembly majority. Affixed onto the end of the plea is part of a letter Cromwell had drawn up on behalf of the Army to the House of Commons. Urging peace and Christian charity, he wrote:

> Presbyterians, Independents, all had here the same Spirit of Faith and prayer, the same presence and answer, they agree here, know no names of difference; pity it is, it should be otherwise any where: All that believe, have the real Unity which is most glorious, because inward and spiritual in the body and to the head. As for being united in forms (commonly called uniformity) every Christian will for Peace's sake, study and do as far as Conscience will permit; And from brethren, in things of the mind, we look for no compulsion, but that of Light and reason.[68]

Cromwell concluded that in other moral matters, however, "God hath put the sword into Parliament's hands, for the terror of Evil doers, and the praise of them that do well."[69]

The pamphlet's author gave the example of the "great and victorious" army to prove that the toleration of differing opinions about church government led not to chaos and disorder but rather to peace and a true spirit of harmony when united with Christian love. Fear of religious and civil chaos had, indeed, for centuries been one great fear motivating good people to advocate uniformity of religion and the brutal punishment of dissent. But now this connection was questioned and, in the author's case, robustly disclaimed. "There is nothing more certain" if a liberty is provided to the people, he asserted, "than that the State shall receive thence its greatest safety, Provided it make good and pertinent Laws against all Treason, Treachery, Vice, and corruption of manners, and withal, appoint good Officers for execution of those Laws."[70] Then "people could not choose but love such a Government, and all errors would be convinced, by reason and demonstration in due time, which is the only just and proper way, for it is a sad thing that any man should suffer imprisonment, or other violent dealing, or punishment, for error in judgment."[71]

In another pamphlet the dissenting brethren within the Assembly accused the majority of the Divines of basing their refusal to find a compromise with the Independents on the supposition that "nothing ought to be tolerated which is unlawful in the judgment of those who are to tolerate," thus claiming some form of oppressive infallibility.[72] Why should honest, godly men be prohibited from enjoying the worship of God in a church that does not trouble their consciences, the Independents asked. "Hath either nature, or the Gospel put such a necessity upon uniformity, in lesser things?"[73]

Apparently, the majority of the divines at the Westminster Assembly concluded that nature or the gospel hath indeed required such coercion. And to a certain degree Parliament agreed with them. "Accommodation" they might have countenanced, but toleration was another story.[74] Even though Vane was succeeding in filling seats in Parliament with sectarian sympathizers, he still lacked a majority. Moreover, Charles's hopes of winning the civil war militarily had been eclipsed by reality, and he was suspected of conducting negotiations with the Scots. Since Scottish support was vital to Parliament, it would need to concede as much as it could to the duplicitous northerners.[75] Presbyterianism was thus established—though far from implemented—as England's official form of church government on March 5, 1646, by a vote of the House of Commons.[76]

The Assembly's "Humble Advice"

The Assembly of Divines completed its first draft of the Westminster Confession of Faith in the fall of 1646. Parliament ordered that copies be printed for members of both Houses and the Assembly to use and critique. This was printed for the Company of Stationers as *The humble Advice of the Assembly of Divines, Now by Authority of Parliament sitting at Westminster.* The next spring, the Assembly completed the scriptural proofs for the confession, as Parliament had requested. The General Assembly of the Scottish Kirk approved this version, as it reflected the views of the Scottish commissioners and Assembly Presbyterians, but the English Parliament was not satisfied.

Before Parliament voted to approve the confession, it made several changes to the Assembly's work. Articles XXX and XXXI were removed or modified because these provisions asserted the idea of the independence of the church from Parliamentary control in strong terms. Parliament, of course, was not too pleased with the affront to its authority contained in these sections, which were implicit statements of church autonomy. In this area the Presbyterians were advocates of religious liberty for the institutional church, while denying liberty for dissenting individuals.

The *Articles* approved by Parliament were also different from the Assembly's *Humble advice* in that the fourth section of Chapter XX, "Of Christian Liberty and Liberty of Conscience," was removed. The Assembly had written:

> And because the Powers which God hath ordained, and the liberty which Christ hath purchased, are not intended by God, to destroy, but mutually to uphold and preserve one another; they, who upon pretense of Christian Liberty, shall oppose any lawful Power, or the lawful exercise of it, whether it be Civil or Ecclesiastical, resist the Ordinance of God. And, for their publishing of such Opinions, or maintaining of such Practices, as are contrary to the light of Nature, or to the known Principles of Christianity, whether concerning Faith, Worship, or Conversation; or, to the Power of Godliness; or, such erroneous Opinions or Practices, as either in their own nature, or in the manner of publishing or maintaining them, are destructive to the external Peace and Order which Christ hath established in the Church, they may lawfully be called to account, and proceeded against by the Censures of the Church, and by the Power of the Civil Magistrate.[77]

No one should mistake this last paragraph of the article as a call for religious liberty. In fact, it plainly declares that it is appropriate to use the power of civil government to punish those who "resist the Ordinance of God" by publishing or speaking in a manner that disagrees with the Westminster Confession. Modern authors who have proclaimed this article to be the first "confessional statement" on liberty of conscience made by a Reformation council apparently failed to understand the historical context as well as the plain meaning of the text.[78] As to civil liberty, there was only one choice offered—agree with this confession or face government sanction.

The Triumph of Independency?

Parliament was nevertheless still hesitant to admit the degree of liberty demanded by the majority of the New Model Army, the multiplying sects, and the growing "Leveller" movement.[79] A bill was introduced in the Commons that established Presbyterianism while nonconformists were granted "liberty to meet for the service and worship of God, and for exercise of religious duties and ordinances in any fit and convenient places," but this effort at compromise was defeated by the Presbyterians.[80] Instead, an ordinance passed aimed at prescribing penalties for heresy and blasphemy. The ordinance required the imprisonment of any person guilty of "Preaching, Teaching, Printing, or Writing" one of the listed unorthodox opinions.[81] If an individual repeated the offence, he might suffer death. For opinions of a less grievous nature, an individual might be imprisoned. This category of erroneous beliefs targeted those who disseminated the views that "man hath by nature free will to turn to God," "the Moral Law of God contained in the ten Commandments is no rule of Christian life," "the baptizing of Infants is unlawful, or such Baptism is void, and that such persons ought to be baptized again," "the Church Government by Presbytery is Antichristian or unlawful," or that the "Magistracy or the power of the Civil Magistrate by law established in England is unlawful."[82] Catholics, Baptists, and various others were thus legally prohibited from spreading their opinions, but they had increased in the nation to such an extent that the ordinance could not be enforced.[83]

Also, by this time the Parliamentary army considered itself invested with the defense of the liberties of England's citizens, whether that meant opposing the Parliament, royalty, or both.[84] Eschewing the traditional approach of assigning military rank according to social standing, the New Model Army was open to new ideas and its members had become allied with sects of various theological stripes who deemed religious coercion and uniformity pointless or damaging to religion since salvation was personal and in no need of assistance from civil power.[85] Pro-toleration groups included the so-called Levellers, who campaigned for the expansion of voting privileges and argued that religious liberty was among the "natural rights and liberties such as men have from birth."[86] These men aimed at redefining freedom by dissociating it from property and educational degrees.[87] From whence did all these demands for religious liberty and greater democracy arise? As Christopher Hill observes, Bibles in the hands of commoners instead of only the elite had a revolutionary effect, for "popular interpretations of the New Testament could overrule the conventionally accepted status and subordination of a hierarchical society."[88]

Impatient and upset with Parliament's response to demands, Cromwell's forces stationed themselves in London one morning in early December 1648 and by force prevented some 121 nonsympathizing members of the House of Commons from taking their seats. "Pride's Purge," as it came to be named, left the Independents in control under the rubric of the "Rump Parliament." By the end of the following month, the Rump had tried and executed Charles outside the Banqueting Hall of Whitehall Palace.

Debate over religious toleration quickly commenced among the members of the Rump. Even among these Independents, there was disagreement over how much latitude to allow. Leveller leader John Lilburne published *Plea for common-right and freedom*, which communicated annoyance with the heavy-handedness of the Commons, which was in the process of carefully outlining the limits of religious divergence and the role of the civil magistrate in demanding orthodoxy and uniformity. "For what freedom is there to Conscientious people," he asked, "where the Magistrate shall be entrusted with a Restrictive power in matters of Religion?"[89]

Lilburne was imprisoned in March during a crackdown on Levellers. In the minds of some, the Levellers were too radical, and their ideas were dangerous to the peace of the already fragile nation. From "causeless captivity" in the London Tower, Lilburne and his associates published their latest version of the *Agreement of the People*, which had been the subject of intense debate in the nation for several years and which Lilburne believed was being butchered by the Rump. This prison edition of the *Agreement* read:

> That we do not empower or entrust our said representatives to continue in force or to make any Laws, Oaths, or Covenants, whereby to compel by penalties or otherwise any person to any thing in or about matters of faith, Religion or God's worship or to restrain any person from the profession of his faith, or exercise of Religion according to his Conscience, nothing having caused more distractions, and heart burnings in all ages, than persecution and molestation for matters of Conscience in and about Religion.[90]

The road to religious freedom remained rocky. Even after nearly a decade of upheaval that was the direct result of intolerance and coercion, fear of religious anarchy and the doctrinal rejection of religious liberty remained ingrained in the most influential Christian minds.

Chapter Fourteen

CALLED HITHER TO SAVE A NATION

The Stirrings of Religious Liberty under Oliver Cromwell

Every sect saith, "Oh! Give me liberty." But give him it,
and to his power he will not yield it to anybody else.

OLIVER CROMWELL

The year 1649 was the climax of England's civil war upheaval. Within the five months spanning January to May, the Rump Parliament demonstrated that it was more than willing to test the limits of its power. It immediately set about executing the king, establishing a Council of State, abolishing the monarchy and the House of Lords, and declaring the nation to be a commonwealth in which supreme authority was vested in the representatives of the people assembled in Parliament.

Although there were overtones of popular sovereignty, the government was anything but representative. The Parliament that entered London in 1650 had been whittled down dramatically: bishops and royalists had been expelled during the war, Presbyterians had been excluded in Pride's Purge, and the House of Lords had been eliminated. As a result, Parliament was less than 20 percent of its original size.[1] This shrunken Rump Parliament claimed its authority "not on popular consent but on the support of the army and on the superstitious reverence which Englishmen paid even to the shadow of a Parliament."[2] There was no legal check on Parliament's power; legislative, executive, judicial, and even military functions were all ultimately subject to parliamentary orders. Furthermore, the Council of State, itself a mere arm of the Rump, had begun vigorously to control the press and erect courts to deal with opponents.

While some in the nation cheered as new leaders took full advantage of their freedom from royal restraint, others viewed the developments with distaste and horror. John Lilburne and his Leveller associates, already famous for their advocacy of the *Agreement of the People*, took initiative in confronting the new government for overextending itself at the expense of the liberty so dearly purchased by the war. Their sentiments were published in February under the title *Englands New-Chaines Discovered*. The work expressed grave disappointment over, among other things, suppression of printing in the manner of "bishops of old" and the censure of a member of Parliament for stating his allegedly unorthodox judgment concerning religion.[3] They thought the sacrifices of the war were for the reclamation of the people's native birthright of freedom, yet they were again being betrayed by what they perceived as the arbitrary exercise of power—which was hardly better than the late king's capricious rule.

When the second part of *Englands New-Chaines* was published in March, Parliament denounced the work for fear it would provoke mayhem and sedition in the army. Parliament could not afford to face rebellion in their armed forces at that moment because there were external enemies with which they had to deal. The biggest threat was a royalist coalition forming in Ireland. Both Catholics and Protestants loyal to the crown were rapidly joining forces there with the intent of putting Prince Charles on the throne. Furthermore, Scotland had already declared the prince to be King Charles II—not only of Scotland but of England and Ireland as well.

Cromwell had been serving as the chairman of the Council of State during the first month of its existence. In light of the recent developments, however, the Council determined that his talents would be better used by putting him in command of the forces designated to suppress the Irish rebellion, so he was nominated to oversee this campaign on March 15. Not being one to take his responsibility lightly, Cromwell made sure that everything was sufficiently provided for before accepting the titles of lord-lieutenant and commander in chief.[4]

Ireland was already an internally divided country, and this worked against the Irish efforts to repel Cromwell's invasion. Cromwell was confident in his own divine commissioning to exercise discipline on ungodliness, much in the manner of Old Testament kings in relation to heathen nations, and Ireland was no exception.[5] After landing in Dublin in August, he quickly conquered and killed thousands at the two Irish strongholds of Drogheda and Wexford. His justification for these "massacres," as they might be called, was simple, religiously motivated, and certain. "I am persuaded," he said, "that this is a righteous judgment of God upon those barbarous wretches" who must "answer the cruelties which they had exercised upon the lives of divers poor Protestants."[6]

By early spring of 1650, the majority of Ireland had been subdued and lay in a devastated state. Parliament was confident that Cromwell's lieutenants could complete the task he had begun, so he was recalled and returned to London in May because war with Scotland was then looming ominously. The Scots were a much more formidable foe, and, unlike the Catholic Irish, the Scots were considered Protestant brethren. Months earlier they had attempted to craft a deal with Charles in exchange for their help in returning him to the throne. They, in turn, wanted his promise to impose Presbyterianism on both England and Ireland. Cromwell deemed the Scots a serious threat because of their military strength and obvious desire for religious dominance.

Parliament responded to these developments by declaring Cromwell commander in chief of all the commonwealth forces in June 1650. He proceeded to wage war with Scotland with the sword and with the pen. With the pen he charged Scotland with falling into Rome's mistake of forcing the specifics of their doctrine on others and prohibiting dissent. He warned, "It will be found an unjust and unwise jealousy to deprive a man of his natural liberty upon a supposition he may abuse it."[7] With the sword Cromwell had achieved the bulk of his military objectives in Scotland by the end of 1651, armed with more than ten thousand foot soldiers and fifty-five hundred horses.[8] Charles II had scampered off to France by hiding, disguising himself in various garbs, and eventually getting aboard a ship bound for the continent.

While Cromwell was gone subduing the royalists in Ireland and Scotland, the English Parliament was busy debating the internal state of the country. Like the commander in chief, the Independent-dominated Parliament was friendly to religious toleration, but members still saw it as their unquestionable duty to prevent the country from degenerating into total doctrinal and moral anarchy. Since there was no established national church at the time, something had to be done to keep the most extreme of religious nonconformists from gaining the upper hand.

A group called the Ranters, for example, was almost universally despised. They were accused of dancing naked, practicing communism, believing in repentance after death and the existence of two gods, refusing to submit to government, disavowing the Scriptures, and holding that Christ's flesh turned into the physical sun at his Ascension.[9] Not surprisingly, people accused Ranters of adhering to "horrid profaneness and blasphemy" and described them as "unclean beasts."[10]

Other groups were more threatening because of their ideology and willingness to use violence to accomplish their conception of the ideal state. The "Fifth Monarchy Men," for example, imagined the downfall of the monarchy and the victories of Cromwell's "army of saints" to be indicative of Christ's imminent thousand-year reign.[11] They based their idea on prophecies in the book of Daniel and prepared for a new phase in history in which righteousness would rule and injustice and oppression would cease.[12] Although they initially hailed Cromwell as a hero, they later saw him as "an apostate and usurper, who had taken the crown from the head of Christ to place it on his own, and whose government was a part of that Fourth Monarchy which it was their duty to destroy" by the sword.[13]

Two acts—one to deal with the delusional and dangerous like the Ranters and Fifth Monarchists, and another to provide legal toleration for honest Christian dissenters—were passed in August and September 1650, shortly after Cromwell had crossed into Scotland. Both acts reflected Cromwell and the Independents' thought of the era.

The first carried the telling title, *An act against several atheistical, blasphemous and execrable opinions, derogatory to the honor of God, and destructive to human society.* Although it was not as extreme as the 1648 blasphemy act, it still proposed to suppress those who were morally questionable or "most monstrous in their opinions."[14] The second act was titled *An Act for Relief of Religious and Peaceable People from the Rigor of former Acts of Parliament in Matters of Religion.* For the first time in recent English history, nonconformists were legally allowed to worship in their own manner in peace since all laws were repealed that mandated penalties for not attending the established church and for not using the Book of Common Prayer. The act only extended to "pious and peaceably minded people," not the "profane and licentious persons" encompassed under the blasphemy act.[15] Citizens were still required on Sundays and holy days to "diligently resort to some public place where the Service and Worship of God is exercised" or be "present at some other place in the practice of some Religious Duty, either of Prayer, Preaching, Reading, or Expounding the Scriptures"—only this time they were given latitude to choose *which* public place they found most conducive to true worship.[16]

Both of these acts were only temporary patches to the problem of nonconformity until the House could make progress on a permanent religious settlement. They did not get around to accomplishing this until early 1652, after Cromwell had already returned from his campaign in Scotland and was becoming actively involved in many affairs of the commonwealth government, even though he often disagreed with the Rump's policies. In February, Parliament followed the advice of a group of prominent Independents led by John Owen and appointed a Committee for the Propagation of the Gospel to provide a solution to the problem that had so long vexed the nation. Owen took the lead in framing the specifics of the proposal, but Cromwell was the committee's most prominent member.[17]

The committee's proposals recommended the establishment of two commissions composed of both laity and clergy to deal with ordination, ejection, and other clerical matters.[18] They also advised that a law should be provided wherein everyone would be required to observe the Sabbath in a public assembly, with an exception for those who preferred to abstain for reasons of conscience. Any dissenters wanting to meet regularly would be able to, provided they give notice to a magistrate.

Anyone who wanted to *teach* or *preach* anything regarding religion, however, was placed under more rigorous guidelines according to the guidelines of the proposals. The Independents as a group were still firmly in favor of requiring the citizenry to adhere to the fundamentals of salvation, even if these were broadly defined, and they did not want to allow anyone to promulgate obviously unbiblical opinions.[19] Rather than defining a "Christian" based on external adherence to the doctrinal tests of an institutional church, Owen and his colleagues gathered passages of Scripture and drew up a list of truths they believed essential to *personal salvation*. Instead of including things like church government and the precise nature of the doctrines of election and predestination as found in the Westminster Confession, the committee of Independents emphasized belief, repentance, rebirth, and Christ's exclusive mediatory role between God and man.[20]

Nevertheless, Cromwell disagreed with the proposition of making Owen's list of sixteen principles binding on anyone who wanted to do more than hold his opinions privately.[21] Cromwell insisted that an established church was a national necessity, although he rejected the notion that an established church should have the prerogative to persecute nonadherents, save those dangerous to the civil state or those who were persecutors in their own right. Therefore, he saw no contradiction between his advocacy of private liberty of conscience and ecclesiastical policies in Ireland and Scotland after his victories, which sent Irish Catholic priests to prison or exile and abolished the General Assembly of the Scottish Kirk.[22]

These debates between Cromwell and those of Owen's stripe over the religious settlement came to a standstill when foreign distractions interfered, and Cromwell had to focus on negotiations with the Dutch because of conflict that was brewing over the competing trade interests of the two countries. He did not want war and made efforts in the summer of 1652 to effect an agreement.[23] This having failed, the commonwealth had to abandon domestic reform efforts and devote the remainder of the year to shoring up the navy, paying the army, and watching fearfully as other countries threatened to become involved on the side of the Dutch.[24] To pay for the war, the Rump resorted to the arbitrary practice of confiscating the property of hundreds of innocent people without compensation, much to Cromwell's dismay.[25]

By August, Cromwell and officers of the army gave vent to their anger in a petition to Parliament, with whom they were frustrated for their tardiness in effecting the long-awaited domestic reforms.[26] This petition was given the customary courtesies, then sent to a committee to languish until it faded from consideration. Cromwell and his officers accused members of Parliament of acting less out of concern for the public good and more on behalf of their own interests.[27] This selfishness was epitomized in their eyes in the bill proposed for a "New Representative," which proposed to allow the existing members of the Rump to keep their seats while arranging for the election of new members whose eligibility would be determined solely by the Rump itself. For the army officers and their eminent Lord General, this desire of a nonrepresentative Parliament to perpetuate itself as the Supreme Authority was too much.

Attempts at compromise over the contested bill ended in failure. On April 20, 1653, when word reached Cromwell that the bill was on the verge of being passed, he rushed to the chamber in which it was being debated—dressed only in "plain black clothes with grey worsted stockings"—and sat down to listen to the debate.[28] After fifteen minutes, the speaker announced that the bill would be put to a vote. Cromwell whispered, "This is the time, I must do it," and rose to address the House. Gesturing toward the members and confronting them for drunkenness, corruption, and self-interest, he declared, "Perhaps you think that this is not Parliamentary language; I confess it is not; neither are you to expect any such from me. . . . I say you are no parliament. Get ye gone! Give way to honester men."[29]

Cromwell then called for the couple dozen musketeers who had been waiting in the lobby. The speaker and the man sitting next to him at first refused to leave, but Cromwell's men laid their hands on the members' hands and shoulders and led them out of the chamber.[30] After the mace was taken away—Cromwell referred to it as a "bauble"—the rest of the members left quietly.[31] Cromwell called after them, "It is you that have forced me to this, for I have sought the Lord night and day, that He would rather slay me than put me upon the doing of this work."[32]

No shots had been fired, but it was without question that Cromwell had acted no more constitutionally than the members of the Rump had been acting since Cromwell left them in power after Pride's Purge less than four years before. As one member of the Council of State warned Cromwell, "You are mistaken to think that the Parliament is dissolved; for no power under heaven can dissolve them but themselves: therefore, take you notice of that."[33]

England had made clear in the civil war that it would not tolerate monarchs on the English throne who leaned toward divine-right absolutism like their counterparts on the continent, and now Parliament's divine-right attitude had been placed under the scrutiny of Cromwell's dutiful eye. Yet, by attacking the *abuse* of parliamentary power through the use of force, he simultaneously undermined the constitutional foundation on which Parliament's *rightful* power had been based. In the words of a historian writing at the dawn of the twentieth century, the Rump

> had all the faults with which Cromwell charged it; but for
> Englishmen it meant inherited rights, "freedom broadening
> slowly down," and all that survived of the supremacy of law.
> With its expulsion, the army flung away the one shred of legal-
> ity with which it had hitherto covered its actions. . . . Henceforth,
> Cromwell's life was a vain attempt to clothe that force in constitu-
> tional forms, and make it seem something else, and so that it might
> become something else.[34]

For this reason, regardless of the sincerity of Cromwell's motives, his efforts were doomed from the beginning, along with his wishes for liberty of conscience. His policies ultimately seemed to hinge on force of arms rather than persuasion based on principle, and the contradictory nature of the ends and the means proved disappointing.

"A Single Person and a Parliament"

A means of replacing the Rump Parliament had not yet been determined when Cromwell strode from his residence at Whitehall to confront the members prepared to pass the "new representative" bill. A small Council of Officers was designated to serve as an interim governing body, which decided after a short period of debate that the nation's congregational churches should recommend individuals from which the council would select 140 to form a new representative assembly. General elections were impractical and dangerous, but funds for the war with the Dutch were desperately needed, and the assembly had to have some form of representative legitimacy that did not rest on military force.[35]

The "Nominated Assembly" convened for the first time in July. Cromwell was not a member; but since he had held a seat at Westminster since 1628, he was clearly making the point that he was now distinct from Parliament.[36] He used Scripture to charge the members, of whom a slight majority consisted of "moderates" and the rest more radical sectarians,[37] with the task of handling affairs justly and equitably, bearing with those who differed and following the call of God to do His work.[38]

It quickly became apparent that the Nominated Assembly was made up of members of a far different character from the well-bred, polished politicians of earlier parliaments. While some may exaggerate the religious zeal, inexperience, and idealism of the assembly—Theodore Roosevelt would say that it was "no more competent to initiate successful self-government in England than a Congress of Abolitionists in 1860 would have been competent to govern the United States"[39]—it was certainly true that many of the new members had not yet learned the skill of legislative compromise. Yet they held the firm conviction that they were going to usher in a new era of freedom and righteousness, the expectation of which had not been "paralleled with any times but those a while before the birth of our Lord and Savior Jesus Christ."[40]

The Parliament focused on both legal and church reforms.[41] They established civil marriage, provided a legal framework for registration of births and burials, and passed an act to secure protection for the mentally ill. They addressed the needs of prisoners and poor debtors. All these things were to their credit. But when it came to the subject of religion, deep divisions began to surface.

The sectarian members tried to abolish the universities as well as the mandatory tithes that went to support the country's ministers, but these schemes were defeated by the Nominated Assembly's more conservative members.[42] The conservatives proposed dividing the nation into districts to be overseen by commissioners who could eject ministers and "maintain a general supervision over the preaching of the Word," but this was defeated by the Sectarians on the basis that it would open the door for renewed religious tyranny.[43] Neither Cromwell nor the nation at large was ready to embrace the kind of drastic proposals the sectarian members wanted, especially in light of a recent spike in radical Fifth Monarchist activity. In December 1653, fearing the possibility of legislative radicalism, the moderate members in Parliament stood up in the middle of debate and marched from Westminster to Whitehall where they resigned in protest and turned their powers over to Cromwell.[44] The Nominated Parliament and its religious proposals had proved a disaster.

The officers of the army urged Cromwell to take control of the situation. Cromwell was reluctant to assume a dictatorial role as he had at the dissolution of the Rump, but the officers prevailed in the end. Months earlier they had written a constitution for a new government, which Cromwell had rejected because it gave him the title of King and would have abolished the Nominated Assembly before its tenure was complete. Since the Parliament's existence was no longer a factor, however, and since the title of King had been changed to Protector, Cromwell again dutifully accepted the charge placed on his shoulders. "I call'd not my self to this place," he said, "of that God is Witness"—and to part from the charge would be to "be false to the Trust that God hath plac'd upon me, and to the Interest of the People of these Nations, if I should."[45]

The *Instrument of Government* was the title of the revised document drafted by the officers to serve as a written constitution for the new "protectorate" government. The document is noteworthy in that England has traditionally operated, even into the twenty-first century, not under a written constitution which outlines a perpetually binding system of government complete with specified powers and limitations, but rather under common law. Common law is based on custom and expressed through the judicial process, which makes it liable to change over time. The *Instrument of Government* was thus a deliberate attempt (some say the first in England) to break with the common law tradition in favor of a single, codified governing document. The American colony in Connecticut had, by this time, adopted a written constitution known as the *Fundamental Orders* that, in 1639, began the process of establishing American law on the foundation of the written word that would one day culminate in the adoption of the United States Constitution.

On December 16, 1653, Cromwell dressed himself in civilian clothing and at one o'clock in the afternoon made his way from Whitehall to Westminster, as he had done so many times before. This time, however, he was accompanied by a great entourage. An oath was read affirming his commitment:

> That he should govern the three Nations of England,
> Scotland, and Ireland, according to the Fundamental Laws
> thereof; That he should maintain the true Orthodox Ministry of
> the Church of England; and that He should extirpate and abolish
> all Popery, Schisms, and Heresy; and maintain and preserve the
> peoples' Rights, Privileges, and Liberty, &c.[46]

After taking the oath, Cromwell gave a speech stating his conviction that his establishment as Protector was indeed "the will of God" as indicated by the desire of the council, to the end that "the Gospel might flourish in its full splendor and purity; and the people enjoy their just Rights and Propriety."[47] The witnesses then proceeded amid "great acclamations of joy" to the Banqueting House to celebrate.[48]

It is obvious from Cromwell's oath that he had a conception of religious liberty different from that of the sectaries who had been so quick to rally around his leadership during the early days of the civil war. An established religion was in his eyes perfectly compatible with liberty of conscience. The *Instrument of Government*, for example, declared Christianity to be the public profession of faith, but it also guaranteed that no one would be coerced into orthodoxy by penalties or otherwise, papists and prelates (i.e., episcopacy) excepted. Those in error were to be won through the teaching of "sound doctrine and the example of a good conversation," and anyone who professed faith in God by Jesus Christ was to be protected in the free exercise of their religion as long as they took care to "abuse not this liberty to the civil injury of others and to the actual disturbance of the public peace."[49] To assist in maintaining an adequate supply of publicly supported preachers, Cromwell issued an ordinance in March establishing a commission to examine and approve ministers qualified to lecture or maintain benefices.[50]

Cromwell described his philosophy of religious liberty in a speech to his first Protectorate Parliament, which convened after elections in the "Painted Chamber" at Westminster on September 4, 1654. Although he had ruled with a relatively free hand since his establishment as Protector in December, the *Instrument of Government* held that "supreme legislative authority" was to reside in "one person and the people assembled in Parliament," and he wanted to make his expectations clear to the assembly with whom he was supposed to work.[51] The distribution of powers between the Protector and Parliament was supposed to "avoid the extremes of Monarchy on the one hand, and Democracy on the other."[52]

Yet within the first week of the Parliament's existence, it attempted to lay claim to sovereignty, and Cromwell felt compelled to confront the members for stepping outside the bounds of some "fundamentals" that he claimed must not be altered. One was that "the Government [be] by a single Person and a Parliament"—not Parliament alone and supreme. Another was that "Parliaments should not make themselves Perpetual." A third asserted liberty of conscience as a fundamental principle. Cromwell asked:

> So long as there is Liberty of Conscience for the Supreme Magistrate, to exercise his Conscience in erecting what Form of Church Government he is satisfied he should set up; why should he not give it to others? Liberty of Conscience is a Natural

Right. . . . Indeed that hath been one of the Vanities of our
Contests. *Every Sect saith, Oh! Give me Liberty. But give him it, and
to his power he will not yield it to any body else.* . . . This, I say, is a
Fundamental. It ought to be so: it is for us, and the Generations to
come. And if there be an absoluteness in the Imposer, without fitting allowances, and exceptions from the Rule, we shall have our
People driven . . . into a vast howling wilderness in *New England,*
where they have for Liberty stripped themselves of all their comfort, and the full enjoyment they had, embracing rather lots of
friends, and want, than to be so ensnared, and in Bondage.[53]

He concluded with a reminder of why he, and they, had been placed
in power: "You have been called hither together to save a Nation" from
all tyrannical impositions whether "upon men as men, or Christians as
Christians."[54]

Cromwell was quickly disappointed. The Parliament seemed intent on
undermining all that Cromwell had asserted as "the fundamentals," especially liberty of conscience. The Independent members had become more
conservative while the Presbyterian members had become more willing to
modify their former ecclesiastical demands; so these two parties were able
to form a majority inclined to trim religious toleration wherever possible.
A committee, for example, drew up articles of faith along with a list of heresies that would have placed a whole array of religious beliefs outside the
bounds of protection, including those held by Quakers.[55] Parliament at first
insisted that the Protector would have no veto power over the definition of
heresy, but a compromise was reached whereby such questions were to be
decided jointly.[56] Still, however, Parliament showed its true colors when it
promptly demanded that a Unitarian named John Biddle be sent to prison
and his books burned.[57]

By January 1655, Parliament had begun to assert its intention to possess
sole control over the army. Cromwell's patience was reaching its limit. The
Instrument permitted Parliament to be dissolved after being in session for
five months, so on Monday, the 22nd, he marched into the Painted Chamber
and rebuked the members for losing "golden opportunities" for effecting
a peaceful civil and religious settlement for the nation.[58] Instead, they had
sought to put shackles on others who, though "different in Judgment on some
lesser matters," nevertheless were true Christians who saw salvation to be
"only by faith in the blood of Christ."[59]

"Is there not yet upon the Spirits of men a strange *itch*?" he asked.
"Nothing will satisfy them, unless they can put their finger upon their

Brethrens' Consciences, to pinch them there."[60] Thus, "bound in *Duty* to God and the People," Cromwell dissolved the first Protectorate Parliament.[61]

In terms of religious liberty, the second Protectorate Parliament, elected in the summer of 1656, was not much friendlier. Cromwell was managing to maintain a relatively moderate stance toward those who did not disturb the civil peace and had no interest in using force against the Anglicans, Catholics, or even Jews, who had been banned from England for centuries.[62] Yet insurrections, threats from both royalists and Levellers, and radical religious expressions had produced a yearning among many in the nation for stability through strict discipline. "I heard the supreme magistrate say it was never intended to indulge such things," one of Cromwell's major-generals moaned, "yet we see the issue of this liberty of conscience. If this be liberty, God deliver me from such liberty. It is to evil, not to good, that this liberty extends."[63]

One example of religious radicalism and efforts to curb it is found in the blasphemy case of a man by the name of James Nayler, which Parliament addressed in December 1656. Nayler began his exodus from religious orthodoxy as a disciple of George Fox, the founder of the Quakers, but later became Fox's rival.[64] The extent of his delusion became apparent on one occasion when, having recently been released from prison, Nayler rode triumphantly into Bristol on a horse while people threw garments in the road ahead of him and shouted, "Holy, Holy, Holy, Lord God of Israel!"[65] His followers also called him such blasphemous names as "the everlasting Son of Righteousness," "the only begotten Son of God," and "the prophet of the Most High."[66]

Some members of Parliament wanted to punish Nayler with death by burning and tried capitalizing on the opportunity to pass some legislation against heresy and religious error. More moderate members acknowledged his error but urged caution and restraint, and the motion to burn him failed by a vote of 96 to 82.

Instead of settling on the penalty of death, Parliament opted for the more "humane" punishment of whipping, branding, public humiliation, torture by hot iron, and imprisonment. On December 17, it was resolved:

> That James Naylor be set on the Pillory . . . [and] whipped
> by the Hangman through the streets from Westminster to the
> old Exchange in the old Exchange London, and there likewise be
> set on the Pillory . . . in each place wearing a paper containing an
> inscription of his crimes; and that at the old Exchange his tongue
> be bored through with a hot iron, and that he be there also stigma-
> tized in the forehead with the letter B, and that he be afterwards

sent to Bristol, and be conveyed into and through the said City on
Horseback bare ridged, with his face backward, and there also publicly whipped the next Market-day after he comes thither & that
from thence he be committed to prison in Breedwell London, &
there be restrained from all society of all people, and there to labor
hard till he shall be released by Parliament, and during that time
be debarred the use of pen, ink, and paper, and shall have no relief,
but what he earns by his daily labor.[67]

Cromwell requested mitigation of Nayler's punishment and demanded
an explanation for the sadistic nature of the punishment, but Parliament
proceeded with its plan, and Nayler met his judgment.

In fact, Cromwell had begun to show increasing reluctance to fight
Parliament's attempts to keep religious radicalism in check. The year after
the Nayler case, Parliament drafted the *Humble Petition and Advice*, to which
Cromwell had little choice but to consent. The *Humble Petition and Advice*,
like the *Instrument of Government*, was a written constitution. It provided
that no one could sit in parliament who was guilty of the 1650 blasphemy
act, "no common scoffer nor reviler of Religion," no person with a Catholic
wife, no morally weak individual, and no one who denied a number of religious tenets.[68] The eleventh article also required that a Confession of Faith
be drafted and approved by Cromwell and Parliament which no one would
be permitted to "by opprobrious words or writing, maliciously or contemp-
tuously . . . Revile or Reproach."[69] On paper the constitution echoed earlier
guarantees for dissenters, but the resurrection of the idea of a national creed
was a frightening proposition for many.

Time and experience would show the *Humble Petition* to be no more
enduring than its predecessor. Both were regarded with insufficient respect
and within a few short years after their adoption were effectively replaced by
military rule. This is hardly surprising, given the fact that they were adopted
not by the common consent of the nation but by imposition from above
by those who had less of a commitment to the rule of law than they did to
accomplishing their own ideas of reform for the nation. By signing the act,
Cromwell "paid for constitutional stability in the coin of religious liberty."[70]
He may have had no other reasonable option, but his willingness to accede to
some of Parliament's less tolerant demands was viewed as a betrayal by some
of his most loyal sectarian allies.

Regardless of what he honestly thought of the *Humble Petition*, Cromwell
was aging, ill, and nearing the end of his life, and stability with limited
concessions seemed a much better option than the twin evils of anarchy and
tyranny that seemed to be lurking in the shadows, awaiting his death. Duty

at this stage, he apparently believed, called for surrender of the principles of religious toleration.

The Return of Old Chains

Cromwell died in September 1658. By the terms of the *Humble Petition and Advice*, he was empowered to choose his successor and did so by selecting his son, Richard, as the next Lord Protector. But Richard was not able to keep things under control as his father had done, and by May 1659 conflicts with army generals resulted in the recalling of members of the Rump. The recalled Parliament immediately voted to end the Protectorate, and Richard resigned.

Yet the chaos continued. In October the Rump was dissolved by Major-General John Lambert, who had been at Oliver Cromwell's side during the first dissolution of the Rump in 1649. In February General George Monck, who had been governing successfully in Scotland for five years, marched into England accompanied by six thousand men to restore the Long Parliament of twenty years prior. All the surviving members reassembled, including those who had been excluded in Pride's Purge.

Now having a thoroughly Presbyterian majority, Parliament nullified all acts passed since Pride's Purge and laid aside matters concerning the militia until "the business concerning Religion" was settled.[71] A frenzy of activity ensued. On March 5, the Westminster Confession was passed as the official confession of the nation and ordered to be printed and published.[72] It was ordered on the same day that all laws against "Popish Recusants, Priests, and Jesuits" be put into "speedy and effectual execution" and that the Solemn League and Covenant "be Printed and Published and set up, and forthwith read in every Church."[73] On March 13, John Owen, the Independent on the Committee for the Propagation of the Gospel during Cromwell's days, was ejected from his position at Christ Church, Oxford, and replaced by the Presbyterian Edward Reynolds, who had held the position prior to Owen's appointment.[74]

With the church established on a firm Presbyterian footing, the Parliament felt confident enough to hold new elections. The outcome was according to prediction: When members of the new Parliament took their seats in April 1660, there was a staunchly royalist majority. Within a month, Charles Stuart had been declared the rightful king.

Champion of Freedom, Epitome of Tyranny

It could be said that Cromwell's "virtuous fault"[75] of committing constitutional travesties and using force to "save his nation" came back to haunt him in his grave; his effort to find a middle way between monarchy and democracy had ironically led to what was essentially an elected monarchy, and his attempt to make liberty of conscience "fundamental" and permanent had led to its curtailment instead.

But it could also be said that had he not done so, England would have plunged into far worse troubles. Cromwell himself had asserted that he did what he did "for the Interest of the people: for the interest of the people alone: and for their good, without respect had to any other Interest,"[76] and it would be foolish to doubt his sincerity. Never once did he betray a selfish motive or ambition.[77] His driving desire was to do more than simply prevent tyranny of the bishops; he wanted to advance the liberty of "all *Species* of *Protestants*" to worship freely without the fingers of brethren straining to pinch their consciences.[78]

As Robert S. Paul writes, "It was the major tragedy of his rule that in defending one liberty he seemed to threaten all the rest, that in standing as the champion of freedom he often appeared as the epitome of tyranny."[79] Cromwell's governance was by no means perfect, but he did more than any king before him to loosen England's spiritual shackles, and the door of hope he had thrust open for freedom would never again be totally shut.

Chapter Fifteen

EXPLICIT FAITH AND SPIRITUAL SWORDS

The Pamphlet Wars, 1640–1660

---

*In vain have English parliaments permitted English Bibles
in the poorest English houses, and the simplest man or
woman to search the Scriptures if yet against their soul's
persuasion from the Scripture they should be forced (as if
they lived in Spain or Rome it self without the sight of a
Bible) to believe as the church believes.*

ROGER WILLIAMS

*B*eginning around 1640, thousands of Englishmen hitherto unable
to proclaim their ideas through the printed word were suddenly given an
opportunity for free expression as royal courts engaged in censorship were
dissolved. Freedom of speech, freedom of assembly, and even procedural
rights became possible as dissenters sought to secure their liberty from an
established church enforced by a tyrannical monarchy.

A Cobbler and the Courts

During the early days of the Long Parliament, a cobbler named Samuel
How preached a sermon to about a hundred people in a tavern. The subject

of his sermon was how human learning can distort the gospel's simplicity and is not necessarily helpful in gaining a spiritual understanding of the Scriptures. It is possible, How said, for men to be always learning and never able to come to a knowledge of the truth.[1] A minister in the audience caused a scene, blasting the poor shoe repairman with accusations of blasphemy, simply because How had dared to imply that the Spirit of God can communicate His truth through a "peddler, tinker, chimney-sweeper, or cobbler" just as well as—if not better than—He can through the highly educated.[2]

If How had lived a little over a century earlier, the anticlerical undertones of his sermon would have undoubtedly resulted in his burning at the stake. Queen Elizabeth had established the Court of High Commission to enforce her religious settlement and punish "heretical" opinions in any form—speech or print—by carrying out ecclesiastical trials. The High Commission could then hand over those convicted to the Star Chamber, which had been empowered to handle criminal trials in 1487 under Henry VII and subsequently used by both Tudors and Stuarts as a piece of political weaponry to deal with enemies of the crown.

Indeed, if the shoemaker How had attempted to exercise his freedom of speech in such a matter only a decade before, during Laud's era, he likely would have been the recipient of brutal torture as Alexander Leighton and William Prynne had been for publishing anti-episcopal sentiments.

The press experienced a similar liberation about this time. The sheer number of publications increased more than threefold between 1640 and 1660 (compared to the previous two-decade period) as authors and publishers became significantly more audacious.[3] When How's friends published a vindication of his teaching—describing how the nation's ministers had set up human learning as a golden calf, then "danc't about it while he (the Cobbler) to their great grief and discontent did cast it down and grind it to Powder, and so blew it away with the Word of God"[4]—the publication and its authors (as far as we know) survived.

Previously, the press had been controlled through the agency of the Stationers Company, a corporate body accountable to the crown. The Stationers Company held monopolistic privileges and was charged with monitoring the press in accordance with royal standards with the help of the Star Chamber and the Court of High Commission. Under an ordinance from 1566, the wardens of the Company were empowered to search without probable cause "in all workhouses, shops . . . and other places of printers, booksellers, and such as bring books into the realm."[5] If any of the works found dealt with suspect ecclesiastical matters, the "offending persons" were to be hauled before the High Commission.[6]

Thus there were numerous opportunities for Stationers Company officials to abuse their privileges, especially since they had a vested interest in eliminating all printing that took place outside their purview. They were hated for their ability to barge into any place where books might be located and seize whatever works they found without any reason to suspect foul play. Furthermore, since the High Commission and the Star Chamber were not typical common law courts and could operate more quickly and arbitrarily, defendants had few protections.

The Long Parliament dissolved both of these hated courts on July 5, 1641. Parliament's motive was founded not so much on devotion to freedom of the press as it was on eliminating a key aspect of royal sovereignty over the nation. Although the two abolition acts paid much lip service to defending the "liberties of the subject" against "abuses, mischiefs, and inconveniences,"[7] Parliament quickly made clear that *it* intended to control the press henceforth. Since one of the primary reasons for putting reins on the press in the first place was to control religion, a subcommittee of the Parliamentary committee on religion was turned into a committee on licensing and printing with the power of "denying license to some books and expunging several passages out of other books."[8]

It became apparent in short order that the new censorship panel had in place none of the enforcement mechanisms it needed to implement its charges. Piracy, counterfeiting, and a barrage of written attacks on both king and Parliament soon overwhelmed the little committee.[9] Exasperated, the committee petitioned Parliament to pay heed to the rights and privileges of the stationers and to consider that "irregular Printing, hath of late been the fuel in some measure of this miserable Civil-War, by deceiving the multitude, and hath brought into Church and State, sundry other mischiefs and miseries."[10] The Lords and Commons agreed that something more needed to be done, so they enlisted the assistance of the stationers company to help with searches and seizures and passed an order "for the Regulating of Printing, and for suppressing the great late abuses and frequent disorders in Printing many false, Scandalous, Seditious, Libelous, and unlicensed Pamphlets, to the great defamation of Religion and Government."[11]

Thus, the printing trade was not formally released from bondage but merely switched masters from the king to the Parliament. Even with the help of the Stationers Company, however, efforts at curtailing the so-called "defamatory" pamphlets were ineffective. Once printers and authors had tasted freedom, they could not easily be suppressed.[12] Streams of thought that had been buried under centuries of accumulated assertions of royal, clerical, and elitist prerogative began to flow into London markets. Before long, they turned into a flood that was difficult to curtail.

Freedom of Association

Part and parcel of religious liberty is the "right of the people peaceably to assemble," otherwise known as freedom of association. This freedom would prove to be of profound importance in the struggle for religious liberty.

Dissenting or unauthorized religious gatherings had been illegal under the Catholic Church and continued to be viewed within Protestantism as subversive of established authority. The church, in its local manifestation, was not understood to be a voluntary association of believers but rather part of a nationwide institution encompassing every subject of the nation and speaking with an authoritative and coercive voice. To disagree with official church teaching and form one's own gathering based on an individual inter-pretation of Scripture was to be considered a schismatic, heretic, or infidel.

Yet once the laity possessed vernacular translations of the Bible and could read the Word for themselves, inevitably entire groups of men and women found themselves struggling with the rectitude of certain doctrines and practices. It was then a short step to form their own voluntary assem-blies of like-minded brethren. Hence there arose the conventiclers of Bloody Mary's reign, the Separatists of Elizabeth's time, and the Baptists of the King James era. Even in a day when religious conformity was the norm and nonconformity seen as somehow inherently sinful, these small groups of dissenters stood on the principle of private judgment and appealed directly to God to sustain them through persecution. "For if God be on our side," Tyndale reminded his readers in *The Obedience of a Christian Man*, "what matter maketh it who be against us, be they bishops, cardinals, popes or whatsoever names they will."[13]

Although the dissenters, in Christopher Hill's words, "carried to its logical conclusion the principle of individualism which rejects all media-tors between man and God," it would be a mistake to think they adhered to an anarchistic notion in which every man was a law unto himself.[14] Congregations formed around common interpretations of Scripture and were bound by the conviction that God, through His Holy Spirit, can and does "say similar things" to His people.[15] Instead of seeking to derive national unity through common university training, long the gateway to ministry in the established church, the dissenters sought unity through the Spirit, which, as the apostle Paul wrote, is the bond of peace. In this they followed in the tradition of Tyndale, who translated the word *ecclesia* in the New Testament as "congregation" instead of "church."

So when the High Commission and Star Chamber fell and the presses started rolling, a nationwide dialogue on the nature of the church—local, national, and universal—commenced. The advocates of religious liberty wrote fervently and at length about the universal church's primarily *spiritual* nature and drew conclusions about how entrance into the church is gained and how ministers are qualified. Yet they could not have done so without a free press, free speech, and freedom of association; and those who opposed independent congregations outside the state church wanted to restrain these free thinkers by suppressing free speech, press, and assembly.

Roger Williams on the Liberty of Conscience

Roger Williams's name is today familiar to students of American history because of his controversial run-ins with the Puritan leadership of New England and his status in colonial affairs as the founder of Rhode Island. However, before he came to New England, Williams was one of the most significant English pamphleteer for religious liberty. He confronted in writing both the Independents and the Scotch commissioners of the Westminster Assembly for arrogating to themselves and to the civil magistrate a power over souls that, in his estimation, should not belong to any human agency.[16] Williams stated in unflinching terms that "a *state Church* (whether *explicit*, as in *Old England*, or *implicit*, as in *New*) is not the *Institution* of the Lord *Jesus Christ*."[17]

Williams contrasted the "national church" of the Jews in the Old Testament with the "spiritual land of Canaan" now possessed by God's people through the gospel.[18] He wrote that the civil sword possessed by ministers of God to enforce external worship under the old law is a "type" of the sword of the Spirit, the Word of God. This spiritual sword alone has the capacity to bring a person to repentance and true worship; the sword of the civil magistrate can do no more than make "a whole nation of hypocrites."[19] How absurd it is, Williams wrote, since Scripture declares that he who "eats and drinks the body and blood of Christ unworthily, eateth and drinketh his own judgment," that every English soul is required by law to take communion at a certain age.[20] Since so many were acknowledged to be "ignorant, impenitent, unregenerate," he concluded that it was illogical and cruel to force them to eat and drink to their own judgment.

Williams reminded his readers that it is equally irrational and ineffective to treat spiritual ailments with physical "remedies." Reformation of the church, he wrote, belongs to "the great and good Physician Christ Jesus, the Head of the Body, and King of the Church," who amply provides "spiritual antidotes and preservatives" against all manner of spiritual ailments in the church.[21] The civil sword, for all its good in protecting the bodies and goods of citizens of civil states, "cannot according to its utmost reach and capacity (now under *Christ*, when all *Nations* are merely *civil* without such typical holy respect upon them, as was upon *Israel* a *National Church*) . . . extend to *spiritual* and *Soul-causes*, Spiritual and Soul *punishment*, which belong to that *spiritual sword* with two edges, the *soul-piercing* (in *soul-saving* or *soul-killing*) the Word of God."[22]

In sum, Williams believed that because of the nature of the church, to charge the civil magistrate with establishing and reforming it is to give Caesar the responsibility to invade an arena where God should possess sole prerogative.

Other figures in the pamphlet war debates were less well-known compared to Williams, Dell, and Richardson, but the works they authored were just as significant. Their thought as "rank and file" members of society, for the first time audible to the whole of England as a result of the opening of the press, was remarkably consistent with the thought on religious toleration expressed by its more prominent advocates.[23] Layman and former member of the army, John Vernon, for example, wrote a pamphlet titled *The swords abuse asserted* and addressed to those who were framing the government of the Commonwealth. He warned that conversion cannot be forced and that the "carnal sword" can never restrain the spirit:[24]

> For I must tell you, though your policy may appear in the managing of the uncertain Affairs of an Early and Politic State, yet, if you intermeddle with matters beyond that sphere, *viz* The ordering of the visible Worship and Service of God, wherein all are alike subject, and your selves as unskillful as any, whereunto no Terrestrial Potentate hath a Grain more Title than the poorest Peasant . . . and in which Kingdom Christ alone should have the Dominion *1 Cor. 1.24.* and wherein it's sin to be the servants of men *1 Cor. 7.23* . . . Beware . . . lest you be judged Infringers of, or Copartners with, what's committed alone to be both governed, ordered, and established for evermore in Justice and Judgment by the Scepter of Christ Jesus, *Isa. 9.7.*[25]

Vernon stressed that such intermeddling is inconsistent with the spirit of the gospel. As he understood it, conviction of the understanding cannot be forced; otherwise, there would have been no reason for the Bereans in the book of Acts to be commended as they were "for refusing to receive [the apostle] implicitly, until they were confirmed in the truth of his Doctrine by scrutiny."[26]

The necessity of this "conviction of the understanding" that Vernon spoke of was often referred to as "conscience" and emphasized many times and in various forms throughout other writings. Advocates of religious liberty disagreed with the long-held notion that conscience can and must be compelled for the good of the state and the glory of God; they asked, how can you *force* someone to believe and do something contrary to what they believe the evidence says without making them sin in the process? Even a so-called erroneous conscience that is forced into compliance, unaccompanied by a willing heart and proceeding from doubt rather than faith, cannot be pleasing to God. An erroneous conscience, they argued, must be instructed from the Word and convicted by the Spirit, not punished by the sword.[27]

Pamphleteers frequently emphasized that voluntary obedience to the truth, springing from love, was the proper mode of operation under the New Covenant, or gospel, and that forced obedience and outward conformity to the letter of the law was a relic of the Old. Therefore, it was not only wrong to disallow individuals from joining other like-minded believers in religious congregations; it was also wrong to make them join a national religious assembly that forced them to adhere to what they disbelieved. In Roger Williams's own passionate words:

> Oh! since the Common-weal cannot without a spiritual rape
> force the consciences of all to one Worship, oh that it may never
> commit that rape, in forcing the consciences of all men to one
> Worship, which a stronger army and Sword may soon (as formerly)
> arise to alter.[28]

John Milton, the legendary poet, understood the terms *conscience* and *religion* to be interchangeable. He described them as "that full persuasion whereby we are assured that our belief and practice, as far as we are able to apprehend and probably make appear, is according to the will of God and his Holy Spirit within us, which we ought to follow much rather than any law of man."[29] The Protestant emphasis on Scripture above—and sometimes even against—the tradition of the institutional church makes persecution for the sake of conscience absurd because the individual believer is urged to examine the Scriptures and make decisions based on an *explicit* faith according to what he or she judges it to say. *Implicit* faith in the teachings of the church, Milton said, destroys Christian liberty, for "who then can plead for such a conscience, as being implicitly enthralled to man instead of God, almost becomes no conscience, as the will not free becomes no will."[30]

Milton asserted that he drew his arguments for religious liberty directly from the Bible. "What I shall argue," he wrote in his *Treatise of Civil Power in Ecclesiastical Causes*, "shall be drawn from the scripture only; and therein from true fundamental principles of the gospel."[31] He said that Scripture is the highest judge in matters of religion and ought to serve as the only authoritative common ground between fellow Christians.[32]

Similar thoughts were expressed by a pastor from Kent named Christopher Blackwood. Blackwood described it as an injustice for a man to be punished for what he thinks is a lie since Christians are admonished in 1 Thessalonians to "test everything, holding fast to what is good." The state, he argued, overthrows Christian liberty when "our faith cannot fix freely upon the object" and we cannot act consistently with what we evaluate to be good, right, and true.[33] Thus, he said, it is far worse to have "a glorious seeming uniformity in a state of self-condemnation" in a single national church than it is to have "conscientious satisfaction" with diversity of opinion and congregations.[34]

In essence, Milton and Blackwood were making arguments for the freedom of private judgment in matters of religion. Private judgment as they and others understood it had been impossible in England prior to Tyndale because the layman was prevented from examining the Bible for himself. Yet in a day when ploughboys and cobblers *could* read and the Scriptures were available to them, how could it be right or consistent in a Protestant country for them to be forced to submit to an interpretation they understood to be false?

The rectitude of the principle of private judgment, however, hinged on the disputed nature of the church. If membership in a "particular" church, to use Barnes's term, should be dependent on personal belief, then it would be wrong for the government or institutional church to mandate participation, especially upon pain of physical torture. As Barnes wrote:

> They that believe that Christ hath washed them from their
> sins, and stick fast unto his merits, and to the promise made to
> them in him only, they be the Church of God . . . whether they
> be Jew or Greek, king or subject, carter or Cardinal, butcher or
> Bishop, tankardbearer or cannelrater, free or bound, friar or fid-
> dler, monk or miller: if they believe in Christ's word, and stick fast
> to his blessed promises, and trust only in the merits of his blessed
> blood, they be the holy Church of God, yea and the very true
> Church of God. . . . Boast, crack, blast, bless, curse till your holy
> eyes start out of your head, it will not help you, for Christ choos-
> eth his church, at his judgment not at yours . . . he will neither be
> bound, to Pope nor Cardinal, Archbishop nor Bishop, Abbot nor
> Prior, Deacons nor Archdeacon, Parson nor Vicar, Nun nor Friar.[35]

"Illiterate, Mechanic Men"

Practically speaking, the realization of religious liberty would be impossible without freedom of association, which allows congregations to be formed based on belief rather than legal requirement. One of the central obstacles to forming such congregations was the legal requirement that local churches be under the authority of "approved" ministers. Only those schooled in Hebrew, Greek, Latin, and possessing a university degree were considered competent enough to interpret and teach from the Bible.[36] Thus ordination was a useful and effective means for maintaining control over the established church.

The tenor of opinion on this matter in the mid-1640s is evident in an ordinance passed by Parliament in October 1644 at the advice of the Assembly of Divines. Lay preaching, such as that of Samuel How, was despised by ordained ministers and evidently feared by officials in Parliament. The old episcopal system that had operated under Laud was despised, but a way was needed temporarily to solve the problem of screening preachers until the Assembly of Divines had worked out a permanent church government arrangement. The Lords and Commons appointed certain individuals to handle the task of ordaining *presbyters*, referred to as elders or ministers. The candidates had to provide proof that they embraced the Solemn League and Covenant, as well as evidence of their university degrees, then be subject to an examination governed by the following enumerated rules:

2. He shall be examined touching his skill in the Original Tongues, and that Trial be made by reading the Hebrew and Greek Testaments, and rendering some portions of them into Latin; and inquiry also shall be made after his other Learning, and whether he hath skill in Logic and Philosophy.

3. What Authors in Divinity he hath read, and is best acquainted with, and trial shall be made of his knowledge in the chief Grounds of Religion, and of his ability to defend the Orthodox Doctrine contained in them against all unsound and erroneous opinions, especially those of the present age: Of his skill, In the sense and meaning of such places of Scripture as shall be proposed unto him, In cases of Conscience, and in the Chronology of Scripture, and of the Ecclesiastical History. . . .

5. He shall in a competent time also frame a Discourse in Latin upon such a common place, or controversy in Divinity, as shall be assigned him, and exhibit to the Ministers appointed to ordain, such Theses as express the sum thereof, and maintain a Dispute upon them.[37]

Upon meeting the requisite qualifications, the candidate was to be ordained "concerning his Faith in Christ Jesus, and his persuasion of the Truth of the Reformed Religion . . . his Zeal, and Faithfulness in maintaining the Truth of the Gospel, and unity of the Church against Error and Schism."[38] By specifically requiring all ordained ministers to reject "schism," it was clear that any person who believed that churches should be voluntary associations was disqualified by definition.

This monopoly on religion held by the educated elite explains the vehement opposition encountered by Samuel How for his daring proposal that formal human learning is not an absolute prerequisite to ministry. How acknowledged that education is "of good use" in its proper place and "so fit for Statesmen, Physicians, Lawyers, and Gentlemen, yea, all men so far as they can attain to it," but if it is allowed to be brought "to the perfecting of the Gospel . . . it will be found to be the spoiling of the right understanding thereof."[39] The "test" How proposed for ministers instead was a spiritual understanding of the Word of God that rested not on private interpretation but on the Spirit of God and the testimony of the Word itself. Under his scheme, even "illiterate mechanick" people—in the sense that they were not university educated—could preach, too.

How and other people like "tailors [who] leap up from the Shop-board to the Pulpit"[40] were frequently attacked in writing for their impudence. Thomas Hall, who possessed a bachelor's degree in divinity and referred to himself as "Pastor of Kings-Norton in Worchester*shire*," wrote a book called *Vindiciae literarum, the schools guarded, or, The excellency and usefulnesse of humane learning in subordination to divinity*. In it he derisively commented on How's analysis of the issue:

> *How* himself confesseth That human learning being sanctified
> is an excellent help to the right understanding of Scripture, and
> that in itself it is a good thing. . . . Well said and well sowed *Sam*:
> these stitches will hold; yet see how like a right sectary he plays
> fast and loose, like the cursed Cow, that having given a good mess
> of milk, knocks down all with her heels again: for mark his follow-
> ing words: But bring it once to be a help to understand the mind
> of God in holy Scriptures, and there its detestable filth, dross, and
> dung, good for nothing but to destroy, and cause men to err.[41]

Both sides were a little extreme in their polemics, but the debate reflects the tension of those turbulent days in England. The contrast between the two "worlds" of the educated and their languages on the one hand, and the laity and their vernacular on the other, can be presented, as one author has put it, "in terms of two different versions of Reformation history."[42] One side equated a lack of university education with heresy, while the other side gloried in the courage and rectitude of the common people in works like Foxe's *Actes and Monuments* (Book of Martyrs).[43]

Like Tyndale, not all of the authors who were on the sectarian laity's side were uneducated themselves; in fact, the opposite was often true. William Dell, for example, held numerous high academic and state positions, including master of Caius College, Oxford.[44] Yet he also was convinced of the power of God's Spirit and Word to work in ordinary men without "proper" training and official ordination. He wrote in *Right Reformation*:

> *Christ* sent [His Disciples] not *forth* with any *power* of *swords*, or *guns*, or *prisons* to *reform* the *world*, or with any *power* of *States*, or *Armies*: but sent forth *poor, illiterate, mechanic* men, and only *armed* them with the *power of the word*; and *behold* what *wonders* they *wrought* by *that* power *alone*: They turned the *world* upside down; they *changed* the *manners, customs, religion, worship, lives*, and *natures* of men . . . they won *many* in *most* Kingdoms unto *Christ*, and *brought* them into *willing* subjection and obedience to *him*: and *all this* they did (I say) not with any *earthly* or *secular* power, but by the *ministry* of the *Gospel* alone, Christ's *great* and *only Instrument* for *conquering, subduing*, and *reforming* of the Nations. And so the *power* appeared to be *God's* only, and not the *creatures'*.[45]

Other writers used the phrase "illiterate mechanic preachers" in a far less conciliatory sense. Thomas Edwards, a Presbyterian minister in London, for example, used it as a term of censure to describe all those laymen who refused to abide by the Parliamentary ordinances against printing without license and preaching without ordination in "unlawful meetings."[46] These sectaries, a friend of Edwards reported, were "very stirred with the Vote passed in Parliament, against Lay-mens meddling with the office of preaching."[47]

William Walwyn frequently took Edwards to task in his writings, just as Edwards had castigated Walwyn in his book *Gangraena, or, A catalogue and discovery of many of the errours, heresies, blasphemies and pernicious practices of the sectaries of this time*. In response to Edwards's arguments against sectaries of all shades, Walwyn sarcastically suggested that Edwards should have been well aware, with all his knowledge of Scripture, that "every one is bound to try all things, the unlearned as well as the learned."[48] If this was the case, Walwyn concluded, how contrary it is to the law of love "to rail, revile, reproach, backbite, slander, or to despise men and women for their weaknesses: their means of trades and callings, or poverty."[49] Here and elsewhere, Walwyn wrote that the crux of the matter was that uniformity in the national church could never be achieved apart from the unity of brotherly love, and brotherly love could never be achieved if the educated were so puffed up with pride that they thought they alone possessed the right to create a mold into which to force the rest of the country.[50]

In a similar vein, the anonymous author of *The Compassionate Samaritane*, published in 1644, asked his readers whether "the most learned, or unlearned men have been the troublers of the World."[51] He then begged his countrymen to consider the presumption and confidence of the Scribes and Pharisees during Jesus' day and how they thought they understood the Scriptures best, yet Christ chose poor fishermen and tent makers to be his apostles and disciples instead.[52] If Christians were forced against their consciences by other Christians to "believe as the Synod would have us," he asked, "what is this but to be brought into their miserable condition that must believe as the Church believes, and so become (as said an honest man) not the Disciples of Christ, but of the Synod?"[53]

Pamphlets like *The Compassionate Samaritane* insisted that placing too much stock in the decisions of "divines" served only to discourage men and women from seeking out the truth for themselves. Robert Barnes had rebuked the bishops of his day, "You are ten times worse than the great Turk: for he regardeth no more but rule and dominion in this world: and you are not therewith content, but you will also rule over men's consciences, yea and oppress Christ and his holy word."[54] Yet by 1645 the Bible and its interpretation still seemed reserved for the educated. This provoked outcries from writers like Roger Williams, who exclaimed:

> In vain have *English Parliaments* permitted *English Bibles* in
> the poorest *English* houses, and the simplest man or woman to
> search the Scriptures, if yet against their soul's persuasion from the
> Scripture, they should be forced (as if they lived in *Spain* or *Rome* it
> self without the sight of a *Bible*) to believe as the Church believes.[55]

Samuel Richardson likewise asked "whether it be not in vain for us to have Bibles in English, if contrary to our understanding of them, we must believe as the Church believes, whether it be right or wrong?"[56]

And perhaps the ever-eloquent Milton said it best when he addressed Parliament in 1644 with this observation:

> Truth is compar'd in Scripture to a streaming fountain; if
> her waters flow not in a perpetual progression, they sick'n into a
> muddy pool of conformity and tradition. A man may be a heretic
> in the truth; and if he believes things only because his Pastor says
> so, or the Assembly so determines, without knowing other reason,

though his belief be true, yet the very truth he holds, becomes his heresy.[57]

Over a century after Tyndale was burned at the stake for his fearless efforts to place the Scriptures in the hands of England's ploughboys, the battle over the Bible was still raging; only this time, instead of prohibiting vernacular translations altogether, those in power found other means of suppressing the ploughboy who endeavored to understand Scripture for himself. As Christopher Hill writes:

> Priests and scholars would have liked to keep interpretation of the Bible the monopoly of an educated elite, as it had been in the days before the vernacular Bible existed. The radical reply was to assert the possibility of any individual receiving the spirit, the inner experience which enabled him to understand God's Word as well as, better than, mere scholars who lacked this grace. . . . For seventeenth century English radicals the religion of the heart was the answer to the pretensions of the academic divinity of ruling-class universities.[58]

The pamphleteers of the 1640s through 1660s echoed the sentiments of Robert Barnes and Tyndale, defending the ploughboys, the cobblers, the tailors, and the bricklayers in their pursuit of knowing God and intent on moving all worldly obstacles out of the way. "And neither the Pope, nor yet his Cardinals be more this Church or of this Church," Barnes affirmed, "than the poorest man on earth. For this Church standeth alone in the spiritual faith of Christ Jesus, and not in dignities nor honors of the world."[59]

The Pamphleteers' Legacy

The authors of religious liberty pamphlets during this period were determined not to undermine the Christian faith but, rather, to restore its vitality. Their authors were dissatisfied with the emphasis on outward conformity in the church and frustrated by those who were content to be "heretics in the truth." Admittedly, some wandered into true heresy and other murky waters—Milton was prone to placing reason above Scripture, while the Quakers were prone to place their "inner lights" above it.[60] Other activists, like the Fifth Monarchists, were somewhat disingenuous in their interpretations of the Bible and had a tendency to create allegorical parallels as a substitution for the Word's plain text. But these were also frequently more interested in creating a utopia than establishing religious freedom, and in this they shared more in common with those against whom they fought.

While these extreme cases caused "respectable" Christians to condemn the whole crowd of "radical" people and their ideas, leading to rigorous persecution under the Restoration government, England would never be the same. Because of free speech and a free press, arguments for religious liberty had been articulated and exposed to all strata of society. Churches and religious assemblies based on belief rather than coercion had begun to gain in numbers and even, occasionally, respectability. And because the pamphleteers' works were based on the truth that only spiritual rebirth, focused study of Scripture, and voluntary obedience by the common man as much as the cleric could ultimately heal the wounds of a nation so torn by religious strife, their work was not ultimately in vain and did not return void—even if it took another century and happened on a continent across the sea.

Chapter Sixteen

A FOUNDATION OF PARADOXES

The Restoration through the Glorious Revolution

*Nothing does more efficaciously dispose and prepare
the minds of men for treason and rebellion than
by force to make them act against their conscience
in matters of religion.*

THE EARL OF CLARENDON

*W*hen news of Cromwell's death reached twenty-eight-year-old Charles Stuart, he was in exile and penniless at Hoogstraeten on the Dutch border— playing tennis, according to some reports. As some royalist friends began celebrating and making dramatic plans for his restoration to the throne, Sir Edward Hyde hurriedly counseled caution and moderation until more favorable circumstances presented themselves.[1] Hyde had been a royal advisor prior to the civil war and possessed the challenging duty of keeping tabs on the young Stuart, who seemed always on the brink of allowing his and his followers' impulsive reactions to ruin Hyde's carefully measured plans.

Hyde's patience proved fruitful in early 1660 when the reconvened Long Parliament dissolved itself and elections were held, resulting in a firm royalist victory in April. To the great delight of some and deep suspicion of others,

Charles issued a declaration from Breda that announced his intention, in the interest of peace and unity, to grant "a free and general pardon" to those who had risen against his father. He also declared a desire to promote religious toleration so as to further bind the wounds of the nation:

> And because the passion and uncharitableness of the times have produced several opinions in religion, by which men are engaged in parties and animosities against each other—which, when they shall hereafter unite in a freedom of conversation, will be composed or better understood—we do declare a liberty to tender consciences and that no man shall be disquieted or called into question for differences of opinion in matter of religion, which do not disturb the peace of the kingdom; and that we shall be ready to consent to such an act of parliament as, upon mature deliberation, shall be offered to us for the full granting of that indulgence.[2]

Although Parliament quickly declared Charles II the rightful king, his promise to grant toleration was easier said than done. He rode triumphantly into London, accompanied by song and celebration, on his thirtieth birthday, May 29, 1660, to face a country still divided.

The Grounds of Revenge

The king's declaration of "liberty to tender consciences" was, at that time, mere words. Ultimately, as he made certain to state, the responsibility for creating a law to that end lay in the hands of Parliament.

Even prior to Charles's return, widespread resentment had been building toward both sectarian dissenters and Presbyterian Puritans. Fairly or not, they were deemed guilty of the bloodshed and chaos of the twenty preceding years.[3] Yet while members of the restored Long Parliament were busily passing bills in March 1660 to settle the established church along firmly Presbyterian lines, they were deceived by their apparent position of strength. By the end of the year, nearly seven hundred Puritan ministers had been ejected from their churches and replaced by Anglicans from the Charles I era.[4]

Some Presbyterians, however, held out hope. As devotees of the idea of an established national church, many recognized that some form of episcopacy was inevitable and that their only option was incorporation within a modified structure. If all had gone according to Charles's inclinations, the Presbyterians might have gotten their wish from the start. He did not share the vindictiveness of many of his royalist and Anglican allies—it did not suit his temper. He was far more interested in political expediency than he was in clinging to principle at all costs. In characteristic fashion, Charles II had sworn to the Solemn League and Covenant to please the Scots in the early 1650s after they declared him king following his father's beheading. It is little wonder, then, that the bishops did not hold much loyalty toward him.[5] As Harvard historian Jeffrey Collins writes, "What had once been a mutual dedication to a unified secular and spiritual order under a godly king was now reduced to a mutually beneficial political alliance, easily dispensed with."[6]

Charles's tendencies were evident in a speech he gave before Parliament in August. He asserted that it should cause "every Religious Heart to bleed" to witness "the perverse Wranglings of passionate and forward Men, the ground of all Animosity, Hatred, Malice and Revenge."[7] How distastefully must the adversaries of Christianity "look upon our sharp and virulent Contentions in the debates of *Christian Religion*, and the Bloody Wars that have proceeded from those Contentions," he quoted Hugo Grotius as saying, "whilst every one pretended to all the Marks which are to attend upon the true Church, except only that which is inseparable from it, *Charity to one another*."[8]

The immediate solution to Presbyterian nonconformity proposed by the king was one of "comprehension,"[9] a view which attempted to expand the parameters of acceptable Anglican belief. Since the potency of Presbyterian support was difficult to measure, Charles and his counselor Hyde hoped that it could be dealt with most safely by offering relatively minor concessions and incorporating them quietly into the establishment.[10] To this end Charles's "Worcester House Declaration" at the end of October explained that he had consulted with "grave and learned" Presbyterian ministers and that he was assured that they were enemies of neither episcopacy nor liturgy. Their moderate requests could be handled by allowing Presbyters to work alongside the bishops within the episcopal structure and by making some slight modifications to the Book of Common Prayer so as to accommodate differences.[11]

The declaration was never made law. Instead, it was defeated in November by Parliament, the majority of which was exhibiting an increasing desire for revenge—typified, perhaps, by a resolution of the Commons in December ordering that Cromwell and three of his associates should be taken from their coffins and displayed in infamy at Tyburn.[12] It should be remembered that Parliament had more than a religious grudge against Cromwell; he had repeatedly interfered with the prerogatives of Parliament.

It was not that Charles necessarily liked Presbyterianism, and his precise motives in wanting to accommodate them are unclear. One fearful possibility in the minds of some Englishmen was that Charles had some sympathy for Catholicism. Since any toleration of Catholics would necessitate keeping the Anglican grip on the national church weak, it seemed to make sense that he would attempt to dilute the bishops' power by infiltrating their ranks with Puritans.[13] And it was a fact that some of Charles's most consistent supporters during his years in exile were Catholics, and he had personal reasons for looking on them favorably. The influence of his mother, Henrietta Maria, and his admiration for Louis XIV of France may also have played a role.[14] He is said to have written to Hyde, "Rebel for rebel, I had rather trust a Papist rebel than a Presbyterian."[15]

On the other hand, Charles did not overtly advocate Catholicism, and some have suggested that Charles and his court never intended for Parliament to follow through on his Worcester promises from the start.[16] Much of the ambiguity may stem from the fact that the king's closest advisors and the Privy Council were not in agreement on how to handle the nation's religious situation,[17] and Charles lacked the kind of serious theological convictions that might be translated into a die-hard political position.

Nevertheless, while many Anglicans began looking to Parliament instead of the king for support, separatist dissenters started looking to the king. The promise of "liberty to tender consciences" was a welcome relief in the midst of severe persecution at the hands of Anglican gentry that had commenced with the downfall of the Protectorate.[18] Baptists in particular bore the brunt of the assault. Only a month after Charles had been declared king, he was presented with a petition that read:

> Being commanded thereto by the Lord, we have met often
> together, to acquaint each other, what God hath done, doth daily,
> and will do for our souls; and what therefore we ought to do
> towards him, each other, and all men. From which assemblings, O
> king! we have been discharged by some in magisterical capacity in
> these parts; although therein, we bless God, none hath ever found
> us with multitude or with tumult. But being taught of God to obey
> him in the things by him commanded, rather than man, though
> in the place of magistracy, when commanding things contrary; we
> therefore durst not receive that discharge. Wherefore some of us
> have been silenced from making mention of the name of the Lord,
> as formerly, by being entangled in bonds, pretendedly imposed
> upon us for this good behavior. Since thus entangled, O king! we
> have been much abused as we pass in the streets, and as we sit in
> our houses; being threatened to be hanged, if but heard praying
> to the Lord in our families, and disturbed in our so waiting upon
> God, by uncivil beating at our doors, and sounding of horns; yea,

we have been stoned when going to our meetings, the windows
of the place where we have been met, struck down with stones;
yea, taken us as evil doers, and imprisoned, when peaceably met
together to worship the Most High, in the use of his most precious
ordinances.[19]

As the year progressed, dissenting congregations continued to be
harassed with banging on their doors, rocks hurled at their windows, and
scorn heaped upon them in public and in private.

John Bunyan is perhaps the most well-known victim of this round of
persecution. In November he was meeting with a group of like-minded
brethren in the country to whom he was going to preach. Their plans
were interrupted when Bunyan was arrested and committed to prison on
the charge of being an "Upholder and Maintainer of Unlawful Assemblies
and Conventicles, and for not conforming to the National Worship of the
Church of England" while "devilishly and perniciously abstain[ing] from
coming to church to hear the Divine service."[20] Bunyan was charged under
the "Act to Retain the Queen's Subjects in Obedience"—also known as the
Act against Sectaries—from Elizabeth's reign[21] and held in prison for twelve
years, during which time he wrote *Pilgrim's Progress.*

The problem intensified further early in January when a Fifth Monarchist
named Thomas Venner led fifty associates in a three-day insurrection in
London on behalf of "King Jesus." The uprising gave credibility to the fears
that many harbored toward dissenters, especially those who met in "private
Congregation[s]," and a royal proclamation was promptly issued "commanding all such persons going under the notion of anabaptists, quakers, and
other sectaries, henceforward not to meet, under pretense of serving God, at
unusual hours, nor in great numbers."[22] As many as four thousand Baptists
and Quakers were arrested and imprisoned before the month had ended,
and Venner was hung, drawn, and quartered—in spite of his insistence that
"what I did was according to the best light I had, and according to the best
understanding the Scripture will afford."[23]

Baptists from London to Lincolnshire immediately began disclaiming
any connection with Venner and his followers. In London thirty individuals published a protestation against the insurrection and an explanation of
their position regarding the civil magistrate. "We should be stupid and
senseless," they wrote, "if we did not deeply resent those black obloquies and
reproaches cast upon those of our profession and practice in the point of
Baptism, by occasion of the late most horrid *Treason* and *Rebellion* in this city
of London."[24] They insisted that their different belief on the doctrine of baptism should imply nothing about their loyalty to the king and that, in fact,

they had been ready to risk their lives to suppress the "few heady and dis-tempered persons" in the "tragical enterprise" who pretended to be acting in the name of Jesus.[25] Their concluding apologetic pleaded for "the quiet and peaceable enjoyment" of their "Religious and Civil Rights and Liberties," as they desired and endeavored to maintain good behavior.[26]

Also in the same month there appeared a publication signed by four indi-viduals "in the name of the Baptists, now prisoners in the gaol at Maidstone." They addressed it to the king as an acknowledgement of his authority in temporal and civil things and yet defended their conclusion that he had no business either as a Christian or a magistrate to dictate "spiritual things or causes." For believing such, they said, their houses had been broken into in the middle of the night and their property confiscated; they had been arrested in their homes and taken from their peaceable congregations; and now they were imprisoned and their families suffering hunger from want of provision. The prisoners concluded, "We beseech thee, O king, that liberty may be given us to worship our God, and such bowels of compassion be in thee, as to give us such speedy relief as may be agreeable to the mind of God: *which made heaven and earth, which executeth judgment for the oppressed, which giveth food to the hungry. The Lord looseth the prisoners.*"

Another "Member of the Baptized People" named John Sturgion made a similar entreaty two months later that makes clear that the persecution had not yet abated. He made note of the Venner incident and insisted that although it had been done under pretence of "liberty of worshipping God apart from the Parochial Assembly," it was a blatant misuse of that freedom and did not merit the crackdown on honest and innocent dissenters.[27] The declaration against conventicles had made "the *Innocent suffer for the Guilty*" and had ruined reputations, harmed families, and resulted in the crowding of prisons—all while those who were truly guilty of debauchery and other various crimes escaped unpunished.[28] After presenting reasons why there should be free exercise of religion, Sturgion emphasized that he and his suffering brethren asked for freedom not for the sake of profit or honor but only desired "that *we may serve the Lord without molestation in that Faith and order which we have Learned in the Holy Scripture;* giving *Honor* to our *King* to whom *Honor belongs; fear* to whom *fear, Tribute* to whom *Tribute* belong, in every thing as far as we have abilities, to *render to God the things that are God's,* and to the *Magistrate* the things that are *His.*"[29]

Even if Charles *had* wanted to make good on his Breda promises and answer this and other petitions favorably, it was becoming increasingly dif-ficult to do so in light of the disposition of Parliament, the church, local officials, and sometimes even the dissenters themselves.

Charles had indicated in the Worcester House Declaration that Anglican and Presbyterian clergy would work together to iron out differences in the Book of Common Prayer and elsewhere. "How much the Peace of the State is concerned in the Peace of the Church, and how difficult a thing it is to preserve Order and Government in Civil, whilst there is no Order or Government in Ecclesiastical Affairs," he said.[30] The Savoy Conference met with this in mind in April 1661—twelve bishops and twelve Presbyterian divines. Yet neither side was willing to compromise, so the effort ended with the Presbyterians largely outside the establishment with other nonconformists.

The conference coincided with the election of a new "Cavalier" Parliament, which convened in May and was even more resolutely determined to restore the old Anglican order. Unlike earlier days when the Commons served as a bulwark for the people's liberties against the tyranny of the king and the church, this time "the Bishops who had been formerly allowed to persecute by favor of the King in spite of the House of Commons" were able "to persecute by favor of the House of Commons in spite of the King."[31] Charles could not be a monarch in the manner of his absolutist continental counterparts, such as Louis XIV, or even as his father had been in *his* early days as king. Especially in regard to religious matters, Parliament was unwilling to allow Charles II's noncommittal attitude to dictate how the country should be run. Before long, coercive church courts had begun operating again, the Solemn League and Covenant was burned in public, and Parliament was undertaking a legislative program—known to posterity as the Clarendon Code—designed to crush dissent into nonexistence.[32]

Clarendon's Code?

The year after Charles came to the throne, Edward Hyde was made the first Earl of Clarendon. Two years before, shortly after the death of Cromwell, Charles had appointed him Lord Chancellor. Hyde was also related by marriage to the royal family; his daughter, Anne, had married Charles's younger brother James. Hyde's respectable English roots, solid education, firm disposition, and commitment to constitutional legality made him a valuable asset to Charles when it came to putting the restoration of the monarchy on a good historical and legal footing.

Historians have debated the Earl of Clarendon's precise role in the series of Parliamentary acts against dissenters that now bear his name, but it is clear that his support extended only so far. His primary goal was to protect royal authority. After living through the conflict over religion and political prerogative during the 1630s through 1650s, he was determined to operate on the principle of expediency and not risk Charles's head (or his own) for the church. Sometimes this meant advocating religious toleration, and at other times it meant helping to restore the privileged status of the Anglican Church and its ability to suppress nonconformity. Either way, the crown needed to retain ecclesiastical supremacy.[33]

One revealing example of Clarendon's perspective is his 1660 work, *Second Thoughts; or the Case of a Limited Toleration, Stated according to the Present Exigence of Affairs in Church and State.* In it he admitted the desirability of unity and universal conformity in matters of national worship but disagreed that it could reasonably be accomplished by force. A refusal to acknowledge the need for some form of religious toleration stemmed, he said, from a desire to enforce a policy "fit [for] an Utopian Kingdom, not England in its present Condition."[34] Expediency and the peace of the nation dictated allowing liberty of conscience, despite assertions to the contrary. In his own words:

> Perhaps you will say, that a wholesome Violence may Cure
> their Obstinacy, and Reduce them to Obedience, and in time
> make them less Numerous, and so less Dangerous. I answer, that
> Compulsion may bring many Hypocrites, but no real Converts
> into our Church: For Conscience is of so Spiritual a Nature, that
> outward Force can have no Influence, nor Dominion over it . . .
> nothing does more Efficaciously dispose and prepare the Minds of
> Men for Treason and Rebellion than by Force to make them Act
> against their Conscience in matters of Religion.[35]

In fact, Clarendon said, the use of force would only provide additional reasons for nonconformists to doubt the veracity of the English Church. It would also contradict the plain dictates of the Scripture's "Gospel rule" regarding brothers living in sin—they are to be put out and avoided, not forced into the church's company.[36]

Lest he be misunderstood, Clarendon made certain to state that the toleration he envisioned was only "a bare Exemption from Penalties."[37] Dissenters would still have civil disabilities and be excluded from places of public trust. This way, the Presbyterians could still "meet in their Halls, the Fanaticks in their Barns, [and] the Papists in their Garrets," while the "Church of England assembled in her Cathedrals" retained its official status.[38] If the only two options for achieving peace in Restoration England were to stamp out all dissent or to allow nonconformists a tightly limited toleration, Clarendon clearly thought the latter more reasonable.

Yet after the election of the Cavalier Parliament, legalization of the degree of toleration proposed by Clarendon began to look increasingly unlikely, although one of the first bills on the topic was not inconsistent with Clarendon's suggestions. Referred to as the Corporation Act, this bill was passed in late 1661. It asserted that no one "forever hereafter" was to be elected or appointed to any municipal position of public trust who had not taken communion according to the rites of the Anglican Church within the preceding year.[39] These same individuals also had to swear that the Solemn League and Covenant was an "unlawful oath" having "no obligation."[40] The burden fell chiefly on the most conscientious Presbyterians, many of whom held offices as aldermen, town clerks, and "common-councilmen" and could not bring themselves to comply.[41]

While the Corporation Act had limited applicability, the second bill of the Clarendon Code—a new Act of Uniformity to replace the one passed under Elizabeth in 1558—had implications for every English soul. All clergy had to declare their assent to the newly revised Book of Common Prayer upon pain of being deprived of their livings, and no one could preach without first being approved and licensed by either the archbishop of the province or the bishop of the diocese upon pain of three months in jail.[42] Furthermore, no religious ceremonies or even prayers were permitted to be used openly except those prescribed by the Book of Common Prayer.[43] Even education was significantly affected. The universities fell under the act, and everyone from the schoolmaster to the private family tutor was prohibited from teaching England's youth until he had first obtained a license from the proper ecclesiastical authorities.[44]

There is some debate over the number of nonconformists living in England at this time, but it appears that the number was somewhere between a quarter and a half million.[45] About half of these were Presbyterians, and the rest were Independents, Baptists, Quakers, and members of other small sects often collectively referred to as "Fanatics."[46] Although the uniformity bill originated in Parliament, Charles found himself obliged to offer his consent by May 1662. He made some efforts to delay its implementation, but the bishop of London and future archbishop, Gilbert Sheldon, hotly refused on the grounds of inevitable "disorders and disturbances."[47] So shortly thereafter close to a thousand Presbyterian ministers were ejected from their posts in addition to the hundreds who had lost their livings during Charles's first year on the throne.[48]

Also accompanying the Act of Uniformity was a licensing act aimed at those who printed and sold "heretical, schismatical, blasphemous, seditious, and treasonable books, pamphlets, and papers . . . to the high dishonor of Almighty God, endangering the peace of these kingdoms, and raising a disaffection to his most excellent majesty and his government."[49] Nothing could be printed that was contrary to either the doctrine or discipline of the

Church of England, and everything of a remotely religious nature had to be licensed by both the archbishop and the bishop of London. The king's representatives and the officials of the Company of Stationers were empowered to search any house or shop suspected of printing sedition books and seize any persons or papers, then haul them before justices of the peace to be imprisoned until trial.

Another blow to dissenters fell in 1664. The Conventicle Act prohibited anyone over the age of sixteen from meeting in any assembly consisting of five or more who met "under colour or pretence of any exercise of religion, in other manner than according to the liturgy and practice of the Church of England."[50] The first two offenses received the penalties of fines and imprisonment, and the third offence merited banishment. A second Conventicle Act with harsher penalties passed in 1670. By its terms any person guilty of preaching or teaching at a conventicle was to forfeit £20 on the first conviction and £40 on each subsequent one. All local officials were allowed by the act to break into "any house or other place" where they suspected that a conventicle met, and failure to comply had a penalty of £100.[51] And to ensure maximum enforcement, no convictions could be thrown out for procedural faults.[52]

The Five Mile Act of 1665 heaped further restrictions on dissenting ministers who had refused to subscribe to the Act of Uniformity and had been ejected from their livings as a result.[53] Unless they swore an oath not to "take arms against the king," not to "at any time endeavor any alteration of government, either in Church or State," and not to "teach [in] any public or private school," the dissenters could not come within five miles of any city, town, or borough that sent representatives to Parliament.[54]

Refusing to consider any adjustments to the Conventicle Act that would ease the burden on dissenters, Archbishop Gilbert Sheldon instead issued a letter to his "Right Reverend" bishops urging them to ensure that every one of the parsons, vicars, and curates within their jurisdictions punished offenders. The Book of Common Prayer, he reminded them, was to be used "without addition to or diminishing from the same, or varying either in substance or ceremony from the order & method which by the said Book is set down," for the glory of God and welfare of the church and kingdom were at stake:

> If we do our parts now at first seriously, by God's help, and the
> assistance of the Civil Power . . . we shall within a few months see
> so great an alteration in the distractions of these times, as
> that the seduced People returning from their seditious and self-
> seeking Teachers, to the Unity of the Church, and Uniformity of
> God's Worship, it will be to the Glory of God, the welfare of the

Church, the praise of his Majesty and Government, the happiness of the whole Kingdom.

To this declaration, we can imagine, the bishops responded, "Amen."

Bloody Hands

It appears that Clarendon was in league with the king in opposing the dramatic severity of the Act of Uniformity, despite the fact that it is part of the code that bears his name. As he told James Butler, the Duke of Ormonde, and another royal advisor, "The very severe execution of the Act of Uniformity which is resolved on may, I fear, add more fuel to the matter that was before combustible enough. But we are in and must now proceed with steadiness."[55] And proceed with steadiness they did.

The Quakers and Baptists suffered the worst treatment in the days that followed, although Presbyterians and Independents also faced imprisonment.[56] The extent of persecution varied by locality and with time, but it was by no means confined to only a handful of vindictive officials. While it is difficult to estimate with certainty how many were subjected to fines, loss of property, imprisonment, whippings, and even death, some have suggested that upward of fifteen thousand Quakers were "prosecuted by imprisonment or otherwise" in the 1660s through 1680s.[57] Hundreds were banished or met their deaths while in prisons of vile condition.[58] "For refusing to swear, and for meeting together, and for refusing to go to public Worship," one 1663 broadside stated, fifty-four hundred individuals had been imprisoned since the king's arrival in England.[59]

While the unwritten practice since the time of James had generally been that no one was to die for heresy by burning, beheading, or the like, this did not mean that death for the sake of religion was a distant threat. In fact, twelve Baptists were convicted and sentenced to death in 1664 under the 1593 act against sectaries, but they were granted a royal pardon that saved their lives.[60] It was also calculated in 1663 that fifty-six people had died "by reason of imprisonment, and hard and cruel usage" during the previous three years.[61]

The following are typical of standard accounts:

> *Anthony Skillington* being at a meeting of the Lord's people
> on the *13th* of the *5th* month 1662. was by the raid Soldiers taken
> out of the meeting, and brought before *R. Brown*, who sent him to
> prison [?]ole, which is the place they put Felons in after they are
> condemned to die; and there eleven of them remained two nights,
> and then were had out, and put in a stinking hole amongst the

common Felons, and *Anthony* often complained of the bad smell before he fell sick; and by reason of want of air, and such a stinking smell, he and several more fell sick and died; and the Jury that viewed his body, concluded that they did believe his close imprisonment, and the stinking smell, surfeited his body, which was the cause of his death, it being in the heat of summer. . . .

Thomas Birkley, Ben. Bromly, John Witlock, William Snowk, being commited to the White-Lyon prison for meeting to worship God, (with several others) they fell sick for want of air and conveniences to lodge; and in the *9th* month 1662. all died in the prison, and gave up their lives for the Truth's sake.

John Dison, John Wostenholm, and Richard Page, being commited to the White-Lyon Prison for the cause aforesaid with about eighty more, were kept in three little Rooms, where by reason of the closeness of the place, they fell sick; and in a short time, being about the *6th* of the *10th* month, they there finished their testimony by death.[62]

Other testimonies recount Quaker and Baptist congregations being raided and their members gathered up and placed in common jails with the felons, sometimes with one hundred to a room.[63]

The common practice was for armed bands to raid conventicles in homes or elsewhere, break up the meetings, and physically punish the members before sending them to prison if need be. Many had property confiscated from them.[64] Some Baptists in Newgate were meeting during the summer of 1662 when, at about four o'clock, a band broke into the room. One of the raiders picked up a Bible, threw it to the ground, and demanded to know why they met. After some of the Baptists were struck with fists and others held at knifepoint, the rest "escaped their bloody hands." Other Baptists were not as fortunate. One group was placed in prison where the jailers threatened that if they prayed or preached, they "had orders to put [them] into the hole, and that they must do it." Some of the felons housed with them taunted the dissenters with similar threats.[65]

Around the same time a Quaker man from a congregation near London was dragged out of their meeting and beaten to such a degree that his body was "black with bruises, and even rotten, and like a Jelly." He died ten days following the incident, and a coroner was called, who summoned a jury to examine the evidence to determine whether the blows were the cause of the man's death. The doctor present testified that they undoubtedly were, but the jury refused to give their verdict on the evidence. The author of the account supposed that their hesitancy was due to the thought that if no one person could be held responsible, the whole city would be liable and risk the displeasure of the king, who was known to be "an enemy in nature to Capital and sanguinary punishments, upon the account of matters of conscience or Religion."[66]

Since the Quakers carried "neither sword nor staff," one wonders why bands were armed and sent on horseback to break up their meetings. A Colchester mayor named William More repeatedly reprimanded a congregation for holding meetings, disbanding the members and sometimes imprisoning them. When the Quakers still determined to meet together, the mayor employed an old man to prevent the Quakers from going to their meeting chamber. Knowing he had no warrant and "was no officer," the Quakers continued their practice until

> upon the 5. of the 10. month, came the troop to this town, and on the 6. day came about 40. of them to the Meeting on horseback in their Armor; and Armed with Swords, Carbines and Pistols, crying, *what a Divel do ye here*, and having their swords drawn, some with swords and others with Carbines did lay on upon old and young, both men and women, until many were exceedingly bruised . . . and in their armor as before they knocked down many in the street in such sort as some lay as dead men, and diverse left their blood on the place, and many had their flesh so bruised, and their Limbs so dissembled as they could not get off their clothes . . . and one trooper beat a Friend with his drawn sword till the blade fell out of the Hilt, which when the friend saw, he said, *I will give it to thee again*, and so giving it to the soldier, said, *I desire the Lord may not lay this day's work to thy charge.*[67]

Other accounts—of jury trials, in particular—are reminiscent of those in Foxe's *Book of Martyrs*. Some of the accused were goaded to incriminate themselves and were denied other basic rights of Englishmen, even by justices of the King's Bench at the Old Bailey in London.[68] This injustice prompted one "Prisoner for the Testimony of Jesus" to write:

> *Ninescore* Prisoners, in *Newgate* now doth lie,
> For Justice, Justice, there aloud do cry;
> Besides many Gaols, in *England* round about,
> God's Heritage are Prisoners without doubt.
> Most Poor, and from our Wives and Children rended,
> And here abus'd, when we should be defended.
> And when unto the Bar we there did come,
> Looking for Justice, but yet finding none,

We call'd to see accusers, face to face,
But met with Violence, to your disgrace.[69]

While most of the persecuted suffered for participating in religious assemblies rather than for heresy, others were indicted on the latter charge. One Benjamin Keach was arraigned in 1664 for publishing a small book called *The Child's Instructor: or, A New and Easy Primer*, all copies of which were seized by the magistrate. Keach was called "a seditious, heretical, and schismatical person, evilly and maliciously disposed" because of his "*damnable positions*, contrary to the Book of Common Prayer and the liturgy of the Church of England" regarding infant baptism.[70] When he was found guilty, Keach was sent to jail without bail and had to stand in the pillory with a sign on his head declaring his offence while his book was burnt in his presence.[71]

The Papists Incognito

Did Charles II ever stand up for the dissenters? Sometimes he did; sometimes he refused. If we are to believe his contemporary Gilbert Burnet, the king thought "an implicitness in religion is necessary for the safety of the government" and saw "all inquisitiveness into these things as mischievous to the state."[72] Another author has said that he "regarded the sects with patrician disdain: they showed what happened when the poor and ignorant were allowed to read the Bible."[73]

Nevertheless, Charles did take some actions early in his reign that showed some measure of pity for nonconformists and were unrelated to his perceived sympathy toward Catholics. As noted earlier, he pardoned three Baptists convicted to death under the Elizabethan Parliament's Act to Retain the Queen's Subjects in Obedience. Charles also issued a proclamation in May 1661 in which he pardoned and ordered the release of all Quakers who had been imprisoned under the Act for the Discovering and Repressing of Popish Recusants from the time of James I, an act mandating the taking of oaths of obedience from Charles I's reign, the royal proclamation against conventicles (intended only for the seditious), or "for any matter referring to their Opinions, or scruples of Conscience."[74] When "several societies" of Baptists from Lincoln petitioned the king because of their imprisonment for refusal to "conform to the Church of England as . . . established," Charles replied that "there should be a speedy and effectual Course taken for the Releasement of Them in Lincolnshire, and the rest throughout the Nation."[75]

Charles was ill at ease with the Act of Uniformity and its accompanying legislation, so he tried to rectify matters in December 1662 through a Declaration of Indulgence. It requested that Parliament enact policies to ease the burden on dissenters by permitting Protestant nonconformists to worship in public with appropriate licenses. Even more controversially, he suggested that Catholics be able to worship, too—provided they did so in private. Parliament reacted with such antagonism to the scheme that Charles was forced to accept its defeat. Members of Parliament cited the tendency of toleration to create schism and endanger the "peace of the kingdom" and made clear to the king that the Act of Uniformity had overruled any promises contained in the Breda Declaration.[76]

A decade later, however, in 1672, the king tried issuing another Declaration of Indulgence that not only promoted tolerance for dissenters but also declared the crown—and not Parliament—to be the "supreme power in ecclesiastical matters."[77] The declaration attributed the "sad experience" of the previous twelve years to the use of coercion in religious matters, which had been shown to be fruitless in promoting the peace of the kingdom. Even though Charles made certain to emphasize that the Church of England would remain the standard of orthodoxy by law and that dissenting preachers and places still had to be licensed, the proposed suspension of all penal laws in ecclesiastical matters made many suspicious. In retrospect it was not unreasonable to question the king's motives.

As it turns out, perhaps the single largest factor that prompted Charles to issue the declaration did indeed have to do with Catholicism—at least in a foreign policy context. The latter half of the 1660s had found England embroiled in an expensive war with the Dutch that resulted in a humiliating defeat for the British. Although England was party to a 1668 alliance with Sweden and the Netherlands to oppose French expansion under Louis XIV, the alliance was negotiated under complex circumstances at home and abroad; and by May 1670, Charles had allied himself with France instead. According to the terms of the secret Treaty of Dover with Louis, Charles was to join in an attack on the Dutch and publicly announce that he had converted to Catholicism. France, for its part, would provide subsidies.

The treaty provision regarding the king's conversion declaration was quietly ignored (and, in fact, did not become public during his lifetime). Instead, it seems, Charles hoped to satisfy France by issuing his Declaration of Indulgence in March 1672. He declared war on the Netherlands two days later, and Louis did the same after three weeks.

Meanwhile, religious dissenters at home were taking advantage of the generous terms of Charles's declaration. More than sixteen hundred dissenting ministers received licenses to preach; homes were approved as nonconformist meeting places; numerous individuals who had been imprisoned for religious offenses received royal pardons, John Bunyan included.[78] Yet this liberality was not to be long-lived. No Parliament had been in session at the time when the declaration was issued, so it was unable to respond until almost a year later. At the start of the new session, when Charles announced his resolution to "stick by [his] Declaration," the Commons promptly retorted, "We find ourselves bound in duty to inform your majesty that penal statutes in matters ecclesiastical cannot be suspended but by act of Parliament."[79]

Before long Charles gave up on sticking by his declaration. On March 8, 1673, "adorned with his crown and regal ornaments," he made a short speech and rescinded it instead.[80] Yet Parliament was not content to rest with this concession and proceeded to hammer out the provisions of a Test Act to ensure that only those who took oaths of supremacy and allegiance, received the Lord's Supper in a local parish church in accordance with the rites of the Church of England, and disclaimed transubstantiation could hold most civil and military offices. Parliament was simultaneously considering a bill to provide some limited relief to Protestant dissenters, indicating its willingness to flex a bit from its earlier intractable Anglicanism, but it could countenance neither allowing potential inroads to popery nor permitting the king to set a precedent of exercising power in the manner he had attempted.

The fear of the return of Catholic dominance lay behind much of the opposition to religious toleration—which could not be justified by any reasonable projection that the country's tiny minority of Catholics might gain ascendancy. The common tenor is aptly captured in the title of a 1673 book by one Anglican divine: *Popery manifested, or, the Papist incognito made known*. England's Catholics were no longer a significant force in themselves, but unlike the Protestant dissenters, there were continental powers who might well have come to their aid.[81] Seething anti-Catholic hysteria had come to the surface in 1666 when the Great Fire of London destroyed the city—13,200 homes and eighty-seven churches were consumed, including St. Paul's Cathedral—and Catholics received the brunt of the blame, almost certainly unfairly.

Charles therefore not only gave his assent to the Test Act but also made peace with the Dutch. This latter concession was significant in that it was the reasonable belief of some that Louis XIV was determined to overcome Protestantism militarily and had enlisted Charles's assistance for this purpose.[82] Many Englishmen considered their nation one of the last holdouts against a devastating tide of Romanism that threatened liberty, Protestant Christianity, and all else worth defending.[83]

Renewed discussion of popery followed in the wake of the Test Act and continued to escalate when James, Duke of York, the king's brother and heir presumptive, resigned from his governmental office before the act was to take effect. This removed any lingering doubts of James's religious convictions. It did not help matters when, in the same year, he married Mary of Modena, an Italian Catholic. (His first wife, Anne Hyde, had died in 1671.) If the Catholic couple were to produce a son, he would follow James in the line of succession since Charles had no legitimate male heirs.

Numerous Catholics included in the king's ministry were now displaced and supplanted by resolute Anglicans. As for Clarendon, he had not been in the picture since 1667, when he had been driven into lifelong exile. Among other perceived offenses, he had served as a convenient scapegoat for the disastrous war with the Dutch.

Charles now associated himself with the antitoleration, antidissenter, and anti-Catholic Earl of Danby as his chief minister in an effort to bolster his Protestant image. A royal proclamation entitled "the True Religion Established" was even issued in February 1675 that ordered all English-born Jesuits and Catholic priests to leave the country and never return.[84] All of these factors sharpened hostility and formed odd and shifting alliances between political "parties" that were still largely divided along religious lines.[85] "Fanatics" closed ranks with or distanced themselves from Catholics; the crown appeared alternately either the friend or foe of uncompromising Anglicanism. The advocates of religious toleration were frequently inconsistent, Charles not the least among them.

Even the liberal philosopher John Locke and his pro-tolerationist patron, the Earl of Shaftesbury, placed dissenting English Catholics in an entirely different category from their Protestant counterparts.[86] Locke's views were not nearly as tolerant as those of the Baptists and Quakers, who advocated a pure theory of religious liberty and included the dreaded Catholics, Turks, infidels, and atheists.

The period of anti-Catholicism inaugurated by the first Test Act paved the way for the adoption of a second more stringent one in 1678. The immediate context for the implementation of the latter was the "Popish Plot," which involved tales of a supposed Jesuit plot to kill Charles and place his Catholic brother on the throne. Legislative attempts to exclude James and his heirs from the monarchy met with final failure when Charles dissolved the Parliament in 1681. It never met again during his reign.

In the streets the pope was burned in effigy on numerous occasions, and Jesuit priests were imprisoned and executed.[87] A panic mode similar to that of the Laudian days kept England on the verge of crisis. In the words of one ballad of the day, written on the occasion of a burning of "several Cart-loads of Popish Books":

As once proud Haman with a curs'd Decree,
Had sign'd God's peoples General Destiny,
So cruel factors now of Hell and ROME,
Resolved on England's universal Doom.
But Heaven's bright Eye Reveal'd the Hellish PLOT,
Which had it prosper'd, boldly might have shot
At the Celestial Throne, put out the Sun,
And made the World back to its Chaos run.[88]

On the same theme, William Prynne's work on "The grand designs of the papists" was reprinted with a typical warning to the reader: "The Papist and Fanatick are of contrary Factions, Interests, and Inclinations; yet it is natural enough, that they may both conspire (though with a different intent) to promote and carry on the very same design."[89]

The Ascendance of James II

The victim of sudden kidney failure, Charles II breathed his last in February 1685 after making a deathbed confession of Catholicism and receiving the sacrament from a priest. He exhibited no desire to claim the throne for any of his illegitimate sons by numerous mistresses, and so James assumed the throne. The great fear had become reality: England once again had a Catholic king.

James II was unlike his brother in many ways, but the Stuart penchant for committing authoritarian constitutional travesties in seeming good faith and alienating former allies remained the standard operating procedure. James had no intention of hiding his Catholicism—the earliest masses of his reign were held at Whitehall with the chapel doors flung open—but he appeared ready to cooperate with the royalists. At minimum, James's ascendency promised more stability than would have been possible under another of questionable legitimacy. These same royalists, however, were also largely the most committed Anglicans, so the two parties did not make a happy match.

The inevitable tension was released following an uprising in June designed to replace James by Charles II's illegitimate Protestant son, the Duke of Monmouth. Although the rebellion was suppressed and Monmouth beheaded, the aftermath put James on the road to confrontation with Parliament over the Test Act and his insistence that Catholic officers be allowed to serve him militarily—flatly contrary to Parliament's desires. With fresh confidence drawn from the victory, James II began to purge his government of opposition and replace them with acknowledged Catholics.

In the context of contemporary European events, this move had fearful implications. Among other considerations, Louis XIV had recently revoked the Edict of Nantes, and the law that had allowed French Protestants to live in relative safety for nearly nine decades was giving way to bitter persecution and religious conflict. The Huguenots—French Calvinists—were now subject to slaughter.

James also began to exercise a hand in church matters by forming a "commission for ecclesiastical causes." When this commission refused to replace the late president and faculty of Magdalen College with loyalists and subjected them to deprivations instead, James began to consider the church as a rather uncooperative support.[90] Instead—and ironically—he turned to the dissenters instead and followed in his brother's footsteps by issuing a Declaration of Indulgence in April 1687.

James's version of the declaration stated his preference for Catholicism, suspended all penal laws for religious nonconformity, gave allowance for dissenting private *and* public worship, and abolished religious tests for office-holders. But the declaration also made the usual pledge that the Church of England would remain protected by law. He stated in no uncertain terms that "conscience ought not to be constrained nor people forced in matters of mere religion."[91] James's stated justification, however, was purely pragmatic and bore little resemblance to the many biblically based arguments for religious liberty that had gone before; in his own words, force "never obtained the end for which it was employed" and, rather, destroyed government "by despoiling trade, depopulating countries, and discouraging strangers."[92]

Ignoring anti-Catholic sentiment and the efforts on the parts of some churchmen to woo the dissenters to their side by offering alternatives, James reissued the declaration a year later but added the further requirement that the declaration be read on set dates from all churches. His attempt to shatter the unity of the Protestants backfired, and the bishops reached agreement with the dissenters to oppose the declaration on procedural grounds—that is, James's shameless misuse of royal prerogative.[93] Those who sided with James—including William Penn, the founder of Pennsylvania—were only a minority.[94]

One of the most influential individuals at the time was the distinguished and experienced George Savile, the Marquis of Halifax. Halifax has been described as among the "least 'hysterical'" men, who chose his sides on specific questions carefully and managed to hold positions in Parliament and in the ministries of three English monarchs.[95] Although he fought vigorously against the Test Acts and the exclusion bills, he disagreed strongly with James's declaration and took it upon himself to warn Anglicans and dissenters in writing against either complying with James's order to read the declaration in churches or taking advantage of its benefits.

Halifax urged dissenters not to rejoice in finding a supposed ally in the king but rather reflect on his ministry's "first Courtships to the Church of England" which were abandoned not on principle but because the church failed to give them what they wanted.[96] "This Alliance," he wrote, "between *Liberty* and *Infallibility*, is bringing together the Two most contrary things that are in the world. . . . Think a little how dangerous it is to build upon a Foundation of Paradoxes."[97] Although Halifax did not voice opposition to the substance of the declaration, he emphasized the illegality of it and cautioned against supporting the breach of one law, lest they "lose the Right of Complaining the breach of all the rest."[98]

With the same political savvy with which he addressed the nonconformists, Halifax also appealed to the Anglican bishops. Reading the declaration publicly, he said, would be like opening their church doors to popery and allowing it to enter at its leisure. If they personally disagreed with the grant of Indulgence, reading it would nevertheless imply "interpretative consent":

> It is to teach an unlimited and universal Toleration, which the Parliament in 72. declared illegal, and which has been condemned by the Christian Church in all Ages. . . . It is to teach my People, that they need never come to Church more, but have my free leave, as they have the King's to go to a Conventicle, or to Mass: It is to teach the dispensing power, which alters, what has been formerly thought, the whole Constitution of this Church and Kingdom: which we dare not do, will we have the Authority of Parliament for it.[99]

Even if "unlimited and universal Toleration" could not be countenanced, Halifax recognized that the bishops as a whole had become more ready and willing to accept limited toleration but not in the manner James had prescribed without hazarding church and state:

> I am sure that tho we were never so desirous that they might have their Liberty, (and when there is opportunity of showing our inclinations without danger, they may find that we are not such Persecutors as we are represented) yet we cannot consent that they should have it this way, which they will find the dearest Liberty that ever was granted.[100]

Halifax argued that Parliament and convocation—not a Catholic king *uno solo*—could provide the lasting liberty the dissenters wanted.

A Letter Concerning Toleration

Some Anglican clergy disagreed with Halifax's assessment and argued that because it was not by all means certain that "this command [of the king's] be altogether unlawful," it would be wrong to disobey the clear command of the king, especially since he appeared to be acting in sincerity by outlawing the persecution of what he considered to be truth.[101] As one minister put it, "Have we robbed the Bishop of Rome of all his Infallibility? . . . I think no man will say, that the King ought in the execution of such laws, to sin against his conscience."[102]

Around the same time this debate over the declaration was occurring in the press, John Locke was in Holland preparing his thoughts in a pamphlet later known as *A Letter Concerning Toleration*. Regardless of the questionable orthodoxy of some of Locke's other works, his arguments for religious liberty in the *Letter* would prove a far cry from the pragmatic arguments popular in his day—perhaps closer in line of reasoning, in some respects, to the pleas of Leveller William Walwyn than to contemporary philosophers like Baruch Spinoza.[103]

To make his case, Locke drew from familiar arguments: the nature of the true church, the dissimilarity between external conformity and true worship, and the arrogance of framing coercive articles of faith on matters based on interpretation rather than the clear dictates of Scripture. He defined a particular church as "a voluntary Society of Men, joining themselves together of their own accord, in order to the public worshipping of God, in such a manner as they judge acceptable to him, and effectual to the salvation of their souls."[104] No one is truly part of any church by virtue of heredity, he wrote; rather, the basis of membership is belief:

> Someone perhaps may object, that no such Society can be said to be a true Church, unless it have in it a Bishop, or Presbyter, with Ruling authority derived from the very Apostles, and continued down unto the present times by uninterrupted Succession. To these I answer: *In the first place*, Let them show me the Edict by which Christ has imposed that Law upon his Church. And let not any man think me impertinent if in a thing of this consequence, I require that the Terms of that Edict be very express and positive. For the Promise he has made us, that *wheresoever two or three are gathered together in his Name, he will be in the midst of them*, seems to imply the contrary.[105]

Would it not be more consistent with the church of Christ, Locke asked rhetorically, to make the "conditions of her Communion consist in such things, and such things only, as the Holy Spirit has in the Holy Scriptures declared, in express Words, to be necessary to Salvation" rather than deductions from Scripture that "Lutherans, Calvinists, Remonstrants, Anabaptists, and other Sects" disagree on?[106]

The crisis in the Church of England over public reading of James's declaration came to a head when the royalist archbishop joined six other bishops in petitioning the king and refusing to comply "because that declaration is founded upon such a dispensing power as hath been often declared illegal in the years 1662 and 1672"—the years of Charles II's declarations of indulgence—"and in the beginning of your majesty's reign," when James issued his first declaration.[107] The petitioners were arrested on June 8, 1688, and put on trial for libel at the King's Bench. Even though James had tried to arrange a court favorable to his likings, he did not have a majority, and the bishops were declared not guilty by the end of the month. The majority concurred that "if there be no such dispensing power in the king, then that can be no libel which they presented to the king, which says that the declaration, being founded upon such a pretended power, is illegal."[108]

The rift in relations between the church and crown had become a gaping breach—with religious toleration being one of the chief catalysts.

The Toleration Act

On the same June day that the seven bishops were acquitted, seven prominent Englishmen sent an invitation to William of Orange, grandson of Charles I and son-in-law of James II, to intervene. A confluence of factors influenced William's decision to accept, but chief among these were undoubtedly the rising fear of an Anglo-French alliance against the Netherlands (assuming that James II and Louis XIV were in cahoots) and reports that James's Catholic wife had given birth to a son earlier in the month. This young prince would almost certainly be raised a Catholic and presumably inherit the throne instead of his older Protestant stepsister Mary, William's wife.

By November 1688, William had arrived in England with his armed forces. By December James had escaped to France. By January a new Parliament had been elected and soon thereafter determined that James had abdicated and declared William III and Mary II joint sovereigns of England. The story of this "Glorious Revolution" has been awash in interpretations and controversies for more than three centuries, but it would never have happened had not James and his "evil counselors" attempted to return England to Catholicism, even if by means of liberty of conscience. As Halifax recognized and William himself acknowledged, the situation both in England

and abroad demanded Protestant unity—and hence a moderate degree of toleration since the dissenters had made clear that they were not going to go away.[109] William proposed that the best means of doing this would be for Parliament to repeal the Test Act and religious penal laws; it would be an "expedient" suitable to the needs of the moment.

Immediately after William and Mary were crowned, Parliament began to debate bills for comprehension and toleration. The comprehension bill that might have brought Presbyterian dissenters back into the established church failed to pass the Commons. Any revisions to the prayer book would have had to be approved by convocation, and neither the Anglican nor the Presbyterian clergy were willing to make the changes that would have been necessary for mutual agreement.[110] Consistent with his opinion of religious tests, William told Parliament, "I doubt not but you will sufficiently provide against papists, so, I hope, you will leave room for the admission of all Protestants that are willing and able to serve. This conjunction in my service will tend to the better uniting you among yourselves, and the strengthening against your common adversaries."[111] But many in Parliament disagreed.

In the end the Toleration Bill that was finally approved by the king was really nothing dramatically new in English history; especially when compared to Cromwell's and even James II's grants of toleration, the Act for Exempting Their Majesties' Protestant Subjects Dissenting from the Church of England from the Penalties of Certain Laws seemed inferior if examined solely on the merits of religious liberty. The major difference was that it bore an incontrovertible stamp of legality from both Parliament and the king.

By the terms of the Toleration Act, the Test Act remained in place along with the whole of the Anglican Church establishment, tithes and ecclesiastical courts included. Dissenting congregations still had to be licensed by a bishop or archdeacon and were required to leave their doors unlocked when they worshipped corporately. Dissenting ministers had to subscribe to the Thirty-Nine Articles, but exceptions to certain articles were admissible, such as those on infant baptism, the traditions of the church, and the consecration of ministers. Quakers also were encompassed by the act, so long as they "sincerely promised and solemnly declared" their belief in the Trinity and the divine inspiration of the Scriptures. On a less generous note, the provisions of the act were specifically denied to "any papist or popish recusant whatsoever" and anyone who denied the Trinity.[112]

Regardless of William's personal opinions, the religious toleration embodied in the act was crafted more out of necessity than principle and a far cry from what most dissenters likely envisioned as desirable. Yet it was nonetheless consistent with the essence of why William and Mary had been invited to take the throne: the restoration and maintenance of England's "laws, liberties, and customs established" that James had proven so adept at subverting by means of "arbitrary and despotic power."[113] Even the coat of arms inscribed above William's declaration regarding his reasons for appearing in England in arms bore testimony to this purpose, the upper inscription being "PROT RELIGION AND LIBERTY" and the lower being a phrase in French meaning "I will maintain." True liberty could not yet be "maintained" since it had not yet been established, but a significant step had indeed been taken.

PART II

AN IRREPRESSIBLE YEARNING

Chapter Seventeen

ENCLOSED GARDENS
OF GOD

The Impossible Dreams of Virginia

---

*The company knew not how to control the members
composing the colony but by religion and law. They
exercised a despotism in both.*

WILLIAM HENRY FOOTE

he Disney film *Pocahontas* depicts the Virginia countryside awaiting the Jamestown settlers in 1607 as an idyllic setting with open vistas,
impossibly beautiful waterfalls, and the romance of a new world beckoning
to all in search of adventure and liberation of the human spirit.

Such thoughts would have been totally foreign to the English settlers of
Virginia—and not just because such waterfalls are impossible in Tidewater
Virginia, where the land is flat and swampy. The settlers' vision for Virginia
was idyllic in their minds, to be sure, but their dreams seem unusually constrained to us today. Their ideal was not a farmstead in a peaceful valley
bordered by mountains but a walled garden in a well-governed town. Nor
was their aspiration for political or religious liberty for the individual soul
but, rather, for ceremonial and doctrinal uniformity rigorously enforced by
a magistrate chosen by the hereditary monarch.

Less than fifty years after the first ship landed at Jamestown, one pastor expressed the hope that "the poor Church (whose plants now grow wilde in that Wildernesse)" would "become like a garden enclosed."[1] Such vineyards would be founded as "the promised fruits of well ordered Towns, under Religious Pastours and Magistrates" which would produce "comely and most ingenious Children like the hopefull plants growing up in Nurseries of learning and piety, and when their time of fruit is come, Transplanted into the enclosed gardens of God, and becoming fruitfull and useful trees of righteousnesse; which is the promised happiness and benefit of well ordered Schooles, in well governed Towns."[2]

In the original charter of Virginia, issued in April 1606, King James I set the tone for such dreams of a religious and utopian settlement:

> We, greatly commending, and graciously accepting of, their
> Desires for the Furtherance of so noble a Work, which may, by
> the Providence of Almighty God, hereafter tend to the Glory of
> his Divine Majesty, in propagating of Christian Religion to such
> People, as yet live in Darkness and miserable Ignorance of the
> true Knowledge and Worship of God, and may in time bring the
> Infidels and Savages, living in those Parts, to human Civility,
> and to a settled and quiet Government, DO, by these our Letters
> Patents, graciously accept of, and agree to, their humble and well-
> intended Desires.[3]

The charter reveals that the English version of the American dream included a clear purpose to bring Christianity to the native population. However, the first words from these "missionaries" to the "infidels and savages" were peculiar if they truly hoped to reach the natives for the cause of Christ; the landing party flatly lied about their purposes. Captain John Smith and others told the local chief, Powhatan, that the English did not intend to settle in Virginia, that they had merely been driven ashore in an attempt to escape a Spanish squadron. Smith reported that Christopher Newport had returned to England to bring back a ship with the help needed to carry the surviving members of the party back home to England.[4]

Decades later one English pastor described a plan for conversion of the Native Americans that seems far more intent on making Englishmen than on creating disciples of Jesus. The pastor decried the "general want of Schooles" which "renders a very numerous generation of Christians' Children born in Virginia (who naturally are of beautiful and comely Persons) . . . unservice-able for any great Employments either in Church or State." Moreover, he defined "the conversion of the Heathen" as:

winning the Heathen to bring in their Children to be taught
and instructed in our Schooles, together with the Children of
Christians. For as it is the Beauty and Glory of Christian Graces,
shining in the lives of Christians, which must make the Heathen
that are men, in love with the Christian Religion; so it is that love,
which can only perswade them to bring in their Children to be
taught and instructed in it.[5]

Once the natives peered over the walls of the "enclosed gardens of God,"
such men reasoned, how could they do anything other than embrace the
society and religion that produced such cultured beauty? The fact that the
English expected complete uniformity of doctrine and practice was thought
to be a mark of culture that would help entice native converts. As one author
wrote:

The Heathen coming in among them, and beholding the
comely order and beauty of their holy worship, perceiving their
unanimity and uniformity in the same faith and worship of the
same God, were so convinced of all and judged of all, that the
secrets of their hearts were made manifest, and they fell down
upon their faces and worship'd God, and confessed that God was
in them of a Truth.[6]

These were expressions of an unrealized dream, not a fulfilled reality.

Despite these repeated declarations of a religious purpose in the founding of the colony, today it is common to view the settlement of Virginia as
essentially nonreligious—a mere secular, commercial endeavor. It was true,
of course, that Virginia was not settled by those seeking to establish religious liberty. For that matter the Massachusetts Puritans were not seeking
religious liberty either, but no one today questions the religiosity of that
northern settlement, founded in 1620. The Puritans, as we will see in a later
chapter, indeed sought religious sanctuary for themselves, but they sought
doctrinal purity and uniformity in a true Genevan spirit, not religious liberty for all. Virginia and Massachusetts differed in some of the particulars
of their doctrinal positions, just as the Puritans and Anglicans differed back
in England. And the trip across the Atlantic did little to change the religious
and political philosophy of either group. Both sets of churchmen steadfastly
believed in compelled religious uniformity, no matter on which side of the
Atlantic they took their stand.

Indeed, the first laws of Virginia in 1610 and 1611 included numerous
coercive religious obligations:

- "Captaines and Officers" were to "have a care that the Almightie God bee duly and daily served, and that they call upon their people to hear Sermons, as that also they diligently frequent Morning and Evening prayer themselves . . . and that such, who shall often and willfully absent themselves, be duly punished according to martial law in that case provided."
- Speaking impiously or maliciously against the Father, Son, or Spirit was punishable by death.
- Derision of God's Word was punishable by death.
- Demeaning any preacher or minister required that the offender "openly be whipt three times, and ask publike forgivenesse in the assembly of the congregation three several Saboth Daies."
- Failing to attend daily services resulted in a loss of daily allowances of food for the first offense, a whipping for the second offense, and for the third offense to be condemned to the "gallies" for "six Moneths."[7]

The ability to guarantee religious uniformity was materially aided by section 33 of these original laws. Every person then in the colony, as well as each new arrival, was required to "repaire unto the Minister, that by his conference with them, he may understand, and gather, whether heretofore they have beene sufficiently instructed, and catechized in the principles and grounds of Religion." Those who needed additional instruction were required to continue to report to the minister. Failure to do so resulted in being "whipt" for the first offense, being whipped twice for the second offense, and, for the third offense, the whippings were to continue every day until the offender relented.[8]

Interestingly, these laws also contained what might be called America's first prohibition of "hate speech":

> No man shall give any disgraceful words, or commit any act
> to the disgrace of any person in this Colonie, or any part thereof,
> upon paine of being tied head and feete together, upon the guard
> everie night for the space of one moneth, besides to bee publikely
> disgraced himselfe, and be made incapable ever after to possesse
> any place, or execute any office in this imployment.[9]

These original Virginia acts of religious coercion were adopted in the emergency conditions that were the life-and-death struggle to settle the swampy environs of the James River. But the colony's coercive tactics and those in place in James I's England differed only in the details, not in basic philosophy.

From the beginning, the Virginia church was driven by the notion that "theire bee a uniformitie throughout this colony both in substance and circumstance to the cannons and constitution of the church of England as neere as may bee,"[10] although it was not until the laws of 1631–32 that this language was formally adopted by the House of Burgesses, the lower house of Virginia's Grand or General Assembly. Yet one central difference between English and Virginian Anglicanism would prove to be enormously important: The Virginia church had no ruling bishops, depriving it of the defining characteristic of episcopacy. Ecclesiastical laws were thus made not by the Convocation of England, composed of an assembly of governing bishops, but by the elected officials of the people with the required approval of the governor, who was initially employed by the proprietary company that controlled the colony but was appointed directly by the king after 1624.

Perhaps the most telling picture of religion in the earliest years of Virginia comes from a description by the secretary and recorder of the colony under the Baron De La Warre, who would come to be known as Lord Delaware and who governed Virginia from 1610 until his death in 1618. Orders were given to repair the local church, which was to have "a Chancell in it of Cedar, and a Communion Table of Black Walnut, and all the pews of Cedar, with faire broad windowes":

> It is so cast as to be very light within, and the Lord Governour and Captain Generall doth cause it to be kept sweete, and trimmed up with divers flowers. . . . Every Sunday wee have Sermons twice a day, and every Thursday a Sermon, having true preachers, which take their weekly turnes. . . . Every Sunday, when the Lord Governour and Captain Generall goeth to Church, hee is accompanied with all the Counsailers, Captaines, other officers and all the Gentlemen, with a guard of Holberdiers, in his Lordship's Liverey, faire red cloakes, to the number of fifty both on each side, and behind him: and being in the Church, his Lordship hath his seat in the Quier, in a greene velvet chair.[11]

Outside the church, with its cedar and flowers and red cloaks and green velvet chairs, the people of Virginia continued to die at a catastrophic rate from disease, starvation, and the occasional Indian attack. How much true comfort the church's showy ceremonies brought to these desperate souls can never be known.

Augustine and the "Savages"

Virginia's first set of laws called for fair treatment for Native Americans. It said, "No man shall rifle or dispoile, by force or violence, take away any thing from any Indian coming to trade, or otherwise, upon paine of death."[12]

The protection provided for in this law was not based on an inherent understanding that the natives were equals of the English, for it was common for the English to view them as barbarian savages comparable to "brute beastes."[13] Yet it was the duty of gentlemen to treat those of more humble station appropriately and in a magnanimous spirit. This spirit of benevolent condescension was clearly manifested in the early attitudes about the prospect for the natives' religious conversion. One leader of the Virginia effort promised to convert the natives to Christianity by "faire and loving meanes,"[14] while an early English pamphlet promoting the Virginia colony called upon the good character of the English to treat the natives well:

> In Virginia the people are savage and incredibly rude, they worship the devil, offer their young children in sacrifice unto him, wander by and down like beasts, having no Art, nor science, nor trade, to employ themselves, or give themselves unto, yet by nature loving and gentle, and desirous to embrace a better condition. Oh how happy were that man which could reduce this people from brutishness, to civility, to religion, to Christianity, to the saving of their souls: happy is that man and blessed of God, to whom God hath endued, either with means or will to attempt this business, but far be it from the nature of the English, to exercise any bloody cruelty among these people; far be it from the hearts of the English, to give them occasion, that the holy name of God should be dishonored among the Infidels, or that in the plantation of that continent, they should give any cause to the world to say that they sought the wealth of that country above or before the glory of God, and the propagation of his kingdom.[15]

Yet these noble sentiments were met by contrary and violent views:

> Moreover, all politicians do with one consent, hold and maintain, that a Christian king may lawfully make war upon a barbarous and savage people, and such as live under no lawful or warrantable government, and may make a conquest of them, so that the war be undertaken to this end, to reclaim and reduce those savages from their barbarous kind of life, and from their brutish and ferine manners, to humanity, piety, and honesty. . . . Saint

Augustine for proof hereof, whose words are these: . . . Those
people are vanquished to their unspeakable profit and gain. . . .
And the same Saint Augustine hath another golden saying to this
purpose: . . . Amongst the true worshippers of God, even that war
is lawful which is undertaken, not for covetousness and cruelty,
but for peace and unity's sake; so that lewd and wicked men may
thereby be suppressed and good men maintained and relieved.[16]

The Native Americans stood condemned under this second view. They
were uncivilized. They had no recognizable government—that is, no government that looked like those of Europe. Thus it was considered by many
altogether just to wage war on such brutes to "reclaim and reduce" them
from their barbarity. And it was none other than Saint Augustine's maxims
that were employed to justify a deadly war against a native population—not
as a defensive measure but as an aggressive tactic designed to rid the land of
the "lewd and wicked." Just as his writings had been employed to sanction
the execution of heretics, Augustine was again employed to provide religious
sanction for the violent coercion of those who differed from the established
church and cultured nations.

But which voice would prevail? The one proclaiming "far be it from the
English" to employ bloody cruelty? Or the one citing Augustine as sanction
for an offensive war conducted for the "good" of the savages? It is important
to note that these two passages—one advocating kindly *noblesse oblige* and the
other advocating noble cruelty—are actually from the same pamphlet. This
dichotomy of thought was typical of an English establishment that was intel-
lectually schizophrenic.[17] In the end the historical record is, unfortunately,
replete with examples that "Jamestown's early colonists made more use of the
sword than the olive branch."[18]

The initial phony story that the colonists were simply awaiting a ship to
rescue them grew thin after a time. In August 1607, a leader of the colony
sent a message to Britain that the natives had treated their men well "until
they found they begann to plant and fortefye, then they fell to skirmishing
and kylled 3 of our people."[19] The tribes led by Powahatan continued to
undertake a series of raids and skirmishes that were apparently designed to
"starve [the settlers] and drive them out."[20] One Indian tactic was to capture
those engaged in exploration of their interior lands. The famous rescue of
John Smith by Pocahontas was the result of one such capture. Yet the English
response could not fairly be described as mere acts of self-defense.

The actions of John Smith are particularly noteworthy:

> On one occasion, he seized Opechancanough, leader of the
> Pamunkey tribe and half-brother of Powhatan, by the hair. "You

promised to fraught my Ship [with corn] ere I departed, and so you shall, or I meane to load her with your dead carkases," he threatened. A few weeks later, Smith grappled with another chief, dragged him into a nearby river, and almost drowned him. He spared the Indian, however, when "having drawne his faucheon to cut off his head, seeing how pittifully he begged his life, he led him prisoner to Iames Towne, and put him in chaynes." Such tactics prevented open warfare. They did not promote cordiality or conversion.[21]

The second wave of colonial leaders, which included George Percy, Thomas Gates, and Thomas Dale, proved even more brutal during the years 1610 to 1614. Provoked by the natives' unfamiliar tactics of war, the colonials lost all pretense of restraint:

> Gates lured some Indians into the open with a music-and-dance act by his drummer, then slaughtered them. Percy routed the Paspahegh tribe, destroyed its village and fields, and allowed his men to throw the Indian queen's children into the river and shoot out their brains for sport. Lord de la Warr wanted to burn the queen; Percy convinced him to let her die by the sword instead.[22]

Even so, a period of relative peace followed the marriage between John Rolfe and Pocahontas. Her conversion to Christianity sparked a desire among the settlers to build schools for the education of Native American youth. Funds were raised and efforts to recruit students were reflected in the laws of 1619, which again noted more noble aims:

> For laying a surer foundation of the conversion of the Indians to Christian Religion, eache towne, citty Borough, and particular plantation do obtaine unto themselves by just means a certaine number of the natives Children to be educated by them in true Religion and civile course of life. Of which children the most towardly boyes in witt and graces of nature [are] to be brought up by them in the firste Elements of literatture, so as to be fitted for the College intended for them, that from thence they may be sent to that worke of conversion.[23]

Understandably, however, most natives refused to turn over their children to be raised by the English. So the governor sought out whole families to be brought in to live among the English by providing them with houses, clothing, cattle, and cornfields.[24] This approach met with limited success.

By 1621, relations with the Native Americans seemed sufficiently cordial that a new governor observed that "the houses [were] generally set open to the Savages, who were always friendly entertained at the tables of the English, and commonly lodged in their bed-chambers."[25] Even though the relations were in a state of general calm, the incursion of more and more English into Virginia began to raise greater Indian concerns about the sanctity of their tribal lands. The Englishmen's apparent desire to assimilate and conquer the indigenous culture through education of the young probably added to the general discomfort of the native population, who had a rational basis for concluding that the English wanted to change their traditional ways of life. Combined with the English propensity toward unprovoked violence in the recent past, an Indian backlash was probably inevitable. Perhaps the only mitigating factor was the catastrophic mortality rate among the settlers. Although 3,750 Europeans arrived in the colony from 1619 to 1622, bringing the total white population to around 4,370, only 1,240 were still alive in early March 1622.[26]

That month an Indian chief lured an Englishman to come to his village to trade with him. The chief, Jack of the Feather, murdered the settler on his way to the village. A few days later two servant boys observed the chief wearing their master's hat and took revenge, killing the native chief. The natives threatened retribution, and the English answered with vicious threats of their own. The natives responded softly, then waited. On March 22, the tribe entered numerous homes, villages, and plantations throughout the English settlements and struck with terrible force. They attacked and killed every white man, woman, and child they could find. At the end of the day, 347 settlers were dead—more than one-fourth of the entire population.[27] John Rolfe, the widower of Pocahontas, was among those killed.[28]

All efforts to build schools for the natives, as well as any realistic hope of converting the natives to Christianity, were abandoned. The Augustinian maxim to "reclaim and reduce those savages from their barbarous kind of life" was put into vigorous effect from that point forward. Self-defense and revenge—not conversion—became the order of the day.

It is impossible to say what might have happened if the English settlers had practiced a form of Christianity that honored the freedom of the will rather than the doctrines of coerced uniformity. Perhaps if the message had been to "become like Christ" rather than "become British," the outcome would have been different. But attempts to entice the natives into the "enclosed gardens of God" was an impossible dream doomed from the outset.

Lest it appear that the English religious policy derived from the Augustinian view was peculiarly vicious toward "savages and brutes," it should be remembered that the English jails under James I were, at the time, full of Baptists and other dissenters whose crime was religious heterodoxy. The fires of Smithfield had recently consumed two English heretics. At least the dominant Anglican philosophy was consistent: If you differed, you were to be coerced or killed for your own good.

The Royal Colony

The proprietary Virginia Company did not last long after the massacre of 1622. By 1624, James was finished with the personalities and policies of those leading Virginia. Virginia was proclaimed a royal colony, with its governor and other leaders answerable solely to the king. Some changes, however, were effected in the laws of the colony even before its proprietary status was officially terminated. The General Assembly enacted a series of laws in 1624 that came to have far-reaching implications.

As might be expected, a number of legislative provisions were enacted in response to the massacre. For example, "All trade for corn with the savages as well publick as private after June next shall be prohibited."[29] Every dwelling house had to "be pallizaded in for defence against the Indians."[30] No one was allowed to "go or send abroad without a sufficient party w[e]ll armed."[31] Workers were required to keep their arms with them while working the fields, and a sentinel was to be posted. Each plantation was to maintain sufficient arms and ammunition at hand and to keep a watch day and night. The use of powder "unnecessarily in drinking or entertainments" was prohibited.[32]

As usual, the first several sections of the Acts of 1623–24 dealt with religion. Each plantation was required to have a room or house that was to be used only for the official worship of God. The churches were to be as "near as may be to the canons in England," and all had to obey the canons upon pain of censure. There was mandatory attendance for Sunday services with a fine of one pound of tobacco for missing a single Sunday and *fifty* pounds of tobacco for those who missed an entire month.[33] Ministers were to be paid in tobacco before any colonist could sell his tobacco to the traders who would carry it on to England. Failure to do so resulted in a double forfeiture. But grumbling against the minister would yield an even greater fine—it would cost a colonist five hundred pounds of tobacco for disparaging a clergyman.

In light of future events, section seven of the acts is especially noteworthy. It decreed that the governor could not "lay any taxes or impositions upon the colony their lands or commodities other way than by the authority of the General Assembly, to be levied and employed as the said Assembly shall appoint."[34] This law was passed 153 years before Thomas Jefferson drafted the Declaration of Independence. The principle that no one could lay taxes upon the colony except its own legislative body was a time-honored practice by the time the Stamp Act and Intolerable Acts would attempt to impose British taxes on American colonies.

While the legacy of American self-government is due in part to this historic rule on taxation, perhaps even more important in the development of democratic traditions was the self-governance of Virginia's churches. Not only were religious laws made by the General Assembly rather than a convocation of bishops, but the day-to-day governance of the churches fell to the leading citizens of the various church congregations. The first office to be recognized in formal acts was that of church warden. The Acts of 1631–32 contain a list of dramatic duties for local church wardens contained in their oath:

> You shall sweare that you shall make presentments [formal charges] of all such persons as shall lead a prophayne or ungodlie life, of such as shall be common swearers, drunkards or blasphemers, that shall ordinarily profane the saboth dayes or contemue Gods holy word or sacraments. You shall also present all adulturers or fornicators, or such as shall abuse theire neighbors by slanderinge tale carryinge or back bitinge, or that shall not behave themselves orderlie and soberlie in the church during devyne servise. Likewise they shall present such maysters and mistresses as shall be delinquent in the catechisinge the youth and ignorant persons. So helpe yow God![35]

In 1643, the vestry system was officially sanctioned by an act of the General Assembly. "The most sufficient and selected men" were chosen by the people of the area to serve as the vestrymen.[36] The vestrymen, however, determined that they would fill all vacancies in office; this made the church leadership a self-perpetuating hierarchy of the most wealthy and influential members of the colony.[37] Even though the vestry selection system lacked a truly republican character, its most important feature was that the church was controlled by local laymen, not distant bishops. And it must be remembered that since the church and state were one united entity, these laymen were exercising what was clearly understood at the time to be political power. The power of the vestry included the ability to name the ministers, except in James-City parish where the governor was given the power to name the minister "for the time being."[38] It is probable that the selection of ministers by the vestry had been the custom for some time prior to 1643, but the practice became official with the adoption of these acts.[39]

Despite the possibility that local control of churches could lead to doctrinal variations and even religious dissent, Virginia remained very much the domain of the established religious order. While Anglicans with Puritan leanings were undoubtedly present in the colony in the earliest years of the settlement, the divide between these two factions was not yet acute in England and never raised itself to create serious dissension in Virginia during this period when the chief goal was simply to survive the elements, disease, and hostile natives. Yet after John Harvey arrived as the new governor of Virginia in 1629, Puritans were no longer to be endured. An associate of the notorious Archbishop Laud, Harvey brought with him a spirit that ended the relative freedom any colonial Puritan clergy had previously enjoyed within the Anglican ranks.[40]

The first significant event approaching a serious episode of religious dissent in Virginia occurred in 1642, just at the threshold of the civil war in England. Seventy-one Virginia colonists sent a written appeal to the General Court of Massachusetts to "send ministers of the gospel into that region, that its inhabitants might be privileged with the preaching and ordinances of Jesus Christ."[41] Three Puritan ministers were dispatched to Virginia from the towns of Watertown, Braintree, and Rowley since each of these places had two ministers serving the local congregation.[42] The ministers' journey by ship took eleven weeks to cover the relatively short distance from Boston. Puritan author Cotton Mather, who was none too friendly to religious dissenters in Massachusetts, would later say of their ministry:

> They had little encouragement from the rulers of the place, but they had kind entertainment with the people; and in the several parts of the country where they were bestowed, there were many persons brought home to God. But as Au[gu]stin[e] told mankind, the devil was never turned Christian yet; the powers of darkness could not count it for their interest, that the light of the gospel powerfully preached, should reach those dark places of the Earth.[43]

The Virginia establishment reacted quickly and expelled the three Puritan ministers from the colony. A law was enacted in 1642–43 that stated that "for the preservation of the puritie of doctrine & unitie of the church" only those ministers ordained by the Church of England could reside in the colony. No others were permitted to teach or preach either in public or private.[44] Violators were to be compelled to leave the colony.

Although few details are known, an old history states that in 1643, "Sir William Berkeley, Royal Governor of Virginia, strove by whippings and brandings, to make the inhabitants of that colony conform to the Established church, and thus drove out the Baptists and Quakers, who found a refuge in the Albemarle country of North Carolina."[45] Virginia generally remained loyal to the church and crown during the English civil war. Charles I had been executed in January 1649; yet in October of that same year Virginia's General Assembly referred to Charles as the "late and most excellent and now undoubtedly sainted king" and expressed dismay at "unparalel'd treasons, perpetrated on the said King."[46] That same year 118 Puritans who had escaped prior notice since the 1643 edict were expelled from the colony. Most migrated to Maryland.[47] According to a 1655 publication in England, a group of people calling themselves Independents was expelled from the colony after some were jailed.[48] It would appear that this is a reference to the same group of dissenters.

In apparent retaliation, Cromwell sent a fleet from the West Indies to Virginia to demand allegiance, and on March 12, 1652, the Old Dominion submitted, albeit inconsistently and reluctantly.[49] It was the last "country belonging to England that submitted to the obedience of the Commonwealth of England."[50]

The Book of Common Prayer, detested by the Puritan element, was not immediately banned in the new Virginia. It was allowed for one year, provided all references to the monarchy were removed. Significantly, no clergyman serving in Virginia was removed from his position as a result of this compelled acquiescence to the Cromwellian Commonwealth.[51] It is noteworthy that a few Anglican ministers fled to Virginia during this period. The loyalist Berkeley said, "The persecution in Cromwells tyranny drove divers worthy men hither."[52]

A few Quakers even dared to enter Virginia during this same period. Though there was no special law against them in force in the colony at the time, at least two Quakers seem to have been imprisoned in the late 1650s, in accordance with the practice back in England under Cromwell.[53]

"Pray Oftener and Preach Less"

A law of 1658 placed all religious control in Virginia in the hands of the local vestries rather than sharing power with the General Assembly.[54] Nevertheless, Virginia's vestries were not likely to become a hotbed of dissent since the self-sustaining vestries were dominated by a class of persons most likely to be loyal to the political and religious established order. After the monarchy was restored in England, the established church was easily reinstalled in Virginia.

Yet the prevalence of laws concerning religion should not be construed to suggest that a robust Christian life was commonplace in the colony either during the Commonwealth or after the Restoration. Conditions and practical considerations made it difficult to maintain ecclesiastical functions among the scattered inhabitants, and by 1660 only two or three parishes out of fifty had established ministers.[55]

For one thing there was the simple economic fact that the living conditions and wages of ministers were far better in England than in Virginia. Few had a missionary spirit that would cause them to depart from their homeland to live in comparatively uncomfortable and dangerous surroundings for low wages. Indeed, the term used to describe ministerial wages—a "living"—suggests the inherent nature of the problem.[56] Under a system similar to the modern form of tenure employed at colleges and universities, once installed a pastor was to receive a permanent "living" regardless of the nature of his teaching or the quality of his spiritual life.

As a consequence, ministers in Virginia tended to be of low quality both in terms of their abilities and character. It was said that "not a few of the Ministers, whose wicked and prophane lives cause the worship of God not only to be slighted, but to be little less than abhorred." On the other hand, those who were "religious and laborious" had "scarce the single honour paid to them that they deserve."[57] Many of the vestries determined to save themselves the expense of incompetent or lazy preachers by appointing lay readers from year to year in lieu of sending the name of a chosen minister who, upon their recommendation, would be appointed to his living for life.[58]

Even though ministers were often of dubious quality, at least they were not dissenters—a fact that enormously pleased Governor Berkeley, who was reinstated after the Restoration. Berkeley was especially pleased by the absence of sources likely to propagate dissenting ideas. "There are forty-eight parishes, and the ministers are well paid," he wrote in his official report of 1671. "The clergy by my consent would be better if they would pray oftener and preach less. But of all commodities, so of this, the worst are sent to us. But I thank God there are no free schools, nor printing, and I hope we shall not have these hundred years."[59]

A few decades later a similar sentiment would be expressed, linking purposeful ignorance as a tool necessary to maintain the established church:

> But as for the children of Negroes and Indians, that are to live
> among Christians, undoubtedly they ought all to be baptized; since
> it is not out of the power of their masters to take care that they
> have a Christian education, learn their prayers and catechism, and
> go to church, and not accustom themselves to lie, swear and steal,
> though such (as the poorer sort in England) be not taught to read
> and write; which as yet has been found to be dangerous upon several political accounts, especially self-preservation.[60]

After the Restoration vigorous measures were adopted to stamp out any form of religious dissent in Virginia—especially those that resembled the forces who supported Cromwell. The Quakers were singled out by Act VI of the General Assembly, which had the straightforward title, "An act for suppressing the Quakers."[61] Since a number of Baptists had supported the Commonwealth, they were a special target of a law adopted in the 1661–62 session of the assembly:

> WHEREAS many scismaticall persons out of their aversenesse to the orthodox established religion, or out of the new fangled conceits of their owne hereticall inventions, refuse to have their children baptized, *Be it therefore enacted by the authority aforesaid*, that all persons that, in contempt of the divine sacrament of baptisme, shall refuse when they may carry their child to a lawfull minister in that county to have them baptized shalbe amerced two thousand pounds of tobacco; halfe to the informer, halfe to the publique.[62]

The fine was disproportionately severe—ten times the amount a law of 1663 imposed upon Quakers or "any other separatists" for the first offense of unlawful assemblies.[63] One member of the General Assembly, John Lower, learned a hard lesson for his kindness to the Quakers and other Anabaptists. Lower, from Norfolk, was accused before the assembly by the high sheriff of his county of being "loving to the Quakers and stood well affected towards them, and had been at their meetings, and was so far an anabaptist as to be against the baptising of children."[64] After he refused to take the oaths of allegiance and supremacy, Lower was dismissed from the House.

Despite efforts to impose a religious orthodoxy on Virginia, the state of religion in the colony still lagged unacceptably to some. One author, generally assumed to be Virginia clergyman Robert Greene, published a utopian plan to repair the colony's religious problems. Even its title is interesting: *Virginia's Cure, or An Advisive Narrative concerning Virginia / Discovering The true Ground of that Churches Unhappiness, and the only true Remedy.*[65] This work was originally delivered as a message to the bishop of London on September 2, 1661, but was published more than a year later on September 15, 1662, the date the work received the necessary "imprimatur" from the Church of England—evidence of the continuing practice of censorship.

In this work the author lamented that the English had allowed plantations in this distant land to be established far away from one another, as such great distances made the outward performance of religious duties impossible to maintain. This, he said, "hath caused them hitherto to rob God in a great measure of that publick Worship and Service, which as a Homage due to his great name, he requires to be constantly paid to him, at the times appointed for it, in the publick Congregations of his people in his House of Prayer."[66] Virginia's "sacrilege" of failing to engage in consistent ceremonial religion the author judged "to be the prime Cause of their long languishing improsperous condition for it puts them under the curse of God."[67]

Moreover, the author contended, the huge distances between many of Virginia's far-flung parishes made it impossible for pastors properly to observe the daily lives of their parishioners and drive out vice in their lives.[68] To the author the solution was obvious: Virginia should be required to build towns. Plantation owners, he said, should maintain an additional, separate residence in town so that they could properly attend to the multiple religious duties demanded by a form of Christianity devoted to the externalities of liturgical worship.[69] Specifically, the author wrote, the correct recourse should be "reducing her Planters into Towns."[70] Previously, the term "reduce" had been used to describe the goal of the coercive conversion of the Native Americans; obviously this suggestion was not a plan for voluntary relocation.

Why would such drastic measures even be contemplated? Because an unprecedented sin was being practiced in this new world. Virginia's planters "were the first considerable numbers of Christians in the whole world," the author wrote, "which first violated this stated Order of Christ."[71] After all, the Bible says that we are to *come into His gates with Thanksgiving*,[72] and that could not conceivably be done except in a compelled, uniform, national church with resplendent ceremonies. Indeed, such proposals had actually been discussed in the General Assembly but were rejected. After all, the Burgesses were "usually such as went over Servants thither, and though by time and industry, they may have attained competent Estates; yet by reason of their poor and mean education they are unskillful in judging of a good Estate either of Church or Common-wealth, or of the means of procuring it."[73]

Others proposed a more traditional solution. Virginia should have its own bishop, they said. The problem was chiefly one of economics and status: no bishop could be induced to leave the splendor of his circumstances in England for the wilderness of Virginia. James Blair, who had previously spent a season as missionary to the colony, was sent to Virginia in 1691 as the commissary of the bishop of London—an attempt to bring a direct representative to exercise proper ecclesiastical control. Blair was a man with clear talent and energy. He succeeded in establishing the College of William and Mary, which was intended for the purpose of educating pastors from among the English settlers to serve congregations in their native Virginia.[74] However, Blair's attempt to demand higher salaries for ministers was not as successful.[75] And neither was his effort to establish further ecclesiastical control through "visitations," a proposition that was utterly rejected because of "the general aversion of the people to everything that looks like a spiritual court."[76]

Blair arrived as commissary three years after the 1689 Act of William and Mary established religious toleration in England. But this act did not have an "extending clause" to make it immediately effective in the American colonies.[77] It was not until 1699 that the General Assembly of Virginia decided it was time to extend this highly attenuated form of toleration to the colony.[78] That same year Francis Makemie, a Presbyterian pastor from Accomack County, applied for and received a license to preach in two separate buildings that he personally owned.[79]

Even though Makemie was clearly the first dissenting pastor to receive a license to preach from the General Assembly, one pastor had previously obtained a license from a local court. In 1692, Josias Mackie appeared before two magistrates in Norfolk County and made the required showing of the narrow nature of his disagreement with the Anglican Church. These local magistrates approved his application and granted him a license,[80] apparently under the mistaken impression that they could do so under the direct authority of the act of Parliament. However, because the 1689 act lacked the extending language, the House of Burgesses needed to act first to validly authorize such preaching licenses.

Looking back in 1850, the great Virginia historian William Henry Foote summarized the state of religious liberty in the colony near the end of the seventeenth century:

> Toleration, in forms of Religion, was unknown in Virginia in 1688. From the commencement of the colony, the necessity of the religious element was felt. The company knew not how to control the members composing the colony, but by religion and law. They exercised a despotism in both.[81]

Nevertheless, these measures were largely ineffective. Church membership in Virginia in the late 1600s hovered around 5 percent, according to some estimates.[82] The "lower classes" were unreached and showed scant concern for religious matters. Both in England and the colonies, "the Established Church had settled down into a deathlike stupor, from which no power seemed to be able to arouse it."[83]

Religious liberty would eventually arise in Virginia but not until a vital form of Christianity was first awakened.

Chapter Eighteen

BETTER HYPOCRITES

Religious Toleration and Persecution in the Northern and Proprietary Colonies

I dare take upon me to be the herald of New England
so far as to proclaim to the world, in the name of our
colony, that all familists, antinomians, anabaptists, and
other enthusiasts shall have free liberty to keep away
from us, and such as will come to be gone as fast
as they can, the sooner the better.

REV. NATHANIEL WARD, PURITAN MINISTER

One early spring day in 1630, John Winthrop stood aboard the *Arbella*, anchored in the harbor in Yarmouth, England, and said his good-byes to his native land. As a "wind Easterly" blew gently overhead, Winthrop and his colleagues in the Massachusetts Bay Company gathered to write a last-minute document before setting sail.[1] They addressed it "to the rest of their Brethren, in and of the Church of *ENGLAND*."[2]

Rumors had begun to spread that the company, New England-bound, was leaving their mother country—and their mother church—on a Separatist mission, not unlike the group of settlers who had set sail across the sea on a small vessel named the *Mayflower* and reached Plymouth some ten years

252

before. Given the current circumstances in England, this was an understandable interpretation. Yet such was not their intent.

The year before, in 1629, members of Parliament had done their best to rally against Anglo-Catholicism. Defying a command by King Charles I, they had pinned the Speaker to his chair and proceeded to pass a resolution declaring that anyone who dared disagree with "the true and orthodox church" by introducing ecclesiastical innovations was a "capital enemy to this kingdom and commonwealth."[3] For such obstinacy Charles had refused to call another Parliament and determined instead to rule England "personally." And so the Church of England continued to be filled with "Anglo-Catholics," infuriating both Puritans and Separatists, though they registered their dissent in different ways.

The Plymouth pilgrims of ten years earlier had been dismissed by some loyal churchmen as looking for heaven on earth. When they failed to find it in England, they searched for it in Holland; and when they failed to find it in Holland, they searched in vain for it in the New World. Uncharitable as this criticism might have been, John Winthrop wanted to make clear that the mission of the Massachusetts Bay Company was not cut from the same cloth. "We are not of those that dream of perfection in this world," the company wrote, "yet we desire you would be pleased to take notice of the principles, and body of our company, as those who esteem it our honor, to call the *Church* of *England*, from whence we rise, our dear Mother."[4] The company of brethren desired to emphasize that they sailed away not in resentment; but with "much sadness of heart, and many tears in [their] eyes" and gratitude for the "common salvation" they had "received in her bosom, and sucked . . . from her breasts."[5] Pray for us, they pleaded, for we are some of your own—"a Church springing out of your own bowels."[6]

Among Puritans, there were differences as to how best to accomplish reformation in the church. To paint with a broad brush, the majority of Puritans who remained in England to fight out the civil war would become devotees of national Presbyterianism while the Puritans who left on their "errand into the Wilderness" were largely "of the Congregational way."[7] England had been infected by "Laodicean lukewarmness in matters of God," they believed, and the church was being seduced into sympathy with popery and its "vain Idolatrous Ceremonies."[8] In the context of these dire straits, the emigrating Puritans believed that God had "raise[d] an Army out of our English Nation, for freeing his people from their long servitude under usurping Prelacy" and so that they might "secure Religion to Posterity, according to the way which they believed was of God."[9] In time, they thought, they would prove to their motherland that indeed this way was best and right. Perhaps England would follow suit, and they would join once again in the same glorious pursuit. But for now Winthrop and the departing Puritans felt they had to escape God's imminent wrath for the nation's sins, and they were willing to suffer the misunderstandings of a few English brethren who thought they were abandoning the cause forever.

While still aboard the *Arbella*, Winthrop articulated their mission in his work *A Modell of Christian Charity*, more popularly known as his "city on a hill" sermon:

> We are a company professing ourselves fellow members of Christ . . . [and] the work we have in hand, it is by mutual consent, through a special overruling providence and a more than an ordinary approbation of the churches of Christ, to seek out a place of cohabitation and consortship, under a due form of government both civil and ecclesiastical. In such cases as this, the care of the public must oversway all private respects by which not only conscience but mere civil policy doth bind us; for it is a true rule that particular estates cannot subsist in the ruin of the public.
>
> The end is to improve our lives to do more service to the Lord, the comfort and increase of the body of Christ whereof we are members, that ourselves and our posterity may be the better preserved from the common corruptions of this evil world, to serve the Lord and work out our salvation under the power and purity of His holy ordinances. . . .
>
> Whatsoever we did or ought to have done when we lived in England, the same must we do, and more also where we go. That which the most in their churches maintain as a truth in profession only, we must bring into familiar and constant practice. . . . We must not look only on our own things but also on the things of our brethren. Neither must we think that the Lord will bear with such failings at our hands as He doth from those among whom we have lived. . . .
>
> Thus stands the cause between God and us: we are entered into covenant with Him for this work; we have taken out a commission, the Lord hath given us leave to draw our own articles.[10]

As is clear from Winthrop's sermon, the Congregational New Englanders conceived of God's interactions with humankind in terms of the *covenant*. The colony, as well as each congregation of "visible saints," was composed of those who voluntarily held to the covenant and their posterity. They were bound by oath to uphold their common mission, and together they would show the world what true reformation looked like. New England would become as a city on a hill, for the "eyes of all people" were upon them.[11]

"Take Ye Us the Foxes"

Prominent members of early New England society expressed the role of the civil magistrate in familiar terms. The aim of the Bay Colony's founders was "a thorough-Reformation of things in the Matters of [God's] Worship," which was a duty incumbent on *both* the "Magistracy in their Sphere" and the "Ministry in theirs."[12] Their civil covenant had a religious end.

Although these Puritans did indeed make a careful theoretical distinction between the civil and ecclesiastical spheres, the civil magistrates and church ministers were considered equally bound to punish any doctrinal heresy. The only difference was the means they could rightfully use to go about it. The church was supposed to discipline using "excommunication or the like," while the magistrate was commissioned by God to inflict "corporal punishments," such as "Imprisonments, Fines, Mulcts, Stripes, Sword, Whip, Fire, Faggot, or the like."[13] The "able Pilots" of the state possessed authority to execute judgment for violations of *both* tables of the law—that is, not only sins chiefly involving man and man but also sins, "errors," and "heresies" between God and man.[14]

Although they considered "the church" to be not a geographical or national entity as in England but, rather, to consist of those "gathered together in Covenant of such a number as might ordinarily meet together in one place," the magistrate nevertheless had jurisdiction over the whole community and any number of gathered Congregational churches as might appear under his care.[15] He was to submit to the definition of *orthodoxy* as concurred to by the visible church of which he was a member.[16] In the opinion of a leading Boston clergyman, John Norton, God armed the magistrate to defend religion for numerous reasons: the vindication of His name and truth, the hope of curing the offenders, the "putting away of evil from Israel," to prevent infection, and to prevent the wrath of God on the people for their violation of the covenant.[17] To support his point, Norton cited three passages of Scripture: Leviticus 24, Deuteronomy 13, and Zechariah 13.[18]

Thomas Cobbet, pastor of the New England congregation at Lynn, likewise made arguments from the Scriptures and other authorities. In the main body of his work titled *The Civil Magistrates Power in matters of Religion Modestly Debated*, Cobbet devoted a significant portion to "that speech, Canticles 2.15. *Take ye us the Foxes, the little Foxes which spoil our vines, for our Vines have tender Grapes.*"[19] Some, he said, would limit this injunction to ecclesiastical officials; but he believed "there is no reason so as to restrain this indefinite speech."[20] He identified the "foxes" either with the "errors, heresies, and other hurtful offences, against the first or second Table" or with the people committing those breaches.[21] Either way, Cobbet concluded:

Evident it is, that this taking of the Foxes there enjoined, is not to be restrained to Church Officers' acts . . . but must be referred to such at least, whose place and work it is, to act in an externally forcible way of taking, or of restraining and punishing such Foxes, which spoil the Vines or Churches of Christ. . . . This is a charge of Christ as Mediator, unto all such, who by place and office under him, are to restrain and punish, not by the use of a spiritual rod, or sword so much, as are Church Officers; but specially by the use of the temporal sword, as our Civil Rulers, who in their political way, are here enjoined forcibly to take such corrupters, and disturbers of Religion, as well as of good manners.[22]

Cobbet scoured the writings of various church fathers and more recent authors for passages buttressing his opinion. One source he cited was Beza's *De Haereticis*, published in defense of the Servetus affair. Cobbett quoted a large chunk of it:

In or by what right did Christ twice take the Whip in hand? . . . By what right did Peter kill Ananias and Sapphira? By what right did Paul strike Elimas blind? What? By that of the Ecclesiastical Ministry? Surely no, unless you would confound the Jurisdictions; therefore by the right of the Civil Magistrate: for there is no third. Yet I acknowledge this power put forth by Ministers of the Word, was in them extraordinary, and the manner of exercising it after a sort divine: but I prove, that though the Lord doth not always make use of the help of the Magistrates, yet in all ages, he doth make use of the Power whereof the Magistrate is the only ordinary Minister, according as himself seeth it meet, for the preservation of his Church.[23]

With a similar emphasis the Reverend Nathaniel Ward, pastor of New England's Ipswich church, cited similar authorities in one of his polemical works aimed at sects who might have found religious toleration appealing. "Ten of the most Christian Emperors," he said, found it best for the magistrate to prosecute religious error, and "five of the ancient fathers persuaded to it, of whom Augustine was one, who for a time argued hard for Indulgency: but upon conference with other prudent Bishops, altered his judgment, as appears in three of his Epistles."[24] Ward further added, "I would be understood, not only an Allower, but an humble Petitioner, that ignorant and tender conscienced Anabaptists may have due time and means of conviction."[25] Boston minister Samuel Willard dismissed the pleas of the

Baptists by quoting Augustine's dictum, also quoted by Calvin, *Causa, non passio, facit Martyrem*—the cause, not the suffering, makes the martyr.[26]

And indeed the Baptists, as usual, bore the brunt of civil and ecclesiastical censures. Reverend Ward went so far as to say that "authority ought to see their Subjects' children baptized though their Parents' judgments be against it."[27] Although the Puritans did make a distinction between "quiet heresy" and "heresy turbulent," even home conventicles were thought to have crossed the border into the latter.[28] Liberty of conscience, they said, all men ought to possess, but "liberty of error" was something entirely different, and those who would not baptize their infants were clearly in error.[29] Ward called the Baptists *Potamides*, the name for freshwater nymphs, and noted that they are "religious men but pernicious heretics, good spirits but very devils."[30] To make room for them in the English Commonwealth was to do no less than invite "Hell above ground."[31]

In brief, religious liberty was utterly contrary to the civil covenant as the Massachusetts founders understood it. As John Norton reminded his readers, "It concerneth N.-E. always to remember, that Originally they are *a Plantation Religious*, not a plantation of Trade. The profession of the purity of doctrine, worship & discipline, is written on her forehead."[32] Edward Johnson likewise counseled, "You are not set up for tolerating times."[33]

Cobbet criticized those who would place restrictions on the magistrate's power over the religious beliefs of citizens, complaining that when such power was "with much ado permitted to come within the range and reach of the first Table, yet they will have it under so short a tether, and lay such strong chains and heavy bolts upon it, that it's there rather as in its prison, than any way as in its privileged place."[34]

Reverend Ward said that among the four things his heart naturally detested were "Tolerations of divers Religions, or of one Religion in segregant shapes"—the other three being the presence of the Apocrypha in the Bible, foreigners in his country, and alchemized coins.[35] Cities where papists, Calvinists, and Lutherans all preach, he said, are possessed by "leopardlike" affections; therefore, "it is far better to live in a State united, though somewhat Corrupt, than in a State, whereof some part is incorrupt, and all the rest divided."[36]

This outlook became codified in New England law. In 1641, the Reverend Nathaniel Ward proposed a code that was later adopted by the colony's General Court under the heading *A Coppie of the Liberties of the Massachusets Collonie in New England*. It is remarkable that this document is regarded by some as the first modern bill of rights, though its codification of rights of due process, the civil liberties of "freemen," and the protections provided for servants against cruel masters are among its commendable aspects. In terms of the liberties of the churches, however, the document blends a statement of the rightful functions of individual congregations of believers and an enunciation of the right of the civil state to define and defend doctrine, discipline, and practice.

The General Court, which ratified the *Coppie of Liberties* with its "sollemne consent," also reserved to itself the sole power of interpretation.[37] This decision had a special significance in light of the fact that only those "people of God within this Jurisdiction" who were "*orthodox in Judgment*" could form a church congregation.[38] The definition of *orthodox* was not codified and left instead to the General Court. Likewise, foreigners and "strangers" outside the covenant and fleeing from persecution or tyranny in their homelands could be entertained but *only* if they professed "the true Christian Religion."[39] Capital punishment applied to anyone who worshipped "any other god, but the Lord God," "consulteth with a familiar spirit," or blasphemed in a "direct express, presumptuous or high handed" manner.[40]

At least one aspect of orthodoxy was defined three years later when the General Court passed a law against those who "have held the baptizing of infants unlawful." The law stated that these individuals opposed the magistracy's "Inspection into any breach of the first Table" and that if this opinion, among others, were "connived at," they would "necessarily bring guilt upon us, infection, & trouble to the Churches & hazard to the whole Commonwealth." Therefore, anyone within the colony's jurisdiction was subject to banishment who either openly or secretly spread their heretical opinion rejecting the baptism of infants, departed from a congregation that practiced infant baptism, or denied that the magistrate could "punish the outward breaches of the first Table of the Ten Commandments."[41]

In sum, the New England Puritans saw themselves as a private religious corporation—or, to put it in more organic terms, a body of which Christ was the head and they the several parts. They were free to define their own rules as He gave them leave. It was legally possible to do so because of a loophole left in the original charter, which enabled the Bay Company to move its governing board to the colony instead of having to keep it in England, where their behavior could be scrutinized by authorities. Other than the colonists' reservation to themselves of the right of corporal discipline through the magistrate, they were constituted in a way similar to many churches today. They should be lauded for their desire to maintain a body of visible saints pure in doctrine and practice. They took significant steps forward in defining, at least in theory, a church as something other than a national or geographical entity; those who disagreed with them did not have to join their covenant, as Reverend Ward emphasized in one of his memorable passages:

We have been reputed a Colluvies[42] of wild Opinionists,
swarmed into a remote wildernes to finde elbow-roome for our
phanatick Doctrines and practices. . . . I dare take upon me, to
bee the Herauld of *New-England* so far, as to proclaime to the
world, in the name of our Colony, that all Familists, Antinomians,
Anabaptists, and other Enthusiasts, shall have free Liberty to keep
away from us, and such as will come to be gone as fast as they can,
the sooner the better.[43]

The problem with this approach did not rear its whole head at the start.
Before long, however, the conflation of church and civil government melded
into their covenant would have unwelcome consequences for both.

Delinquents for Doctrine

The theory of the Puritan commonwealth was challenged by the birth
of the second generation. Some of the children of the initial believers did not
share their parents' faith. Thus, a significant source of religious dissent arose
from an unlikely source. Massachusetts was intended to be like Virginia—
a "closed garden." Appearance of unity was all-important, as minister John
Cotton expressed when he stated emphatically that if magistrates make men
hypocrites by compelling them to do that which they disbelieve "yet better
be hypocrites than profane persons."[44]

All things were well and good until people who disagreed with the
founders either arrived in the colony by way of the sea or were born to
members of the original covenant. Difficulties stemming from the former
appeared almost immediately.

On February 5, 1631, Winthrop recorded that the ship *Lyon*, which had
set sail from Bristol, England, on December 1, reached Nantucket. Although
"she had a very tempestuous passage," she landed safely "through God's
mercy" with her passengers, among whom was one "Mr. Williams a godly
man with his wife."[45] By April 18, however, Roger Williams had already
begun to stir up trouble. The church in Salem had asked Williams to fill
the office of "teacher," but a court in Boston wrote to Captain John Endicott
of Salem, telling him to "forbear" until the Court had given the situation
further consideration. These were Williams's offenses:

Williams had refused to join with the churches at Boston,
because they would not make a public declaration of their repentance for having communion with the churches of England while
they tarried there; and besides had declared his opinion that the

magistrate might not punish the breach of the Sabbath nor any
other offence that was a breach of the first table.[46]

This began a series of run-ins with the Massachusetts officialdom. The
next was over Williams's circulation of a work contesting James I's original
patent for the land comprising Massachusetts as illegitimate (since the land
really belonged to the Native Americans) and taking issue with the king's
reference to Europe as "Christendom" and the rest of the world as "heathen" (since the "true spiritual Jew" becomes one by his regeneration, not
his outward christening into a national church).[47] Mr. Williams responded
to officials' objections to the work "very submissively," and the matter was
dismissed for a time.[48] However, when he began to teach this material again
publicly, Williams was called to answer before the General Court.[49]

Foremost among Williams's "divers dangerous opinions" was that the
civil magistrate ought not to punish breaches of the first table of the Ten
Commandments except those that disturbed the civil peace.[50] This was
called "a great contempt of authority" and "heinous sin," and in late 1635,
an authority was sent to seize him and put him aboard the next ship leaving for England.[51] Having been forewarned, Williams left his home and
fled with some companions beyond the border of the land comprising the
Massachusetts grant. They settled in an area that would become known as
Providence and began the colony that would soon bear the name Rhode
Island. Nevertheless, Bay Company leaders wrung their hands in fear that
the "infection" of Williams's dangerous opinions would "easily spread."[52]

Williams insisted that "the Scriptures of Truth and the Records of Time
concur in this, that the first Churches of Christ Jesus, the lights, patterns,
and precedents to all succeeding Ages, were gathered and governed without
the aid, assistance, or countenance of any Civil Authority"; the civil authority, rather, had been the chief cause of "great persecutions for the name of
the Lord Jesus professed amongst them."[53] On this point Williams met with
fierce resistance.

John Cotton wrote a tract that would start a polemical pamphlet battle
between himself and Williams over the issue of religious freedom. It started
when Cotton was given a short document by "a witness of Jesus Christ close
prisoner in Newgate, against persecution in cause of conscience," and was
asked for his opinion of it.[54] This prisoner, who had written it "long since,"
was probably John Murton, Thomas Helwys's English Baptist colleague.[55]
(It is said that Murton wrote the "Scriptures and Reasons" in milk, as he
was not allowed ink while in prison.[56]) Cottons's critique of the Murton
piece prompted Williams to pen a rebuttal saying that Murton had been
answered in blood: "*bloudy* to the *souls* of all men, forc'd to the *Religion* and

Worship which every civil State or Common-weale agrees on, and compels all subjects to in a dissembled *uniformitie*."[57] Cotton returned fire, citing Calvin's discourse against Servetus and *"Beza his Book de Haereticis a Magistratu puniendis"* in a manner typical of his Presbyterian contemporaries in Scotland and England.[58]

Williams was a dissenter among dissenters, and Rhode Island would be characterized by his hallmark beliefs about the civil magistrate. In Providence's 1640 governing document, it was agreed that "as formerly hath been the liberties of the town, so still, to hold forth liberty of conscience," which was later elucidated as "none shall be accounted a Delinquent for *Doctrine*: Provided, it be not directly repugnant to ye Government or Laws established."[59] When Charles II finally granted Rhode Island a charter in 1663, it spoke of the friendly relations and agreements between the Narragansett Indians and the settlers, then stated:

> And whereas, in their humble address, they have freely
> declared, that it is much on their hearts (if they may be permitted),
> to hold forth a livelie experiment, that a most flourishing civil state
> may stand and best bee maintained, and that among our English
> subjects, with a full libertie in religious concernments; and that
> true piety rightly grounded upon gospell principles, will give the
> best and greatest security to sovereignty, and will lay in the hearts
> of men the strongest obligations to true loyalty. . . . Our royal
> will and pleasure is, that no person within the said colony, at any
> time hereafter, shall bee any wise molested, punished, disquieted,
> or called in question, for any differences in opinion in matters of
> religion, and does not actually disturb the civil peace of our said
> colony; but that all and every person and persons may, from time
> to time, and at all times hereafter, freely and fully have and enjoy
> his and their own judgments and consciences, in matters of reli-
> gious concernments, throughout the tract of land.[60]

Already, however, Rhode Island had begun to collect numerous "heretics" who somehow never managed to keep themselves outside the Bay Company's jurisdiction. One of the first was Mistress Anne Hutchinson.

"Corrupt and Dangerous Opinions"

Anne Hutchinson took to shore in New England after "the Lord spake" to her through diverse passages of Scripture about the corrupt state of the churches in her native land.[61] Although she remained in England for some time thereafter under the preaching of John Cotton and her brother-in-

law, John Wheelwright, she followed them when they made their way to
Massachusetts. It did not take long for church authorities to recognize that
Wheelwright and his sermons and Hutchinson and her "wonted meetings"
were among the little foxes ruining their vineyard, so they endeavored to
catch and destroy them first by ecclesiastical means. When this proved
ineffective, officials determined in October 1637 that it was high time "to
suppress them by the civil authority."[62]

The immediate pretense for bringing the pair before the General
Court was a publication titled *A Remonstrance or Petition*, written by some of
Wheelwright's supporters as a plea to the Court to reassess their accusations
of sedition. "We beseech your Worships to consider, that either the person
condemned must be culpable of some seditious fact, or his doctrine must be
sedition, or must breed sedition in the hearts of his hearers," the petition
explained. Its authors were unaware of any action leading to the first; the
second reason was certainly not true; and the third was also patently false, in
their eyes, since Wheelwright had "not drawn the sword" and, in fact, had
taught his followers "rather to become humble suppliants to your Worships."
They recited examples of men in Scripture who had been accused of troubling Israel—Elijah, Amos, Christ Himself—and urged the court to consider
"the danger of meddling against the Prophets of God" and "whether that old
serpent work not after his old method, even in our days."[63]

Since one person on the General Court admitted that he agreed with
the sentiments of the petition, even though he did not sign it, and since
another had actually subscribed to it himself, these two were disqualified
from the court even before the trial began. Once proceedings finally got
underway, Wheelwright denied that he was guilty of sedition or "contempt
of authority," the charges that had been brought against him. The court
responded hotly that his doctrine and declarations "tend[ed] to sedition: for
whereas before he broached his opinions, there was a peaceable and comely
order in all affairs in the Churches, and civil state, &c." Now, they asserted,
Wheelwright had provoked differences in doctrine "whereby one party is
looked at as friends to Christ, and the other as his enemies. . . . All things
are turned upside down among us."[64] When it was argued that disturbance of
unity is not necessarily sedition, Winthrop and the court insisted that such
an argument was patently false because any time the people looked on their
rulers as enemies or persecutors, it hindered the public good.[65]

The following day the court declared Wheelwright guilty of "his seditious Sermon," "corrupt and dangerous opinions," and obstinate maintenance of "his said errors and offences." Since Wheelwright would not leave
voluntarily, the court disenfranchised and banished him. For him to remain
in their midst would tend to "the ruin of the whole." Wheelwright appealed

to the king, but the court denied that he had such a right of appeal since the king had given into *their* hands full authority "to hear and determine all causes without any reservation."[66] And thus they continued to do.

One William Aspin was also charged with putting his hand to the petition and justifying Wheelwright's sermon. When Aspin argued "that it is lawful for Subjects to Petition," the court denied that the so-called petition was actually a petition and insisted instead that it was libel. In any case, the court added, "It was great arrogance of any private man thus openly to advance his own judgment of the Court." The debate concluded when Aspin "desired the Court to show a rule in Scripture for banishment," whereupon the General Court disenfranchised and banished him after reminding him "that Hagar and Ishmael were banished for disturbance."[67] Another "honest poor man" named Richard Gridly was also disenfranchised, as he "was very apt to meddle in public affairs, beyond his calling or skill."[68]

The real affair, however, did not begin until Mistress Anne was brought before the court. Winthrop readily acknowledged that her good works in the colony from her arrival in 1636 began in "wholesome truth," but then her strong and charismatic personality got the better of her, and she began to "set forth her own stuffe."[69] Her corrupting influence had to be dealt with, for she had begun to hold lectures at her home which drew as many as eighty women two days a week. After "repeating the sermon," she would expound and comment upon it. This, it was alleged, produced public disturbance because of her propagation of opinionative doctrinal error.

The trial proceeded in this manner:

> COURT: Have you countenanced, or will you justify those seditious practices which have been censured here in this Court?
>
> HUTCH: Do you ask me upon point of conscience?
>
> COURT: No, your conscience you may keep to your self, but if in this cause you shall countenance and encourage those that thus transgress the Law, you must be called in question for it, and that is not for your conscience, but for your practice.
>
> HUTCH: What Law have they transgressed? The Law of God?
>
> COURT: Yes, the fifth Commandment, which commands us to honor Father and Mother, which includes all in authority, but these seditious practices of theirs, have cast reproach and dishonor upon the Fathers of the Commonwealth.[70]

When asked by what authority she upheld her meetings, Hutchinson answered that it was by Titus 2, which commands older women to teach the younger. The court responded that they had a plain command against what she was doing: "I permit not a woman to teach." When she contested that this passage referred to teaching men, the court answered that it forbade women from teaching *anyone* in public.

Hutchinson denied that she taught in a public congregation, then insisted, "The men of Berea are commended for examining Paul's Doctrine: we do no more but read the notes of our teachers Sermons, and then reason of them by searching the Scriptures."

To this the court retorted, "You do not as the Bereans search the Scriptures for their confirming in the truths delivered, but you open your teachers points, and declare his meaning, and correct wherein you think he hath failed, &c. and by this means you abase the honor and authority of the public Ministry."[71]

Deliberation continued in this way, but it soon became clear to the court that there was then "an inevitable necessity to rid her away" for their own sake and the sake of the gospel, so she was committed to the marshall until a season arrived suitable to her banishment. And Winthrop breathed a sigh of relief. He rejoiced that "peace and truth may again flourish in *New England, Amen.*"[72]

But not for long. For in 1651, three men took lodgings at a house two miles outside the town of Lynn in Massachusetts Bay. The owner, a blind man named William Witter, was a Baptist, as were his three guests. When the Sabbath arrived, the men resolved to hold a private service in their home instead of repairing to public worship. One of them, John Clark, preached from Revelation 3:10 on keeping "the Word of his Patience" and being preserved from "the hour of temptation." As he spoke, two town police arrived and announced that they had authority to apprehend the participants by virtue of a warrant from the magistrate, Robert Bridges. The three men were thereupon brought by force into the meeting of the local congregation. When Clark entered the church, he removed his hat to salute all, then sat down at his appointed seat, returned his hat to his head, and fell to reading his book. Much annoyed, Bridges commanded that the constable remove Clark's hat from his head. Clark sat until the praying, singing, and preaching had concluded, then rose to address the congregation, noting that "wisdom that is from above" is first pure, then "peaceable, gentle, and easy to be entreated." Upon pausing for a moment to wait for their response, Mr. Bridges interjected that if the congregation did not want to give him leave, Clark would have to be silent, for they would "have no Objections made against what is delivered."[73]

Clark and his companions were taken to prison. During the ensuing trial, Clark disowned the name of "Anabaptist," which the magistrates attempted to foist upon them, saying that he had never "*re*-baptized" anyone.

"You deny the former Baptism," then, the Governor shot back, "and make all our worship a nullity." Clark did not deny this and thus was sentenced for his "contempt to Authority" and denial of "the lawfulness of Baptizing of Infants."[74] The judge thereupon pronounced that such contempt and denial "tends to the dishonor of God, the despising the ordinances of God among us, the peace of the Churches, and seducing the Subjects of this Commonwealth from the truth of the Gospel of Jesus Christ, and perverting the straight ways of the Lord." Clark was to be fined twenty pounds as surety for good behavior or else be whipped and kept in prison until such fine was paid.[75] Clark's companions, Obadiah Holmes and John Crandall, were likewise ordered to pay fines or be whipped.

Clark pleaded that he be given a chance to defend his positions publicly and asked to be shown under what law he had been convicted. When both of these requests were ignored, he framed four "conclusions" to present his beliefs in clear form, the last of which dealt with religious liberty:

> I testify that no such believer, or Servant of Christ Jesus hath
> any liberty, much less Authority, to smite his fellow servant, nor
> yet with outward force, or arm of flesh, to constrain or restrain
> his Conscience, no nor yet his outward man for Conscience sake,
> or worship of his God, where injury is not offered to the person,
> name or estate of others, every man being such as shall appear
> before the judgment seat of Christ, and must give an account of
> himself to God, and therefore ought to be fully persuaded in his
> own mind, for what he undertakes, because he that doubteth is
> damned if he eat, and so also if he act, because he doth not eat or
> act in Faith, and what is not of Faith is sin.[76]

No one listened. When some kind well-wishers paid Clark's bond, he refused to accept it on principle and determined yet again to have a public hearing. Crandall paid his bond so as to return to his family, but "his Spirit [being] unsatisfied in what he had done," he turned himself back in to the jailer because he did not want to confess guilt by choosing his punishment.[77]

When at length it was clear that Clark would remain until forcibly whipped, the jailor was sent to fetch him. John Cotton had just concluded a sermon justifying the sentences of the three Baptists in which he argued that denial of infant baptism was an offense worthy of death because those who believed such were "soul-murtherers."[78] Nevertheless, the lesser offense had been agreed upon. So Clark "besought the Lord earnestly" and was so comforted by the assurance that he could leave the affair in His hands that when the jailor approached, "even cheerfulness did come upon" him as he took his Bible in his hands and went to the place where he was to be whipped.[79]

Although the magistrate's judgment had specified that he speak nothing during the proceedings, Clark appealed to the onlookers, saying that he was ready to defend his beliefs "by the Word" and seal them with his own blood. The whipper was instructed to do his office quickly before Clark proceeded to delude the people, but Clark insisted, "That which I am to suffer for, is for the Word of God, and testimony of Jesus Christ."

"No," the magistrate replied, "it is for your Error, and going about to seduce the people."[80]

Clark asked why no one tried to convince him of his error, then, or at least let him dispute publicly. But it was no use. Even while his clothes were being removed, Clark continued to speak.

"I told them," he later wrote, "the Lord having manifested his love towards me, in giving me repentance towards God, and Faith in Jesus Christ, and so to be baptized in water by a Messenger of Jesus into the name of the Father, Son, and Holy Spirit, wherein I have fellowship with him in his death, burial, and resurrection, I am now come to be baptized in afflictions by your hands, that so I may have further fellowship with my Lord, and am not ashamed of his sufferings, for by his stripes am I healed."[81] Being bound to a post, Clark was whipped thirty times with a three-cord whip. Clark said his flesh almost failed him, but he was then filled with "such a spiritual manifestation of God's presence" that he told the magistrates, "You have struck me with Roses."

"Although the Lord hath made it easy to me," he continued, "yet I pray God it may not be laid to your charge."[82]

Some onlookers were incensed by this behavior, which Holmes and Crandall had likewise displayed. Two men, a Mr. Cole and Mr. Buttolph, even made deposition before the court that they had seen one John Spur meet Obadiah Holmes after his whipping, "laughing in his face, saying, *Blessed be God for thee Brother*, and so did go with him, laughing upon him up towards the prison."

Mr. Cole testified that it "was very grievous to me to see him harden the man in his sin, and showing much contempt of Authority by that carriage, as if he had been unjustly punished, and had suffered as a righteous man, under a tyrannical Government."[83]

Tyrannical government or not, incidents of this sort continued to proliferate in New England's holy vineyards.

"These Rigid Ways Have Laid You Low"

In early July 1656, Mary Fisher and Ann Austin were waiting aboard a boat in Boston Harbor when the deputy governor, Richard Bellingham, caught wind of their arrival and ordered that they not be allowed to come ashore. Their books were taken forcibly from them, which were then burnt in the Boston marketplace, and all their boxes, trunks, and chests were searched thoroughly. Once they were in prison, the jailor even "rob[bed] them of their Bible, and so debarr'd them the use of the Scriptures."[84] Boards were nailed up over their jailhouse window to prevent people from coming to visit them, and they were not allowed to confer with any other person. When one old man, an inhabitant of Boston, tried to get provisions to them, he could only do so by bribing the jailor at a rate of five shillings a week. They were even "stript stark naked" in order to be searched.[85]

The heinous crime these two women had committed? Put simply, they were Quakers. And that was crime enough.

Ann Austin was a married woman and mother of five. Mary Fisher had hitherto been a missionary to the Turks.[86] At their trial Reverend Norton and Governor Endicott warned them, "Take heed yet break not Our Ecclesiastical Laws." So Austin and Fisher asked to see a copy of the law, but their request was rejected because no such law against Quakers had yet been codified.[87] So Austin and Fisher were banished. Eight other "Quakers" remained in prison for eleven weeks and were banished the day after a new law was finally published.

The law originally required banishment for the first offense and the chopping off of the ears for the second, but this proved too weak a penalty to prevent exiles from returning, so Massachusetts passed a second Quaker law demanding death for the second offense. "Ye are in a bad state, to become Persecutors your selves who fled Persecution," some objected, asking, "May not an English man come into an English Jurisdiction?"[88] The answer was apparently no, because the new, more stringent code soon found victims.

Mrs. Mary Dyer was passing through Massachusetts, on her way to Rhode Island to meet her husband, when she was arrested and imprisoned.[89] Her husband came to get her, and only after paying a large penalty and promising not to let her lodge anywhere or speak to anyone within the Bay Company's jurisdiction could he take her home. Mrs. Dyer was safe until 1659, when a merchant from London named William Robinson and a farmer from Yorkshire named Marmaduke Stevenson[90] crossed over into Massachusetts from Rhode Island. They were immediately apprehended and sent to prison to wait until the next session of the General Court. Having pity on them, Mary Dyer visited the men in prison. All three were banished upon pain of death, but this did not keep them away from the colony. Some four months later Mrs. Dyer returned to Boston on another visit to imprisoned Quakers. Five days after she arrived, Robinson and Stevenson joined her, accompanied by a small band "in the *Moving* and *Power* of the Lord, as

One Man, to look [their] Bloody Laws in the face, and to try *them*, and to accompany *those* who should suffer by *them*."[91]

Predictably, every one of the company was imprisoned and the three returnees brought before the court. Robinson requested to read a paper he had written explaining "his Call to Boston," but the governor refused and instead announced, "Hearken to your Sentence of Death,—You shall be had back to the Place from whence you came, and from thence to the place of Execution to be hanged on the Gallows till you are dead."[92] Stevenson and Dyer received similar sentences. At the time of their hanging, the two men were led amid loud banging of drums to prevent them from speaking to the people. Yet "with great cheerfulness of heart; and having taken Leave of each other with the dear Embraces of one anothers Love in the Love of the Lord," the two men were hanged.[93]

Meanwhile, at Mary Dyer's appointed time, the people cried out, "Pull her down!"—for, as one author noted, "Her Death they were against."[94] Dyer was bound, arms and legs, with "the Halter about her Neck, and her Face covered with a Handkerchief." As she stood upon the ladder, waiting for it to be pulled from beneath her, an order came to give her a reprieve because of the clamor of the people.[95] Dyer was returned to prison, where she wrote to the General Court:

> Even as before, my Life is not accepted, neither availeth me,
> in comparison of the Lives, and Liberty of the Truth and Servants
> of the living God; for whom, in the bowels of Love and Meekness
> I sought you: Yet nevertheless, with wicked hands have you put
> two of them to Death; which makes me to feel that the mercies of
> the wicked, are cruelty. I rather choose to die than live, as from
> you (who are guilty of their innocent blood). Therefore seeing
> my request is hindered, I leave you to the Righteous Judge, and
> Father of all Hearts. . . . For, He is my Life, and the length of my
> days: And as I said before, I came at His Command, and go at His
> Command.[96]

Dyer was finally executed in 1660.[97]

This practice of strict "discipline" did not sit well with the Puritans' brethren in England. New England dissenters urged the colony authorities to "consider their Brethren of the Congregational Way in England lest they justify those that trouble them there,"[98] and those English brethren concurred. John Cotton received a letter from Richard Saltonstall, one of the original members of the Bay Company who had returned to Europe, after it became known in England how dissenters were suffering under the whips of New England magistrates. Saltonstall wrote:

It doth not a little grieve my spirit to hear what sad things are reported daily of your tyranny and persecution in New England. . . . These rigid ways have laid you very low in the hearts of the saints. I do assure you I have heard them pray in the public assemblies that the Lord would give you meek and humble spirits, not to strive so much for uniformity.[99]

If internal religious struggles within the colony had not deflected attention away from external threats, it is likely that enforcement of religious uniformity would have continued with increasing vigor. But as it happened, by the time of Dyer's death, it had been three decades since Winthrop first arrived on the *Arbella*, and the original members of the covenant no longer held sway over the majority as they once had. The colony was slowly slipping away from those tenets that had defined it at its inception. And in some ways such slippage was inevitable.

Restricting the right to vote to church members was intended to preserve the religious character of the colony, but serious confusion resulted as churches became filled with the unconverted children and grandchildren of the "owners" of the original covenant. From the beginning of the colony, although ministers themselves could not hold civil offices, no adult could become a member of a church without the express approbation of the minister,[100] and this enabled the ministers to serve as the gatekeepers to both the civil realm and religious life of the community. Those who were not members of the church were not considered "freemen," and even juries gathered to judge nonmembers were composed solely of church members.[101] Thus the all-important question was, who is a church member?

In 1662, the Massachusetts ministers gathered in synod to address the matter. The proposal they adopted would become infamously known as the "Half-Way Covenant." The new arrangement made clear that children and grandchildren of members were "children" as opposed to "strangers" of the covenant upon their infant baptisms.[102] Such baptism was the only requisite for an individual to partake of the civil benefits of church membership. Partaking of the Lord's Supper was among those benefits reserved for those who exhibited both internal adherence to the "Covenant of Grace" and external adherence to the "covenant of the church." Yet if baptized-yet-unconverted adults wanted their own children baptized, they were simply required to give assent to the latter.[103]

Roger Williams, of course, had seen this compromise coming when he exhorted New England's true Christians not to seek to encompass the unregenerate in outward forms and ceremonies but instead take seriously the understanding that God's church is based on spiritual rather than geographical boundaries. Williams was considered a fanatic for insisting that internal spiritual and external ecclesiastical covenants should coincide.[104] His views never went very far in a place where forced worship was not only acceptable but a Christian duty. For, as John Cotton had said, "If it do make men hypocrites, yet better be hypocrites than profane persons. Hypocrites give God part of his due, the outward man, but the profane giveth God neither outward nor inward man."[105]

Whitewashed tombs, it was supposed, were better than no tombs at all.

The Noble Experiments of Baltimore and Penn

When the Puritans who were living in Virginia at the time of Charles I's beheading in 1649 were expelled from the royalist colony, most of them transplanted themselves in Maryland. In some respects, it seemed an unlikely place for Puritans to settle, since it was owned and governed by Roman Catholics, whom the Puritans considered allies of the Antichrist.

When Virginia became a royal colony in 1624, part of its territory was granted to Sir George Calvert. Calvert, a prominent Englishman who had been a member of Parliament and the secretary of state, possessed an entrepreneurial spirit that motivated him to undertake a variety of colonial and trading ventures. His sincerity in his conversion to Roman Catholicism prevented Calvert from establishing himself in Virginia because of its requirement that inhabitants subscribe to the Oath of Supremacy, so the proprietary grant enabled him to settle a colony within wide parameters.

Charles I, of course, had no particular antipathy toward Catholics and even made Calvert "Lord Baltimore" after he announced his conversion and resigned from political office on that account. After Calvert died in 1632, his son, Cecil Calvert, the second Lord Baltimore, gained possession of the land his father had been granted by virtue of the hereditary nature of the proprietorship. Charles, for whom Christianity was not limited to Protestantism, issued a charter in June 1632 that favorably described Cecil as "treading in the Steps of his Father, being animated with a laudable, and pious Zeal for extending the Christian Religion, and also the Territories of our Empire."[106]

By reason of necessity, although Catholics dominated governance of Maryland until 1648, the colony was home to a large number of Protestants, and Lord Baltimore instructed his Catholic colonists not to give offense to Protestants nor make the exercise of their faith too showy an ordeal.[107] Governors were required to take an oath that had the express purpose of protecting religious toleration:

I will not myself or any other, directly or indirectly, trouble, molest, or discountenance any person professing to believe in Jesus Christ, for or in respect to religion: I will make no difference of persons in conferring offices, favors, or rewards, for or in respect of religion: but merely as they shall be found faithful and well deserving, and endued with moral virtues and abilities: my aim shall be public unity, and if any person or officer shall molest any person professing to believe in Jesus Christ, on account of his religion, I will protect the person molested, and punish the offender.[108]

These sentiments were codified further in Maryland's Toleration Act of 1649—predating its English counterpart by forty years—when Protestants had achieved the majority in the legislative assembly and William Stone had recently been appointed as Maryland's first Protestant governor. Even though the act proscribed anyone from molesting another within the province "for or in respect of his or her religion or the free exercise thereof," it nonetheless maintained stiff penalties for anyone who blasphemed God, denied Jesus Christ as the Son of God, denied the Godhead or unity of the Trinity, used reproachful language concerning the Trinity, the Virgin Mary, the apostles, or the evangelists.[109] First-time offenders were to be fined five pounds sterling or be publicly whipped and imprisoned if they did not have adequate funds; second-time offenders would pay ten pounds sterling or be *severely* whipped and imprisoned if they were too poor to pay; and third-time offenders would forfeit *all* their lands and goods and be forever banished from the colony. If these penalties have a familiar ring to them, it is because they were intended to bring the act more in line with the Long Parliament's 1648 heresy and blasphemy law.[110] There was also a hate speech provision which leveled similar discipline on anyone using "*heritick, Scismatick, Idolator, Puritan, Independent, Prespiterian popish prest, Jesuite, Jesuited Papist, Lutheran, Calvenist, Anabaptist, Brownist, Antinomian, Barrowist, Roundhead, Sepatist* [sic], or any other name or term in a reproachfull manner relating to matter of religion."[111]

Lord Baltimore probably got more than he bargained for when he had set out purposely to attract Puritans to Maryland in order to prevent a group of overzealous Jesuits from taking control of the colony. Things got out of hand during the Commonwealth and Protectorate eras, leading to conflict between the more or less royalists who upheld the Proprietor's full authority and the increasing numbers of Puritans of Ann Arundel and Kent Counties who rallied behind the newly formed Commonwealth's claim to power.[112] In the miniature civil war that resulted, the Protestants spoke reproachfully of those who purported to be upholding Lord Baltimore's authority, saying the group of "Romish Catholicks, Malignants, and disaffected persons," along with "a great number of Heathen" acted under pretence and actually planned to execute a "bloody design" against the "poor oppressed" Puritans.[113] It did not help matters that Baltimore's defenders blatantly violated the Toleration Act by shouting out such epithets as *Rogues, and Round-headed Rogues!* and *"God bless the Lord Proprietary!"* and *"Hey for St. Maries!"* during their assaults.[114]

Baltimore and his allies failed to hold the fine line between appeasing the royalists and keeping the favor of Cromwell's government, and the Puritans gained ascendancy in Maryland until Charles II's restoration in 1660. Meanwhile, Jesuits were plundered, some were executed, and fines were exacted on Protestant "enemies."[115] Even though the Calverts regained control during the reigns of Charles II and James II, they lost their proprietorship forever in 1692 when William and Mary declared Maryland a royal colony and the Church of England was established there. Baltimore's experiment with religious toleration in the colony, though founded largely on grounds of expedience, ended in defeat—ironically, at the hands of Protestants.

Another proprietor did not fare much better. His name was William Penn. Like Baltimore, Penn was a prominent Englishman who managed a significant concession from the Stuart kings despite his status as a dissenter. After the Dutch colonies of New Netherlands and New Amsterdam were captured by the English in 1664, Charles II granted them to the Duke of York, his brother and the future James II. Whereas previously there were harsh laws prohibiting dissent from the established Dutch Reformed Church, the duke insisted that liberty of conscience be allowed under a system of coexistent "multiple establishments."[116] After some further exchanges, sales, and negotiations, "West Jersey" landed in the hands of Quaker proprietors, one of whom was Penn, who had definite inclinations toward religious liberty for settlers.[117]

In 1681, Charles II, ever strapped for cash, granted William Penn the territory now known as Pennsylvania as a payment for a £16,000 debt owed to him by the crown. Not unlike the Massachusetts founders, Penn had an expressly religious and theistic mission in establishing his colony—a "holy experiment."[118] But entirely unlike the Massachusetts founders, Penn also believed in ecclesiastical liberty.

The "frame of government" agreed to by Penn and the freemen of the colony in 1682, in accordance with royal procedural dictates, contains a detailed explanation written by Penn establishing why government is "a part of religion itself, a thing sacred in its institution and end."[119] In it he emphasized that "any government is free to the people under it (whatever be the frame) where the laws rule, and the people are a party to those laws" and declared that the people hold the ultimate responsibility for being good, since "Governments, like clocks, go from the motion men give them."[120] Article 35 clearly established the principle that there would be no ecclesiastical hegemony in the Pennsylvania colony, even though any form of atheism could not be tolerated:

> That all persons living in this province, who confess and acknowledge the one Almighty and eternal God, to be the Creator, Upholder and Ruler of the world . . . shall, in no ways, be molested or prejudiced for their religious persuasion, or practice, in matters of faith and worship, nor shall they be compelled, at any time, to frequent or maintain any religious worship, place or ministry whatever.[121]

The reason for this section was articulated in the Act for Freedom of Conscience, which was passed some months after the frame of government and spoke of the colony's desire to give "due reverence to [God's] sovereignty over the souls of mankind."[122] The act recognized the need for God "to have his due, Caesar his due, and the people their due," and referred to "Almighty God" as the "only Lord of conscience" who alone can "enlighten the mind and persuade and convince the understandings of the people."[123] Penn had served time in prison in England for his religious beliefs and actions, so he understood firsthand what it meant to face persecution for conscience's sake.

Everything progressed pleasantly until Penn's desire to abolish religious tests was rebuffed by English officials, to whom Charles had reserved the right to review Pennsylvania's legislation. At the onset of William and Mary's reign, the charter was temporarily suspended. During this time all Pennsylvania officials were to comply with the 1689 Toleration Act, which of course was far more stringent than Penn's original designs. The Toleration Act was even reinstated after Penn repealed its application when he returned to the colony in 1700.[124]

Thus, as with Maryland, the founders' liberal aims were defeated by the crown in the name of "toleration," even though the two colonies continued to provide a safer haven to dissenters who found themselves entirely unwelcome in places like Virginia. And, as with the Massachusetts Puritans, even religious life among the Quakers in Pennsylvania declined because of "birthright membership," which changed Quaker congregations from "church[es] of believers" to associations of "unconverted."[125]

Interestingly, today it is widely understood that the religious liberty later to become part and parcel of the American experience came not chiefly from

Maryland or Pennsylvania or even Rhode Island, but from the Anglican stronghold of Virginia. If no one was executed in the Old Dominion as in New England, Thomas Jefferson later noted, it was certainly "not owing to the moderation of the church, or spirit of the legislature."[126] Yet the steadfast conviction in the minds of a few that God alone possesses authority over the human soul was enough to demand respect and shake the establishment forever. The Supreme Court would state three centuries hence in the 1983 case *Marsh v. Chambers* that Virginia "took the lead in defining religious rights," chiefly through the adoption of its Declaration of Rights in 1776.[127] And as John Adams wrote from Massachusetts to Patrick Henry, "We all look up to Virginia for examples."[128]

So from this point forward we will turn to Virginia.

Chapter Nineteen

A NEW LIGHT IN HANOVER

The Virginia Presbyterians

*To bind men to a particular minister, against their
judgment and inclinations when they are more edified
elsewhere, is . . . a cruel oppression of tender consciences.*

GILBERT TENNANT

he Tidewater and Piedmont regions of Virginia are noted for
their distinguished families. Historically, these families were planters who
epitomized southern colonial aristocracy with their cultivated gardens,
expansive estates, refined cultural tastes, and stately mansions built along
the James River, upstream from Jamestown and within traveling distance of
Williamsburg.

The more modest portions of the area also have a strong agricultural
bent. The landscape of the counties of Hanover and New Kent still consists
largely of swatches of farmland cut out of thick deciduous forests, canopied
byways, and small rural towns with remnants of centuries-old courthouses,
churches, and jails. The pace of life is noticeably slower than in nearby met-
ropolitan centers like Richmond or the ever-encroaching Washington, D.C.,
suburbs of northern Virginia.

It is a place steeped in history. Historical markers abound. Here George Washington crossed with General Rochambeau as they headed to victory at Yorktown; there the Marquis de Lafayette escaped from General Cornwallis; slightly to the southwest is where Henry Clay was born in 1777. Dolley Madison lived in the county for a time. And it was the home of Patrick Henry.

We take up our story in the early 1730s, when religious dissent was yet a rarity in Virginia. By some accounts few found reason to take the dangerous risk of forming separate congregations. One such account is by George Webb, a justice of the peace in New Kent County. In a 1736 book designed as a practical legal manual on how to deal with problems ranging from drunkenness to forgery to pickpockets, Webb resolutely reported:

> This Government has hitherto enjoyed the singular
> Happiness, that all the Subjects here agree in Uniformity of
> Worship, according to the Doctrine of the Church of *England*,
> which is here by Law established: and we have among us no
> Conventicles, or Meetings, of professed Dissenters, except
> Quakers: All other Persons agree in a decent and uniform Exercise
> of the Protestant Religion, in their Parish Churches.[1]

Agreement or not, there was certainly no legal incentive for dissent. Webb recited the standard laws and procedures for handling religious misconduct: Those who denied the Trinity or inspiration of the Scriptures were to be disabled from all official civil capacities on the first offense and imprisoned on the second; those who absented themselves from divine service at the local parish church were to be fined and perhaps whipped; those who refused to have their children baptized by a minister of the established church were required to pay a stiff fine of two thousand pounds of tobacco.[2] Protestant dissenters could be tolerated within strict limits if they jumped through some hoops to get there, but no one was exempt from paying parish taxes.[3] The less conscientious perhaps often got away with absenting themselves from parish services without any serious penalties, but enforcement was bound to vary by locale. Inhabitants of the less-settled, westernmost portions of the colony were, in fact, left to worship largely unmolested; they seemed in a different category altogether.[4]

Ten years before Webb's account, the rector of St. Peter's parish in New Kent, John Lang, sent a mixed report to the bishop of London that likewise mentioned minimal nonconformity but also referred to the moral and spiritual degeneracy he observed in this generation:

I observe the people are very zealous for our Holy Church, as
it is established in England, so that (except some few inconsiderable
Quakers) there are scarce any Dissenters from our communion,
and yet at the same time supinely ignorant in the very principles of
religion, and very debauched in morals.[5]

If the laity were indeed guilty of immorality as Lang asserted, they were
only partly to blame. Clergymen of the Anglican Church in neighboring
counties had been charged with fornication, lying, negligence, and drunkenness.[6] Lang himself attributed the poor religious state of the colony to its
dissolute clergy, who were typically either sober and slothful or lewd and
debauched.[7] A fellow minister in nearby Isle of Wight County concluded
that their scandalous behavior was "such that it greatly tend[ed] to confirm
Atheists in their Infidelity and contempt of Religion, yea, to make Proselytes
thereto, or to any party besides the Church of England."[8]

The root of the problem, however, seems not to have been loose living;
despite some immoral colleagues, other ministers like Lang were known
explicitly for their "harangues on morality" and attempts to induce the
people to good behavior.[9] Rather, the real problem was a widespread failure
to feed and care for the internal spiritual life of the individual.

As required by Virginia law, aristocratic planters and vestrymen attended
the weekly reading of the homily, but Sabbath meetings of the parish church
were often more like business and political meetings, or "Drowsyland," in
the words of one author.[10] The common people did not fare much better
under the preaching, which contemporaries said was conspicuously lacking
fundamental evangelical doctrines and was dominated instead by "insipid
speculations."[11] As closely as the functions of church and state intertwined
in society, there appears to have been a pronounced disconnect between
the truly spiritual aspects of the church and the people. This was certainly
the case in St. Paul's parish in Hanover County, where Patrick Henry Sr. was
named rector in 1737.

The standard complaint against the established church was similar to
that of John Champneys, the English conventicler who had posited that the
clergy were unregenerate, and that of Samuel How, the cobbler who had
boldly asserted the uselessness of educated ministers who lacked the power
of the Spirit. In the words of Presbyterian minister Samuel Blair, who would
be instrumental in spreading revival from Pennsylvania to Virginia through
his pupil, Samuel Davies, "dead formality in religion" had begun to dominate
colonial society. Even churchgoers were content to aim at outward duty,
"stupidly indifferent about the great concerns of Eternity" and carelessly

ignorant of every individual's need to be reborn into "vital Union" with Christ.[12]

The chief proponent of the message of "new birth," both in England and the colonies, was a man raised in none other than Gloucestershire, the birthplace of William Tyndale.

"Market Language" to Common People

George Whitefield was born to a Gloucester businessman and his wife on December 16, 1714. His parents were the proprietors of the Bell Inn, a popular tavern that frequently served as a trading post for itinerant merchants.[13] Even after the death of her husband, George's mother continued to run the inn, often putting the young boy to work in a blue apron, cleaning rooms and washing mops. He was expected to become a tradesman like his older brother Richard, who eventually took on the responsibility of the family business. Young George even abandoned his Latin studies for a time by using the excuse that since family circumstances did not permit him to receive a university education, it would be useless to waste his time studying the classics. Yet God had other plans, and Whitefield ended up a student at Oxford University.[14]

During his time as a student, George read a book by Charles Wesley that dramatically changed his life. He later described his conversion in his autobiography:

> At my first Reading [of the book], I wondered what the Author meant by saying, That "some falsely placed Religion in going to Church, doing Hurt to no one, being constant in the Duties of the Closet, and now and then reaching out their Hands to give Alms to their Neighbors." Alas! thought I, *if this be not Religion, What is?* GOD soon showed me: For reading in a few Lines following, *That TRUE Religion was an Union of the Soul with GOD, and CHRIST formed within us;* a Ray of divine Light broke in upon my Soul, and from that Moment, but not till then, did I know that I must be a *New-Creature.*[15]

This theme became the animating feature of Whitefield's life. Before long, he was drawing large crowds who thronged to hear his sermons. Thousands at a time would gather to hear multiple sermons a day. When he was not preaching, he visited prisoners in Newgate and "expounded the Scriptures" to various societies.[16] Civil and religious authorities were distressed and wondered what to do with him. When Whitefield returned to

Oxford in 1739, the vice chancellor sent word to him not to preach and to get out of the place.[17]

If new birth was his theme, the vernacular was his medium. Whitefield's boyhood experiences at the inn helped bridge the gap between his scholarly pursuits and a desire to communicate gospel truth, not just to fellow learned men but also to the tradespeople and ordinary consumers who used to crowd the inn on market days. In the words of one observer, Whitefield "preached in what [was] called MARKET-LANGUAGE," the kind of speech "most likely to be understood and remembered by the common people."[18] He stood up for the least among citizens—whether prisoners, slaves, or "Mechanicks about Town."[19] Thus, in more ways than one, Whitefield was an heir of Tyndale's mantle.

In 1738, Whitefield made the first of his thirteen trans-Atlantic crossings to preach in the American colonies. Among those whom he would inspire there was Gilbert Tennent, son of the Irish-born Presbyterian minister who had founded what became known as the Log College in Neshaminy, Pennsylvania. Gilbert shared his father's evangelistic zeal, and he was eventually convinced to join Whitefield on his preaching tour of New England in 1740 and 1741. Although the young Presbyterian evangelists who graduated from the Log College were previously sent only to parishes where ministers were needed, Whitefield motivated them not to pay undue attention to physical boundaries and instead to preach even where uninvited.[20] Gilbert Tennent made this practice his own and boldly preached against the laws and officials that would have prevented the itinerants from disregarding parish boundaries. In doing so, he made a rousing case for liberty of conscience:

> To bind Men to a particular Minister, against their Judgment
> and inclinations, when they are more edified elsewhere, is carnal
> with a Witness; a cruel Oppression of tender Consciences, a com-
> pelling of Men to Sin: For he that doubts, is damn'd if he eat; and
> whatsoever is not of Faith, is Sin.[21]

As is evident from his relationship with the Tennents, Whitefield showed little concern for denominational differences and seemed unaffected by the disapproval toward itinerancy within Anglicanism. Of church government, he wrote, "I am persuaded there is no such form of church government prescribed in the book of God as excludes a toleration of all other forms whatsoever."[22] Although his communion with the Anglican Church was never formally broken, Whitefield was a hero in the eyes of dissenters. Although he purportedly declined an invitation to preach at a meeting house of the dissenters and told a man who entreated him to baptize his child to go to his parish minister instead, Whitefield later commented, "'Twas a silly scruple, and that this would be a means of bringing persecution on the people of God, and that not for righteousness' sake, either."[23]

When the evangelist passed through Virginia in late 1739 and preached on *What think ye of Christ?* at Williamsburg's Bruton Parish Church, few were in attendance to hear the sermon, perhaps due to a lack of publicity.[24] By the following year, however, copies of Whitefield's sermons were being reprinted in Williamsburg and began to circulate.[25] Other copies were brought over from Scotland with the wave of Scotch-Irish immigrants who were settling in large numbers in Hanover and further west in the Shenandoah Valley. One of these landed in the hands of a Hanover bricklayer by the name of Samuel Morris.

The Morris Reading Houses

As late as 1743, the series of religious revivals in Old and New England that would later be called the Great Awakening had not yet had any significant impact on the colony of Virginia. By nearly all accounts, the colony was not in the best spiritual condition. Religious persecution had died out to a degree, partly because there were so few dissenters in the eastern counties to threaten the establishment. As in George Whitefield's early experience, however, few parishioners of Saint Paul's in Hanover knew what they were missing.

That all changed one day when Samuel Morris managed to procure a book of sermons Whitefield had given in Glasgow that were transcribed by an onlooker and subsequently published. After reading them and finding them to be of great and unusual insight, Morris told his neighbors to come join him at his house where they could read and listen together. "The Plainness, Popularity, & Fervency of the Discourses, being peculiarly fitted to affect our unimproved Minds, and the Lord rendering the Word efficacious," he later recounted, "many were convinced of their undone Condition, and constrained to seek Deliverance with the greatest Solicitude."[26] Before long Morris's house was crowded beyond capacity as the people met to read the Bible, Whitefield, Luther (particularly his commentary on Galatians), and Bunyan, among others.

Although those who attended the "reading houses" at first had no intention of absenting themselves from worship at St. Paul's, they evidently found it more spiritually satisfying to listen to the simple readings than to sit through a service under Patrick Henry Sr., so they began meeting on Sunday mornings as well as weekdays. None of them had ever sung or prayed extemporaneously before, and they had no formal minister to lead them for some time. Morris simply continued his practice of reading the sermons aloud, and, as word spread, he was even invited to read at locations some distance away. In the words of one account:

> Numbers were pricked to the heart,—the word became sharp and powerful,—"what shall we do," was the general cry. What to do or say the principal leaders knew not. They themselves had been led by a small still voice, they hardly knew how, to an acquaintance with the truth; but now the Lord was speaking as on Mount Sinai, with a voice of thunder, and sinners, like that mountain itself, trembled to the centre. And it was not long before they had the happiness to see a goodly little number healed by the same word that had wounded them, and brought to rejoice understandingly in Christ.[27]

Word inevitably reached the ears of the civil authorities that these sundry meetings were occurring. Morris and his companions were summoned before the General Court, composed of the governor and the council, to explain their reasons for violating Virginia law. When asked to identify what denomination they belonged to, they did not know what to answer. Remembering that they had read some Luther and had agreed with his doctrines, the little band stated that they were Lutherans.[28] According to another story, perhaps apocryphal, one of their number was driven by a storm on his way to Williamsburg to take shelter in the home of a poor man, who happened to possess an old, dusty religious book. The traveler was impressed by its contents, which he thought corresponded perfectly with his own doctrinal understanding, so he and his friends presented it to the governor as a summary of their beliefs. The governor identified the volume as the Confession of Faith of the Scottish Kirk.[29]

Fortunately for the men from Hanover, the colonial governor (or lieutenant governor, to be precise) at that time was Sir William Gooch. Gooch had already promised religious toleration to the immigrants who had begun to settle to the west in the largely unsettled "Valley of Virginia," the fertile strip of land between the Blue Ridge and Allegheny mountains. Because of the desirability of settling the valley to provide a buffer against incursions from the west, Gooch was liberal in allowing German Lutherans, Quakers, and Scotch-Irish Presbyterians to establish settlements according to their liking.[30]

In 1738, some Presbyterians "about to settle in the back parts of Virginia" petitioned to the Synod of Philadelphia to gain a hearing with Governor Gooch and the council and to request accommodation for those of their persuasion. The synod accordingly addressed the governor to ask him to allow them "the liberty of their consciences, and of worshipping God in a way agreeable to the principles of their Education." Gooch replied that he indeed wished to show favor to those settling to the west and would not interfere with their ministers—as long as "they conform[ed] themselves to the rules prescribed by the Act of Toleration in England, by taking the oaths enjoined thereby, and registering the place of their meeting, and behav[ing] themselves peaceably towards the government."[31]

There is no indication that Morris or any of his friends knew of the governor's promise or of the terms of the Toleration Act. Neither did they know of anyone besides themselves who conscientiously absented themselves from parish services. With the possible exception of some Quakers, Hanover was Anglican through and through. Nevertheless, Gooch maintained that Presbyterians were tolerated within the colony even to the east of the mountains, and the reading house meetings continued unabated.[32]

Gooch's pronouncement was somewhat prophetic. Shortly thereafter, the New Castle Presbytery sent a minister named William Robinson on an evangelistic trip to the backwoods of Pennsylvania, Virginia, and North Carolina. The New Castle Presbytery had separated from the "Old Side" Synod of Philadelphia and was referred to derogatorily as part of the "New Lights" because of its hearty approval of the revivals begun by Whitefield and other itinerant preachers. Although another presbytery by the same name had remained allied with the Synod of Philadelphia, this New Castle Presbytery was associated with the Tennents and remained largely independent before joining the New Light Synod of New York in 1745.[33]

Hearing of Robinson's travels and the tendency of his preaching "to awaken people," the Hanover dissenters invited him to come preach to a gathering at their meeting house. They were concerned about how to examine his doctrine before he gave his sermon, so as a "test of orthodoxy," they decided to ask him what he thought of a number of books.[34] Robinson far exceeded their expectations. His first sermon was on Luke 13:3: "I tell you, nay: but except ye repent ye shall all likewise perish." The congregation continued to increase during the three subsequent days, and Robinson took pains to instruct his listeners in doctrine and to advise them in adding prayer and hymn-singing to their services.[35]

Even though Morris and his friends believed that God had blessed them in their simple practice of reading sermons, their exposure to Robinson's teaching caused them to seek help from the New Castle Presbytery in finding a more permanent minister. The presbytery answered their request in late 1744 by sending them John Roan. Reverend Roan was noticeably less temperate in denouncing the "degeneracy of the clergy," and it was only a matter of time before word reached Reverend Patrick Henry (uncle of the famous revolutionary leader) and his fellow parishioners, who made an effort to suppress the dissenters. Eventually, some "perfidious Wretch" (as Morris referred to him) made a deposition in which he claimed that Roan had spoken blasphemy and was denigrating the established church. Sensing danger brewing, Roan escaped from the colony.[36]

It was not a moment too soon. An indictment was drawn up against Roan, and some of the individuals whose houses he had preached at were told to appear before the General Court. Governor Gooch abandoned his typically tolerant stance and addressed the Grand Jury in a speech later published in the *Virginia Gazette*. He was willing to put up with those who were properly licensed under the Toleration Act, but neither the Hanover meeting houses nor their preachers had been properly sanctioned, and they even endeavored to lead innocent people astray:

> And therefore, gentlemen, since the workers of a deceitful work, blaspheming our sacraments, and reviling our excellent liturgy, are said to draw disciples after them, and we know not whereunto this separation may grow, but may easily foretell into what a distracted condition, by long forbearance, this colony will be reduced, we are called upon by the rights of society, and what, I am persuaded will be with you as prevailing an inducement, by the principles of Christianity, to put an immediate stop to the devices and intrigues of these associated schismatics, who having, no doubt, assumed to themselves the apostasy of our weak brethren, we may be assured that there is not any thing so absurd but what they will assert and accommodate to their favorite theme, railing against our religious establishment; for which in any other country, the British dominions excepted, they would be very severely handled. . . .
>
> I must, as in duty bound to God and man, charge you in the most solemn manner, to make strict enquiry after those seducers, and if they, or any of them, are still in this government, by presentment or indictment to report them to the court, that we, who are in authority under the Defender of the faith, and the appointed guardians to our constitution and state, exercising our power in this respect for the protection of the people committed to our care, may show our zeal in the maintenance of the true religion.[37]

In accordance with the charge given them, the grand jury made three presentments: one against Roan for saying such things as, "All your ministers preach false doctrine . . . and all who follow them, are going to hell," one against Joshua Morris (undoubtedly a relation of Samuel's, possibly his son) for permitting Roan to preach to "very many people" assembled "in an unlawful manner at his house," and one against one Thomas Watkins for saying, "Your churches and chapels are no better than the synagogues of Satan."[38]

The following month, the Synod of Philadelphia sent a letter to Governor Gooch affirming their approval of his speech to the grand jury and distancing themselves from "those persons" who had been sent out as missionaries not under their approbation but, rather, under "divisive, censorious, and uncharitable" New Light auspices.[39] Meanwhile, Morris and a companion traveled to a joint meeting of the New Light presbyteries of New Castle and New Brunswick (soon to be joined as the Synod of New York) in order to request that they dispatch an advocate to represent them in the proceedings. The presbyteries granted their petition by sending them Gilbert Tennent and Samuel Finley, whom Gooch willingly accepted as legitimately licensed. Tennent and Finley were granted liberty to preach.

The tactic proved successful for a while, and Morris and the others cited for religious misdemeanors escaped from whippings, imprisonment, and banishment, allthough they still had to pay significant fines. Morris later recounted:

> While my Cause was upon Trial, I had Reason to rejoice that
> the Throne of Grace is accessible in *all Places*, and that helpless
> Creatures can waft up their Desires unseen, to God, in the midst
> of a Crowd. Six Evidences were cited to prove the Indictment
> against Mr. *Roan*; but their Depositions were in his Favour;
> and as for the Evidence mentioned just now, who accused him
> of Blasphemy against God and the Church, when he heard of
> Messirs. *G. Tennent*'s and *S. Finley*'s Arrival, he fled, and has not
> returned since; so that the Indictment was drop'd. I had Reason to
> fear being banished the Colony, and all Circumstances seem'd to
> threaten the Extirpation of Religion among the Dissenters in these
> Parts.[40]

Morris faced repeated indictments and fines for continuing to hold meetings and for failing to attend parish services after Tennent and Finley left. One Sunday morning he awoke to find a proclamation by the governor posted at their meeting house "strictly requiring all Magistrates to suppress & prohibit, as far as they lawfully could, all itinerant Preachers, &c."[41] Before the week had passed, however, good news arrived from the north.

Samuel Davies

It has been said that when William Robinson was preparing to depart from Hanover in the summer of 1743, Morris's congregation offered him money as a token of thanks for his ministry and service to them. He refused, so they hid it in his saddlebags, which he discovered and again refused. After some conversation about whether to accept the gift, Robinson finally agreed to take it and give it to one young man "studying divinity to the North; whose parents are very hard scuffed." His name was Samuel Davies. When he was done with his studies and fully licensed, Robinson promised, Davies could return to be their preacher. And that is precisely what he did.[42]

Davies's arrival in Hanover was a cause for rejoicing among the Hanover dissenters. He immediately sought a license from the General Court to perform ministerial functions at four different meetinghouses, which was granted within a tolerable amount of time after he had taken the requisite oaths, declarations, and subscriptions. Yet this good will did not last for long. When Davies returned to Williamsburg the following year to help his friend and pastoral assistant, John Rodgers, become licensed, the court rejected his application. The court also determined that Rodgers would be imprisoned and fined five hundred pounds if he dared to preach anywhere within the colony.[43] Rodgers had no recourse or opportunity for appeal—save one to the king himself—since the General Court had taken away all matters pertaining to licensing from the jurisdiction of county courts and intended to exercise sole control. When the county court of New Kent subsequently tried to license a meeting house for dissenters within their county, the General Court revoked the grant.[44]

Regardless of what the governor intended or desired, the council was certainly interested in stepping up the heat on the dissenters. After a fire ravaged the capitol, the council recommitted themselves to defending the Church of England and pressing forward with a "Reformation of Manners" as an act of gratitude to God.[45] They pointedly addressed Gooch and reminded them of his duty in regard to religion in the colony:

> It is with Hearts full of the most unfeigned Concern, that
> we observe a Spirit of Enthusiasm introduced among the People
> by itinerant Preachers; a Spirit more dangerous to the com-
> mon Welfare, than the furious Element, which laid the Royal
> Edifice in Ashes; a Spirit productive not only of Confusion, but
> of Blasphemy, Profaneness, and the most wicked and destructive
> Doctrines and Practices, which, in the Days of their Forefathers,
> utterly subverted our excellent Constitution in Church and State.
> The Prevention of these shocking and prodigious Mischiefs, the
> Maintenance of Ecclesiastical as well as Civil Peace and Order, and
> the best Support of both, the Doctrine of the Church of *England*,
> demand our most hearty and unanimous Concurrence with your

Honour, in discouraging such Teachers, by what Name soever
known and distinguished, from settling, or even preaching, in this
Colony.[46]

Although Rodgers's case had been lost and the council was resolutely
against him, Davies did not give up. Only six months later, in November
1748, he was somehow successful in obtaining licenses for three more meeting houses in the counties surrounding Hanover.[47] Davies split his time
between all seven houses, traveling between them and preaching both on
Sundays and during the week. People who at first hesitated to depart from
the parish church went to hear Davies on weekdays, and many were soon
members of his congregations.[48] Some families traveled as far as thirty or
forty miles; and as the congregations and bystanders grew into the hundreds,
it became an increasing hardship for both Davies and his congregations to
be limited to one minister. Davies had a special concern for the "Negroes"
whom he baptized but lamented, "While my Charge is so extensive, and my
Labours parceled out among so many, I cannot take sufficient Pains with
them for their Instruction; which often oppresses my Heart."[49]

Colonial and ecclesiastical officials looked on the dissenters with
increasing suspicion. Speaking to an ally, Davies wrote, "Were your Soul,
Sir, contracted with the narrow Spirit of a Bigot, you would no doubt indulge
an ignoble Joy at the Tho't, that there are now some *Hundreds* of Dissenters
in a place where a few Years ago there were not *ten* that I know of within
a hundred miles."[50] And some narrow-spirited bigots there indeed were. In
1750, the commissary of London, William Dawson, wrote a letter to the
bishop asking for his advice regarding Davies's multiple congregations. Have
we erred and gone beyond the intent of the king's instructions[51] and the Act
of Toleration, Dawson asked, in granting Davies permission to teach at more
than one house?

Davies caught wind of the scheme to involve the bishop of London and
requested help from the eminent English nonconformist Philip Doddridge.[52]
Doddridge decided that, as an acquaintance of the bishop's, he would write
a letter to him and enclose a portion of a letter written by Davies regarding the state of dissenters in Hanover and elsewhere. The bishop responded
to Doddridge with courtesy but made clear that if anyone interpreted the
Act of Toleration to mean that "every body has a natural right to propagate
their opinions in religion in such manner as they approve themselves," he
was deeply mistaken.[53] Under a clause of a law passed under Queen Anne in
1711, dissenting ministers were able to preach *occasionally* in a county other
than where they resided and were licensed. The bishop pointed this out and
insisted that the Toleration Act "was never intended to permit [dissenters]

to set up itinerant preachers, to gather congregations where there was none before."[54]

Even though Doddridge seemed to imply that some nonconformist ministers in England got away with preaching consistently in locations other than where they were licensed, colonial authorities were not about to let Davies slip by without a fight. Peyton Randolph, the attorney general, stuck to his argument that just as Anglican ministers were legally confined to their parishes except for occasional visits elsewhere, so too dissenting ministers were legally confined to the place where they were originally licensed. "One man, one pulpit" would have been a fitting maxim. This, of course, placed the legitimacy of Davies's multiple licenses in doubt, but Davies's repeated skill in defending himself outdid even the distinguished attorney general.[55]

Davies countered his opposition with the claim that he was *not* acting as an itinerant but as a settled minister for several congregations and that the Act of Toleration was ineffectual in its purpose of relieving tender consciences if the people had to travel an impractical distance to the place where their preacher was licensed.[56] He insisted that the bishop had misinterpreted his actions and that his purported "intrusive schismatical itinerations" were nothing of the sort; he desired only "to preach repentance towards God, and faith towards our Lord Jesus Christ."[57] It was true that he abstained from denigrating the established clergy and exalting his own denomination; his chief concern was for Christianity, whatever denominational form that might take.[58] Far from desiring to subvert church and state, Davies maintained that he could be considered orthodox and loyal, as proved by his belief in the doctrines in the Westminster Confession and catechism and his compliance with the law's oath requirements.[59]

Davies took extra measures to convince Reverend Patrick Henry by going point by point through the Thirty-Nine Articles and explaining those parts where he differed—all of which were reservations permitted under the Toleration Act. One of the foremost was article 37, stating that the kings and queens of England have the chief government over ecclesiastical matters as well as civil:

> I readily concede, That Principles subversive of Civil Society, & of the Foundations of N[atu]ral and reveal[e]d Religion, then propagated, may justly be checked by Civil Authority, & the Propagators of them punished with condign Punishment. But I cannot grant, That civil Rulers have Authority to preside in, and determine Controversies about Matters of Faith, & Affairs that Peculiarly concern the Church: The Determination of these, I humbly conceive, belongs ultimately to God speaking in his word,

& subordinately to Church Judicatures; not excluding the invio-
lable right of private Judgment.[60]

Reverend Henry may not have been listening, but other people were—
his own nephew among them.

Parson's Cause

When the words "Give me liberty, or give me death!" echoed through
St. John's Church in Richmond, Virginia, in 1775, they did not spring from
untaught lips. Patrick Henry, who was named after his uncle, had no formal
college education, but the training he received in its place proved no less
effective.

He was born to John and Sarah Henry in 1736 in Hanover. John and
his brother had emigrated from Scotland after completing their educations
at Aberdeen University, and both quickly established themselves in respectable positions in the colony. John married a Hanover native, Sarah Winston
Syme, after the death of her first husband. While John and his brother were
staunch supporters of the established church, the Winstons were involved
in the activities of the Hanover dissenters.[61] Sarah followed in her family's
footsteps and frequently took her son Patrick with her to one of the meeting
houses in the vicinity to hear Samuel Davies preach.[62]

Davies was known for his extraordinary oratorical skills. One individual
described his sermons as the epitome of "sublimity and elegance, plainness and
perspicuity, and all the force and energy that the language of mortals could
convey . . . in a word, whatever subject he undertook, persuasive eloquence
dwelt upon his tongue; and his audience was all attention."[63] As the story goes,
Sarah Henry would take her double gig to and from the meeting house. On the
way home she would make young Patrick, on the seat beside her, repeat Davies's
sermons to her as they drove. The Winstons were said to possess an exceptional
gift in the way of public speaking to begin with, but Patrick's portion was
undoubtedly nurtured and inspired by the example of Pastor Davies.[64]

A number of years would pass before Patrick was given the opportunity
to demonstrate his skill to the public. While he was occupied with starting his family and business, trying his hand at farming, and getting his law
license, the situation of the Hanover dissenters began to improve substantially. The number of well-educated and upright ministers increased, and the
government began to lighten its hand after failing to receive any instructions
(contrary or otherwise) from the bishop of London. It was the outbreak of
the French and Indian War, however, which perhaps had the greatest effect
on the dissenters' status in the colony.[65]

As in England following the Restoration, fear of French Catholicism—this time from the Louisiana Territory to the west—had forced colonial Anglican authorities to accommodate nonconformists. The French and British were now at war in North America, and as many of the Virginia dissenters lived farthest to the west, they had to endure the brunt of attacks by French and Native American forces. The dissenters were just as interested in defending the colony as their eastern neighbors, and the governor and other officials were not about to interfere with their religious practices at a time when the British forces and Virginia militia needed all the help they could get.

Furthermore, Davies was a sterling recruiter. He gave two "war sermons" in Hanover during the conflict—one in 1755 to Captain Overton's Independent Company of Volunteers called "Religion and Patriotism, the Constituents of a Good Soldier" and another in 1759 to Hanover County's militia, aimed at raising a company for Captain Samuel Meredith, called "The Curse of Cowardice." "Our Territories are invaded by the Power and Perfidy of *France*," Davies cried. "Our Frontiers are ravaged by merciless Savages, and our Fellow-Subjects there murdered with all the horrid Arts of *Indian* and Popish Torture."[66] Following depictions of "mangled Limbs" and "ript-up Women," Davies asked:

> And shall these Ravages go on unchecked? Shall *Virginia* incur
> the Guilt and the everlasting Shame, of tamely exchanging her
> Liberty, her Religion, and her All, for arbitrary *Gallic* Power, and
> for Popish Slavery, Tyranny and Massacre? Alas! are there none
> of her Children, that enjoyed all the Blessings of her Peace, that
> will espouse her Cause, and befriend her now in the Time of her
> Danger?[67]

Davies emphasized that peace with men was one of the principal truths of Christianity but also that when an enemy would "enslave the free-born Mind" and seek to tear away "your Religion, the pure *Religion of Jesus*, streaming uncorrupted from the sacred Fountain of the Scriptures," it was time for arms.[68]

Although the clearest echoes of Davies's style in Patrick Henry's speeches would appear later, on the eve of American independence, a speech Henry gave one day at the Hanover Courthouse in 1763 stunned the ears of his listeners. The event was a legal case that came to be known as Parson's Cause. Events in the case were precipitated by the passage of the so-called Two Penny Acts in the House of Burgesses in 1755 and 1758. For many years, each parish minister's stipend had been fixed by law at 16,000 pounds of tobacco. When droughts produced meager tobacco crops in 1755 and 1758, added to losses caused by the war, the colonial legislature overwhelmingly passed relief measures allowing tobacco farmers to pay their debts in currency at a fixed rate equivalent to two pence per pound, far below the market rate, for a set period of time. Reverend Patrick Henry and other members of the Virginia clergy had responded to the first act by sending a letter to the bishop of London requesting that the act be repealed. They complained that the act would make it extremely difficult for the colony to attract good ministers, especially when dissenters were increasing and "gaining ground." "Here then," the ministers wrote, "is the best opportunity for them to exult & triumph" by seeing the reduction of the established clergy's privileges.[69] An agent of the clergy was sent to England and returned over a year later with a royal disallowance of the act.

Among the clergy who sued the parish collectors for damages and back pay was James Maury,[70] who succeeded in getting the Hanover County Court to declare the 1758 act null and void. A jury was then selected to determine damages. Although Maury objected to the jury selection, he could not provide good proof of the reasons, other than the fact that there were no "gentlemen" on it. So none other than Samuel Morris, founder of the reading houses, and two other dissenters joined the jury of twelve. The counsel for the defendants had already abandoned the case, so Patrick Henry was hired in his place.

Henry argued with amazing rhetorical effectiveness, basing his case on the grounds that government is a conditional contract. The king had illegitimately annulled an act of the people, and he was thereby guilty of tyranny. Furthermore, Patrick contended, an established church existed in order to "enforce obedience to civil sanctions," so by failing to uphold the duly passed acts and, in fact, contradicting them, the clergy "ought to be considered as enemies of the community" and Reverend Maury should be penalized rather than compensated. The jury was overawed and awarded damages of *one penny*.[71]

This case was one of the final straws in cementing the wedge between the established clergy and the people of the colony. As Reverend Henry and his fellow parishioners feared, it was a triumph not only for the colonial legislature but also for the dissenters.

A Well-Paved Road

Although Samuel Davies never went so far as to campaign for disestablishment and full-blown religious liberty, he "paved the way."[72] As an archivist for the Virginia State Library once wrote in a special report:

The setting-up of a rival sect in the colony, with a form of government responsive to popular wishes, broke in upon the autocracy of the old regime. It is true that in a few years the Presbyterians, with their natural conservatism, ceased actively to antagonize the establishment and settled down to a quiet existence, but they had paved the way for other dissenters who would demand a further extent of liberty. The crust of privilege was broken and democratic ideas in religion and politics spread and strengthened. At the same time the moral and spiritual life of the colony was deeply influenced, and the foundation was laid for the conquest of Virginia to evangelical Christianity.[73]

While he lived, Davies never failed to encourage the dissenters to be politically active in defense of their right to worship freely. Only a few years after Davies's arrival in Hanover, Samuel Morris became involved in campaigns for the House of Burgesses in Hanover. Morris and his friends had made a practice of screening the candidates and getting them to state in writing, with bond, whether they would support the division of St. Paul's into two separate parishes. The dissenters, of course, objected to the division because it would mean higher taxes for them when they already had their own minister to support besides those of the established church. The elections were later declared invalid, supposedly because they had been improperly influenced by money. One Virginia planter surmised that the real reason was that the dissenters had dared to interject their voice into colony politics.[74]

Today among the trees in eastern Hanover is a place counted in the National Register of Historic Places—little noticed but of great significance. It is the site of a meetinghouse where Samuel Davies preached to one of his congregations. Here was the birthplace of religious revival in eighteenth-century Virginia—revival that began with both planters and ploughboys in the home of a bricklayer. As in England in the days of Tyndale, there was an irrepressible yearning for spiritual instruction that few even realized they possessed until they received it—outside the established church.

Chapter Twenty

BE YE SEPARATE

The Virginia Baptists

*Convince us by argument that we are misled with error,
and I trust we will repent and reform. But until then, we
crave the freedom to go in the way which we verily believe
is most agreeable to the New Testament.*

DAVID THOMAS, BAPTIST PASTOR

For Virginians of the mid-eighteenth century, the *Virginia Gazette* out of Williamsburg contained a wealth of information. The publisher, William Parks, was an adventurous entrepreneur who had started the paper in 1736.[1] Petitions, advertisements, bits of gossip from England, reports from the legislature, and even some entertainment-oriented pieces found their way into public print for the first time in the colony. This was quite an accomplishment in a place where Governor Berkeley had previously thanked God "there are no free schools nor printing [in Virginia] . . . for learning has brought disobedience, and heresy, and sects into the world, and printing has divulged them. . . . God keep us from both!"[2] Even though Parks was to be hauled before the General Court on occasion for printing particular items that rankled the authorities, the *Gazette* provided a forum in which Virginians could read not only about shipwrecks in Cadiz and duels in London but also what was happening with dissenters at home and abroad.

In 1752, Parks printed some accounts from Norwich, England, where Methodists and Baptists were still being molested, not necessarily by city magistrates but by angry mobs. One day in January, a cobbler-turned-Welsh Methodist preacher was splashed with mud while some in the crowd banged on drums to distract him. The following month, a rowdy group broke into a Baptist meeting house, staged a mock service, shattered windows, and "very much abused" the members of the congregation. As the irritated crowd grew into thousands, officials tried to intervene, but the rioters shouted all the more, "Church and King, down with the Meetings!"[3]

Earlier, in the late 1730s, Parks had reported that Quakers were taking records of their sufferings to members of Parliament and pleading for relief.[4] He also obliged Quakers in Virginia by publishing a petition they addressed to the colonial governor, council, and House of Burgesses, lamenting their imprisonment and the confiscation of their property for their failure to pay parish levies because of "conscientious refusal."[5] In the following issue, however, Parks printed a piece of satire submitted by a reader to ridicule the Quakers. It was titled "Instructions how to make a perfect QUAKER." The piece began, "First, take a handful of the Herb of Deceit, and a few Leaves of Folly, and a little of the Rose of Vain-Glory . . . and stew them altogether in a stony-hearted Jugg, over the Fire of cold Zeal . . . and suck every Morning thro' a Spout of Ignorance."[6]

More than thirty years later, well after Parks's death, a strikingly similar piece appeared that instructed readers on how to make "an ANABAPTIST PREACHER in two Days Time." It read:

> Take the Herbs of Hypocrisy and Ambition, of each one
> Handful, of the Spirit of Pride two Drams, of the Seed of
> Dissention and Discord one Ounce . . . bruise them altogether in
> the Mortar of Vain-Glory, with the Pestle of Contradiction, put-
> ting amongst them one Pint of the Spirit of Self-Conceitedness.
> When it is luke-warm let the dissenting Brother take two or three
> spoonfuls of it. . . . This will make the Schismatic endeavor to
> maintain his Doctrine, wound the Church, delude the People, jus-
> tify their Proceedings of Illusion, foment Rebellion, and call it by
> the Name of Liberty of Conscience.[7]

By the 1760s, the Baptists of Virginia had become the colony's most-persecuted sect, and the harassment and obloquies against them far exceeded anything the Hanover dissenters had endured. Presbyterian congregations typically contained a fair share of educated, upper-class individuals who were respected in their communities, and this status coupled with the congregations' willingness to apply for licenses greatly minimized the amount of persecution that denomination might have otherwise suffered.[8]

But the Baptists seemed to be a different breed altogether. Many were caricatured as little more than country bumpkins who could not be bothered to do so much as *apply* for licenses for their preachers and meetinghouses, much less receive them. In 1772, the *Gazette* devoted its entire front page and part of the second to a piece addressed to some Baptists imprisoned in Caroline County, just to the north of Hanover. The author explained that the Baptists were perfectly free to hold their private opinions, but when it came to preaching publicly, the legislature was likewise perfectly within its rights to establish religion and set bounds to its toleration; everything outside of what the government established should be considered heresy and schism. The world has been acquainted with the Scriptures "for upwards of seventeen Hundred Years," the author quipped, so why should you think you have anything more to offer by explaining them according to your understanding?[9]

In the eyes of authorities, it was the epitome of obstinacy and stubborn ingratitude for unlicensed Baptists to preach. Yet in the eyes of many Baptists, merely to apply for a license was to acknowledge the legitimacy of the government's control over religion, which they decried as a surrender of God's sole prerogative to Caesar.

Persuasion and Persecution

In a brief history of religion in Virginia, a Virginia Baptist named John Leland once reflected on the humble origins of his denomination. "About the year 1765," he recorded, "the Baptists began to spread in Virginia. Several ministers came from the Northern States, and some rose in the South, and preached, *Repent for the kingdom of God is at hand.*" Yet persecution followed immediately on the heels of their success. In Leland's words, "the Baptists met with great opposition: The Ministers were imprisoned, and the disciples were buffeted; but God preserved them amidst all their foes."[10] And, in fact, they not only were preserved but flourished.

Although the Hanover reading house congregations had already been established for more than twenty years when Baptists began to meet in homes up and down the Virginia Piedmont, both movements had their roots in the preaching of George Whitefield.

One individual touched by the revival that followed in Whitefield's wake was a man by the name of Shubal Stearns.[11] After his conversion, Stearns remained a member of the established church in his home of Tolland, Connecticut, for several years before forming a so-called "Separate" congregation—outside the establishment—of which he was pastor. The church was based on principles of congregational autonomy and had a membership of only the "regenerate." It was not long before Stearns began to question whether there was, in fact, a biblical basis for the practice of infant baptism, and after deciding in the negative, he became a Baptist in 1751. Many others in both Connecticut and New England followed a similar path, transitioning from membership in the Congregational establishment to becoming members of "Separate" congregational churches and, later, of "Separate Baptist" churches.[12]

Stearns and some of his friends set out from Connecticut in 1754, headed south in response to what they believed the clear calling of God. They stopped in northwestern Virginia but then continued journeying through the backwoods after receiving letters from friends there who said that the people were in desperate need of a preacher. In November 1755, Stearns and fifteen other people formed a church at Sandy Creek, North Carolina. Within a short time the congregation had grown to more than six hundred. It became a kind of missionary base from which these Separate Baptists could take their message north into Virginia.

Among the original sixteen members was Daniel Marshall, Stearns' brother-in-law. Marshall had been a missionary to the Native Americans prior to joining Stearns on his journey to North Carolina but soon found a mission field among his own countrymen. His untiring efforts reaped rich rewards as he planted churches and sometimes baptized as many as forty-two people at a meeting. Samuel Harris, a Hanover native whom Marshall baptized in 1758, proved to be a faithful compatriot. Like Marshall, Harris traveled and preached extensively.

One day in 1765, while Harris was giving a message in southern Virginia's Pittsylvania County, a man named Allen Wyley "providentially" ran across the meetinghouse while on a mission to fetch a preacher for a congregation further north in Culpeper. After some deliberation Harris agreed to go with Wyley.[13] On the way they stopped at various houses, "exhorting and praying" at each one.[14] Harris finally reached Wyley's home, where he preached for two days. On the second day a mob appeared bearing whips, sticks, and clubs with which to harass the congregation gathered for worship. Another time in neighboring Orange County, a man named Benjamin Haley took it upon himself to pull Harris down from the platform and drag him about by the hand, leg, and hair, until some friends rescued Harris and scurried him off to hide in the loft of a nearby house.[15] Despite such inhospitable welcomes, Harris continued to preach at various locations, drawing large crowds of willing hearers, as well as the usual indignant hecklers.[16]

Most of Harris's opposition came from "gangs" of dubious authority, though sometimes the county courts were involved. Once, Harris was arrested in Culpeper on accusations of being "a vagabond, a heretic, and a mover of sedition everywhere." He told the court that he lived hundreds of miles south and would not preach within that county again for a year. But a few days later Harris's conscience began to bother him and "the word of God began to burn" in his heart. Not able to brush the conviction aside, he told the congregation with whom he was worshipping, "I partly promised the devil, a few days past, at the court-house, that I would not preach in this county again for the term of a year; but the devil is a perfidious wretch, and covenants with him are not to be kept, and therefore I will preach."[17]

So he did. And the Separate Baptists continued to multiply and spread. In 1769, there were only seven Separate Baptist churches in Virginia—three to the north of the James River and four to the south. Five years later the number of established congregations had reached fifty-four, and the number of recorded members reached nearly four thousand.[18]

Pockets of Baptists had been scattered throughout Rhode Island, Pennsylvania, South Carolina, and New England for many decades prior to the so-called "New Light Stir" of the 1740s, but they differed in a few significant ways from their Congregationalist-turned-Separate Baptist counterparts. Many of these newer congregations, for instance, had direct connections to their English counterparts, some adopting a confession of faith that had been drawn up by a group of English Baptists in and around London some sixty-five years earlier. Indeed, many of the congregations were pastored by English Baptist immigrants. One of these was a Pennsylvania church founded in 1688 by Elias Keach, son of the English Baptist minister Benjamin Keach who was put in the pillory and had his book, *The Child's Instructor*, burned before his eyes after the Restoration.[19]

Within the colonies Baptists were sometimes differentiated by the names "Regular" and "Separate." The Separates grew out of the revivals of the 1740s, while the Regulars had been established for some time, chiefly in those colonies with less stringent religion laws. Both groups began to appear and multiply in Virginia in the 1760s. Although neither was able to avoid persecution, the Separates bore the brunt of the harassment since the Regulars were more willing to apply for licenses under the Toleration Act and exhibited less "enthusiasm" in their preaching and worship services.[20]

Whereas the Regulars often required members to adhere to a confession of faith or carefully defined doctrinal system, the Separates "took the Bible alone for their guide."[21] In 1808, William Fristoe, a Regular Baptist pastor in northern Virginia, described the difference in these terms:

The regular Baptists were jealous of the separate Baptists because, as yet, they never formed nor adopted any system of doctrine, or made any confession of their faith, more than verbally; and it was thought unreasonable, that if they differed from all other denominations, why they should not in a fair, open and candid manner, make known their principles to the world, and in so doing, act as children of the light; and on the other hand, the separate Baptists supposed the adopting a confession of faith would only shackle them; that it would lead to formality and deadness, and divert them from the Bible.[22]

Simply put, it was primarily fear of confessions of faith becoming vehicles of coercion that made the Separates averse to adopting one. When the Separates formed their first association in Virginia in 1771, members unanimously agreed that it would possess "no power or authority to impose anything upon the churches" but, rather, serve only an advisory role.[23]

By 1787, however, the Regulars and Separates in Virginia joined under one banner when they realized, as Leland wrote, that "all agreed in repentance towards God, and faith in our Lord Jesus Christ . . . [and] that none were subjects of baptism but believers."[24] Even their pronounced doctrinal differences (for example, over predestination) did not prevent them from jointly adopting a confession of faith but only with a proviso to satisfy the Separates:

But to prevent [the confession from] usurping a tyrannical power over the consciences of any, we do not mean that every person is to be bound to the strict observance of everything therein contained, yet that it holds forth the essential truths of the gospel and the doctrine of salvation by Christ, and free unmerited grace alone, which ought to be believed by every Christian, and maintained by every minister of the Gospel.[25]

In the end much more united the two groups than divided them. Both had separated from the established church, and both faced heated opposition. England separated from Rome first for "the love of a woman"[26] and afterwards gave better reasons, they noted; why should we not be able to separate first for conscience's sake?[27] The chief reason for their separation was tied directly to religious liberty. In the words of one of their own, "No national church can, in its organization be the gospel church. A national church takes in the whole nation, and no more; whereas the gospel church, takes in no whole nation, but those who fear God and work righteousness in every nation."[28] For this reason, the Virginia Baptists concluded, no civil magistrate can rightfully interfere with religion in his official capacity, and "the notion of a Christian commonwealth, should be exploded forever"— unless, of course, all members were "real Christians."[29]

The right of private judgment was a concept central to the Baptist mind-set. As David Thomas, a Regular Baptist pastor, wrote:

> No man is, or can be safe in a blind submission to the deter-mination of others, tho' ever so right in themselves. The apostolic rule in disputable points is this, "Let every man be fully persuaded in his own mind." *Rom.* 14.5. And indeed without such a persua-sion, I can't perceive how we could expect acceptance with *GOD.* . . . Convince us by argument that we are misled with error, and I trust we will repent and reform. But until then, we crave the freedom, to go in the way which we verily believe is most agreeable to the New Testament.[30]

Despite their emphasis on the individual believer, the Baptists formed tightly knit communities with strict accountability. Even the acting gov-ernor, John Blair, in 1768 acknowledged that the Baptists' seriousness in practicing church discipline had been remarkably effective in encouraging good behavior.[31] Members were confronted for everything from failing to provide adequately for their families to defending themselves in an angry and disorderly, or "irregular," manner.[32] "If this be their behavior," Blair wrote to the Spotsylvania County attorney, "it were to be wished, we had some of it among us."[33]

Although the Baptists were in some ways more strict about who could enter their communion, in other ways they were also less so. Even slaves were not excluded from becoming coequal brethren.[34] Social rank mattered little to the Baptists, and the many common folk in their number made them despised as "an ignorant illiterate set—and of the poor and contemptible class of people."[35] Even though the College of Rhode Island (later Brown University), founded by Baptists in 1764, did some to remove the stigma of intellectual inferiority, the Baptists still lacked a classically educated minis-try during their period of greatest growth in Virginia. They did not neces-sarily see this, however, as a liability. As David Thomas asserted, "That we deny the use of human learning, is a mistake. Though we don't approve of it as a mistress; yet we esteem it as a serviceable handmaid. It is one thing to respect literature in its proper place, and another to idolize it."[36]

This outlook, especially in terms of wealth and rank, was in stark con-trast to Virginia high society.[37] When members of the gentry came to check in on Baptist meetings, normally to disperse them, they were not necessarily met with the deferential and respectful greetings they were accustomed to receiving elsewhere. A story is told about a colonel and his men who interrupted John Leland during his sermon "under the pretence of civil authority." Leland stomped the floor and answered back, "In the name of God *forbear!*" Returning home with injured pride, the colonel told his mother, "Why he stamped at me and made no more of me than if I had been a dog! I'll have no more to do with them."[38]

But other authorities were more vindictive. And if Baptist preachers were not being disturbed by the "half drunken strolls" who were paid to beat drums to prevent people from hearing sermons, then the pastors were hauled into prison and harassed by the fumes of "pepper pods" burnt at their cell doors.[39]

"Most Dreadful Accusations"

A common accusation against the Baptists was that their meetings diverted the people from their work. Some with ill intent are said to have sneaked into the worship services, counted the men, then multiplied the number by a day's wage. After coming up with an impressive-sounding number, they would bemoan, "All this loss is sustained by the wretched new-Lights, had it not been for them all this might have been saved, and our country much enriched; we fear times will grow worse and worse, without a stop can be made to the career, and some preventative devised that may bring them to silence."[40]

A favorite tactic of the Baptists' opponents was to sing obscene songs in the middle of sermons or engage in lewd jesting to divert the listeners' attentions, but fines and imprisonment were popular among the more "genteel."[41] Although it was reported that Virginians could whittle away their days "card playing, horse racing, cock fighting, fish frying, barbecuing, shooting matches, and other fashionable vices" without the interference of a magistrate, Baptists met with repeated fines for nonattendance at the established church.[42] Some were brought to court on charges of holding conventicles, preaching without Episcopal ordination, failing to qualify themselves in accordance with the Act of Toleration, and teaching doctrines "to the subversion of all Religious Establishments."[43]

Sometimes, the arrests and trials served only to create new converts. John Waller was in his thirties when he served on a jury during the trial of a Spotsylvania County Baptist preacher named Lewis Craig. Prior to that time, Waller had been notorious for his frivolous lifestyle (financed by gambling), crude speech (earning him the name of "Swearing Jack"), and furious contempt for the Baptists (which he expressed by presenting them in court as nuisances). When Craig was declared guilty of preaching and fined as punishment, Waller was astounded by Craig's response. Craig said, "I thank you, gentlemen, for the honor you did me. While I was wicked and injurious you took no notice of me; but now having altered my course of life, and endeavoring to reform my neighbors you concern yourselves much about me." Waller began to ponder the "absurdity of his conduct," began attending the Baptist meetings, repented, and was baptized in 1767. He was ordained a minister three years later.[44]

Only a year after Waller's baptism, he and Craig landed in jail together. They were at a meetinghouse in Spotsylvania in early June 1768 when a sheriff came and took them, along with a few others, outside where three officials were waiting. They made the men promise to appear in court two days later upon pain of heavy fines. Once they were in court, a lawyer named Oliver Towles made "most dreadful accusations" against them, one of which was, "May it please your worships, these men are great disturbers of the peace, they cannot meet a man upon the road, but they must ram a text of scripture down his throat." But Waller made such an impressive defense that the court said he could be released if he promised to quit preaching for the space of a year plus a day.

Waller and his associates refused to comply with the stipulation, convinced that they would rather obey God than man. So the five men were escorted through the streets of Fredericksburg to the jail, singing an Isaac Watts hymn that begins, "Broad is the road that leads to death" and ends with the stanza:

> Lord, let not all my hopes be vain
> Create my heart entirely new;
> Which hypocrites could ne'er attain,
> Which false apostates never knew.

While in prison, the Baptists preached through the windows in the jail. People "flocked" to listen, and the preaching "made very serious impressions" on eleven men and many in their families. Craig was released first and went straight to Williamsburg to petition the acting governor, John Blair. Blair wrote the Spotsylvania County attorney and told him he hoped to see the Baptists left alone until the General Court convened and could decide whether to grant their preachers licenses under the Toleration Act. For whatever reason, Waller and the rest were finally released, and the officials were glad "to get rid of him."[45]

In early 1771, Waller was leading the singing of a psalm during a service in Caroline County, probably held outdoors, when they were interrupted by Mr. Morten, the parish minister, and Thomas Buckner, Morten's clerk. Morten rode up to the platform Waller was standing on and used his whip to flip the pages of the hymnbook in an effort to make Waller lose his place. When this proved unsuccessful, Morten shoved the end of his whip into Waller's mouth, and Buckner yanked Waller over to the sheriff, who stood nearby. The sheriff completed the injustice by whipping Waller twenty times, then let him go free. Waller triumphantly remounted the stage "in a gore blood" and "preached a most extraordinary sermon, thereby showing that *beaten oil* is best for the sanctuary."[46]

Craig and Waller, of course, were not the only ones to receive appalling treatment from mobs and authorities. When the Chesterfield County court indicted William Webber and Joseph Anthony for itinerant preaching and demanded that they cease, Webber and Anthony refused, knowing they could not comply in good conscience, and so were cast into jail.[47] Another time, Webber was preaching from James 2:8 in Middlesex County when a county magistrate, the parish minister, and some others ran into the congregation and dragged a number of them into a flea-infested jail while they waited for a trial. One man was severely whipped, and Webber fell sick while in prison. Twenty-eight of the prisoners' friends signed a petition to the Middlesex County court which pleaded:

> That whereas your worships made an order last Court for the Baptist Preachers now in our Prison Bounds to enter into Recognizance not to preach or teach in the County for six months under Certain penalties and they being Conscientious and fearing God Could not Consent to the said Conditions . . . We therefore pray your Worships would Reconsider their Case, supersede the aforesaid Order, and release them from their imprisonment to Return home to their Distressed Families.[48]

The men were eventually released, their practice of preaching to the people outside the jail walls making their adversaries "desirous to be rid of them."[49]

On occasion, the Baptists had advocates. When "Elder" Jeremiah Moore was arrested while preaching and placed on trial in Alexandria, after the justice warned "you shall lay in jail until you rot," tradition has it that Patrick Henry defended him with the expression, "Great God, gentlemen, a man in prison for preaching the gospel of the Son of God?!"[50] Typically, however, the Virginia Baptists were left to fend for themselves.

Redress of Grievances

Starting in 1770, Baptists from all over Virginia began petitioning the House of Burgesses for relief from discrimination and persecution. As with Samuel Davies, even those Baptist ministers who applied for licenses and received them were still legally limited to one meetinghouse, which caused considerable hardships for people who lived great distances away from the nearest settled minister of their persuasion and therefore had to rely on itinerant preachers instead.

The most notable wave of requests to the House of Burgesses came in early 1772, immediately after the House had convened in Williamsburg on Wednesday, February 10, "in the twelfth Year of the Reign of our Lord *George* the Third, by the Grace of God . . . Defender of the Faith, &c."[51] Appointments to the Committee of Religion were made after a vote on the customary "humble address" to the royal governor to thank him for his "obliging speech" at the opening of the session. Patrick Henry of Hanover was among those appointed to "take under their Consideration all Matters and Things relating to Religion and Morality."[52]

The following day a petition was read from Baptists in Lunenburg County. In the minutes of the House of Burgesses, it was recorded that these Baptists found themselves "restricted in the Exercise of their Religion, their Teachers imprisoned under various Pretences, and the Benefits of the Toleration Act denied them." The petition was referred to committee.[53] On February 22, another petition was read with the same grievances and requests for "kind Indulgence in religious Matters" from Baptists in the county of Mecklenburg.[54] Two days later two Baptist petitions were read: one from Sussex County and another from Amelia, the latter of which explained the "severe Persecution" the Baptists endured and requested "Liberty of Conscience may be secured to them."[55]

On February 27, a bill was reported out of the committee on religion "for extending the Benefit of the several Acts of Toleration to his Majesty's Protestant Subjects, in this Colony, dissenting from the Church of England."[56] On March 17, the Committee reported an amendment,[57] and the bill was published the following week in the *Virginia Gazette*. Although the bill made the guarantee that all Protestant dissenters in Virginia "shall have and enjoy this full and free Exercise of their Religion, without Molestation or Danger of incurring any Penalty whatsoever," it mandated that they could not meet at night, nor with locked doors, and that the county courts were empowered to summon any dissenting minister and require him, upon pain of imprisonment, to take oaths of allegiance and a declaration of belief in the Scriptures.[58]

The governor repeatedly prorogued the House of Burgesses, so that they were prevented from voting on the bill. As soon as the assembly reconvened in May 1774, one of the first items of business was a Baptist petition expressing concern that the bill's prohibition of worship at night was "inconsistent with the laws of *England*, as well as the Practice and Usage of the Primitive

Churches, and even of the English Church itself."[59] A few days later a petition from Baptist ministers all over the colony arrived, asking that it be made
expressly clear that dissenting ministers could preach "in all proper places,
and at all Seasons, without restraint."[60] For whatever reason, the toleration
bill never came to a final vote.

By August 1775, the first shots in the war for American independence
had been fired, and Virginia was in the thick of the colonies' mobilization
efforts against the British. The Baptists were "to a man" in favor of American
independence and saw in the war an opportunity to achieve the religious liberty they had always desired.[61] With this in mind, representatives of Baptist
churches in the state joined together at a central location, Du Puy's meetinghouse in what is now Powhatan County, on the second Saturday of the
month. They selected Samuel Harris as a moderator. Their purpose in meeting was to coordinate efforts for religious liberty. As Robert Baylor Semple
wrote in his 1810 *History* of the Baptist denomination in Virginia:

> They had known from experience that mere toleration was not
> a sufficient check, having been imprisoned at a time when that law
> was considered by many as being in force. It was therefore resolved
> at this session to circulate petitions to the Virginia Convention
> or General Assembly throughout the State in order to obtain sig-
> natures. The prayer of these was that the church establishment
> should be abolished, and religion left to stand upon its own merits,
> and that all religious societies should be protected in the peaceable
> enjoyment of their own religious principles and modes of
> worship.[62]

Encouraged by Patrick Henry's call for liberty five months earlier in
his famous speech before the Second Virginia Convention, the delegates to
the Baptist gathering petitioned the Third Convention to include religious
liberty in the conduct of the American effort.

John Waller, as the clerk, transcribed the petition in his own hand on
behalf of the association of Baptist churches. The members of the Virginia
Convention were addressed as "the Guardians of the Rights of [their]
Constituents" and acknowledged as holding the responsibility for protecting
the freedom of the American people in Virginia. The Baptists wrote first and
foremost of their commitment to stand against British tyranny:

> Alarmed at the shocking oppression, which in a British cloud
> hangs over the American Continent, we as a society and part
> of the distressed state, have in our Association considered what
> part might be most prudent for the Baptists to act in the present

unhappy contest. After we had determined "that in some cases it was lawful to go to war—and also for us to make a military resistance against Great-Britain, in regard to their unjust invasion, and tyrannical oppression of, and repeated hostilities against America," our people were all left to act at discretion with respect to enlisting, without falling under the censure of our community—And as some have enlisted and many more likely so to do, who will have earnest desires for the ministers to preach to them during the campaign, we therefore delegate and appoint our well-beloved brethren in the ministry, Elijah Craig, Lewis Craig, Jeremiah Walker and John Williams, to present this address and to petition you that they may have free liberty to preach to the troops at convenient times without molestation or abuse: And as we are conscious of their strong attachment to American liberty, as well as their soundness in the principles of the Christian religion, and great usefulness in the work of the ministry, we are willing that they may come under your examination, in any matters you may think requisite. We conclude with our earnest prayers to Almighty God, for his Divine Blessing on all your patriotic and laudable resolves, for the good of mankind and American freedom, and for the success of our colonies in defense of our lives, liberties, and properties. Amen.[63]

Two days after the petition was presented, on Wednesday, August 16, 1775, Patrick Henry recorded the following resolution of the Third Virginia Convention:

Resolved that it be an instruction to the commanding officers of the regiments or troops to be raised to permit dissenting clergymen to celebrate divine worship and to preach to the soldiers or exhort from time to time as the various operations of the military service may admit for the ease of such scrupulous consciences, as may not choose to attend divine worship as celebrated by the chaplain.[64]

For the first time in Virginia history, the Baptists had been recognized favorably by a representative governing body and promised the free exercise of religion while they served the cause of American freedom.

Chapter Twenty-One

"VERY EARLY AND STRONG IMPRESSIONS"

James Madison at the College of New Jersey

That diabolical, hell-conceived principle of persecution rages among some and to their eternal infamy the clergy can furnish their quota of imps for such business.

JAMES MADISON

he College of New Jersey was chartered in 1748 with strict instructions to posterity not to deny "any person of any religious denomination whatsoever from free and equal liberty and advantage of Education or from any of the liberties, Privileges, or immunities . . . on account of his or their being of a religious profession different from the said trustees."[1] The trustees, a majority of whom were ministers, contained in their number the most ardent of New Light Presbyterians—Gilbert and William Tennent, Samuel Blair, and Samuel Finley.[2] The college was founded as an educational alternative to the establishment institutions like New England's Congregationalist Harvard (theologically liberal) and Virginia's Anglican William and Mary (with dissolute administrators); it had ties not to Oxford and Cambridge but to English academies founded by dissenters who still found themselves unwelcome at the mother country's foremost universities.[3]

305

At the college's inception, classes met at the home of Jonathan Dickinson, its first president. Dickinson was a New England Presbyterian who had been one of the first to voice opposition to the decisions of what would become the "Old Side" in the Philadelphia Synod. Prior to 1729, when a majority of the synod voted to require that all ministers formally subscribe to the Westminster Confession, Dickinson preached strongly against subscription.[4] He argued that the Scriptures were entirely sufficient in themselves "to make the *Man of GOD* perfect in, and thoroughly furnish him for, the whole Work of his Ministry."[5] No human, Dickinson warned, possesses power or authority "to impose *Interpretations* of Scripture" and thereby usurp Christ's *"absolute legislative Power."*[6]

Regardless of Dickinson's cautions that "human inventions" in the church become the "source of innumerable Michiefs and Confusions,"[7] the synod continued to press for stricter qualifications for ministerial candidates. Educational credentials became an integral part of the licensing process, as they had been in England, and this issue came to a climax in 1738 when the synod mandated that ministers within its jurisdiction possess degrees from either New England (i.e., Harvard or Yale) or European educational institutions.[8] For those like Dickinson and the Tennent brothers, the latter of which had been schooled in their father's Log College, this was yet another sign of the great need to establish a college with a distinctive New Light bent.

The Doctor

James Madison Sr., of Orange County, Virginia, was an Anglican vestryman at his local parish church, but the College of New Jersey nevertheless seemed to offer the most promising education for his son, James Jr. The closest option was the College of William and Mary in Williamsburg, not too many miles southeast of the family plantation. All other considerations pointed north.

For one, James Jr. had been taught by a Presbyterian and a College of New Jersey alumnus from the time he was twelve. The first was a Scotsman named Donald Robertson who ran a boarding school in King and Queen County.[9] After a few years with Robertson, James moved backed home to be tutored by the Anglican minister Thomas Martin. Martin served briefly as a parish minister after his graduation from the College of New Jersey, and his brother, Alexander—a revolutionary patriot and future governor of North Carolina and United States senator—had also attended the college. The Martin brothers, by James's own admission, had a great deal to do with convincing the Madisons that the College of New Jersey was the best choice.[10] Also, not incidentally, the president of William and Mary at the time was known to be a "High Church Tory" who had aspirations of becoming the first American bishop—something that even some devout Anglicans resisted furiously.[11] Perhaps less significantly, the Virginia Tidewater was known to be ill suited for the health of individuals from more mountainous regions.

By the time young Madison arrived in Princeton, New Jersey, in the summer of 1769 after a long, hot, and dusty journey north from Orange County through Philadelphia, accompanied by the Martin brothers and a faithful slave named Sawney, the college had developed into a thriving center of educational rigor, missionary spirit, and patriotic fervor. No longer meeting for classes in the president's parlor, students studied, slept, ate, participated in recitations and disputations, attended morning and evening prayers, researched in the library, and listened to lectures and chapel messages in Nassau Hall. Named after William III, of the House of Orange-Nassau, Nassau Hall was a stately structure that had been constructed in Princeton after Samuel Davies conducted a successful fund-raising trip in England and Scotland during the early 1750s. The college was also entering a phase of relative stability, with a new president, John Witherspoon, having arrived from Scotland the year before to replace a series of presidents after Dickinson, all of whom died within a few years of assuming their position.

John Witherspoon was a good fit for the still-young school. He was essentially a compromise candidate between the Old and New Light factions, which had officially reunited in 1758 but still possessed some residual differences and competitiveness.[12] Witherspoon had not been privy to the squabbling between the two groups that had existed for decades while he was engaged in ministerial work in his native Scotland, and thus was not hindered by prior alliances and arguments. He was warm-hearted yet commanded respect and demanded strict discipline, staunchly orthodox yet never afraid to explore science and philosophy to its limits, dogmatic to the point of causing offense yet an advocate of liberty. In Witherspoon the evangelical, civic, and academic aims that had motivated the founding of the college blended easily together.

Samuel Davies had originally discovered Witherspoon when he was in England fundraising for the school. The work that caught his eye was Witherspoon's *Ecclesiastical Characteristics*, a satirical piece exposing the dangerous faults of the "Moderates" who were then gaining ground within the Scottish Kirk.[13] Davies wrote in his journal after visiting Edinburgh that "a great number of the clergy and laity have of late carried church-power to an extravagant height, deny to individuals the right of judging for themselves, and insist upon absolute universal obedience to all the determinations of the General Assembly."[14] Additionally, in Witherspoon's opinion, the Moderates placed too high a premium on intellectual and societal respectability—

at the expense of orthodox doctrine and preaching that convicted rather than entertained with fashionable rhetorical tropes. According to *Ecclesiastical Characteristics*, among the maxims of the "moderate men" with whom many young Scottish men had become "smitten" were the following:

> His authorities must be drawn from heathen writers, NONE, or as few as possible, from Scripture. . . .
>
> He must be very unacceptable to the common people. . . .
>
> A minister must endeavor to acquire as great a degree of politeness, in his carriage and behavior, and to catch as much of the air and manner of a fine gentleman, as possibly he can. . . .
>
> In church-settlements . . . the only thing to be regarded is, who is the patron and the great and noble heritors are for; the inclinations of the common people are to be utterly despised. . . .
>
> A moderate man is to have great charity for Atheists and Deists in principle, and for persons that are loose and vicious in their practice; but none at all of those that have a high profession of religion, and a great pretence to strictness in their walk and conversation.[15]

From this and other more academic works, the College of New Jersey's board of trustees recognized that Witherspoon was a man of conviction who would have no trouble standing against roughly comparable "moderate men" in America who then thrived at places like Harvard.

Once in Princeton, Witherspoon began immediately to shape the curriculum, classes, discipline, and general tenor of the college in the direction he thought best. His philosophical bent, which has been the source of endless comment and critique over the years, defies precise categorization. What *is* clear is that he fought vigorously against the philosophical idealism which had crept into the college during the presidency of Jonathan Edwards, primarily via the systematic thought and writings of Anglican bishop George Berkeley.[16] In brief, the tendency of this brand of idealism was to posit that knowledge is derived from ideas and that ideas themselves constitute reality.[17] This grated on President Witherspoon's conviction, commonly associated with Scottish "common sense" thinkers, that "our senses are to be trusted in the information they give us."[18] In the words of Ashbel Green, a student and future president of the college, Witherspoon "reasoned against the system" and then later "ridiculed it till he drove it out of the college"—along with a handful of tutors who resigned within a year of his arrival.[19]

When Samuel Blair wrote as president in 1764 that the mission of the college was "to train up our youth in the paths of piety and erudition, for the future service of their country," he meant what he said. Witherspoon also took this literally and led by example. A total of 469 young men graduated from the college during the time of his presidency, including a future United States president, a vice president, six members of the Continental Congress, twenty U.S. senators, twenty-three members of the House of Representatives, thirteen state governors, and three Supreme Court justices—not to mention ministers, college presidents and professors, attorneys general and judges in lower courts, poets and writers, and even medical doctors.[20] Witherspoon himself signed the Declaration of Independence and was elected to the Second Continental Congress and the legislature of New Jersey.

Witherspoon's passion for American liberty—religious (to a degree) as well as civil—was undoubtedly translated to his students. He lectured to seniors in his hallmark class, "Moral Philosophy," on subjects ranging from personal and civic virtue to the holiness of God to the role of the civil magistrate. The express aim of the course was to inquire into the "the nature and grounds of moral obligation by reason, as distinct from revelation," which enabled students to meet their philosophical opponents on their own turf, so to speak.[21] In doing so, Witherspoon took pains to emphasize that "there is nothing certain or valuable in moral philosophy, but what is perfectly coincident with the scripture."[22] He did not hesitate to voice loudly his opinion of all manner of writers and thinkers who did not meet his standard of orthodoxy or reasonableness.[23]

Thus, in Moral Philosophy, Madison likely was listening with attention when Witherspoon categorized the right (or duty) of a man to "judge for himself in all matters of religion" as something that should never be surrendered.[24] Witherspoon told his class that at their moment in history, "one of the most important duties of the magistracy is to protect the rights of conscience" and that "we ought in general to guard against persecution on a religious account as much as possible."[25] He combated the idea of "infidels" that Christians are necessarily persecutors by reminding his students that Christians were, in fact, some of the first to *be* persecuted for claiming "that the gods of the heathens were no gods."[26] Elsewhere, although he counseled that "he is the best friend to American liberty, who is most sincere and active in promoting true and undefiled religion," Witherspoon warned, "Do not suppose, my brethren, that I mean to recommend a furious and angry zeal for the circumstantials of religion, or the contentions of one sect with another about their peculiar distinctions. I do not wish you to oppose any body's religion, but every body's wickedness."[27]

For his part, Madison looked upon "the Doctor," as he fondly referred to him, with deep respect.[28] Besides taking his courses, Madison joined his fellow students every morning after six o'clock prayers to listen to Witherspoon preach a message on a Scripture passage after the members of the senior class translated the verses from the original Hebrew or Greek into English.[29] Madison also probably partook of meals frequently with the president, who often joined students in the dining hall to sup on simple and moderate dishes of whatever "fish and flesh" the market happened to afford.[30] And it was no large campus community—in Madison's graduating class, only twelve bachelor's degrees were granted.[31] After finishing his course of study in September 1771, only two years after being admitted, Madison stayed on at the college until the following April to study Hebrew and theology with Witherspoon.

Time and Eternity

Madison worked so hard during college, in fact, that he damaged his health. He had no clear direction as yet in regard to his vocation, but it seems that Madison entertained thoughts of going into the ministry and following in the footsteps of those men who had taught him and whom he seemed to admire most.[32] And he certainly might have headed that direction if he thought he possessed adequate physical stamina. Sometime either during his two and a half years in New Jersey or shortly thereafter when he returned home to recover and tutor his younger siblings, Madison copied verse-by-verse, nearly verbatim notes from Proverbs and a commentary series on the Gospels and the book of Acts. Among these:

[Acts 22] Carnal Reason, when against the command of God, should be laid by. v. 19

[Acts 23] Conscience[:] it should be inform'd as well as followed. v. 1 . . . Magistrates must do nothing blindfold or blindly. Should know a Cause before they give sentence or Judgment about it. v. 35

[Acts 24] Persecution, a persecuting Spirit claps Wings to a Person[.] It makes him swift in his Motions & Zealous in his application & Endeavours. v. 1

[Acts 25] Politicians (Carnal) do not so much consider what is Just & Righteous in its own nature as what is of use & Advantage to themselves be it Right or Wrong v. 9 &c

[Acts 26] Ministers[:] great is the dignity of Gospel Ministers they are God's Messengers v. 16. &c

[Matthew 10] Lost Sheep, the Israelites so call'd because they were lost in themselves & were in great Danger of being eventually & finally lost, by the Ignorance & Wickedness of their spiritual Guides v. 6. Preachers, must not be strikers v. 10.

[John 20] Angels to be desired at our feet as well as at our head—not an angelical understanding and a diabolical conversation—not all our religion in our brains and tongue, and nothing in our heart and life.[33]

Writing of the Bereans in Acts 17 who "searched the Scriptures daily, whether these things were so," Madison scribbled, "a noble example for all succeeding Christians to imitate and follow."[34] Of course, both Madison and the author of the commentary, William Burkitt, read from the Tyndale-influenced King James Version of the Bible.

Around the same time Madison was reading Burkitt at home in Orange County, he began corresponding with William Bradford, son of a prominent Philadelphia family, who probably began college at Princeton at the same time Madison did but received his bachelor's degree after the usual three years instead of Madison's two.[35] In their correspondence, both men wrote fondly about their college experiences and old acquaintances, and Madison—four years Bradford's senior—often threw in a fair share of counsel to his younger friend.

"My dear Billey," he wrote in November 1772, "a watchful eye must be kept on ourselves lest while we are building ideal monuments of Renown and Bliss here we neglect to have our names enrolled in the Annals of Heaven." Madison confided that his illness had prompted him "to not expect a long or healthy life" and that he therefore had "little spirit and alacrity to set about any thing that is difficult in acquiring and useless in possessing after one has exchanged Time for Eternity."[36]

Bradford wrote back, "My dear Jemmy," reminding Madison of Witherspoon's prayer, "[God] spare useful lives."[37] And in Madison's case indeed He would.

Throughout the following year, Madison's mood remained much the same. In their letters he and Bradford chiefly discussed Bradford's choice of a career. Bradford was waffling between going into divinity, law, or possibly even "physic" or "merchandize." Although he had always wanted to be a minister, he felt himself unqualified, and law seemed to have a reputation for being "prejudicial to morals." He comforted himself in the latter option, however, with Dr. Witherspoon's comment that "a man of known probity will have great weight with the Judges and his very appearing in a cause will influence them in its favour."[38] Madison responded with a hint of disappointment, recommending to Bradford that he "always keep the Ministry obliquely in View whatever your profession be." Madison then added:

I have sometimes thought there could not be a stronger testimony in favor of Religion or against temporal Enjoyments even

the most rational and manly than for men who occupy the most
honorable and gainful departments and are rising in reputation and
wealth, publicly to declare their unsatisfactoriness by becoming
fervent Advocates in the cause of Christ, & I wish you may give in
your Evidence in this way. Such Instances have seldom occurred,
therefore they would be more striking and would be instead a
"Cloud of Witnesses.["] . . . I greatly commend your determined
adherence to probity and truth in the Character of a Lawyer but
fear it would be impracticable. . . . Though it must be allowed
there are a thousand cases in which your rule would be safe and
highly commendable.[39]

Although Madison concluded his letter with the determined statement,
"I do not meddle with Politicks," within three months, he would begin to
indicate an increasing interest in current affairs—almost against his will.
Cries for liberty and American independence were in the air.

In with Politicks

Madison would write late in life that he was "under very early and strong
impressions in favor of Liberty both Civil & Religious."[40] If by "early" he
meant from his childhood, he may have been referring in part to his eager
reading of *The Spectator*, past volumes of which were probably lying around
his family's home for perusal even before he was born. He copied some of it
into his commonplace book when he was a young teenager and told someone
after his presidency that it was "one of the earliest books which engaged his
attention" and "peculiarly adapted to inculcate in youthful minds, just sentiments[,] an appetite for knowledge, and a taste for the improvement of the
mind and manners."[41]

The essays in this English daily periodical were chiefly written by author
and politician Joseph Addison, who was described as "a zealous advocate for
Virtue and Religion against Profaneness and Infidelity."[42] Addison wrote on
one occasion:

In that disputable Point of Persecuting Men for Conscience
Sake, besides the embittering their Minds with Hatred,
Indignation, and all the Vehemence of Resentment, and ensnaring
them to profess what they do not believe; we cut them off from the
Pleasures and Advantages of Society, afflict their Bodies, distress
their Fortunes, hurt their Reputations, ruin their Families, make
their Lives painful, or put an End to them. Sure when I see such
dreadful Consequences arising from a Principle, I would be as fully

convinced of the Truth of it, as of a Mathematical Demonstration, before I would venture to act upon it, or make it a Part of my Religion.

In this Case the Injury done to our Neighbor is plain and evident, the Principle that puts us upon doing it, of a dubious and disputable Nature. Morality seems highly violated by the one, and whether or no a Zeal for what a Man thinks the true System of Faith may justify it, is very uncertain. I cannot but think, if our Religion produces Charity as well as Zeal, it will not be for showing it self by such Cruel Instances. But, to conclude with the Words of an Excellent Author, *We have just enough Religion to make us hate, but not enough to make us love one another.*[43]

Whether Addison's words influenced Madison to any degree is not known. What is clear is that by January 1773, Madison had arrived at a decided opinion on the topic.

Immediately after Bradford announced his final decision to study law, which he began by eagerly reading William Blackstone's *Commentaries on the Laws of England*, Madison jotted down, "Here allow me to propose the following Queries. Is an Ecclesiastical Establishment absolutely necessary to support civil society in a supreme Government? & how far it is hurtful to a dependent State?"[44]

The question was at the forefront of Madison's mind. Without waiting for Bradford's answer, Madison commented in a subsequent letter on the revolutionary activities then occurring in Boston. He then stated with surprising certitude and conviction:

If the Church of England had been the established religion in all the Northern Colonies as it has been among us here and uninterrupted tranquility had prevailed throughout the Continent, It is clear to me that slavery and Subjection might and would have been gradually insinuated among us. Union of Religious Sentiments begets a surprising confidence and Ecclesiastical Establishments tend to great ignorance and Corruption all of which facilitate the Execution of mischievous projects. But away with Politicks![45]

And yet he could not help himself. After warning Bradford yet again about avoiding "dirty and unprofitable Companions," Madison returned to the subject toward the end of his letter:

Poverty and Luxury prevail among all sorts: Pride ignorance and Knavery among the Priesthood and Vice and Wickedness

among the Laity. This is bad enough But it is not the worst I have
to tell you. That diabolical Hell conceived principle of persecution rages among some and to their eternal Infamy the Clergy
can furnish their Quota of Imps for such business. This vexes me
the most of any thing whatever. There are at this [time?] in the
adjacent County not less than 5 or 6 well meaning men in close
G[ao]l for publishing their religious Sentiments which in the main
are very orthodox. I have neither patience to hear talk or think of
any thing relative to this matter, for I have squabbled and scolded
abused and ridiculed so long about it, [to so lit]tle purpose that
I am without common patience. So I [leave you] to pity me and
pray for Liberty of Conscience [to revive among us].[46]

Madison's personal encounters appear to have ultimately stirred his soul
and made him eager to take action against persecution. He was not a typically passionate person—more inclined to sit, study, ponder, and write than
to take sides in a public debate or draft legislation; indeed, he preferred good
literature to law, musing that to study the latter instead of the former was
like "leaving a pleasant flourishing field for a barren desert."[47] But at a time
when he was still young and wondering what his future held, Madison took
notice of the outrageous treatment of Virginia dissenters and saw in them a
cause worth fighting for.

Chapter Twenty-Two

FREE EXERCISE OF RELIGION

The Virginia Declaration of Rights

That religion, or the duty which we owe to our Creator,
and the manner of discharging it, can be directed
only by reason and conviction, not by force or violence; and
therefore, that all men are equally entitled to
the free exercise of religion . . .
THE VIRGINIA DECLARATION OF RIGHTS, ARTICLE XVI

ewis Craig, the Baptist preacher who suffered numerous imprisonments and was instrumental in John Waller's conversion, had a younger brother named Elijah.[1] Elijah Craig became a Baptist in the mid-1760s at about the age of twenty. He and other young Baptists began meeting in a building used for storing crops, which served as their chapel most evenings after the day's work was complete.[2] In 1768, Elijah was arrested—some accounts say at his plow, for he was a "plowman"[3]—and confined to jail after refusing to stop teaching his "schismatick doctrines."[4] Yet he continued preaching through the bars of the jail window. Authorities built a high wall around the prison to keep people from hearing and confined Elijah to an "inner dungeon" where there was only a small hole through which he was fed bread and water.[5]

After his release, Elijah Craig became pastor of the Blue Run Baptist congregation and preached at a church planted by Samuel Harris in Rapidan.[6] The Blue Run church, composed of four hundred families from the surrounding Orange County area, was located just a few miles from the Madison family's vast plantation, which would later be given the name Montpelier.

From the time James Madison was but a lad running about the sloping hills of the Virginia Piedmont, the area had been home to many relatives and cousins from both parents' families. One of these was Francis Taylor, his second cousin on his father's side. James and Francis were roughly the same age and boarded together at the Robertson school.[7]

Even when James and Francis grew up and went their separate ways, their interests converged over American independence. Both were members of the Orange County Committee of Safety, organized in late 1774—James Madison Sr. was the chairman, and Francis Taylor, his cousin's son, was the clerk.[8] During the war with Britain, Francis served as officer for two Virginia regiments, eventually attaining the position of colonel.[9]

Interestingly, a "Francis Taylor" also appears in a list of founding members of the Baptist church in Rapidan compiled by Morgan Edwards in the late 1700s.[10] Although it ostensibly could be referring to Francis's father, Francis Taylor II, it is more likely that it was James's second cousin. Either way, Madison almost certainly had personal connections with the Rapidan Baptist minister, Elijah Craig. As time passed, his interactions with Craig and other Virginia dissenters would play a key role in his own fight for religious liberty in the colonies.

Madison's Public Service Begins

By April 1774, Madison was making no apologies to Bradford for interjecting commentaries on politics into his letters. Virginia and her sister colonies were buzzing with talk of tyranny, liberty, and Boston's recent defiance of the English Parliament's Tea Act. Madison had started keeping up with affairs at Williamsburg, where it was well-known that the House of Burgesses would be pressed to address numerous petitions from dissenters when the new session opened at the beginning of May. Previous attempts had been made to pass the Bill to Extend the Act of Toleration but to no avail. Ever since one of the first versions of the bill made its way into the *Virginia Gazette* in March 1772—the month before Madison returned home from New Jersey—the paper had published a number of front-page editorials by individuals who were both for and against relieving the burdens on Protestant dissenters.[11] Even in England, the *Gazette* reported, Newgate prison had turned into a "French Bastile" for dissenting ministers who had to be fetched from the countryside, sixty or seventy miles away.[12]

On this subject Madison wrote to Bradford:

> Our Assembly is to meet the first of May When It is expected something will be done in behalf of the Dissenters: Petitions I hear are already forming among the Persecuted Baptists and I fancy it is in the thoughts of the Presbyterians also to intercede for greater liberty in matters of Religion. For my part I can not help being very doubtful of their succeeding in the Attempt. The Affair was on the Carpet during the last Session; but such incredible and extravagant stories were told in the House of the monstrous effects of the Enthusiasm prevalent among the Sectaries and so greedily swallowed by their Enemies that I believe they lost footing by it and the bad name they still have with those who pretend too much contempt to examine into their principles and Conduct and are too much devoted to the ecclesiastical establishment to hear of the Toleration of Dissentients, I am apprehensive, will be again made a pretext for rejecting their requests. The Sentiments of our people of Fortune & fashion on this subject are vastly different from what you have been used to. That liberal catholic and equitable way of thinking as to the rights of Conscience, which is one of the Characteristics of a free people and so strongly marks the People of your province is but little known among the Zealous adherents to our Hierarchy. We have it is true some persons in the Legislature of generous Principles both in Religion & Politicks but number not merit you know is necessary to carry points there. Besides[,] the Clergy are a numerous and powerful body[,] have great influence at home by reason of their connection with & dependence on the Bishops and Crown and will naturally employ all their art & Interest to depress their rising Adversaries; for such they must consider dissenters who rob them of the good will of the people and may in time endanger their livings & security.[13]

Both the Baptists and Presbyterians had indeed petitioned the House of Burgesses, contending that the Bill to Extend the Act of Toleration would not provide adequate protection. The Baptists pointed out that the regulations still placed upon them were "inconsistent with . . . the Practice and Usage of the Primitive Churches," and the Presbytery of Hanover made the case that the licensing requirements and limitations on where ministers could preach prevented them from following "the Example of our blessed Saviour, 'who went about doing good,' and the example of his apostles who not only 'taught in the Temple, but in every hour where they came they ceased not to teach and preach Jesus Christ.'"[14]

Madison was proven right in his estimation that the requests of the persecuted dissenters would be rejected in Williamsburg that spring. Nevertheless, he continued looking for avenues of relief for "the sect of Baptists" in particular. At some point, according to a brief autobiography written late in life, he even "spared no exertion to save them from imprisonment & to promote their release from it."[15] Even so, there was a long road ahead.

In the northern colonies the Baptists were not faring well either. In November 1774, Madison informed Bradford that a Quaker from Philadelphia had reported to him that "a complaint of being persecuted in New-England was laid before the Congress by the People called baptists."[16] In all likelihood, that "Quaker gentleman" was referring to a meeting in which leading Baptists and Quakers from New England and Pennsylvania petitioned members of the Continental Congress for help and relief.[17] Among those present at a meeting on October 14 at Carpenter's Hall in Philadelphia were Samuel Adams and John Adams as delegates from Massachusetts. The ringleader of the Baptists was a man named Isaac Backus.

Backus's testimony of his conversion—as well as his testimony of opposition from the Congregational establishment—was similar to that of many other New England Baptists. In 1741, Backus was living in Norwich, Connecticut, when some itinerant New Light preachers visited his parish church. One day shortly thereafter, he was out mowing his fields when he became deeply convicted of his sinful state. But then, as he later related, God "shined into [his] heart with such a discovery of that glorious righteousness which fully satisfied the law that [he had] broke[n], and of the infinite fullness that there is in Christ to satisfy the wants of such a helpless creature."[18] Backus and many in his family built a meetinghouse on "Bean Hill," near their property, and started worshipping there instead.

Although the parish minister had been the first to invite the itinerants into his parish, he soon began vigorously to oppose the practice as more and more people like Backus began to form their own "separate" congregational churches. Backus was a farmer by trade and shy by nature, but he believed God wanted him to preach. About five years after his conversion experience, he answered his calling by going on preaching tours in Connecticut, parts of Massachusetts, and Rhode Island. While in Massachusetts, some "moderate New Lights" began to pressure him to become ordained in accordance with the colony's ecclesiastical laws and become the parish minister. Backus refused, and he and the "radicals" formed their own church. Backus was ordained by some fellow Separate ministers—not in accordance with legal requirements. Later, when an official showed up at his boarding house to collect a five-pound tax to pay for the construction of a building for the established church, Backus told him that "they were going on in an unscriptural way to support the Gospel."[19] Backus was not taken to jail because someone intervened and paid for him, but other people from his congregation were jailed or had their property confiscated. This event had precipitated Backus's lifelong fight for religious liberty.[20]

By 1773, the New England Baptists had become exasperated by injustice. Baptists in Mendon, Massachusetts, had property confiscated, even though they had applied for exemption from the government, because their exemption certificates did not specifically state that each of the individuals had a *conscientious* objection. Baptists in Chelmsford, Massachusetts, were also jailed despite having properly completed certificates and were kept in confinement for nine months while the unscrupulous lawyers hired to defend them purposely allowed their cases to be drawn out. A year later, in February 1774, eighteen Baptists from Warwick were arrested and imprisoned on a semantic technicality—namely, not specifically stating that they "belonged to" a Baptist church.[21]

So, at the Carpenter's Hall meeting in October 1774, Backus and his colleagues felt they had a good case. James Manning, the Baptist president of the newly established College of Rhode Island (now Brown University), presented to the delegates a memorial which contained familiar echoes of arguments for liberty made during the previous century in England:

> The free exercise of private judgment, and the unalienable
> rights of conscience are of too high a rank and dignity to be sub-
> jected to the decrees of councils, or the imperfect laws of fallible
> legislators. The merciful Father of mankind is alone the Lord of
> conscience. Establishments may be enabled to confer worldly dis-
> tinctions and secular importance. They may make hypocrites, but
> cannot create Christians. They have been reared by craft
> or power, but liberty never flourished perfectly under their
> control. . . . The care of souls cannot belong to the civil magis-
> trate, because his power consists only in outward force; but pure
> and saving religion consists in the inward persuasion of the mind,
> without which nothing can be acceptable to God. . . . It may now
> be asked—*What is the liberty desired?* The answer is; as the kingdom
> of Christ is not of this world, and religion is a concern between
> God and the soul with which no human authority can intermeddle;
> consistently with the principles of Christianity, and according to
> the dictates of Protestantism, we claim and expect the liberty of

worshipping God according to our consciences, not being obliged
to support a ministry we cannot attend, whilst we demean ourselves as faithful subjects.[22]

Despite these pleas, the delegates countered with long and defensive
arguments that conscience had nothing to do with "paying a little money"
and that, in any case, the establishment that existed was "a very slender
thing."[23]

The Baptists were not particularly pleased by this response, so the
Grievance Committee of the Philadelphia Baptist Association voted to give
Isaac Backus's work, *An Appeal to the Public for Religious Liberty Against the
Oppressions of the Present Day*, to every delegate to the Continental Congress.
Backus's sixty-two-page pamphlet contained an eclectic mix of arguments
drawn readily from Scripture, history, Roger Williams, John Locke, and
colonial and English laws. He contended that mankind has "no more warrant
from divine truth, for any people on earth to constitute any men their representatives, to make laws, to impose religious taxes, than they have to appoint
Peter or the Virgin Mary to represent them before the throne above."[24] In
ecclesiastical matters, God's people were commanded to be subject to Him,
not to the doctrines and commandments of men. "By the law of Christ,"
Backus wrote, "*every man*, is not only allowed, but also required, to judge for
himself, concerning the circumstantials as well as the essentials, of religion,
and to act according to the *full persuasion of his own mind*; and he contracts
guilt to his soul if he does the contrary. Rom. 14. 5, 23."[25]

Congressional delegates also received a copy of Manning's memorial.

Like John Witherspoon, James Manning taught his students well. The
College of Rhode Island had been established with the guarantee that members of all Protestant denominations "shall forever enjoy full, free, absolute,
and uninterrupted liberty of conscience."[26] At the annual commencement
ceremony the month prior to the Carpenter's Hall meeting, the valedictory
oration was given by a graduate named Barnabus Binney on the topic "A plea
for the right of private judgment in religious matters." Binney highlighted
Tyndale's era, the time of Henry VIII, and quoted a passage by an English
historian about what Cardinal Wolsey might have told the king about the
pernicious effects of allowing the common people to read the Bible for
themselves:

> His holiness could not be ignorant what diverse effects this
> new invention of printing had produced . . . men began to call in
> question the present faith and tenets of the *church*, and to exam-
> ine how far religion is departed from its primitive institution.
> And that, which particularly was most to be lamented, they had

exhorted *lay* and *ordinary men* to read the scriptures, and to pray in their vulgar tongue; and if this was suffered, besides all other dangers, the common people at last might come to believe, that there was not so much use for the clergy. For if men were persuaded once, they could make their own way to God, and that prayers in their native and ordinary language might please heaven as well as Latin; how much would the authority of the mass fall! For this purpose, since printing could not be put down, it were best to set up learning against learning; and by introducing able persons to dispute, to suspend the laity between fear and controversy.[27]

In the words of a vicar quoted by Binney as an example of clerical tyranny, "We must root out Printing, or Printing will root us out!"[28] Binney commented, "Blessed be God! In *this* land, the human mind is not so enervated and depressed as to shudder at the brandishing of the raw steel; the clanking of the heavy chains; or, the mock solemnity of *sacerdotal* anathemas. The people, the *common* people, still dare to think, to speak, to write."[29] It was when "the first printed copies of the Bible got loose" that the established clergy began to shake with fear that the common people were being empowered to find out what it actually said.[30]

In the print version of his oration, Binney frequently quoted excerpts from what he called the *5th Vol. of Dr. Blackstone's Commentaries.* He noted that this work was worthy of greater attention, despite the fact that it was known at the time generally only among lawyers. Binney was referring to an American publication of letters by Philip Furneaux, a Presbyterian minister in London, to Sir William Blackstone, the great English common law jurist who was then becoming popular in America. Furneaux had taken issue with Blackstone's interpretation of the Toleration Act of 1689, which Blackstone interpreted as removing the *penalties*, but not the *crime* of nonconformity.[31] Furneaux wrote to Blackstone in response to the latter's contention that the only thing wrong with the civil laws against heresy was that "heresy is not defined in them with sufficient precision":

> In your opinion, it is fit, that heresy should be punished with temporal penalties; only care should be taken, that what is heresy, be first settled by proper authority. But here the question occurs, What is proper authority? and where is it lodged? . . . If the scripture is to determine for us, the point, I think, is clearly decided. For our blessed Saviour hath commanded his disciples not to be "called masters; for," saith he, "one is your Master, even Christ, and all ye are brethren;" [Matth. Xxiii. 8, 10] and this he said in opposition to the authority which the Jewish rabbis assumed, in

deciding questions of their law. And the apostles, who certainly, if any persons, might have pretended to authority in matters of faith, declared "that they had no dominion over the faith" of Christians, but were "only helpers of their joy." [2 Cor. i. 24] They appealed to reason and conscience, and referred the final decision to every man's own private judgment: "We speak as unto wise men; judge ye what we say." [I Cor. x. 15] The Bereans are commended for "searching the scriptures" of the Old Testament daily, to see, "whether the things" which the apostles declared to them "were so" as they reported. [Acts xvii. 11] And it is the duty of every Christian to endeavor, for himself, to understand the sacred oracles, as well as he is able, in the use of all the means and helps which divine providence puts in his power.

Human helps and assistances, while they are only employed to open and inform the understanding, are very desirable and useful. But human authority, sitting in judgment on points of faith, and deciding cases of heresy, and controlling, without enlightening, our understandings, is a very different thing. There is, surely, sufficient room for our receiving instruction and assistance in matters of religion, without being deprived of our right of judging, in the last resort, for ourselves. And that we must do in opposition to all human authority, in whatsoever hands it be lodged, and with whatsoever venerable titles it comes recommended; or else we violate our allegiance to Christ, the only lawgiver and king in his church.[32]

Interestingly, back in Orange County, Virginia, a work by Philip Furneaux had caught James Madison's attention as well. Madison wrote to Bradford on July 28, 1775, requesting that he tell one of their mutual friends to bring him a copy of Furneaux's *An Essay on Toleration: with a particular view to the late application of the Protestant Dissenting Ministers to Parliament, for amending and rendering effectual the Act of the first of William and Mary, commonly called the Act of Toleration*, published in London in 1773. According to one author, this book was "regarded on both sides of the Atlantic as the leading statement of the principles of religious liberty."[33]

Furneaux was writing on behalf of dissenting English ministers (of which he was one) who found themselves outside the protection of the Toleration Act of 1689 because they did not "scruple subscription" to both the doctrinal and disciplinary aspects the law required.[34] "It is their principle," Furneaux explained, "that it is not consistent with the regard due to the authority of Christ, by which alone they acknowledge themselves to be bound in matters of religion, to subscribe any human explications of scripture, as a condition of religious liberty."[35] Furneaux buttressed this statement under seven sections, explaining why the government's demand of subscription was a violation of divine law, why the duties of the civil magistrate do not extend to religion, why "an essential branch of Toleration" is that parents have the right to direct the upbringing of their children, and how mere "connivance ought not by any means to be considered as amounting to toleration."[36] Although Furneaux used the term "toleration," he emphasized that the religious liberty of which he was speaking had nothing to do with the "forbearing of the Magistrate, but in the right of the subject," which had been woven into the fabric of his being by God.[37]

By the time Madison requested Furneaux's work, he had been on the Orange County Committee of Safety for more than six months. He, along with his father and second cousin, were busy watching developments between Britain and the colonies, and they took especial care to congratulate Patrick Henry and his "Gentlemen Independents of Hanover" for their courageous action in arming themselves against Governor Dunmore and demanding that he make restitution for the gunpowder he took "fraudulently" from the Williamsburg magazine.[38] Madison even served a short stint in a company of militia but quickly realized that his health was not adequate for the task and turned his efforts to the political arena instead. But, as John Witherspoon would almost certainly have said, this was providential.

Substantial and Equal Liberty

On May 6, 1776, members of the Virginia House of Burgesses "met, but did neither proceed to Business nor adjourn."[39] Thus it happened that the nearly sixteen decades of meetings of the crown's colonial assembly came to an abrupt end. In the words of Edmund Pendleton, remaining members rendered it best just to "let that body die."[40] The royal governor had disappeared into hiding, tensions with Britain had reached a stage when reconciliation no longer seemed possible, and at the tall brick capitol in Williamsburg where the burgesses normally gathered in the lower east wing, no members of the Council of State met in their upstairs chamber.[41]

James Madison had been elected as a delegate to the Fifth Virginia Convention the previous month. So, when the former burgesses exited the capitol, the twenty-five-year-old delegate from Orange joined the group of men who entered or reentered the building not at the bidding of Lord Dunmore but solely as "representatives of the good people of Virginia, assembled in full and free Convention."[42] It was a moment to be remembered. In the words of an onlooker, they were "not quite so well dressed, nor so politely Educated, nor so highly born," perhaps, compared to some previous assemblies under the crown, but "full as honest, less intriguing, more sincere."[43] And they were ready for business.

Among the approximately one hundred delegates in attendance were a few heavyweights like Patrick Henry—others, like Richard Henry Lee, were in Philadelphia with the Continental Congress—but also lesser-known individuals like Madison. Young and inexperienced though he was, Madison had connections. Another family relation in the Taylor line, Edmund Pendleton,[44] was chosen president of the convention, and Pendleton's fellow delegate from Caroline County was James Taylor IV,[45] who was a brother of Francis Taylor II.

On Wednesday, May 15, the convention resolved unanimously, "appealing to the SEARCHER OF HEARTS," that they had "no alternative left but an abject submission to the will of those over-bearing tyrants, or a total separation from the crown and government of Great Britain," and therefore that Virginia's delegates to the Continental Congress should vote to "declare the United Colonies free and independent states absolved from all allegiance to or dependence upon the crown or Parliament of Great Britain."[46] On the same day Pendleton appointed a committee to prepare a Declaration of Rights that would "secure substantial and equal liberty to the people."[47] This significant committee was twenty-eight members large and included delegates from twenty-four different counties, Williamsburg, and the College of William and Mary. Madison was not included.

It is not known whether Madison spoke with Pendleton on the evening of the fifteenth about his desire to be included on the Declaration committee, but Pendleton appointed his young cousin the following day.[48] Knowing that the committee would undoubtedly be discussing religious liberty, Madison was probably overjoyed; of all committees to be on, this was the one. George Mason, who had not been able to arrive until May 18 due to "a smart fit of gout," was also appointed as soon as he took his seat.[49] Mason quickly gained "ascendancy" on the committee, which he complained was "overcharged with useless members."[50]

By Monday, May 27, chairman Archibald Cary reported out of committee a draft of a Declaration of Rights prepared by George Mason, with only a few minor word changes. After being read a second time, it was ordered that the draft be committed to a committee of the whole for debate on a future date. Meanwhile, copies were ordered to be printed for members, and one ended up in the *Virginia Gazette* by June 1 before spreading to newspapers in Philadelphia and other colonies.[51]

The last article of eighteen was the one on religion. Like the other seventeen, it was unambiguous and girded by resolute purpose and conviction:

Biographical information derived from
the Madison Papers; Meade, Old
Churches, Ministers, and Families of
Virginia; Brewer, From Log Cabins to
the White House, Ketcham, James
Madison; and the R. Bolling Batte
Papers Biographical Card Files, Library
of Virginia.

Madison's Pendleton & Taylor Family Connections

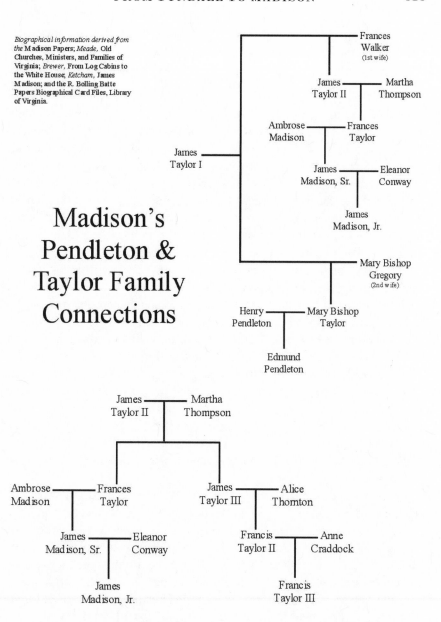

That religion, or the duty which we owe to our CREATOR, and the manner of discharging it, can be directed only by reason and conviction, not by force or violence; and therefore, that all men should enjoy the fullest toleration in the exercise of religion, according to the dictates of conscience, unpunished and unrestrained by the magistrate, unless, under colour of religion, any man disturb the peace, the happiness, or safety of society. And that it is the mutual duty of all to practice Christian forbearance, love, and charity, toward each other.[52]

Madison, being the quiet-natured person he was—Edmund Randolph said his "lips were never unsealed, except to some member who happened to sit near him"[53]—did not participate in debates on the floor but did more than his duty by coming up with amendments. Regardless of Mason's intent, Madison thought the elder statesman's wording was insufficient.

Sometime during the debates on a handful of days between the twenty-ninth of May and the eleventh of June, Madison pondered how to rectify Mason's article. In his estimation the problem was that freedom of conscience was still not declared to be "a *natural and absolute* right."[54] "Toleration" implied that the government was the one granting some sort of limited indulgence or permission; it implied that the civil authority had the rightful power to take its grant away, but was simply choosing not to. And as Virginia's persecuted dissenters knew well, the *tolerance* granted them by the Toleration Act of 1689 fell far short of providing protection. The true religious *liberty* they desired did not include having to pay heavy taxes to the established church in addition to supporting their own ministers, being jailed for preaching the gospel, leaving their meetinghouse doors unlocked and meeting only during the day, facing demeaning interviews from courts deciding whether to grant exemption certificates, and being considered second-class in the eyes of the law because they dared to obey what they believed the Bible commanded instead of the parish minister.

Madison knew what he had to do.

Beyond question it was a bold move. Madison drafted a new article.[55] He jotted down a new version on the bottom half of the second page of his printed copy of the Declaration. He began by substituting "violence or compulsion" for Mason's "force or violence" and shuffling a few of the surrounding words. Then, instead of Mason's "All men should enjoy the fullest toleration in the exercise of religion," he wrote, "all men are equally entitled to the full and free exercise of it." No duties to the Creator should be placed under the arbitrary of human tribunals; religion came from Him, not the government. So Madison furthermore added, "And therefore that no man or class of men ought, on account of religion to be invested with peculiar emoluments or privileges; nor subjected to any disabilities." Liberty was not achieved if the established church was still being forcibly supported by dissenters. As Thomas Paine would later say, intoleration "is the Pope, armed with fire and faggot," while toleration "is the Pope selling or granting indulgences. . . . The former is church and state, and the latter is church and traffic."[56]

Somehow, Madison convinced Patrick Henry to introduce the revision for him.[57] Henry had made the successful motion at the Third Virginia Convention in Richmond to allow the Baptist ministers Elijah Craig, Lewis Craig, Jeremiah Walker, and John Williams to preach freely to the troops who so desired it,[58] and it seemed reasonable to think he would be a good advocate in this instance.

Once the bill was on the table for debate, however, some members bristled. One gentleman queried whether the words were indeed as they sounded—whether Mr. Henry actually intended his amendment "as a prelude to an attack on the Established Church." Suddenly realizing what he had gotten himself into, Henry quickly "disclaimed such an object," and the amendment died.[59]

Madison realized with a sigh that his attempt had failed and did not attempt to speak in its defense. But returning to his printed copy of the Declaration, he set to work once again—perhaps in a hurry—scribbling down a way that the article could be changed so as not to explicitly disestablish the church but to banish forever religious *toleration* and all it implied. His change was succinct and direct; instead of "That all men should enjoy the fullest toleration in the exercise of religion," he wrote, "that all men are equally entitled to enjoy the free exercise of religion," leaving the rest of Mason's version intact.[60]

It has long been believed from manuscript evidence that Edmund Pendleton himself introduced Madison's second amendment on the floor— perhaps as a simple favor to his young cousin.[61] It is unlikely that he had carefully considered why Madison was so insistent; Pendleton was as devoted a man to the establishment as any man in the room. Undoubtedly his reputation as a "conservative churchman" helped reassure members who had become uneasy after the introduction of Henry's amendment that the established church would be safe and sound.[62]

But there is another reason Madison might have chosen Henry to be his first sponsor, why Pendleton agreed to be his second, and even why Madison had worked so hard and boldly on this particular occasion to defeat religious toleration once and for all. During the first couple weeks of June, Madison sent a packet of information home to his father in Orange County via "Mr. Crig," who was probably the Baptist pastor Elijah Craig.[63] Craig had been active in the Separate Baptist Association since its inception, and it is reasonable to conclude that he would have been sent to Williamsburg to lobby for religious liberty during the time when the convention was drafting a Declaration of Rights.

Knowing that Henry had been the one to make the motion to allow him and his fellow Baptist ministers to preach to the troops at the Third Virginia Convention, Elijah Craig may have suggested that Madison ask Henry to introduce it for him. Pendleton, as well, had connections to the Craig brothers—albeit connections of a different sort.[64] Pendleton was both a vestryman and judge in Caroline County during 1771, when the Baptists were just beginning to multiply there. In August, Elijah's brother, Lewis, had been arrested and pleaded guilty before Pendleton for preaching the gospel "not having Episcopal Ordination." For this Lewis was sent to jail where he joined five other Baptists already there for the same offense.[65] One of Pendleton's friends later wrote that Pendleton supported these persecutions, which ended up backfiring and kindling a flame that ended up destroying the established church, "though its friends soon endeavoured to extinguish it by the tears of repentance." Then Mr. Pendleton's friend added, "But this event did neither shake Mr. Pendleton's popularity, nor deprive him of the friendship of those individuals, who were the objects of a severity, administered with a sympathy so unaffected, as to convince the injured of the purity of his motives."[66]

Perhaps upon seeing Elijah at the convention which spoke so much of defending liberty in the face of tyranny, Pendleton's conscience was pricked for the imprisonments to which he had given his assent, and he sought to make amends. Madison's change seemed to please the dissenters, but it appeared to Pendleton harmless enough. As time would show, Pendleton was perhaps willing to concede free exercise of religion on that momentous June day in 1776 but was nowhere near countenancing disestablishment. So he introduced the amendment, little knowing where it would lead.

It passed. So did the entire Declaration—*nemine contradicente*, i.e., unanimously, with no one speaking against it. Article XVI of the final version of the Declaration of Rights bore Madison's strategic handiwork:

> That religion, or the duty which we owe to our CREATOR, and the manner of discharging it, can be directed only by reason and conviction, not by force or violence; and therefore, that all men are equally entitled to the free exercise of religion, according to the dictates of conscience; and that it is the mutual duty of all to practice Christian forbearance, love, and charity, towards each other.[67]

Virginia would never be the same.

Chapter Twenty-Three

THE RISING SUN OF LIBERTY

The Virginia Act for Establishing Religious Freedom

*Millions of innocent men, women, and children, since
the introduction of Christianity, have been burnt,
tortured, fined, imprisoned; yet we have not advanced one
inch towards uniformity. What has been the
effect of coercion? To make one half the world fools,
and the other half hypocrites.*

THOMAS JEFFERSON

he day after the Continental Congress in Philadelphia voted to
adopt the Declaration of Independence, the Fifth Virginia Convention, still
meeting in Williamsburg following its adoption of the Declaration of Rights,
dissolved itself and reorganized into Virginia's first House of Delegates. A
weary yet undoubtedly exultant Madison was given leave to return home,
along with his fellow delegates, until the assembly convened in October.

Once back in his legislative chamber seat that fall, one week after
deliberations had gotten underway, Madison was immediately added to the
Committee of Religion.[1] Edmund Pendleton had been unanimously elected
as speaker. It was an easy choice, for, as Thomas Jefferson described him,

he was "the ablest man in debate . . . cool, smooth, and persuasive" as well as "one of the most virtuous and benevolent of men, the kindest friend, the most amiable and pleasant of companions."[2] Jefferson himself had returned from Philadelphia and was also on the committee assigned to the task of considering "all matters and things relating to religion and morality."[3] The House gave him special recognition for the "diligence, ability, and integrity" he had displayed at the Continental Congress and rewarded his desire by allowing him to exercise his talents in a small committee charged with the incredibly influential task of revising all the existing laws of Virginia.[4] Patrick Henry, probably the most popular man in Virginia at the time, had been thrust into the governor's chair during the waning days of June as the new government was beginning to take shape.

Even before Madison's arrival, the committee had already been assigned the task of inquiring into and reporting on petitions from Virginia's religious dissenters. The first was signed by "sundry inhabitants," probably Presbyterians, a few weeks prior in Prince Edward County. Some say it was written by Samuel Stanhope Smith, Madison's good friend and another young Witherspoon protégé, or even drafted by Madison himself.[5] And it was indeed a statement of sentiments on a topic near to Madison's heart. Handwritten in a hasty script, it pled eloquently for the full realization of the religious liberty promised in Article XVI:

> The last article of the Bill of Rights, we also esteem as the rising Sun of religious Liberty, to relieve us from a long night of ecclesiastical bondage: and we do most earnestly request and expect that you would go on to complete what is so nobly begun; raise religious as well as civil Liberty to the Zenith of Glory, and make Virginia an Asylum for free enquiry, knowledge, and the virtuous of every Denomination. Justice to ourselves and our Posterity, as well as a regard to the honour of the Common Wealth, makes it our indispensable Duty, in particular to intreat, that without Delay, you would pull down all Church Establishments [and] abolish every Tax upon Conscience and private judgment. . . . The whole account of what we desire, is, That our Honorable Legislature would blot out every vestige of British Tyranny and Bondage, and define accurately between civil and ecclesiastic Authority; then leave our Lord Jesus Christ the Honour of being the Sole Lawgiver and Governor in his Church.[6]

For the next decade, regardless of what the rest of the honorable legislature did, Madison made the pursuit of this objective his own indispensable duty.

Morning had certainly dawned following a "long night of ecclesiastical bondage," but it was not yet high noon.

Inching Toward Freedom

The Prince Edward petition was only the first of many that landed in the Committee of Religion during the fall session. In fact, a few that had not been addressed during the May-June session were carried over and discharged from the Committee of Propositions and Grievances to Madison's first committee. One of these was from Baptists in Prince William County who were ahead of the game in asking for more than toleration. They requested full liberty to worship without interruption, freedom from religious taxes so they might be able to support their own ministers only, and the ability to marry, bury their dead, "and the like" without having to go through the established church's ministers.[7]

But even during the summer months, the dissenters had been busy collecting signatures and rallying their forces. In the words of Daniel Dreisbach, Article XVI had turned into a "vehicle for reform."[8] Volunteers were riding up and down the sloping hills and backwoods of the Piedmont, in and out of the swampy marshlands of the Tidewater, carrying their parchments from congregation to congregation. Jubilantly and expectantly, one of them presented to the House of Delegates a petition of impressive length on October 16. The petition was formatted as a booklet of some 250 pages with ten thousand signatures arranged in columns in the posterior pages. The Baptist drafters referenced Madison's language in the Declaration of Rights, focusing on the promise of equal entitlement to the free exercise of religion:

> The hopes of your petitions have been raised and confirmed
> by the Declarations of [this] Honorable House with regard to
> equal liberty. Equal Liberty! that invaluable blessing which though
> it be the birthright of every good member of the State, is what
> [your petitioners] have been deprived of, in that, by taxation, their
> property hath been wrested from them and given to those from
> whom they receive no equivalent . . . having long groaned under
> the burden of an ecclesiastical establishment [pray that this] as well
> as every other yoke may be broken, and that the oppressed may
> go free, that so every religious Denomination being on a Level,
> Animosities may cease, and that Christian Forbearance, Love, and
> Charity may be practiced towards each other.[9]

This was not the only petition. For two weeks in late October, the House of Delegates and Committee of Religion were swamped with petitions from various regions: one from a German congregation in Culpeper asking for deliverance from religious disabilities and taxation since their fathers "ventured their Lives and Fortunes to come into a Land of Liberty from a European Egypt, to an American Canaan, to enjoy those Sweets of Freedom, which God created for all men"[10]; a number from dissenters in Amherst, Albemarle, and Buckingham counties who expressed their "real Concern" that there were "many who were still violent for a re-establishment of the Episcopal church";[11] some asking for the fulfillment of the declaration's promise of equal liberty from hundreds of dissenters in Berkeley County and elsewhere.[12] There was also a multiple-page petition from the Presbytery of Hanover in elegant language and script, setting forth the proposition that being forced to support the establishment was a violation of Article XVI. Echoes of Samuel Davies's heart for "the pure Religion of Jesus" are embedded the carefully considered language of one of the appeals:

> Neither can it be made to appear that the Gospel needs any such civil aid. We rather conceive that when our Blessed Savior declares his *kingdom is not of this world*, he renounces all dependence upon State Power; and as his *weapons are spiritual*, and were only designed to have influence upon the judgment & heart of man, we are persuaded that if mankind were left in the quiet possession of their unalienable religious privileges, Christianity, as in the days of the Apostles, would continue to prevail and flourish in the greatest purity, by its own native excellence, and under the all-disposing providence of God.[13]

Yet for all ecclesiastical dependence on civil power to be renounced and for yokes to be fully broken and the oppressed to be set free, the proponents of religious liberty on the Committee of Religion would have to get to work. As the dissenters knew well enough, they were still counted as criminals under the statutory law. Nothing less than an overthrow of the establishment and the repeal of all religious disabilities would ensure enduring freedom for themselves and their descendants.

Article XVI of the Declaration of Rights did not result in an automatic overthrow of the statutory provisions that had been used to persecute and prosecute the Baptists and other religious dissenters. The declaration was considered, at least in practice, to be more a statement of a political maxim that ought to be followed by the legislature rather than a constitutional rule that trumped any inconsistent legislative enactment. This limited understanding of the nature of a bill of rights significantly shaped Madison's long-term thinking on the efficacy of such documents.

Advocates of the establishment were a little behind the game, with the first of their two petitions arriving after the first firestorm of requests from the dissenters and the second not reaching the House until November 8. The first was from the General Convention of Methodists, not a particularly well-liked group among the establishment clergy, emphasizing that they were not dissenters and rather were sure that there would arise "very bad Consequences" if disestablishment were to occur.[14] The second petition was from the established church's ministers themselves. It was perhaps a little more than disingenuous in speaking of the "mild & tolerating Spirit of the Church established, which with all Christian Charity & Benevolence has regarded dissenters of every Denomination, & has shewn no Disposition to restrain them in the Exercise of their Religion."[15]

Debate in the Committee of Religion had been contentious enough already, but with the arrival of these two petitions, deliberations reached an impasse.[16] On November 9, the committee was discharged from the consideration of the religious petitions, and the matter was referred instead to a committee of the whole House.[17] Jefferson prepared a set of resolutions with an ambitious goal. The drafts of these resolutions were aimed at "totally and eternally restraining the civil magistrate from all pretensions of interposing his authority or exercise in matters of religion" by repealing all laws associated with three categories: (1) those rendering religious opinions and exercises criminal or prescribing punishments for them, (2) those establishing the Church of England, and (3) those related to levying involuntary contributions (i.e., religious taxes).[18]

Madison was unusually silent during this period, probably watching the elder and more experienced statesman Jefferson with admiration as he battled on the floor with Pendleton and other eloquent advocates of the established church. Madison, however, did his part, expertly tweaking the phrasing of committee documents, which Jefferson took special notice of and later commented on in his autobiography.[19] These two hit it off immediately, and the long days sitting around the committee table wrangling over the meaning of religious liberty marked the start of a lifelong friendship.

Knowing he would face certain opposition, Jefferson prepared a detailed outline supporting his resolutions for use in debate. He painstakingly catalogued all the laws passed by both the Parliament and Virginia Assembly which infringed on religious liberty. Some were familiar, like the 1662 act against persons refusing to have their children baptized; others were more arcane. Regardless of Jefferson's unorthodox and supposedly deist views on other matters of religion, it must be recognized that he grounded his arguments for religious liberty on the nature of the church, the relationship of an individual to God, and even Scripture. Madison was his confederate and, of course, was prone to discussions of political philosophy, but his ideas about religious liberty certainly did not arise from an atheistic, purely secularist, or even deistic context.

The first time Jefferson wrote anything noteworthy on the subject of the relationship between church and state was during the fall session of the Virginia House of Delegates in 1776, when he drafted a set of resolutions in response to the great number of petitions from dissenters.[20] As he wrote later in life, these pleas "to abolish spiritual tyranny" from all over the Commonwealth were what "brought on the severest contests in which [he had] ever been engaged."[21] Jefferson had been a member of the House of Burgesses' religion committee in 1772 when the Baptists started petitioning for the free "exercise of their religion," long before he had made the issue his own.[22]

Based on Jefferson's notes and the arguments most commonly presented by the opposition, though there is no verbatim transcript, we can infer the course of argument employed on November 19, 1776, when the whole House of Delegates met to discuss the petitions that had been discharged from the Committee of Religion.

Jefferson first questioned whether the state had a right to adopt an opinion in matters of religion. When individuals enter society, he contended, they ought to surrender as little as possible to the civil government. A man cannot surrender those religious rights for which he is responsible only to God. God requires every act to be done according to belief, founded on the evidence offered to a man's mind. In reply, the advocates of the establishment contended that all nations have national churches and religious establishments.

Jefferson then demanded to know why churches should be defined by national boundaries. Christ has said, he noted, that "wheresoever two or three are gathered together in His name He will be in the midst of them"—this was *His* definition. And haven't these governing powers of the earth assumed some kind of infallibility by establishing a particular form of religion? Examine the effects of it, Jefferson challenged his opponents. Look at England herself! How many laymen have had their lives destroyed by the acts of Elizabeth's reign,[23] or those of King James,[24] or the 1705 Act against Arians and Jews. Furthermore, Jefferson demanded, has God stamped *us* in particular with some kind of earmark from whence comes our confidence?

To this, establishment forces likely replied, as they had elsewhere, that plain reason reveals the truth. Jefferson conceded that every man's reason must judge for himself: one man judges Presbyterianism best for himself, another Episcopalianism. Suppose, for instance, there are two churches in Constantinople, he suggested. One is Arminian and the other Calvinist. Has either any right over the other? Will it be said the orthodox one has the superior right? But then, which is the orthodox one since every church is to itself orthodox, to others erroneous or heretical?

The advocates of the status quo contended that religion would decline if not supported by the state, and the church would be ruined! Jefferson replied that Jesus Himself said that the gates of hell could not prevail against His church. How demeaning to think that the church of Christ must depend on the civil magistrate! His opponents might argue that disestablishment would give free reign to heresy and blasphemy and shatter the unity of the church; but the goal they were seeking was *uniformity*, not unity, Jefferson told his listeners, and is uniformity even desirable? There would have been no glorious Reformation if private judgment had not been set up against the public opinion, which was then surrounded by the darkness of monkish impositions.

Then Jefferson delivered his famous line:

> Millions of innocent men, women, and children, since the introduction of Christianity, have been burnt, tortured, fined, imprisoned; yet we have not advanced one inch towards uniformity. What has been the effect of coercion? To make one half the world fools, and the other half hypocrites.

Even our Savior chose not to propagate his religion by temporal punishments or civil incapacitation, as was in His almighty power to do, Jefferson continued. And the apostles, in 2 Corinthians 1:24, declared that even they had no dominion over the faith of the people.

The establishment replied that a simple, fixed contribution to the established clergy did not infringe on the dissenters' liberty of conscience. After all, the dissenters themselves benefited from the services offered by the establishment to society. And wasn't the concern of the House supposed to be the good of the *whole*?

Jefferson was incredulous that anyone could contend that the religious taxes did not infringe on liberty of conscience. The Declaration of Rights promises the people of Virginia *freedom of religion*, he reminded them. And how is it freedom of religion to force men to take contributions that might otherwise have been given to their own teachers and use them instead to support what they consider heresy?[25]

After further debate in this manner—Edmund Randolph later wrote that "the severest persecutions in England" and longstanding ecclesiastical laws were "ransacked for colors in which to paint the burdens and scourges of freedom in religion" in order to beckon "so many demons hovering over every scrupulous conscience not bending to the church"[26]—the Speaker resumed his chair. It was reported that the committee had framed six resolutions.

The majority of the committee resolved that "publick assemblies of societies for divine worship ought to be regulated, and that proper provision should be made for continuing the succession of the clergy, and superintending their conduct." This, of course, was nothing new. But they also took the momentous steps of allowing dissenters to obtain exemptions from religious taxes and of repealing all laws that either rendered certain religious opinions criminal or demanded the performance of certain religious duties, such as "repairing to church."[27] In the end, the bill adopted—styled "the bill *For exempting the different societies of dissenters from contributing to the support and maintenance of the church as by law established and its ministers*"—placed religion on a voluntary basis while still asserting the special rights and privileges of the established church and reserving to civil magistrates the ambiguous ability to "regulate" public expressions of religious worship. Because the religious tax exemptions for dissenters would undoubtedly place a heavy burden on members of established churches, the mandatory fixed salaries of their ministers were suspended until the next session. Significantly, the final text also left the door open for a future legislature to levy a "general Assessment."[28] Time would show that this was a deliberate reservation.

The exemption act that finally passed was not entirely what Jefferson had in mind. We can imagine that he, along with Madison, were somewhat more piqued than delighted by the final outcome of their efforts. Complete disestablishment would have to wait for another session.

"Yea, Farewell to Free Exercise!"

Within weeks word had gotten out to dissenters of what the legislature had devised as a halfway compromise measure. Jefferson added to his stock of ammunition against the establishment a Baptist petition to the House of Delegates protesting the impending general assessment and, for good measure, a list of Baptists enlisted in military service for the American cause.[29]

The "general assessment" was a euphemism for a religious tax. Unlike the former religious taxes that were paid solely to the established churches, a general assessment would have levied a tax that the taxpayers could supposedly designate to the minister of their choosing, even if he was a dissenter. As Jefferson and the Baptists immediately recognized, this opened the door for all manner of unwelcome interference and kept religion in a subordinate position under the state, thus usurping God's rightful prerogative. The

Virginia Association of Baptists adopted a resolution on December 25, 1776, which passionately summed up their view on the matter:

> We believe that Preachers should be supported only by *voluntary Contributions* from the People, and that a general Assessment (however harmless, yea useful some may conceive it to be) is pregnant with various Evils destructive to the Rights and the Privileges of religious Society.
>
> [Article IV of the Declaration of Rights says,] "No Man or set of men are entitled to exclusive or separate Emoluments or Privileges from the Community but in consideration of public Services." If, therefore, the State provides a Support for Preachers of the Gospel, and they receive it in Consideration of their Services, they must certainly when they Preach act as Officers of the State, and ought to be Accountable thereto for their Conduct, not only as Members of civil Society, but also *as Preachers*. The Consequence of this is, that those whom the State employs in its Service, it has a Right to *regulate* and *dictate to*; it may judge and determine *who* shall preach; *when* and *where* they shall preach; and *what* they must preach. The *mutual Obligations* between Preachers and the Societies they belong to, should this be the Case, must be evidently weakened—Yea, farewell to the last Article of the Bill of Rights! Farewell to "the free exercise of Religion," if civil Rulers go so far out of their Sphere as to take the Care and Management of *religious Affairs* upon them!
>
> Sorry should we be to see the *Seeds of Oppression* sown by the Hand of Power among us, and as we think it our Duty, to our utmost *in a legal Way*, to retard, or if possible, to prevent the luxuriant Growth of a Plant that has always brought forth the most *bitter and baneful Fruit* wherever it has been cultivated, should a general Assessment take place, the Preachers of our Communion, unitedly agree (and we doubt not but the Conduct of *every dissenting Minister in the Commonwealth* will be *uniform* on such an Occasion) to give *Discharges in full* to every Person who shall direct the Payment of his Quota of the Assessment to them, leaving all such with respect to Contributions, to the *Freedom* of their own Will.[30]

Pregnant with evils. Destructive to the rights of society and the free exercise of religion. Seeds of oppression. Bitter and baneful fruit. The Baptists could not have been clearer. The Presbytery of Hanover also memorialized the possibility of a religious assessment as an "injury" and a violation of those principles upon which "the gospel was first propagated, and the reformation from popery carried on."[31]

Such unequivocal statements riled supporters of the establishment, both in the legislature and at large, and they began to pull their forces together in response. Churchmen from Cumberland County were among the first of these to register their opinion with the House of Delegates, "praying the church may be maintained in all its legal rights" but nevertheless indulging the "sectaries" with "such a regulated toleration as shall be thought reasonable."[32] Inhabitants of Mecklenburg County employed rather contradictory language by insisting that they were of the opinion that "an established church in any State" supported by tax dollars of every citizen constitutes no less than "one of the great bulwarks of liberty, the cement of society, the bond of union, and an asylum for the persecuted to fly to."[33] Article XVI may have legally enshrined religious liberty in Virginia law, but religious toleration was still part of the public understanding and practice. The decade following the article's adoption was spent attempting to resolve this ambiguity.

Opportunity for clarification came as a result of Jefferson's appointment by the House of Delegates to the committee responsible for revising Virginia's legal code. For more than two years, Jefferson slaved over the task. Undoubtedly, among the most important component bills was "No. 82," which was the bill "for establishing religious freedom."[34] This was presented to the House in mid-June of 1779, but Jefferson had been appointed to the governorship on the first of the month and was not in attendance to defend it or at least push for its consideration. The bill was referred to the next session.[35]

Religious petitions continued to descend ominously upon the Virginia legislature. Some requests were more particular—such as the one from a group of Presbyterians conscientiously opposed to the kissing of the Bible in court and the one from Baptist Jeremiah Walker asking for reconsideration of his imprisonment for preaching back in 1773 and 1774[36]—but most registered an opinion on either a general assessment or Jefferson's religious freedom bill. At root, it was a belated debate over whether Virginia would continue the old English and colonial policy of religious toleration or, to use Jefferson's terminology, establish religious liberty and thereby keep the promise of the Declaration of Rights.

Seeds of oppression latent in the general assessment proposal became glaringly apparent in the fall of 1779 when advocates of the establishment capitalized on a recent wave of public support for their cause and introduced a bill "concerning Religion" on October 25. As with many of the pro-state church petitions, the bill contained a somewhat misleading header line: "For the encouragement of Religion and virtue, and for removing all restraints on the mind in its inquiries after truth." The proposal's opening paragraph read, *"Be it enacted by the General Assembly*, that all persons and Religious Societies who acknowledge that there is one *God*, and a future State of rewards and punishments, and that *God* ought to be publicly worshipped, shall be freely tolerated."[37]

After declaring Christianity the established religion of the Commonwealth, the bill then proceeded to stipulate that for a religious "society" to constitute a "church" and be tolerated under the law, it would have to subscribe to five articles:

> *First*, That there is one Eternal God and a future State of
> Rewards and Punishments.
> *Secondly*, That God is publicly to be Worshiped.
> *Thirdly*, That the Christian Religion is the true Religion.
> *Fourthly*, That the Holy Scriptures of the old and new
> Testament are of divine inspiration, and are the only rule of Faith.
> *Fifthly*, That it is the duty of every Man, when thereunto called
> by those who Govern, to bear Witness to truth.[38]

In addition, ministers were required to subscribe to a two-hundred-word paragraph promising the state fidelity in their religious, domestic, and public duties.[39] In these requirements the bill was overtly modeled after the constitution of South Carolina, passed in 1778. The Virginia version was more liberal in the sense that it did not limit "tolerable Christianity" to Protestants.[40] On the other hand, the delegates of the Old Dominion added to South Carolina's more moderate formula the dreaded general assessment.

Neither Jefferson's bill nor the general assessment passed that fall. The real controversy would not start, in fact, until the spring of 1784, after Madison had returned to the House. He had not been reelected in 1777—he attributed this failure to his resolute refusal to engage in the typical pandering that involved submitting voters to "the corrupting influence of spirituous liquors, and other treats"[41]—and in the interim served some time on the Council of State under Patrick Henry and then as a member of the Continental Congress.

These positions, held during the height of the Revolution, gained Madison much-needed experience for the battle awaiting him when he arrived in Richmond in his old position as a delegate from Orange. This time he was equipped not simply to participate quietly by suggesting textual amendments behind the scenes but rather to *lead* the dissenters' fight for religious liberty in Virginia, even on the House floor. Madison's newly acquired status as a leader among his freshman delegates has been described as a "woodwind counterpoint to the stereophonic contrast between the two older rival oratorical brass bands, Patrick Henry and Richard Henry Lee."[42] This battle would pit Madison unhappily against the strongest of the strong in the Old Dominion. But he had a weapon at his disposal that he—or, rather, the people of Virginia—soon found could defeat even the "steamrollers" of the establishment.[43]

Showing Their Teeth and Fangs

In the autumn of 1779, the House of Delegates continued to receive petitions, but a lesser percentage than usual came from dissenters. Many were from the pro-establishment forces, including one from Culpeper predicting the dreadful "evils" that would result if the religious freedom bill were adopted, one from Essex lamenting the "great confusion and discord" that had transpired since the Old Establishment had been "interrupted" and requesting the legislature to do away with such "diabolical schemes," and one from Amherst expressing that "toleration" should at best be "guarded and limited."[44] Visible public opinion on the topic was "clearly weighted against Jefferson's bill."[45] Perhaps this was because so many dissenters were too busy fighting for American independence; they, of all people, had reasons to fight that went far deeper than taxes on tea.

After the spring session had closed, Madison reported to Jefferson (who was two days from sailing away from American soil as a minister to France) that the Committee of Religion had given its nod of approval to several petitions on behalf of a general assessment. "The friends of the measure did not choose to try their strength in the House," though, he noted.[46] The Episcopal clergy had also put their requests on the table. Their "notable project" aimed, in Madison's estimation, at establishing themselves perpetually independent of the laity and the vestries. They would achieve this by becoming legally incorporated, vested with all church property, and empowered by the legislature to have virtually unopposed authority in dictating the matters of the church. The proposal was too extreme to make significant headway before the session ended, but "it was preserved from a dishonorable death by the talents of Mr. Henry" and was carried over for consideration in the fall.[47]

Having caught wind of the general assessment proposals, the Virginia Baptist General Committee met in Dover to consider "all the political grievances of the whole Baptist Society in Virginia."[48] They resolved to oppose both the general assessment and the incorporation schemes, and submitted a petition to the House of Delegates pleading "that every grievous Yoke be broken, and that the Oppressed go free; And that in every Act, the bright beams of equal Liberty, and Impartial Justice may shine."[49] But this sentiment was exceptional among the many autumn petitions expressing concern "to see the countenance of the civil power wholly withdrawn from religion, and the people left without the smallest coercion to contribute to its support."[50] These latter petitioners believed that the church would not survive without the financial support that came from religious taxes.

This time, even the Presbytery of Hanover disappointed Madison with its petition. The wording left open the possibility that its adherents were in favor of some sort of assessment—or at least not entirely opposed to it so long as it was "done on the most liberal plan."[51] Madison wrote to James Monroe from Richmond on the day the petition arrived, saying that the Presbyterian clergy "indirectly favor[ed] a more comprehensive establishment."[52] He referenced the matter again the following April, calling it "shameful" that they would remonstrate against establishments that left them out but support a multiple establishment that promised them a share of the loot.[53] In the opinion of some historians, Madison perhaps was overreacting.[54] And yet he had good reason to be frustrated with this lack of support. Madison already knew things did not look good when the religious petitions in favor of assessment began to be referred to a committee of the whole House on November 8.[55] Patrick Henry worked his oratorical magic on November 11, and the House voted by a vote of 47 to 32 to adopt a resolution "that the people of this Commonwealth . . . ought to pay a moderate tax or contribution annually for the support of the Christian religion, or of some Christian church, denomination, or communion of Christians, or of some form of Christian worship."[56]

Jefferson wrote Madison from Paris on December 8 and took the opportunity to comment on Henry's indubitable and indomitable influence, which had become a sore point for both of them. "What we have to do, I think," Jefferson lamented, "is devo[u]tly to pray for his death."[57] Choosing to look on the brighter side, Jefferson then added, "I am glad the *Episcopalians* have again shown their teeth & fangs. The *dissenters* had almost forgotten them."[58]

But Madison had already begun to negotiate his own arrangements on both fronts. To deal with the problem of Mr. Henry, he chose the less sinister route of supporting Henry's election as governor in late November. To get him out of the House and into the governor's chair was the equivalent of taking the wind out of the pro-assessment and pro-incorporation sails although the effect of it was not fully evident until the next session. Henry's residual influence was enough to carry the general assessment bill up to its third reading on Christmas Eve. Madison was convinced that postponing the final vote on the bill until a subsequent session would constitute a big enough threat to rouse dissenters into a frenzy, while providing them enough time to register their opposition. In the meantime he would get to work finding effective ways to help them and continue fighting in the House.

The version proposed was not as extensive as the one from 1779, which had required subscription to doctrinal articles. But the 1784 assessment bill still contained the hallmark of a religious establishment in that it placed religion under the purview of the civil authority. Having already lost the fight to establish specific doctrines, advocates turned instead to promoting Christianity in the name of proper manners and morals.[59] Surely no one could object to that, they reasoned. Everyone was required to pay a compulsory religious tax though they could designate it for the "Christian teacher" of their choice. Yet what exactly "Christian" meant was left undefined. The measures disallowed congregations from relying on the freewill contributions of their members, who were left at the mercy of the local sheriffs charged with levying the tax.

Madison was probably reminiscing about his experience in Williamsburg during the sessions of 1776 when he prepared a couple of outlines not dissimilar from, but less detailed than, Jefferson's outlines from eight years before. Madison's speeches on the floor on the days leading up to Christmas touched on definition, doctrine, and history. We must ask ourselves, he advised, how the bill defines Christianity. Since it is left *un*defined, Madison argued, the courts of law are left to be the ultimate judge! Accordingly, the judges will have to ask, "What edition of the Scriptures shall I hold canonical—the Hebrew, Septuagint, or Vulgate? Or, for that matter, what copy? What translation? What books? And in what light are they to be viewed? As dictated every letter by inspiration, or the essential parts only?"

Then Madison turned to the matter of doctrine. If some doctrines are essential to Christianity within the meaning of the bill, which ones shall they be? Is salvation by faith or works also? By free grace or free will? What clue will guide a judge through this labyrinth when faced with the question of which religious societies may be properly considered Christian? Madison pointed out the logical conclusion of such a system: Judges would be left free to define orthodoxy and heresy according to their own interpretations. And how dreadfully that would open the door to destroying the promise of free exercise of religion!

Madison argued that religion neither was nor ever would be within the rightful purview of the civil authority. The true question was never, "Is religion necessary?" but rather, "Are religious establishments necessary for religion?" Madison contended that the answer was an unequivocal no. To the contrary, experience shows that religion is corrupted by establishments, he explained. Consider how Christianity flourished in primitive times without the aid of the state; consider how Christianity flourished during the Reformation; consider the case of Virginia's own dissenters! In fact, Madison reminded his listeners, dissenters were more often on the side of good morals than many in the establishment.

He concluded by charging his fellow delegates to action. He said that they must make it their duty to administer justice, provide good personal example, educate our youth, enact laws that cherish virtue . . . and *by their present votes cut off hope of a General Assessment*. If enacted, he warned them, the assessment would fail to achieve the ends they desired and promised to do much damage to the Declaration of Rights in the process.[60]

The motion to postpone the third reading of the "Bill establishing a provision for the teachers of the Christian religion" until the fourth Thursday in November 1785 passed by a vote of 45 to 38.[61] The bill was tabled for the moment. Madison had done what he could. The rest was up to the dissenters.

Gospel of Liberty

The bared fangs of the establishment during the 1784 sessions of the Virginia General Assembly indeed jolted the dissenters into action.

As winter gave way to spring, and the spring warmed into summer, dissenters gathered in meetinghouses to sign broadsides declaring their opposition to the proposed general assessment and announcing their desire to see the House of Delegates establish religious liberty at last. Once again, over the highways and byways of the commonwealth, word spread from east to west and south to north, county by county; and petition drafts were passed from hand to hand. Contemporary observers noted that although a majority of the county representatives favored the assessment—they were, after all, almost entirely from the gentry class with few dissenters among them—"a great majority of the people" were against it.[62] One of Madison's friends told him that if this great public majority did not make known their opinion, their opponents would deny it, and the cause would be lost. Madison already knew this, of course, but he took his friends' suggestion to help the dissenters out by anonymously drafting *A Memorial and Remonstrance*.[63]

It had been over twelve years since Madison had first broached the topic of religious liberty in his letters to William Bradford. He now drew on his rich experiences, long evenings of careful pondering, and interactions with dissenters to craft a bold document with the prayer that "the Supreme Lawgiver of the Universe" would turn the legislature "from every act which would affront his holy prerogative." It is clear that Madison's youthful convictions still reverberated through his soul:

It is the duty of every man to render to the Creator such homage and such only as he believes to be acceptable to him. This duty is precedent, both in order of time and in degree of obligation, to the claims of Civil Society. Before any man can be considered as a member of Civil Society, he must be considered as a subject of the Governor of the Universe. . . .

Who does not see that the same authority which can establish Christianity, in exclusion of all other Religions, may establish with the same ease any particular sect of Christians, in exclusion of all other Sects? . . .

Whilst we assert for ourselves a freedom to embrace, to profess and to observe the Religion which we believe to be of a divine origin, we cannot deny an equal freedom to those whose minds have not yet yielded to the evidence which has convinced us. If this freedom be abused, it is an offence against God, not against man: To God, therefore, not to man, must an account of it be rendered. . . .

The Bill implies either that the Civil Magistrate is a competent Judge of Religious Truth; or that he may employ Religion as an engine of Civil policy. The first is an arrogant pretension falsified by the contradictory opinions of Rulers in all ages, and throughout the world: the second an unhallowed perversion of the means of salvation. . . .

The establishment proposed by the Bill is not requisite for the support of the Christian Religion. To say that it is, is a contradiction to the Christian Religion itself, for every page of it disavows a dependence on the powers of this world. . . .

Experience witnesseth that ecclesiastical establishments instead of maintaining the purity and efficacy of Religion, have had a contrary operation. During almost fifteen centuries has the legal establishment of Christianity been on trial. What have been its fruits? More or less in all places, pride and indolence in the Clergy, ignorance and servility in the laity, in both, superstition, bigotry and persecution . . .

If Religion be not within the cognizance of Civil Government how can its legal establishment be necessary to Civil Government? . . .

Torrents of blood have been spilt in the old world, by vain attempts of the secular arm, to extinguish Religious discord, by proscribing all difference in Religious opinion.[64]

Madison transmitted the petition, in his own hand, to George Mason with strict instructions not to identify its author. Mason granted his request and hurried to a printer in Alexandria where the *Memorial and Remonstrance* could be typeset and distributed throughout Northern Virginia with greater ease.[65]

As valiant as Madison and Mason's efforts were, the Baptists and Presbyterians needed little help. Madison wrote to Monroe of the "very warm opposition" of the commoners in the Piedmont and "back Counties" who did "not scruple to declare [the bill] an alarming usurpation of their fundamental rights."[66] On August 13, the General Committee of the Virginia Baptist Association met in Powhatan County at "Du Puy's meeting-house" to discuss what part they should play at the next session of Virginia's General Assembly. They unanimously adopted the following resolution:

> *Resolved*, That it be recommended to those counties which have not yet prepared petitions to be presented to the General Assembly against the engrossed bill for a general assessment for the support of the teachers of the Christian religion, to proceed thereon as soon as possible;
>
> that it is believed to be *repugnant to the spirit of the Gospel* for the Legislature thus to proceed in matters of religion;
>
> that no human laws ought to be established for this purpose; but that every person ought to be left entirely free in respect to matters of religion;
>
> that the holy Author of our religion needs no such compulsive measures for the promotion of His cause;
>
> that the Gospel wants not the feeble arm of man for its support;
>
> that it has made, and will again through divine power, make its way against all opposition;
>
> and that should the Legislature assume the right of taxing the people for the support of the Gospel, it will be destructive to religious liberty.
>
> Therefore, This committee agrees unanimously that it will be expedient to appoint a delegate to wait on the General Assembly with a remonstrance and petition against such assessment.[67]

And wait on the assembly they did. The various counties did as they had been instructed.

On October 26, two days after a quorum was reached in the House of Delegates and business got underway, petitions from three counties were announced in opposition to the general assessment. The text was substantially the same in all three. Unlike the one short pro-assessment petition that arrived from Mecklenburg—applauding the past legislature's "Disposition to patronize and protect the Concerns of our holy Religion" and citing the "Peace & Prosperity of Civil Government" as the reason behind the proposed religious tax—the three antiassessment petitions cited the peace and prosperity of the *gospel* as their chief motivating factor. They reminded legislators that "the Blessed Author of our Religion supported and maintained his Gospel in the World for several Hundred Years, not only without aid of civil power, but against all the powers of the Earth" and that the church of Christ was none the better when Constantine established Christianity by the force of human law. How soon afterward, they exclaimed, "was the church Overrun with error, superstition and Immorality, how unlike were Ministers then, to what they were in time past, both in orthodoxy of principle, and purity!"

Noting with regret that although "Deism with its baneful Influence" was spreading in popularity, it was not because of lack of establishment, and perhaps even because of it; the most effective method of putting deism to "open shame" would be through faithful ministers independent of any desire for the emoluments of the state. Therefore, they concluded:

> If such Tax is against the Spirit of the Gospel of Christ for several Hundred Years; not only without aid of Civil power, but against all the powers of the world supported it, If Establishment has never been a means of Prospering the Gospel, If no more faithful Men would be call'd into the Ministry by it; If it would not revive decayed Religion and Stop the Growth of Deism, or secure the purposes of government and if against the Bill of Rights; which your Petitioners believe—They trust the wisdom and uprightness of your Honorable House will leave them entirely free in matters of Religion and the manner of Supporting its ministers, and they shall ever pray.[68]

The message was simple and clear: The gospel is prospered not by civil establishment and monetary allurements but by the power of God and the call of the "Holy Ghost" in the lives of faithful ministers. Backwoodsmen though they were, the subscribers understood something important about the essential nature of Christianity—something that most of the legislature's educated elite had yet to grasp. As another of the Baptist petitions phrased it, "The Proud Greeks, the Stubborn Jews, and the wild Barbarians were made to bow to the Scepter of Gospel Grace, not by the force of human Laws, nor the Carnal Weapons of Sword and Spear, but by the Spiritual Weapons of Grace and Mercy held out in the Divine doctrines of the Gospel."[69]

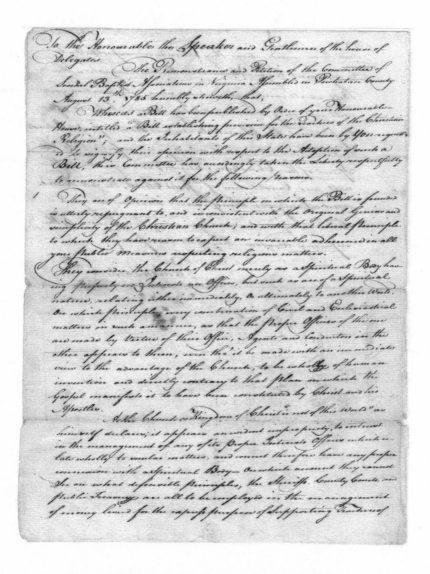

A page from a petition of the Baptist Association in Powhaton
County, 3 November 1785, courtesy of The Library of Virginia,
Early Virginia Religious Petitions.

During the month leading up to the fourth Thursday in November,
petitions continued to land on the clerk's table. As many as eight arrived
in a single day. There was one from the Orange County Baptist churches
claiming that the bill would have the tendency not of "upholding Religion in

its native purity," but rather corrupting and depraving it.[70] There was also a memorial from Presbyterian ministers and lay leaders, assembled in convention, which decried the "evil" and "manifest disposition" of the state "to consider itself as possessed of Supremacy in Spirituals as well as Temporals" by supporting a bill that "revives the principle which our Ancestors contested to blood, of attempting to reduce all Religions to one Standard, by the Force of Civil Authority"; as "servants of One Common Master . . . Jesus Christ," they declared themselves "wholly opposed to the exercise of Spiritual powers by Civil Rulers."[71] There was even one from predominantly Episcopal gentry in Dinwiddie County, who declared that they were as "decidedly opposed to a General assessment, as they were formerly in favor of it," because it now appeared to them "injurious to the liberties of the people, destructive to true Religion, and . . . fatal to the happiness and prosperity of the Commonwealth."[72] Nowhere among the scores of broadsides was found one hostile to religion, or even neutral to Christianity; all upheld religious liberty *on the basis of* Christianity. If anything, the petitions in favor of the assessment had the least to say about religion and appealed to less noble, temporal benefits of a religious tax, except in general terms.

The petitions bypassed the Committee of Religion and were referred directly to the committee of the whole on the state of the commonwealth. By November 2, more than two dozen had been read in opposition to the assessment, while only five had been read in support of it.

The effect was overwhelming. By the time the number of signatures reached eleven thousand in opposition to the general assessment—including the 1,552 on Madison's *Memorial* and nearly five thousand on the twenty-nine "spirit of the Gospel" petitions[73]—members of the House of Delegates who had supported the assessment previously were feeling uneasy. No oratorical fireworks from Patrick Henry or smooth talk from Edmund Pendleton, even if they had been present, could compete with the united voices of so many. On Thursday, November 24, 1785, the day appointed for the third reading of the assessment bill, no mention of it was made. It was quietly allowed to die.

Not one to let a golden opportunity slip by, Madison seized the momentum to resurrect Jefferson's long-dormant bill, No. 82, the one establishing religious freedom. Jefferson had entrusted to Madison the task of shepherding through the legislature the whole set of revised laws. Hearty opposition and the passing of time had made it impossible for Madison even to hope that the code would be passed in its entirety before the end of the session, so he plucked No. 82 from the pile and brought it forward on December 14.

On the third day of debate, after votes to modify it significantly and delay it until the next session were defeated, bill No. 82 passed the House of

Delegates by a vote of seventy-four to twenty.[74] It was signed by the Speaker on January 19, following unsuccessful attempts by the Senate to amend it beyond recognition. Madison recounted the story to Jefferson, with unusually breathless enthusiasm, the day after the session ended,[75] and he later wrote in his autobiography that "the number of Copies & signatures prescribed displayed such an overwhelming opposition of the people, that the proposed plan of a genl assessmt was crushed under it; and advantage taken of the crisis to carry thro' the Legisl: the Bill above referred to, establishing religious liberty."[76]

The final version read, in part:

> Whereas Almighty God hath created the mind free; that all attempts to influence it by temporal punishments or burthens, or by civil incapacitations, tend only to beget habits of hypocrisy and meanness, and are a departure from the plan of the Holy author of our religion, who being Lord both of body and mind, yet chose not to propagate it by coercions on either, as it was in his Almighty power to do; that the impious presumption of legislators and rulers, civil as well as ecclesiastical, who being themselves but fallible and uninspired men, have assumed dominion over the faith of others, setting up their own opinions and modes of thinking as the only true and infallible, and as such endeavouring to impose them on others, hath established and maintained false religions over the greatest part of the world, and through all time; that to compel a man to furnish contributions of money for the propagation of opinions which he disbelieves, is sinful and tyrannical; that even the forcing him to support this or that teacher of his own religious persuasion, is depriving him of the comfortable liberty of giving his contributions to the particular pastor, whose morals he would make his pattern, and whose powers he feels most persuasive to righteousness, and is withdrawing from the ministry those temporary rewards, which proceeding from an approbation of their personal conduct, are an additional incitement to earnest and unremitting labours for the instruction of mankind. . . .
>
> Be it enacted by the General Assembly, That no man shall be compelled to frequent or support any religious worship, place, or ministry whatsoever, nor shall be enforced, restrained, molested, or burthened in his body or goods, nor shall otherwise suffer on account of his religious opinions or belief; but that all men shall be free to profess, and by argument to maintain, their opinion in

matters of religion, and that the same shall in no wise diminish, enlarge, or affect their civil capacities.[77]

Success in extinguishing religious coercion forever in Virginia, as Madison recognized, ultimately had little to do with him. It was the petitions from faithful dissenters that carried the statute establishing religious freedom to victory. Liberty was won by the common man. In fact, all of the votes for the general assessment came from delegates in the southeastern portion of the state, long the bastion of planter aristocracy.[78] As noted Virginia historian Rhys Isaac has observed, the battle was "primarily a struggle over the Word and the appropriation of the Word." It pitted the vast majority of Virginia's gentleman—who "insisted that only a man qualified by higher learning" could fulfill the station of minister—against the slighted, back-country Baptists, Presbyterians, and a few allies who "defiantly practiced their belief that any man, however humble, if his neighbors recognized 'a gift' in him, could preach, bringing home the Word of God."[79]

This was the gospel of liberty.

Chapter Twenty-Four

BATTLE FOR THE BILL
OF RIGHTS

Part I

---

*Nothing is more evident, both in reason and the Holy
Scriptures, than that religion is ever a matter between
God and individuals; and, therefore, no man or men can
impose any religious test without invading the essential
prerogatives of our Lord Jesus Christ.*

ISAAC BACKUS

reat difficulties often arise when dissenters become the ruling majority because it is far easier to proclaim philosophical principles than it is
to govern. Adopted by the Second Continental Congress in 1777, the Articles
of Confederation were, by any fair-minded assessment, a dismal failure. The
nation lacked the structural capacity to pay the national debts incurred in the
War for Independence, to collect tax revenues for this or any other purpose,
and to regulate commerce so that retaliatory measures imposed by England
on the new nation could be met with a measured response. It was not easy to
modify the Articles so as to accomplish structural change, however, since the
document required unanimous approval of any amendment.

In January 1786, under the leadership of the young James Madison, the Virginia General Assembly called for a meeting of the states to be held in Annapolis, Maryland, in September of that year. The stated purpose was to discuss the need for better regulation of commerce. Although nine states appointed representatives, only twelve men from five states actually came to Annapolis. Among these were James Madison and Edmund Randolph of Virginia, Alexander Hamilton of New York, and John Dickinson of Delaware. New Jersey and Pennsylvania were also represented. New Hampshire, Massachusetts, Rhode Island, and North Carolina had appointed commissioners who failed to arrive to the meeting in time, while Connecticut, Maryland, South Carolina, and Georgia had taken no action at all. Lacking any semblance of proper national representation, the convention wisely petitioned the Congress of the United States to call for a second convention, this time not limited to the issue of commerce.

On February 21, 1787, Congress considered two motions relative to the calling of such a convention. The first motion was based on the request issued by the Annapolis convention. A substitute motion offered by the delegates from New York to postpone consideration of the matter failed.

A second motion was then introduced on much sounder legal basis. Rather than relying on the request from the Annapolis Convention, Congress noted the fact that it possessed the authority to recommend amendments under the Articles of Confederation and that a convention could be called to make a recommendation back to Congress. By these means Congress could retain the authority to approve or disapprove the work of such a convention as it was, in effect, nothing more than an outside committee called to assist Congress in the performance of a specific task. This latter motion passed without a recorded vote.[1]

Since the government under the Articles of Confederation was nearly powerless, there had been no material threat to personal liberty from the confederation government during the six years the Articles had been in effect. Consequently, it is unlikely that the desire to provide better protection for personal liberty was a consideration in the minds of those who called what would come to be known as the Constitutional Convention.

The Fatal Objection

With General George Washington serving as convention president, the Philadelphia Convention of 1787 set out ostensibly to revise the Articles of Confederation. As the proceedings got underway, however, it soon became apparent that what was called for was not a repair job but the creation of a whole new government.

George Mason, the chief draftsman of the Virginia Declaration of Rights, was nearly a lone voice at the Constitutional Convention advocating the inclusion of a "bill of rights" as a part of the new constitution. Early in the proceedings he urged the convention to "attend to the rights of every class of people" and added that he favored a policy that "would provide no less carefully for the rights—and happiness of the lower than the highest orders of citizens."[2]

The prevailing view in the convention was that the guarantees of personal liberty offered by existing state constitutions and bills of rights provided sufficient protection. Mason was not satisfied. Together with Charles Pinckney, Elbridge Gerry, and Roger Sherman, Mason introduced a number of propositions for the inclusion of a bill of rights. A few of these were eventually adopted, albeit in piecemeal fashion. Article I, Section 9, became the locus of the rule prohibiting bills of attainder or ex post facto laws. Sherman's motion to ban any religious test for holding public office was appended to the rule in Article VI that all office holders must take an oath to support the United States Constitution.

Most delegates gave little thought to the need for a bill of rights. One of the reasons it was possible to overlook such a matter was that the convention met in absolute secrecy. There is little doubt that if the convention's actions had been known to the public Patrick Henry and others would have taken up the hue and cry of a need for a bill of rights prior to the completion of the work of the convention. However, it is probably equally true that if the convention had had to subject itself to widespread public criticism in the process of fashioning a constitution, the necessary compromises on governance issues would have become far more difficult, if not impossible, to resolve.

But the failure to heed George Mason's call for a bill of rights not only lost his support—he was one of three delegates who refused to sign the final version of the Constitution—but he also left the convention determined to defeat the ratification of the Constitution. Madison wrote to Thomas Jefferson in France, "Col. Mason left Philada. in an exceeding ill humour indeed." Adding, "He returned to Virginia with a fixed disposition to prevent the adoption of the plan if possible. He considers the want of a Bill of Rights as a fatal objection."[3]

With the able aid of Patrick Henry, Mason nearly succeeded.

Was the Constitution Illegally Adopted?

As written, the new constitution required that only nine states ratify it before it could be adopted, despite the fact that the Articles of Confederation required unanimous consent of the thirteen states for any amendment. This disparity in the required number of states, together with the assertion that the Philadelphia Convention was given the authority only to amend the Articles, not to replace them with an entirely different document, form the basis of a still-circulated criticism that the U.S. Constitution was illegally adopted.

This erroneous conclusion is based on the common omission of any consideration of the two intervening steps between the Philadelphia Convention where the document was drafted and the ratification conventions held in each of the states. In keeping with the instructions given to it by Congress, the Philadelphia Convention sent its final product not to the states, but back to the Confederation Congress meeting in New York. This very body had authorized the Philadelphia Convention and defined the scope of its work. If Congress believed that the convention had strayed too far from its assigned mission, it was clearly the institution with the most at stake in the process and could have rejected the work of the convention as being *ultra vires*, or beyond its power. More importantly, it must be remembered that the convention served no purpose other than to make a recommendation to the Confederation Congress. If the Congress rejected its work, that would have ended the matter—at least in an official sense. But the Congress not only approved the work of the convention but also adopted it as its own, for only Congress actually had the authority to promulgate proposed amendments to the Articles of Confederation. There is no merit in the idea that the Confederation Congress lacked the authority to recommend a wholesale amendment to the Articles in the form of the proposed constitution.

Then there is the matter of the number of states required for ratification. The Articles of Confederation required that all thirteen states approve changes. The newly drafted constitution said that nine would be sufficient. But an even more fundamental change had been called for by the proposed document. According to the Articles, amendments were to be ratified by thirteen *state legislatures*, whereas the constitution specified ratification by nine *state ratification conventions*. This was a completely new ratification process, which, to be legal under the Articles, had to be approved by all thirteen state legislatures.

Yet when a legislature called for the convening of a state ratification convention and the election of delegates, it necessarily approved the new process. It is generally conceded that eleven state legislatures called for constitutional ratification conventions, and this is the number of states that ratified the Constitution before it became the law of the land. Two states were holdouts: North Carolina and Rhode Island.

North Carolina may be counted in the column of state legislatures that approved the new process. Even though on August 2, 1788, the convention in North Carolina tabled the constitution—which was an effective rejection of ratification—the North Carolina legislature had to have previously approved the new process for a convention to have been held.

Rhode Island's actions in regard to the Constitution are less well-known. In February 1788, the Rhode Island legislature agreed to hold an unusual ratification convention. Every voter in the state was appointed as a delegate to a ratification convention. Each town was to hold a separate meeting to vote on the issue of ratification. On March 24, the voters of Rhode Island overwhelmingly rejected the constitution by a vote of 2,708 to 237. Again this rejection of the constitution was by the town conventions, not by the Rhode Island legislature. Even though the legislature was no friend of the new constitution, it had, nonetheless, voted to approve the new process for amending the Articles of Confederation by approving the convening of these town-based ratification conventions.

Although the form of the change in the amending process might be considered tacit rather than explicit, it is clear that, in substance, the Articles of Confederation were obeyed. Congress proposed this new process for ratification, and all thirteen state legislatures approved it. Any suggestion that the Constitution was illegally adopted elevates form over substance in the extreme.

Early Ratifications

On September 28, 1787, the secretary of the Confederation Congress formally transmitted the proposed Constitution to the governors of the states who would then submit the issue to their state legislatures. Each legislature then was able to authorize, if it chose to do so, the selection of delegates for a ratifying convention to be held at a time specified by the legislature.

Given all the steps that had to be taken and the relative slowness of communications and transportation systems available in that era, five of the states acted with remarkable speed. On December 7, a mere sixty-nine days after the letter was dispatched from Congress, Delaware ratified the constitution by a unanimous vote of 30 to 0. Five days later Pennsylvania ratified by a closer vote, 46 to 23, but the margin was still 2 to 1 in favor of the new constitution. New Jersey's unanimous vote came on December 18. On January 9, 1788, Connecticut ratified by a lopsided vote of 128 to 40. Georgia's unanimous vote came on February 2.

Massachusetts, one of the largest states in the union, was next in line; and the vote was incredibly close. After a compromise was reached with the help of John Hancock and Samuel Adams—the latter had been critical of the constitution—Massachusetts ratified on February 6 by a vote of 187 to 168. Rather than reject the constitution because of perceived defects, the convention voted to ratify it with a list of desired amendments. These were to be transmitted to the new Congress that would convene under the constitution. Some structural changes were requested concerning congressional district size, jurisdiction of the federal courts, and the elimination of direct taxation unless states refused to pay their allotment. There were also a few requests that paralleled certain provisions in the eventual Bill of Rights, particularly those regarding the procedural rights of those accused of crimes. But there was no mention of freedom of religion, speech, press, or assembly in the nine amendments requested by Massachusetts. Importantly, Massachusetts demanded an amendment to make clear that all powers not delegated to the federal government were to be reserved for the states.

At the time of its ratification of the United States Constitution, the Massachusetts Constitution of 1780 still imposed a religious test for public office and levied taxes for the benefit of churches. The provision in Article VI prohibiting a religious test for office drew some criticism at the ratification convention. Major Lusk complained that Catholics would be allowed to hold office if this provision were ratified and that this could usher in a new Inquisition. In reply, the renowned Baptist leader Isaac Backus, also a ratification delegate, replied:

> I shall begin with the exclusion of any religious test. Many appear to be much concerned about it; but nothing is more evident, both in reason and the Holy Scriptures, than that religion is ever a matter between God and individuals; and, therefore, no man or men can impose any religious test, without invading the essential prerogatives of our Lord Jesus Christ.[4]

Rhode Island's town-based ratification conventions were the next to act, rejecting the constitution on March 24. The following month, Maryland easily ratified without any mention of amendments.

South Carolina ratified by a two-to-one margin, although certain amendments were requested relating to direct taxation and a declaration that the states were to retain all power not specifically delegated. Interestingly, South Carolina requested an amendment to the "religious test" provision in Article VI. Apparently, the purpose of this provision was to allow South Carolina to apply its existing religious test to federal elections of South Carolina's representatives to Congress. The state's constitution of 1778 contained the requirement that all office holders be of the Protestant Christian religion and specifically limited all new religions to Protestant Christian denominations that could pass a broad, five-part doctrinal test.

On June 21, New Hampshire ratified by a comparatively close vote of fifty-seven to forty-seven. This ratification took place near the end of the monthlong Virginia ratification convention. New Hampshire requested twelve amendments. The first nine were almost identical to the Massachusetts list. The three additional items were:

> X. That no standing army shall be kept up in time of peace, unless with the consent of three fourths of the members of each branch of Congress; nor shall soldiers, in time of peace, be quartered upon private houses, without the consent of the owners.
>
> XI. Congress shall make no laws touching religion, or to infringe the rights of conscience.
>
> XII. Congress shall never disarm any citizen, unless such as are or have been in actual rebellion.[5]

News over the battle for a bill of rights in the Virginia convention had no doubt reached the convention in New Hampshire. Indeed, Virginia political debate had been extremely intense prior to the commencement of the formal work of the convention. All eyes in America were now on Virginia, the nation's largest and most influential state.

The Battle of the Giants

Patrick Henry and George Mason had a simple plan. They would demand that certain amendments be made to the constitution as a prior condition to Virginia's ratification. Two thoughts were uppermost on their minds—the elimination of direct taxation by Congress and the establishment of a bill of rights.

Their idea was not without precedent. Maryland had delayed the ratification of the Articles of Confederation for several years until Virginia and New York met its demand to give up their claims to western lands—in Virginia's case, a claim that spanned the continent from sea to sea. However, there was a crucial procedural difference. The Articles were not operative until unanimously ratified; the Constitution required only nine states to operate. In fact, Rhode Island and North Carolina were left out of the original government under the Constitution. They did not participate in the first election of George Washington as president, and they played no role in the drafting of the Bill of Rights.

American history might be radically different if Virginia had joined them in rejecting the Constitution. George Washington was the unanimous choice for president of the members of the electoral college chosen by the eleven states that ratified the Constitution. Yet if Virginia had refused to ratify until prior amendments were obtained, Washington would have been ineligible to serve since his state of residence had not joined the union under the Constitution. Moreover, it is highly unlikely that the Bill of Rights would have been adopted by the First Congress without the personal leadership of James Madison—representative from Virginia.

Patrick Henry's strategy began with the selection of the date for the ratification convention. As the undisputed leader of the Virginia General Assembly, Henry obtained a relatively late date for the convening of the convention. This allowed the Anti-federalists, those opposed to the ratification of the Constitution, sufficient time to organize a campaign to elect anti-Constitution delegates from the vast state that included counties which now belong to the states of West Virginia and Kentucky.

Henry's electoral tactics included an effort to keep Madison from being selected to serve as a delegate to Virginia's ratification convention. At first, Madison planned to exclude himself,[6] as he believed it was improper for members of the convention that had drafted the Constitution to sit in judgment on the validity of their own work. Some friends implored him to change his mind. "For gods sake do not disappoint the Anxious expectations of yr friends & let me add of yr Country," Archibald Stuart wrote to Madison on November 2.[7]

Madison was eventually persuaded that his personal presence was needed to explain and defend the text of the Constitution—and no one knew it like the man who played a leading role at the Constitutional Convention, had kept the detailed minutes of the debates in Philadelphia, and was a co-author with John Jay and Alexander Hamilton of the published defense of the Constitution that became known as *The Federalist Papers*.

Madison's willingness to serve at the ratification convention did not, in his mind, necessarily involve any duty to return home from the Confederation Congress in New York to campaign personally; he viewed such tactics as lacking appropriate dignity. However, both Edmund Randolph and Madison's father sent him letters pleading with him to come home and make his case in person. Both of them noted that significant opposition had arisen in Orange County. His father noted, "The Baptists are now generally opposed to it."[8]

The Baptist opposition to the Constitution became solidified at a March 7 meeting of the Virginia Baptist General Committee, where it was unanimously agreed that the document did not make "sufficient provision for the secure enjoyment of religious liberty."[9] In fact, Madison's longtime friend John Leland, an acknowledged leader among the Baptists, had written a list of ten objections to the Constitution at the request of Thomas Barbour—one of the two Anti-federalist candidates opposing Madison in Orange County. His objections began with the fact that there was no bill of rights and included a specific reference to the need to protect the liberty of the press. Barbour raised objections to the proposed structure of the Congress and a few other more technical matters, such as concern that the people's House of Representatives had no vote in the ratification of treaties which are to be "some of the Supreme Laws of the Land."[10] He concluded with his main point:

> [Tenthly]. What is dearest of all—Religious Liberty, is
> not Sufficiently Secured, No religious test is required as a
> Qualification to fill any office under the United States, but if a
> Majority of Congress with the precedent favour one System more
> than another, they may oblige all others to pay to the Support of
> their System as Much as they please, & if Oppression does not
> ensue, it will be owing to the Mildness of Administration & not to
> any Constitutional defense, & if the Manners of People are so far
> Corrupted, that they cannot live by republican principles, it is Very
> Dangerous leaving religious Liberty at their Mercy.[11]

Madison was advised by a friend, Joseph Spencer,[12] of the necessity of dealing with the Baptist opposition, with a special request that he talk with John Leland. "[T]herefore as Mr. Leeland Lies on your Way home from Fredericksburg to Orange would advise you'll call on him & spend a few Hours in his Company." Spencer believed that Madison's election to the ratification convention might depend on the outcome of this meeting. He wrote, "My fears are that Except you & yr friends do Exert yr selves Very much you'll not obtain yr Election in Orange Such are the prejudices of the people for in short there is nothing so Vile, but what the Constitution is Charged with, hope to See you in Orange in a few days."[13]

Madison arranged to meet with Leland, with whom he had worked closely in securing three previous victories for religious liberty in Virginia. It is believed that the meeting took place on March 22, just two days before the election of delegates. Leland had every reason to trust Madison's core convictions, even more than those of Patrick Henry—since Henry had been on the opposite side of the assessment controversy. But at the same time Leland clearly believed that an explicit provision protecting religious liberty needed to be added to the Constitution, a view that Madison did not share. Madison consistently contended that since the enumerated powers given to Congress contained no authority over religion, religious liberty was safe.

It is not known what assurances Madison gave to Leland at this meeting. While Madison was capable of confidential political promises, all of his private correspondence during this period indicates a consistent view that no explicit provision to protect religious liberty was necessary. Madison did, on occasion, say that if amendments proved to be necessary over time, he would lead the effort to secure them. It would have been consistent with his other statements at the time for him to have made this conditional promise to Leland. It should be understood, however, that such statements were a long step away from a promise that he would seek a bill of rights *after* the Constitution was ratified. It is most probable that Leland simply decided to trust Madison's record and his personal character.

With Leland's endorsement, Madison and the other Federalist candidate won convincingly—202 and 187 for Madison and James Gordon, respectively, to 56 and 34 for the Anti-federalist candidates, Thomas Barbour and Charles Porter. These results are recorded in the diary of Madison's cousin and ally, Francis Taylor.[14]

Preconvention Suspicion

The tone of the debate over the ratification of the Constitution should not be skewed too heavily by reading the scholarly expositions contained in *The Federalist Papers*. Much of the public debate over the ratification of the Constitution was just plain ugly, and this is equally true of both sides of the debate. Ridicule, sarcasm, and imputing bad motives to the opposition were commonplace. Even heroes such as George Washington and Patrick Henry were not exempt. Both men were the objects of such attacks, and, sadly, both men engaged in some form of these attacks as well—although Washington kept his criticism in the form of private correspondence to his trusted allies.

Washington wrote that the clamor for a bill of rights, which was being led by Henry, was a smoke screen designed to cover other motives for the opposition which could not withstand examination "in open day."[15] In the early days of the convention, Henry responded to such charges that had apparently made their way into the public square, although it is highly doubtful that Washington's name was ever attached to the critiques:

> Is it necessary for your liberty that you should abandon those
> great rights by the adoption of this system? Is the relinquishment
> of the trial by jury and the liberty of the press necessary for your
> liberty? Will the abandonment of your most sacred rights tend
> to the security of your liberty? Liberty, the greatest of all earthly

blessing—give us that precious jewel, and you may take every thing else! But I am fearful I have lived long enough to become an old-fashioned fellow. Perhaps an invincible attachment to the dearest rights of man may, in these refined, enlightened days, be deemed old-fashioned; if so, I am contented to be so. I say, the time has been when every pulse of my heart beat for American liberty, and which, I believe, had a counterpart in the breast of every true American; but suspicions have gone forth—suspicions of my integrity—publicly reported that my professions are not real.[16]

Despite Washington's private aspersions, there is no reason to believe that Henry's demand for a bill of rights, or his demand for reforms on taxation and the theory of representation, were not completely sincere. Likewise, the Anti-federalist clamor that the Constitution was designed to usurp personal liberties and usher in a monarchy were equally unfair.

Washington's own explanation for the lack of a bill of rights in the Constitution, contained in a letter to the Marquis de Lafayette (the French hero of the American Revolution) just a little more than a month before the ratification convention, was straightforward:

> There was not a member of the convention, I believe, who had the least objection to what is contended for by the Advocates for a Bill of Rights and Trial by Jury. The first, where the people evidently retained every thing which they did not in express terms give up, was considered nugatory as you will find to have been more fully explained by Mr. Wilson [James Wilson of Pennsylvania] and others:—And as to the second, it was only the difficulty of establishing a mode which should not interfere with the fixed modes of any of the States, that induced the Convention to leave it, as a matter of future adjustment.[17]

The intemperate nature of the public debate can best be seen in a few selections from the press. A Richmond newspaper, the *Virginia Independent Chronicle*, contained a reply to George Mason written by "Civis Rusticus" and dated January 30, 1788:

> The proposed government is thoroughly popular. . . . A government thus constituted stands in need of no bill of rights: the liberties of the people never can be lost, until they are lost to themselves, in a vicious disregard of their dearest interests, a sottish indolence, a wild licentiousness, a dissoluteness of morals, and contempt of all virtue.[18]

Federalist and future lexicographer Noah Webster, using the pen name Giles Hickory, wrote in a February edition of a New York publication:

> The contest for *perpetual bills of rights* against future tyranny resembles Don Quixotes fighting windmills; and I never can reflect on the declamation about an *unalterable constitution* to guard certain rights, without wishing to add another article as necessary as those that are generally mentioned; viz, "that no future Convention of Legislature shall cut their own throats, or those of their constituents."[19]

One writer in a Pennsylvania paper ridiculed the idea of a bill of rights, claiming that Americans were becoming as attached to forms of government in a way "that has obtained among the Hollanders upon the subjects of foot-stoves and houses." This writer declared that a bill of rights was a British idea that degraded the thoughtful American. "Let these truths sink deep into our hearts: that the people are masters of their rulers . . . and that a master reserves to himself the exclusive care of all property, and *every thing else* which he has not committed to the care of those servants."[20]

These themes would soon be explored at length in the crucial Virginia ratification convention.

Chapter Twenty-Five

BATTLE FOR THE BILL
OF RIGHTS

Part II

*You are not to inquire how your trade may be increased,
nor how you are to become a great and powerful people, but
how your liberties can be secured; for liberty ought to be the
direct end of your government.*

PATRICK HENRY

June 2, 1788 was the opening day of what proved to be a long, hot four weeks at the ratification convention in Richmond, Virginia. A few housekeeping matters were attended to that first day, including the election of Edmund Pendleton as the presiding officer. At the suggestion of George Mason, the convention voted to move their proceedings to the New Academy on Shockoe Hill—a much more spacious facility for the nearly 170 delegates than could be accommodated in the state legislative chamber.

On the second day the convention agreed to debate the Constitution section by section. This agreement would be repeatedly breached by all sides but especially by Patrick Henry, who gave numerous lengthy, wide-ranging speeches attacking the Constitution and demanding that a number of amendments be obtained prior to Virginia's ratification.

The first substantive debates began on June 4. The honor of giving the first speech on the merits of the document was accorded to George Nicholas, who, as a military leader in the War for Independence, had personally fired the first shot at British troops when they invaded Virginia territory. Anticipating the attacks that were soon to come from Henry and Mason, Nicholas introduced the theme that, in a democratically controlled government, the people were the best guardians of their own liberties and a bill of rights was, accordingly, unnecessary. "An enlightened people will never suffer what was established for their security to be perverted to an act of tyranny," he said.[1]

The next four speakers, in order, were Patrick Henry, Edmund Randolph, George Mason, and James Madison. In addition to these, John Marshall, the future chief justice of the Supreme Court, and future president James Monroe were among the more vocal contributors. A relatively small number of the 168 delegates who would cast votes ever addressed the convention. Of all the state conventions, only Virginia kept a stenographic record of all the speeches in the course of the debate—save for one day when the shorthand reporter was unavailable.

Perhaps it seems strange in retrospect that these famous Virginian patriots should be aligned on opposite sides of the two most crucial issues of the day. Nicholas, Randolph, Madison, and Marshall favored immediate ratification of the Constitution. Indeed, Madison, Marshall, and Nicholas *opposed* the idea of the adoption of a bill of rights. Their opposition during the convention was not merely that it was better to approve a bill of rights *after* the Constitution was ratified; they flatly rejected the idea that a bill of rights was appropriate for the federal Constitution. Henry, Mason, and Monroe, of course, demanded a bill of rights as a prior condition to ratification.

The position of Edmund Randolph is of particular interest. As a delegate to the Constitutional Convention, Randolph had originally proposed the key elements of the Constitution that would frame much of the debate at the convention. But in the end he joined George Mason as one of only three delegates who refused to sign the Constitution, and he later published a public letter declaring why he opposed the document. Yet, less than a year later, Randolph had become one of the chief supporters of ratification. His change of position was the subject of bitter exchanges between Randolph and Henry. On the subject of amendments, Randolph stated his willingness to consider subsequent amendments *after* ratification had been secured.

Why did he change his mind? His own words on that first day of substantive debate provide the most succinct answer. "[I rise] to repeat my earnest endeavors for a firm, energetic government," he told the convention, "[and] to enforce my objections to the Constitution, and to concur in any practical scheme of amendments; but I never will assent to any scheme that will oper- ate a dissolution of the Union, or any measure which may lead to it."[2]

This was to become the overarching theme of the Federalists. If we do not ratify, they argued, the Union will be destroyed. The Anti-federalists responded with an equally cataclysmic claim: If we do ratify, liberty will be destroyed. And the tone of debate was, far too often, anything but temperate.

Patrick Henry's first speech began with an unwise questioning of the actions, if not the character, of those who had drafted the Constitution:

> I have the highest respect for those gentlemen who formed
> the Convention, and, were some of them not here, I would express
> some testimonial of esteem for them. America had, on a former
> occasion, put the utmost confidence in them—a confidence which
> was well placed; and I am sure, sir, I would give up any thing to
> them; I would cheerfully confide in them as my representatives.
> But, sir, on this great occasion, I would demand the cause of their
> conduct. Even from that illustrious man who saved us by his valor,
> I would have a reason for his conduct: that liberty which he has
> given us by his valor, tells me to ask this reason; and sure I am,
> were he here, he would give us that reason. But there are other
> gentlemen here, who can give us this information. The people
> gave them no power to use their name. That they exceeded their
> power is perfectly clear. It is not mere curiosity that actuates me:
> I wish to hear the real, actual, existing danger, which should lead
> us to take those steps, so dangerous in my conception. Disorders
> have arisen in other parts of America; but here, sir, no dangers, no
> insurrection or tumult have happened; every thing has been calm
> and tranquil.[3]

The allusion to Washington was plain to all—and it brought forth a stinging rebuke from Henry "Light Horse Harry" Lee of Westmoreland.[4] Speaking of Henry's aforementioned speech, Lee said:

> He was pleased to pass a eulogium on that character who is the
> pride of peace and support of war; and declared that even
> from him he would require the reason of proposing such a system.
> I cannot see the propriety of mentioning that illustrious character
> on this occasion; we must be all fully impressed with a conviction
> of his extreme rectitude of conduct. But, sir, this system is to be
> examined by its own merit.[5]

Lee then took Henry to task for his attack on the character of the Philadelphia delegates. Henry's speech, Lee asserted, was "inapplicable, strange, and unexpected," and "it was a more proper inquiry whether such evils existed as rendered necessary a change of government."[6]

Perhaps it is not surprising that Lee was the one to defend Washington's character. Not only had he served with Washington during the war, but their friendship was so close that upon Washington's death nearly twenty years later, Lee was asked by Congress to deliver the now-famous eulogy of Washington: "First in war, first in peace, and first in the hearts of his countrymen."

Henry versus Randolph

But the most vicious exchanges at the convention were between Patrick Henry and Edmund Randolph. Randolph drew first blood in these verbal volleys. Mocking Henry's most famous speech, Randolph answered Henry's earlier demand that proof of the danger to the nation be established before taking the monumental step of changing from a confederation to a national government:

> We are told that the report of dangers is false. The cry of peace, sir, is false: say peace, when there is peace; it is but a sudden calm. The tempest growls over you: look round—wheresoever you look, you see danger. Where there are so many witnesses in many parts of America, that justice is suffocated, shall peace and happiness still be said to reign? Candor, sir, requires an undisguised representation of our situation. Candor, sir, demands a faithful exposition of facts.[7]

Randolph then turned to an impugn Henry's actions, and even his character. The essence of the claim was that when Henry was governor during the war, the legislature had ordered the execution of a man named Josiah Philips without any semblance of a fair trial. Yet Randolph was doing more than merely mocking Henry's conduct in light of Henry's arguments that the right to a jury trial was not sufficiently protected by the Constitution. Randolph's point was actually an important one for the Federalist camp, even if made in the context of an unnecessary personal attack on Henry.

One of the central arguments raised by the Federalists against a bill of rights was that such documents, to use the words of Madison, were little more than "parchment barriers." This argument was based on an understanding of the concept of a bill of rights that is far different from the modern view.

The English Bill of Rights of 1689 had been written as a statement of principles intended to be a barrier against acts of abuse by the monarchy. But the provisions of this bill of rights were not self-enforcing. In other words, no one could go to court and sue the king for violation of the Bill of Rights. It was up to Parliament to check the unlawful actions of the king by the enactment of appropriate legislation. Under the British system, the idea of judicial review to enforce individual rights never existed.

The Federalists thought it strange to argue for a bill of rights to protect the people from legislative abuses by Congress since it was the legislative branch that had historically been the enforcement mechanism for the English Bill of Rights. Today, it is understood that the American Bill of Rights can prevent even Congress from violating the rights of the individual. But to the Federalists of the time, a bill of rights was utterly useless as a barrier against tyrannical action by the legislature. (This is somewhat like the thinking of many modern Americans of the futility of trying to stop the Supreme Court from violating the Constitution.)

Randolph announced the principle, followed by his personal attack on Henry:

> We not only see violations of the constitution, but of national principles in repeated instances. How is the fact? The history of the violations of the constitution extends from the year 1776 to this present time—violations made by formal acts of the legislature: every thing has been drawn within the legislative vortex.
>
> There is one example of this violation in Virginia, of a most striking and shocking nature—an example so horrid, that, if I conceived my country would passively permit a repetition of it, dear as it is to me, I would seek means of expatriating myself from it.[8]

Randolph went on to discuss the case of Josiah Philips, claiming that all men, even the most notorious, had the right to a fair trial and should not be executed by a bill of attainder passed by the legislature. While the details of the Philips case were not mentioned during the convention, there was little doubt that every man present knew exactly what Randolph was talking about.

Philips was a Tory renegade who had been operating a guerilla band out of Virginia's aptly named Dismal Swamp. Henry clearly viewed the case of Philips as being governed by the laws of war, rather than the common law concerning crimes. Years later Thomas Jefferson, who had drafted the Bill of Attainder against Philips, commented that "the censure of Mr. E. Randolph on Mr. Henry in the case of Philips, was without foundation."[9] Nonetheless, several Federalist speakers throughout the convention followed Randolph's lead and continued to return to the Philips case in an effort to discredit and embarrass Henry. Like so many of the speeches at the convention, the goal was simply to change the minds of those delegates who were perceived as uncommitted.

After Henry jabbed Randolph for referring to the lower classes of society as a "herd," Randolph exploded with unguarded anger:

> I find myself attacked in the most illiberal manner by the honorable gentleman (Mr. Henry). I disdain his aspersions and his insinuations. His asperity is warranted by no principle of parliamentary decency, nor compatible with the least shadow of friendship; and if our friendship must fall, *let it fall, like Lucifer, never to rise again!* Let him remember that it is not to answer him, but to satisfy his respectable audience, that I now get up. He has accused me of inconsistency in this very respectable assembly. Sir, if I do not stand on the bottom of integrity, and pure love for Virginia, as much as those who can be most clamorous, I wish to resign my existence. Consistency consists in actions, and not in empty, specious words.[10]

Randolph's last statement was yet another reference to the Josiah Philips case. Randolph may be fairly accused of inconsistency in the form of changing his mind; but Henry, it was clearly implied, was guilty of hypocrisy—saying one thing and doing another.

Henry tried to calm the situation with an apology, but Randolph was slow to relent. The transcript of the convention records the following:

> When Mr. Henry arose, and declared that he had no personal intention of offending any one; that he did his duty, but that he did not mean to wound the feelings of any gentleman; that he was sorry if he offended the honorable gentleman without intending it; and that every gentleman had a right to maintain his opinion. His excellency then said that he was relieved by what the honorable gentleman said; that, were it not for the concession of the gentleman, he would have made some men's hair stand on end, by the disclosure of certain facts. Mr. Henry then requested that, if he had any thing to say against him, he would disclose it. His excellency then continued, that as there were some gentlemen there who might not be satisfied by the recantation of the honorable gentleman, without being informed, he should give them some information on the subject; that his ambition had ever been to promote the Union; that he was no more attached to it now than he

always had been; and that he could in some degree prove it by the
paper which he held in his hand, which was his public letter. . . .

He then read part of a letter which he had written to his
constituents on the subject, which was expressive of sentiments
amicable to a union with other states. He then threw down the letter on the clerk's table, and declared that it might lie there for the
inspection of the curious and malicious.[11]

Other Federalists later made the same argument—that bills of rights
were nearly worthless protections against legislative violations—albeit without any of the fireworks that characterized the exchanges between Randolph
and Henry.

George Nicholas proclaimed:

But it is objected to for want of a bill of rights. It is a principle
universally agreed upon, that all powers not given are retained.
Where, by the Constitution, the general government has general
powers for any purpose, its powers are absolute. Where it has powers with some exceptions, they are absolute only as to those exceptions. In either case, the people retain what is not conferred on
the general government, as it is by their positive grant that it has
any of its powers. In England, in all disputes between the king and
people, recurrence is had to the enumerated rights of the people,
to determine. Are the rights in dispute secured? Are they included
in Magna Charta, Bill of Rights, &c.? If not, they are, generally speaking, within the king's prerogative. In disputes between
Congress and the people, the reverse of the proposition holds. Is
the disputed right enumerated? If not, Congress cannot meddle
with it.[12]

Enumerated Powers

None of the Federalists seemed to believe that if a bill of rights were
attached to the Constitution, its provisions would become judicially enforceable limitations on the power of government to protect the liberties of
citizens—this despite the fact Federalist delegate John Marshall had offered
the opinion that under this constitution the judges would have the power to
declare acts of Congress to be "unconstitutional" for exceeding their enumerated powers, something that Marshall himself would be the first to do

in the case of *Marbury v. Madison*. Speaking of Congress's legislative power, he said:

> Can they make laws affecting the mode of transferring property, or contracts, or claims, between citizens of the same state? Can they go beyond the delegated powers? If they were to make a law not warranted by any of the powers enumerated, it would be considered by the judges as an infringement of the Constitution which they are to guard. They would not consider such a law as coming under their jurisdiction. They would declare it void.[13]

But Marshall did not allow that this same logic would apply to allow judicial enforcement of a bill of rights if Congress enacted laws invading the rights of freedom of religion, speech, or press. It must be kept in mind, however, that not only was the Constitution a new document, but the whole idea of written constitutions in a republican form of government with enumerated powers was still in the experimental stages. There was no relevant prior human experience to draw upon to understand how the system they were creating would really work.

Madison clearly held this same low view of the efficacy of bills of rights. Addressing Henry's claims that the Constitution would be dangerous to liberty, Madison demanded proof:

> Let the dangers which this system is supposed to be replete with be clearly pointed out: if any dangerous and unnecessary powers be given to the general legislature, let them be plainly demonstrated; and let us not rest satisfied with general assertions of danger, without examination. If powers be necessary, apparent danger is not a sufficient reason against conceding them.[14]

Moreover, Madison argued, any encroachments on liberty would be rebuffed and resolved by the federal legislature—the historic protector of the liberties of the people. He still had no concept of a judicially enforceable bill of rights. He spoke even more bluntly on the ineffectiveness of bills of rights in a letter to Thomas Jefferson in the months following the convention:

> Experience proves the inefficacy of a bill of rights on those occasions when its control is most needed. Repeated violations of these parchment barriers have been committed by overbearing majorities in every State. In Virginia I have seen the bill of rights violated in every instance where it has been opposed to a popular current. Notwithstanding the explicit provision contained in that instrument for the rights of Conscience it is well known that a

religious establishment wd. have taken place in that State, if the legislative majority had found as they expected, a majority of the people in favor of the measure; and I am persuaded that if a majority of the people were now of one sect, the measure would still take place and on narrower ground than was then proposed, notwithstanding the additional obstacle which the law has since created. Wherever the real power in a Government lies, there is the danger of oppression. In our Governments the real power lies in the majority of the Community, and the invasion of private rights is *chiefly* to be apprehended, not from acts of Government contrary to the sense of its constituents, but from acts in which the Government is the mere instrument of the major number of the constituents.[15]

A second argument key to the Federalist opposition to a bill of rights was that it was simply not needed since the federal government possessed only enumerated powers and therefore lacked authority to touch any subject within the rights of the people. The official reporter of the convention, writing in the third person, recorded Henry Lee's argument to this effect:

He observed, that, if a man delegated certain powers to an agent, it would be an insult upon common sense to suppose that the agent could legally transact any business for his principal which was not contained in the commission whereby the powers were delegated; but that, if a man empowered his representative or agent to transact all his business except certain enumerated parts, the clear result was, that the agent could lawfully transact every possible part of his principal's business except the enumerated parts; and added, that these plain propositions were sufficient to demonstrate the inutility and *folly* (were he permitted to use the expression) of bills of rights.[16]

Madison urged this same point in arguing that even religious freedom, something he clearly cherished, was safe from encroachments by the federal government:

I confess to you, sir, were uniformity of religion to be introduced by this system, it would, in my opinion, be ineligible; but I have no reason to conclude that uniformity of government will produce that of religion. This subject is, for the honor of America, perfectly free and unshackled. The government has no jurisdiction over it: the least reflection will convince us there is no danger to be feared on this ground.[17]

Answering a later charge made by Patrick Henry that religious liberty was at risk, Madison declared:

> The honorable member has introduced the subject of religion. Religion is not guarded; there is no bill of rights declaring that religion should be secure. Is a bill of rights a security for religion? Would the bill of rights, in this state, exempt the people from paying for the support of one particular sect, if such sect were exclusively established by law?[18]

This was as pointed as Madison was in his interchanges with Henry. Virginia's Declaration of Rights had established religious freedom in 1776. Yet the General Assessment bill—supported by Henry—had been a real possibility until Madison and the Baptists rallied to defeat it ten years later. The point was a fair one: It was legislative action, not a Bill of Rights, that had protected religious freedom in Virginia. However, it should be remembered that Madison's own wording in the Declaration of Rights had stopped short of disestablishing the Anglican Church. Thus, the Virginia Declaration of Rights [is] properly understood to protect only what is today termed the "free exercise" of religion, rather than enacting a prohibition against religious establishments. The General Assessment bill clearly had been more in the nature of a religious establishment than a violation of free exercise, and Article XVI did not specifically address the egregious practice of paying for all the expenses of the state church through coerced taxation.

Although the demand for amendments—particularly for a bill of rights—dominated the Virginia convention, the Federalists tried to make their case in chief: that the nation was in economic distress from the failure of the Articles of Confederation and ultimately the Union would be destroyed if something were not done to rectify the problems.

Patrick Henry attempted to turn even this argument into an opportunity to assert the priority of the establishment of protection of liberty of individual citizens as the chief goal of government:

> The rights of conscience, trial by jury, liberty of the press, all your immunities and franchises, all pretensions to human rights and privileges, are rendered insecure, if not lost, by this change, so loudly talked of by some, and inconsiderately by others. Is this tame relinquishment of rights worthy of freemen? Is it worthy of that manly fortitude that ought to characterize republicans? It is said eight states have adopted this plan. I declare that if twelve states and a half had adopted it, I would, with manly firmness, and in spite of an erring world, reject it. You are not to inquire how

your trade may be increased, nor how you are to become a great and powerful people, but how your liberties can be secured; for liberty ought to be the direct end of your government.[19]

One of the most effective Anti-federalist replies was to point out the presence of a guarantee of a jury trial in criminal cases contained in Article III. If all rights were implicitly protected, why was it necessary to enumerate this particular right? And if a specific provision was needed to protect the right to a jury in a criminal case, why wasn't it equally necessary to protect the right to a jury in a civil case with explicit language? Moreover, if it was necessary to enumerate the right to a jury in criminal cases, how could any other right—including religious liberty, free speech, and freedom of the press—be protected by mere implication and the argument that Congress had been delegated no power in the matter? The Federalists could not produce an effective reply to the opposition's constant hammering on this theme.

It is beyond question that Patrick Henry and George Mason feared more than the absence of a bill of rights. They believed that the national government would grow in power and eventually obliterate both any semblance of state sovereignty and any true notion of individual liberty. They especially feared that direct federal taxes would end up dominating the lives and liberties of most Americans. Mason made one argument against the federal courts that would indeed prove prophetic—that the federal courts would be the chief instruments in the demise of state authority and autonomy. He said, "When we come to the judiciary, we shall be more convinced that this government will terminate in the annihilation of the state governments: the question then will be, whether a consolidated government can preserve the freedom and secure the rights of the people."[20]

Henry and Mason clearly had the stronger case that at least some amendments to the Constitution were necessary. The Federalist refrain that bills of rights were ineffective and that the new government possessed only enumerated authority and was incapable of violating the rights of the people was no match for the relentless argument that the rights of the people needed to be protected in the explicit text of the Constitution. And if it had been in the power of the Virginia Convention to unilaterally amend the Constitution and add a bill of rights, there is no doubt it would have been done. In the words of John Tyler, "Previous and subsequent amendments are now the only dispute."[21]

The strongest Federalist arguments relative to amendments concerned the difficulties and consequences that would result if Virginia insisted on amendments prior to the adoption of the Constitution. Madison questioned the practicality of prior amendments in light of the prior actions of the states that had already ratified the Constitution:

> I am persuaded that the gentlemen who contend for previous amendments are not aware of the dangers which must result. Virginia, after having made opposition, will be obliged to recede from it. Might not the nine states say, with a great deal of propriety, "It is not proper, decent, or right, in you, to demand that we should reverse what we have done. Do as we have done; place confidence in us, as we have done in one another; and then we shall freely, fairly, and dispassionately consider and investigate your propositions, and endeavor to gratify your wishes. But if you do not do this, it is more reasonable that you should yield to us than we to you. You cannot exist without us; you must be a member of the Union."[22]

One late-arriving delegate, James Innes, got to the heart of the matter: "Upon the whole, this is the question—Shall it be adopted or rejected? With respect to previous amendments, they are equal to rejection."[23] Innes left no doubt as to his opinion relative to prior amendments. "They are abhorrent to my mind," he said. "I consider them as the greatest of evils. I think myself bound to vote against every measure which I conceive to be a total rejection, than which nothing, in my conceptions, can be more imprudent, destructive, and calamitous."[24] The danger that Innes saw, and which was repeatedly echoed by a succession of Federalist speakers, was that the insistence on prior amendments would keep Virginia out of the Union and possibly destroy the Union permanently.

Tyler clearly stated the Anti-Federalists' preferred path for attaining amendments: "Another Convention ought to be had."[25]

From the opening of this Richmond convention, the Anti-federalists argued that once power had been delegated to Congress, there was every reason to believe that the new government would be satisfied with its powers and refuse to consider subsequent amendments. Even this Anti-Federalist argument would have likely been persuasive if there was a practical path for obtaining prior amendments other than calling a second Constitutional Convention. The Federalists argued that such a convention would likely result in more discord and no better resolution or, at worst, result in a decision to disband the Union.

When the closing arguments of the Virginia convention were presented, news had not yet reached the gathering that New Hampshire had already become the ninth state to ratify the Constitution just four days earlier.

The Edge of Resolve

Patrick Henry and Edmund Randolph addressed the convention once more as the concluding speakers for each side.

> Mr. HENRY: I beg pardon of this house for having taken up more time than came to my share, and I thank them for the patience and polite attention with which I have been heard. If I shall be in the minority, I shall have those painful sensations which arise from a conviction of being overpowered in a good cause. Yet I will be a peaceable citizen. My head, my hand, and my heart, shall be at liberty to retrieve the loss of liberty, and remove the defects of that system in a constitutional way. I wish not to go to violence, but will wait with hopes that the spirit which predominated in the revolution is not yet gone, nor the cause of those who are attached to the revolution yet lost. I shall therefore patiently wait in expectation of seeing that government changed, so as to be compatible with the safety, liberty, and happiness, of the people.
>
> Gov. RANDOLPH: Mr. Chairman, one parting word I humbly supplicate. The suffrage which I shall give in favor of the Constitution will be ascribed, by malice, to motives unknown to my breast. But, although for every other act of my life I shall seek refuge in the mercy of God, for this I request his justice only. Lest, however, some future annalist should, in the spirit of party vengeance, deign to mention my name, let him recite these truths—that I went to the federal Convention with the strongest affection for the Union; that I acted them in full conformity with this affection; that I refused to subscribe, because I had, as I still have, objections to the Constitution, and wished a free inquiry into its merits; and that the accession of eight states reduced our deliberations to the single question of Union or no Union.[26]

Randolph's comments did not amount to a general concession by the Federalists that there should be subsequent amendments as the first act of the new government. Both Madison and John Marshall had clearly stated that they would be open to subsequent amendments only if they proved to be necessary over time and if they were not dangerous to the necessary powers of the government. The principal Federalist position to the very end was that a bill of rights was unnecessary and would prove to be ineffective.

The first vote taken was taken on Patrick Henry's motion, which read:

Resolved, That, previous to the ratification of the new
Constitution of government recommended by the late federal
Convention, a declaration of rights, asserting, and securing from
encroachment, the great principles of civil and religious liberty,
and the unalienable rights of the people, together with amendments to the most exceptionable parts of the said Constitution of
government, ought to be referred by this Convention to the other
states in the American confederacy for their consideration—[27]

The vote was extremely close. Eighty delegates voted for this resolution,
knowing full well that it was being portrayed as a veritable danger to the
Union. Eighty-eight delegates voted against the resolution.

The next vote was a near mirror image of the first. Would Virginia ratify
the Constitution of the United States? The resolution to ratify contained a
preamble drafted by Randolph that attempted to accomplish much of what
the Anti-Federalist critics had sought to secure:

We, the delegates of the people of Virginia, duly elected in
pursuance of a recommendation from the General Assembly, and
now met in Convention, having fully and freely investigated and
discussed the proceeding of the federal Convention, and being
prepared, as well as the most mature deliberation hath enabled us,
to decide thereon, Do, in the name and in behalf of the people
of Virginia, declare and make known, that the powers granted
under the Constitution, being derived from the people of the
United States, be resumed by them whensoever the same shall be
perverted to their injury or oppression, and that every power, not
granted thereby, remains with them, and at their will; that, therefore, no right, of any denomination, can be cancelled, abridged,
restrained, or modified, by the Congress, by the Senate or House
of Representatives, acting in any capacity, by the President, or
any department or officer of the United States, except in those
instances in which power is given by the Constitution for those
purposes; and that, among other essential rights, the liberty
of conscience and of the press cannot be cancelled, abridged,
restrained, or modified, by any authority of the United States.[28]

With this attempt at assuaging the fears of those who believed that the
Constitution was dangerous to liberty, the final vote was eighty-nine for
the Constitution and seventy-nine against. The only person to switch sides
between the two votes was Benjamin Harrison, a signer of the Declaration
of Independence, former governor of Virginia, and the father of the ninth

president of the United States, William Henry Harrison ("Ole Tippecanoe"). The other representative from Harrison's county was John Tyler, father of John Tyler Jr., Tippecanoe's vice president (who became the tenth president of the United States when Harrison died). The senior Tyler, who would be elected governor of Virginia in 1809, voted for Henry's resolution for prior amendments and against the ratification of the Constitution.

A committee was then formed to consider a list of proposed amendments that would be sent to Congress as a suggestion for them to consider under the process outlined in the Constitution for obtaining amendments. Henry had drafted a list that he submitted shortly before the voting began, and the final list adopted by the committee was essentially the same as Henry's. It contained forty amendments; twenty denominated a bill of rights, while twenty proposed structural changes to the government. A motion was made to strike the proposed amendment eliminating direct taxation unless a state refused to comply with its requisition, but it failed by a vote of sixty-five to eighty-five. But the delegates knew that they were only suggesting changes and Congress could deal with the problem of sorting through all the various states' proposals. The vote to approve the whole list of amendments was done by a voice vote without a recorded division of the house.

On the two primary motions—prior amendments and ratification of the Constitution—former governors of Virginia, former delegates to the Constitutional Convention in Philadelphia, and future presidents of the United States voted on opposite sides of both questions. If just five delegates had changed their votes, Virginia would have required that amendments be made to the Constitution before it would consider ratifying. Yet the Union was already created at this point. Virginia would have been, like North Carolina and Rhode Island, sitting on the outside, waiting to see if Congress would propose acceptable amendments. George Washington would not have been eligible to become the first president of the United States. James Madison could not have been a member of the first Congress. And the subsequent history of the United States would have been radically different.

Madison's Difficult Campaign

Having secured victory for Virginia as the tenth ratifying state, and with New York following suit a month later by the close vote of thirty to twenty-seven, James Madison's next challenge was to secure his place in the first Congress. He knew that he would have no chance of being selected for the Senate since the original Constitution called for senators to be chosen by the state legislatures. Forces loyal to Patrick Henry controlled the Virginia General Assembly, which is to say that the people had elected a clear majority that shared Henry's views. Anti-federalists Richard Henry Lee and William Grayson were selected for Virginia's two seats in the Senate. Madison was nominated but came in third in the balloting among the legislators.

Madison's only hope and real desire was to be elected to the House of Representatives. But the Virginia legislature was in charge of drawing legislative district lines, and they included Orange County in a district with several well-known pockets of Anti-federalist voters.[29] The candidate recruited to oppose Madison was a young man who showed much promise, James Monroe.

Madison left the ratification convention with the public posture that a bill of rights was unnecessary but could be agreed to over time if the need for such protections was demonstrated. The editor of Madison's collected writings described his position between the convention and the campaign for his seat in Congress by noting that he "preferred to let the Constitution operate a few years before making alterations or additions."[30] It was not a position Madison could sustain, however—not because of a change in ideology but because of pure political pragmatism.

On October 17, Madison wrote a lengthy letter to Jefferson in Paris discussing at length his views on proposed amendments, especially a bill of rights. On the one hand, Madison claimed that he had always favored a bill of rights if adopted by subsequent amendment but quickly added that this was motivated not because he thought it was truly necessary but because it was "anxiously desired" by others. "I have favored it because I supposed it might be of use, and if properly executed could not be of disservice. I have not viewed it in an important light," he wrote.[31] Again, his negative view of the value of bills of rights was heavily colored by their ineffectiveness in stopping a legislature from violating their provisions; they were mere "parchment barriers."

Jefferson's reply was prescient. He advised his younger compatriot, "In the arguments in favor of a declaration of rights, you omit one which has great weight with me, the legal check which it puts in the hands of the judiciary."[32]

As his campaign against James Monroe wore on, Madison would be forced to declare his public support for a bill of rights that would be adopted in the first session of Congress. He did so not because he was convinced by Jefferson's argument—he seemed to pass it by in silence—but because it became politically necessary to do so. The greatest source of pressure on this issue once again came from the Baptists in his own district who were insistent that the protection of religious liberty demanded a wide-ranging bill of rights. Madison needed little reminder of how effective the Baptists could be in mounting grassroots political activity.

In a letter to Baptist pastor George Eve dated January 2, 1789, Madison wrote:

> Being informed that reports prevail not only that I am opposed to any amendments whatever to the new federal Constitution; but that I have ceased to be a friend to the rights of Conscience; and inferring from a conversation with my brother William, that you are disposed to contradict such reports as far as your knowledge of my sentiments may justify, I am led to trouble you with this communication of them.[33]

Citing the change of circumstances that the Constitution had been safely ratified, and stating with admirable candor that he sought to satisfy the concerns that have "alarmed many respectable citizens," Madison wrote that it was his "sincere opinion" that the Constitution needed revision. "The first Congress meeting under it," he said, "ought to prepare and recommend to the States for ratification, the most satisfactory provisions for all essential rights, particularly the rights of Conscience in the fullest latitude, the freedom of the press, trials by jury, security against general warrants &c."

Madison then revealed another important factor in his decision to support a bill of rights as amendments to be proposed by Congress: It would be safer and more expeditious to charge Congress with the task since it would probably be the body most "careful not to destroy or endanger" the Constitution and the form of government that it established.[34]

Although Eve appeared to be willing to help forward Madison's candidacy, George Nicholas wrote to Madison that another influential Baptist pastor could be sitting on the sidelines: "Your county man Leland has great influence in Louisa, and Goochland cannot be prevailed to exert himself."[35] Another supporter, Benjamin Johnson, wrote to Madison a few days later, on January 12, telling him of an attempted meeting with Reverend Leland. The pastor's wife had informed him that he was riding the circuit for his preaching duties. He also learned of a political meeting of the Baptist ministers to be held in Louisa. Although Mrs. Leland did not know the specific time or place, she did state her belief that Madison's opponent, James Monroe, was certain to attend.[36]

On January 19, Johnson wrote again to Madison, giving him the results of the Baptist meeting. One of the pastors claimed that Madison was opposed to all amendments. George Eve, armed with a direct communication from Madison, defended his candidacy and argued that the Baptists owed their loyalty to him as a result of "the many important Services which you have rendered their Society, in particular for the Act for establishing Religious Liberty."[37] Johnson concluded that Eve appeared to have been effective in turning the Baptists in a renewed loyalty to Madison. Absent Madison's public change of position on a bill of rights, the Baptist community likely would have shifted their loyalty to Monroe.

On February 2, 1789, James Madison defeated James Monroe for a seat in the first Congress by a total of 336 votes out of 2,280 votes cast. There is no doubt that the Baptist vote had made the difference in the election. One major work of a modern historian says of the contest: "Madison's stand won over influential churchmen, including Baptist John Leland; and his exertions enabled him to defeat Monroe despite the Anti-federalist rumors and the gerrymander."[38]

Leland wrote to congratulate Madison shortly after his election. He modestly asserted, "If my Undertaking in the Cause conduced Nothing else towards it, it certainly gave Mr. Madison one Vote." Leland told Madison that he only expected one thing from him: "that if religious Liberty is anywise threatened, that I shall receive the earliest Intelligence."[39]

The First Congress

Upon his arrival at the first Congress in New York, Madison faced two problems in securing a series of amendments to protect the liberties of the people. First, the Congress was dominated by his fellow Federalists who believed the party line that amendments were unnecessary since the government possessed only enumerated powers. Second, there was still much to do to secure the basic organization of the government. Amendments could wait awhile, many believed.

Madison waited as long as he thought he could. While he recognized that it was necessary to secure organization of the basic departments of government and to enact a tax program, his desire to secure a bill of rights had grown to be more than a willingness to fulfill a campaign promise. He perceived a growing threat that impatient state legislatures would call for another constitutional convention—the other means allowed by the Constitution to secure amendments.[40]

Indeed, on May 26, Congressman Theodorick Bland of Virginia formally presented a resolution from the Virginia General Assembly calling for such a convention. The following day, a similar request was presented from the legislature in New York. Madison recognized that other states might well follow suit, especially since Henry and Mason and their allies were likely to begin working to secure support in other states. It was not a risk that Madison was willing to take.

Despite the outright objections of Roger Sherman and many others, Madison finally prevailed upon the House to take up the matter of a proposed series of amendments. For his part, Madison did not envision a distinct document to be called a bill of rights. Rather, he wanted the House to propose a series of amendments to be inserted into various provisions of the Constitution. This approach was born, in part, out of a concern that a separate document would not be accorded the same standing as the Constitution itself. In other words, Madison was not interested in creating yet another "parchment barrier" that could be ignored.

Roger Sherman, however, persisted in the idea of a separate document, rather than a series of interlineations. Finally, Sherman's suggestion that the Bill of Rights would be treated as "a supplement" to the Constitution was adopted.[41] This approach apparently satisfied Madison in that the Bill of Rights promised to have the Constitutional stature he desired.

Madison shepherded a list of seventeen proposed amendments through the House. Several of his proposed amendments were consolidated into a more tightly worded amendment containing several clauses. Madison's personal favorite, a proposition that had not been requested by any state ratification convention, provided: "No state shall infringe on the right of trial by jury in criminal cases, nor the rights of conscience, nor the freedom of speech, or of the press." This provision should not be understood to have been an attempt to disestablish the remaining state churches. Rather, it would have simply required that all states guarantee the free exercise of religion. Madison was too pragmatic a politician to believe that he could have succeeded in banning state religious establishments, as much as he would have liked to do so.

But it was not to be. This proposed amendment was rejected by the Senate, which, after some editing of Madison's language, reduced the list to twelve proposed amendments. A conference committee hammered out the final wording; and on September 24, 1789, twelve amendments were approved by the necessary two-thirds of Congress and sent to the states for ratification.

With only two dissenting votes, the following day Congress approved a resolution to ask President Washington to "recommend to the people of the United States a day of public thanksgiving and prayer, to be observed by acknowledging, with grateful hearts, the many signal favors of Almighty God."[42] Washington did just that on October 3.

The first two proposed amendments failed to attain ratification—at least during Madison's era.[43] The proposed first amendment changed the theory of congressional apportionment in line with many of the criticisms made by Patrick Henry and others during the various ratification conventions. The proposed second amendment prohibited any congressional pay raise from taking effect until an intervening election of the House had occurred. This provision was directly requested by Henry as one of the proposed structural amendments that had been approved by the Virginia convention. What we know as the First Amendment was the proposed third amendment, the Second Amendment was the fourth amendment, and so on.

In the meantime, both Rhode Island and North Carolina ratified the Constitution. Vermont was inducted as the new fourteenth state in the Union, settling a territorial dispute between New York and Connecticut. Accordingly, eleven state legislatures were required to ratify the Bill of Rights. Virginia was the first state to take up debate on the matter. But true to form, Virginia debated longer than any other state. On December 15, 1791, Virginia supplied the necessary vote to approve the Bill of Rights for the Constitution of the United States.

Madison's role had been crucial at every step of the process. Fisher Ames, who was no particular friend of Madison, labeled him "the first man" in the first Congress by common consent.[44]

The role of Patrick Henry cannot be denied either. Had he succeeded in defeating Virginia's ratification, again, Madison would not have been a member of the first Congress and, without him, the Bill of Rights would almost certainly not have emerged at that time. Yet if Henry had not objected so strenuously to the lack of a bill of rights, it is highly unlikely that Madison would have ever been willing to move off his position that the Constitution should be allowed to operate for a few years before any amendments were considered.

Likewise, the role of Virginia's Baptists cannot be overlooked. Without their support, Madison might not have been elected to the Virginia ratification convention, though it is hard to know whether the Federalists could have emerged victorious without his leadership and detailed knowledge of the Constitution as it had been written. Even more clearly, Baptist support for Madison had made the difference in his election to Congress. Like Tyndale's ploughboys, the Baptists had often been ridiculed for their ignorance and common ways. Motivated to fight for liberty because of the principles they read from the Word of God, these "common" people were central to the adoption of the Bill of Rights.

Epilogue

THE LESSONS OF LIBERTY

oday the United States State Department maintains a Web site with the goal of teaching the principles of democracy to the entire world. What does our State Department say about the origin of the Bill of Rights?

> Two historic declarations of human rights were approved in the summer and fall of 1789, less than a month apart—France's Declaration of the Rights of Man and the Citizen on August 26, and America's Bill of Rights on September 25. Both drew upon the doctrine of natural rights and other philosophical wellsprings of the Enlightenment at a time when French and American attitudes were close and compatible.[1]

This statement reflects what amounts to the "party line" among most modern academic elite. The assertion that the Enlightenment is responsible for the American Bill of Rights may be common, but it is devoid of any meaningful connection to the actual historical account.

History reveals a different story.

The eyes of history see William Tyndale in his study at Little Sodbury Manor reading the Word of God. He reads Acts 17:11, which says, in the words of Tyndale's translation: "These were the noblest of byrth amonge them of Thessolonia which receaved the Word with all dylygence of mynde / and searched the Scriptures daily whether those thynges were even so." Based on this and many other passages from the Word of God, Tyndale was convinced that the Bible needed to be made available in English to every person in the land, from the king to the ploughboy. He repeatedly asserted the central idea of religious liberty—private judgment—in his writings and his actions. In the marginal notes of his New Testament, Tyndale wrote: "Searche the scriptures for by them may ye trye all doctrine." Believers who measured the official doctrines of the established church against the plumb line of Scripture were the inherent opponents of religious oppression. Tyndale's beliefs led him to action, and he paid with his life.

History sees Robert Barnes, likely armed with Tyndale's translation of the Word of God, defy the ostentatiously powerful Cardinal Wolsley, only to be told to "abjure or burn." First Corinthians 1 taught Barnes that God "will destroy the wisdom of the wise," and from this he concluded that the true nature of God's church is spiritual and universal:

> Whether they bee Jew or Greeke, kyng or subject, carter or Cardinall, butcher or Byshop, tancardbearer or cannelrater, free or bounde, frier or fidler, Monke or miller: if they believe in Christes word, and sticke fast to his blessed promises, and trust onely in the merits of his blessed bloud, they be the holy Church of God, yea and the very true church afore God. And you with all your spiritual tokens, and with all your exterior cleanness, remaine in your filthynes of sinne . . . the Church is a spiritual thing, and no exterior thing . . . the holy Church is the congregation of faithful men wheresoever they be in the world.[2]

Barnes's belief that the church was spiritual and universal, not political and national, was utterly incompatible with the policies of repression inherent in a nationally established church. Eventually, Queen Mary I took his life for his contributions to the cause of liberty.

The Kent Coventiclers, also known as the Freewillers, read Isaiah 29:13-14, which teaches that the wicked honor God with their lips "taught by the commandment of men" and that "wisdom of the wise men shall perish." These individuals, including men like Henry Hart and John Champneys, concluded that they were better off with small churches in homes taught by ordinary men who studied the Scriptures for themselves. Protestants and Catholics alike opposed them, saying they needed instead to heed the teaching of the educated and ordained who were sanctioned by church and crown. But Hart boldly asserted:

> Woe be to those bishops, pastors / and lawyers / of what name and place so ever they be, which boast of power and authority to rule and govern another / and yet have no respect to their own souls: for . . . miserably shall they be rewarded that bear the name of christian people which seek holiness only by outward sacraments

and signs, not regarding what the heart and inward conscience be / and also say in your selves, tush we be well enough, for the holy laws ceremonies / and Sacraments of god are remaining among us and thereby we are known to be his people. Nevertheless be thou of good comfort, O thou little worm Jacob, and thou despised Israel, for thy redeemer liveth: fear neither the proud boasting nor threatening of thine enemies.[3]

These families were the first to challenge the idea of an established church—not by ideas alone but with their actions. For this they were threatened and jailed, and many were executed. The educated elite could not silence them using their human wisdom, so they turned to the sword and the faggot.

Sebastian Castellio, in hiding in Bern, Switzerland, but never far from the shadow of Geneva, dared to read the parable of the wheat and tares found in Matthew 13 and not rely exclusively on the contorted interpretation of that passage in the writings of Augustine. One of Augustine's later disciples, John Calvin, believed that it was his job, not God's, to separate the wheat from the tares by the execution of heretics. Castellio's arguments for religious liberty were not based on a rejection of Scripture but on its proper interpretation: Christ gave a direct command to leave the tares until the harvest, not to root them out; Ananias and Sapphira were killed by a direct act of God, not church or civil officials; and Deuteronomy 13 says that the test for false prophets is whether their predictions come true, not whether their interpretation of Scripture agrees with that of the ruling authority. Castellio's words, cited by later English dissenters, still ring true today. "It is absurd to wage spiritual war with earthly arms," he said. "The office of the doctor is not to be committed to the executioner, nor the outside of the cup to be cleansed before the inside."[4]

Thomas Helwys and the other early Baptists in England were moved by the words of John 4:24: "God is spirit, and they that worship him, must worship him in spirit and truth." From this Helwys concluded that coerced worship is not acceptable to God because it does not flow from the heart of the compelled worshipper and thus is necessarily riddled with hypocrisy.[5] Because Helwys read in the Scriptures that God demands true worship from a willing heart, he advocated religious liberty and dared to convey his plea for freedom to King James. Helwys would die in Newgate Prison, but his ideas would not perish because they were not his alone but flowed from his dedicated reading of the Word of God.

Samuel How, a simple cobbler, dared to preach in the early days of the English Civil War. His preaching was grounded in Scripture. He placed particular reliance on 1 Corinthians 2, which taught him that spiritual knowledge is given freely, as believers have the mind of Christ. How argued that the formal blessing of the state and church is no guarantee of spiritual wisdom and that "the natural man," or "carnal reason," cannot perceive the things of God. Therefore, a university degree and proficiency in classical languages is no guarantee that an individual is a spiritual leader, and these qualifications should certainly not form the test of whether an individual can understand and interpret for himself the Word of God. How told his listeners that God can and still does communicate His truth to peddlers, tinkers, chimney sweepers, and cobblers.[6]

William Dell, chaplain in the New Model Army, saw the potential for liberty evaporate as both Anglicans and Presbyterians battled for ecclesiastical supremacy in England. During the crucial days of the Westminster Assembly, Dell defied the call for coerced uniformity to the Confession. Rather, reasoning from Galatians 5–6, he called for a spiritual unity based on new birth in Christ in lieu of coerced uniformity arising from a national doctrine:

> As in Christ's kingdom neither Circumcision availeth any thing, nor uncircumcision, but a new creature, so in this same kingdom of Christ, neither Presbytery availeth anything nor Independency, but a new creature: and that the kingdom of God stands not in Presbytery or Independency, but in righteousness, and peace, and joy in the holy Ghost.

The spiritual distinctions that matter, he said, "Lie only there, where God hath made it," between those born after the flesh and those born after the Spirit.[7]

Roger Williams was greatly influenced by Hebrews 4:12, which proclaims that the Word of God is the sword that God uses to judge the hearts of men. This meant, in his mind, that there was no rightful place for the sword of government in spiritual matters. The civil sword, he insisted, "cannot according to its utmost reach and capacity . . . extend to *spiritual* and *Soul-causes*, Spiritual and Soul *punishment*, which belong to that *spiritual sword* with two edges, the *soul-piercing* (in *soul-saving* or *soul-killing*) the Word of God."[8] Williams's advocacy of religious liberty is found not merely in his writings but in the founding of Rhode Island, the first colony with a commitment to liberty.

Christopher Blackwood, a Baptist pastor from Kent, writing during the Pamphlet Wars of the mid-seventeenth century, contended that true belief in the Christian faith is utterly inconsistent with compulsion and forced conformity. Blackwood took his understanding of Scripture to the logical conclusion that God cannot be pleased with national churches. It is a violation of Christian liberty, he said, to force a man to act according to what he believes is a lie. And, likewise, it is never better to have "a glorious seeming uniformity in a state of self-condemnation" in a single national church than it is to have "conscientious satisfaction" with diversity of opinion and congregations.[9]

John Sturgion's 1660 response to repression by vindictive Anglican officials proclaimed the theme that would echo in America a century later: namely, that mankind has different duties to both God and the state, and the state has no right to interfere with God's prerogative. His only desire, as he expressed it, was "that *we may serve the Lord without molestation in that Faith and order which we have Learned in the Holy Scripture; giving Honor to our King* to whom *Honor belongs; fear* to whom *fear, Tribute* to whom *Tribute* belong, in every thing as far as we have abilities, to *render to God the things that are God's,* and to the *Magistrate* the things that are *His.*"[10] Sturgion, a "member of the Baptized People," found his ideas of liberty in the pages of the Word of God.

Even John Locke reasoned largely from Scripture when it came to religious liberty. He contested the idea that a national church could ever be found within the pages of the Gospels:

> Someone perhaps may object, that no such Society can be said to be a true Church, unless it have in it a Bishop, or Presbyter, with Ruling authority derived from the very Apostles, and continued down unto the present times by uninterrupted Succession. To these I answer: *In the first place,* Let them show me the Edict by which Christ has imposed that Law upon his Church. And let not any man think me impertinent if in a thing of this consequence, I require that the Terms of that Edict be very express and positive. For the Promise he has made us, that *wheresoever two or three are gathered together in his Name, he will be in the midst of them,* seems to imply the contrary.[11]

Locke understood that Christ is found among the faithful few—an idea he got expressly from a faithful application of the teaching of Matthew 18:30.

Gilbert Tennent, son of a Presbyterian minister, traveled up and down the American colonies with the great George Whitefield during the mid-1700s. He preached that it was improper for the state to demand the right to license ministers. This idea came from his reading of Romans 14:23, which says that "whatever does not proceed from faith is sin." Tennent concluded that it was therefore *sin*—an idea not fashionable among the Enlightenment philosophers—to compel a man to confess doctrine he does not genuinely believe:

> To bind Men to a particular Minister, against their Judgment and inclinations, when they are more edified elsewhere, is carnal with a Witness; a cruel Oppression of tender Consciences, a compelling of Men to Sin: For he that doubts, is damn'd if he eat; and whatsoever is not of Faith, is Sin.[12]

Soon after the birth of the United States of America, Baptist and Presbyterian petitioners reasoned from the Gospels and the book of Acts to proclaim that the established church's licensing requirements were unscriptural. Licensing requirements and overbearing regulation of their churches, they said, were "inconsistent with . . . the Practice and Usage of the Primitive Churches," contrary to "the Example of our blessed Saviour, 'who went about doing good,' and the example of his Apostles who not only 'taught in the Temple, but in every hour where they came they ceased not to teach and preach Jesus Christ.'"[13]

John Leland, the influential Virginia Baptist preacher and associate of James Madison, focused on Christ's final judgment as one of his many scriptural arguments for religious liberty. "Every man must give an account of himself to God," he wrote, "and therefore every man ought to be at liberty to serve God in that way that he can best reconcile it to his conscience. If Government can answer for individuals at the day of judgment, let men be controlled by it, in religious matters; otherwise, let men be free."[14] Leland, like so many of the historic advocates of religious liberty, was not simply a philosopher or author. He thought and wrote *and* acted. He did not just talk about religious liberty; he was an actor on the stage of history, turning ideas into reality.

James Madison played a key role in the founding of America and in the establishment of religious liberty and clearly deserves to be known as the Father of the Constitution. But the true heroes of our story are the common people whom Tyndale inspired and Madison marshaled for political victory. These individuals read the Word of God for themselves and truly understood both the liberty of the soul and the liberty of the mind. And the test of liberty has never been whether one asked for liberty for himself, but whether he wished liberty for all of humankind.

Historian Perez Zagorin has examined the supposed role played by the Enlightenment in the development of the ideals of religious liberty. He found little evidence of a direct influence. Instead, Zagorin looked to the era of the

Kent conventiclers and Thomas Helwys and concluded, "The intellectual changes . . . , since they occurred only gradually, cannot possibly account for the theories and defenses of toleration that appeared in the second half of the sixteenth century." Rather, religious freedom was wrought "not of minds inclined to religious indifference or unbelief" among "nearly all the major theorists of toleration in the seventeenth century."[15]

W. K. Jordan said much the same in the opening pages of his acclaimed four-volume work on the history of religious toleration in England written in the 1930s. "It cannot be denied that skepticism and indifference have been powerful agents in weakening the theory and practice of persecution. But it is an error to say that the indifferent man can be tolerant of a religious belief; he is simply indifferent to it." Jordan continued, "There can be little doubt that the modern tolerance towards religious diversity has a large content of indifference, but religious toleration was achieved, at least in England, before public indifference to theological questions had attained a place of dominant influence."[16]

It is one thing to talk about religious liberty as an abstract concept. It is quite another to enter into the lists of battle and be willing to fight for religious liberty—sometimes at a great personal cost. Those willing to engage in such a battle are not the indifferent but those whose personal faith is at the core of their life.

Ideas matter. And not all religious ideas are equal. The ideals of religious liberty were found in the Word of God by those who believed that salvation was individual and personal, and that the church was first and foremost a spiritual institution. The advocates of freedom did not believe in religious liberty in spite of their Christianity, but explicitly *because* of their individual faith in Christ, which had been molded and instructed by the Bible. The greatest evidence of the truth of the inner reality of their commitment to liberty can be found in their willingness to support the cause of liberty for those different from themselves.

This leads us to one final story from among the Virginia Baptists of the late 1700s. Even as the Bill of Rights was being debated and ratified, the Virginia General Baptist association held yet another political meeting, this in Richmond on May 8, 1790. One of the resolutions emerging from the meeting concerned the issue of slavery. A committee was appointed to consider the matter, but it could not agree on the wording of any resolution. But, as the official minutes record, they "agreed to lay the weight thereof, on the Reverend John Leland who brought forth in a resolution which was agreed to and is as followeth":

Resolved, That slavery, is a violent deprivation of the rights of nature, and inconsistent with a republican government; and therefore recommend it to our Brethren to make use of every legal measure, to extirpate the horrid evil from the land, and pray Almighty God, that our Honourable Legislature may have it in their power, to proclaim the general Jubilee, consistent with the principles of good policy.[17]

Leland had read the Bible and understood the principle of Jubilee—a declaration of freedom for all encumbered by debt and servitude.

The Virginia Baptists were ahead of their time on the issue of slavery. But then again, on matters of liberty, the ploughboys were consistently in front of the educated elite. Today we have a Bill of Rights in the United States because countless ploughboys like John Leland believed the Bible and took to heart its truth and teaching. Indeed, the Word of God is the source of our liberty.

Now the Lord is the Spirit;
and where the Spirit of the Lord is,
there is liberty.
(2 CORINTHIANS 3:17)

NOTES

Introduction

1. "Remarks by Firuz Kazemzadeh" in "The State of Religious Freedom," *World Affairs* 147, no. 4 (1985): 246.

2. "Jefferson and Religious Freedom," *The Atlantic Monthly* 274 (December 1994): 113.

3. Recorded Books, *His Excellency by Joseph J. Ellis*, performed by Nelson Runger (Prince Frederick, MD: Recorded Books, LLC, 2004).

4. *A Patriot's History of the United States, From Columbus's Great Discovery to the War on Terror* (New York: Sentinel, 2004), 70.

5. Introduction, *Freedom: A History of US* (New York: Oxford UP, 2003).

Chapter 1

1. John Foxe, *Actes and monuments of matters most speciall and memorable*, 982.

2. Bobrick, *Wide as the Waters*, 36.

3. Foxe, *First volume of the ecclesiasticall history*, 1224–25.

4. Tyndale, "To the Reader," [4].

5. Daniell, *William Tyndale*, 78; Bobrick, *Wide as the Waters*, 90.

6. Strype, *Memorials*, 3.

7. Moynahan, *God's Bestseller*, 89.

8. Ibid., 83.

9. Monahayan convincingly argues that Tyndale was naïve in his later dealings with representatives of the crown; see *God's Bestseller*, 45, 229–34. Daniell defends the reasonableness of Tyndale's request to Tunstall; see *William Tyndale*, 85.

10. Daniell, *William Tyndale*, 11, 92–93.

11. Moynahan, *God's Bestseller*, 12.

12. *History of . . . K. Henry VIII*, 24–25.

13. Some historians assert that the entire book was written by Thomas More. More's biographer and defender, Peter Ackroyd, writes on page 226 of *The Life of Thomas More*, "It is not at all certain that Henry himself composed every word." He ascribes a relatively modest role to More. The viciousness of language used against Luther is one reason to suspect More's greater involvement. However, since the viciousness lacks the

additional quality of vulgarity, More either restrained himself when writing for the king or was less involved than some suggest.

14. Daniell, *William Tyndale*, 255.

15. Ibid., 254.

16. Ibid., 258, quoting R. Marius, *Thomas More: A Biography*, 281; Marius also coedited *The Complete Works of Thomas More*, vol. 8 (New Haven, CT: Yale UP, 1973).

17. Lewis, *English Literature*, 175.

18. Tyndale, "To the Reader," [6].

19. Moynahan, *God's Bestseller*, 91.

20. David Daniell has given us unparalleled analysis to understand the excellence of Tyndale's work. In addition to his superb biography, Daniell's massive treatise, *The Bible in English*, thoroughly documents the overall accuracy of Tyndale's translation.

21. Daniell, *William Tyndale*, 177–78.

22. Ibid., 171.

23. Tyndale, *Wicked Mammon*, [Avir]; spellings have been modernized here and wherever needed for clarity's sake throughout the book.

Chapter 2

1. Travitsky, "Reprinting Tudor History," 165–66; Vives, *Instructio[n] of a Christen woma[n]*, [Bivr].

2. Moynahan, *God's Bestseller*, 128.

3. Pollard, *Wolsey*, 12.

4. Ibid., 12–14.

5. John Rendle-Short, *Journey of the Bible Text and the Division of the Ways*, "Chapter 17: The Scriptures Translated into English by William Tyndale," www.journeyofbible text.org/chap_17.htm; Professor Rendle-Short is Professor Emeritus at the University of Queensland.

6. *New Advent Catholic Encylopedia*, s.v. "Thomas Wolsey," http://www.newadvent.org/cathen/15685a.htm.

7. Thomas Smith, *Select Memoirs*, "Thomas Cranmer: Archbishop of Canterbury" (Glasgow: n.p., 1836), www.apuritansmind.com/Reformation/MemoirsReformers/MemoirsThomasCranmer.htm.

8. Strype, *Memorials*, 4.

9. Ibid.

10. Bobrick, *Wide as the Waters*, 140.

11. Strype, *Memorials*, 9.

12. Ibid., 5.

13. Ibid.

14. Ibid., 14–15.

15. Ibid., 1–3.

16. Ibid., 9.

17. This book was published in Latin in 1530 and in English in 1531.

18. I.e., money paid by the clergy to the pope. All Catholic clergymen had to pay the pope the salary from their first year in any new or advanced position. The new act

reduced this amount to 5 percent of the salary, which was a far more realistic figure, but also a drastic reduction from the perspective of Rome.

19. The relevant portion of the text from "The Submission of the Clergy, 1532" follows:

First, the clergy will not meet in convocation and will not pass any new canons without the king's consent. First, do offer and promise, on our priestly word, here unto your highness, submitting ourselves most humbly to the same, that we will never from henceforth enact, put in use, promulge, or execute any new canons or constitutions provincial, or any other new ordinance, provincial or synodal, in our convocation or synod in time coming, which convocation is, always has been, and must be, assembled only by your highness' commandment of writ, unless your highness by your royal assent shall license us to assemble our convocation, and to make, promulge, and execute such constitutions and ordinances as shall be made in the same; and thereto give your royal assent and authority.

Secondly, the clergy approve of a revision of all the existing laws of the church by the king and a royal commission. Secondly, that whereas divers of the constitutions, ordinances, and canons, provincial or synodal, which have been heretofore enacted, be thought to be not only much prejudicial to your prerogative royal, but also overmuch onerous to [p. 341] your highness' subjects, your clergy aforesaid is contented, if it may stand so with your highness' pleasure, that they be committed to the examination and judgment of your grace, and of thirty-two persons, whereof sixteen to be of the upper and nether house of the temporalty, and the other sixteen of the clergy, all to be chosen and appointed by your most noble grace. So that, finally, whichsoever of the said constitutions, ordinances, or canons, provincial or synodal, shall be thought and determined by your grace and by the most part of the said thirty-two persons not to stand with God's laws and the laws of the realm, the same to be abrogated and taken away by your grace and the clergy; and such of them as shall be seen by your grace, and by the most part of the said thirty-two persons, to stand with God's laws and the laws of your realm, to stand in full strength and power, your grace's most royal assent and authority once impetrate and fully given to the same.

(Quoted in Edward Potts Cheyney, ed., *Readings in English History Drawn from the Original Sources: Intended to Illustrate a Short History of England* [Boston: Ginn, 1922, 1935], 340–41, Original Sources.)

Chapter 3

1. Lewis, *English Literature*, 176.

2. More, *Complete Works*, 12–13.

3. Daniell, *William Tyndale*, 226.

4. Tyndale, *Obedience*, 61.

5. This page count is in the modern printed version, *The Complete Works of Thomas More*—in the original, this preface is 37 pages in length.

6. Quoted in More, *Complete Works*, 258.

7. Ibid., 259.

8. Ibid.

9. Tyndale, *Obedience*, 15.

10. Ibid.
11. Ibid.
12. Ibid., 16.
13. Ibid.
14. Ibid.
15. Quoted in *God's Bestseller*, 193.
16. Tyndale, *Obedience*, 17.
17. Ibid.
18. Ibid.
19. Ibid., 18.
20. Ibid. 64.
21. Ibid.
22. Ibid.
23. Ibid., 65.
24. Moynahan, *God's Bestseller*, 169.
25. More, *Complete Works*, 7.
26. Ibid., 383. More's perspective is not obsolete. Henry G. Graham's book, *Where We Got the Bible: Our Debt to the Catholic Church*, was written in the early twentieth century and recently republished by Catholic Answers with a laudatory forward from the organization's president. In Graham's text we read:

"Please observe that, while the Church approves of the people reading the Scriptures in their own language, she also claims the right to see that they really have a true version of the Scriptures to read and not a mutilated or false or imperfect or heretical version. She claims that she alone has the right to make translations from the original languages (Hebrew or Greek) in which the Bible was written, the right to superintend and supervise the work of translating, the right of appointing certain priests or scholars to understand the work, the right of approving or condemning versions and translations which are submitted to her for her judgment. She declares that she will not tolerate that her children should be exposed to the danger of reading copies of Scripture which have changed or falsified something of the original apostolic writing, which have added something or left out something, which have notes and explanations and prefaces and prologues that convey false doctrine or false morals. *Her people must have the correct Bible or no Bible at all.*

"Rome claims that the Bible is her book, that she has preserved it and perpetuated it, that she alone knows what it means, that nobody else has any right to it whatsoever or any authority to declare what the true meaning of it is. She therefore has declared that the work of translating it from the original languages, of explaining it, and of printing it and publishing it, belongs strictly to her alone and that, if she cannot nowadays prevent those outside her fold from tampering with it and misusing it, at least she will take care that none of her own children abuse it or take liberties with it, and hence she forbids any private person to attempt to translate it into the common language without authority from ecclesiastical superiors and also forbids the faithful to read any editions but such as are approved by the bishops" (78–79, emphasis added).

Thus, Graham concludes that Tyndale's translation was riddled with "the Lutheran heresy" and asserts Thomas More and Bishop Tunstall's opinion of its multitudinous errors (89–91).

27. Ibid., 7. Those who defend More might point out that he was arguing that it is only because of the misuse of the Bible that the suggestion was made, that he was not seriously contending that Scripture should not have been written. While this point deserves some recognition, it must be remembered that More was using deadly force to keep the English Bible out of the hands of the people. Any suggestion that he was only using hyperbole in argument must be discounted in light of More's vicious enforcement actions. Moreover, there are some arguments that are simply out of bounds for any true Christian. Christians should never suggest that it would be better if the Bible had never been written—even with the limitations expressed by More.

28. Ibid., 144.

29. Ibid.

30. Ibid, 145.

31. Moynahan, *God's Bestseller*, 238.

32. Bobrick, *Wide as the Waters*, 27.

33. Quoted in Daniell, *Tyndale*, 52.

34. More, *Complete Works*, 38.

35. Ibid., 270.

36. Lollards, the followers of the teaching of John Wycliffe, persisted in the face of unrelenting persecution up until the time Lutheranism or Protestantism emerged with essentially the same teaching. Between 1506 and 1519, the years immediately before the era formally recognized as the Reformation, twenty-two English Lollards were burned at the stake (Moynahan, *God's Bestseller*, 9).

37. Jordan, *Development of Religious Toleration*, I:42–43.

38. That is, "Christ-man" or Christian.

39. More, preface to the *Confutation*, [Biii^r].

40. Ibid., [Biii^v].

41. Ibid., [Biv^r].

42. It is interesting to note that in the Bodleian Library's copy of More's *Confutation*, the word *pope* is often blotted out but not completely, so it is still readable. Nonetheless, it is the only word on the page suffering from such defacement.

43. Ibid., [Biv^r–Biv^v].

44. Ibid., [Biv^v].

Hitton's argument is based on an obvious reference to 2 Peter 3:9: "The lorde is not slake to fulfill hys promes as some men count slackness but is patient to us warde / and wolde have no man lost / but wolde receave all men to repentaunce" (Tyndale, *The New Testament*). Even if Hitton's argument against the death penalty might not agree with the majority view among modern evangelicals, he nonetheless based his argument on a scriptural principle, which was a novel approach to theological reasoning.

45. Ibid.

46. Ibid.

47. Ibid., 30–31. Despite More's contention that Christians must always obey the law, as Lord Chancellor he violated the procedural rights of those accused of heresy—

which, in its essence, was a violation of the rule of law. As Brian Moynahan demonstrates, the law of Henry IV gave those accused of heresy certain limited procedural rights. More disregarded all those laws within his first couple months in office in his prosecution of a London leather seller named Thomas Philips. He repeatedly interrogated Philips in private, which was illegal, and pressured him to confess his guilt, even though the jury had neither convicted him nor given him a sentence. Philips spent several years unjustly suffering in the Tower (*God's Bestseller*, 208–10).

48. Ibid., 14–26.

49. Ibid., 22.

Chapter 4

1. "The First Act of Succession," quoted in George Burton Adams and Henry Morse Stephens, eds., *Select Documents of English Constitutional History* (New York: Macmillan Company, 1916), 236 (http://members.shaw.ca/reformation/1534succession.htm).

2. Ackroyd, *Life of Thomas More*, 356.

3. Quoted in Ackroyd, *Thomas More*, 360–61.

4. Ibid., 361.

5. Roper, *Mirrour of Virtue*, 126–28.

6. Quoted in Daniell, *Tyndale*, 365.

7. Daniell, *Tyndale*, 379.

8. Ibid., 379–80; However, Benson Bobrick, 134, *Wide as the Waters*, suggests that Tyndale *did* receive some of the materials in prison that enabled him to translate Joshua through 2 Chronicles.

9. This is the date of execution as observed by the Anglican Church. If Tyndale was literally jailed for one year and 135 days, as one record suggests, his execution would have been on October 3.

10. Foxe, *Actes and monuments of matters most speciall*, 985.

11. Daniell, *The Bible in English*, 193.

12. Ibid., 194.

13. The Great Bible bears the distinction of being the only Bible in English records ever to be officially authorized by a king of England. See chapter 11 for a discussion of the claim that King James "authorized" the version of the Bible bearing his name. David Daniell provides a complete account of both the Great Bible and the King James Bible in *The Bible in English*, chapters 13 and 25.

14. Cranmer, *The Judgment of Archbishop Cranmer*, 1–2.

15. Ibid., 4.

16. Ibid., 7.

17. Ibid., 9.

18. Ibid., 9.

19. Daniell, *Tyndale*, 280.

Chapter 5

1. Many people know that the jingle "Divorced, beheaded, died; divorced, beheaded, survived" refers to Henry VIII's six wives. Fewer, perhaps, are aware of the circumstances

surrounding their estrangements from the king. Anne, like Catherine before her, could not please the king by giving birth to a son. To make matters worse, Thomas Cromwell and others in the court realized that political expediencies favored dissolving the king's marriage with Anne because the Boleyn family's French connections hindered negotiations with Spain. Jane Seymour was a better candidate for queen, and Henry was all too ready to agree. Anne was accused of adultery, incest, and conspiracy, then beheaded in May 1536. Jane remained in the king's favor, especially after she gave birth to the future Edward I, but died within a year of her marriage to the king. Henry's relationship with his next wife, Anne of Cleves, was the result of a political alliance that Cromwell had contrived with the Protestant League of Schmalkalden. Henry never liked Anne, so he was quick to divorce her and marry Katherine Howard, the young and spirited first cousin of Anne Boleyn, as soon as Cromwell was beheaded on diverse charges. Katherine too was beheaded (after revelations of infidelity), but the proceedings were initiated by the council rather than the king himself. Henry's last wife was a widow named Catherine Parr. She survived the king, caring for him in his final days.

2. Hayward, *Life and Raigne of King Edward*, 35.

3. Strype, *Memorials*, 141.

4. Ibid., 142.

5. Quoted in ibid., 144.

6. Ibid.

7. Ibid., 145.

8. Ibid., 148–49.

9. Ibid., 217.

10. Ibid., 218.

11. Ibid., 149.

12. Thomas Cranmer, *Certayne sermons appoynted by the kinges Majestie, to be declared and reade, by al persons, vicars, or curates, euery Sonday and holy daye in theyr churches where they haue cure*, 4; the 1549 edition at the Bodleian Library at Oxford, which appears to be unchanged in content from the 1547 edition, is much more legible than the available copies of the 1547 printing.

13. Strype, *Memorials*, 185.

14. Ibid.

15. Ibid., 186.

16. Anon., *[Ballad on the defeat of the Devon and Cornwall rebels of 1548]*, (London: n.p., 1549), reproduction of original at the British Library, Early English Books Online.

17. Strype, *Memorials*, 156.

18. Ibid., 146–47.

19. Ibid., 150.

20. Ibid., 173.

21. Ibid., 208.

22. Ibid., 179.

23. Ibid., 181.

24. Ibid.

25. Ibid., 211–16.

26. Ibid.

27. E.g., see Edmund Becke, *A brefe confutatacion of this most detestable, [and] Anabaptistical opinion, that Christ dyd not take hys flesh of the blessed Vyrgyn Mary nor any corporal substaunce of her body* (London: 1550).

28. Cranmer, *Memorials*, 194–98.

29. Ibid., 206.

30. Ibid., 207.

31. Ibid.

Chapter 6

1. Ridley, *Bloody Mary's Martyrs*, 47.

2. Ibid., 48.

3. Ibid.

4. Ibid.

5. Ibid., 51.

6. Ibid.

7. For example, the Twenty-Second Session of the Council of Trent (1562) declared in Canon 3 of the Doctrine on the Most Holy Sacrifice of the Mass:

"If anyone says that the sacrifice of the Mass is merely an offering of praise and thanksgiving, or that it is a simple commemoration of the sacrifice accomplished on the cross, but not a propitiatory sacrifice, or that it benefits only those who communicate; and that it should not be offered for the living and the dead, for sins, punishments, satisfaction and other necessities, *anathema sit*."

(Quoted in Dupuis, *The Christian Faith*, 630.)

8. Zagorin, *Idea of Religious Toleration*, 55–56; Lecler, *Toleration and the Reformation*, 124–28.

9. Strype, *Memorials*, 312.

10. Ibid.

11. Ibid., 307.

12. Ibid., 323.

13. Ibid., 344.

14. Ibid., 348.

15. Penny, *Freewill or Predestination*, 106, quoting P. L. Hughes and J. F. Larkin, eds., *Tudor Royal Proclamations* (New Haven: Yale UP, 1964, 1969), II: 6.

16. Strype, *Memorials*, 349.

17. Ridley, *Bloody Mary's Martyrs*, 65.

18. Foxe, *Actes and monuments of these latter and perilous days*, 1036.

19. Ridley, *Bloody Mary's Martyrs*, 67.

20. Brown, *Life of Rowland Taylor*, 1959.

21. Penny, *Freewill or Predestination*, 105.

22. Brown, *Life of Rowland Taylor*, 10–11.

23. Ridley, *Bloody Mary's Martyrs*, 69.

24. Brown, *Life of Rowland Taylor*, 10.

25. E.g., see Mary Taylor Brewer, *From Log Cabins to the White House*.

26. Brown, *Life of Rowland Taylor*, 106.

27. Foxe, *Actes and monuments of these latter and perilous days*, 1062.

28. Ibid.

29. Foxe, *Book of Martyrs*, 419; Ridley, *Bloody Mary's Martyrs*, 152.

30. Foxe, *Actes and monuments of these latter and perilous days*, 1606, 1609–10.

31. Latimer, *Frutefull sermons*, 195.

32. Ibid.

33. Foxe, *Book of Martyrs*, 346.

34. Strype, *Memorials*, 373.

35. By this time Mary had married Philip of Spain. He was designated the king of England, but Mary continued to rule.

36. Ibid., 374.

37. Ibid., 376.

38. Ridley, *Bloody Mary's Martyrs*, 128.

39. Ibid., 384–89.

Chapter 7

1. Dickens, *English Reformation*, 189–90; see also Martin, *Religious Radicals*, 71–72.

2. Martin, *Religious Radicals*, 72.

3. Ibid.

4. Ibid., 73.

5. Foxe, *First volume of ecclesiasticall history*, 2073; this account is described in *Religious Radicals* on page 73, but Martin gives Maundrel the first name of William rather than John. The earliest versions of Foxe contain neither Maundrel's first name nor the account of his becoming a disciple of Tyndale.

6. Ibid.

7. Foxe, *Actes and monuments of these latter and perillous dayes*, 1734.

8. Ibid., 1504; Spicer is alternately referred to as "Robert Spicer."

9. Strype, *Memorials*, 350.

10. Freeman, "Dissenters from a dissenting Church," 131.

11. Champneys, *Harvest is at hand*, [Aiiii^v].

12. Ibid., [Bv^{r-v}, Cviii^v].

13. Hart, *A consultorie*, [Ciiii^r].

14. Ibid., *A Godlie exhortation*, [Avii^r].

15. Ibid., *A consultorie*, [Dvii^v–Dviii^r, Fi^{r-v}].

16. Quoted in Martin, *Religious Radicals*, 41.

17. Freeman, "Dissenters from a dissenting Church," 129; see also an entire book devoted to this group by Andrew Penny titled *Freewill or Predestination: The Battle over Saving Grace in Mid-Tudor England*.

18. Penny, *Freewill or Predestination*, 51.

19. Ibid.

20. Ibid., 52–55.

21. Bradford, *Treatise on Predestination*, 14.

22. See, e.g., Martin, *Religious Radicals*, 67, and Penny, *Freewill or Predestination*, 117ff.

23. Freeman, "Dissenters from a Dissenting Church," 134.

24. Ibid.

25. Bradford, *Godlie meditations*, [Oviii^v–Pi^r].

26. Trewe, *Cause of contention*, 45–46.

27. Ibid.

28. Ibid., 15.

29. Trewe, *Cause of Contention*, 44–45, 53–54.

30. Veron, *A fruteful treatise*, [Fii^r].

31. Penny, *Freewill or Predestination*, 72; see also Cole, *A godly and frutefull sermon*, Dii^{r–v}.

32. Knox, *Answer*, 191, quoted and interpreted in Freeman, "Dissenters from a dissenting Church," 149–50.

33. Bradford, *Writings*, 165.

34. Trewe, *Cause of Contention*, 56–57. Emphasis added.

35. Penny, *Freewill or Predestination*, 105, quoting W. Stanford Reid, *Trumpeter of God: A Biography of John Knox* (New York: Charles Scribner's Sons, 1974), 100.

36. Knox, *Answer*, 193.

37. Ibid.

38. Ibid., 193–94.

39. Ibid., 194.

40. Ibid., 196–97.

41. Ibid., 208–209.

42. Ibid., 215–16.

43. Ibid., 212.

44. Ibid., 206.

Chapter 8

1. Calvin, *Institutes*, 3.19.15.

2. Ibid., 4.20.4, 4.20.3.

3. Witte, "Moderate Religious Liberty," 83; Adams, *Works*, 6: 313.

These comments by John Adams are found in his *Disourses on Davila*, a compilation of essays on political history and philosophy. The balance of his comments on Geneva are as follows:

"After Martin Luther had introduced into Germany the liberty of thinking in matters of religion, and erected the standard of reformation, John Calvin, a native of Noyon, in Picardie, of a vast genius, singular eloquence, various erudition, and polished taste, embraced the cause of reformation. In the books which he published, and in the discourses which he held in the several cities of France, he proposed one hundred and twenty-eight articles in opposition to the creed of the Roman Catholic church. These opinions were soon embraced with ardor, and maintained with obstinacy, by a great number of persons of all conditions. The asylum and the centre of this new sect was Geneva, a city situated on the lake anciently called *Lemanus*, on the frontiers of Savoy, which had shaken off the yoke of its bishop and the Duke of Savoy, and erected itself into a republic, under the title of a free city, for the sake of liberty of conscience."

(See Essay XIX, *Works*, 6:313–14. A footnote Adams added in 1813 contains his admonition not to forget or despise Geneva.)

4. Calvin, *Sermons*, 536–37.

5. Ibid., 545.

6. Ibid., 537.

7. Bainton, *Travail of Religious Liberty*, 74; Goldstone, *Out of the Flames*, 48, 55–56.

8. Ibid., 74.

9. Ibid.; Schaff, *The Swiss Reformation*, 740.

10. Bainton, *Travail of Religious Liberty*, 79.

11. Servetus' work was first published in Latin under the title, *De Trinitatis Erroribus*.

12. Bainton, *Hunted Heretic*, 118ff.; Schaff, *The Swiss Reformation*, 724.

13. Bainton, *Travail of Religious Liberty*, 83.

14. Lecler, *Toleration and the Reformation*, 326, quoting Calvin's *Opera*.

15. Bainton, *Travail of Religious Liberty*, 87.

16. Schaff, *The Swiss Reformation*, 764–65; Rilliet, *Calvin and Servetus*, 87, quoting Calvin's *Declaration*.

17. Bainton, *Travail of Religious Liberty*, 88; cf., Rilliet, *Calvin and Servetus*, 126.

18. Rilliet, *Calvin and Servetus*, 106.

19. Bainton, *Hunted Heretic*, 197.

20. Bainton, *Travail of Religious Liberty*, 92.

21. Jordan, *Religious Toleration*, I:310.

22. Hillar, *Case of Michael Servetus*, 359.

23. Bainton, *Travail of Religious Liberty*, 98; Zagorin, *Idea of Religious Toleration*, 98.

24. Zagorin, *Idea of Religious Toleration*, 98.

25. Ibid., 99.

26. See Calvin, *Institutes*, 2.21.11–12, footnotes 25, 29, and 31.

27. Zagorin, *Idea of Religious Toleration*, 100.

28. See ibid., 101.

29. Castellio, "Preface to the French Bible," in Bainton's translation and compilation of *Concerning Heretics*, 257–58.

30. Ibid., 258–59.

31. Calvin, "Prefatory Address to King Francis," in the *Institutes*, 14.

32. Ibid., 12.

33. Ibid., 11–12.

34. Castellio, "Preface to the French Bible," in Bainton's translation and compilation of *Concerning Heretics*, 260.

35. Ibid., 263–64.

36. Some authors view this work as being of questionable origin, but the vast majority agree that Castellio had a primary hand in compilation and partial authorship. Even Calvin and Beza had no doubts. For a discussion of authorship, see the introduction to Bainton's translation of *Concerning Heretics*, 3–11; Jordan, *Religious Toleration*, I: 312; and Lecler, *Toleration*, 337.

37. Castellio, *Concerning Heretics*, 121–22.

38. Ibid., 122–23.

39. Ibid., 124–25.

40. Ibid., 126.

41. Ibid., 214–15.

42. For Augustine, see Christenson, "Political Theory of Persecution," 422–23; Zagorin, *Idea of Religious Toleration*, 27; Augustine, "Letter XCIII," chapter 17, 388. For Luther, see Zagorin, *Idea of Religious Toleration*, 73, citing W. J. Cargill Thompson, *The Political Thought of Martin Luther* (Brighton: Harvester Press, 1984), chapter 9; Acton, *Study and Writing of History*, 101ff; Lecler, *Toleration and the Reformation*, chapter titled "Luther: From 'Christian Liberty' to Established Church." For Calvin, in addition to what has already been discussed, see Witte, "Moderate Religious Liberty," 86. Another individual who found himself in a similar position was Thomas More. For an account of More's change in theory and perspective, see Jordan, *Religious Toleration*, I: 43.

43. Castellio, *Concerning Heretics*, 127.

44. Lecler, *Toleration and the Reformation*, 344–45, citing numerous sources for various opinions and further investigation.

45. Castellio, *Concerning Heretics*, 227–28.

46. Calvin, *Sermons*, 528–29, 537.

47. Castellio, *Concerning Heretics*, 230.

48. Ibid., 234.

49. Ibid., 235, quoting Calvin, *Institutes*, 4.11.3.

50. The Donatists abandoned the Catholic Church because of local bishops who had compromised with pagan religions during an early persecution by the Roman emperor. These Donatists contended that baptisms conducted by such compromisers were not valid, and a proper baptism required a faithful priest. Augustine viewed such people as heretics primarily because they rejected the authority of the Roman Church.

51. Quoted in Lecler, *Toleration and the Reformation*, 55; the quotation is from Augustine's *Contra epistulam Parmeniani*.

52. Zagorin, *Idea of Religious Toleration*, 29.

53. Ibid.

54. Castellio, *Concerning Heretics*, 220.

55. Lecler, *Toleration and the Reformation*, 152, 163.

56. Calvin, *Sermons*, 536.

57. For Calvin's original Latin edition, see his *Opera*, VIII: cols. 457ff. Partial English translations appear in Zagorin, *Idea of Religious Toleration*, 80ff.; Schaff, *The Swiss Reformation*, 791–92; Hillar, *Case of Michael Servetus*, 320.

The author of this book obtained the complete Latin version of Calvin's work and employed numerous Latin students from Patrick Henry College to provide a translation.

58. Schaff, *The Swiss Reformation*, 793.

59. Calvin, *Defensio*, 479.

60. Schaff, *The Swiss Reformation*, 793.

61. Calvin, *Defensio*, 477.

62. Ibid.

63. Ibid., 478.

64. Ibid., 466.

65. Hall, *The Genevan Reformation and the American Founding*, 116–17.

66. Bainton, *Travail of Religious Liberty*, 94; why else would Calvin write a defense of putting heretics to death by the sword?

67. Schaff, *The Swiss Reformation*, 768; Schaff records, "'From the time Servetus was convicted of his heresy,' says Calvin, 'I have not uttered a word about his punishment, as all honest men will bear witness.' . . . One thing only he did: he expressed for a mitigation of his punishment. And this humane sentiment is almost the only good thing that can be recorded to his honor in this painful trial." Calvin wrote in a letter to Farel on August 20, 1553, "*Spero capitale saltem judicium fore; poenae vero atrocitatem remitti cupio.*"

68. Calvin, *Defensio*, 479.

69. Ibid.

70. Castellio, "Reply to Calvin's Book" (Bainton's translated excerpts of *Contra libellum Calvini*), *Concerning Heretics*, 271.

71. Ibid., 267.

72. E.g., William Prynne in *The sword of Christian magistracy supported: or, A full vindication of Christian Kings and Magistrates Authority under the Gospell, to punish Idolatry, Apostacy, Heresie, Blasphemy, and obstinate Schism, with Pecuniary, Corporall, and in some Cases with Banishment, and Capitall Punishments*, George Gillespie in *Wholesome Severity reconciled with Christian Liberty. Or, The true Resolution of a present Controversy concerning Liberty of Conscience*, and John Cotton in *The bloudy tenent, washed, and made white in the bloud of the Lambe*.

73. Castellio, "Reply to Calvin's Book" (Bainton's translated excerpts of *Contra libellum Calvini*), *Concerning Heretics*, 213.

Chapter 9

1. Camden, *Elizabeth*, 12.

2. Jordan, *Religious Toleration*, 1: 82.

3. Barrowe, *Brief Discoverie*, 10.

4. Jordan, *Religious Toleration*, 1: 91.

5. "Queen Elizabeth's Proclamation to Forbid Preaching," in Gee, *Documents of English Church History*, 416.

6. Ibid.

7. Ibid., 417.

8. Quoted in Strype, *Annals*, 78.

9. Ibid., 79.

10. Ibid.

11. "Elizabeth's Supremacy Act, restoring Ancient Jurisdiction," in Gee, *Documents of English Church History*, 442.

12. Ibid., 449.

13. "Elizabeth's Act of Uniformity," in ibid., 463.

14. Ibid., 462.

15. Quoted in Jordan, *Religious Toleration*, 1: 90.

16. Ibid., 84.

17. Ibid.

18. Ibid., 95.

19. Ibid., 96.

20. Ibid., 110.

21. See, e.g., Rafael E. Tarrago, "Bloody Bess: The Persecution of Catholics in Elizabethan England," *Logos: A Journal of Catholic Thought and Culture*, 7, no. 1 (Winter 2004).

22. "England (since the Reformation)," *The Catholic Encyclopedia*, vol. 5 (Robert Appleton Co., 1909; K. Knight, 2003), available at http://www.newadvent.org/cathen/05445a.htm.

23. Ibid.

24. Jordan, *Religious Toleration*, 1: 84–85.

25. Ibid., 118, n1.

26. "Robert Persons," *The Catholic Encyclopedia*, vol. 11 (Robert Appleton Co., 1909; K. Knight, 2003), available at http://www.newadvent.org/cathen/11729a.htm.

27. Evans, *Early English Baptists*, 1: 140.

28. Amy Butler, "A Strange Allegiance," sermon given on 4 July 2004 at Calvary Baptist Church in Washington, D.C., available at http://www.calvarydc.com/sermons04july4.html.

29. Collinson, *Elizabethan Puritans*, 36.

30. Evans, *Early English Baptists*, 1: 135.

31. Collinson, *Elizabethan Puritans*, 36.

32. Jordan, *Religious Toleration*, 1: 244.

33. Collinson, *Elizabethan Puritans*, 25.

34. Ibid.

35. Jordan, *Religious Toleration*, 1: 246–47, quoting Dudley Fenner, *A Defense of the Godlie ministers*.

36. Ibid., 249.

37. Ibid., 179.

38. Collinson, *Elizabethan Puritans*, 47.

39. Evans, *Early English Baptists*, 1: 142.

40. Quoted in Collinson, *Elizabethan Puritans*, 42.

41. Quoted in Evans, *Early English Baptists*, 143.

42. Collinson, *Elizabethan Puritans*, 428; cf., "The Act Against Recusants," in Gee, *Documents of English Church History*, 498ff.

43. Quoted in Evans, *Early English Baptists*, 148

44. Ibid.

45. Cramp, *Baptist History*, 280.

46. Quoted in Evans, *Early English Baptists*, 141.

47. Quoted in Jordan, *Religious Toleration*, 1: 296–97.

48. Cramp, *Baptist History*, 270. Cramp calls this group Baptists. However, they appear to hold to the doctrine of the celestial flesh (Cramp, 271), which would remove them from the Baptist camp and place them squarely with Anabaptists.

49. Ibid., 273.

50. Ibid.

51. Ibid., 276.

52. Ibid.

53. Ibid., 275.

54. Ibid., 263.

55. Browne, *Reformation without tarying for anie*, [A3].

56. Barrow, *A true description*, [A2].

57. Jordan, *Religious Toleration*, 1: 288.

58. Ibid., 289.

59. Ibid., 290.

60. Ibid., 289.

61. Ibid., 287.

62. Ibid., 286–87, n5.

63. Ibid., 299.

64. Browne, *Reformation without tarying for anie*, [K].

65. Ibid.

Chapter 10

1. Jordan, *Religious Toleration*, 2: 17–18.

2. Ibid., 32.

3. Ibid., 18.

4. Lindsay, *History of the Reformation*, 289.

5. Dawson, *Politics of Religion*, 89.

6. Knox, *Copie of a letter*, [Biii^r].

7. Quoted in Hart, "John Knox," 270–71.

8. Cameron, *The European Reformation*, 386.

9. Lindsay, *History of the Reformation*, 300.

10. Ibid., 305.

11. Dawson, *Politics of Religion*, 115.

12. Knox, *Ecclesiastical History*, 310.

13. Knox, *First Blast*, 9^v.

14. The preceding account of the conference was derived from Knox's *Ecclesiastical History*, pages 310–15.

15. Zweig, *Mary Queen of Scotland*, 55.

16. Bergeron, *Letters*, 32ff.

17. "The Millenary Petition, A.D. 1603," in Gee, *Documents*, 509.

18. Ibid.

19. Ibid.

20. Barlow, *Summe of the Conference*, 4–5.

21. Ibid., 5–6.

22. Ibid., 6.

23. Ibid., 7.

24. Ibid.

25. Ibid., 11.

26. Ibid., 11–12.

27. In a later discussion about baptisms performed by women in cases of necessity when no qualified man could be found, the assurance of salvation that the Calvinist-Anglicans found in baptism is clearly stated: "As if God, without Baptism could not save

the child; but the case put, that the state of the Infant, dying unbaptized, being uncertain, and to God only known; but if it die baptized, there is an evident assurance, that it is saved, who is he, that having any Religion in him, would not speedily, by any mean, procure his Child to be baptized, and rather ground his action upon Christ's promise, then his omission thereof upon Gods secret judgment" (*The Summe of the Conference*, 16). James replied to this by saying that it seemed that baptism was a necessity but that at times the Scottish ministers seemed to place too little emphasis on it, while the Anglicans seemed to place too much emphasis. He told a story of a Scottish minister who asked, "If I thought Baptism so necessary, that if it were omitted, the child should be damned? I answered him no: but if you, being called to baptize the child, though privately should refuse to come, I think you shall be damned" (ibid., 17).

28. Ibid., 20.

29. Ibid., 21.

30. Ibid., 22–23.

31. Ibid., 24.

32. Ibid., 29.

33. Ibid., 30.

34. Ibid., 36.

35. Ibid., 37.

36. Ibid., 73.

37. Ibid., 77.

38. Ibid., 71.

39. Ibid.

40. Ibid., 83.

41. Ibid., 95.

42. Ibid., 46.

43. Ibid., 47–46.

44. Daniell, *The Bible in English*, 428–29.

45. Ibid.

46. Barlow, *Summe of the Conference*, 48.

47. See Daniell, *Bible in English*, 136ff, 448.

48. Collinson, *Elizabethan Puritans Movement*, 461.

49. Jordan, *Religious Toleration*, 2: 21.

50. Ibid., 20.

51. Ibid., 25.

52. Ibid.

53. Ibid., 24–25.

54. Ibid., 26, quoting Gardiner, *History of England, 1603–1642*, 1: 197–98, fn2; Collinson contends that the number was closer to ninety Puritans who left the ministry (*Elizabethan Puritans*, 464–65).

55. Daniell, *Bible in English*, 432.

56. Jordan, *Religious Toleration*, 2: 31.

57. *Proceedings and Debates of the House of Commons in 1620 and 1621*, 1: 6, quoted in ibid., 31, fn1.

58. "A declaration against Vortius," in James I, *The Works*, 349.

59. Jordan, *Religious Toleration*, 2: 37–38.

60. Ibid., 38.

61. Osborne, *Works*, 534–35.

62. David M. Bergeron's *King James and Letters of Homoerotic Desire* provides a comprehensive and well-documented account of three of King James' "favorites." Although Bergeron clearly holds the opinion that James had homosexual tendencies, the original sources he quotes from are difficult to refute or explain away.

63. E.g., seventeenth-century historian Arthur Wilson wrote in his *History of Great Britain* (London, 1653): "But whether from an apprehension that the king's love and company was alienated from her [i.e., the queen], by this *Masculine conversation* and *intimacy*, or whether the man's [i.e., Carr's] *insolence*, (thus high mounted) had carried him too near the *Beams* of *Majesty* . . . or whether from that *natural inclination* that makes every one oppose *Pride* in others . . . I know not. But she became the head of a great *Faction* against him" (79).

The Historicall Narration of the first Fourteen years of King James (1651) describes Carr's rise to power after he came to the king's attention due to a riding accident:

"This Accident being no less strange than sudden, in such a place, causes the *King* to demand who it was, answer was made him his name was *Carr*, he taking notice of his name . . . caused him to be had into the *Court*, and there provides for him, until such time as he was recovered of his hurt: After in process of time, the *young man* is called for, and made one of his *Majesty's Bed-Chamber*, where he had not long continued in that place before (by his good endeavors, and diligent service in that office) the *King* showed extraordinary favor unto him, doubling the value of every action in estimation, so that many were obscured that he might be graced and dignified" (8).

64. These were republished in Bergeron's work.

65. E.g., see "To George Villier, Marquess of Buckingham [December 1622?]" and "To Prince Charles and the Marquess of Buckingham [27 February 1623?]," in Bergeron, *Letters*, 150–51; E. Cobham Brewer, "Steenie," *Dictionary of Phrase and Fable* (Philadelphia: Henry Altemus, 1898; Bartleby.com, 2000).

66. Bergeron, *Letters*, 139.

67. Wilson, *History of Great Britain*, 79–80.

68. Ibid., 104–105.

69. Osborne recorded, "I have heard that Sir *Henry Rich*, since *Earl of Holland*, and some others refused his Majesty's favor upon those conditions they subscribed to, who filled that place in his Affection; *Rich* losing that opportunity his curious Face and Complexion afforded him, by turning aside and spitting after the King had slabbered his mouth" (*Works*, 535).

70. Ibid.

71. Ibid., 73.

72. Ibid., 73–74.

73. Bruce Robinson, "The Gunpowder Plot" (BBC, 2001), at http://www.bbc.co.uk/history/.

74. Jordan, *Religious Toleration*, 2: 78.

75. Fuller, *Church-History*, 10: 63.

76. Ibid., 64.

77. Jordan, *Religious Toleration*, 2: 49.

78. Ibid.

79. Ibid., 50.

80. Ibid.

81. Fuller, *Church-History*, 10: 64.

Chapter 11

1. W. J. McGlothlin says, "With the exception of the Anabaptists, all parties of reformers were Augustinian, emphasizing predestination and personal election, a limited atonement, the final perseverance of the saints, and related doctrines" (*Baptist Confessions*, 50). Also, A. C. Underwood says of the early Anabaptists, "They were, however, opposed to the Augustinian theology, which had so powerfully influenced Luther and Calvin. They insisted strongly on the freedom of the human will, for it seemed to them that Augustinian doctrines of unconditional election and irresistible grace were damaging to the interests of practical piety" (*A History of the English Baptists*, 22).

2. See previous chapters for a fuller discussion of Augustine's theory on this point.

3. Augustine's views on election changed over time, but his work *A Treatise on the Predestination of the Saints* (written in 428–29) may be seen as his final and ultimately most influential understanding of the topic (see especially, chapters 7 [III], 11 [VI], and 14 [VIII]).

4. A later chapter will address some of the writings of these individuals; e.g., George Gillespie quoted from Augustine against the Donatists, Calvin against Servetus, and Beza against Castellio to support his view of "pernicious, God-provoking, Truth-defacing, Church-ruinating, & State-shaking toleration" (*Wholesome Severity*, [A3ʳ]).

5. Jordan, *Religious Toleration*, 2: 258–59.

6. Ibid., 259.

7. Ibid., 261.

8. "Opposed to the notion of a territorial or State Church composed of all baptized in infancy and now living in a certain district, the Anabaptists formed churches of truly converted persons, on a basis of voluntary membership. They rejected infant-baptism because it was without Scriptural warrant and also because it implied an all-inclusive, non-ethical basis of church membership" (Underwood, *History of the English Baptists*, 22).

9. Ibid., 23.

10. Ibid., 24.

11. Underwood disagrees with this analysis, claiming that "Anabaptism in England was never organized and lacked a real leader. For this reason it cannot be regarded as the seed-ploy of the English Baptist movement whose origin must be sought elsewhere, and is to be found among those native Englishmen who, in a spirit of radicalism and with their eyes on the New Testament, carried the principles of the English Reformation to their logical conclusion" (*History of the English Baptists*, 27). While there is a certain element of truth in this assertion, and while it is difficult to say with absolute certainty how the chain of religious ideas is transmitted from group to group, the strongest evidence against this claim is the plain fact that the first English Baptists were launched from

a group who had been living in Holland, where there was unquestionably some direct Anabaptist contact and influence.

12. McGlothlin, *Baptist Confessions*, 51.

13. Ibid.

14. Ibid.

15. Underwood, *History of the English Baptists*, 35.

16. Ibid., fn3.

17. Ibid., 37–38.

18. Ibid., 38–39.

19. Ibid., 39, 47.

20. Ibid., 46.

21. Ibid.

22. Jordan, *Religious Toleration*, 2:274.

23. Helwys, *A Short Declaration*, 69.

24. Underwood, *History of the English Baptists*, 51.

25. *A Declaration of Faith of English People*, in McGlothlin, *Baptist Confessions*, 88. The first article reads, "[We believe and confess] That there are THREE which bear record in heaven, the FATHER, the WORD, and the SPIRIT; and these THREE are one GOD, all in equality, 1 Jno. 5.7; Phil. 2.5, 6. . . ." (86).

26. Ibid., 86.

27. Ibid., 88–89.

28. Ibid., 89.

29. Ibid.

30. Ibid., 90–91.

31. Ibid., 91.

32. Ibid.

33. Helwys, *A short declaration*, i.

34. Ibid., iv.

35. Ibid., 69.

36. Ibid., 70–71.

37. Ibid., 73.

38. Ibid., 75.

39. Ibid., 77.

40. Ibid., 76.

41. Ibid., 77.

42. Ibid., 79.

43. Ibid., 80.

44. Ibid.

45. Busher, *Religions Peace*, 1.

46. Ibid., 3.

47. Ibid., 4.

48. Ibid.; 1 John 4:1–3.

49. Busher, *Religions Peace*, 6.

50. Castellio had written, "Let not the Jews or Turks condemn the Christians, nor let the Christians condemn the Jews and Turks, but rather teach and win them by true

religion and justice, and let us, who are Christians, not condemn one another, but, if we are wiser than they, let us also be better and more merciful" (*Concerning Heretics,* "Dedication to Duke Christoph," 132–33).

51. *Objections Answered,* 2–3.

52. Ibid., 6.

53. Ibid., 6–7.

54. Ibid., 8.

55. Ibid., 10.

56. Ibid.

57. Ibid., 16.

58. Ibid., 17.

Chapter 12

1. 1 Kings 12:10–11 NIV.

2. 1 Kings 12:16 NIV.

3. Elizabeth married Frederick V, Elector of Palatine—a hereditary throne of a district within present-day Germany, subject to the overlordship of the Holy Roman Emperor. Frederick was briefly the king of Bohemia for three months during the winter of 1614–1615. Elizabeth would have merited little more than a historical footnote in Anglo-American history had it not been for a 1707 treaty between England and Scotland requiring a Protestant always to hold the throne of Great Britain. Upon the death of Queen Ann in 1714, Elizabeth's grandson, Elector George Ludwig of Hanover, was the closest Protestant in the line of succession and was therefore crowned King George I of Great Britain. His grandson, George III, ruled Britain during the American Revolution.

4. Jordan, *Religious Toleration,* 2:93.

5. *"Marc" Antonio Morosini to Doge and Senate,* September 13, 1624, quoted in ibid., 112.

6. Ibid., 110.

7. The Palatinate refers to two German regions that are historically related but geographically separate. In 1619, Bohemia's Protestant diet had deposed the Holy Roman Emperor, the Catholic Ferdinand II. Frederick was offered the crown in Ferdinand's place, which he accepted. He was soon defeated by the Spanish and Bavarian armies, however, and failed to receive needed help from fellow Protestants.

8. The Anglo-Catholic movement was also labeled "Arminianism" or "the Popish faith" by contemporaries (e.g., Anthony Wotton's book *A Dangerous Plot Discovered,* 1626). The term "Arminianism" in this context, however, refers not *just* to a doctrinal position on predestination but rather to a broader framework of thought in which Roman Catholic theology, practice, and hierarchy were integrated into Anglicanism as much as possible without eradicating the latter's English identity.

9. Ibid., 123–24.

10. No copies of this composition are known to exist, but as in other similar cases, its content can be surmised from various works written in response to it.

11. Montagu[e], *New Gagg,* "To the Reader," n.p.

12. See ibid., 1–30; Bernard, *Rhemes against Rome,* 29–53.

13. This was an English Catholic translation completed in 1582 and followed by its Old Testament counterpart, published in Douai, France, in 1610. Both translations were taken from the Latin Vulgate rather than from the original languages. Unlike other English translations, the Douai-Rheims translation was not intended for mass consumption or to aid in private understanding. Tyndale had been motivated by the goal of enabling each individual, no matter how "ordinary," to search the Scriptures for himself without an intermediary such as a bishop or priest. In contrast, the right of private judgment in spiritual matters posed too great a threat to the ecclesiastical authorities responsible for the Rheims New Testament. In fact, its benefactors were downright derogatory toward common people. The preface read, "The poor ploughman, could then in labouring the ground, sing the hymns and psalms whether in known or unknown languages, as they had heard them in the holy Church, *though they could neither read nor know the sense, meaning and mysteries of the Same.*" (See Daniell, *Bible in English*, 359–61.)

14. Bernard, *Rhemes against Rome*, 50–53; Bernard notes, "Jesus Christ saw how Satan abused Scripture, yet he did use it, and exhorted other [sic] to search the Scriptures" (53).

15. Montague rejected the Gagger's assertion that Anglican Protestants rely "only upon the written Word" and quoted the Eleventh Article to support his argument that in "controversies of faith," the "Church hath authority" to judge and determine (*New Gagg*, 13–30). Archbishop William Laud believed this as well: "And while the one faction [i.e., Catholics] cries up the Church above the Scripture: and the other the Scripture to the neglect and Contempt of the Church, which the Scripture it self teaches men both to honour, and obey. . . . Whereas, according to Christ's Institution, The Scripture, where 'tis plain, should guide the Church: And the Church, where there's Doubt or Difficulty, should expound the Scripture; yet so, as neither the Scripture should be forced, nor the Church so bound up, as that upon Just and farther Evidence, She may not revise that which in any Case hath slipped by Her" (Preface to the *Relation of the Conference*, n.p.).

16. See Montague, *Appello Caesarem*, "The Epistle Dedicatory," [Ai^v].

17. "Resolutions on Religion Presented by a Committee of the House of Commons, A.D. 1629," in Gee, *Documents*, 521, 524, 527.

18. Montague, *Appello Caesarem*, "The Epistle Dedicatory, [Aii^r–Aiii^r].

19. Ibid., [Aii^v].

20. Murphy, *Conscience and Community*, 79.

21. Jordan, *Religious Toleration*, 2: 168.

22. Ibid., 118–19.

23. Charles I, *Instructions*, [Aii^v].

24. Ibid., [Bi^v].

25. It is ironic that Parliament insisted on due process since they had enacted a bill of attainder convicting Montague and imposing penalties without any semblance of a trial.

26. "Resolutions on Religion Presented by a Committee of the House of Commons, A.D. 1629," quoted in Gee, *Documents*, 522.

27. Ibid, 522–23.

28. "Resolutions of the Commons (1629)," in Stephenson and Marcham, *Sources*, 454.

29. Ibid.

30. Tyacke, "Puritanism," 55–56.

31. *Appeal of the Orthodox Ministers*, 3; "Brief Supplication of the Ministers of the Church of Scotland," *Appeal*, 33–35.

32. Murphy, *Conscience and Community*, 83.

33. Laud, *Speech delivered in the Starre-Chamber*, 3.

34. Murphy, *Conscience and Community*, 83–84; see also, Collins, "The Restoration Bishops and the Royal Supremacy," 553, for more on Laud's "deference to royal authority."

35. Montague, *Appello Caesarem*, 113.

36. Jordan, *Religious Toleration*, 116.

37. Zagorin, *Idea of Religious Toleration*, 171.

38. Jordan, *Religious Toleration*, 116.

39. Ibid.

40. Laud, *Relation of the Conference*, in the dedication to Charles, n.p.

41. Ibid.

42. Lyon, *Theory of Religious Liberty*, 68.

43. Jordan, *Religious Toleration*, 2: 177; see also 171, 182–83.

44. Ibid., 138.

45. Ibid., 161.

46. Ibid., 141, 164–65.

47. "High Commission Reports (1631), [3 May 1632]," in Stephenson and Marcham, *Sources*, 469–70.

48. Ibid., 138; Leighton, *An Appeal*, 3.

49. See the full title of Prynne's *Histrio-mastix*; Cheyney, "The Court of the Star Chamber," 747–48.

50. Cheyney, "The Court of the Star Chamber," 748.

51. Jordan, *Religious Toleration*, 160.

52. Laud, *Speech delivered in the Starre-Chamber*, 2.

53. "Resolutions on Religion Presented by a Committee of the House of Commons, A.D. 1629," quoted in Gee, *Documents*, 527.

54. Jordan, *Religious Toleration*, 2: 179–80.

55. Ibid., 139, 156.

Chapter 13

1. "The Root and Branch Petition, A.D. 1640," in Gee, *Documents*, 537–38.

2. Ibid., 543, 538, 541.

3. Fletcher, "Episcopacy," 92.

4. Ibid., 111–15; Jordan, *Religious Toleration*, 3: 34–35, 368.

5. Ibid., 30–31.

6. In 1604, the dictionary definition of a *sect* was "a diversitie in opinion from others," and a *sectarie* was defined as "one whom many other doe followe in opinion" (Cawdrey, *A Table Alphabeticall*). For our purposes the term *sectaries* simply means those dissenters who cannot be classed as Catholics, Anglicans, or Presbyterians.

7. Quoted in ibid., 31.

8. Jordan, *Religious Toleration*, 3: 25–27.

9. Ibid., 37.

10. "Selections from the Petition and the Grand Remonstrance, A.D. 1641," in Gee, *Documents*, 561.

11. Ibid.

12. Ibid., 561–62.

13. "The Militia Ordinance (1642)," in Stephenson and Marcham, *Sources*, 486.

14. "Royal Proclamation (27 May 1642)," in ibid., 487.

15. "Declaration of the Lords and Commons (27 May 1642)," in ibid., 488.

16. "The Nineteen Propositions (1 June 1642)," in ibid., 489–90.

17. Ibid., 90.

18. Kenyon, *Stuart England*, 151.

19. Ibid., 152–53.

20. Paul, *Assembly of the Lord*, 66.

21. Ibid.

22. Ibid., 66–67.

23. Jordan, *Religious Toleration*, 3: 43–44.

24. "The Solemn League and Covenant, A.D. 1643," in Gee, *Documents*, 571.

25. Ibid., 570–71, emphasis added.

26. Paul, *Assembly of the Lord*, 97; Jordan, *Religious Toleration*, 3: 45–46.

27. Unlike the English members, who were elected by Parliament and possessed voting privileges in the Assembly, the Scotch divines declined the opportunity to become full members and were selected by the General Assembly of the Church of Scotland. As commissioners, they could take part in committee action and debate at will within the boundaries prescribed for all members while still maintaining an independent status accompanied by fewer restraints, especially in dealings with the government (see Paul, *Assembly of the Lord*, 116).

28. Hetherington, *History of the Westminster Assembly*, 136.

In the words of one analyst, "The Scottish commissioners cannot with propriety be regarded as forming a party in the Westminster Assembly, as they and the English Presbyterians were in all important matters completely identified" (Hetherington, *History of the Westminster Assembly*, 144). This identification between the two groups is remarkable if Richard Baxter's observations from the era are indeed true. He wrote, "When the War was first raised, there was but one Presbyterian known in all the Parliament; There was not one Presbyterian among all the General Officers of the Earl of Essex Army; nor one among all the English Colonels, Majors, or Captains, that ever I could hear of. . . . The truth is, Presbytery was not then known in England, except among a few studious Scholars, nor well by them" (*Reliquiae Baxterianae*, 3: 41).

29. Jordan, *Religious Toleration*, 47.

30. These divines are also referred to as Congregationalists, since they advocated a larger degree of autonomy for individual congregations within the national church.

31. Murphy, *Conscience and Community*, 101, quoting Alexander Henderson, one of the Scotch commissioners.

In the Independents' own words: "We believe the truth to lie and consist in a *middle way* betwixt that which is falsely charged on us, *Brownism* [i.e., sectarianism in the tradition of Robert Browne, who was discussed in the chapter on Elizabeth]; and that which is the contention of these times, the *authoritative Presbyteriall Government* in all the subordinations and proceedings of it" (*Apologeticall Narration*, 24).

32. Baillie, Public Letter, quoted in Paul, *Assembly of the Lord*, 132.

33. Warfield, *Westminster Assembly*, 40.

34. The title on the first page of text is *An Apologeticall Narration of Some Ministers Formerly in Exile: Now Members of the Assembly of Divines.*

35. Goodwin, *Apologeticall Narration*, 5, 3.

36. Ibid., 12–13.

37. Ibid., 14.

38. Ibid., 10–11.

The Independents objected to three particular propositions debated and voted on in the Assembly. Some years later Parliament directed that all the debates between the Independents and their opponents in the Assembly be published in one work under the title *The Grand Debate Concerning Presbytery and Independency by the Assembly of Divines convened at Westminster by the authority of Parliament* (1652). The propositions the dissenting brethren found objectionable were reprinted in the preface to the compilation of writings by both sides. In abbreviated form the first concerned presbyterial government:

The Scripture doth hold forth that many particular Congregations may be under one Presbyterial Government. This proposition is proved by instances.

1. Instance, Of the Church of Jerusalem, which consisted of more Congregations than one, and all those Congregations were under one

2. Presbyterial Government.

Instance, Of the Church of Ephesus.

The second proposition dealt with the subordination of synods. The Assembly had determined:

It is lawful and agreeable to the word of God, that there be a Subordination of Congregational, Classical, Provincial, and National Assemblies: that so appeals may be made from the inferior to the superior, respectively. Proved from Mat. 18. which holding forth the subordination of an offended Brother, to a particular Church, it doth also, by a parity of reason hold forth the subordination of a Congregation to superior Assemblies.

The third concerns ordination and reads, in part,

It is very requisite that no single Congregation that can conveniently Associate, do assume to it self all and sole power in Ordination.

1. Because there is no example in Scripture, that any single Congregation which might conveniently associate, did assume to it self all and sole power in ordination; neither is there any rule which may warrant such a practice.

2. Because there is in Scripture an example of an Ordination in a Presbytery over divers Congregations; as in the Church of Jerusalem, where were many Congregations; these many Congregations were under one Presbytery, and this Presbytery did ordain.

39. Ibid., 12.

40. Ibid., 31.

41. Ibid.

42. For example, Prynne wrote *The sword of Christian magistracy supported: or A full vindication of Christian kings and magistrates authority under the Gospell, to punish idolatry, apostacy, heresie, blasphemy, and obstinate schism, with pecuniary, corporall, and in some cases with banishment, and capitall punishments* (1647). Its unflinching title gives clear indication of his argument.

43. Prynne, *Twelve Considerable Serious Questions*, 2, 6–7.

44. Thomas Goodwin, *Apologeticall Narration*, 23.

45. Ibid., 23–24.

46. *Letter of the Ministers of London*, 1.

47. Ibid., 2–3.

48. Ibid., 3–4.

49. Ibid., 5.

50. Ibid., 6.

51. Gillespie, *Sermon*, 16.

52. Gillespie, *Wholesome Severity*, [A3ʳ].

53. E.g., ibid., 1.

54. Ibid., [A3ᵛ].

55. Ibid., [A2ᵛ, A3ʳ].

56. Ibid., 2–4, 6–7, 26–27.

57. Ibid., 25.

58. Ibid., 26–27.

59. Rutherford, *A Free Disputation*, 50.

60. Ibid., 51.

61. Jordan, *Religious Toleration*, 3:50–52.

62. As Westminster chronicler Robert S. Paul observes, it is dangerous to use the terms "Independent" and "Presbyterian" interchangeably to refer to the parties by those names in the Assembly and the parties by those names in Parliament (*vide*, Appendix V, *Assembly of the Lord*). This has been a source of intense debate among historians, and there is no need to cover it in depth here. For our purposes it is sufficient to recognize that divines and their political counterparts under the same title were not necessarily of one mind on any number of subjects.

63. Ibid., 65; Baxter, *Reliquiae Baxterianae*, 1: 47.

64. Baxter, *Reliquiae Baxterianae*, 1: 48.

65. Ibid., 47.

66. Jordan, *Religious Toleration*, 3: 67.

67. Other examples

68. Cromwell, "The conclusion of Lieuten. Generall Cromwells letter to the House of Common[s]," in *Strong Motives*, 7–8.

69. Ibid., 8.

70. Ibid., 6.

71. Ibid.

72. Ibid., 32.

73. Ibid., 38.

74. Jordan, *Religious Toleration*, 3: 79.

75. Ibid., 83.

76. Ibid., 80.

77. *Humble Advice*, 33–34; cf., *Articles*, 33.

78. Van Til, *Liberty of Conscience*, 86.

79. Murphy, *Conscience and Community*, 90ff.

80. Quoted in Rushworth, *Historical Collections*, 7: 840, in Jordan, *Religious Toleration*, 3: 103.

81. *An ordinance . . . for the punishing of blasphemies and heresies*, 1.

Those convicted under this section might be guilty of holding the opinions, *inter alia*, "that there is no God, or that God is not present in all places, doth not know and foreknow all things, or that he is not Almighty, that he is not perfectly Holy, or that he is not Eternal, or that the Father is not God, the Son is not God, or that the Holy Ghost is not God. . . . That Christ did not Die, did not rise from the Dead, nor is ascended into Heaven bodily, or that shall deny his death is meritorious in the behalf of Believers . . . or that the holy Scripture . . . is not the Word of God, or that the Bodies of men shall not rise again after they are dead, or that there is no day of Judgment after death" (*An ordinance . . . for the punishing of blasphemies and heresies*, 1–3).

82. Ibid., 4–5.

83. Jordan, *Religious Toleration*, 3: 114–15.

84. Murphy, *Conscience and Community*, 91.

85. Ibid., 94.

For example, Leveller leader John Lilburne wrote, "God has revealed the way of eternal salvation only to the individual faith of each man, and demands of us that any man who wishes to be saved should work out his beliefs for himself" (quoted in Hill, *The Revolutionary Bible*, 200).

86. Thomas Edwards, *Gangraena*, 3: 20, quoted in Hill, *The Revolutionary Bible*, 178; these ideas were articulated in the "Putney Debates" of 1647 but were opposed even by some leading members of the Army (see Hill, *The Revolutionary Bible*, 190).

A distinction is often made between Levellers like Lilburne and more radical, "true" Levellers (a.k.a., "Diggers") who had socialist tendencies. Lilburne despised the name and said that it was unfairly used by enemies to refer to those "who are against any kind of tyranny, whether in King, Parliament, Army, Councel of State, &c" (*Second part of Englands New-Chaines*, 7).

87. Hill, *The Revolutionary Bible*, 178.

88. Ibid.

89. Lilburne, *A plea*, 3.

90. Lilburne, *Agreement*, 5.

Chapter 14

1. Firth, *Oliver Cromwell*, 230.

2. Ibid., 231.

3. Lilburne, *Englands new chains*, [Aiii^v^–Aiv^r^].

4. Firth, *Oliver Cromwell*, 253.

5. D'Aubigne, *The Protector*, 107–108.

6. Quoted in Firth, *Oliver Cromwell*, 255.

7. Quoted in ibid., 279.

8. Firth, *Oliver Cromwell*, 274.

9. Roulston, *The Ranters Bible*, 2–6.

10. Firth, *Last Years of the Protectorate*, 83–84.

11. Zagorin, *Political Thought in the English Revolution*, 96.

12. Ibid., 98, 101.

13. Firth, *Last Years of the Protectorate*, 207.

14. *An act against several atheistical . . . opinions*, 979.

According to the terms of the *Act against several atheistical . . . opinions*, Anyone who affirmed or maintained any of the clearly heretical opinions listed was to be convicted on the testimony of two witnesses. If convicted, he or she would be sent to prison for six months or longer without bail. A second conviction for the same offense merited banishment.

15. *Act for Relief of Religious and Peaceable People*, 1024.

16. Ibid., 1024–25.

17. Firth, *Oliver Cromwell*, 300.

18. See *Proposals for the . . . propagation of the gospel*, 2ff.

19. Ibid., 5ff.

20. See, e.g., ibid., Principles V and XII, which begin, "That Jesus Christ is the only Mediator between God and man, without the knowledge of whom there is no salvation" (10), and "That all men by Nature are dead in trespasses and sins, and no man can be saved unless he be born again, repent and believe" (16).

21. Firth, *Oliver Cromwell*, 300–301.

22. Ibid., 262–63, 289.

23. Ibid., 308.

24. Ibid., 309.

25. Ibid., 309–10.

26. See *The humble Petition of the Officers of the Army*, [n.p.].

27. Cromwell, et al., *Declaration of the Lord Generall*, 2.

28. Firth, *Oliver Cromwell*, 316.

29. Quoted in ibid., 317; D'Aubigne, *The Protector*, 153.

30. Ibid., 317.

31. D'Aubigne, *The Protector*, 154.

32. Firth, *Oliver Cromwell*, 317.

33. Quoted in ibid., 318.

34. Ibid.

35. Paul, *The Lord Protector*, 276–77.

36. Ibid., 278.

37. As mentioned previously, the dictionary definition of a *sect* in 1604 was "a diversitie in opinion from others," and a *sectarie* was defined as "one whom many other doe followe in opinion" (Cawdrey, *A Table Alphabeticall*). By the late 1650s, the terms had taken on a more negative connotation due to the excesses of groups like the Ranters. One dictionary from 1656 defined *sectary* as "one that follows private opinions in Religion, a Ring-leader of a Sect, a seditious, factious person," and one from 1658 defined it as "one of a Sect, a follower of new opinions in matters of religion" (Blount, *Glossographia*; Phillips, *New world of English words*). Again, for our purposes, the term *sectaries* simply

means those dissenters who cannot be classed as Catholics, Anglicans, or Presbyterians. Some Independents to the left of the spectrum might be considered sectaries, too, but typically only if they advocated disestablishment of the national church.

38. Ibid., 279.

39. Roosevelt, *Oliver Cromwell*, 192.

40. Paul, *The Lord Protector*, 290; Firth, *Oliver Cromwell*, 324.

41. Firth, *Oliver Cromwell*, 325.

42. Paul, *The Lord Protector*, 290–91.

43. Jordan, *Religious Toleration*, 3: 150.

44. Firth, *Oliver Cromwell*, 332; Paul, *The Lord Protector*, 291–94.

45. Cromwell, "His Highnesse the Lord Protectors Speech to the Parliament . . . on Tuesday the 12. of September," in *His Highnesse the Lord Protector's Two Speeches*, 16–17.

46. *A Declaration concerning the Government of the Three Nations*, 4–5.

47. Ibid., 5.

48. Ibid.

49. "The Instrument of Government (1653)," in Stephenson and Marcham, *Sources*, 528.

50 Cromwell, "An Ordinance appointing Commissioners for Approbation of Publick Preachers," *Catalogue and collection*, 52–55.

51. "The Instrument of Government (1653)," in Stephenson and Marcham, *Sources*, 525.

52. Cromwell, *His Highness Speech to the Parliament . . . at their Dissolution*, 12.

53. Cromwell, "His Highnesse the Lord Protectors Speech to the Parliament . . . on Tuesday the 12. of September," in *His Highnesse the Lord Protector's Two Speeches*, 26–27 [emphasis added].

54. Ibid., 29–30.

55. Firth, *Oliver Cromwell*, 404; D'Aubigne, *The Protector*, 162.

56. Paul, *The Lord Protector*, 308.

57. Ibid.

58. Cromwell, *His Highness Speech to the Parliament . . . at their Dissolution*, 9.

59. Ibid., 10.

60. Ibid.

61. Ibid., 20.

62. Jordan, *Religious Toleration*, 3: 193–94, 203, 218.

63. Quoted in Firth, *Last Years of the Protectorate*, 88–89.

64. Ibid., 84.

65. Ibid., 85.

66. *A true narrative . . . of James Nayler*, 17–18, 20.

67. Ibid., 34–35.

68. *Humble Petition and Advice*, 6–7.

69. Ibid., 12–14.

70. Jordan, *Religious Toleration*, 3: 250.

71. Oliver Williams, *An Exact Accompt*, Thursday, 1 March 1660, 720; cf., Jordan, *Religious Toleration*, 3: 266.

72. Ibid., Monday, 5 March 1660, 747.

73. Ibid., 747–49.

74. Ibid., Tuesday, 13 March 1660, 765.

75. D'Aubigne, *The Protector*, 165.

76. Cromwell, "His Highnesse the Lord Protectors Speech to the Parliament . . . on Monday, the 4th of September," in *His Highnesse the Lord Protector's Two Speeches*, 10.

77. Paul, *The Lord Protector*, 391–92.

78. Cromwell, *His Highness Speech to the Parliament . . . at their Dissolution*, 10.

79. Paul, *The Lord Protector*, 392.

Chapter 15

1. How's sermon was later published under the title *Sufficiency of the Spirits Teaching without Humane Learning* (1655). Some of How's friends published *The Vindication of the Cobler*, being a brief publication of his doctrine in 1640 to immediately dispel the untruths that were circulating about what he taught.

2. How, *Sufficiency of the Spirits Teaching*, 37.

3. Taking into account all works recorded in Redgrave and Pollard's (covering 1475–1640) and Wing's (covering 1641–1700) *Short Title Catalogues* and the *Thomason Tracts*, as contained in the Early English Books Online database, 9337 records have publication dates between the years 1620 to 1639, while 34, 642 records have dates from 1640 to 1660.

4. *Vindication of the Cobler*, [n.p.].

5. "Ordinance of the Star Chamber for the Censorship of the Press," Document 173 in George Burton Adams and Henry More Stephens, eds., *Select Documents of English Constitutional History* (New York: Macmillan Co., 1916), OriginalSources.com.

6. Ibid.

7. "Act for the Abolition of the Court of Star Chamber," Document 199, and "Act for the Abolition of the Court of High Commission," Document 200 in George Burton Adams and Henry More Stephens, eds., *Select Documents of English Constitutional History* (New York: Macmillan Co., 1916), OriginalSources.com.

8. "Orders of the Commons with Regard to Printing [13 February 1641]," in Stephenson and Marcham, *Documents*, 485.

9. Siebert, *Freedom of the Press*, 173–74.

10. Stationers' Company, *The humble remonstrance*, [n.p.].

11. *An order . . . for the regulating of printing* (1643), [title page].

12. Siebert, *Freedom of the Press*, 176.

13. Tyndale, *Obedience*, 6.

14. Hill, *World Turned Upside Down*, 34, 301.

15. Ibid., 301.

16. See Williams, *Queries of the Highest Consideration, proposed to the five Holland Ministers and the Scotch Commissioners (so called) upon occasion of their late Printed Apologies for themselves and their Churches* (1643/44).

17. Williams, *Bloudy Tenet*, 104.

18. Ibid., 171–72.

19. Ibid., 64.

20. Williams, *Queries*, "The Epistle," [Aiii^r].

21. Williams, *Bloudy Tenet*, 58.

22. Ibid., 79–80.

23. Jordan, *Religious Toleration*, 4: 332.

24. Vernon, *Swords abuse asserted*, 6.

25. Ibid., 3–4.

26. Ibid., 6.

27. For example, in John Goodwin's words, "Service cannot be acceptable to God which is not performed with a willing mind, and a curse lies on him that does the work of the Lord negligently, which must inevitably happen if this course were taken, to tyrannize over men's Consciences" (*Independencie God's Veritie*, 5). Jeremy Taylor wrote in *Theologia eklektike. A discourse of the liberty of prophesying. Shewing the unreasonableness of prescribing to other mens faith, and the iniquity of persecuting differing opinions*, "And although we *must contend earnestly for the faith*, yet *above all things we must put on charity which is the bond of perfectness:* And therefore this contention must be with arms fit for the *Christian warfare, the sword of the Spirit, and the shield of Faith, and preparation of the Gospel of peace instead of shoes, and a helmet of salvation*, but not with other arms, for a Church-man must not be . . . *a striker, for the weapons of our warfare are not carnal but spiritual*, and the persons who use them ought to be *gentle, and easy to be entreated*, and we *must all give an account of our faith to them that ask us with meekness and humility, for so is the will of God, that with well doing ye may put to silence the ignorance of foolish men*" (8).

28. Williams, *Queries*, 3.

29. Milton, *Treatise of Civil Power*, 4–5.

30. Ibid., 35–36.

31. Ibid., 2.

32. Ibid., 5, 7–8, 32–33.

Some of the many verses Milton quoted are: "*Act.* 4.19. *Whether it be right in the sight of God, to hearken to you more than to God, judge ye*" (5), "And therefore those Bereans are commended, *Act.* 17.11, who after the preaching even of S. Paul, *searched the scriptures daily, whether those things were so*" (6), "Whereas we find, James 4.12, *there is one lawgiver, who is able to save and to destroy: who art thou that judgest another?* That Christ is the only lawgiver of his church and that it is here meant in religious matters, no well grounded Christian will deny" (10), "2 *Cor.* 1.24. *not that we have dominion over your faith, but are helpers of your joy*" (13), "1 *Pet.* 5.2, 3. *feed the flock of God not by constraint &c. neither as being lords over God's heritage*" (13), "*Joh.* 18.36. *if my kingdom were of this world, then would my servants fight, that I should not be delivered to the Jews*" (41), "2 *Cor.* 10.3, 4, 5, 6. *for though we walk in the flesh, we do not war after the flesh: for the weapons of our warfare are not carnal; but mighty through God to the pulling down of strong hold; casting down imaginations and every high thing that exalts itself against the knowledge of God; and bringing into captivity every thought to the obedience of Christ: and having in a readiness to avenge all disobedience*" (42–43), "John 4.21, 23. *neither in this mountain nor yet at Jerusalem. In spirit and in truth, for the father seeketh such to worship him*" (56), "*Rom.* 14.5. *Let every man be fully persuaded in his own mind*" (66), and "If after excommunion he be found intractable, incurable, and will not hear the church, he becomes as one never yet within her pale, *a heathen or a publican, Mat.* 18.17; not further to be judged, no not by the magistrate, unless for civil causes;

but left to the final sentence of that judge, whose coming shall be in flames of fire; that *Maran atha,* 1 *Cor.* 16,22" (76).

33. Blackwood, *Storming of Antichrist,* 19.

34. Ibid., 27.

35. Barnes, *What the Churche Is,* in Foxe, *Whole Works,* 244.

36. McDowell, *English Radical Imagination,* 34.

37. *An Ordinance . . . for the Ordination of Ministers,* 5–7.

The remainder of the eight "rules for examination" are as follows:

1. That the party Examined be dealt with in a Brotherly way, with mildness of spirit, and with special respect to the gravity, modesty, and quality of every one. . . .

4. If he hath not before Preached in public, with approbation of such as are able to judge, he shall, at a competent time assigned him, and before the Ministers appointed to Ordain, expound such a place of Scripture as shall be given him. . . .

6. He shall Preach before the People, and Ministers appointed to Ordain, or some of them.

7. The proportion of his gifts, in relation to the place, unto which he is called, shall be considered.

8. Besides the Trial of his gifts in preaching he shall undergo an Examination in the Premises, two several days, or more, if the Ministers appointed to Ordain, shall judge it necessary (5–8).

Interestingly, the only qualification concerning moral character mentioned in the ordinance is a vague reference to "holiness of life" (4).

38. Ibid., 10.

39. How, *Sufficiency of the Spirits Teaching,* 17.

40. Featley, "To the Reader" in *Dippers dipt,* [n.p.].

41. Hall, *Vindiciae Literarum,* 9–10.

42. McDowell, *English Radical Imagination,* 32.

43. Ibid., 32–38.

44. Jordan, *Religious Toleration,* 3: 506–507.

45. Dell, *Right Reformation,* 15–16.

46. Edwards, "Epistle to the Reader" in *Gangraena,* [n.p.].

47. Ibid., 97.

48. Walwyn, *A prediction of Mr Edwards,* 4.

49. Ibid.

50. See, e.g., Walwyn's 1643 work, *The power of love.*

51. *Compassionate Samaritane,* 33; William Walwyn is often credited as being the author.

52. Ibid.

53. Ibid., 42–43.

54. Barnes, *It is lawfull for all men to reade holy Scripture,* in Foxe, *Whole Works,* 284.

55. Williams, *Bloudy Tenet,* "To every courteous reader," [Bii^v].

56. Richardson, *The necessity of Toleration,* 8.

57. Milton, *Areopagitica,* 26.

58. Hill, *World Turned Upside Down,* 76.

59. Barnes, *What the Churche Is,* in Foxe, *Whole Works,* 245.

60. See Hill, "Samuel Fisher and the Bible," Chapter 11 in *World Turned Upside Down*.

Chapter 16

1. Bryant, *King Charles II*, 62–63; Airy, *Charles II*, 134.

2. "The Declaration of Breda (1660)," in Stephenson and Marcham, *Sources*, 533.

3. Zagorin, *Idea of Religious Toleration*, 241; Coffee, *Persecution and Toleration*, 167; Schochet, "From Persecution to 'Toleration,'" 131–32.

4. Coffee, *Persecution and Toleration*, 167.

5. Collins, "Restoration Bishops," 572–73.

6. Ibid., 572.

7. "His Majesties Gracious Speech to Both Houses of Parliament, On the 29th day of August 1660," in Charles II, *Collection*, 81.

8. Ibid., 83.

9. Andrew Murphy offers a helpful explanation of the differences within this context between the terms *toleration, indulgence,* and *comprehension,* all of which will appear frequently in this chapter. *Toleration* refers to the freedom from legal penalties granted to any nonconformist outside the established church; *indulgence* refers to "how such liberty would likely come about: through a royal grant (rather than Parliamentary legislation)"; and *comprehension* refers to the "movement to enlarge the parameters of acceptable Anglican belief and practice to encompass [other] orthodox Protestants" (*Conscience and Community*, 128, n8). *Indulgence*, however, can also mean the suspension of the penal laws, even if by Parliament; in the words of one author in 1689, "Comprehension without Indulgence destroys the Separatist, that is both the Papists and Sectaries. Indulgence without Comprehension depopulates the Church. Comprehension with Indulgence Unites the Protestants, secures the Church of England, and gives Ease and Safety to all People" (*King William's Toleration*, 16).

10. Seaward, *The Restoration*, 46, 48.

11. "His Majesties Declaration to all His Loving Subjects . . . Concerning Ecclesiastical Affairs," in Charles II, *Collection*, 86–109.

12. Ogg, *Reign of Charles II*, 167.

13. Airy, *Charles II*, 174–77.

14. Seaward, *The Restoration*, 64.

15. Airy, *Charles II*, 175; Schochet, "From Persecution to 'Toleration,'" 138.

16. Ogg, *Reign of Charles II*, 165–66; cf., Collins, "Restoration Bishops," 556.

17. Coffee, *Persecution and Toleration*, 166–67.

18. Ibid., 167–68.

19. Underhill, "Introductory Notice" to "The Humble Petition and Representation of the Sufferings of several Peaceable, and Innocent Subjects, called by the Name of Anabaptists," in *Tracts*, 291–92.

20. Bunyan, *Grace Abounding*, 159; Evans, *Early English Baptists*, 2: 267.

21. Coffee, *Persecution and Toleration*, 169; cf., "Act Against Sectaries (1593)," in Stephenson and Marcham, *Sources*, 354.

22. [Venner], *Last speech and prayer*, 3; quoted in Underhill, "Introductory Notice" to "A Plea for Toleration," in *Tracts*, 313.

23. Coffee, *Persecution and Toleration*, 167; [Venner], *Last speech and prayer*, 4.

24. [Kiffen], *Humble Apology*, 5.

25. Ibid., 7–8, 13.

26. Ibid., 20.

27. Sturgion, *A Plea for Tolleration*, 5.

28. Ibid., 5–7.

29. Ibid., 17–18.

30. "His Majesties Declaration to all His Loving Subjects . . . Concerning Ecclesiastical Affairs," in Charles II, *Collection*, 86.

31. Dudley, "Nonconformity Under the 'Clarendon Code,'" 66.

32. Collins, "Restoration Bishops," 555; Schochet, "From Persecution to 'Toleration,'" 139.

33. See Collins, "Restoration Bishops," 574–78.

34. Clarendon, *Second Thoughts*, 2.

35. Ibid., 3.

36. Ibid., 9.

37. Ibid., 7.

38. Ibid., 9–10.

39. "Corporation Act (1661)," in Stephenson and Marcham, *Sources*, 543.

40. Ibid.

41. Ibid.; Coffee, *Persecution and Toleration*, 168.

42. "The Uniformity Act, A.D. 1662," in Gee, *Documents*, 603, 612.

43. Ibid., 610–11.

44. Ibid., 608, 610–11.

45. Coffee, *Persecution and Toleration*, 168; cf., 192, n8.

46. Dudley, "Nonconformity Under the Clarendon Code," 72.

47. Quoted in Samuel Parker, *Bishop Parker's History of His Own Time* (London: 1727), 32–33, in Schochet, "From Persecution to 'Toleration,'" 141.

48. Schochet, "From Persecution to 'Toleration,'" 141; Coffee, *Persecution and Toleration*, 168.

49. "Licensing Act (1662)," in Stephenson and Marcham, *Sources*, 548.

50. See "The Second Conventicle Act, A.D. 1670," in Gee, *Documents*, 624; Coffee, *Persecution and Toleration*, 169.

51. Ibid., 624, 628.

52. Ibid., 628.

53. Seaward, *The Restoration*, 49.

54. "The Five Mile Act, 1665," in Gee, *Documents*, 621.

55. Coltman, *Private Men*, 120; cf., Seaward, *The Restoration*, 49.

56. Dudley, "Nonconformity Under the Clarendon Code," 67; Coffee, *Persecution and Toleration*, 170.

57. Coffee, *Persecution and Toleration*, 170.

58. Ibid.

59. *For the King . . . Being a brief, plain, and true Relation of . . . [the] Quakers*, n.p.

60. Coffee, *Persecution and Toleration*, 169.

61. *For the King . . . Being a brief, plain, and true Relation of . . . [the] Quakers*, n.p.

62. Ibid.

These and other detailed reports were bequeathed to us through the record-keeping practices of the Quakers, who meticulously transcribed instances of suffering and often sent them to their national "headquarters" at Devonshire House for compilation. They even kept a running list of their persecutors, which at one time numbered 3,898 (see Dudley, "Nonconformity Under the Clarendon Code," 66–67). It is highly unlikely that their accounts are exaggerated or untruthful, given the tremendous risk anyone took to publish such things without a license.

63. [Burrough], *A Brief Relation of the . . . Quakers in and about the City of London*, 21.

64. See, e.g., *A Short relation of some part of the sad sufferings and cruel havock and spoil, inflicted on the persons and estates of the people of God . . . Contrary to the Laws of God, of Nature, and of the Land.*

65. Evans, *Early English Baptists*, 2: 279–80.

66. *For the King . . .Being a brief, plain, and true Relation of . . . [the] Quakers*, n.p.; [Burrough], *A Brief Relation . . . Quakers in and about the City of London*, 1–5; *A True and Faithful Relation from the . . . Quakers in Colchester*, 19.

67. *A True and Faithful Relation from the . . . Quakers in Colchester*, 6–7.

Some of these marauding bands may not have been express agents of any church or government official, as Quakers were careful to note, but they were nevertheless allowed to do their work (cf., *A True and Faithful Relation from the . . . Quakers in Colchester*, 6). Others appear to have acted out of anything besides righteous indignation:

"Between 30. & 40. Horsemen, who said they were the Kings soldiers, quartering in *Southwark*, went to a Friend's House near *London*, & broke open the doors, notwithstanding there was one there that would have open'd any door to them, & under pretence of searching for Arms, robbed a poor serving-man who was left to look to the house, and took away two pair of Stockins from him, and a pair of Shoes, and a Bible and Knife, and drank four or five Bottles of Wine up, and swore God damn him, and called him son of a Whore, and so went away" (*A Brief Relation . . . Quakers in and about the City of London*, 21).

68. E.g., [Crook, John.] *The Cry of the innocent for justice being a relation of the tryal of John Crook, and others, at the general sessions, held in the Old Bayley, London.*

69. [Blackborow], *The oppressed prisoner's complaint*, n.p.

70. Keach's position, as recorded in his trial, can be summed up as: "*Ques.* Who are the right subjects of baptism? *Ans. Believers*, or godly men and women only who can make confession of their faith and repentance."

71. Evans, *Early English Baptists*, 2: 307–10.

72. Quoted in Miller, *Bourbon and Stuart*, 187.

73. Ibid.

74. Charles II, *A proclamation of grace*, n.p.

75. *The fourth humble address of . . . baptized believers*, n.p.

76. Schochet, "From Persecution to 'Toleration,'" 141–42.

77. "Charles II's Declaration of Indulgence," in Adams and Stephens, *Select Documents*, 434.

78. Coffee, *Persecution and Toleration*, 172; some estimate the number of licenses to be much higher, e.g., Mullett, "Toleration and Persecution," 26.

79. Schochet, "From Persecution to 'Toleration,'" 145; "On the Declaration of Indulgence (1673)," in Stephenson and Marcham, *Sources*, 567.

80. "On the Declaration of Indulgence (1673)," in Stephenson and Marcham, *Sources*, 569.

81. Seaward, *The Restoration*, 62–63.

82. Ibid., 67.

83. Ibid., 63.

84. *A proclamation . . . at Whitehall, the fifth day of February 1674/5*, n.p.

85. Mark Goldie, "Danby, the Bishops, and the Whigs," 78–79, chapter 4 in Harris, *Politics of Religion*.

86. Coffee, *Persecution and Toleration*, 186.

87. Ibid., 186–87.

88. *Horrid Popish Plot*, n.p.

89. "To the Reader," in *Grand designs of the papists*, n.p.

90. Seaward, *The Restoration*, 130–31.

91. "The Declaration of Indulgence, 1687," in Gee, *Documents*, 641.

92. Ibid., 642.

93. Murphy, *Conscience and Community*, 135–36.

94. Ibid., 136.

95. Jonathan Scott, "England's Troubles: Exhuming the Popish Plot," 118, chapter 5 in Harris, *Politics of Religion*; Clark, *The Later Stuarts*, 102.

96. Halifax, *Letter to a dissenter*, 1–2.

97. Ibid., 2.

98. Ibid., 4.

99. Halifax, *Letter from a Clergy-man*, 5–6.

100. Ibid., 8.

101. *Letter from a clergy-man in the country*, 40.

102. Ibid., 40, 26.

103. See Schochet, "From Persecution to 'Toleration,'" 125; cf., John Christian Laursen, "Spinoza on Toleration: Arming the State and Reining in the Magistrate," chapter 10 in *Difference and Dissent*.

104. Locke, *Letter concerning Toleration*, 9.

105. Ibid., 9, 11.

106. Ibid., 12, 60.

Elsewhere, Locke emphasized that the beliefs essential to salvation are not so extensive and complicated that only the most educated can understand them and thereby decide who belongs to the true church and who does not: "The Writers and Wranglers in Religion fill it with niceties, and dress it up with notions; which they make necessary and fundamental parts of it; As if there were no way into the Church, but through the Academy or Lyceum. The bulk of Mankind have not leisure for Learning and Logick and superfine distinctions of the Schools. Where the hand is used to the Plough, and the Spade, the head is seldom elevated to sublime Notions, or exercised in mysterious reasonings. . . . Had God intended that none but the Learned Scribe, the disputer or wise of this World, should be Christians, or be Saved, thus Religion should have been prepared for them; filled with speculations and niceties, obscure terms, and abstract notions. But men of that expectation, Men furnished with such acquisitions, the Apostle tells us, 1 *Cor. I.* are rather shut out from the simplicity of the Gospel; to make way for those poor, ignorant, illiterate, Who heard and believed promises of a Deliverer; and believed Jesus to be him" (*Reasonableness of Christianity*, 303–4).

107. "The Case of the Seven Bishops (1688)," in Stephenson and Marcham, *Sources*, 584.

108. Ibid., 586.

One minority justice argued, "And shall or ought anybody to come and impeach that as illegal which the government has done? Truly, in my opinion, I do not think he should or ought; for by this rule may every act of the government be shaken when there is not a parliament" ("The Case of the Seven Bishops," in Stephenson, *Sources*, 586).

109. See, e.g., William III, *The declaration . . . of the reasons inducing him, to appear in armes in the kingdome of England, for preserving of the Protestant religion, and for restoring the lawes and liberties of England, Scotland and Ireland.*

110. Schochet, "From Persecution to 'Toleration,'" 152; Mullett, "Toleration and Persecution," 39–40.

111. Quoted in Mullett, "Toleration and Persecution," 39.

112. "The Toleration Act, A.D. 1689," in Gee, *Documents*, 654–63.

113. William III, *The declaration*, 1, 4.

Chapter 17

1. [Greene], *Virginia's Cure*, 19.

2. Ibid., 19–20,

3. "First Charter of Virginia," in William MacDonald, ed., *Documentary Source Book of American History, 1606–1913* (New York: The Macmillan Company, 1916), 2, OriginalSources.com.

4. Vaughan, "Expulsion," 63.

5. [Greene], *Virginia's Cure*, 5.

6. Ibid., 14.

7. "Articles, Laws, and Orders, Divine, Politic, and Martial for the Colony in Virginia, 1610–1611," in Lutz, *Colonial Origins*, 316.

8. Ibid., 324.

9. Ibid., 319.

10. Hening, ed., *Statutes at Large*, 1: 155.

11. Quoted in Sweet, *Story of Religion*, 29.

12. "Articles, Laws, and Orders, Divine, Politic, and Martial for the Colony in Virginia, 1610–1611," in Lutz, *Colonial Origins*, 319.

13. Vaughan, "Expulsion," 60.

14. Ibid., 61.

15. Gray, *Good Speed*, [Cii^v].

16. Ibid., [Ciii^{r-v}].

17. Vaughan, "Expulsion," 58.

18. Ibid., 62.

19. Quoted in ibid., 63.

20. Ibid., 64.

21. Ibid., 65, quoting Smith.

22. Ibid., 67.

23. Quoted in ibid., 69–70.

24. [Edward Waterhouse], *A Declaration of the State of the Colony and Affaires in Virginia* (London: 1622), quoted in ibid., 70.

25. Ibid.

26. Ibid., 75.

27. Ibid., 75–76.

28. Sweet, *Story of Religion*, 4.

29. Hening, ed., *Statutes at Large*, 1:126.

30. Ibid., 127.

31. Ibid.

32. Ibid.

33. Ibid., 122–23.

34. Ibid., 124.

35. Ibid., 156.

36. Ibid., 1: 240.

37. Jones, *Present State*, 96.

38. Hening, ed., *Statutes at Large*, 1: 242.

39. Eckenrode, *Separation*, 10.

40. Ibid., 8.

41. Sweet, *Story of Religion*, 36.

42. Foote, *Sketches*, 30.

43. Quoted in ibid, 30–31.

44. Hening, ed., *Statutes at Large*, 1: 277.

45. James, *Documentary History*, 18.

46. Hening, ed., *Statutes at Large*, quoted in Seiler, "Church of England," 487.

47. Little, *Imprisoned Preachers*, 4.

48. Hammond, *Leah and Rachel*, 21

49. Little, *Imprisoned Preachers*, 4.

50. Hammond, *Leah and Rachel*, 21.

51. Seiler, "Church of England," 488.

52. Foote, *Sketches*, 33.

53. McIlwaine, *Struggle of . . . Dissenters*, 20.

54. Lambert, *Founding Fathers*, 54.

55. Eckenrode, *Separation*, 12.

In his special report for the Virginia State Library, H. J. Eckenrode wrote: "Measures were indeed necessary to instill some vitality into the church of Virginia. The chief impediment to the growth of religion was the sparseness of the settlement. Virginia was a land of great plantations lying along the main tidal rivers in long narrow strips, with an uncultivated hinterland. The planters consequently tended to neglect religious service because of the distances to be traveled, and to lose, in some part, the religious instinct. Ministers were difficult to obtain, as the work of supervising the immense, thinly-populated parishes was great."

(*Separation of Church and State in Virginia*, 12).

56. Sweet, *Story of Religion*, 37.

57. Eckenrode, *Separation*, 14.

58. Sweet, *Story of Religion*, 37.

59. Ibid.

60. Jones, *State of Virginia*, 99.

61. Hening, ed., *Statutes at Large*, 1: 532.

62. Ibid., 2: 165–66.

63. Ibid., 2: 181.

64. Ibid., 2: 198.

65. Note that Virginia was referred to as a Church. The state was coextensive with the church.

66. [Greene], *Virginia's Cure*, 3.

67. Ibid.

68. Ibid., 5.

69. Ibid., 8–9.

70. Ibid., 17.

71. Ibid., 16.

72. Ibid.

73. Ibid., 18.

74. Eckenrode, *Separation*, 16.

In the 1728 statutes of William and Mary College, three aims were delineated for the school: (1) "that the Youth of Virginia should be well educated to Learning and good Morals," (2) "that the Churches of America, especially Virginia, should be supplied with good Ministers after the Doctrine and Government of the Church of England," and (3) "that the Indians of America should be instructed in the Christian Religion, and that some of the Indian Youth that are well-behaved and well-inclined, being first well prepared in the Divinity School, may be sent out to preach the Gospel to their Countrymen in their own Tongue, after they have duly been put in Orders of Deacons and Priests." The last section aimed to avoid "the Danger of Heresy, Schism, and Disloyalty" among the president and masters by making them take the oaths of allegiance and "give their Assent to the Articles of the Christian Faith, in the same Manner, and in the same Words, as the Ministers in England, by Act of Parliament are obliged to sign the Articles of the Church of England"—all "under the Penalty of being deprived of their Office and Salary." (See Statutes of 1728, "William & Mary," in Gaustad, *Documentary History*, 202–3.)

75. Ibid.

76. Ibid., 18.

Eckenrode described Blair's era in this way: "The people were accustomed to take their religion formally; there were few enthusiasts, few deeply zealous in the colony. Furthermore, the plantation system, by isolating colonists and depriving them of community interests, weakened their religious instincts. And, besides, the church had no healthy government. It was neither Episcopal, Presbyterian nor Congregational; it was peculiar and colonial. The union of church and state put the church under a political control, and that control took its character from existing political conditions. Vestrymen were usually politicians and frequently burgesses. The church was thoroughly subordinated to the state" (*Separation*, 14).

77. Seiler, "Church of England," 496.

78. Hening, ed., *Statutes at Large*, 3: 171.

79. James, *Documentary History*, 20.

80. Little, *Imprisoned Preachers*, 10.

81. Foote, *Sketches*, 25.

82. Sweet, *Story of Religion*, 38.

83. Ibid.

Chapter 18

1. Winthrop, *Journal*, 3; *Arabella* is sometimes used as an alternate spelling.

2. Winthrop, et al., *Humble Request*, 1.

3. "Resolutions of the Commons (1629)," in Stephenson and Marcham, *Sources*, 454; see chapter 12.

4. Winthrop, *Humble Request*, 3.

5. Ibid., 4.

6. Ibid., 6.

7. See Danforth, "To the Christian Reader," *New Englands Errand*, n.p.; Willard, *Brief Animadversions*, 4.

8. Danforth, "To the Christian Reader," *New Englands Errand*, n.p.; Johnson, *History*, 1.

9. Johnson, *History*, 1; Willard, *Brief Animadversions*, 4.

10. Winthrop, "A Model of Christian Charity," in Miller, ed., *The American Puritans*, 81–82.

11. Ibid., 83.

12. Danforth, "To the Christian Reader," *New Englands Errand*, n.p.

13. Cobbet, *Civil Magistrates Power*, 13.

14. Johnson, *History*, 8, 21.

15. Johnson, *History*, 3.

16. Cobbet, *Civil Magistrates Power*, 13–14.

17. Norton, *Heart of N-England Rent*, 49–50.

18. Ibid., 48–49.

19. Cobbet, *Civil Magistrates Power*, 20.

20. Ibid.

21. Ibid., 21.

22. Ibid., 21–22.

23. Ibid., 9.

24. Ward, *The Simple Cobler*, [Bi^v]

25. Ibid.

26. Willard, *Brief Animadversions*, 9; in quoting Augustine, however, Calvin used the Latin word for "penalty" rather than "suffering."

27. Ward, *The Simple Cobler*, [Bii^r].

28. Norton, *Heart of N-England Rent*, 52.

29. Ibid., 51, for a description of the distinction.

30. Ward, *The Simple Cobler*, [Aiv^v].

31. Ibid.

32. Norton, *Heart of N-England Rent*, 58.

33. Johnson, *History*, 7.

34. Cobbet, "To the Reader," *The Civil Magistrates Power*, n.p.

35. Ward, *The Simple Cobler*, [Aiii^r].

36. Ibid., [Aiv^r].

37. "The Massachusetts Body of Liberties, December 1641," in Lutz, *Colonial Origins*, 71, 87.

38. Ibid., article 95.1, 85; emphasis added.

39. Ibid., article 89, 82.

40. Ibid., article 94.1–3, 83.

41. See "The Laws and Liberties of Massachusetts: Ana-Baptists," 100–1.

42. Ward used the term "Colluvies" as the plural for the Latin noun *colluvium*, which refers to the dregs or rock debris that collects at the base of slopes or cliffs after being drawn downward by the force of gravity or being washed downhill by rainwater.

43. Ward, *The Simple Cobler*, [Aii^v].

44. Quoted in McLoughlin, *New England Dissent*, 1: 93.

45. Winthrop, *Journal*, 23.

46. Ibid., 25–26.

47. Ibid., 60; Garrett, *Roger Williams*, 15–16; cf., Williams, *Christenings make not Christians*.

48. Winthrop, *Journal*, 60.

49. Ibid., 76, 84.

50. Ibid., 84.

51. Ibid., 91–92.

52. Ibid., 92.

53. Quoted in Pfeffer, *Church, State, & Freedom*, 78.

54. Cotton, *The controversie*, 1; Williams, *Bloudy Tenet*, 7ff.

55. Watts, *The Dissenters*, 1:104–5.

56. Ibid.; Philip Schaff, *The New Schaff-Herzog Encyclopedia of Religious Knowledge*, vol. 1 (Grand Rapids, Mich.: Baker Book House, 1951), 460; Williams, *Bloudy Tenet*, 18–19.

57. Williams, *Bloudy Tenet*, 19.

58. Cotton, *Bloudy Tenent Washed*, 181.

59. "Plantation Agreement at Providence," August 27, 1640, and "[Organization of the Government of Rhode Island]," March 16–19, 1642, in Lutz, *Colonial Origins*, 169, 173.

60. "Charter of Rhode Island and Providence Plantations," in William MacDonald, ed., *Documentary Source Book of American History, 1606–1913* (New York: Macmillan, 1916), 68–69, OriginalSources.com.

61. Winthrop, *Proceedings*, 38.

62. Ibid., 21.

63. Quoted in ibid., 22.

64. Ibid., 23–24.

65. Ibid., 57–58.

66. Ibid., 26–27.

67. Ibid., 29–30.

68. Ibid., 31.

69. Ibid.

70. Ibid., 34.

71. Ibid., 35.

72. Ibid., 41–43.

73. Clarke, *Ill Newes*, 1–4.

74. Ibid., 5.

75. Ibid., 5–6.

76. Ibid., 10.

77. Ibid., 10–11, 14–15.

78. Ibid., 26–27.

79. Ibid., 20.

80. Ibid., 21.

81. Ibid.

82. Ibid., 22.

83. Ibid., 28.

84. Bishope, *New England Judged*, 6–7.

85. Ibid., 8–9.

86. When brought before "the Great Turk" and questioned "what she thought of their Prophet Mahomet," Fisher responded, "That she knew him not, but the Christ, the true Prophet, the Son of God, Who was the Light of the World, and enlighteneth every man that cometh into the World, Him she knew. . . . they might judge [of Mahomet] to be true or false, according as the Words and Prophesies he spake were either true or false, Saying, 'If the Word that the Prophet speaketh come to pass, then shall ye know that the Lord hath sent that Prophet, but if it come not to pass, then shall ye know that the Lord never sent him.'—To which they confessed and said, 'It was truth'" (Bishope, *New England Judged*, 19–20).

87. Ibid., 10.

88. Ibid., 35.

89. Ibid., 38; "Dyar" is an alternate spelling.

90. Stevenson wrote from Boston prison that on one day in early 1655, he was walking "after the Plough" at his home in Yorkshire when he was suddenly "filled with the Love and Presence of the Living God." After "it did increase and abound in [him] like a Living Stream," he was quiet for a time and then sensed that God was sending him as a missionary. This was why, he explained, he was willing even to die for his call. (See Bishope, *New England Judged*, 107–8.)

91. Ibid., 97.

92. Ibid., 90.

93. Ibid., 93.

94. Ibid., 109.

95. Ibid., 109–10.

96. Ibid., 195–96.

97. Today in Boston, a statute of Dyer stands in front of the State House with the inscription, "Mary Dyer: Quaker, Witness for Religious Freedom," and her words, "*My life not availeth me in comparison to the liberty of the truth.*"

98. Willard, *Brief Animadversions*, 6.

99. McLoughlin, *New England Dissent*, 1: 103.

100. Sweet, *Story of Religion*, 51.

101. Lechford, *Plain Dealing*, 23.

102. Miller, *New England Mind*, 95.

103. Ibid., 96.

104. See Murphy, *Conscience and Community*, 56–57, 64–66.

105. Quoted in McLoughlin, *New England Dissent*, 1: 93.

106. "Charter of Maryland," in William MacDonald, ed., *Documentary Source Book of American History, 1606–1913* (New York: Macmillan, 1916), OriginalSources.com.

107. Cecilius Calvert, "Instructions to Colonists (1633)," in Albert Bushnell Hart, ed., *American History Told by Contemporaries*, vol. 1 (New York: Macmillan, 1897), 247, OriginalSources.com; Sweet, *Story of Religion*, 78.

108. Sweet, *Story of Religion*, 79.

109. "[Maryland Toleration Act], April 21, 1649," in Lutz, *Colonial Origins*, 309–12.

110. Andrews, *Colonial Period*, 2: 310–11.

111. "[Maryland Toleration Act], April 21, 1649," in Lutz, *Colonial Origins*, 310–11.

112. See Andrews, *Colonial Period*, 2: 319.

113. Heaman, *Additional Brief Narrative*, 2.

114. Ibid., 9–10.

115. Andrews, *Colonial Period*, 2: 320.

116. Pfeffer, *Church, State, & Freedom*, 70.

117. Sweet, *Story of Religion*, 97–98.

"The Charter or Fundamental Laws, of West New Jersey, Agreed Upon," chapter XVI reads, "That no men, nor number of men upon earth, hath power or authority to rule over men's consciences in religious matters, therefore it is consented, agreed and ordained, that no person or persons whatsoever within the said Province, at any time or times hereafter, shall be any ways upon any pretence whatsoever, called in question, or in the least punished or hurt, either in person, estate, or privilege, for the sake of his opinion, judgment, faith or worship towards God in matters of religion. But that all and every such person, or persons may from time to time, and at all times, freely and fully have, and enjoy his and their judgments, and the exercises of their consciences in matters of religious worship throughout all the said Province" (in "Concessions and Agreements of West New Jersey, 1677," in Schwartz, *Bill of Rights*, 1: 127).

118. Quoted in Murphy, *Conscience and Community*, 185.

119. "Charter of Liberties and Frame of Government of the Province of Pennsylvania in America, May 5, 1682," in Lutz, *Colonial Origins*, 272–73.

120. Ibid., 273–74.

121. Ibid., 285.

122. "An Act for Freedom of Conscience, December 7, 1682," in Lutz, *Colonial Origins*, 288.

123. Ibid., 287–88.

124. Murphy, *Conscience and Community*, 183.

125. Sweet, *Story of Religion*, 99–101.

126. Jefferson, *Notes*, 157.

127. 463 U.S. 783 at 788.

128. *Works of John Adams*, quoted in Buckley, *Church and State*, 6.

Chapter 19

1. Webb, *Office and Authority*, 133.

2. Ibid., 61, 128–29, 268.

3. Ibid., 130–33.

Legally, Protestant dissenters had to present proof of their membership and presence in a duly allowed congregation and, if necessary, had to take a declaration of fidelity to the king, make a profession of belief in the Trinity and inspiration of the Holy Scriptures, and deny transubstantiation, among other things. Upon refusal to take the oaths, dissenters were to be treated as popish recusants.

4. Speaking of Virginia, one individual writing in 1705 recorded, "The people are generally of the Church of England, which is the religion established by law in the country, from which there are very few dissenters. Yet liberty of conscience is given to all other congregations pretending to Christianity, on condition they submit to all parish duties. . . . They have no more than five conventicles amongst them, namely, three small meetings of Quakers, and two of Presbyterians. 'Tis observed, that those counties where the Presbyterian meetings are, produce very mean tobacco, and for that reason can't get an orthodox minister to stay amongst them; but whenever they could the people very orderly went to church" (Beverly, *History and Present State of Virginia*, quoted in Foote, *Sketches of Virginia*, 50–51). The clergy of the established church were paid in tobacco. A 1689 law fixed their salaries at sixteen thousand pounds per year.

5. "Mr. Lang to the Bishop of London," 1 February 1725/6, in Perry, *Papers*, 346.

6. Bidwell, "Morris Reading-Houses," 25–27; cf., Gewehr, *Great Awakening*, 36–37.

7. "Mr. Lang to the Bishop of London," 7 February 1725/6, in Perry, *Papers*, 347.

8. "Mr. Forbes' Account of the State of the Church in Virginia," 21 July 1724, in Perry, *Papers*, 332.

9. Gewehr, *Great Awakening*, 34.

10. Ibid., 33–34.

11. Ibid., 38, quoting Devereux Jarratt; cf., "Letter from the Reverend Mr. Sam. Davies in Hanover County, Virginia, to Dr. Doddridge, dated Oct 2nd, 1750," in Perry, *Papers*, 368, in which he remarks, "Religion, alas! was just expiring and a strict form of godliness was very rare."

12. Blair, *Short and faithful narrative*, 8–10.

13. Lambert, *"Pedlar in Divinity,"* 37.

14. Whitefield, *Brief Account*, 1, 7, 12, 16.

15. Ibid., 20–21.

16. *The Boston Weekly News-Letter*, 12–19 April 1739.

17. *Virginia Gazette*, 27 July 1739.

18. Quoted in Lambert, *"Pedlar in Divinity,"* 47–48.

19. *Virginia Gazette*, 8 September 1739.

Whitefield even wrote a letter to the inhabitants of the Southern Colonies, published in the *New England Weekly Journal* on 29 April 1740, confronting the wealthy plantation owners of enjoying ease and luxury while their slaves "had neither convenient Food to eat or proper Raiment to put on." He accused slave owners of deliberately keeping their "Negroes ignorant of Christianity," much to their shame and disrepute. Whitefield predicted that God would send his judgment for their hard-heartedness, then ended with the rebuke, "And whatever Quantity of Rum there may be, yet I fear but very few Bibles are annually imported into your different Provinces. God has already begun to visit for this as well as for other wicked things."

20. Heimert, *The Great Awakening*, 71–72.

21. Tennent, "The Danger of an Unconverted Ministry," in Heimert, *The Great Awakening*, 89.

22. Quoted in Bidwell, "Morris Reading-Houses," 122.

23. *Virginia Gazette*, 18 October 1745; it is possible, however, that Whitefield actually said something quite to the contrary. Reverend Patrick Henry wrote to William Dawson, Commissary of the Bishop of London, reporting that when the parents brought the child to Whitefield, he told them "that by their senseless, singular and [?] they laid themselves open to prosecution, but not for righteousness sake" (Letter from Patrick Henry to William Dawson, 13 February 1745, in "Letters of Patrick Henry," *William and Mary Quarterly*, 267).

24. *Virginia Gazette*, 21 December 1739.

25. *Virginia Gazette*, 11 January 1740.

26. Quoted in Davies, *State of Religion*, 10.

27. Quoted in Foote, *Sketches of Virginia*, 122.

28. Quoted in Davies, *State of Religion*, 11.

29. Foote, *Sketches of Virginia*, 124.

30. Elsewhere in Virginia dissenters were apparently allowed to worship in accordance with the Toleration Act as well. Considering the case of some dissenters and their minister from Richmond County (in the Northern Neck region of the colony), the Council concluded that upon applying for licenses in their county and taking the prescribed oaths and declarations, the dissenters "have the free exercise of their religion at such place of public worship in the said county as they shall desire to be recorded by the county court for that purpose, so as they also observe the directions of the said act of Parliament at their meetings at such place of public worship set apart as aforesaid" (*Executive Journals, Council of Colonial Virginia*, 4 May 1725).

31. All three documents quoted in ibid., 103–4.

32. Ibid., 124.

33. See Payne, "New Light in Hanover," 668.

34. Davies, *State of Religion*, 12.

35. Ibid., 13–14.

36. Quoted in ibid., 15.

37. Quoted in Foote, *Sketches of Virginia*, 136–37 (the original apparently no longer exists).

Gooch also explained his understanding of the Toleration Act and its application in Virginia:

"However, not meaning to inflame your resentment, as we may without breach of charity pronounce, that 'tis not liberty of conscience, but freedom of speech, they so earnestly prosecute; and we are very sure that they have no manner of pretense to any shelter under the acts of toleration, because, admitting they have had regular ordination, they are by those acts obliged, nor can they be ignorant of it, not only to take the oaths, and with the test to subscribe, after a deliberate reading of them, some of the articles of our religion, before they presume to officiate. But that in this indulgent grant, though not expressed, a covenant is intended, whereby they engage to preserve the character of conscientious men, and not to use their liberty for a cloak of maliciousness,—to that I say, allowing their ordination, yet as they have not, by submitting to those essential points, qualified themselves to gather a congregation, or if they had, in speaking all manner of evil against us, have forfeited the privilege due to such compliance; insomuch, that they are entirely without excuse, and their religious professions are very justly suspected to be the result of Jesuitical policy, which also is an iniquity to be punished by the judges."

(Quoted in Foote, *Sketches of Virginia*, 136–37.)

38. Records of the General Court, 19 April 1745, quoted in Foote, *Sketches of Virginia*, 137–38. Records of the General Court from this period were housed at Richmond during the Civil War and were lost in the fires that ravaged the city, so fragments of official documents such as these can only be found in secondary sources.

39. *Pennsylvania Gazette*, 26 September 1745.

40. Quoted in Davies, *State of Religion*, 15.

41. Ibid., 18.

On 3 April 1747, the Council ordered a proclamation to be issued to restrain the itinerant preachers. The text from the governor was entered in the executive minutes on the 28th of the same month:

"Whereas It is represented to me that several Itinerant Preachers have lately crept into this Colony and that the Suffering these Corruptors of our Faith and true Religion to propagate their shocking Doctrines may be of mischievous consequences. I have therefore thought fit by and with the Advice of his Majesty's Council to issue this Proclamation strictly requiring all Magistrates and Officers to discourage and prohibit as far as they legally can all Itinerant Preachers whether New-Light Men Moravians, or Methodists, from Teaching Preaching or holding any Meeting in this Colony: And that all Persons be enjoined to be aiding and assisting to that Purpose."

(*Executive Journals, Council of Colonial Virginia*, 5: 227–28, 490.)

42. Pilcher, "Samuel Davies," 8–9; Foote, *Sketches of Virginia*, 129.

43. Gewehr, *Great Awakening*, 70.

44. Ibid., 72.

45. Virginia Colonial Council, *Humble Address* [in reply to his speech of 13 March 1747], 1.

46. Ibid.

47. Gewehr, *Great Awakening*, 72.

48. Ibid., 73.

49. Davies, *State of Religion*, 24.

50. Ibid., 28.

51. In 1692, William III had first instructed the governor of New York, "And you are to permit a liberty of conscience to all persons, except papists, so they be contented with a quiet and peaceable enjoyment of the same, not giving offence or scandal to the government" ("Instructions to the Governor of New York [1692]," in Stephenson and Marcham, *Sources*, 648).

52. Foote, *Sketches of Virginia*, 174.

53. "The Bishop of London to Rev'd Dr. Doddridge," 11 May 1751, in Perry, *Collections*, 371–2.

54. "Bishop of London to Doddridge," 25 December 1750, quoted in "Doddridge to Davies," 1751, in Pilcher, "Samuel Davies," 54.

55. Cobb, *Rise of Religious Liberty*, 105–6; cf., Pilcher, "Samuel Davies," 50–52.

56. "Davies to the Bishop of London," quoted in Foote, *Sketches of Virginia*, 189; Davies, *State of Religion*, 43–44.

57. Ibid., 183, 194.

58. Gewehr, *Great Awakening*, 86.

59. "Extract of a letter from the Reverend Mr. Sam. Davies . . . to Dr. Doddridge," 2 October 1750, in Perry, *Collections*, 371.

60. Davies to Rev. Henry, 21 April 1747, in Henry, "Letters," 269.

61. Samuel Davies purportedly once said that John Henry knew his Horace better than he knew the Bible (Henry, *Patrick Henry*, 4). Isaac Winston, certainly a relation of Sarah if not her father, was one of those individuals cited in the 1745 General Court record for hosting Roan in his house and allowing him to preach there. In 1747, the Jury concluded that even though a congregation did assemble there, it was "not in a riotous manner" and "not against the canons of the Church of England" (quoted in Foote, *Sketches of Virginia*, 141–42, 161).

62. Henry, *Patrick Henry*, 15.

63. David Bostwick, "Character of the Author," lxvii–lxviii, in Davies, *Sermons on important subjects*.

64. Wirt, *Sketches*, 21.

65. Pilcher, "Samuel Davies," 65.

66. Davies, *Religion and Patriotism*, 3.

67. Ibid., 4–5.

68. Davies, *Curse of Cowardice*, 1; ibid., 13.

69. "The Clergy of Virginia to the Bishop of London," 25 February 1756, in Perry, *Collections*, 445.

70. In a letter requesting his ecclesiastical superior to do something to stop Davies's itinerant preaching, Maury had written in 1755, "I trust I am far from the inhuman & uncharitable Spirit of Persecution. No Man either professes or thinks himself a warmer Advocate for Liberty of Conscience, that natural Right of Mankind. But when Men under Pretence of asserting & exercising this Right, sow the Seeds of Discord & Confusion: when they so industriously propagate heterodox opinions in a Manner, inconsistent with & repugnant to the formal Sanctions of Government & Law; none, surely, not their most

zealous adherents, nor even themselves, can justly complain, should they be laid under just & equitable restraints" (in Henry, et al., *Letters*, 278).

71. Henry, *Patrick Henry*, 39–41.

72. Gewehr, *Great Awakening*, 105.

73. Eckenrode, *Separation of Church and State*, 34.

74. *Journal of the House of Burgesses*, 26 March 1752; Isaac, *Transformation of Virginia*, 153.

Chapter 20

1. William Parks was also the grandfather of Sarah Shelton, Patrick Henry's wife. He purchased the Hanover Tavern, across the street from the Hanover Courthouse, and bequeathed it to his daughter and son-in-law, John and Elizabeth Shelton. The Sheltons employed Patrick at the tavern for some time while he was a young man.

2. William Berkeley, quoted in Sloan, *The Early American Press*, 98.

3. *Virginia Gazette*, 8 May 1752.

4. *Virginia Gazette*, 6 May 1737.

5. *Virginia Gazette*, 17 November 1738.

6. *Virginia Gazette*, 24 November 1738.

7. Purdie and Dixon's *Virginia Gazette*, 31 October 1771.

8. Isaac, *Transformation of Virginia*, 154.

9. Purdie and Dixon's *Virginia Gazette*, 20 February 1772.

10. Leland, *Virginia Chronicle . . . with judicious and critical remarks*, 4.

11. Morgan Edwards, one of the better educated Baptists from the north who undertook a massive effort to compile information on Baptists in all the colonies, wrote that Stearns "was but a little man, but a man of good natural parts and sound judgment. Of learning he had but a small share, yet was pretty well acquainted with books. . . . His character was indisputably good, both as a man, a Christian, and a preacher" (*Materials*, 148–49).

12. Semple, *History*, 12–13.

13. Ibid., 20.

14. Ibid.

15. Edwards, *Materials*, 59–60.

16. Little, *Imprisoned Preachers*, 47–49.

17. Benedict, *General History*, 2: 335–36.

18. Gewehr, *Great Awakening*, 117; cf., Isaac, *Transformation of Virginia*, 173.

19. Williams, "Colonial Baptists," 30–31; cf., *Confession of Faith . . . of Christians (baptized upon Profession of their Faith) in London and the Country*.

20. Gewehr, *Great Awakening*, 115.

21. Benedict, *General History*, 1:274.

22. Fristoe, *Concise History*, 22.

23. Semple, *History*, 71.

24. Leland, *Virginia Chronicle*, 4.

25. Fristoe, *Concise History*, 23.

26. I.e., Henry VIII for Anne Boleyn.

27. Leland, *Virginia Chronicle . . . with judicious and critical remarks*, 25.

28. Ibid.

29. Ibid., 25–26.

30. Thomas, *Virginian Baptist*, 42.

31. John Blair to John Lewis, 16 July 1768, in Little, *Imprisoned Preachers*, 100–1.

32. Ibid.; Isaac, *Transformation of Virginia*, 169–70.

33. Ibid.

34. Isaac, *Transformation of Virginia*, 171–72.

35. Fristoe, *Concise History*, 63.

36. Thomas, *Virginian Baptist*, 56.

Thomas also wrote, "The greater part of every denomination, are as poor, and as unlearned as we. And would our having some wealthy and well-learned persons on our side, prove our Religion to be true, I might soon put an end to the controversy. But riches, and honor and carnal wisdom, are no badges of the Christian Religion. Judas had the bag; Mahomet obtained the largest empire on earth; and the Pope has the greatest revenue of perhaps any monarch in Europe. Porphyry, and Julian, and Arius, and the worst of Heretics were and still are good scholars" (*Virginian Baptist*, 55).

37. E.g., see Semple, *History*, 43–44.

38. Gewehr, *Great Awakening*, 134.

39. Leland, *Virginia Chronicle . . . with judicious and critical remarks*, 24.

40. Fristoe, *Concise History*, 69.

41. Once when David Thomas was preaching, a "parcel of Virginia bucks" arrived and began a conversation as they watched Thomas:

"*That is he,*" quoth one.

"*Yes,*" said a second, "*it is he that stole my neighbor Johnson's bull.*"

"*Did he eat it?*" said a third.

"*No,*" replied a fourth, "*for I saw him riding the bull about the country to preach.*"

"*Yes,*" added a fifth, "*and I saw him ride the bull last night to Moll Heerley's baudy-house.*"

Here followed a great horse-laugh with the ensuing epilogue: "*I have heard that the king of Morocco, is the devil's bull-rider, but now the de-l come he to employ Old Thomas in bull-riding and preaching.*"

Then the band headed off whistling to themselves—undoubtedly leaving the congregation frustrated and uncomfortable (Edwards, *Materials*, 26; cf., 75).

42. Gewehr, *Great Awakening*, 128.

43. Arrest warrant for John Waller, Robert Ware, James Greenwood, William Webber, Richard Faulkner, and Thomas Wafer, Middlesex County, 10 August 1771, in ibid., 123–24.

44. Edwards, *Materials*, 73–74; cf., Little, *Imprisoned Preachers*, 53–54.

45. Accounts drawn from Edwards, *Materials*, 74–75; Semple, *History*, 29–32; Little, *Imprisoned Preachers*, 93–102.

46. Edwards, *Materials*, 75; cf., parallel account in Isaac, *Transformation of Virginia*, 162–63.

Edwards also commented, "Pity that the Bishop of London and the king do not know this that they may see what *Virginia-crackers* they employ instead of ministers of the gospel and an officer of justice!" (*Materials*, 75).

47. Little, *Imprisoned Preachers*, 210–11; Semple, *History*, 32–33.

48. Ibid., 273–85.

49. Semple, *History*, 35–36.

50. See Little, *Imprisoned Preachers*, 385–91.

51. *Journal of the House of Burgesses*, 10 February 1772.

52. *Journal of the House of Burgesses*, 11 February 1772.

53. *Journal of the House of Burgesses*, 12 February 1772.

54. *Journal of the House of Burgesses*, 22 February 1772.

55. *Journal of the House of Burgesses*, 24 February 1772.

56. *Journal of the House of Burgesses*, 27 February 1772.

57. *Journal of the House of Burgesses*, 17 March 1772.

58. Rind's *Virginia Gazette*, 26 March 1772.

The Declaration read, "I A. B. do solemnly declare my unfeigned Assent and Consent to all and every Article and Thing contained in the Holy Scriptures of the Old and New Testament, and I do acknowledge, profess, testify and declare, that I do firmly believe that the said Scriptures of the Old and New Testament were given by Divine Inspiration" (reprinted in the *Virginia Gazette*, 26 March 1772).

59. *Journal of the House of Burgesses*, 12 May 1774.

An identical petition was presented and read in the House of Burgesses on Tuesday, 13 June 1775.

60. *Journal of the House of Burgesses*, 16 May 1774.

61. Semple, *History*, 85.

62. Ibid., 85.

63. Minutes of the Virginia Convention, 14 August 1775, *Revolutionary Virginia*, 3: 441–42.

64. Minutes of the Virginia Convention, 16 August 1775, *Revolutionary Virginia*, 3: 450–51.

Chapter 21

1. Blair, *Account of the College*, 9; College of New Jersey, *Laws of the College of New Jersey*, 10; the original charter was not issued until fall 1748.

2. College of New Jersey, *A General Account . . . of the College*, 5.

3. E.g., see Sloan, *The Scottish Enlightenment*, 65–70.

4. Hoeveler, *Creating the American Mind*, 103.

5. Dickinson, *Sermon preached at the . . . Synod at Philadelphia*, 8.

6. Ibid., 19.

Dickinson recognized that his position on scriptural interpretation had clear implications for religious liberty:

"THE *Ministers of Christ* do come to us in his name, and by his Authority, when they preach nothing but what is contain'd in his Word, and we are under indispensable Obligation to receive the manifest *Truths* of God by them preached, *not as the Word of Man, but as (it is in truth) the Word of God* [I Thes. II. 13]. But they have no Commission to teach us to observe any thing [See Mat. XXVIII. 20]. And when they teach any other Doctrine, they come in their own Names, and not in Christ's.—So, then, we are to esteem them as *Christ's Ambassadors*, and with awful Reverence to attend their preaching, *as if Christ was speaking to us by them*, when we are convinced that they declare the *Counsel of God*: But are not bound to an implicit Faith, against contrary Convictions. It concerns them therefore, to justify their *Interpretations* of God's Word, by clear Scripture Evidence, to the Conviction of the Hearers; and thereby lay 'em under Obligations to Observance and Obedience. . . .

"THOUGH some plain and comprehensive Creed or Confession of Faith (for distinguishing such as receive, from those who reject *the Faith once delivered to the Saints*) may be useful and necessary, since the worst of heresies may take shelter under the express Words of Scripture. Yet we are by no means to force these *credenda*, upon any of differing Sentiments.

"WE may not so much as shut out of Communion, any such Dissenters, as we can charitably hope Christ won't shut out of Heaven: But should open the *Doors of the Church* as wide, as Christ opens the *Gates of Heaven*; and *receive one another, as Christ also received us, to the Glory of God* [Rom. XV. 7].

"AND tho' we ought to reject both the Heresy and the Communion of those, who deny what we esteem the Fundamental Truths of our holy Religion; yet even these essential Articles of Christianity, may not be imposed by Civil Coercions, temporal Penalties, or any other way whatsoever."

(*Sermon preached at the . . . Synod at Philadelphia*, 21–23.)

7. Ibid., 11.

8. Hoeveler, *Creating the American Mind*, 105.

9. Later in life, Madison described Robertson as "a man of extensive learning, and a distinguished teacher." For Robertson's part, he called Madison simply "Mr. Jamie" ("Accounts of the Donald Robertson School," 194). Robertson taught Madison English, Latin, and Greek, written French, arithmetic, geography, algebra, geometry, and "miscellaneous literature," which included works by Horace, Justinian, and Sallust. Among the other students at the school during the same time were James's second cousins (Francis Taylor—about whom we will have more to say later—and his brother, James Taylor IV) and John Tyler, father of the future president by the same name. (See "James Madison's Autobiography," 197; "Accounts of the Donald Robertson School," 291–92; Ketcham, *James Madison*, 19–21.)

10. "James Madison's Autobiography," 197.

11. Adair, "James Madison's Autobiography," 193n9; Brant, *The Fourth President*, 10.

12. Hoeveler, *Creating the American Mind*, 117.

13. Ibid., 121.

14. Foote, *Sketches of Virginia*, 262.

15. Witherspoon, *Ecclesiastical Characteristics*, 14, 23, 34, 52.

16. See, e.g., Witherspoon, *Lectures on Moral Philosophy*, 14–15.

17. For discussions of Berklean Idealism in the context of the eighteenth-century College of New Jersey, see Noll, *Princeton and the Republic*, 36–43; Sloan, *The Scottish Enlightenment*, 126–31; Hoeveler, *Creating the American Mind*, 122–26.

18. Witherspoon, *Lectures on Moral Philosophy*, 14.

19. Noll, *Princeton and the Republic*, 37; Sloan, *The Scottish Enlightenment*, 114–15.

20. Maclean, *History of the College*, 402–403.

21. Witherspoon, *Lectures on Moral Philosophy*, 1.

22. Ibid., 141.

23. E.g., Sloan, *The Scottish Enlightenment*, 133.

24. Witherspoon, *Lectures on Moral Philosophy*, 56.

25. Ibid., 112.

26. Ibid., 111.

27. Witherspoon, "The Dominion of Providence over the Passions of Men," 17 May 1776, in Sandoz, *Political Sermons*, 1: 554.

In a similar vein Witherspoon also said in a sermon that elected officials "are under the strongest obligations to do their utmost to promote religious sobriety, industry, and every social virtue, among those who are committed to their care." He defined this, however, in a way quite different from those who placed the civil magistrate in a position of using force to compel citizens into doctrinal orthodoxy: "If you ask me what are the means which civil rulers are bound to use for attaining these ends, further than the impartial support and faithful guardianship of the rights of conscience; I answer that example itself is none of the least" (*Works*, 2: 473). In the preface to his multivolume set of sermons and speeches, he likewise wrote of the relationship between liberty and religion: "the great decay of religion . . . is chiefly owing to a departure from *the truth as it is in JESUS*, from those doctrines which chiefly constitute the substance of the gospel. . . . At present, if a man shall write or speak against certain principles, and style them pernicious, it will be thought a sufficient vindication of them to make a beaten common-place encomium on liberty of conscience and freedom of inquiry. Blessed be God, this great and sacred privilege is well secured to us in this nation: But pray, is it not mine as well as yours? And is it not the very exercise of this liberty, for every man to endeavor to support those principles which appear to him to be founded in Reason and Scripture, as well as to attack without scruple every thing which he believes to be contrary to either[?]" (*Works*, 1: 3).

28. E.g., "To William Bradford," 10 June 1773, *Madison Papers*, 1: 89.

29. See Blair, *Account of the College*, 27.

30. Ibid., 38; Ketcham, *James Madison*, 33.

31. Maclean, *History of the College*, 313.

32. E.g., see *Madison Papers*, "To William Bradford," 25 September 1773, 1: 95–97.

33. *Madison Papers*, "Commentary on the Bible," 1: 52–58.

34. Ibid., 58.

In the spirit of Tyndale, William Burkitt also wrote of this section of Scripture:

"*Note*: I. That the Scriptures then were in the vulgar tongue. 2. That, as they were in their own tongue, so the laity had them in their own hands. 3. That the common people did read them, and heard them read, searched, and examined them. . . . From the whole, *note*. That a diligent reading of and daily searching into the holy scriptures, is a duty incumbent upon all those in whose hands are, or may be found. These Christians at Berea searching the scriptures, were a noble pattern for all succeeding Christians to imitate and follow."

(*Expository notes, with practical observations upon the New Testament of our Lord and Saviour Jesus Christ*, New York: T. Dunning and W.W. Heyer, 1796, Evans Early American Imprints, no. 30085, 488.)

He also exhorted his readers in the preface of the commentary:

"My design in preparing and giving these *notes* into your hands is to oblige you to read a part of the Holy Scriptures in your families every day; and to invite you thereunto, the sacred text is here at large recited, and controversies declined. And I do most affectionately request you, not to suffer the *holy word of* GOD, which is in all your hands, to lie by you as a neglected book; but daily to read it in and to your families, with a simplicity of mind to be directed and instructed by it."

("Address to Family Governors," ibid., iv.)

35. Bradford's father of "the London Coffee-House" was the printer responsible for reprinting the first American version of Witherspoon's *Ecclesiastical Characteristics* in 1767.

36. Ibid., "To William Bradford," 9 November 1772, 1: 75.

37. Ibid., "From William Bradford," 1 March 1773, 1: 80, 81n7.

38. Ibid., "From William Bradford," 12 August 1773, 1: 91–92.

39. Ibid., "To William Bradford," 25 September 1773, 1: 96.

40. "James Madison's Autobiography," 198.

41. *Madison Papers*, 1: 32n103; ibid., 197.

42. Preface to Joseph Addison, *The Evidences of the Christian Religion* (Boston: Bumstead for Larkin, 1795), Evans Early American Imprints, no. 28150, iii.

43. Addison, *The Spectator*, 16 August 1712, in Joseph Addison and Richard Steele, *The Spectator*, 4 vols., ed. Gregory Smith (Reprint, N. Y.: E. P. Dutton & Co., Inc., 1958), 3: 419.

44. "To William Bradford," 1 December 1773, *Madison Papers*, 1: 101.

45. Ibid., "To William Bradford," 24 January 1774, 105.

46. Ibid., 1: 105–6.

47. Ibid., 1: 105.

Chapter 22

1. Semple, *History*, 472.

2. Semple, *History*, 1810 edition, 415.

3. Ibid.; Morgan Edwards, quoted in Little, *Imprisoned Preachers*, 134.

4. Orange County Order Book, 28 July 1768, quoted in Little, *Imprisoned Preachers*, 136.

5. Edwards, *Materials*, 82.

6. Ibid., 82, 117; Semple, *History*, 238, 240.

7. *Madison Papers*, 1: 125n7; "Accounts of the Donald Robertson School," 291–92.

8. Charles Washington Coleman, "The County Committees of 1774–'75 in Virginia: II," *William and Mary College Quarterly Historical Magazine* 5 (April 1897): 247; *Madison Papers*, 1: 147.

9. *Madison Papers*, 1: 174, n7.

10. Edwards, *Materials*, 82.

11. The "Massachusetts Spy" wrote an open letter to Virginia's royal governor, Lord Dunmore, published in the *Gazette* on May 21, 1772, crying, "My Lord, set at Liberty the persecuted for Religion's Sake, and *let the Prisoners go free* who are confined

in some of your loathsome jails for preaching the *everlasting Gospel.* Supposing them to hold some Errours, *let those of their Persecutors who are without Sin cast the first stone.*"

On June 10 and 17, 1773, the *Gazette* published an exchange between Robert Carter Nicholas, the Virginia treasurer, and "Hoadleianus," the latter of which insisted that Locke's doctrine of religious toleration rested on the foundation of "THE NATURAL AND UNALIENABLE RIGHTS OF HUMAN NATURE."

On July 1 of the same year, the *Gazette* published a debate on a religious toleration bill from the House of Commons in London. One member of Parliament argued eloquently against those who would have clamped the chains around England's dissenter's even tighter. "What, Sir," he asked, "is Liberty by Connivance by a temporary Relaxation of Slavery?" Then he continued:

"Granting that the Dissenters do now enjoy a Sort of Liberty by Connivance, a Liberty which hath this for its Dependence is precarious, may exist today, and be annihilated tomorrow. . . When the Romish Church cast aside its Toleration, and betook itself to Threatenings, Slaughter, and Persecution, Commotions ensued, Ecclesiastical Anarchy prevailed, and the Kingdom of Darkness was erected on the Ruins of Christian Charity and mutual Forbearance. Instead of combating the common Foe, Christians fought and combated each other; instead of taking arms against the grand Deceiver, they strove, by every deceptious Art, to harass and torment those to whom they ought to have loved as Brethren."

The bill passed, but as noted above, this did not prevent dissenting ministers from being imprisoned.

12. *Virginia Gazette,* 16 February 1776.

13. Ibid., "To William Bradford," 1 April 1774, 1: 112.

14. *Journal of the House of Burgesses,* 12 May 1774; Petition from the Presbytery of Hanover, 5 June 1775, *Early Virginia Religious Petitions.*

15. "James Madison's Autobiography," 198.

16. "To William Bradford," 26 November 1774, *Madison Papers,* 1: 130.

17. Cf., ibid., 131n11.

18. Quoted in McLoughlin, *Revivals,* 64.

19. Backus, quoted in McLoughlin, *Isaac Backus,* 7.

20. Ibid., 6–7.

21. McLoughlin, *New England Dissent,* 1: 547–50.

22. Quoted in Hovey, *Memoir,* 204–5, 210.

23. McLoughlin, *New England Dissent,* 1: 560; ibid., 210.

24. Backus, *Appeal to the public,* 43.

25. Ibid., 47.

Backus also spoke of English history and both the impact of the vernacular Bible and the reformation yet to complete: "As the high priest's sentence in the Jewish state, divided matters both for prince and people, the same deceitful philosophy that had gone so far, never left plotting till they had set up an ecclesiastical head over kingdoms as well as churches, who with Peter's keys was to open and shut, bind and loose, both in spiritual and temporal affairs. But after many generations groaned under this hellish tyranny, a time came when England renounced that head, and set up the king as their head in ecclesiastical as well as civil concernments; and though the free use of the Scriptures which was then introduced by a divine blessing, produced a great reformation, yet still the *high places* were not taken away, & the *lord bishops* made such work in them, as drove our fathers from thence into America. The first colony that came to this part of it [the Separatist Pilgrims] carried the reformation so far, as not to make use of the civil power to save the people to support religious ministers . . . but the second colony, who had not taken up the cross so as to separate from the national church before they came away, now determined to pick out all that they thought was of universal and moral equity in Moses' laws, and so to frame a Christian common-wealth here. . . .And as the Jews were required to inflict corporal punishments, even unto death, upon non-conformers to their worship, this common-wealth did the like to such as refused to conform their way; and they strove very hard to have the church govern the world" (*An appeal to the public*, 14–16).

26. Rhode Island General Assembly, *Act for the Establishment of a College.*

27. Lord Herbert, *Life of King Henry VIII*, in Binney, *An oration*, 7.

28. Ibid.

29. Ibid.

30. Ibid., 6.

31. See Blackstone, *Commentaries*, Book IV, chapter 4; Blackstone, "A Reply to Dr. Priestley's Remarks," in *An Interesting Appendix*, 40; Furneaux, "Letter I," *Letters*, 2ff.

32. "Letter II," in Furneaux, *Letters*, 18–20.

33. Bonwick, *English Radicals*, 205.

34. Furneaux, *Essay on Toleration*, 358.

35. Ibid., 359.

36. Ibid., 362, 366, 379, 384.

37. To quote Furneaux directly:

"And from [man] being thus accountable to God alone, it follows, that as his judging and acting for himself in matters of religion is, with respect to his fellow men, a right which he holds independent of them; so, with respect to God, it is a duty which he owes to him: a duty, which he is bound to discharge, notwithstanding every attempt to induce him to profess opinions, which he doth not believe; or adopt practices, which he doth not approve or acknowledge any authority, or any law, in the mere concerns of religion, except the divine authority, and the divine law.

"Absolute liberty, therefore, in the affair of religion, belongs to us, as reasonable creatures, dependent on, and subject to, the universal Sovereign and Judge. It is a right essential to our nature: whatsoever other rights, therefore, we are supposed to resign on entering into society, this we cannot resign; we cannot do it, if we would; and ought not, if we could. . . .

"I think, it appears, that Toleration cannot be complete; nor the natural inherent rights of mankind, with respect to religion, be preserved inviolate; and maintained in that degree, in which it is the duty of the Magistrate to maintain them . . .

"Some persons talk with much seeming liberality of the right of private judgment, who yet, by the restrictions which they at last throw in, appear to mean nothing more by it than that judgment, which is to be *kept private*, and to be locked up in a man's own bosom. For, though they will allow him the right of private judgment, they will not allow him to publish that judgment, with the reasons and grounds of it, to others. . . .

"Now, if I worship God according to the dictates of my own conscience; and give, or receive, such religious instructions, as I judge most agreeable to reason and scripture, and consequently most conducive to my own, or others deification; how does that prevent my neighbor from doing the same; or the Magistrate from encouraging, if he is so inclined, those sentiments which are agreeable to his judgment: or how does it injure either the one, or the other, in any of their respective rights?"

(*An Essay on Toleration,* 364, 371, 374.)

38. "Address to Captain Patrick Henry and the Gentlemen Independents of Hanover," 9 May 1775, *Madison Papers,* 1: 146–47.

39. *Journal of the House of Burgesses,* 6 May 1776, in *Revolutionary Virginia,* 5: 19.

40. Tarter and Scribner, *Revolutionary Virginia,* 5: 1.

41. Ibid.

42. Dixon's *Virginia Gazette,* 1 June 1776.

43. Tarter and Scribner, *Revolutionary Virginia,* 5: 1.

44. Edmund Pendleton and James Madison Jr. had James Taylor I as a common ancestor. James Taylor I was Pendleton's maternal grandfather and Madison's great-great-grandfather. This would make them first cousins, twice removed.

45. This James Taylor also married Elizabeth Fitzhugh after his first two wives died. Elizabeth was the widow of Francis Conway III, one of Madison's first cousins on his mother's side. (See "Taylor, J," cards 7 and 8, R. Bolling Batte Papers Biographical Card Files, Library of Virginia.)

46. Records of the Fifth Virginia Convention, 15 May 1776, in *Revolutionary Virginia,* 5: 143; *Proceedings of the Convention,* 15 May 1776, 32.

47. Ibid.

48. Records of the Fifth Virginia Convention, 16 May 1776, in ibid., 5: 158.

49. Records of the Fifth Virginia Convention, 18 May 1776, in ibid., 5: 182–83, n1.

50. Ibid., 5: 186n22.

51. Records of the Fifth Virginia Convention, 27 May 1776, in ibid., 5: 270–72, 276–77.

52. See *Revolutionary Virginia,* 5: 272; "Committee's Proposed Article on Religion," *Madison Papers,* 1:173.

53. Randolph, *History of Virginia,* 235.

54. "James Madison's Autobiography," 199.

55. See "Madison's Amendments to the Declaration of Rights," *Madison Papers,* 1: 174.

56. Thomas Paine, *Rights of Man,* Part 1, in *Thomas Paine: Collected Writings* (New York: Literary Classics of the United States, 1995), 482.

57. Tarter and Scribner, *Revolutionary Virginia,* 5: 457n33.

58. Records of the Third Virginia Convention, 16 August 1775, in *Revolutionary Virginia,* 3: 451, 453n3.

59. Randolph, *History of Virginia,* 254; Tarter and Scribner, *Revolutionary Virginia,* 5: 457, n33.

60. See "Madison's Amendments to the Declaration of Rights," *Madison Papers,* 1: 174.

61. See, e.g., Tarter and Scribner, *Revolutionary Virginia*, 5: 457–58, n33; Hutchinson and Rachal, *Madison Papers*, 1: 179, n9; Brant, *The Fourth President*, 34.

62. Tarter and Scribner, *Revolutionary Virginia*, 5: 458n33.

63. "To James Madison, Sr.," [1–15 June 1776], *Madison Papers*, 1: 182–83, n7; cf., Ketcham, *James Madison*, 57.

64. Remember that Pendleton was also a first cousin, twice removed, to the Francis Taylor (III) who was a member of Elijah Craig's Rapidan congregation. Pendleton's fellow delegate, James Taylor IV, was Francis' uncle.

65. Mays, *Edmund Pendleton*, 1: 264–65.

It was to these men that the anonymous disparaging editorialist in the *Virginia Gazette* wrote, "You must perform the Condition [of the Act of Toleration—namely, receiving a license from the General Court of the colony, which was no easy task] before you can claim the Exemption; that is, among other Qualifications, you must preach and assemble at registered of licensed Houses only" ("An ADDRESS to the ANABAPTISTS imprisoned in CAROLINE County, August 8, 1771," *Virginia Gazette* [Purdie and Dixon], 20 February 1771).

66. Quoted in ibid., 265.

67. Virginia Convention, *Proceedings of the Convention of Delegates*, 12 June 1776, 102–3.

Chapter 23

1. *Journal of the House of Delegates*, 14 October 1776.

2. Dumas Malone, ed., *The Autobiography of Thomas Jefferson*, quoted in Ketcham, 76.

3. *Journal of the House of Delegates*, 11 October 1776.

4. Dreisbach, "Church-State Debate," 147; ibid., 12 October 1776.

5. Ketcham, *James Madison*, 75; for an interpretation of Smith's views contrary to Ketcham's portrayal, see Buckley, *Church and State*, 53–55.

6. Petition from Prince Edward, October 11, 1776, *Early Virginia Religious Petitions*.

7. Petition from Prince William, 20 June 1776, *Early Virginia Religious Petitions*.

8. Dreisbach, "Church-State Debate," 146.

9. Miscellaneous "Ten-thousand name" petition, 16 October 1776, *Early Virginia Religious Petitions*; *Journal of the House of Delegates*, 16 October 1776; Isaac, "The Rage of Malice," 146.

10. Petition from Culpeper, 22 October 1776, *Early Virginia Religious Petitions*; *Journal of the House of Burgesses*, 22 October 1776.

11. Petitions from Albemarle, Amherst, Buckingham, 22 October 1776 and 1 November 1776, *Early Virginia Religious Petitions*; *Journal of the House of Burgesses*, 22 October 1776.

12. *Journal of the House of Delegates*, 25 October 1776; *Petition from Berkeley*, 25 October 1776, *Early Virginia Religious Petitions*.

13. Petition from the Presbytery of Hanover, 24 October 1776, *Early Virginia Religious Petitions*; *Journal of the House of Burgesses*, 24 October 1776.

14. Buckley, *Church and State*, 27–28; Petition from the General Convention of Methodists, 28 October 1776, *Early Virginia Religious Petitions*.

15. Petition from the Clergy of the Established Church, 8 November 1776, *Early Virginia Religious Petitions; Journal of the House of Delegates*, 8 November 1776.

16. Buckley, *Church and State*, 30.

17. *Journal of the House of Delegates*, 9 November 1776.

18. *Jefferson Papers*, 1: 530–31.

19. Hutchinson and Rachal, eds., *Madison Papers*, 1: 186–87.

20. Boyd, ed., *Jefferson Papers*, 1: 531, n1.

21. Ibid., 1: 589.

22. Ibid., 1: 525.

23. Among those Jefferson cited were 5.6.E.6.c.1, where he noted, "Every person to resort to church every Sunday . . . Ecclesiasticl. courts to punish offenders . . . if any one hear & be present at any form of prayer but 'the book of Common prayer imprisonmt. For 6. months 1st. offfnce.—2d. ditto.—3d imprisonmt. for life"; 1.El.c.1, "heresies defined 'such as have heretofore been determined heresy by the authority of the Canonical scripture, or by the first 4 general councils, or any of them, or by any other general council [wherein] it was declared heresy . . . Ecclesiastical Commissrs. to correct. Diocesan may burn the heretic 1.Hale.P. C. 405, 2. Arians burnt under this law in 17.El. & 9.Jac.—repd in Engld. By 29.Car.2. c.9. but not here"; and 35.El.c.1., "Every person absenting from place of the Common prayer one month without lawful excuse, & by printing, writing, or express words or speeches move or persuade any one to deny, withstand & impugn the Queen's supremacy ecclesiastical, or to abstain from church to the service accdg. to law, or to come to or be present at any unlawful assemblies, conventicles or meetings under colour of exercise of religion contrary to the statutes . . . shall be committed to prison till conformity: and if they do not conform in three months & make public recantation, they shall abjure the realm: & if he does not depart, or if he returns, shall suffr. death witht. clergy."

24. Jefferson noted 1.Jac.1.c.4 and 3.Jac.1.c.1, *inter alia*.

25. See the extensive set of Jefferson's notes in *Jefferson Papers*, 1: 535–58 and his *Notes on the State of Virginia*, 160.

26. Randolph, *History of Virginia*, 264.

27. *Journal of the House of Delegates*, 19 November 1776.

28. See *Jefferson Papers*, 1: 532–35; *Journal of the House of Delegates*, 30 November 1776ff; Buckley, *Church and State*, 35–36; Eckenrode, *Separation*, 49–53.

29. "Declaration of the Virginia Association of Baptists" and "Memorandum concerning Military Service of Baptists" in *Jefferson Papers*, 1: 660–62.

30. "Declaration of the Virginia Association of Baptists" in *Jefferson Papers*, 1: 660–61.

31. Petition from the Presbytery of Hanover, 3 June 1777, *Early Virginia Religious Petitions*.

32. Petition from Cumberland, 21 May 1777, *Early Virginia Religious Petitions*.

33. Petition from Mecklenburg, 29 May 1777, *Early Virginia Religious Petitions;* see also the same petition signed by inhabitants of Lunenburg County, 11 December 1777, and Westmoreland County, 9 October 1778, *Early Virginia Religious Petitions*.

34. House of Delegates, *Report of the Committee of Revisors*, 5.

35. See Dreisbach, "Church-State Debate," 144, 147; *Journal of the House of Delegates*, 12 June 1779 and 18 June 1779.

36. Petitions from Seceding Presbyterians, 29 October 1778, and from Jeremiah Walker, 14 November 1778, *Early Virginia Religious Petitions*.

37. "'A Bill concerning Religion,' 1779," Appendix I in Buckley, *Church and State*, 185.

38. Ibid., 186.

39. Ibid., 187.

40. Miller, *The First Freedom*, 18–21.

41. *Madison Papers*, 1: 193.

42. Miller, *The First Freedom*, 32.

43. Rutland and Rachel, eds., *Madison Papers*, 8: 196.

44. Petitions from Culpeper, Essex, and Amherst Counties, 21 October 1779, 22 October 1779, and 10 November 1779, *Early Virginia Religious Petitions*.

45. Buckley, *Church and State*, 50.

46. "To Thomas Jefferson," 3 July 1784, *Madison Papers*, 8: 93.

47. Ibid., 93–94.

48. Semple, *History*, 94.

49. Petition from the Baptist Association assembled at Dover Meeting-House, 11 November 1784, *Early Virginia Religious Petitions*.

50. Petition from Isle of Wight County, 4 November 1784, *Early Virginia Religious Petitions*.

51. Petition of the Presbytery of Hanover, 12 November 1784, *Early Virginia Religious Petitions*.

52. "To James Monroe," 14 November 1784, *Madison Papers*, 8: 137.

53. "To James Monroe," 12 April 1785," in ibid., 8: 261.

54. Eckenrode, *Separation*, 88–91.

55. *Journal of the House of Delegates*, 8 November 1784.

56. Ibid., 11 November 1784.

57. "From Thomas Jefferson," 8 December 1784, *Madison Papers*, 8: 178.

58. Ibid.

59. The preamble read, "Whereas the general diffusion of Christian knowledge hath a natural tendency to correct the morals of men, restrain their vices, and preserve the peace of society, which cannot be effected without a competent provision for learned teachers, who may be thereby enabled to devote their time and attention to the duty of instructing such citizens, as from their circumstances and want of education, cannot otherwise attain such knowledge; and it is judged that such provision may be made by the Legislature, without counteracting the liberal principle heretofore adopted and intended to be preserved by abolishing all distinctions of preeminence amongst the different societies or communities of Christians" ("A Bill 'Establishing a Provision for Teachers of the Christian Religion,' 1784," Appendix 1 in Buckley, *Church and State*, 188).

60. See "Outline A" and "Outline B" in *Madison Papers*, 8: 197–99.

61. House of Delegates, *Friday, the 24th* of December, 1784.

62. "From George Nicholas," 22 April 1785, *Madison Papers*, 8: 264.

63. Ibid.

64. Ibid., 298–304.

65. Hutchinson and Rachal, eds., in ibid., 296.

66. "To James Monroe," 21 June 1785, in ibid., 306.

67. Semple, *History*, 96, emphasis added.

68. Petition from Surry County, 26 October 1785, *Early Virginia Religious Petitions*.

69. Petition from Powhatan, Baptist Association, 3 November 1785, *Early Virginia Religious Petitions*.

70. Petition from Orange, Baptist Association, 17 November 1785, *Early Virginia Religious Petitions*.

71. Petition from Presbyterians assembled in Augusta County, 2 November 1785, *Early Virginia Religious Petitions*.

72. Petition from Dinwiddie County, 28 November 1785, *Early Virginia Religious Petitions*.

73. Hutchinson and Rachal, eds., *Madison Papers*, 8: 297–98; Banning, *Sacred Fire*, 96.

74. *Journal of the House of Delegates*, 14–17 December 1785.

75. Madison wrote: "The steps taken throughout the Country to defeat the Genl, Assessment, had produced all the effect that could have been wished. The table was loaded with petitions & remonstrances from all parts against the interposition of the Legislature in matters of Religion. A General convention of the Presbyterian church prayed expressly that the bill in the Revisal might be passed into law, as the best safeguard short of a constitutional one, for their religious rights. The bill was carried thro' the H of Delegates, without alteration. The Senate objected to the preamble, and sent down a proposed substitution of the 16th art: of the Declaration of Rights. The H. of D. disagreed. The Senate insisted and asked a Conference. Their objections were frivolous indeed. In order to remove them as they were understood by the Managers of the H. of D. the preamble was sent up again from the H. of D. with one or two verbal alterations. As an amendment to these the Senate sent down a few others; which as they did not affect the substance though they somewhat defaced the composition, it was thought better to agree to than run further risks, especially as it was getting late in the Session and the House growing thin. The enacting clauses past [sic] without a single alteration, and I flatter myself have in this Country extinguished for ever the ambitious hope of making laws for the human mind" ("To Thomas Jefferson," 22 January 1785, *Madison Papers*, 473–74).

76. Madison, "Detached Memoranda," 556.

77. Hening, ed., *Statutes at Large*, 12: 84–86.

78. Map in Buckley, *Church and State*, 160.

79. Isaac, "The Rage of Malice," 156.

Chapter 24

1. *Journals of the Continental Congress*, 21 February 1787.

2. Ibid., 30 May 1787.

3. Madison to Jefferson, October 24, 1787.

4. Elliot, *Debates*, 2: 148ff.

5. Ibid.

6. "James Madison to Ambrose Madison," 8 November 1787, in Merrill, et al., eds., *Documentary History*, 9: 596–97.

7. "Archibald Stuart to James Madison," 2 November 1787, in ibid., 596.

8. "Edmund Randoph to James Madison," 3 January 1788, and "James Madison Sr., to James Madison," 30 January 1788, in ibid., 598–99.

9. "From Joseph Spencer," 28 February 1788, in *Madison Papers*, 10: 541.

10. "Joseph Spencer to James Madison," 28 February 1788, in Merrill, et al., eds., *Documentary History*, 8: 424.

11. Ibid., 426.

12. It is thought that the Spencer who penned this letter was the same Joseph Spencer who served as a captain in the Continental Army and later as a delegate from Orange County to the Virginia General Assembly in 1780–81. A Baptist pastor named Joseph Spencer from Orange County was imprisoned for preaching without a license in 1773. Whether all of these are the same person cannot be determined with the resources at hand. But it is clear that this Spencer who wrote to Madison possessed all the sentiments that would be consistent with this biography. (See Merrill, et al., eds, *Documentary History of the Constitution*, 8: 426n1.)

13. Ibid., 424–25.

14. "Francis Taylor Diary," 24 March 1788, in Merrill, et al., eds., *Documentary History*, 9: 602.

15. Rutland, *Birth of the Bill of Rights*, 134.

16. Elliot, *Debates*, 3: 45.

17. "George Washington to Lafayette," 28 April 1788, in Farrand, *Records*, 3: 297–98.

18. "Reply to Mason's 'Objections': 'Civis Rusticus,'" *Virginia Independent Chronicle* (Richmond), 30 January 1788, in Bailyn, *Debate on the Constitution*, 1: 357.

19. "Giles Hickory," *American Magazine* (New York), February 1788, in Bailyn, *Debate on the Constitution*, 2: 311.

20. Rutland, *Birth of the Bill of Rights*, 150–51.

Chapter 25

1. Elliot, *Debates*, 3: 10.

2. Ibid., 24.

3. Ibid., 22–23.

4. There were two Henry Lees at this convention. The other was from Bourbon County [Kentucky]. Henry Lee of Westmoreland should not be confused with Richard Henry Lee of Westmoreland who was an ardent Anti-Federalist and colaborer with Patrick Henry in efforts to defeat the Constitution. Richard Henry Lee was not a delegate to the ratification convention.

5. Ibid., 42.

6. Ibid.

7. Ibid., 65–66.

8. Ibid., 66.

9. "To William Wirt," 14 August 1814, in Paul L. Ford, ed., *The Works of Thomas Jefferson* (New York: G.P. Putnam's Sons, 1904–1905).

10. Elliot, *Debates*, 3: 187–88.

11. Ibid., 188.

12. Ibid., 246.

13. Ibid., 553.

14. Ibid., 87.

15. "James Madison to Thomas Jefferson," 17 October 1788, in *Madison Papers*, 11: 297–300.

16. Elliot, *Debates*, 3: 186.

17. Ibid., 93.

18. Ibid., 330.

19. Ibid., 44–45.

20. Ibid., 33.

21. Ibid., 639.

22. Ibid., 622.

23. Ibid., 637.

24. Ibid.

25. Ibid., 640.

26. Ibid., 652.

27. Ibid., 653.

28. Ibid., 656.

29. Rutland, et al., *Madison Papers*, 11: 302.

30. Ibid.

31. "To Thomas Jefferson," 17 October 1788, in ibid., 11: 297.

32. "From Thomas Jefferson," 15 March 1789, in ibid., 12: 13.

33. "To George Eve," 2 January 1789, in ibid., 11: 404–05.

34. Ibid., 405

35. Ibid., 408.

36. Ibid., 414–15

37. Ibid., 423–24.

38. Rutland, *Birth of the Bill of Rights*, 196.

39. "From John Leland," [ca. 15 February 1789], in *Madison Papers*, 11: 443.

40. Rutland, *Birth of the Bill of Rights*, 198–99.

41. Ibid., 207–8.

42. Hutson, *Religion and the Founding*, 80.

43. In 1992, the amendment, which was proposed as the original Second Amendment relative to congressional pay raises, was ratified by three-fourths of the state legislatures. Congress has subsequently gutted the meaning of this provision by enacting automatic pay raises adjusted by the cost of living index without any need for a future vote.

44. Quoted in Rutland, et al., eds., *Madison Papers*, 12: 53.

Epilogue

1. "The Bill of Rights and the Rights of Man," International Information Programs, U.S. Department of State, available at http://usinfo.state.gov/products/pubs/whatsdem/whatdm12.htm [accessed 26 July 2006].

2. Barnes, *What the Churche Is*, in Foxe, *Whole Works*, 244.

3. Hart, *A consultorie*, [Dvii^v–Dviii^r, Fi^{r-v}].

4. Castellio, *Concerning Heretics*, 214–15.

5. [Helwys], *Objections Answered*, 2.

6. How, *Sufficiency of the Spirits Teaching*.

7. Dell, *Building and Glory*, "To the Reader," [Aiv^r].

8. Williams, *Bloudy Tenet*, 79–80.

9. Blackwood, *Storming of Antichrist*, 19.

10. Sturgion, *A Plea for Tolleration*, 5.

11. Locke, *Letter Concerning Toleration*, 9, 11.

12. Tennent, "The Danger of an Unconverted Ministry," in Heimert, *The Great Awakening*, 89.

13. *Journal of the House of Burgesses*, 12 May 1774; "The Petition of the Presbytery of Hanover," 5 June 1775, *Early Virginia Religious Petitions*.

14. Leland, *Virginia Chronicle . . . with judicious and critical remarks*, 25–26.

15. Zagorin, *Idea of Religious Toleration*, 9.

16. Jordan, *Development of Religious Toleration*, 1: 1–2.

17. Virginia Baptist General Committee, *Minutes*, 6–7.

BIBLIOGRAPHY

I. Primary Sources

A. Original Printed Material

An appeale of the orthodox ministers of the Church of England against Richard Mountague late bishop of Chichester, now bishop of Norwich. . . . Wherein his dangerous heresies are revealed; and the character of an Arminian or Mountaguists is added. Edinburgi [i.e., London?: B. Alsop and T. Fawcet], 1629. Reproduction of the original at the Bodleian Library. STC (2nd ed.) / 18040. Early English Books Online.

Backus, Isaac. *An appeal to the public for religious liberty, against the oppressions of the present day.* Boston: Printed by John Boyle in Marlborough-Street, 1773. Reproduction of the original, Evans Early American Imprints, 1st series, no. 12654.

―――. *A Fish caught in his own net. . . .* Boston: Printed by Edes and Gill, in Queen-Street, 1768. Reproduction of the original, Evans Early American Imprints, 1st series, no. 10823.

―――. *Government and liberty described; and ecclesiastical tyranny exposed.* Boston: Printed by Powars and Willis, and sold by Philip Freeman, in Union-Street, 1778. Reproduction of the original, Evans Early American Imprints, 1st series, no. 15727.

―――. *Policy, as well as honesty, forbids the use of secular force in religious affairs.* Boston: Printed by Draper and Folsom, and sold by Phillip Freeman, in Union-Street, 1779. Reproduction of the original, Evans Early American Imprints, 1st series, no 16195.

―――. *A seasonable plea for liberty of conscience, against some late oppressive proceedings.* . . . Boston: Philip Freeman, in Union-Street, 1770. Reproduction of the original, Evans Early American Imprints, 1st series, no. 11556.

Barlow, William. *The svmme and svbstance of the conference which, it pleased his excellent Maiestie to haue with the lords, bishops, and other of his clergie, (at vvhich the most of the lordes of the councell were present) in his Maiesties priuy-chamber, at Hampton Court. Ianuary 14. 1603. . . .* London: imprinted by Iohn Windet [and T. Creede] for Mathew Law, and are to be sold at his shop in Paules Churchyeard, neare S. Austens Gate, 1604. Reproduction of the original at Folger Shakespeare Library. STC (2nd ed.) / 1456.5. Early English Books Online.

Barrow[e], Henry. *A Brief Discoverie of the False Church.* [Dort?]: n.p., 1590. Reproduction of the original at Yale University Library. STC (2nd ed.) / 1517. Early English Books Online.

————. *A true description out of the Worde of God of the visible church.* [Amsterdam: n.p.], 1589. Reproduction of the original at the Lambeth Palace Library. STC (2nd ed.) / 1526.5. Early English Books Online.

Baxter, Richard. *Reliquiae Baxterianae, or, Mr. Richard Baxters narrative of the most memorable passages of his life and times faithfully publish'd from his own original manuscript by Matthew Sylvester.* London: Printed for T. Parkhurst, J. Robinson, F. Lawrence and F. Dunton, 1696. Reproduction of the original at the British Library. Wing / B1370; Arber's Term cat. / II 601. Early English Books Online.

Becke, Edmund. *A brefe confutatacion of this most detestable, [and] Anabaptistical opinion, that Christ dyd not take hys flesh of the blessed Vyrgyn Mary nor any corporal substaunce of her body.* London: By Iohn Day dwellynge ouer Aldersgate and Wylliam Seres dwellynge in Peter Colledge, 1550. Reproduction of the original at Bodleian Library. STC (2nd ed.) / 1709. Early English Books Online.

Bernard, Richard. *Rhemes against Rome: or, The remoouing of the gagg of the new Gospell, and rightly placing it in the mouthes of the Romists, by the Rhemists in their English translation of the Scriptures.* . . . London: Imprinted by Felix Kingston, for Ed. Blackmore, and are to be sold at his shop at the great south doore of Pauls, 1626. Reproduction of the original at the Cambridge University Library. STC (2nd ed.) / 1960. Early English Books Online.

Binney, Barnabus. *An oration delivered on the late public commencement at Rhode-Island College in Providence; September 1774. Being a plea, for the right of private judgment in religious matters; or, for the liberty of choosing our own religion. Corroborated by the well-known consequences of priestly power.* . . . Boston: John Kneeland, 1447. Reproduction of the original, Evans Early American Imprints, 1st series, no. 13153.

Bishop, George. *New England judged, not by man's, but the spirit of the Lord: and the summe sealed up of New-England's persecutions being a brief relation of the sufferings of the people called Quakers in those parts of America* . . . London: Robert Wilson, 1661. Reproduction of the original at the Henry E. Huntington Library. Wing / B3003. Early English Books Online.

[Blackborow, Sarah.] *The oppressed prisoners complaint of their great oppression: with a loud call to Englands magistrates for the exercise of impartial justice* . . . [London: n.p.], 1662. Reproduction of the original at the Folger Shakespeare Library. Wing (CD-ROM, 1996) / B3064A. Early English Books Online.

Blackwood, Christopher. *The storming of Antichrist, in his two last and strongest garrisons; of compulsion of conscience, and infants babptisme [sic]. Wherein is set down a way and manner for church [sic] constitution; together with markes to know right constituted churches, from all other societies in the world.* . . . London: n.p., 1644. Reproduction of the original at the British Library. Wing (2nd ed.) / B3103; Thomason / E.22[15]. Early English Books Online.

Blair, Samuel. *A short and faithful narrative, of the late remarakable [sic] revival of religion in the congregation of New-Londonderry, and other parts of Pennsylvania* . . . Philadelphia: Printed and sold by William Bradford at the Sign of the Bible in Second-Street, 1744. Reproduction of the original, Evans Early American Imprints, 1st series, no. 5342.

————. *An account of the College of New-Jersey* . . . Woodbridge, N. J.: James Parker, 1764. Reproduction of the original, Evans Early American Imprints, 1st series, no. 9752.

The booke of common prayer, and administration of the sacraments and other rites and ceremonies of the Church of England. London: Robert Barker, printer to the kings most excellent Maiestie, 1603. Reproduction of the original at the British Library. STC (2nd ed.) / 16326. Early English Books Online.

The booke of common prayer, and administration of the sacraments and other rites and ceremonies in the Church of England. London: By the Deputies of Christopher Barker, Printer to the Queenes most excellent Maiestie, 1596. Reproduction of the original at the British Library. STC (2nd ed.) / 16321. Early English Books Online.

Bradford, John. *Godlie meditations vpon the Lordes prayer, the beleefe, and ten commaundementes with other comfortable meditations, praiers and exercises. Whereunto is annexed a defence of the doctrine of gods eternall election and predestination, gathered by the constant martyr of God Iohn Bradford in the tyme of his imprisonment.* [London]: Nowe fyrst prynted by Rouland Hall, dwellyng in gutter lane at the signe of the halfe Egle and key, 1562. Reproduction of the original at Folger Shakespeare Library. STC (2nd ed.) / 3484. Early English Books Online.

Bray, Thomas. *A memorial representing the present state of religion, on the continent of North-America* . . . London: Printed by William Downing for the author, 1700. Reproduction of the original at the Henry E. Huntington Library. Wing / B4294; Sabin / 7479. Early English Books Online.

A Brief Confession or Declaration of Faith: Set forth by many of us, who are (falsely) called Ana-Baptists, to inform all Men (in these days of scandal and reproach) of our innocent Belief and Practise; for which we are not only resolved to suffer Persecution, to the loss of our Goods, but also Life it self, rather than to decline the same. . . . London: Printed by G. D. for F. Smith, at the Elephant and Castle, near Temple-Barr, 1660. Reproduction of the original at the British Library. Wing (2nd ed., 1994) / B4559; Thomason / E.1017[14]. Early English Books Online.

Browne, Robert. *A booke which sheweth the life and manners of all true Christians and howe vnlike they are vnto Turkes and Papistes, and heathen folke.* . . . *Also there goeth a treatise before of reformation without tarying for anie, and of the wickednesse of those preachers, which will not refourme them selues and their charge, because they will tarie till the magistrate commanude and compell them.* Middelburgh: Imprinted by Richarde Painter, 1582. Reproduction of the original at Yale University Library. STC (2nd ed.) / 3910.3. Early English Books Online.

Bunyan, John. *Grace abounding to the chief of sinners* . . . London: Printed for Nath. Ponder . . ., 1688. Reproduction of the original at the British Library. Wing / B5526. Early English Books Online.

[Burrough, Edward.] *A brief relation of the persecutions and cruelties that have been acted upon the people called Quakers in and about the city of London* . . . London: n.p., 1662. Reproduction of the original at the Huntington Library. Wing / B4629. Early English Books Online.

Burroughs, Jeremiah. *Irenicum, to the lovers of truth and peace. Heart-divisions opened in the causes and evils of them: with cautions that we may not be hurt by them, and endeavours to heal them.* London: Printed for Robert Dawlman, 1645. Reproduction of the original at the British Library. Wing (2nd ed., 1994) / B6088; Thomason / E.306[9]. Early English Books Online.

Burton, Henry. *Truth, still truth, though shut out of doores: or, A reply to a late pamphlet entituled The doore of truth opened: published in the name and with the consent of the whold church of Aldermanbury. With some animadversions upon a late letter of the ministers of London to the Reverend Assembly, against toleration.* London: Printed for Giles Calvert, at the black spread-Eagle, at the west end of Pauls, 1646. Reproduction of the original at the British Library. Wing (2nd ed., 1994) / B6174; Thomason / E.315[6]. Early English Books Online.

Busher, Leonard. *Religions peace: or, A plea for liberty of conscience. Long since presented to King James, and the High Court of Parliament then sitting . . . Wherein is contained certain reasons against persecution for religion, also a designe for a peaceable reconciling of those that differ in opinion.* Amsterdam: n.p., 1614. Reprint, London: Printed for John Sweeting at the Angel in Popes-head-alley, 1646. Reproduction of the original at British Library. Wing (2nd ed., 1994) / B6251; Thomason / E.334[7]. Early English Books Online.

————. *Religions peace or A reconciliation, between princes & peoples, & nations (by Leonard Busher: of the county of Gloucester, of the towne of Wotton, and a citticen, of the famous and most honorable citty London, and of the second right worshipfull Company) supplicated (vnto the hygh and mighty King of great Brittayne: etc: and to the princely and right Honorable Parliament) with all loyalty, humility and carefull fidelity.* Amsterdam, n.p., 1614. Reproduction of the original at Henry E. Huntington Library. STC (2nd ed.) / 4189. Early English Books Online.

Calvin, Jean. *The sermons of M. Iohn Caluin vpon the fifth booke of Moses called Deuteronomie faithfully gathered word for word as he preached them in open pulpet; together with a preface of the ministers of the Church of Geneua, and an admonishment made by the deacons there. . . .* Translated by Arthur Golding. London: Printed by Henry Middleton for George Bishop, 1583. Reproduction of the original at the Henry E. Huntington Library. STC (2nd ed.) / 4442. Early English Books Online.

Camden, William. *The historie of the life and reigne of the most renowmed [sic] and victorious Princesse Elizabeth, late Queene of England contayning the most important and remarkeable passages of state, during her happy, long and prosperous raigne / composed by way of annals.* London: Printed for Benjamin Fisher and are to be sold at his shop in Aldersgate streete, at the signe of the Talbot, 1630. Reproduction of the original at Harvard University Library. STC (2nd ed.) / 4500.5. Early English Books Online.

Champneys, John. *The harvest is at hand, wherin the tares shall be bound, and cast into the fyre and brent.* London: By Humfrey Powell, dwellyng aboue Holvurne Conduit, 1548. Reproduction of the original at the British Library. STC (2nd ed.) / 4956. Early English Books Online.

Charles I. *Instructions directed from the Kings Most Excellent Maiestie vnto all the Bishops of this Kingdome and fit to be put in execution, agreeable to the necessitie of the time.* London: Printed by Bonham Norton and Iohn Bill, Printers to the Kings most Excellent

Maiestie, 1626. Reproduction of the original at the Henry E. Huntington Library. STC (2nd ed.) / 9247; McAlpin, / vol. 1, p. 383. Early English Books Online.

Charles II. *A collection of His Majestie's gracious letters, speeches, messages, and declarations since April 4./14. 1660.* London: Printed by John Bill, Printer to the Kings most excellent Majesty, 1660. At the King's Printing-house in Black-Friers, 1660. Reproduction of the original at the British Library. Wing (2nd ed.) / C2937; Thomason / E.191[1]. Early English Books Online.

—————. *A proclamation . . .* [*"Given at our court at Whitehall, the fifth day of February 1674/5, in the seven and twentieth year of our reign."*]. London: Printed by the assigns of John Bill and Christopher Barker, 1675. Reproduction of the original at the Harvard University Library. Wing / C3598A. Early English Books Online.

—————. *A proclamation of grace, for the inlargement of prisoners called Quakers.* London: Printed by the assigns of John Bill and Christopher Barker, 1661. Reproduction of the original at the University of Illinois, Urbana-Champaign. Wing / C3523; Steele / 3301. Early English Books Online.

—————. *A proclamation prohibiting the seizing of any persons, or searching houses without warrant, except in time of actual insurrections.* London: Printed by John Bill, printer to the King's Most Excellent Majesty, 1661. Reproduction of the original at the Henry E. Huntington Library. Wing (2nd ed.) / C3553. Early English Books Online.

Church of England. Convocation. *Articles whereupon it was agreed by the archbishoppes and bishoppes of both prouinces and the whole cleargie, in the conuocation holden at London in the yere of our Lorde God. 1562. according to the computation of the Churche of Englande for the auoiding of the diuersities of opinions, and for the stablishyng of consent touching true religion.* London: In Poules Churchyard, by Richarde Iugge and Iohn Cawood, printers to the Queenes Maiestie, 1571. Reproduction of the original at the British Library. STC (2nd ed.) / 10039.3. Early English Books Online.

Clarendon, Edward Hyde, Earl of. *Second thoughts, or, The case of a limited toleration, stated according to the present exigence of affairs in church and state.* [London]: n.p., 1660. Reproduction of the original at the Henry E. Huntington Library. Wing / C4425. Early English Books Online.

Clarke, John. *Ill newes from New-England, or, A nar[r]ative of New-Englands persecution wherin is declared that while old England is becoming new, New-England is become old . . .* London: Henry Hills, 1652. Reproduction of the original at the Henry E. Huntington Library. Wing / C4471. Early English Books Online.

Cobbet, Thomas. *The civil magistrates povver in matters of religion modestly debated . . .* London: Printed by W. Wilson for Philemon Stephens at the Gilded Lion in Paul's Churchyard., 1653. Reproduction of the original at the British Library. Wing (2nd ed., 1994) / C4776; Wing (2nd ed., 1994) / B4541; Thomason / E.687[2]; Thomason / E.687[3]. Early English Books Online.

Cockerham, Henry. *A table alphabeticall conteyning and teaching the true writing, and vnderstanding of hard vsuall English wordes, borrowed from the Hebrew, Greeke, Latine, or French, &c. With the interpretation thereof by plaine English words, gathered for the benefit & helpe of ladies, gentlewomen, or any other vnskilfull persons. Whereby they may the more easilie and better vnderstand many hard English wordes, vvhich they shall heare or read in scriptures, sermons, or elswhere, and also be made able to vse the same aptly themselues.* London: Printed by I. R[oberts] for Edmund Weauer, & are to be sold at his shop at the great North dore of Paules Church, 1604. Reproduction of the original at the Bodleian Library. STC (2nd ed.) / 4884. Early English Books Online.

Cole, Thomas. *A godly and frutefull sermon, made at Maydestone in the county of Kent the fyrst sonday in Lent, in the presence of the most reuerend father in God Thomas archbishop of Canterbury. &c. / by M. Thomas Cole scholemayster there, againste dyuers erronious opinions of the Anabaptistes and others.* London: [by Reginalde Wolfe], 1553. Reproduction of the original at Folger Shakespeare Library, 1553. STC (2nd ed.) / 5539. Early English Books Online.

College of New Jersey. *Laws of the College of New-Jersey reviewed, amended and finally adopted, by the Board of Trustees, in April 1794.* . . . Trenton, N. J.: Isaac Collins, 1794. Reproduction of the original, Evans Early American Imprints, no. 27392.

A Confession of Faith Of seven Congregations or Churches of Christ in London, which are commonly (but unjustly) called Anabaptists. Published for the vindication of the truth, and information of the ignorant; likewise for the taking off of those aspersions which are frequently both in pulpit and print unjustly cast upon them. The second impression corrected and enlarged. . . . London: Printed by Matth. Simmons, and are to be sold by John Hancock in Popes-head Alley, 1646. Reproduction of the original at the British Library. Wing (2nd ed., 1994) / C5780; Thomason / E.319[13]. Early English Books Online.

A Confession of Faith Put forth by the Elders and Brethren Of many Congregations of Christians (baptized upon Profession of their Faith) in London and the Country. London: Printed for Benjamin Harris and are to be sold at his shop, 1677. Reproduction of the original at Henry E. Huntington Library. Wing / C5794A. Early English Books Online.

Cotton, John. *The bloudy tenent, washed, and made white in the bloud of the Lambe: being discussed and discharged of bloud-guiltinesse by just defence. Wherein the great questions of this present time are handled, viz. how farre liberty of conscience ought to be given to those that truly feare God? And how farre restrained to turbulent and pestilent persons, that not onely raze the foundation of godlinesse, but disturb the civill peace where they live? Also how farre the magistrate may proceed in the duties of the first table? And that all magistrates ought to study the word and will of God, that they may frame their government according to it.* . . . London: Printed by Matthew Symmons for Hannah Allen, at the Crowne in Popes-Head-Alley, 1647. Reproduction of the original at the British Library. Wing (2nd ed., 1994) / C6409; Thomason / E.387[7]. Early English Books Online.

———. *The controversie concerning liberty of conscience in matters of religion* . . . London: Printed by Robert Austin, for Thomas Banks, and are to be sold at Mrs. Breaches shop in Westminster-Hall, 1649. Reproduction of the original at the British Library. Wing (2nd ed., 1994) / C6421; Thomason / E.578[8]. Early English Books Online.

Cranmer, Thomas. *Certayne sermons appoynted by the kinges Majestie, to be declared and reade, by al persons, vicars, or curates, euery Sonday and holy daye in theyr churches where they haue cure.* London: In Fletestrete at the signe of the Sunne, by Edwarde whitchurche, 1549. Reproduction of the original at the Bodleian Library. STC (2nd ed.) / 13644. Early English Books Online.

———. *The judgment of Archbishop Cranmer concerning the peoples right to, and discreet use of the H. Scriptures.* London: Printed for John Taylor, at the Ship in St. Paul's

Church-Yard, 1689. Reproduction of the original at Cambridge University Library. Wing / C6827; Arber's Term cat. / II 244. Early English Books Online.

Cromwell, Oliver. *A catalogue and collection of all those ordinances, proclamations, declarations, &c. which have been printed and published since the government was established in His Highness the Lord Protector (viz.) from Decem. 16, 1653 unto Septemb. 3, 1654* . . . London: Printed by William Du-Gard and Henry Hills . . ., 1654. Reproduction of the original at the Bodleian Library. Wing (2nd ed., 1994) / C7045. Early English Books Online.

―――. *A declaration concerning the government of the three nations of [brace] England, Scotland, and Ireland, by His Highness the Lord Protector Cromwel* . . . London: R. Wood, 1653. Reproduction of the original at the British Library. Wing (2nd ed., 1994) / C7057; Thomason / E.725[2]. Early English Books Online.

―――. *[Friday, April 22. 1653.] The declaration of the Lord Generall, and his Councell of Officers, shewing the grounds and reasons for the dissolution of the Parliament, April 20. 1653.* [n.p.: n.p.], 1653. Reproduction of the original at the British Library. Wing (2nd ed.) / D703; Thomason / E.693[3]. Early English Books Online.

―――. *A proclamation prohibiting the disturbing of ministers and other Christians in their assemblies and meetings.* London: Printed by Henry Hills and John Field, Printers to His Highness, 1655. Reproduction of the original at the British Library. Wing (2nd ed., 1994) / C7163; Steele, I, 3045. /; Thomason / 69.f.19[68]. Early English Books Online.

―――. *[His Highness'] speech to the Parliament in the Painted Chamber at their dissolution, upon Monday the 22d. of Ianuary 1654.* [Dublin]: Reprinted at Dublin, by William Bladen, 1654. Reproduction of the original at Dr. Williams' Library. Wing (2nd ed.) / C7174. Early English Books Online.

―――. *[His Highnesse the Lord Protector's] two speeches to the Parliament in the Painted Chamber the one on Monday the 4. of September; the other on Tuesday the 12. of September, 1654.* [Leith]: Printed at London, and reprinted at Leith, 1654. Reproduction of the original at the William Andrews Clark Memorial Library. Early English Books Online.

[Crook, John.] *The Cry of the innocent for justice* . . . 1662. Reproduction of the original at the Huntington Library. Wing / C7200. Early English Books Online.

Danforth, Samuel. *A brief recognition of New-Englands errand into the wilderness made in the audience of the General Assembly of the Massachusetts Colony at Boston in N.E. on the 11th of the third moneth, 1670, being the day of election there.* Cambridge, Mass.: Printed by S.G. and M.J., 1671. Reproduction of the original at the Huntington Library. Wing / D175. Early English Books Online.

Davies, Samuel. *The curse of cowardice. A sermon preached to the militia of Hanover county in Virginia at a general muster, May 8, 1758. With a view to raise a company, for Captain Samuel Meredith.* Woodbridge, N. J.: James Parker, 1759. Reproduction of the original, Evans Early American Imprints, 1st series, no. 8333.

―――. *Religion and patriotism the constituents of a good soldier. A sermon preached to Captain Overton's Independent Company of Volunteers, raised in Hanover County, Virginia, August 17, 1755.* Philadelphia: James Chattin, 1755. Reproduction of the original, Evans Early American Imprints, 1st series, no. 7403.

―――. *Sermons on important subjects, by the late Reverend and pious Samuel Davies.* . . . Edited by Samuel Finley and Thomas Gibbons. New York: T. Allen, 1792. Reproduction of the original, Evans Early American Imprints, 1st series, no. 24248.

————. *The state of religion among the Protestant dissenters in Virginia; in a letter to the Rev. Mr. Joseph Bellamy, of Bethlem, in New-England.* Boston: Printed and sold by S. Kneeland, in Queen-Street, opposite the prison, 1751. Reproduction of the original, Evans Early American Imprints, 1st series, no. 6657.

A declaration of the faith and order owned and practised in the Congregational Churches in England; agreed upon and consented unto by their elders and messengers in their meeting at the Savoy, Octob. 12. 1658. London: printed for D.L. and are to be sold in Paul's Church-yard, Fleet-Street, and Westminster-Hall, 1659. Reproduction of the original at the British Library. Wing (2nd ed.) / N1488; Thomason / E.968[4]. Early English Books Online.

Dell, William. *The building and glory of the truely Christian and spiritual church. Represented in an exposition on Isai. 54, from vers. 11. to the 17. Preached to His Excellency Sir Tho. Fairfax and the general officers of the army, with divers other officers, and souldiers, and people, at Marston, being the head-quarter at the leaguer before Oxford, June. 7. 1646.* London: Printed for G. Calvert, at the Black Spread-Eagle at the West-end of Pauls, 1646. Reproduction of the original at the British Library. Wing (2nd ed., 1994) / D918; Thomason / E.343[5]; Madan 1894. /. Early English Books Online.

————. *Right reformation: or, The reformation of the church of the New Testament, represented in Gospell-light. In a sermon preached to the Honourable House of Commons, on Wednesday, November 25. 1646. . . .* London: Printed by R. White, for Giles Calvert, at the Black-spred-Eagle, near the West end of Pauls, 1646. Reproduction of the original at the British Library. Wing (2nd ed., 1994) / D927; Thomason / E.363[2]. Early English Books Online.

————. *Vniformity examined, whether it may be found in the gospel, or, in the practice of the churches of Christ.* London: Printed by Matthew Simmons for Henry Overton in Popes-head Alley, 1646. Reproduction of the original at the British Library. Wing (2nd ed.) / D936; Thomason / E.322[12]. Early English Books Online.

D'Ewes, Simonds. *The primitive practise for preserving truth. Or An historicall narration, shewing what course the primitive church anciently, and the best reformed churches since have taken to suppresse heresie and schisme. And occasionally also by way of opposition discovering the papall and prelaticall courses to destroy and roote out the same truth; and the judgements of God which have ensued upon persecuting princes and prelates.* London: Printed by M.S. for Henry Overton, and are to be sold at his shop in Popes-head Alley, 1645. Reproduction of the original at the British Library. Wing (2nd ed.) / D1251; Thomason / E.290[9]. Early English Books Online.

Dickinson, Jonathan. *A sermon, preached at the opening of the synod at Philadelphia, September 19, 1722. Whererein [sic] is considered the character of the man of God, and his furniture for the exercise both of doctrine and discipline, with the true boundaries of the churches power.* Boston: Printed by T. Fleet, for S. Gerrish, at his shop in Corn-hill., 1723. Reproduction of the original, Evans Early American Imprints, 1st series, no. 2428.

Dillingham, John, ed. *The moderate intelligencer impartially communicating martiall affaires to the kingdom of England.* London: Printed by R.W., 1645–1649. Reproduction of the original at the British Library. Thomason / 48:E.294[16]. Early English Books Online.

Edwards, Morgan. *Materials toward a history of Baptists in the provinces of Maryland, Virginia, North Carolina, South Carolina, and Georgia, 1772.* Microfilm of original manuscript housed in the Baptist Historical Collection of the Furman University Library.

Edwards, Thomas. *Gangraena, or, A catalogue and discovery of many of the errours, heresies, blasphemies and pernicious practices of the sectaries of this time, vented and acted in England in these four last years . . .* London: Printed for Ralph Smith, 1646. Reproduction of the original at the British Library. Wing / E229. Early English Books Online.

Elizabeth I. *Iniunctions geuen by the Quenes Maiestie.* London: In Powles Church yarde by Rychard Iugge and Iohn Cawood, printers to the Quenes Maiestie, 1559. Reproduction of the original at the British Library. STC (2nd ed.) / 10099.5. Early English Books Online.

England. Parliament. *An act against several atheistical, blasphemous and execrable opinions, derogatory to the honor of God, and destructive to humane society. Die Veneris, 9 Augusti,, [sic] 1650. Ordered by the Parliament, that this act be forthwith printed and published. . . .* London: Printed by Edward Husband and John Field, Printers to the Parliament of England, 1650. Reproduction of the original at the British Library. Thomason / E.1061[14]. Early English Books Online.

———. *An ordinance of the Lords and Commons assembled in Parliament after advice had with the assembly of divines for the ordination of ministers pro tempore according to the directory for ordination and rules for examination therein expressed.* London: Printed for Ralph Smith. Reproduction of the original in the Thomason Collection, British Library. Wing / E1801. Early English Books Online.

———. *An order of the Lords and Commons assembled in Parliament. For the regulating of printing, and for suppressing the great late abuses and frequent disorders in printing many false, scandalous, seditious, libellous and unlicensed pamphlets, to the great defamation of religion and government. . . .* London: Printed for I. Wright in the Old-baily, 1643. Reproduction of the original at the British Library. Wing (2nd ed.) / E1711; Thomason / E.106[15]. Early English Books Online.

———. *An ordinance of the Lords and Commons assembled in Parliament, for the punishing of blasphemies and heresies : with the severall penalties therein expressed. Die Martis, 2 Maii 1648.* London: for John Wright at the Kings Head in the old Bayley, 1648. Reproduction of the original at the British Library. Wing (2nd ed., 1994) / E2006; Thomason / E.437[29]. Early English Books Online.

———. *Articles of Christian religion, approved and passed by both houses of Parliament, after advice had with the Assembly of Divines by authority of Parliament sitting at Westminster.* London: Printed for Edward Husband, Printer to the Honorable House of Commons, and are to be sold at his shop at the sign of the golden Dragon in Fleetstreet, near the Inner-Temple, 1648. Reproduction of the original at the British Library. Wing (2nd ed., 1994) / E1233A; Thomason / E.449[4]. Early English Books Online.

Falkland, Lucius Cary. *A speech made to the House of Commons concerning episcopacy.* London: Printed for Thomas Walkely, 1641. Reproduction of the original at the British Library. Wing (2nd ed.) / F324; Thomason / E.196[36]. Early English Books Online.

Fenner, Dudley. *A defence of the godlie ministers, against the slaunders of D. Bridges, contayned in his ansvvere to the preface before the discourse of ecclesiasticall gouernement with a declaration of the bishops proceeding against them. Wherein chieflie, 1 The lawfull authori-*

tie of her Maiestie is defended by the Scriptures, her lawes, and authorised interpretation of them, to be the same which we haue affirmed, against his cauilles and slaunders to the contrarie. . . . [Middelburg: Richard Schilders], 1587. Reproduction of the original at the Henry E. Huntington Library. STC (2nd ed.) / 10771. Early English Books Online.

For the King and both Houses of Parliament being a brief, plain, and true relation of some of the late sad sufferings of the people of God called Quakers for worshipping God and exercising a good conscience towards God and man . . . [London?]: n.p., 1663. Reproduction of the original at the Huntington Library. Wing / F1431. Early English Books Online.

The fourth humble address of several societies of baptized believers (commonly called Anabaptists) in the county of Lincoln . . . [London: n.p.], 1663. Reproduction of the original at the Universität Göttingen Bibliothek. Wing (2nd ed.) / F1687A. Early English Books Online.

Foxe, John. *Actes and monuments of matters most speciall and memorable, happening in the Church with an universall historie of the same: wherein is set forth at large the whole race and course of the Church from the primitive age to the later times . . . with the bloody times . . . and great persecutions against the true martyrs of Christ.* London: Printed for the Company of Stationers, 1610. Reproduction of the original at Henry E. Huntington Library. STC (2nd ed.) / 11227. Early English Books Online.

———. *Actes and monuments of these latter and perillous dayes touching matters of the Church, wherein ar comprehended and decribed the great persecutions [and] horrible troubles, that haue bene wrought and practised by the Romishe prelates, speciallye in this realme of England and Scotlande, from the yeare of our Lorde a thousande, vnto the tyme nowe present.* . . . London: By John Day, dwelling over Aldersgate, 1563. Reproduction of the original at Henry E. Huntington Library. STC (2nd ed.) / 11222. Early English Books Online.

———. *The first volume of the ecclesiasticall history contaynyng the actes and monumentes of thynges passed in euery kynges tyme in this realme . . . with a full discourse of such persecutions, horrible troubles, the sufferyng of martyrs, and other thinges incident . . . from the primitiue tyme till the reigne of K. Henry VIII.* London: Iohn Daye, dwellyng ouer Aldersgate [these bookes are to be sold at hys shop vnder the gate], 1570. Reproduction of the original at Harvard University Library. STC (2nd ed.) / 11223. Early English Books Online.

———, ed. *The vvhole workes of W. Tyndall, Iohn Frith, and Doct. Barnes, three worthy martyrs, and principall teachers of this Churche of England collected and compiled in one tome togither, beyng before scattered, [and] now in print here exhibited to the Church. To the prayse of God, and profite of all good Christian readers.* London: Printed by Iohn Daye, and are to be sold at his shop vnder Aldersgate, 1573.

Furneaux, Philip. *Letters to the Honourable Mr. Justice Blackstone, concerning his exposition of the Act of Toleration, and Some positions relative to religious liberty in his celebrated Commentaries on the Laws of England. In An Interesting appendix to Sir William Blackstone's Commentaries on the laws of England* . . . Philadelphia: Bell, 1772. Reproduction of the original, Evans Early American Imprints, 1st series, no. 12328.

Gillespie, George. *A sermon preached before the Right Honourable the House of Lords, in the Abbey Church at Westminster, upon the 27th. of August. 1645. Being the day appointed for solemne and publique humiliation.* . . . London: Printed for   Robert Bostock dwelling in

Pauls Church-yard at the sign of the Kingshead, 1645. Reproduction of the original at the British Library. Wing (2nd ed.) / G758; Thomason / E.298[12]. Early English Books Online.

————. *Wholesome severity reconciled with Christian liberty. Or, the true resolution of a present controversie concerning liberty of conscience. Here you have the question stated, the middle way betwixt popish tyrannie and schismatizing liberty approved, and also confirmed from Scripture, and the testimonies of divines, yea of whole churches . . . And in conclusion a paraenetick to the five apologists for choosing accommodation rather then toleration.* London: Printed for Christopher Meredith, and are to be sold at the Signe of the Crane in Pauls Churchyard, 1645. Reproduction of the original at the British Library. Wing (2nd ed.) / G765; JCB Lib. cat., pre-1675 II 331. /; Thomason / E.24[5]. Early English Books Online.

Goodwin, John. *M. S. to A. S. with a plea for libertie of conscience in a church way, against the cavils of A. S. and observations on his considerations, and annotations upon the apologeticall narration, humbly submitted to the judgements of all rationall, and moderate men in the world.* . . . London: Printed by F. N. for H. Overton, 1644. Reproduction of the original at the British Library. Wing (2nd ed.) / S116A; Thomason / E.45[3]. Early English Books Online.

————. *Independencie Gods veritie: or, The necessitie of toleration. Unto which is added the chief principles of the government of independent churches.* London: Printed for William Ley, 1647. Reproduction of the original at the British Library. Wing (2nd ed.) / G1173; Thomason / E.410[24]. Early English Books Online.

————. *Theomachia; or The grand imprudence of men running the hazard of fighting against God, in suppressing any way, doctrine, or practice, concerning which they know not certainly whether it be from God or no. Being the substance of two sermons, preached in Colemanstreet, upon occasion of the late disaster sustain'd in the west.* . . . London: Printed for Henry Overton, and are to be sold at his shop entering into Pope's-head-Alley out of Lumbard-street, 1644. Reproduction of the original at the British Library. Wing (2nd ed.) / G1206; Thomason / E.12[1]. Early English Books Online.

————. *Thirty queries, modestly propounded in order to a discovery of the truth, and mind of God, in that question, or case of conscience; whether the civil magistrate stands bound by way of duty to interpose his power or authority in matters of religion, or worship of God.* London: Printed by J. M. for Henry Cripps and Lodowick Lloyd, 1653. Reproduction of the original at the British Library. Wing (2nd ed.) / G1208; Thomason / E.689[4]. Early English Books Online.

Goodwin, Thomas, Philip Nye, William Bridge, Jeremiah Burroughes, and Sidrach Simpson. *An apologeticall narration, humbly submitted to the Honourable Houses of Parliament.* London: Printed for Robert Dawlman, 1643. Reproduction of the original at the British Library. Wing (2nd ed.) / G1225; Thomason / E.80[7]. Early English Books Online.

Gray, Robert. *A good speed to Virginia.* London: Printed by Felix Kyngston for VVilliam Welbie, and are to be sold at his shop at the signe of the Greyhound in Pauls Churchyard, 1609. Reproduction of the original at the Henry E. Huntington Library. STC (2nd ed.) / 12204. Early English Books Online.

[Greene, Robert.] *Virginia's cure, or, An advisive narrative concerning Virginia discovering the true ground of that churches unhappiness, and the only true remedy* . . . London: Printed by W. Godbid for Henry Brome, 1662. Reproduction of the original at the Henry E. Huntington Library. Wing / G1624; Sabin / 26274. Early English Books Online.

Halifax, George Savile, Marquis of. *A letter from a clergy-man in the city, to his friend in the country, containing his reasons for not reading the declaration.* [London?]: n.p., 1688. Reproduction of the original at the Henry E. Huntington Library. Wing / H308; McAlpin Coll. / IV 305. Early English Books Online.

Hammond, John. *Leah and Rachel, or, the two fruitfull sisters Virginia and Mary-land: their present condition, impartially stated and related. VVith a removall of such imputations as are scandalously cast on those countries, whereby many deceived souls, chose rather to beg, steal, rot in prison, and come to shamefull deaths, then to better their being by going thither, wherein is plenty of all things necessary for humane subsistance.* London: Printed by T. Mabb, and are to be sold by Nich. Bourn, neer the Royal Exchange, 1656. Reproduction of the original at the British Library. Wing (2nd ed.) / H620; Thomason / E.865[6]. Early English Books Online.

Hart[e], Henry. *A consultorie for all Christians Most godly and ernestly warnyng al people, to beware least they beare the name of christians in vayne.* Worcester: John Oswen, 1549. Reproduction of the original at Cambridge University Library. STC (2nd ed.) / 12564. Early English Books Online.

———. *A godlie exhortation to all suche as professe the Gospell, wherein they are by the swete promises thereof prouoked [and] styrred vp to folowe the same in liuing, and by the terrible threates, feared from the contrary.* London: By Iohn Day, and William Seres, dwellyng in Sepulchres parish, at the signe of the Resurrection, a litle aboue Holbourne conduite, 1549. Reproduction of the original at Emmanuel College (University of Cambridge) Library. STC (2nd ed.) / 12887.3. Early English Books Online.

Heaman, Roger. *An additional brief narrative of a late bloody design against the Protestants in Ann Arundel county, and Severn, in Maryland in the country of Virginia. As also of the extraordinary deliverance of those poor oppressed people.* London: Printed for Livewell Chapman at the Crown in Popes-Head-Alley, 1655. Reproduction of the original at the British Library. Wing (2nd ed.) / H1305; Thomason / E.850[5]. Early English Books Online.

Helwys, Thomas. *A Short Declaration of the mistery of iniquity.* [Amsterdam?]: n.p., 1612. Reproduction of the original at Bodleian Library. STC (2nd ed.) / 13056. Early English Books Online.

[Helwys, Thomas, and John Murton.] *Obiections: answered by way of dialogue wherein is proved by the Law of God: by the law of our land: and by his Maties many testimonies that no man ought to be persecuted for his religion, so he testifie his allegeance by the Oath, appointed by law.* [The Netherlands?]: n.p., 1615. Reproduction of the original at Bodleian Library. STC (2nd ed.) / 13054. Early English Books Online.

———. *Persecution for religion judg'd and condemned in a discourse between an anti-christian and a Christian: proving by the law of God and of the land, and by King James his many testimonies, that no man ought to be persecuted for his religion, so he testifie his allegiance by the oath appointed by law. . . .* Printed in the years 1615 and 1620 and now reprinted for the establishing some and convincing others. [London]: n.p., 1662. Reproduction of the original at Harvard University Library. Wing / H1413A. Early English Books Online.

The history of the life, victorious reign, and death of K. Henry VIII . . . London: Printed and are to be sold by H. Rodes, next door to the . . . Tavern, near Bride Lane, in Fleetstreet, 1682. Reproduction of the original at the British Library. Wing (2nd ed.) / H2168A. Early English Books Online.

The Horrid Popish Plot happily discover'd, or, The English Protestants remembrancer a poem on the never-to-be-forgotten powder-treason, and late burning of several cart-loads of popish books at the Royal Exchange. London: R. G., 1678. Reproduction of the original at the Harvard University Library. Wing / H2866. Early English Books Online.

How, Samuel. The sufficiency of the spirits teaching without humane learning a treatise tending to prove humane learning to be no help to the spirituall understanding of the word of God. . . . 1639. [London]: Newly printed, and are to be sold by William Larnar, 1655. Reproduction of the original at the British Library. Wing / H2952. Early English Books Online.

[To the supreame authoritie the Parliament of the Common-vvealth of England.] The humble petition of the officers of the army. . . . London: Printed by M. Simmons for L. Chapman in Popes-head-Alley, 1562. Reproduction of the original at the British Library. Wing (2nd ed.) / T1748B; Thomason / 669.f.16[62]; Steele I, 2972. /. Early English Books Online.

An Interesting appendix to Sir William Blackstone's Commentaries on the laws of England. Containing, I. Priestley's Remarks on some paragraphs in the fourth volume of Blackstone's Commentaries, relating to the dissenters. II. Blackstone's Reply to Priestley's Remarks. III. Priestley's Answer to Blackstone's Reply. IV. The case of the late election of the county of Middlesex considered on the principles of the Constitution and the authorities of law. V. Furneaux's Letters to the Hon. Mr. Justice Blackstone concerning his Exposition of the Act of Toleration, and some positions relative to religious liberty, in his celebrated Commentaries on the laws of England. VI. Authentic copies of the argument of the late Hon. Mr. Justice Foster in the Court of Judges Delegates, and of the speech of the Right Hon. Lord Mansfield in the House of Lords, in the cause between the city of London and dissenters. Philadelphia: Printed for the subscribers, by Robert Bell, at the late Union-Library, in Third-Street, 1773. Reproduction of the original, Evans Early American Imprints, 1st series, no. 12684.

James I. A proclamation for the authorizing and vniformitie of the Booke of Common Prayer to be vsed throughout the realme. London: Robert Barker, printer to the Kings most excellent Maiestie, 1603. Reproduction of the original at the Harvard University Library. STC (2nd ed.) / 8344. Early English Books Online.

———. The vvorkes of the most high and mightie prince, Iames by the grace of God, King of Great Britaine, France and Ireland, defender of the faith, &c. London: Printed by Robert Barker and Iohn Bill, printers to the Kings most excellent Maiestie, 1616. Reproduction of the original at the British Library. STC (2nd ed.) / 14344. Early English Books Online.

Johnson, Edward. A history of New-England. From the English planting in the yeere 1628. untill the yeere 1652. Declaring the form of their government, civill, military, and ecclesiastique. Their wars with the indians, their troubles with the Gortonists, and other heretiques. Their manner of gathering of churches, the commodities of the country, and description of the principall towns and havens. . . . London: printed for Nath: Brooke at the Angel in

Corn-hill, 1653. Reproduction of the original at the British Library. Wing (2nd ed.) / J771; Thomason / E.721[4]. Early English Books Online.

The iudgement of the synode holden at Dort, concerning the fiue Articles as also their sentence touching Conradus Vorstius. London: Iohn Bill, 1619. Reproduction of the original at the Folger Shakespeare Library. STC (2nd ed.) / 7066. Early English Books Online.

[Kiffen, William, et al.] *The humble apology of some commonly called Anabaptists, in behalf of themselves and others of the same judgement with them: with their protestation against the late wicked and most horrid treasonable insurrection and rebellion acted in the city of London* . . . London: printed by Henry Hills, and are to be sold by Francis Smith, at the sign of the Elephant and Castle without Temple-Bar, 1660. Reproduction of the original at the British Library. Wing (2nd ed.) / H3404; Thomason / E.1057[1]. Early English Books Online.

Knox, John. *An answer to a great number of blasphemous cauillations written by an Anabaptist, and aduersarie to Gods eternal predestination. And confuted by Iohn Knox, minister of Gods worde in Scotland. Wherein the author so discouereth the craft and falshode of that sect, that the godly knowing that error, may be confirmed in the trueth by the euident Worde of God.* [Geneva]: Printed by Iohn Crespin, 1560. Reproduction of the original at the Henry E. Huntington Library. STC (2nd ed.) / 15060. Early English Books Online.

———. *The copie of a letter, sent to the ladye Mary dowagire, Regent of Scotland, by Iohn Knox in the yeare. 1556. Here is also a notable sermon, made by the sayde Iohn Knox, wherin is euydentlye proued that the masse is and alwayes hath ben abhominable before God and idolatrye.* [Wesel?: Printed by H. Singleton?], 1556. Reproduction of the original at the Cambridge University Library. STC (2nd ed.) / 15066. Early English Books Online.

———. *The first blast of the trumpet against the monstruous regiment of women.* [Geneva: J. Poullain and A. Rebul], 1558. Reproduction of the original at the Henry E. Huntington Library. STC (2nd ed.) / 15070. Early English Books Online.

———. *The historie of the reformation of the Church of Scotland containing five books: together with some treatises conducing to the history.* Edited by David Buchanan. London: Printed by John Raworth for George Thomason and Octavian Pullen, 1644. Reproduction of the original at the Henry E. Huntington Library. Wing / K738. Early English Books Online.

Latimer, Hugh. *Frutefull sermons preached by the tight [sic] reuerend father, and constant martyr of Iesus Christ M. Hugh Latymer, newly imprinted: with others, not heretofore set forth in print, to the edifying of all which will dispose them selues to the readyng of the same.* . . . London: by John Day, dwelling over Aldersgate, 1575. Reproduction of the original at the Henry E. Huntington Library. STC (2nd ed.) / 15278. Early English Books Online.

Laud, William. *A relation of the conference betweene William Lawd, then, Lrd. Bishop of St. Davids; now, Lord Arch-Bishop of Canterbury: and Mr. Fisher the Jesuite by the command of King James of ever blessed memorie. With an answer to such exceptions as A. C. takes against it.* . . . London: Printed by Richard Badger, printer to the Prince his Highnes, 1639. Reproduction of the original at the British Library. STC (2nd ed.) / 15298. Early English Books Online.

———. *A speech delivered in the Starre-Chamber, on VVednesday, the XIVth of Iune, MDCXXXVII. at the censure of Iohn Bastwick, Henry Burton, and VVilliam Prinn;*

concerning pretended innovations in the Church. Reproduction of the original at the New York Public Library. STC (2nd ed.) / 15308. Early English Books Online.

Lechford, Thomas. *Plain dealing, or, Nevves from New-England a short view of New-Englands present government, both ecclesiasticall and civil, compared with the anciently-received and established government of England in some materiall points : fit for the gravest consideratin in these times.* London: Printed by W. E. and I. G. for Nath. Butter . . . , 1642. Reproduction of the original at the British Library. Wing / L810. Early English Books Online.

Leighton, Alexander. *An appeal to the Parliament; or Sions plea against the prelacie The summe wheroff is delivered in a decade of positions. In the handling whereoff, the Lord Bishops, and their appurtenances are manifestlie proved, both by divine and humane lawes, to be intruders vpon the priviledges of Christ, of the King, and of the common-weal: and therefore vpon good evidence given, she hartelie desireth a iudgement and execution.* [Amsterdam]: [by the successors of Giles Thorp], 1629. Reproduction of the original at the British Library. STC (2nd ed.) / 15428.5. Early English Books Online.

Leland, John. *The rights of conscience inalienable, and therefore religious opinions not cognizable by law: or The high-flying church-man, stript of his legal robe, appears a Yaho.* 2nd ed. Richmond, Va.: T. Nicolson, 1793. Reproduction of the original, Evans Early American Imprints, 1st series, no. 25717.

―――. *The Virginia Chronicle.* [Norfolk, Va.: Prentis and Baxter, 1789.] Reproduction of the original, Evans Early American Imprints, 1st series, no. 21920.

―――. *The Virginia chronicle: with judicious and critical remarks, under XXIV heads.* Fredericksburg, [Va.]: T. Green, 1790. Reproduction of the original, Evans Early American Imprints, 1st series, no. 22617.

A letter of the ministers of the city of London, presented the first of Ian. 1645. to the reverend Assembly of Divines sitting at Westminster by authority of Parliament, against toleration. London: Printed for Samuel Gellibrand at the Brasen Serpent in Pauls Church-yard, 1646. Reproduction of the original at the British Library. Wing (2nd ed.) / L1578; Thomason / E.314[8]. Early English Books Online.

Lilburne, John, et al. *Englands new chains discovered; or The serious apprehensions of a part of the people, in behalf of the Commonwealth; (being presenters, promoters, and approvers of the large petition of September 11. 1648.) Presented to the supreme authority of England, the representers of the people in Parliament assembled.* . . . [London: n.p.], 1649. Reproduction of the original at the British Library. Thomason / 84:E.545[27]. Early English Books Online.

―――. *A plea for common-right and freedom. To His Excellency, the Lord General Fairfax, and the commission-officers of the armie. Or, the serious addresses, and earnest desires of their faithful friends, inhabiting in the cities of London and Westminster, the borough of Southvvark, Hamblets, and places adjacent: promoters and presenters of the late large-petition of the eleventh of September, MDCXLVIII. As it was presented to his Excellency, Decemb. 28. 1648.* London: Printed by Ja. and Jo. Moxon, for Will. Larnar, at the signe of the Black-Moor neer Bishops-gate, 1648. Reproduction of the original at the British Library. Wing (2nd ed.) / L2159; Thomason / E.536[22]. Early English Books Online.

Lilburne, John, William Walwyn, Thomas Prince, and Richard Overton. *An agreement of the free people of England. Tendered as a peace-offering to this distressed nation. By Lieutenant Colonel Iohn Lilburne, Master William Walwyn, Master Thomas Prince, and*

Master Richard Overton, prisoners in the Tower of London, May the 1. 1649. London: Printed for Gyles Calvert at the black spread-Eagle at the West end of Pauls, 1649. Reproduction of the original at the British Library. Wing (2nd ed.) / L2079; Thomason / E.552[23] and E.571[10]; Goldsmiths' 1001. /. Early English Books Online.

Locke, John. *The reasonableness of Christianity as delivered in the Scriptures.* London: Printed for Awnsham and John Churchil, 1695. Reproduction of the original at the Henry E. Huntington Library. Wing / L2751; Arber's Term cat. / II 568. Early English Books Online.

――――. *A Second Letter concerning Toleration.* London: Printed for Awnsham and John Churchill, 1690. Reproduction of the original at Bristol Public Library. Wing / L2755. Early English Books Online.

――――. *A Letter concerning Toleration humbly submitted, etc. Translated by William Popple.* London: Printed for Awnsham Churchill, 1689. Reproduction of the original at Bristol Public Library. Wing / L2747; Arber's Term cat. / II 284. Early English Books Online.

Milton, John. *Areopagitica; a speech of Mr. John Milton for the liberty of vnlicens'd printing, to the Parlament of England.* London: n.p., 1644. Reproduction of the original at the British Library. Wing (2nd ed.) / M2092; Thomason / E.18[9]; Pforzheimer / 707; Shawcross, J. Milton / 61. Early English Books Online.

――――. *A treatise of civil power in ecclesiastical causes shewing that it is not lawfull for any power on earth to compell in matters of religion.* London: Printed by Tho. Newcomb, 1659. Reproduction of the original at the Henry E. Huntington Library. Wing / M2185; Grolier. Wither to Prior / 596. Early English Books Online.

Minister of the Church of England. A letter from a clergy-man in the country to the clergy-man in the city, author of a late letter to his friend in the country shewing the insufficiency of his reasons therein contained for not reading the declaration. [London]: Printed by Edw. Jones and published by Randal Taylor, 1688. Reproduction of the original at the Harvard University Library. Wing / L1369A. Early English Books Online.

Montagu[e], Richard. *A gagg for the new Gospell? No: a nevv gagg for an old goose VVho would needes vndertake to stop all Protestants mouths for euer, with 276. places out of their owne English Bibles. Or an ansvvere to a late abridger of controuersies, and belyar of the Protestants doctrine.* London: Printed by Thomas Snodham for Matthew Lownes and William Barret, 1624. Reproduction of the original at the University of Illinois at Urbana-Champaign library. STC (2nd ed.) / 18038. Early English Books Online.

More, Sir Thomas. *The co[n]futacyon of Tyndales answere made by syr Thomas More knyght lorde chau[n]cellour of Englonde.* London: Wyllyam Rastall, 1532. Reproduction of the original at Bodelian Library at Oxford University. STC (2nd ed.) / 18079. Early English Books Online.

Nichols, Josias. *The plea of the innocent wherein is auerred; that the ministers & people falslie termed puritanes, are iniuriouslie slaundered for enemies of troublers of the state. Published for the common good of the Church and common wealth of this realme of England as a countermure against all sycophantising papsts, statising priestes, neutralising atheistes, and satanising scorners of all godlinesse, trueth and honestie. . . . * [London: J. Windet?], 1602. Reproduction of the original at the British Library. STC (2nd ed.) / 18541. Early English Books Online.

Norton, John. *The heart of N-England rent at the blasphemies of the present generation.* . . . [Cambridge, Mass.:] Samuel Green, 1659. Reproduction of the original at the Henry E. Huntington Library. Wing (2nd ed.) / N1318. Early English Books Online.

An Orthodox Creed: or, A Protestant Confession of Faith, being An Essay to Unite, and Confirm all true Protestants in the Fundamental Articles of the Christian Religion against the Errors and Heresies of the Church of Rome. London: n.p., 1679. Reproduction of the original at Cambridge University Library. Wing / O503. Early English Books Online.

Osborne, Francis. *Historical memoires on the reigns of Queen Elizabeth and King James.* London: Printed by J. Grismond, and are to be sold by T. Robinson, 1658. Reproduction of the original at the British Library. Wing / O515; Madan / 2401. Early English Books Online.

—————. *The works of Francis Osborne . . . divine, moral, historical, political in four several tracts.* . . . London: Printed for R. D. and are to be sold by Allen Bancks, 1673. Reproduction of the original at the Cambridge University Library. Wing / O505. Early English Books Online.

[Overton, Richard.] *The araignement of Mr. Persecution presented to the consideration of the House of Commons, and to all the common people of England: wherein he is indicted, arraigned, convicted, and condemned of emnity (sic) against God, and all goodneese, of treasons, rebellion, bloodshed, &c. and sent to the place of execution.* . . . Europe [London]: Printed by Martin Clawe-Clergie, printer to the Reverend Assembly of Divines, for Bartholomew Bang-Preist, 1645. Reproduction of the original at the Henry E. Huntington Library. Wing / O621. Early English Books Online.

Owen, John, et al. *Proposals for the furtherance and propagation of the gospel in this nation. As the same were hubly presented to the Honourable Committee of Parliament by divers ministers of the gospell, and others. As also, some principles of Christian religion, without the beliefe of which, the Scriptures doe plainly and clearly affirme, salvation is not to be obtained. Which were also presented in explanation of one of the said proposals.* London: Printed for R. Ibbitson dwelling in Smith-field neer Hosier Lane, 1652. Reproduction of the original at the British Library. Wing (2nd ed.) / O799; Thomason / E.683[12]. Early English Books Online.

Penn, William. *The great case. Of liberty of conscience once more debated & defended with some brief observations on the late Act, presented to the Kings consideration.* [Dublin]: Printed [by Josiah Windsor], 1670. Reproduction of the original at the Henry E. Huntington Library. Wing (2nd ed.) / P1298B. Early English Books Online.

—————."To the Supreme Authority of England." *The great case of liberty of conscience once more briefly debated & defended ... which may serve the place of a general reply to such late discourses as have oppos'd a toleration.* 1670. Reproduction of the original at the Henry E. Huntington Library. Wing / P1299; Smith, J. Friends' books / II 286. Early English Books Online.

[Poulton?]. *An answer to a letter from a clergyman in the city, to his friend in the country containing his reasons for not reading the declaration. With a reply to an answer to the city-minister's letter from his friend in the country.* London: Printed for J. O., 1688. Reproduction of the original at the British Library. Wing (2nd ed.) / P3039A. Early English Books Online.

Prynne, William. *The grand designs of the papists, in the reign of our late sovereign, Charles the I and now carried on against His Present Majesty, his government, and the Protestant religion.* Reprint, London: Henry Hills, 1678. Reproduction of the original at the Union Theological Seminary Library, New York. Wing / H163. Early English Books Online.

————. *Histrio-mastix The players scourge, or, actors tragaedie, divided into two parts. Wherein it is largely evidenced, by divers arguments, by the concurring authorities and resolutions of sundry texts of Scripture . . . That popular stage-playes . . . are sinfull, heathenish, lewde, ungodly spectacles, and most pernicious corruptions; condemned in all ages, as intolerable mischiefes to churches, to republickes, to the manners, mindes, and soules of men. . . .* London: Printed by E[dward] A[llde, Augustine Mathewes, Thomas Cotes] and W[illiam] I[ones] for Michael Sparke, and are to be sold at the Blue Bible, in Greene Arbour, in little Old Bayly, 1633. Reproduction of the original at the Henry E. Huntington Library. STC (2nd ed.) / 20464a. Early English Books Online.

————. *The sword of Christian magistracy supported: or A full vindication of Christian kings and magistrates authority under the Gospell, to punish idolatry, apostacy, heresie, blasphemy, and obstinate schism, with pecuniary, corporall, and in some cases with banishment, and capitall punishments. . . .* London: Printed by John Macock for John Bellamie, and are to be sold at his shop at the three Golden Lyons in Cornhill, neer the Royall Exchange, 1647. Reproduction of the original at the British Library. Wing (2nd ed.) / P4098; Thomason / E.514[1]. Early English Books Online.

————. *Twelve considerable serious questions touching church government: sadly propounded (out of a reall desire of vnitie, and tranquillity in church and state) to all sober-minded Christians, cordially affecting a speedy setled reformation, and brotherly christian vnion in all our churches and dominions, now miserably wasted with civill vnnaturall wars, and deplorably lacerated with ecclesiasticall dissentions.* London: Printed by F.L. for Michael Sparke, Senior, and are to bee sold at the Blew-Bible in Green-Arbour., 1644. Reproduction of the original at the British Library. Wing (2nd ed.) / P4116; Thomason / E.257[1]. Early English Books Online.

Rhode Island. General Assembly. *An Act for the Establishment of a College, or University, Within this Colony.* Newport, R. I.: n.p., 1764. Reproduction of the original, Evans Early American Imprints, no. 9823.

Richardson, Samuel. *Some briefe considerations on Doctor Featley his book, intituled, The dipper dipt, wherein in some measure is discovered his many great and false accusations of divers persons, commonly called Anabaptists, with an answer to them, and some brief reasons of their practice. . . .* London: [n.p.], 1645. Reproduction of the original at the British Library. Wing (2nd ed.) / R1414; Thomason / E.270[22]. Early English Books Online.

————. *The necessity of toleration in matters of religion, or, Certain questions propounded to the Synod, tending to prove that corporall punishments ought not to be inflicted upon such as hold errors in religion, and that in matters of religion, men ought not to be compelled, but have liberty and freedome.* London: n.p., 1647. Reproduction of the original at the British Library. Wing (2nd ed.) / R1409; Thomason / E.407[18]; Thomason / E.407[19]. Early English Books Online.

————. *Fifty questions propounded to the Assembly, to answer by the Scriptures: whether corporall pnnishments [sic] may be inflicted upon such as hold different opinions in religion.*

London: [n.p.], 1647. Reproduction of the original at the British Library. Wing (2nd ed.) / R1407; Thomason / E.388[11]. Early English Books Online.

Robinson, Henry. *John the Baptist, forerunner of Christ Iesvs, or, A necessity for liberty of conscience as the only meanes under heaven to strengthen children weake in faith, to convince hereticks mis-led in faith, to discover the gospel to all such as yet never heard thereof, and establish peace betweene all states and people throughout the world, according unto which were both our Saviour commission, and the apostles practice for the propagation of it peaceably : as appeares most evidently by sundry scriptures digested into chapters. . . .* [London]: n.p., 1644. Reproduction of the original in the Thomason Collection, British Library. Wing / R1673. Early English Books Online.

———. *Liberty of conscience: or The sole means to obtaine peace and truth. Not onely reconciling His Majesty with His subjects, but all Christian states and princes to one another, with the freest passage for the gospel. Very seasonable and necessary in these distracted times, when most men are weary of war, and cannot finde the way to peace.* [London]: n.p., 1643. Reproduction of the original at the British Library. Wing (2nd ed.) / R1675; Thomason / E.39[1]. Early English Books Online.

Robinson, John. *Of religious communion private, & publique With the silenceing of the clamours raysed by Mr Thomas Helvvisse agaynst our reteyning the baptism receaved in Engl: & administering of Bapt: vnto infants. As also a survey of the confession of fayth published in certayn conclusions by the remaynders of Mr Smithes company.* [Amsterdam?]: n.p., 1614. Reproduction of the original at British Library. STC (2nd ed.) / 21115. Early English Books Online.

Roper, William. *The mirrour of vertue in worldly greatnes. Or The life of Syr Thomas More Knight, sometime Lo. Chancellour of England.* Paris [i.e., Saint-Omer: Printed at the English College Press], 1626. Reproduction of the original at the Harvard University Library. STC (2nd ed.) / 21316. Early English Books Online.

Roulston, Gilbert. *The ranters bible or, Seven several religions by them held and maintained. With the full particulars of their strange sects and societies; their new places of meetings, both in city and countrey; the manner of their life and conversation; their blasphemous opinion of our Lord and Saviour Jesus Christ, and their burning of his blessed word, and sacred Scriptures* . . . London: Printed by J. C. and are to be sold in Cornhil, near the Exchange, and at Temple-Bar, 1650. Reproduction of the original at the British Library. Wing (2nd ed.) / R2006; Thomason / E.619[6]. Early English Books Online.

Rutherford, Samuel. *A free disputation against pretended liberty of conscience tending to resolve doubts moved by Mr. John Goodwin, John Baptist, Dr. Jer. Taylor, the Belgick Arminians, Socinians, and other authors contending for lawlesse liberty, or licentious toleration of sects and heresies.* London: Printed by R. I. for Andrew Crook, and are to be sold at his shop, at the signe of the Green Dragon in St. Pauls Church-yard, 1649. Reproduction of the original at the British Library. Wing (2nd ed.) / R2379; Thomason / E.567[2]. Early English Books Online.

Servetus, Mordecai. *The mystic's plea for universal redemption, as held forth, and preached by Mr. Elhanan Winchester; being an occasional answer to his persecutors, in a number of letters to the Rev. William Rogers, &c.* Philadelphia: Printed [by Benjamin Towne?], 1781. Reproduction of the original, Evans Early American Imprints, 1st series, no. 17439.

A Short relation of some part of the sad sufferings and cruel havock and spoil, inflicted on the persons and estates of the people of God, in scorn called Quakers for meeting together to worship God in spirit and truth since the late act against conventicles . . . [London: n.p.], 1670. Reproduction of the original at the Harvard University Library. Wing / S3619. Early English Books Online.

Smith, John. *The generall historie of Virginia, New-England, and the Summer Isles with the names of the adventurers, planters, and governours from their first beginning. ano: 1584. to this present 1626.* . . . London: Printed by I[ohn] D[awson] and I[ohn] H[aviland] for Michael Sparkes, 1626. Reproduction of the original at the Henry E. Huntington Library. STC (2nd ed.) / 22790b; Sabin 82823. /. Early English Books Online.

Sparke, Michael. *The narrative history of King James, for the first fourteen years in four parts.* . . . London: Printed for Michael Sparke, 1651. Reproduction of the original at the British Library. Wing / S4818. Early English Books Online.

Stationers' Company. *To the High Court of Parliament: the humble remonstrance of the Company of Stationers, London.* [London: n.p.], 1643. Reproduction of the original at the British Library. Wing (2nd ed.) / P425; Thomason / E.247[23]. Early English Books Online.

Strong motives, or Loving and modest advice, vnto the petitioners for presbiterian government. That they endeavour not the compulsion of any in matters of religion, more then they wish others should endeavour to compell them. But with all love, lenitie, meekenesse, patience, & long-suffering to doe unto others, as they desire others should doe unto them. Whereunto is annexed the conclusion of Lieuten. Generall Cromwells letter to the House of Common tending to the same purpose. London: [n.p.], 1645. Reproduction of the original from the British Library. Wing (2nd ed.) / S6016; Thomason / E.304[15]. Early English Books Online.

Strype, John. *Memorials of the Most Reverend Father in God, Thomas Cranmer sometime Lord Archbishop of Canterbury wherein the history of the Church, and the reformation of it, during the primacy of the said archbishop, are greatly illustrated: and many singular matters relating thereunto: now first published in three books: collected chiefly from records, registers, authentick letters, and other original manuscripts.* Printed for Richard Chiswell, at the Rose and Crown in St. Paul's Church-Yard, 1694. Reproduction of the original at the University of Illinois Library. Wing / S6024; Arber's Term. cat. / II 475; McAlpin Coll. / IV 505. Early English Books Online.

Sturgion, John. *A plea for tolleration of opinions and perswasions in matters of religion, differing from the Church of England. Grounded upon good authority of Scripture, and the practice of the primitive times. Shewing the unreasonablenesse of prescribing to other mens faith, and the evil of persecuting differing opinions.* London: Printed by S. Dover, for Francis Smith, at the Elephant and Castle near Temple-Bar, 1661. Reproduction of the original at the British Library. Wing (2nd ed.) / S6093; Thomason / E.1086[3]. Early English Books Online.

Taylor, Jeremy. *Theologia eklektike. A discourse of the liberty of prophesying. Shewing the unreasonablenes of prescribing to other mens faith, and the iniquity of persecuting differing opinions.* London: Printed for R. Royston, at the Angel in Ivie-lane, 1647. Reproduction of the original at the British Library. Wing (2nd ed.) / T400; Thomason / E.395[2]. Early English Books Online.

Thomas, David. *The Virginian Baptist: or A view and defence of the Christian religion, as it is professed by the Baptists of Virginia. In three parts: containing a true and faithful account I[.] Of their principles. II. Of their order as a church. III. Of the principal objections made against them, especially in this colony, with a serious answer to each of them.* Baltimore, Md.: Printed by Enoch Story, living in Gay-Street, 1774. Reproduction of the original, Evans Early American Imprints, 1st series, no. 13651.

Travers, Walter. *A directory of church-government anciently contended for, and as farre as the times would suffer, practised by the first non-conformists in the daies of Queen Elizabeth / found in the study of the most accomplished divine, Mr. Thomas Cartwright, after his decease, and reserved to be published for such times as this.* London: Printed for John Wright, 1644. Reproduction of the original at the British Library. Wing / T2066. Early English Books Online.

A True and faithful relation from the people of God (called) Quakers, in Colchester . . . [London:] Printed for M., 1664. Reproduction of the original at the William Andrews Clark Memorial Library, University of California, Los Angeles. Wing (2nd ed.) / T2475. Early English Books Online.

Tyndale, William, trans. *The new Testament as it was written, and caused to be written, by them which herde yt Whom also oure Saueoure Christ Iesus commaunded that they shulde preach it vnto al creatures.* Antwerp: By me wyddowe of Christoffel [Ruremond] of Endhoue[n], 1534. Reproduction of the original at the British Library. STC (2nd ed.) / 2825. Early English Books Online.

―――. *The parable of the wycked mammon Compiled in the yere of our lorde .M.d.xxxvi.* W.T. London: By Jhon daye, dwellyng in Sepulchres Paryshe at the signe of the Resurrectio[n], a litle aboue Holbourne Co[n]duit, 1547. Reproduction of the original at the Bodleian Library. STC (2nd ed.) / 24457. Early English Books Online.

―――. *The prayer and complaynt of the ploweman vnto Christ writte[n] nat longe after the yere of our Lorde. M. [and] thre hu[n]dred.* [London: T. Godfrey, ca. 1532] Reproduction of the original at the Bodleian Library. STC (2nd ed.) / 20036.5. Early English Books Online.

―――. "To the Reader." [Prologue to] *The Pentateuch. Marlborow in the lande of Hesse* [i.e., Antwerp]: Hans Luft [i.e., Johan Hoochstraten], 1530. Reproduction of the original at Cambridge University Library. STC (2nd ed.) / 2350. Early English Books Online.

Vane, Henry. *A healing question propounded and resolved upon occasion of the late publique and seasonable call to humiliation, in order to love and union amongst the honest party, and with a desire to apply balsome to the wound, before it become incurable.* London: Printed for T. Brewster at the sign of the three Bibles at the west-end of Pauls, 1656. Reproduction of the original at the British Library. Wing (2nd ed.) / V68; Thomason / E.879[5]. Early English Books Online.

Venner, Thomas. *The last speech and prayer with other passages of Thomas Venner, the chief incourager and promoter of the late horrid rebellion . . .* London: [n.p.], 1660. Reproduction of the original at the University of Illinois Library. Wing / V194A. Early English Books Online.

Vernon, John. *The swords abuse asserted: or, A word to the Army; shewing, the weakness of carnal weapons in spiritual warfare. The sword an useless tool in temple work: and the bearer thereof an unfit builder. Tendred to the serious consideration of His Excellency, the Lord Fairfax, and his General Councel, upon occasion of their late debates about the clause concerning religion in the promised agreement.* [London]: Imprinted for John Harris, 1648. Reproduction of the original at the British Library. Wing (2nd ed.) / V252; Thomason / E.477[3]. Early English Books Online.

_____. *A fruteful treatise of predestination and of the diuine prouidence of god with an apology of the same, against the swynyshe gruntinge of the epicures and atheystes of oure time. Whereunto are added, as depending of it a very necessary boke againste the free wyll men, and an other of the true iustification of faith, and of the good workes proceadynge of the same. . . .* London: By Iohn Tisdale, and are to be solde at his shop in the vpper end of Lombard strete, in Alhalowes churchyard, nere vnto grace church, 1561. Reproduction of the original at the Henry E. Huntington Library. STC (2nd ed.) / 24681. Early English Books Online.

The Vindication of the cobler, being a briefe publication of his doctrine, or, Certaine tenents [sic] collected out of the sermon of Samuel How, a cobler in Long Ally in Morefields which sermon he preacht in the Nags-head Tavern neare Coleman-street, in the presence of aboue a hundred people ... : this sermon lately printed and intituled, The sufficiency of the Spirits teaching, without humane learning, for the light and information of the ignorant. . . . London: Printed by R. Oulton, for John Wright the younger, and are to be sold at his Shop in the Old-Bayly, 1640. Reproduction of the original at the Harvard University Library. STC (2nd ed.) / 13855.4. Early English Books Online.

Virginia. Colonial Council. *To the Honourable William Gooch, Esq; His Majesty's lieutenant-governor, and commander in chief of the colony and dominion of Virginia, the humble address of the Council.* [Williamsburg, Va.: William Parks, 1747]. Reproduction of the original, Evans Early American Imprints, 1st series, no. 40445.

Virginia. Convention (1776). *Proceedings of the Convention of Delegates, held at the Capitol, in the city of Williamsburg, in the colony of Virginia, on Monday the 6th of May, 1776.* Williamsburg, Va.: Alexander Purdie, 1776. Reproduction of the original, Evans Early American Imprints, 1st series, no. 15198.

Virginia. General Assembly. Committee of Revisors. *Report of the Committee of Revisors appointed by the General Assembly of Virginia in MDCCLXXVI.* [Richmond, Va.:] Dixon & Holt, 1784. Reproduction of the original, Evans Early American Imprints, 1st series, no. 18863.

Virginia. General Assembly. House of Delegates. *Journal of the House of Delegates.* [October 1776] Williamsburg, Va.: Alexander Purdie, 1776. Reproduction of the original, Evans Early American Imprints, 1st series, no. 15204.

———. *Journal of the House of Delegates.* [May 1779] Williamsburg, Va.: John Clarkson and Augustine Davis, 1779. Reproduction of the original, Evans Early American Imprints, 1st series, no. 16659.

———. *Journal of the House of Delegates.* [October 1784] [Richmond: Thomas Nicholson and William Prentis, 1785.] Reproduction of the original, Evans Early American Imprints, 1st series, no. 19353.

———. *Journal of the House of Delegates.* [24 December 1784] [Richmond: n.p., 1784 or 1785] Reproduction of the original, Evans Early American Imprints, 1st series, no. 44619.

Virginia. House of Burgesses. *Journal of the House of Burgesses.* [February 1752] Williamsburg, Va.: William Hunter, 1752. Reproduction of the original, Evans Early American Imprints, 1st series, no. 6943.

―――. *Journal of the House of Burgesses.* [February 1772] Williamsburg, Va.: William Rind, 1772. Reproduction of the original, Evans Early American Imprints, 1st series, no. 12592.

―――. *Journal of the House of Burgesses.* [May 1774] Williamsburg, Va.: Clementina Rind, 1774. Reproduction of the original, Evans Early American Imprints, 1st series, no. 13749.

Virginia Baptist General Committee. *Minutes of the Baptist General Committee, at their yearly meeting, held in the city of Richmond, May 8th, 1790.* Richmond, Va.: T. Nicolson, 1790. Reproduction of the original, Evans Early American Imprints, 1st series, no. 45820.

Vives, Juan Luis. *A very frutefull and pleasant boke called the instructio[n] of a Christen woma[n], made fyrst in Laten, and dedicated vnto the quenes good grace, by the right famous clerke mayster Lewes Vives, and turned out of Laten into Englysshe by Rycharde Hyrd. . . .* [Imprynted at London: In Fletestrete, in the house of Thomas Berthelet nere to the Cundite, at the signe of Lucrece], 1529. Reproduction of the original at the British Library. STC (2nd ed.) / 24856. Early English Books Online.

[Walwyn, William.] *The compassionate Samaritane unbinding the conscience, and powring oyle into the wounds which have beene made upon the separation: recommending their future welfare to the serious thoughts, and carefull endeavours of all who love the peace and unity of Commonwealths men, or desire the unanimous prosecution of the common enemie, or who follow our Saviours rule, to doe unto others, what they would have others doe unto them.* 1644. Reproduction of the original at the British Library. Wing (2nd ed.) / W681B; Thomason / E.1202[1]. Early English Books Online.

―――. *The power of love.* London: Printed by R. C. for John Sweeting, at the signe of the Angell in Popes-head Alley, 1643. Reproduction of the original at the British Library. Wing (2nd ed.) / W690A; Thomason / E.1206[2]. Early English Books Online.

―――. *A prediction of Mr. Edvvards his conversion and recantation.* London: Printed by T[homas] P[aine] for G. Whittington and N. Brookes, at the signe of the Angell in Cornhill, below the Exchange, 1646. Reproduction of the original at the British Library. Wing (2nd ed.) / W691; Thomason / E.1184[5]. Early English Books Online.

Ward, Nathaniel. *The simple cobler of Aggavvam in America Willing to help mend his native country, lamentably tattered, both in the upper-leather and sole, with all the honest stitches he can take. And as willing never to be paid for his work, by old English wonted pay. It is his trade to patch all the year long, gratis. Therefore I pray gentlemen keep your purses. By Theodore de la Guard.* London: printed by John Dever & Robert Ibbitson, for Stephen Bowtell, at the signe of the Bible in Popes Head-Alley, 1647. Reproduction of the original at the British Library. Wing (2nd ed., 1994) / W786A. Early English Books Online.

Webb, George. *The office and authority of a justice of peace. . . . Collected from the common and statute laws of England, and acts of Assembly, now in force; and adapted to the constitution and practice of Virginia.* Williamsburg, Va.: William Parks, 1736. Reproduction of the original, Evans Early American Imprints. 1st series, no. 4101.

Westminster Assembly. *The humble advice of the Assembly of Divines, now by authority of Parliament sitting at Westminster, concerning a confession of faith, presented by them lately to both houses of Parliament. A certain number of copies are ordered to be printed only for the use of the members of both houses and of the Assembly of Divines, to the end that they may advise thereupon.* London: Printed for the Company of Stationers, 1646. Reproduction of the original at the British Library. Wing (2nd ed.) / W1427; Thomason / E.368[3]. Early English Books Online.

Whichcote, Benjamin. *Select sermons of Dr. Whichcot [sic] in two parts.* London: Printed for Awnsham and John Churchill, 1698. Reproduction of the original at the Henry E. Huntington Library. Wing / W1642; Arber's Term cat. / III 105. Early English Books Online.

Whitefield, George. *A brief and general account, of the first part of the life of the Reverend Mr. George Whitefield, from his birth, to his entring [sic] into holy-orders.* Philadelphia: Printed and sold by Andrew and William Bradford at the Sign of the Bible in Second-Street., 1740. Reproduction of the original, Evans Early American Imprints, 1st series, no. 4627.

Whitgift, John. *An ansvvere to a certen libel intituled, An admonition to the Parliament.* London: By Henrie Bynneman, for Humfrey Toy, 1572. Reproduction of the original at the Henry E. Huntington Library. STC (2nd ed.) / 25427. Early English Books Online.

Willard, Samuel. *Ne sutor ultra crepidam, or, Brief animadversions upon the New-England Anabaptists late fallacious narrative wherein the notorious mistakes and falshoods [sic] by them published are detected.* Boston, Ma.: Printed by S. Green upon assignment of S. Sewall and are to be sold by Sam. Philips ..., 1681. Reproduction of the original at the Harvard University Library. Wing / W2288. Early English Books Online.

William III. *The declaration of His Highnes William Henry, by the grace of God Prince of Orange, &c. of the reasons inducing him, to appear in armes in the kingdome of England, for preserving of the Protestant religion, and for restoring the lawes and liberties of England, Scotland and Ireland.* Printed at the Hague: by Arnout Leers, by His Highnesses special order, 1688. Reproduction of the original at the Henry E. Huntington Library. Wing (2nd ed.) / W2328. Early English Books Online.

Williams, Oliver. *An exact accompt of the daily proceedings in Parliament. With occurrences from foreign parts.* London: John Redmayne, 1660. Reproduction of the original at the British Library. Nelson and Seccombe / 491.053; Thomason / E.773. Early English Books Online.

Williams, Roger. *The bloody tenent yet more bloody: by Mr Cottons endevour to wash it white in the blood of the lambe; of whose precious blood, spilt in the blood of his servants; and of the blood of millions spilt in fromer and later wars for conscience sake, that most bloody tenent of presecution for cause of conscience, upon a second tryal, is found now more apparently and more notoriously guilty. In this rejoynder to Mr Cotton, are principally I. The nature of persecution, II. The power of the civill sword in spirituals examined, III. The Parliaments permission of dissenting consciences justified. . .* London: Printed for Giles Calvert, and are to be sold at the black-spread-Eagle at the West-end of Pauls, 1652. Reproduction of the original at the British Library. Wing (2nd ed.) / W2760; Thomason / E.661[6]. Early English Books Online.

————. *The bloudy tenet, of persecution, for cause of concience [sic], discussed, in a conference betweene truth and peace, who, in all tender affection, present to the high court of Parliament, (as the result of their discourse) these, (amongst other passages) of highest consideration.* London: n.p., 1644. Reproduction of the original at the John Carter Brown Library. Wing (2nd ed.) / W2759. Early English Books Online.

————. *Christenings make not Christians . . .* London: Iane Coe, for I. H., 1645. Reproduction of the original at the British Library. Wing (2nd ed.) / W2761; Thomason / E.1189[8]. Early English Books Online.

————. *Queries of highest consideration, proposed to the five Holland ministers and the Scotch Commissioners (so called) upon occasion of their late printed apologies for themselves and their churches. In all humble reverence presented to the view of the Right Honourable the Houses of the High Court of Parliament.* London: n.p., 1644. Reproduction of the original at the British Library. Thomason / E.32[8]. Early English Books Online.

Wilson, Arthur. *The history of Great Britain being the life and reign of King James the First, relating to what passed from his first access to the crown, till his death.* London: Richard Lowndes, 1653. Reproduction of the original at the Henry E. Huntington Library. Wing / W2888. Early English Books Online.

Winthrop, John. *Antinomians and familists condemned by the synod of elders in Nevv-England: with the proceedings of the magistrates against them, and their apology for the same. . . .* London: Printed for Ralph Smith at the signe of the Bible in Cornhill neare the Royall Exchange, 1644. Reproduction of the original at the British Library. Wing (2nd ed.) / W3094; Thomason / E.251[10]. Early English Books Online.

————. *The humble request of His Majesties loyall subjects, the governour and the company late gone for Nevv-England to the rest of their brethren, in and of the Church of England. For the obtaining of their prayers, and the removall of suspitions, and misconstructions of their intentions.* London: Iohn Bellamie, 1630. Reproduction of the original at the Henry E. Huntington Library. STC (2nd ed.) / 18485. Early English Books Online.

————. *A journal of the transactions and occurrences in the settlement of Massachusetts. and the other New-England colonies, from the year 1630 to 1644 . . . now first published from a correct copy of the original manuscript.* Edited by Noah Webster. Hartford, CT: Elisha Babcock, 1790. Reproduction of the original, Evans Early American Imprints, 1st series, no. 23086.

Witherspoon, John. *Ecclesiastical Characteristics: or, the arcana of church policy. Being an humble attempt to open the mystery of moderation. . . .* 7th ed. Philadelphia: William and Thomas Bradford, 1767. Reproduction of the original, Evans Early American Imprints, 1st series, no. 10804.

————. *The Works of the Rev. John Witherspoon, D.D. L.L.D. Late President of the College, at Princeton New-Jersey. To Which is Prefixed An Account of the Author's Life, in a Sermon occasioned by his Death, by the Rev. Dr. John Rodgers, of New York.* Philadelphia: William W. Woodward, no. 17, Chestnut near Front Street, 1800. Reproduction of the original, Evans Early American Imprints, 1st series, nos. 39128 and 43595.

Wotton, Anthony. *A dangerous plot discovered By a discourse, wherein is proved, that, Mr. Richard Mountague, in his two bookes; the one, called A new gagg; the other, A iust appeale: laboureth to bring in the faith of Rome, and Arminius: vnder the name and pretence of the doctrine and faith of the Church of England. A worke very necessary for all them which haue received the truth of God in loue, and desire to escape errour.* . . . London: Printed [by John Dawson] for Nicholas Bourne, at the Exchange, 1626. Reproduction of the original at the Henry E. Huntington Library. STC (2nd ed.) / 26003. Early English Books Online.

B. Reprints, Collections, Records

Adams, John. *The Works of John Adams, Second President of the United States: With a Life of the Author, Notes and Illustrations.* Vol. 6. Boston: Little, Brown, & Co., 1851.

Alley, Robert S, ed. *James Madison on Religious Liberty.* Buffalo, N. Y.: Prometheus Books, 1985.

Augustine, Saint. "Letter XCIII," in *The Confessions and Letters of St. Augustin, with a Sketch of His Life and Work,* vol. 1, A Select Library of the Nicene and Post-Nicene Fathers of the Christian Church. Edited by Philip Schaff. New York: Christian Literature Publishing Co., 1886. Grand Rapids, Mich.: Christian Classics Ethereal Library.

Backus, Isaac. *Isaac Backus on Church, State, and Calvinism: Pamphlets, 1754–1789.* Edited by William G. McLoughlin. Cambridge, Mass.: Belknap Press of Harvard University Press, 1968.

Bailyn, Bernard, ed. *The Debate on the Constitution: Federalist and Antifederalist Speeches, Articles, and Letters During the Struggle over Ratification.* 2 vols. New York: Library of America, 1993.

Blackstone, William. *Commentaries on the Laws of England: A Facsimile of the First Edition of 1765–1769,* vol. 4, Of Public Wrongs (1769). Introduction by Thomas A. Green. Chicago: The University of Chicago Press, 1979.

Bradford, John. *A Treatise on Predestination, with an Answer to Certain Enormities Calumniously Gathered of One to Slander God's Truth.* [London]: n.p., 1554. Reprinted in Richard Laurence, *Authentic Documents Relative to the Predestinarian Controversy, which Took Place Among Those Who Were Imprisoned For their adherence to the Doctrines of the Reformation by Queen Mary.* Oxford: W. Baxter, 1819.

―――. *The Writings of John Bradford, M.A. . . . Containing Letters, Treatises, Remains.* Edited by Aubrey Townsend. Cambridge: The University Press, 1853. Reprint, New York: Johnson Reprint Corporation, 1968.

Calvin, Jean. *Institutes of the Christian Religion,* 2 vols. Edited by John T. McNeill. Translated by Ford Lewis Battles. Louisville, Ky.: Westminster John Knox Press, 1960.

―――. *Opera quae supersunt omnia. . . .* vol. 8. Edited by G. Baum, August Eduard Cunitz;, Eduard Reuss, Alfred Erichson, Paul Lobstein, Wilhelm Baldensperger, and Ludwig Horst. Brunswick: C. A. Schwetschke, 1870. Reprint, New York: Johnson Reprint Corporation, 1964.

Castellio, Sebastian. *Concerning Heretics, Whether they are to be persecuted and how they are to be treated, A collection of the opinions of learned men both ancient and modern. An anonymous work attributed to Sebastian Castellio. Now first done into English, together with excerpts from other works of Sebastian Castellio and David Joris on religious liberty.* Translated and edited by Roland H. Bainton. New York: Columbia University Press, 1935. Reprint, New York: Columbia University Press, 1965.

Dupuis, Jacques, ed. *The Christian Faith in the Doctrinal Documents of the Catholic Church,* 7th ed. New York: Alba House, 2001.

Early Virginia Religious Petitions. *A collaborative project between the Library of Congress and the Library of Virginia.* Available at http://memory.loc.gov/ammem/collections/petitions/.

Elliot, Jonathan, ed. *The Debates in the Several State Conventions on the Adoption of the Federal Constitution, as Recommended by the General Convention at Philadelphia, in 1787 . . .* 5 vols. Philadelphia: J. P. Lippincott & Co., 1836–59. Available at American Memory, Library of Congress, http://memory.loc.gov/ammem/amlaw/lwed.html.

Estep, William R., ed. *Anabaptist Beginnings (1523–1533): A Source Book.* Nieuwkoop: B. de Graff, 1976.

Executive Journals of the Council of Colonial Virginia. 6 vols. Edited by H. R. McIlwaine, Wilmer Lee Hall, and Benjamin J. Hillman. Richmond, Va.: Virginia State Library, 1976.

Executive Journals of the Council of Colonial Virginia. Vols. 1 and 2. Edited by H. R. McIlwaine. Richmond, Va.: Virginia State Library, 1925–1927.

Farrand, Max, ed. *The Records of the Federal Convention of 1787.* 3 vols. New Haven, Conn.: Yale University Press, 1911. Available at American Memory, Library of Congress, http://memory.loc.gov/ammem/amlaw/lwfr.html.

Foote, William Henry. *Sketches of Virginia, Historical and Biographical.* 1850. Reprint, Richmond, Va.: John Knox Press, 1966.

Foxe, John. *Book of Martyrs; or, A History of the Lives, Sufferings, and Triumphant Deaths, of the Primitive as well as Protestant Martyrs: From the Commencement of Christianity, to the Latest Periods of Pagan and Popish Persecution. . . .* Edited by Charles A. Goodrich. New York: William W. Reed & Co., 1831.

Fristoe, William. *A Concise History of the Ketocton Baptist Association, 1766–1808.* Staunton, Va.: William Gilman Lyford, 1808. Reprint, San Antonio, Tex.: Primitive Baptist Heritage Corporation, 2002.

Furneaux, Philip. *An Essay on Toleration: With a particular View to the late application of the Protestant Dissenting Ministers to Parliament, for Amending, and rendering Effectual, the Act of the first of William and Mary, commonly called the Act of Toleration.* London: Printed for T. Cadell, in the Strand, 1773. Edited by Mark Goldie. The Reception of Locke's Politics. Volume 5, *The Church, Dissent and Religious Toleration, 1689–1773.* London: Pickering & Chatto, 1999.

Gaustadt, Edwin S. *A Documentary History of Religion in America to the Civil War.* 2nd ed. Grand Rapids, Mich.: William B. Eerdmans, 1993.

Gee, Henry, and William John Hardy. *Documents Illustrative of English Church History, Compiled from Original Sources.* London: Macmillan and Co., 1910. Reprint, New York: Kraus Reprint Corporation, 1966.

Hayward, John. *The Life and Raigne of King Edward the Sixth.* 1630. Edited by Barrett L. Beer. Kent, Ohio: Kent State University Press, 1993.

Heimert, Alan, and Perry Miller. *The Great Awakening: Documents Illustrating the Crisis and Its Consequences.* Indianapolis, Ind.: The Bobbs-Merrill Company, 1967.

Hening, William Waller, ed. *The Statutes at Large; being a collection of all the laws of Virginia, from the first session of the Legislature in the year 1619.* 13 vols. New York: Printed for the editor, 1819–23. Charlottesville: University Press of Virginia, 1969.

Henry, Patrick, Sr., Samuel Davies, James Maury, Edwin Conway, and George Trask. "Letters of Patrick Henry, Sr., Samuel Davies, James Maury, Edwin Conway, and George Trask." *William and Mary College Quarterly Historical Magazine*, 2nd series, 1 (October 1921): 261–81.

Jefferson, Thomas. *Notes on the State of Virginia*. Edited by William Peden. Chapel Hill, N. C.: University of North Carolina Press, 1954.

———. *The Papers of Thomas Jefferson*. 31 vols. Edited by Julian P. Boyd, L. H. Butterfield, Charles T. Cullen, and John Catanzariti. Princeton, N. J.: Princeton University Press, 1950–.

Jensen, Merrill, John P. Kaminski, and Gaspare J. Saladino. *The Documentary History of the Ratification of the Constitution*. Vols. 1–10, 13–21. Madison, Wis.: State Historical Society of Wisconsin, 1976–2005.

Jones, Hugh. *The Present State of Virginia from Whence is Inferred a Short View of Maryland and North Carolina. 1724*. Reprinted with introduction by Richard L. Morton. Chapel Hill, N. C.: University of North Carolina Press, 1956.

Journals of the Continental Congress, 1774–1789. 34 vols. Washington, D.C.: GPO, 1904–37. Available at American Memory, Library of Congress, http://memory.loc. gov/ammem/amlaw/lwjc.html.

Laurence, Richard. *Authentic Documents Relative to the Predestinarian Controversy, which Took Place among Those Who Were Imprisoned for Their Adherence to the Doctrines of the Reformation by Queen Mary. . . .* Oxford: W. Baxter, 1819.

Lutz, Daniel S., ed. *Colonial Origins of the American Constitution: A Documentary History*. Indianapolis, Ind.: Liberty Fund, 1998.

Madison, James. "Detached Memoranda." Edited by Elizabeth Fleet. *The William and Mary Quarterly* 3 (October 1946): 534–68.

———. *James Madison: A Biography in His Own Words*. Edited by Merrill D. Peterson. New York: Newsweek, 1974.

———. "James Madison's Autobiography." Edited by Douglas Adair. *The William and Mary Quarterly* 2 (April 1945): 191–209.

———. *The Papers of James Madison*. 17 vols. Edited by William T. Hutchinson, William M. C. Rachal, and Robert Allen Rutland. Chicago: The University of Chicago Press, 1962–1991.

McGlothlin, William J. *Baptist Confessions of Faith*. Philadelphia: American Baptist Publication Society, 1911.

McIlwain, Charles Howard, ed. *The Political Works of James I*. Vol. 1 of Harvard Political Classics. Cambridge: Harvard University Press, 1918.

Miller, Perry. *The American Puritans: Their Prose and Poetry*. New York: Columbia University Press, 1956.

Milton, John. *Areopagitica and Other Political Writings of John Milton*. Indianapolis, Ind.: Liberty Fund, 1999.

———. *The Complete Poems of John Milton*. Edited by Charles W. Eliot. New York: P. F. Collier & Son Co., 1909.

More, Thomas. *Complete Works of St. Thomas More*. Edited by Louis A. Schuster, Richard C. Marius, James P. Lusardi, and Richard J. Schoeck. Vol. 8, The Confutation of Tyndale's Answer, Part I, The Text, Books I–IV. New Haven, Conn.: Yale University Press, 1973.

Patrick, John J. and Gerald P. Long, eds. *Constitutional Debates on Freedom of Religion: A Documentary History*. Primary Documents in American History and Contemporary Issues series. Westport, Conn.: Greenwood Press, 1999.

Pendleton, Edmund. *The Letters and Papers of Edmund Pendleton, 1734–1803*. 2 vols. Edited by David John Mays. Charlottesville, Va.: University Press of Virginia, 1967.

Perry, William Stevens, ed. *Papers relating to the history of the church in Virginia, A.D. 1650–1776. 1870*. New York: AMS Press, 1969.

Peterson, Merrill D., ed. *James Madison: A Biography in His Own Words*. New York: Newsweek, 1974.

Randolph, Edmund. *History of Virginia*. Edited by Arthur H. Shaffer. Charlottesville, Va.: The University Press of Virginia, 1970.

Sandoz, Ellis. *Political Sermons of the American Founding Era, 1730–1805*. Vol. 1. 2nd ed. Indianapolis, Ind.: Liberty Fund, 1998.

Schaff, Philip. *The Creeds of Christendom, with a History and Critical Notes*. 3 vols. 6th ed. Revised by David S. Schaff. Grand Rapids, Mich.: Baker Books, 1998.

Schwartz, Bernard. *The Bill of Rights: A Documentary History*. Vol. 1. New York: Chelsea House Publishers, 1971.

Smyth, John. *The Works of John Smyth, Fellow of Christ's College, 1594–8*. 2 vols. Edited by W. T. Whitley. Cambridge: University Press, 1915.

Stephenson, Carl, and Frederick George Marcham, eds. *Sources of English Constitutional History: A Selection of Documents from A.D. 600 to the Present*. New York: Harper & Brothers, 1937.

Strype, John. *Annals of the Reformation and Establishment of Religion and other various occurrences in the Church of England during Queen Elizabeth's happy reign, together with an appendix of original papers of state, records, and letters*. Vol. 1. 1708, 1824. Reprint, New York: B. Franklin, 1968.

Trewe, John. *John Trewe, the unworthy marked Servant of the Lord, being in bands for the testimony of Jesu, signifieth the cause of contention in the King's Bench, as concerning sects in religion, the 30th of January, Anno Dom. 1555. Reprinted in Richard Laurence, Authentic Documents Relative to the Predestinarian Controversy, which Took Place Among Those Who Were Imprisoned For their adherence to the Doctrines of the Reformation by Queen Mary*. Edited by Richard Laurence. Reprint, Oxford: W. Baxter, 1819.

Tyndale, William. *The Obedience of a Christian Man*. First published in Antwerp, 1528. Edited by David Daniell. New York: Penguin Books, 2000.

Underhill, Edward B. *Tracts on Liberty of Conscience and Persecution: 1614–1661*. London: Hanserd Knollys Society, 1846. Reprint, New York: Burt Franklin, 1966.

Van Schreeven, William J., Robert L. Scribner, and Brent Tarter, eds. *Revolutionary Virginia: The Road to Independence*. 7 vols. [Charlottesville, Va.]: University Press of Virginia, 1973–1983.

The Virginia Gazette. *Colonial Williamsburg Foundation, Past Portal*. Available at http://www.pastportal.com/browse/vg/.

Witherspoon, John. *Lectures on Moral Philosophy*. Edited by Varnum Lansing Collins. Princeton, N. J.: Princeton University Press, 1912

II. Secondary Sources

"Accounts of the Donald Robertson School." *Virginia Magazine of History and Biography* 33 (1925): 194–95, 288–92.

Ackroyd, Peter. *The Life of Thomas More*. New York: Anchor Books, 1998.

Acton, John E. E. D. *Essays in the Study and Writing of History*. Vol. 2. Edited by J. Rufus Fears. Indianapolis: Liberty Classics, 1986.

Adams, George Burton. *Constitutional History of England*. Revised by Robert L. Schuyler. New York: Henry Holt and Company, 1934.

Andrews, Charles M. *The Colonial Period of American History*. New Haven, Conn.: Yale University Press, 1936.

Armstrong, O. K. and Marjorie M. *The Indomitable Baptists: A Narrative of Their Role in Shaping American History*. Garden City, N. Y.: Doubleday & Company, Inc., 1967.

Auski, Peter. "Tyndale on the Law of Reason and the Reason of Law." Chapter 4 in *William Tyndale and the Law*. Vol. 25, *Sixteenth Century Essays & Studies*. Edited by John A. R. Dick and Anne Richardson. Kirksville, Mo.: Sixteenth Century Journal Publishers, Inc., 1994.

Bailyn, Bernard. *The Ideological Origins of the American Revolution*. Enlarged Edition. Cambridge, Mass.: Belknap Press of Harvard UP, 1992.

Bainton, Roland H. *Hunted Heretic: The Life and Death of Michael Servetus, 1511–1553*. Boston: Beacon Press, 1953.

———. *The Travail of Religious Liberty: Nine Biographical Studies*. Philadelphia: Westminster Press, 1951.

Banning, Lance. *The Sacred Fire of Liberty: James Madison & the Founding of the Federal Republic*. Ithaca, N. Y.: Cornell University Press, 1995.

Beliles, Mark A. "The Christian Communities, Religious Revivals, and Political Culture of the Central Virginia Piedmont, 1737–1813." Chapter 1 in *Religion and Political Culture in Jefferson's Virginia*. Edited by Garrett Ward Sheldon and Daniel L. Dreisbach. Lanham, Mass.: Rowman & Littlefield Publishers, Inc., 2000.

Benedict, David. *A General History of the Baptist Denomination in America, and other parts of the world*. 2 vols. 1813. Reprint, Freeport, N. Y.: Books for Libraries Press, 1971.

Bergeron, David M. *King James & Letters of Homoerotic Desire*. Iowa City, Iowa: University of Iowa Press, 1999.

Bidwell, Robert Leland. "The Morris Reading-Houses: A Study in Dissent." M.A. Thesis, College of William and Mary, 1948.

Bobrick, Benson. *Wide as the Waters: The Story of the English Bible and the Revolution It Inspired*. New York: Penguin Books, 2001.

Bonomi, Patricia U. *Under the Cope of Heaven: Religion, Society, and Politics in Colonial America*. New York: Oxford University Press, 1986.

Bonwick, Colin. *English Radicals and the American Revolution*. Chapel Hill, N. C.: University of North Carolina Press, 1977.

Brant, Irving. *The Fourth President: A Life of James Madison*. Indianapolis, Ind.: The Bobbs-Merrill Co., 1970.

———. "Madison: On the Separation of Church and State." *The William and Mary Quarterly*, 3rd ser., 8 (January 1951): 3–24.

Brewer, Mary Taylor. *From Log Cabins to the White House: A History of the Taylor Family.* Wooton, Ky.: M. T. Brewer, 1985.

Brown, William James. *The Life of Rowland Taylor LL.D., Rector of Hadleigh in the Deanery of Bocking.* London: The Epsworth Press, 1959.

Bryson, Gladys. *Man and Society: The Scottish Inquiry of the Eighteenth Century.* 1945. Reprint, New York: Augustus M. Kelley, 1968.

Buckley, Thomas E. *Church and State in Revolutionary Virginia.* Charlottesville, Va.: University Press of Virginia, 1977.

Butler, Jon. "Enthusiasm Described and Decried." Essay 6b in *Taking Sides: Clashing Views on Controversial Issues in American History, Volume 1, The Colonial Period to Reconstruction.* 10th ed. Edited by Larry Madaras and James M. SoRelle. Guilford, Conn.: McGraw-Hill/Dushkin, 2003.

Butterfield, Herbert. *Historical Development of the Principle of Toleration in British Life.* Robert Waley Cohen Memorial Lecture, 1956. London: Epworth Press, 1957.

Cameron, Euan. *The European Reformation.* Oxford: Clarendon Press, 1991.

Cheyney, Edward P. "The Court of the Star Chamber." *The American Historical Review* 18 (July 1913): 727–50.

Christenson, Ronald. "The Political Theory of Persecution: Augustine and Hobbes." *Midwest Journal of Political Science* 12 (August 1968): 419–38.

Clark, Sir George. *The Later Stuarts, 1660–1714.* 2nd ed. Oxford: Clarendon Press, 1956.

Cobb, Sanford H. *The Rise of Religious Liberty in America: A History.* 1902. Reprint, New York: Cooper Square Publishers, Inc., 1968

Collins, Jeffrey R. "The Restoration Bishops and the Royal Supremacy." *Church History* 68 (September 1999): 549–80.

Collinson, Patrick. *The Elizabethan Puritan Movement.* London: Jonathan Cape, 1967. Reprint, New York: Oxford University Press, 1991.

Coltman, Irene. *Philosophy and Politics in the English Civil War.* London: Faber and Faber, 1962.

Cramp, J. M. *Baptist History: From the Foundation of the Christian Church to the Close of the Eighteenth Century.* Philadelphia: American Baptist Publication Society, 1869.

Curry, Thomas J. *The First Freedoms: Church and State in America to the Passage of the First Amendment.* New York: Oxford University Press, 1986.

Cuthbertson, David. *A Tragedy of the Reformation: Being the Authentic Narrative of the History and Burning of the "Christianismi Restitutio," 1553, with a succinct account of the theological controversy between Michael Servetus, its author, and the reformer, John Calvin.* Edinburgh: Oliphant, Anderson & Ferrier, 1912.

Daniell, David. *The Bible in English: Its History and Influence.* New Haven, Conn.: Yale   UP, 2003.

———. *William Tyndale: A Biography.* New Haven, Conn.: Yale University Press, 1994.

Dawson, Jane E. A. *The Politics of Religion in the Age of Mary, Queen of Scots: The Earl of Argyll and the Struggle for Britain and Ireland.* Cambridge: Cambridge University Press, 2002.

Dawson, Joseph Martin. *Baptists and the American Republic*. Nashville, Tenn.: Broadman Press, 1956.

Dickens, A. G. *The English Reformation*. New York: Schocken Books, 1964.

Drakeman, Donald L. "Religion and the Republic: Madison and the First Amendment." Essay in *James Madison on Religious Liberty*. Edited by Robert S. Alley. Buffalo, N. Y.: Prometheus Books, 1985.

Dreisbach, Daniel L. "Church-State Debate in the Virginia Legislature: From the Declaration of Rights to the Statute for Establishing Religious Freedom." Chapter 7 in *Religion and Political Culture in Jefferson's Virginia*. Edited by Garrett Ward Sheldon and Daniel L. Dreisbach. Lanham, Mass.: Rowman & Littlefield Publishers, 2000.

————. *Real Threat and Mere Shadow: Religious Liberty and the First Amendment*. Vol. 5, *The Rutherford Institute Report*. Westchester, Ill.: Crossway Books, 1987.

Eckenrode, H. J. *Separation of Church and State in Virginia: A Study in the Development of the Revolution*. Virginia State Library. Special Report of the Department of Archives and History. Richmond: Davis Bottom, 1910.

Erickson, Carolly. *Bloody Mary*. New York: St. Martin's Press, 1978.

Estep, William R. *The Anabaptist Story: An Introduction to Sixteenth Century Anabaptism*. 3rd ed. Grand Rapids, Mich.: William B. Eerdmans Publishing Company, 1996.

————. *Revolution within the Revolution: The First Amendment in Historical Context, 1612–1789*. Grand Rapids, Mich.: William B. Eerdmans Publishing Company, 1990.

Evans, B. *The Early English Baptists*. 2 vols. London: J. Heaton & Son, 1862. Reprint, Greenwood, S. C.: Attic Press, 1977.

Firth, Charles Harding. *The Last Years of the Protectorate, 1656–1658*. Vol. 1. New York: Longmans, Green, 1909.

————. *Oliver Cromwell and the Rule of the Puritans in England*. Reprint, London: Oxford University Press, 1961.

Fletcher, Anthony. "Episcopacy and the Liturgy." Chapter 3 in *The Outbreak of the English Civil War*. New York: New York University Press, 1981.

Fogarty, Gerald. "Catholics in Colonial Virginia." Paper presented at the 154th Annual Meeting (Spring) of the American Society of Church History. April 1–4, 1993. Williamsburg, Va.

Foster, Stephen. "New England and the Challenge of Heresy, 1630 to 1660: The Puritan Crisis in Transatlantic Perspective." *William and Mary Quarterly* 38 (October 1981): 624–60.

Freeman, Thomas. "Dissenters from a Dissenting Church: The Challenge of the Freewillers, 1550–1558." Chapter 6 in *The Beginnings of English Protestantism*. Edited by Peter Marshall and Alex Ryrie. Cambridge: Cambridge University Press, 2002.

Fristoe, William. *A Concise History of the Ketocton Baptist Association, 1766–1808*. Staunton, Va.: William Gilman Lyford, 1808. Reprint, San Antonio, Tex.: Primitive Baptist Heritage Corporation, 2002.

Garrett, John. *Roger Williams: Witness Beyond Christendom, 1603–1683*. New York: The Macmillan Company, 1970.

Gaustad, Edwin S. "Colonial Religion and Liberty of Conscience." Chapter 2 in *The Virginia Statute for Religious Freedom: Its Evolution and Consequences in American*

History. Edited by Merrill D. Peterson and Robert C. Vaughan. Cambridge Studies in Religion and American Public Life series. Edited by Robin W. Lovin. 1988. Reprint, Cambridge: Cambridge University Press, 2003.

Gewehr, Wesley M. *The Great Awakening in Virginia, 1740–1790.* Duke University Press, 1930. Reprint, Gloucester, Mass.: Peter Smith, 1965.

Goen, C. C. *Revivalism and Separatism in New England, 1740–1800: Strict Congregationalists and Separate Baptists in the Great Awakening.* New Haven, Conn.: Yale University Press, 1962.

Goldstone, Lawrence and Nancy. *Out of the Flames: The Remarkable Story of a Fearless Scholar, a Fatal Heresy, and One of the Rarest Books in the World.* New York: Broadway Books, 2002.

Guggisberg, Hans R. "Religious Freedom and the History of the Christian World in Roger Williams' Thought." *Early American Literature* 12, 1:36–48.

Guy, John. *Tudor England.* New York: Oxford University Press, 1988.

Gwaltney, L. L. *Heralds of Freedom.* Nashville, Tenn.: Broadman Press, 1939.

Hall, David W. *The Genevan Reformation and the American Founding.* Lanham, Md.: Lexington Books, 2003.

———. *Windows on Westminster: A look at the men, the work, and the enduring results of the Westminster Assembly (1643–1648).* Norcross, Ga.: Great Commission Publications, 1993.

Hammond, Gerald. "Law and Love in Deuteronomy." Chapter 5 in *William Tyndale and the Law.* Vol. 25, Sixteenth Century Essays & Studies. Edited by John A. R. Dick and Anne Richardson. Kirksville, Mo.: Sixteenth Century Journal Publishers, Inc., 1994.

Harkness, R. E. E. *Roger Williams—Prophet of Tomorrow.* Introduction in Oscar S. Straus, *Roger Williams: The Pioneer of Religious Liberty.* Freeport, N. Y.: Books for Libraries Press, 1970.

Harris, Tim, Paul Seaward, and Mark Goldie, eds. *The Politics of Religion in Restoration England.* Oxford: Basil Blackwell, 1990.

Hart, Albert Bushnell. "John Knox as a Man of the World." *The American Historical Review* 13 (January 1908): 259–80.

Hart, Freeman H. *The Valley of Virginia in the American Revolution, 1763–1789.* Chapel Hill, N. C.: University of North Carolina Press, 1942.

Hetherington, William M. *History of the Westminster Assembly of Divines.* Reprint, Edmonton, AB Canada: Still Waters Revival Books, 1991.

Hill, Christopher. *The English Bible and the Seventeenth-Century Revolution.* New York: Penguin Books, 1993.

———. *The World Turned Upside Down: Radical Ideas during the English Revolution.* New York: Viking Press, 1972.

Hillar, Marian. *The Case of Michael Servetus (1511–1553): The Turning Point in the Struggle for Freedom of Conscience.* Lewiston, N. Y.: Edwin Mellen Press, 1997.

Hoeveler, J. David. *Creating the American Mind: Intellect and Politics in the Colonial Colleges.* Lanham, MD: Roman & Littlefield Publishers, 2002.

Hovey, Alvah. *A Memoir of the Life and Times of the Rev. Isaac Backus.* Boston: Gould and Lincoln, 1859.

Howell, Robert Boyle C. *The Early Baptists of Virginia*. Philadelphia: The Bible and Publication Society, 1876.

Hutson, James H. *Religion and the Founding of the American Republic*. Washington, D.C.: Library of Congress, 1998.

Isaac, Rhys. "'The Rage of Malice of the Old Serpent Devil': The Dissenters and the Making and Remaking of the Virginia Statute for Religious Freedom." Chapter 6 in *The Virginia Statute for Religious Freedom: Its Evolution and Consequences in American History*. Edited by Merrill D. Peterson and Robert C. Vaughan. Cambridge Studies in Religion and American Public Life series. Edited by Robin W. Lovin. 1988. Reprint, Cambridge: Cambridge University Press, 2003.

―――. "Religion and Authority: Problems of the Anglican Establishment in Virginia in the Era of the Great Awakening and the Parsons' Cause." *The William and Mary Quarterly*, 3rd series, 30 (January 1973): 3–36.

―――. *The Transformation of Virginia, 1740–1790*. Chapel Hill, N. C.: The University of North Carolina Press, 1982, 1999.

James, Charles F. *Documentary History of the Struggle for Religious Liberty in Virginia*. Lynchburg, Va.: J. P. Bell Co., 1900.

Johnson, Thomas Cary. *Virginia Presbyterianism and Religious Liberty in Colonial and Revolutionary Times*. Richmond, Va.: Presbyterian Committee of Publication, 1907.

Jones, J. R., ed. *Liberty Secured? Britain Before and After 1688*. Stanford, Calif.: Stanford University Press, 1992.

Jordan, W. K. *Development of Religious Toleration in England*. 4 vols. Cambridge: Harvard University Press, 1932–40.

Kenyon, J. P. *Stuart England*. 2nd ed. New York: Penguin Books, 1985.

Ketcham, Ralph. "The Dilemma of Bills of Rights in Democratic Government." Chapter 1 in *The Legacy of George Mason*. Edited by Josephine F. Pacheco. Fairfax, Va.: George Mason University Press, 1983.

―――. *James Madison: A Biography*. Charlottesville, Va.: University Press of Virginia, 1990.

―――. "James Madison and Religion: A New Hypothesis." Essay in *James Madison on Religious Liberty*. Edited by Robert S. Alley. Buffalo, N. Y.: Prometheus Books, 1985.

Lambert, Frank. *The Founding Fathers and the Place of Religion in America*. Princeton, N. J.: Princeton University Press, 2003.

―――. *Inventing the "Great Awakening."* Princeton, N. J.: Princeton University Press, 1999.

―――. *"Pedlar in Divinity": George Whitefield and the Transatlantic Revivals, 1737–1770*. Princeton, N. J.: Princeton University Press, 1994.

Lecler, Joseph S. J. *Toleration and the Reformation*. 2 vols. Translated by T. L. Westow. New York: Associated Press, 1960.

Leibiger, Stuart. "James Madison and Amendments to the Constitution, 1787–1789: 'Parchment Barriers.'" *The Journal of Southern History* 59 (August 1993): 441–68.

Levy, Leonard W. *Origins of the Bill of Rights*. New Haven, Conn.: Yale Nota Bene, 2001.

Lewis, C. S. *English Literature in the Sixteenth Century, Excluding Drama*. Oxford: Clarendon Press, 1954.

Lindsay, Thomas. "James Madison on Religion and Politics: Rhetoric and Reality." *The American Political Science Review* 85 (December 1991): 1321–37.

Lindsay, Thomas M. *A History of the Reformation.* Vol. 2, *The Reformation in Switzerland, France, the Netherlands, Scotland and England; The Anabaptist and Socinian Movements; The Counter-Reformation.* New York: Charles Scribner's Sons, 1913.

Little, Lewis Peyton. *Imprisoned Preachers and Religious Liberty in Virginia: A Narrative Drawn Largely from the Official Records of Virginia Counties, Unpublished Manuscripts, Letters, and Other Original Sources.* Lynchburg, Va.: J. P. Bell Co., 1938.

Loades, David. *Mary Tudor: A Life.* Cambridge, Mass.: Basil Blackwell, Inc., 1989.

Lorenzo, David J. "Tradition and Prudence in Locke's Exceptions to Toleration." *American Journal of Political Science* 47 (April 2003): 248–58.

Lyon, T. *The Theory of Religious Liberty in England, 1603–39.* Cambridge: Cambridge University Press, 1937.

Macaulay, Thomas Babington, Lord. *The History of England from the Accession of James II.* Vol. 3. Philadelphia: Lippincott, 1884.

Maclean, John. *History of the College of New Jersey, 1746–1854.* 2 vols. Philadelphia: J. B. Lippincott & Co., 1877. Reprint, New York: Arno Press & The New York Times, 1969.

Marnell, William H. *The First Amendment: The History of Religious Freedom in America.* Garden City, N. Y.: Doubleday & Company, 1964.

Marshall, Peter, and Alex Ryrie, eds. *The Beginnings of English Protestantism.* Cambridge: Cambridge University Press, 2002.

Martin, J. W. *Religious Radicals in Tudor England.* London: The Hambledon Press, 1989.

Mathew, David. *The Age of Charles I.* London: Eyre & Spottiswoode, 1951.

Mays, David John. *Edmund Pendleton, 1721–1803: A Biography.* 2 vols. Cambridge, Mass.: Harvard University Press, 1952.

McIlwaine, Henry R. *The Struggle of Protestant Dissenters for Religious Toleration in Virginia.* Volume 4 of Johns Hopkins University Studies in Historical and Political Science. Edited by Herbert B. Adams. Baltimore: The Johns Hopkins Press, 1894.

McLoughlin, William G. "Enthusiasm for Liberty." Essay 6a in *Taking Sides: Clashing Views on Controversial Issues in American History, Volume 1, The Colonial Period to Reconstruction.* 10th ed. Edited by Larry Madaras and James M. SoRelle. Guilford, Conn.: McGraw-Hill/Dushkin, 2003.

———. *Isaac Backus on Church, State, and Calvinism.* Cambridge, Mass.: Belknap Press, 1968.

———. *New England Dissent, 1630–1833: The Baptists and the Separation of Church and State.* 2 vols. Cambridge, Mass.: Harvard University Press, 1971.

———. *Revivals, Awakenings, and Reform: An Essay on Religion and Social Change in America, 1607–1977.* An essay in the series *Chicago History of American Religion.* Edited by Martin E. Marty. Chicago: University of Chicago Press, 1978.

Meade, Bishop William. *Old Churches, Ministers, and Families of Virginia.* 2 vols. Reprint, Baltimore, Md.: Genealogical Publishing Company, 1966.

Meeter, H. Henry. *The Basic Ideas of Calvinism,* 6th ed. Reprint, Grand Rapids, Mich.: Baker Books, 1997.

Meyer, Arnold Oskar. *England and the Catholic Church Under Queen Elizabeth.* Translated by J. R. McKee. London: Kegan Paul, Trench, Trubner & Co., Ltd., 1916.

Miller, John. *Bourbon and Stuart: Kings and Kingship in France and England in the Seventeenth Century.* New York: Franklin Watts, 1987.

Miller, Perry. *The New England Mind: From Colony to Province.* Cambridge, Mass.: Harvard University Press, 1953.

———. "Religion and Society in the Early Literature: The Religious Impulse in the Founding of Virginia." *The William and Mary Quarterly* 6 (January 1949): 24–41.

Miller, William Lee. *The First Liberty: Religion and the American Republic.* New York: Alfred A. Knopf, 1987.

Moore, R. Walton. "George Mason, The Statesman." *William and Mary College Quarterly Historical Magazine,* 2nd ser., 13 (January 1933): 10–17.

Morison, Samuel Eliot, Henry Steele Commager, and William E. Leuchtenburg. *The Growth of the American Republic.* 7th ed. Vol. 1. New York: Oxford University Press, 1980.

Moynahan, Brian. *God's Bestseller: William Tyndale, Thomas More, and the Writing of the English Bible—a Story of Martyrdom and Betrayal.* New York: St. Martin's Press, 2002.

Mullett, Charles F. "Toleration and Persecution in England, 1660–89." *Church History* 18 (1949): 18–43.

Murphy, Andrew R. *Conscience and Community: Revisiting Toleration and Religious Dissent in Early Modern England and America.* University Park, Pa.: Pennsylvania State University Press, 2001.

———. "The Uneasy Relationship between Social Contract Theory and Religious Toleration." *The Journal of Politics* 59 (May 1997): 368–92.

Nederman, Cary J., and John Christian Laursen, eds. *Difference and Dissent: Theories of Toleration in Medieval and Early Modern Europe.* Lanham, Md.: Rowman & Littlefield, Inc., 1996.

Nicolson, Adam. *God's Secretaries: The Making of the King James Bible.* New York: HarperCollins, 2003.

Noll, Mark A. *Princeton and the Republic, 1768–1822: The Search for a Christian Enlightenment in the Era of Samuel Stanhope Smith.* Princeton, N. J.: Princeton University Press, 1989.

Noonan, John T. *The Lustre of Our Country: The American Experience of Religious Freedom.* Berkeley, Calif.: University of California Press, 1998.

"The Northern Neck of Virginia." *William and Mary College Historical Magazine,* 6 (April 1898): 222–26.

Paffenroth, Kim, and Kevin L. Hughes, eds. *Augustine and Liberal Education.* Burlington, Vt.: Ashgate Publishing Co., 2000.

Paul, Robert S. *The Assembly of the Lord: Politics and Religion in the Westminster Assembly and the "Grand Debate."* Edinburgh: T. & T. Clark Ltd., 1985.

———. *The Lord Protector: Religion and Politics in the Life of Oliver Cromwell.* Grand Rapids, Mich.: William B. Eerdmans Publishing, 1964.

Payne, Rodger M. "New Light in Hanover County: Evangelical Dissent in Piedmont Virginia, 1740–1755." *The Journal of Southern History* 61 (November 1995): 665–94.

Penny, D. Andrew. *Freewill or Predestination: The Battle Over Saving Grace in Mid-Tudor England.* Woodbridge, England: Boydell Press, 1990.

Peterson, Merrill D., and Robert C. Vaughan, eds. *The Virginia Statute for Religious Freedom: Its Evolution and Consequences in American History.* Cambridge Studies in Religion and American Public Life series. Edited by Robin W. Lovin. 1988. Reprint, Cambridge: Cambridge University Press, 2003.

Pfeffer, Leo. *Church, State, and Freedom.* Boston: The Beacon Press, 1953.

Pilcher, George William. "Samuel Davies and Religious Toleration in Virginia." *The Historian: A Journal of History* 28 (1965): 48–71.

———. *Samuel Davies: Apostle of Dissent in Colonial Virginia.* Knoxville, Tenn.: University of Tennessee Press, 1971.

Reichley, A. James. *Religion in American Public Life.* Washington, D.C.: The Brookings Institution, 1985.

Reid, James. *Memoirs of the Westminster Divines.* Reprint, Edinburgh: The Banner of Truth Trust, 1982.

Reynolds, Noel B., and W. Cole Durham, eds. *Religious Liberty in Western Thought.* Atlanta, Ga.: Scholars Press, 1996.

Richardson, Anne. "William Tyndale and the Bill of Rights." Chapter 2 in *William Tyndale and the Law.* Vol. 25, Sixteenth Century Essays & Studies. Edited by John A. R. Dick and Anne Richardson. Kirksville, Mo.: Sixteenth Century Journal Publishers, 1994.

Ridley, Jasper. *Bloody Mary's Martyrs: The Story of England's Terror.* New York: Carroll & Graf Publishers, 2001.

———. *Statesman and Saint: Cardinal Wolsey, Sir Thomas More, and the Politics of Henry VIII.* New York: The Viking Press, 1982.

Rilliet, Albert. *Calvin and Servetus: The Reformer's Share in the Trial of Michael Servetus Historically Ascertained. From the French: with notes and additions.* Translated by W. K. Tweedie. Edinburgh: J. Johnstone, 1846

Roosevelt, Theodore. *Oliver Cromwell.* New York: C. Scribner's Sons, 1900.

Rosenmeier, Jesper. "The Teacher and the Witness: John Cotton and Roger Williams." *The William and Mary Quarterly* 25 (July 1968): 408–31.

Rutland, Robert Allen. *The Birth of the Bill of Rights, 1776–1791.* 1955. Reprint, Boston: Northeastern University Press, 1991.

———. "George Mason and the Origins of the First Amendment." Chapter 1 in *The First Amendment: The Legacy of George Mason.* Edited by T. Daniel Shumate. Fairfax, Va.: George Mason University Press, 1985.

Ryland, Garnett. *The Baptists of Virginia, 1699–1926.* Richmond, Va.: The Virginia Baptist Board of Missions and Education, 1955.

Schaff, Philip. *Church and State in the United States, or, The American Idea of Religious Liberty and Its Practical Effects, with Official Documents.* Papers of the American Historical Association, Vol. 2, No. 4. New York: G. P. Putnam's Sons, 1888. Reprint, New York: Arno Press, 1972.

———. *The Creeds of Christendom, with a History and Critical Notes.* 3 vols. 6th ed. Revised by David S. Schaff. Grand Rapids, Mich.: Baker Books, 1998.

————. *The German Reformation: the Beginning of the Protestant Reformation up to the Diet of Augsburg, 1517–1530.* Vol. 7, *History of the Christian Church.* 1888. Reprint, Peabody, Mass.: Hendrickson Publishers, 1996.

————. *The Swiss Reformation: The Protestant Reformation in German, Italian, and French Switzerland up to the Close of the Sixteenth Century, 1519-1605.* Vol. 8, *History of the Christian Church.* 1892. Reprint, Peabody, Mass.: Hendrickson Publishers, 1996.

Schochet, Gordon J. "From Persecution to 'Toleration.'" Chapter 4 in *Liberty Secured? Britain Before and After 1688.* Edited by J. R. Jones. Stanford, Calif.: Stanford University Press, 1992.

Schwartz, Bernard. *The Roots of Freedom: A Constitutional History of England.* New York: Hill and Wang, 1967.

Seaward, Paul. *The Restoration.* New York: St. Martin's Press, 1991.

Seiler, William H. "The Church of England as the Established Church in Seventeenth-Century Virginia." *The Journal of Southern History* 15 (November 1949): 478–08.

Semple, Robert Baylor. *History of the Baptists In Virginia.* 1810. Revised and extended by G. W. Beale. Reprint, Lafayette, Tenn.: Church History Research and Archives, 1976.

Shumate, T. Daniel, ed. *The First Amendment: The Legacy of George Mason.* Fairfax, Va.: George Mason University Press, 1985.

Siebert, Fredrick Seaton. *Freedom of the Press in England, 1476–1776: The Rise and Decline of Government Control.* Urbana, Ill.: University of Illinois Press, 1965.

Singleton, Marvin K. "Colonial Virginia as a First Amendment Matrix: Henry, Madison, and Assessment Establishment." Essay in *James Madison on Religious Liberty.* Edited by Robert S. Alley. Buffalo, N. Y.: Prometheus Books, 1985.

Sloan, Douglas. *The Scottish Enlightenment and the American College Ideal.* Columbia, N. Y.: Teachers College Press, 1971.

Sloan, Wm. David, and Julie Hedgepeth Williams. *The Early American Press, 1690–1783.* Westport, Conn.: Greenwood Press, 1994.

Stohlman, Martha Lou Lemmon. *John Witherspoon: Parson, Politician, Patriot.* Philadelphia: The Westminster Press, 1976.

Stokes, Anson Phelps, and Leo Pfeffer. *Church and State in the United States.* New York: Harper & Row, 1964.

Straus, Oscar S. *Roger Williams: The Pioneer of Religious Liberty.* Freeport, N. Y.: Books for Libraries Press, 1970.

Swanson, Mary-Elaine. "James Madison and the Presbyterian Idea of Man and Government." Chapter 6 in *Religion and Political Culture in Jefferson's Virginia.* Edited by Garrett Ward Sheldon and Daniel L. Dreisbach. Lanham, Mass.: Rowman & Littlefield Publishers, Inc., 2000.

Sweet, William Warren. *Revivalism in America: Its Origin, Growth, and Influence.* New York: Abingdon Press, 1944.

————. *The Story of Religion in America.* New York: Harper & Row, 1950.

Tait, L. Gordon. *The Piety of John Witherspoon: Pew, Pulpit, and Public Forum.* Louisville, Ky.: Geneva Press, 2001.

Tarter, Brent. "Virginians and the Bill of Rights." Chapter 1 in *The Bill of Rights: A Lively Heritage*. Edited by Jon Kukla. Richmond, Va.: Virginia State Library and Archives, 1987.

Thom, William Taylor. *The Struggle for Religious Freedom in Virginia: The Baptists*. Series XVIII, nos. 10–11–12 in Johns Hopkins University Studies in Historical and Political Science. Edited by Herbert B. Adams. Baltimore: The Johns Hopkins Press, 1900.

Todd, Margo, ed. *Reformation to Revolution: Politics and Religion in Early Modern England*. New York: Routledge, 1995.

Travitsky, Betty S. "Reprinting Tudor History: The Case of Catherine of Aragon." *Renaissance Quarterly* 50 (Spring 1997): 164–74.

Tyacke, Nicholas. "Puritanism, Arminianism, and Counter-Revolution." Chapter 3 in *Reformation to Revolution: Politics and Religion in Early Modern England*. Edited by Margo Todd. New York: Routledge, 1995.

Underhill, Edward B. *Tracts on Liberty of Conscience and Persecution: 1614–1661*. London: Hanserd Knollys Society, 1846. Reprint, New York: Burt Franklin, 1966.

Underwood, A. C. *A History of the English Baptists*. London: Carey Kingsgate Press, 1947. Reprint, London: Unwin Brothers, 1961.

Van Til, L. John. *Liberty of Conscience: The History of a Puritan Idea*. Nutley, N. J.: Craig Press, 1972. Reprint, Phillipsburg, N. J.: P & R Publishing, 1992.

Vaughan, Alden T. "'Expulsion of the Salvages': English Policy and the Virginia Massacre of 1622." *The William and Mary Quarterly* 35 (January 1978): 57–84.

Walker, William. "Force, Metaphor, and Persuasion in Locke's *A Letter Concerning Toleration*." Chapter 11 in *Difference and Dissent: Theories of Toleration in Medieval and Early Modern Europe*. Edited by Cary J. Nederman and John Christian Laursen. Lanham, Md.: Rowman & Littlefield, 1996.

Warfield, Benjamin B. *The Westminster Assembly and Its Work*. Reprint, Edmonton, AB Canada: Still Waters Revival Books, 1991.

Watts, Michael. *The Dissenters*. 2 vols. Oxford: Clarendon Press, 1978, 1995.

Whipple, Leon. *Our Ancient Liberties: The Story of the Origin and Meaning of Civil and Religious Liberty in the United States*. New York: The H. W. Wilson Company, 1927.

Williams, Michael E. "The Influence of Calvinism on Colonial Baptists." *Baptist History and Heritage* (Spring 2004): 26–39.

Wilson, Douglas. *For Kirk and Covenant: The Stalwart Courage of John Knox*. Leaders in Action series, edited by George Grant. Nashville, Tenn.: Highland Books, 2000.

Wirt, William. *Sketches of the Life and Character of Patrick Henry*. 15th ed. 1857. Reprint, Purcellville, Va.: Home School Legal Defense Association, 1998.

Zagorin, Perez. *A History of Political Thought in the English Revolution*. London: Routledge & Paul, 1954.

———. *How the Idea of Religious Toleration Came to the West*. Princeton, N. J.: Princeton University Press, 2003.

Zweig, Stefan. *Mary Queen of Scotland and the Isles*. [*Maria Stuart*. Vienna: Herbert Reichner Verlag, 1935.] Translated by Eden and Cedar Paul. New York: Viking Press, 1935.